# *CHRISTIAN CONVERSATIONS WITH JEHOVAH'S WITNESSES*

Biblical Answers
to Questions
Jehovah's Witnesses Ask

**Christina R. (Harvey) Darlington**

**Second Edition**

**Updated and Expanded**

Witnesses for Jesus Inc
PO Box 50911
Colorado Springs, CO 80949 USA
4witness.org * 4jehovah.org * 4mormon.org

ISBN: 1480004022
ISBN-13: 978-1480004023

## DEDICATION

It has been said that a Jehovah's Witness can leave the Watchtower religion over night, but it can take months and even years to overcome the confusion of Watchtower thinking.

This book is dedicated to the countless spiritual lives lost and deceived by the literature of the Watchtower Society of Jehovah's Witnesses and to their Christian loved-ones who care enough about them to learn how to effectively present Biblical truth in love.

The dialogues in this book between a Christian and a Jehovah's Witness are designed to expose the deceptive thinking behind many of the unique beliefs held by Jehovah's Witnesses and to present new ways of thinking about these doctrines that will deprogram their minds with the truth of God's Word.

Our goal is to help free Jehovah's Witnesses from mental and spiritual bondage so that they can embrace true Christian freedom in Christ.

# TABLE OF CONTENTS

# FORWARD

*Are Jehovah's Witnesses Christians? What do they believe? Does the message they take door-to-door set them apart as the one true religion? If not, is there another religion I should seek? If Jehovah's Witnesses are Christians (as they claim), why do they persist in distributing their literature to those who already belong to a Christian denomination? What drives them to remain devoted to the Watchtower organization that has a history of changing its doctrines and making false predictions regarding the end of the world? Is there anything I can say to open the minds of these people who come knocking on my door?*

You may be asking the above questions because you have a friend or a loved-one who has begun to study with Jehovah's Witnesses and is expressing an interest in becoming one of them. Because you are concerned for the safety and spiritual well-being of your friend or loved-one, you may be seeking to know more about Jehovah's Witnesses in an attempt to respond to your friend or loved-one who is studying with them.

While this book is not a full, comprehensive exposition on all of the unique doctrines, policies, and historical background of the Jehovah's Witness religion, the dialogues in this book address the major aspects of these areas and will give you an inside perspective into the mental framework of Jehovah's Witness thinking on these key issues. This book will give you insight into what attracts individuals to the Watchtower organization and the dialogues will help you prepare yourself to answer the common questions raised by Jehovah's Witnesses. This book not only provides creative arguments to use when discussing these topics with Jehovah's Witnesses, it provides the necessary photocopied documentation needed to constructively challenge the devotion of your Jehovah's Witness loved-ones to the Watchtower organization.

If you are not in the category above of someone who is trying to learn about Jehovah's Witnesses, you may be in the other category of people who ask the above questions because they have been or are currently associated with Jehovah's Witnesses. While outwardly you may be embracing this religion as "the truth"—devoting your time and energy to furthering the purposes of the Watchtower organization—you may have observed situations that have caused you to inwardly question whether this organization is truly being led by Jehovah God. If you are in this situation, please realize that you are not alone. **Statistics reveal that nearly 50% of the annual number of Jehovah's Witnesses that come into the Watchtower organization, leave by becoming inactive or disfellowshipped during the year.**[1] In your search for truth, may you be comforted by the following promise in Scripture:

> " 'For I know the plans that I have for you,' declares the LORD [Jehovah], 'plans for welfare and not for calamity to give you a future and a hope. Then you will call upon Me and come and pray to Me, and I will listen to you. And you will seek Me and find *Me,* when you search for Me with all your heart."—Jeremiah 29:11-13[2]

Although I have never been baptized as one of Jehovah's Witnesses, I know about the fear that active Jehovah's Witnesses have toward reading literature from "apostate" or Ex-Jehovah's Witness sources. So, I have taken the necessary precautions in this book to ensure that all claims are documented and substantiated from the official publications of the Watchtower and secular sources available in most university libraries. The student of Jehovah's Witnesses is encouraged to verify all the information presented in this book by cross-referencing all quotes to the photocopied documentation provided in the back of this book.

With the exception of the first two dialogues, all of the rest take place between Cindy, a Jehovah's Witness, and Karen, a Christian Householder, who discuss the teachings expressed in the 1996 Watchtower brochure publication *What Does God Require of Us?* (WDGR). I chose this brochure as the basis for my book because it lays out the beliefs of Jehovah's Witnesses in a concise way, making it easy to address their key beliefs in a simple dialogue format.

Although this brochure is no longer the primary booklet used by Jehovah's Witnesses to present their beliefs to potential converts, **it is still very relevant as it addresses nearly every significant doctrinal belief held by Jehovah's Witnesses today**. Therefore, if you learn the specific technique and evangelistic questions given in these dialogues, you will be equipped to address nearly all significant doctrines presented in the current literature of Jehovah's Witnesses.

This book is the product of the **many years that I have spent talking to active and former Jehovah's Witnesses** who have been involved at all levels of leadership. As I was researching the information for this book, I regularly attended meetings at a local Kingdom Hall and participated in their studies. In an attempt to make these dialogues as realistic as possible, **I have patterned most of these**

---

[1] Because the Watchtower does not maintain a "membership" list, the only way to track the growth of their membership is through the monthly reports turned in by active Jehovah's Witnesses in the door-to-door ministry. Every year the January 1st issue of *The Watchtower* publishes the total number of Jehovah's Witnesses baptized during the year and the largest number of "Peak Publishers" (Highest number of active Jehovah's Witnesses placing Watchtower literature during a given month of the year). A comparison of the number of Jehovah's Witnesses baptized during 1996-2000 (1,670,940) with the growth of "Peak Publishers" between the year 1995 (5,199,895) and 2000 (6,035,564), reveals a difference of 835,271 between the number of individuals baptized into the Watchtower organization (1,670,940) and the actual increase of active Jehovah's Witness publishers (835,669) during that period. Thus 49.98% became inactive during that period.

[2] Scripture quotation is taken from the *New American Standard Bible.* Brackets enclose words added to complete the context of the passage.

**dialogues between Cindy and Karen after the real-life conversations I and others have had with active Jehovah's Witnesses.**

Since these dialogues are designed to equip the student of Jehovah's Witnesses with the most effective research that debunks the main tenants of the doctrinal system of the Watchtower Society, they are arranged topically and do not correspond to the chronological order given in this Watchtower brochure. To make the reader's research easier, they are broken down into the following three topical categories, referred to as "sections" in this book:

1. EXAMINING THE AUTHORITY OF THE WATCHTOWER SOCIETY
2. ANALYZING THE ISSUES RELATING TO ETERNAL LIFE
3. EVALUATING JEHOVAH'S WITNESS CONSCIENCE ISSUES

**EDITORIAL NOTE:**

Each dialogue discussion within each section is represented by a question title that provides a preview into the content of each dialogue. Since these dialogues were originally used as scripts for a recorded telephone message ministry to Jehovah's Witnesses, each dialogue is designed to be read easily in less than 15 minutes.

At the end of the book, you will find photocopies of the supporting documentation referenced in each dialogue. The copies are arranged according to the order in which they were presented within each dialogue. These photocopies have been reproduced to validate the claims made in each dialogue discussion. Due to copyright constraints, the *WDGR* brochure has not been reproduced in the photocopied documentation provided.

You will notice that except for the citations from other documents, all pronoun references to Jesus Christ in Karen's response and the comments section of this book are capitalized to denote Deity, while all of Cindy's responses and any other statement discussing the Jehovah's Witness position do not have the pronoun capitalized because Jehovah's Witnesses deny the Deity of Jesus Christ.

# SECTION ONE:

# *EXAMINING THE AUTHORITY OF THE WATCHTOWER SOCIETY*

*Conversations inside the Watchtower organization and Conversations in door-to-door ministry with a Christian Householder and One of Jehovah's Witnesses discussing the Watchtower Publication, "What Does God Require of Us?"*

*"But you are not to be called 'Rabbi,' for you have only one Master and you are all brothers. And do not call anyone on earth 'father,' for you have one Father, and he is in heaven.* ***Nor are you to be called 'teacher,' for you have one Teacher, the Christ****."—Matthew 23:8-11, New International Version*

# THE PURPOSE OF SECTION ONE:

# EXAMINING THE AUTHORITY OF THE WATCHTOWER SOCIETY:

Whether they realize it or not, the minds of Jehovah's Witnesses have been conditioned to believe the faulty concept that the Watchtower Society (Governing Body) of Jehovah's Witnesses holds all spiritual authority over the followers of Jehovah God. Thus, a person within the Jehovah's Witness religion is not allowed to question any of the doctrines and practices of this organization without being judged as an "apostate" or "opposer" of Jehovah God and His ways.

In order to help free the minds of Jehovah's Witnesses so that they can consider alternate ways of interpreting Biblical Scripture and practicing Christian freedom, it is essential to examine the core authority claims of the Watchtower Society to determine if in fact this organization is what it claims to be—"God's Organization."

As you will see proved through the dialogues in this section, the Watchtower Society does not speak for Jehovah God and all authority claims made by this organization are invalid. When a Christian presents the documentation provided in this section to an honest, thinking Jehovah's Witness, it can be a powerful tool to remove the mental barriers to effective dialogue about alternative Christian beliefs and practices.

The first two dialogues in this section (Dialogue 1A and 1B) stand out from the rest of the dialogues in this book because they are completely separate and unrelated to the Karen and Cindy dialogues in the rest of the book. Because the stigma of leaving the Watchtower organization is so great, I wrote these first two dialogues to help Jehovah's Witnesses face the opposition they will encounter from devoted friends and family members when they make known their decision to leave this religion. Christians will likewise learn from these first two dialogues how shunning operates in the Watchtower organization and what they can do to help an Ex-Jehovah's Witness face this opposition.

## DIALOGUE ONE A: Can You Serve Jehovah Without The Watchtower "New Light"?

*A concerned Father challenges his son about his decision to leave the Watchtower. The son responds by questioning the organization's "new light from Jehovah" defense for doctrinal changes and flip-flops.*

**FATHER:** Johnny, don't turn your back on Jehovah. I raised you in the Truth. How can you turn your back on us and on Jehovah by leaving His organization?

**SON:** Dad, I **love** Jehovah! That's why I'm leaving the Watchtower organization; because it isn't His. It's just a group of men **claiming** to represent God.

**FATHER:** I happen to know that it is God's organization, Son. I proved it to myself when I left the Catholic Church before you were born. The Truth is so precious to me, Johnny. Please don't turn your back on us and Jehovah by leaving His organization!

**SON:** But, Dad, didn't you tell me Grandpa said the same thing to you when you left the Church – that you were 'leaving God'?

**FATHER:** Yes, Son, but this is different. You know apostate Christendom doesn't have the Truth! Aren't the churches worse than some of the faults you see in our brothers? Why don't you just have patience with the organization? If something is wrong, Jehovah will send "new light" to clear it up in His timing. Our responsibility is to patiently remain **loyal** to His "channel" of communication.[1]

**SON:** Dad, you say to have patience with the organization, but the organization doesn't have patience. If ninety percent of Russell's teachings were wrong and much of what the Jehovah's Witnesses **now** call "the Truth" has changed in the last fifty years, how can we point our finger at Christendom when we didn't have the truth all those years either?

**FATHER:** I wouldn't say we didn't have the truth, Son. It's just that the truth needed refining. We should be grateful that the Society is humble enough to admit its mistakes and receive "new light" from Jehovah. This is proof that Jehovah is leading us.[2]

**SON:** But Dad, do you remember the Watchtower article on the Society's "Progressive Understanding of 'the Superior Authorities' " in **Romans 13:1**? In that article, the Society explained how back in 1886, Charles Russell "correctly identified 'the higher powers,' or 'the superior authorities,' mentioned by the apostle Paul, as human governmental authorities."[3] Then in 1929, the Society received "new light" and changed their interpretation of this passage to teach that "the higher powers must be Jehovah God and Jesus Christ." And then again in 1961, the Society's "new light" caused them to change back to the **original** view that Jehovah's Witnesses believed

---

[1] See *The Watchtower,* October 1, 1967, p. 590
[2] See *The Watchtower,* March 15, 2000, pp. 12, 14
[3] *The Watchtower* May 1, 1996, p. 13

before 1929 and which they currently teach—"that the term *'superior* authorities' referred, not to the *Supreme* Authority, Jehovah, and to His Son, Jesus, but to *human governmental authorities.*"[4] How can "truth" change back and forth like this? When they go back to the original view and call it "new light," how can this be evidence that Jehovah is leading them? Rather than being "new light," Dad, this sounds to me like the "light" is flicking on and off.

**FATHER:** Son, do you remember the Watchtower article on how "new light" is like a ship "tacking into the wind"? In this article, the Society states: "At times explanations given by Jehovah's visible organization have shown adjustments, **seemingly to previous points of view**. **But this has not actually been the case**."[5] The Society went on to explain that just like a ship swerves right and left as it is progressing toward its destination in spite of contrary winds, the "new light" they receive is like "tacking into the wind" of spiritual truth. So you see, Son, these changes **are** evidence that Jehovah is leading us.

**SON:** Dad, when a ship is tacking into the wind, does it ever turn **one hundred eighty degrees** and go in the total **opposite** direction?

**FATHER:** Well, no, Son, but the Society has never changed their view so much that they taught the opposite of their original position, have they?

**SON:** Yes, they have, Dad. Did you ever notice the change between the Society's 1982 and 1989 editions of the book *You Can Live Forever in Paradise on Earth*? On page 179 of the 1982 edition, they state: "By saying this, Jesus showed that at **least some of the unrighteous people** of ancient Sodom and Gomorrah **will be present** on earth during Judgment Day. Although they had been very immoral, we can expect **that some of them will be resurrected**." So in the 1982 edition, the Society is saying that the Sodomites would be resurrected, but now we turn to the same page in the 1989 edition and it reads: "Will such terribly wicked persons be resurrected during Judgment Day? The Scriptures indicate that **apparently they will not**....Yes, for their excessive immorality the people of Sodom and of the surrounding cities suffered a destruction from which **they will apparently never be resurrected**." So, Dad, which is it? Will the Sodomites be resurrected or will they not? You call this "tacking in to the wind"?

**FATHER:** OK, Son, so they did teach the total opposite of their original position, but couldn't this be "new light"?

**SON:** Well, maybe we could call this "new light" if they weren't returning to their old light taught way back in 1952. In the Watchtower article of June 1, 1952, page 338, the Society stated that the Sodomites fate was sealed and that there would be no "future judgment" in which they would be resurrected. So, can you see, Dad, how the Society is actually putting forth old light and calling it "new light" to excuse their doctrinal flip-flops?

---

[4] *The Watchtower* May 1, 1996, p. 14

[5] *The Watchtower* December 1, 1981, p. 27

**FATHER:** I - I don't know, Son. . . All I know is that Jehovah has always used an organization to lead His people. Just look at the Israelites. Jehovah God appointed Moses and the priests of Aaron to lead His people and when that organization became corrupt at the time of Christ, He organized a governing body of anointed Christians to take its place. You see, Jehovah always takes care of His **loyal** people, even if an organization becomes corrupt.

**SON:** Dad?

**FATHER:** Yes, Son?

**SON:** If the disciples had been **loyal** to Jehovah's organization of their day, would they have followed Jesus?

**COMMENTS:**

*Friends,* ***loyalty*** *to a counterfeit is* ***disloyalty*** *to Jehovah God. Just as the disciples of Jesus' day had to make a decision between following an organization or following the One who is "the Truth" — Jesus Himself—so today the "Truth" is not found in a religious organization, but in the One who said: "****I am*** *the Way, and* ***the Truth****, and the Life; no one comes to the Father, but through* ***Me****."*[6]

*Throughout history, God's prophets have found themselves outcasts, reproved and disfellowshipped by governmental and priestly organizations. The prophet Jeremiah was accused of disloyalty when he urged his fellow brothers to leave the "organization" of his day and told them that "everyone remaining in Jerusalem would die...but anyone surrendering to the Babylonians would live."*[7] *Those loyal to the organization viewed Jeremiah as an apostate rebel and turned a deaf ear to his advice. Rather than join with the Babylonians as God commanded, they felt safer staying within Jerusalem, the headquarters of Jehovah's organization. But the prophet Jeremiah warned them: "Do not put trust in lying phrases, 'Jehovah's Temple...they are.' "*[8]

*The fulfillment of Jeremiah's words proved that there are times when men must chose between loyalty to an organization and loyalty to God Himself. So, while Jehovah has always had faithful individuals on earth, the organizations claiming to represent Him have often failed to live up to their names. In fact, such self-serving power structures have often become the persecutors of individuals faithful to God. An organization did not die to pay your sin debt, nor will an organization intercede before Jehovah God on your behalf.*

---

[6] John 14:6, *New American Standard Bible*
[7] Jeremiah 38:2, *The Living Bible*
[8] Jeremiah 7:4, *Byington Bible*

*Where you spend eternity depends on your relationship with a* ***person*** *— Jesus Himself—not an organization. You* ***can*** *indeed serve Jehovah without the Watchtower.*[9]

[9] Closing comments for this dialogue were taken from the *Comments from the Friends* article entitled "Don't Leave Jehovah…", Comments from the Friends, January-March 1998, vol. XVII. No. 1, pages 2-4 (Comments from the Friends - www.cftf.com)

## DIALOGUE ONE B: Love Our Brother And Shun Our Mother?

*Two Jehovah's Witness sisters discuss the Watchtower policy of shunning those who leave this religion and contrast the difference between the lack of love shown among the devoted followers of the Watchtower with the brotherly love shown among Christian followers of Jehovah who serve Him outside the organization.*

**JULIE:** Sarah, how could Brother Anderson be so cruel to Sister Jones? It's as if she couldn't do anything right. I understand he had to correct her for wearing slacks out in service, but then to embarrass her in front of the whole congregation like that, I think that was totally uncalled for. I just don't understand why Jehovah allows elders who are so lacking in brotherly love to be in leadership like this.

**SARAH:** I know, Julie, but you must not blame Jehovah God for faults we see in our brothers. In His time, He will cleanse His organization. You just need to have patience.

**JULIE:** But, Sarah, doesn't this hypocrisy upset you? How can we point at Christendom and talk about how they are so judgmental and condemning of each other, when we do the same thing to our brothers in the congregation? Doesn't the Bible say the world will know we are Christians by our love for each other?

**SARAH:** Yes. . .

**JULIE:** Brother Anderson is anything but loving. Do you remember the way he acted when mom disassociated herself from the Watchtower organization? You would have thought she had cursed Jehovah God.

**SARAH:** I know, Julie, I had a hard time with that too, but we must not forget that our love for Jehovah needs to be greater than our love for our earthly mother. By rejecting the Watchtower organization, mom has rejected the truth, and we must not associate with her or Jehovah may reject us too.

**JULIE:** I know she had a hard time with the hypocrisy she saw in the congregation and for some reason she thinks she can serve Jehovah without the Watchtower. I don't understand her, but that doesn't seem like a good reason we should refuse to speak to her.

**SARAH:** Yes, Julie, but our loyalty to Jehovah's organization requires us to not associate with her anymore. If Sister Brown had seen you two together the other day and turned you into Brother Anderson, you know what he'd have done.

**JULIE:** I know, but don't you realize how hard it was for me to try to resist saying "Hello" to her when I saw her in the store yesterday? She hasn't seen the grandchildren since Joey was two years old! Why would a loving God require us to shun our mom like this?

**SARAH:** Julie, don't you remember the Watchtower article on how we are to treat those who leave the organization? In that article, the question was asked: "Would upholding God's...disfellowshiping arrangement mean that a Christian should not speak at all with an expelled person, not even saying 'Hello'?"[1] In answer, the Society said: "...we all know from our experience over the years that a simple 'Hello' to someone can be the first step that develops into a conversation and maybe even a friendship. Would we want to take that first step with a disfellowshiped person?...Consequently, Christians related to such a disfellowshiped person living outside the home should strive to avoid needless association, even keeping business dealings to a minimum."[2] So you see, Julie, Jehovah requires us to keep the Congregation clean and you know what that means!

**JULIE:** What that means! Why, I'm to love Brother Anderson who tramples anyone who dares stand in his way, but at the same time, I'm to shun my mom who left the organization of her own accord but still loves Jehovah God and would never do anything to hurt anyone. You call this a loving organization? Where in the Bible does it state we are to shun those who leave the Watchtower because they believe they can serve Jehovah better outside of the organization?

**SARAH:** Julie, doesn't 2 John 10 say: "If anyone comes to YOU and does not bring this teaching, never receive him into YOUR homes or say a greeting to him."?[3] Doesn't this mean we shouldn't talk with someone who has left the organization?

**JULIE:** Sarah, look at the context of that passage here in 2 John. This letter is addressed "to the chosen lady and to her children."[4] In the Watchtower book "All Scripture is Inspired of God and Beneficial," the Society notes that "...it is thought by some that John was writing to a Christian congregation, referring to it as 'the chosen lady.' This may have been done in order to confuse persecutors."[5] So, you can see, Sarah, this letter was likely written to a congregation that met in the brothers' homes. Due to the many false teachers that were traveling from congregation to congregation, John admonished the brothers to prevent these false teachers from entering their house-congregations and deceiving the flock. But this says nothing about how Christians should treat a sister who wants to serve Jehovah outside of the organization.

**SARAH:** But, Julie, doesn't 2 Thessalonians 3:14 say: "...if anyone is not obedient to our word through this letter, keep this one marked, stop associating with him, that he may become ashamed."?[6]

**JULIE:** Yes, Sarah, but look at the next verse. Verse15: "And yet do not be considering him as an enemy, but continue admonishing him as a brother."[7] Mom did not leave the

---

[1] *The Watchtower* September 15, 1981, pp. 24
[2] *The Watchtower* September 15, 1981, pp. 25, 29
[3] *New World Translation*
[4] 2 John 1, *New World Translation*
[5] *"All Scripture is Inspired of God and Beneficial,"* 1963, 1990, p. 259
[6] *New World Translation*
[7] *New World Translation*

organization because she wanted no part in Jehovah's table. She left because she loves Jehovah God and feels that serving Him outside of a hypocritical organization was the best way she could remain loyal to God. All of the Scriptures I've researched on apostasy have to do with leaving Jehovah God—not an organization!

**SARAH:** I know, Julie, but hasn't Jehovah always worked through an organization? Doesn't loyalty to Jehovah God require loyalty to His organization?

**JULIE:** I'm not so sure, Sarah. Wasn't the prophet Jeremiah accused of disloyalty and apostasy when he urged his fellow brothers to leave the "organization" of his day and told them that "everyone remaining in Jerusalem would die...but anyone surrendering to the Babylonians would live."?[8] And what about those disciples who followed Jesus instead of staying with the priestly organization they were taught was of Jehovah? Why does it seem like people who choose loyalty to Jehovah over loyalty to an organization end up being persecuted by the very organizations that claim to represent God?

**COMMENTS:**

*Friends, there are times when one must choose between loyalty to an organization and loyalty to God. Just as Jesus noted: "You will know them by their fruits.... "*[9] *So, the apostle John stated: "If someone says, 'I love God,' and hates his brother, he is a liar; for the one who does not love his brother whom he has seen, cannot love God whom he has not seen."*[10] *An organization did not die to pay our sin debt, nor will an organization intercede before Jehovah God on our behalf. Where we spend eternity depends on our relationship with a* ***person*** *— Jesus Himself—not an organization. John 8:32, 36 states: "and you shall know the truth, and the truth shall make you free....If therefore the Son shall make you free, you shall be free indeed."*[11] *You* ***can*** *indeed serve Jehovah without the Watchtower.*

---

[8] Jeremiah 38:2, *Living Bible*
[9] Matthew 7:16, *New American Standard Bible*
[10] 1 John 4:20, *New American Standard Bible*
[11] *New American Standard Bible*

## DIALOGUE TWO: Is Spiritual Adoption Only For 144,000 People?

(WDGR LESSON 1: "How You Can Find Out What God Requires")

*Karen asks Cindy why Jehovah's Witnesses read the Bible when the majority of Jehovah's Witnesses today do not believe the New Covenant Scriptures about going to heaven, being spiritually adopted, and being born again apply to them.*

**CINDY:** Knock, Knock…

**KAREN:** I'm coming… Who is it?

**CINDY:** It's me, Cindy. Do you remember the Bible study we started last week?

**KAREN:** Oh, yes! Come on in. I'm so glad you are willing to study with me.

**CINDY:** So how was your week?

**KAREN:** Pretty good. I didn't have much time to look over the Watchtower brochure you gave me *What Does God Require of Us?*, but I've been thinking about what we discussed on how the Bible is like God's love letter to us,[1] and I have a question.

**CINDY:** Yes, Karen?

**KAREN:** A friend of mine was telling me that Jehovah's Witnesses don't believe that all of the Bible applies to them. He said the Watchtower teaches that only 144,000 people are in the New Covenant and will go to Heaven and that because most Witnesses don't believe they are in that group, they don't believe that they can be "born again".[2] Is this true?

**CINDY:** Well, yes, Karen, but that is what the Bible teaches and besides, as you progress in the truth, you'll come to see that later. For now let's just work on the basics.

**KAREN:** But I don't understand, Cindy. Didn't Jesus say: "…no one can see the kingdom of God unless he is born again."?[3] Since the theme of the Bible is about God's Kingdom, why do Jehovah's Witnesses study about it if they do not believe Jesus' words apply to them? Isn't this like dreaming about something you can't have?

**CINDY:** Karen, I wouldn't say the Kingdom isn't something we can't have. We'll be under the rulership of that Kingdom even though we won't be in it. After all, a Kingdom needs subjects to rule over. If we are all in the Kingdom in Heaven, who will we rule over?[4]

---

[1] *What Does God Require of Us?,* 1996, p. 3:1

[2] *Jehovah's Witnesses—Who Are They? What Do They Believe?,* 2000, p. 13; *The Watchtower,* February 1, 1998, p. 20; *The Watchtower,* February 15, 1998, p. 20

[3] John 3:3, *New International Version*

[4] *Reasoning From the Scriptures,* 1985, 1989, p. 79

**KAREN:** Cindy, doesn't the Bible say there will be people during Christ's Millennium Kingdom on earth that have not made a decision for or against God? Couldn't we be ruling over them?

**CINDY:** Maybe, Karen, but we will study about that later. Right now we need to focus on what we should do in order to please God. Wouldn't you agree that, "The Bible **alone** tells us what we must do to please God"?[5]

**KAREN:** Yes, Cindy. I know we read that in the brochure, and I agree, but that brings up another question. I was reading in Galatians 4:4-6: "But when the fulness of the time came, God sent forth His Son…in order that…we might receive the adoption as sons. And because you are sons, God has sent forth the Spirit of His Son into our hearts, crying, Abba! Father!"[6] Isn't this Scripture saying that we must become adopted before we can have the Holy Spirit working in our lives?

**CINDY:** Well, Karen, I guess it does... "because you are sons, God has sent forth the Spirit..." But you must realize that these verses don't apply to us. They apply only to those who are going to heaven. I'm not going to heaven, so I don't need to be adopted into God's family as it talks about here.

**KAREN:** And since you're not "adopted," you can't be "anointed" with the Holy Spirit either, can you, Cindy?

**CINDY:** No, I can't, but that doesn't bother me, Karen. As long as I gain Jehovah's approval upon my life through obedience to His Word, that is all that I need to do.

**KAREN:** But Cindy, that is my concern. You just told me that you believe that, "the Bible alone tells us what we must do to please God,"[7] and now you're telling me that those verses in the Bible do not apply to us. I'm confused! If we can't have God's Spirit, how can we please God? Let's read Romans 8:8-9 in your Bible—*The New World Translation:* "So those who are in harmony with the flesh **cannot please** God. However, YOU are in harmony, not with the flesh, but with the spirit, if God's spirit truly dwells in YOU. But if anyone does not have Christ's spirit, this one does **not** belong to him." Isn't this Scripture saying that we are in "harmony with the flesh" and "cannot please God" if we do not have God's Holy Spirit?

**CINDY:** Well, yes, but I have God's Spirit, Karen. I may not be adopted, but I have some kind of measure of God's Spirit.

**KAREN:** You do, Cindy? Where does it say in the Bible you can have God's Spirit apart from adoption? Even the Hebrew Patriarch David had to be adopted as God's son in order to receive God's Spirit.[8] And just a few verses down from this Scripture we are reading

---

[5] *What Does God Require of Us?,* 1996, p. 3:1

[6] *New International Version*

[7] *What Does God Require of Us?,* 1996, p. 3:1

[8] At Psalm 89:20, Jehovah God declared that finding David to be a faithful servant, He had "anointed him" with His

here in Romans 8, it states that, "all those who are led by God's spirit, these are God's sons."[9] You just told me you can't be adopted as one of God's children, so how can you be led by God's Spirit at all?

**CINDY:** Well, I don't know. . .

**KAREN:** Cindy, let's read verse 9 again.

**CINDY:** "However, YOU are in harmony, not with the flesh, but with the spirit, **if** God's spirit truly dwells in YOU. But if anyone does not have Christ's Spirit, this one **does not belong** to him." I never noticed that before. It does say that I can't even belong to Christ unless I have God's Spirit. I guess that's why the Watchtower Society says these verses don't apply to us. For if they did, we'd all be in trouble.

**KAREN:** Cindy, if these verses don't apply to you, why do Jehovah's Witnesses read the Bible? Isn't that like reading somebody else's love letter?

**COMMENTS:**

*Friends, Satan wins a great victory when he can get us to doubt the validity of God's Word. "Is it **really** so that God said you must not eat. . .?"[10] questioned Satan as he tempted Eve in the Garden. While the Bible talks about a group of 144,000 people, nowhere does it state that this is the **only** group that will be in heaven, nor does it say that the promises given to the Christians by means of the New Covenant apply only to 144,000 people. Rather, to the contrary, the Bible says: "For no matter how **many** promises God has made, they are 'Yes' in Christ."[11] For those of us who are in Christ Jesus, **all** of the promises of God apply to us. John 1:12 says: "But as many as received Him, to them He gave the right" [authority] "to become children of God, even to those who believe in His name."— New American Standard Bible*

---

"holy oil." It was at this anointing, that "the spirit of Jehovah began to be operative upon David from that day forward."—1 Samuel 16:13, *NWT* Just as Galatians 4:6 reveals that those who have been "adopted" into God's spiritual family are able to call God "Abba! Father!" so David, having been anointed with God's Holy Spirit and spiritually adopted into His family, cried out to God saying: "You are my Father...."—Psalm 89:26, *NWT* As a result, in a figurative way and as a picture of Christ, God appointed David to the position of "firstborn." (Psalm 89:27) Calling David "firstborn" would hardly be logical if David was not adopted as a part of God's spiritual family.

[9] Romans 8:14

[10] Genesis 3:1, *New World Translation*

[11] 2 Corinthians 1:20, *New International Version*

## DIALOGUE THREE: Is The Watchtower Organization A Cult? —*Part I*

(WDGR LESSON 4: "Who is the Devil?")

*Are personal opinions and independent thinking condemned by God? How can Christian unity exist in a religion that allows its members to disagree on spiritual issues? Do true Christians need the guidance of an organization to understand the Bible? What are the mental manipulation techniques of a cult?*

**CINDY:** Hi, Karen. How was your week?

**KAREN:** Oh, it was all right. It's just that my mom is giving me a hard time because I'm studying with Jehovah's Witnesses. I guess she's afraid that I'm going to end up in a cult.

**CINDY:** Karen, we hear that a lot from people who don't understand our religion. Just like usual we'll be studying today in the Watchtower brochure *What Does God Require of Us?:* "Satan may use *persecution* or *opposition* to get you to leave Jehovah." As you are seeing, Karen, "Some of your loved ones may become very angry because you are studying the Bible....Satan wants to frighten you so that you will stop learning about Jehovah."[1] You won't let Satan win by listening to your mom, will you Karen?

**KAREN:** Cindy, my mom is not upset that I'm studying the Bible. It's just that she's worried that I'm studying **with** Jehovah's Witnesses. She thinks that the Jehovah's Witness religion is a cult and she doesn't want me to end up in it.

**CINDY:** Karen, do you know what a "cult" is? A few years ago, in the February 15, 1994 issue of *The Watchtower,* the Society described what a "cult" is. Let me read some of the things they said in that article: "Cult leaders are known to use manipulative methods to control the minds of their followers. Is there any evidence that Jehovah's Witnesses do this? ...Outstanding is a recent ruling by the European Court of Human Rights. It declared that the Witnesses should enjoy freedom of thought, conscience, and religion and that they have the right to speak about their faith and teach it to others. This would hardly be the case if Jehovah's Witnesses ...used manipulative methods to control the minds of their followers."[2] Karen, you see what we are like. Do you think we use "manipulative methods" to control your mind?

**KAREN:** I'm not sure, Cindy. My mom said that Jehovah's Witnesses are not allowed to question any of the doctrines and policies of the Watchtower organization and that if they don't believe absolutely everything the Society teaches, they will be disfellowshipped from the organization. She said that fear of being rejected by the organization, manipulates many Witnesses into not accepting blood transfusions,[3]

[1] *What Does God Require of Us?,* 1996, p. 9:7

[2] *The Watchtower,* February 15, 1994, pp. 4, 6

refusing any kind of political activities,[4] and not participating in anything that is disapproved of by the Watchtower organization. Is this true that the Watchtower manipulates its members in this way?

**CINDY:** I wouldn't call it "manipulation," Karen. The Watchtower Society doesn't tell us what to believe. Based on our conscience, we make our own personal decision in regard to blood transfusions and politics.

**KAREN:** Really, Cindy? You are allowed to make your own personal decision? So what happens if the conscience of a Witness permits him to vote; are you saying he wouldn't be disfellowshipped for such an action?

**CINDY:** Well, no, Karen. He would be disfellowshipped if he persists in this action because a Jehovah's Witness must believe and act in harmony with the Watchtower organization.

**KAREN:** Then are you saying, Cindy, that a Witness' personal conscience is determined by the Watchtower organization's doctrine and policies?

**CINDY:** Well, I guess so. . .

**KAREN:** Listen to this Watchtower article and tell me how this is not mental "manipulation" in controlling what people think and believe. The Society said: "…Satan called into question God's way of doing things. He promoted independent thinking.…How is such independent thinking manifested? A common way is by questioning the counsel that is provided by God's visible organization…Why is it so dangerous? Such thinking is an evidence of pride… Really, can we get along without the direction of God's organization? No, we cannot!"[5] Cindy, when personal judgment of determining Scriptural truth is viewed as pride against God, how can this not be a means of controlling what people believe? If a person is not allowed to question the doctrines of an organization, how can he follow the Biblical command to "make sure of all things"?[6]

**CINDY:** That's a good question, Karen, but once we prove that this is Jehovah's organization, we must not question its doctrines any longer. Jesus told us that we must be "one" even as he and the Father are one,[7] and the apostle Paul exhorted the Corinthian believers to: "all speak in agreement, and that there should not be divisions" so that they would be "united in the same…line of thought."[8] So in order to have unity of thought, we must not question the counsel provided by the organization.

**KAREN:** Cindy, is unity the same thing as uniformity or is there a difference?

---

[3] *The Watchtower,* January 15, 1961, p. 64
[4] *The Watchtower,* November 1, 1956, p. 648
[5] *The Watchtower,* January 15, 1983, pp. 22, 27
[6] 1 Thessalonians 5:21, *New World Translation*
[7] John 17:21
[8] 1 Corinthians 1:10, *New World Translation Bible*

**CINDY:** What do you mean by "is there a difference" between unity and uniformity? Aren't they the same thing, Karen?

**KAREN:** Not exactly, Cindy. Let me explain. Notice that in the passage you referenced, 1 Corinthians 1:10, Paul does not tell the believes to have uniformity of belief, but rather, as he put it, to be: "united in the **same**...**line of** thought." Do you think it is possible for a group of people to be "united in the same...line of thought" without having absolute uniformity in beliefs? For example, Cindy, suppose you and your husband were to have a disagreement on whether you should eat apples for breakfast. Now the Bible says that husbands and wives, by being united in marriage, are as "one," but does this mean that you are required to like apples as much as your husband does?

**CINDY:** Of course, not, Karen. I'm in unity with my husband, but that doesn't mean that we do not have our differences of opinion on certain issues. He may like certain kinds of food or clothing that I'm not particularly fond of, but that doesn't affect our relationship. We exercise unity in our marriage by working together in spite of our differences. When an issue comes up that we don't see eye to eye on, I defer to his leadership and support him in his decision, even if I disagree with his viewpoint. Is this what you mean by the difference between unity and uniformity?

**KAREN:** Yes, Cindy, that's exactly what I'm talking about. What you just described about your relationship with your husband, is a beautiful picture of what being "one" in unity is all about. While uniformity requires absolute conformity in every aspect of life and thought; unity, on the other hand, is more concerned about working together in the midst of diversity. Given the context of the passage in which the Corinthian believers were so divided that they could not work together, can you see why Paul exhorted the believers to lay aside their differences in order to unite for the cause of the Kingdom?

**CINDY:** Yes, I see your point, Karen, but I don't understand how Christians can work together in unity if they disagree on spiritual issues?

**KAREN:** Cindy, do you remember how the Corinthian believers had a dispute over whether a Christian should be allowed to eat meat that was offered in sacrifice to idols? What was Paul's advice to the believers? Did he make the eating of idolatrous meat used in false worship a disfellowshipping offense?

**CINDY:** No, he didn't, Karen. In fact at 1 Corinthians chapters 8 and 10, Paul seemed to be more concerned about offending the conscience of a weak brother, than he was about settling the dispute by an organizational policy.

**KAREN:** You are right, Cindy, and look at how Paul addressed this issue at Romans 14:1-3: "Now accept the one who is weak in faith, but not for the purpose of passing judgment on his opinion. One man has faith that he may eat all things, but he who is weak eats vegetables only. Let not him who eats regard with contempt him who does not eat, and let not him who does not eat judge him who eats, for God has accepted him."[9] Did you

[9] *New American Standard Bible*

notice, Cindy, how Paul specifically told the Christians not to judge a brother who has a different opinion on an issue?

**CINDY:** Yes, that's a good point. Oh, and look at verse five! It says: "One [man] judges one day as above another, another [man] judges one day as all others, let each [man] be fully convinced in his own mind."[10] Is this saying that Christians have the freedom to disagree on what days to regard as holy?

**KAREN:** That's right, Cindy. Some of the believers observed all of the Jewish holidays and others didn't. Paul's response to this was to "let each [man] be fully convinced in his own mind." Can you see how, far from enforcing organizational conformity to a uniform system of beliefs, true Christianity allows for freedom on peripheral issues as long as there is unity on the central teachings pertaining to the Kingdom?

**CINDY:** Yes, I see your point, Karen.

**KAREN:** Since the Watchtower organization does not allow for freedom in disagreeing with any of its doctrines and policies, can you see why my mom is concerned that the Watchtower organization is a cult?

**CINDY:** I can see why she'd be concerned, Karen, but I wouldn't be so quick to view Jehovah's Witnesses as a cult. There are many other points the Society examined in that 1994 Watchtower article. Could we discuss the others next week?

**KAREN:** Sure, Cindy. I'll be here.

**COMMENTS:**

*Friends, Colossians 2:16-17 warns: "Therefore do not let anyone judge you by what you eat or drink, or with regard to a religious festival, a New Moon celebration or a Sabbath day. These are a shadow of the things that were to come; the reality, however, is found in Christ."*[11]

---

[10] *New World Translation*

[11] *New International Version*

## *DIALOGUE THREE: Is The Watchtower Organization A Cult? —Part II*

(CONTINUED FROM THE PREVIOUS DIALOGUE)

**CINDY:** Karen, last week, you mentioned that your mom is concerned about the fact that you are studying with Jehovah's Witnesses because she is afraid that the Watchtower organization is a cult. I showed you the February 15, 1994 issue of *The Watchtower* in which the Society describes what cults are and proves that Jehovah's Witnesses are not a cult.

**KAREN:** Yes, Cindy. You had brought up the fact that the Society states: "Cult leaders are known to use manipulative methods to control the minds of their followers"[1] and we had discussed how even though the Watchtower denies using manipulative methods to control the minds of their followers, they control what Jehovah's Witnesses think and believe by claiming that "independent thinking is evidence of pride."[2] I had asked, if personal judgment of determining Scriptural truth is viewed as pride against God, how can this **not** be a means of controlling what people believe?

**CINDY:** Yes, Karen. Last week we had a good discussion on that, but there are other issues in this *Watchtower* article that we still need to cover. One of them is found here on pages 4 and 7. The Society states: "Many of these cultic groups actually isolate themselves in communes. Their devotion to a self-proclaimed human leader is likely to be unconditional and exclusive. Often these leaders boast of having been **divinely chosen**... Is there evidence that Jehovah's Witnesses do this?... It is precisely because of this close adherence to Bible teachings that the veneration and idolization of human leaders so characteristic of cults today is not to be found among Jehovah's Witnesses... They follow Jesus Christ as their Leader and as Head of the Christian congregation."

**KAREN:** Cindy, is the Society saying that they are not a cult because they teach the Bible and are not "following...a human leader"?

**CINDY:** That's right, Karen. While cults often follow the teachings of a man, Jehovah's Witnesses do not look to a human to lead them, but rather to Jesus Christ.

**KAREN:** Cindy, does the Watchtower Society discourage Jehovah's Witnesses from reading and studying the Bible apart from their literature?

**CINDY:** Well, yes, Karen, they do. The Society says: "...the Bible is an organizational book and belongs to the Christian congregation as an organization, not to individuals, regardless of how sincerely they may believe that they can interpret the Bible. For this reason the Bible cannot be properly understood without Jehovah's visible organization in mind."[3]

---

[1] *The Watchtower,* February 15, 1994 p. 4

[2] *The Watchtower,* January 15, 1983 pp. 22, 27

**KAREN:** Cindy, why does the Watchtower teach that Christians cannot understand the Bible apart from their literature?

**CINDY:** Well, it's because the Society says that: "We all need help to understand the Bible, and we cannot find the Scriptural guidance we need outside the 'faithful and discreet slave' organization."[4] You see, Karen, the Watchtower leadership of Jehovah's Witnesses is not just some ordinary group of men who study the Bible. Back in 1914 when "Jesus Christ was enthroned in heaven" the Society says: "Jehovah poured out his spirit upon them and assigned them the responsibility of serving as his **sole visible channel**, through whom **alone** spiritual instruction was to come."[5]

**KAREN:** That's very interesting, Cindy. Is the Watchtower teaching that the leadership of their organization was "appointed" by God to serve as His only "visible channel" of "spiritual instruction"?

**CINDY:** Why, yes, Karen. The Society claims that the facts prove that: "...Jehovah's organization must henceforth be **guided** and directed by Jehovah's spirit **through** the visible governing body made up of those servants whom Jehovah himself would **appoint**."[6]

**KAREN:** Cindy, how is this any different from cults whose "leaders boast of having been divinely chosen" and whose leaders require "exclusive" devotion to their teachings?

**CINDY:** I - I don't know, Karen, but doesn't the Bible teach in Matthew 24, that Jehovah would appoint a "faithful and discreet slave" organization to give His people spiritual "food at the proper time"?

**KAREN:** Cindy, if you look at the context of these verses here in Matthew 24, you will see that this passage is not talking about an organization being setup to dispense spiritual food, but rather, it is talking about every individual Christian who is faithful in sharing the Word of God to the people God has placed in his life. It is because of their service, that in the last days Jesus will call them "faithful servants" of His kingdom and give them more responsibility. But do you see anything in this passage that suggests that these believers belong to an organization that requires of its followers "exclusive devotion" to its teachings?

**CINDY:** Well, no, Karen, but what about the story of Philip and the Ethiopian eunuch at Acts 8? Why would Jehovah send Philip to teach the Bible to the eunuch if he didn't need help in understanding the Bible?

**KAREN:** Cindy, was the eunuch a Christian at the time when Philip went to teach him the Bible?

---

[3] *The Watchtower,* October 1, 1967, p. 587

[4] *The Watchtower,* February 15, 1981, p. 19

[5] *The Watchtower,* October 1, 1967, p. 590

[6] *The Watchtower,* June 1, 1965, p. 352

**CINDY:** No, Karen, but what difference does that make?

**KAREN:** It makes a **big** difference when you consider the fact that according to the Bible, a person receives the spiritual guidance of the Holy Spirit only **after** he accepts Christ. Of course, the eunuch at Acts 8 needed help in understanding the Bible because he was not a Christian yet. But notice, Cindy, after Philip baptized the eunuch, what does the Bible say happened to the eunuch?

**CINDY:** In Acts 8:39, it says: "When they had come up out of the water, Jehovah's spirit quickly led Philip away, and the eunuch did not see him anymore…"

**KAREN:** Cindy, if true Christians need someone other than God's Holy Spirit to teach them the Bible, why did God choose to leave the eunuch all alone without his teacher after he became a follower of Jesus Christ?

**CINDY:** I don't know, Karen. That's a good question.

**KAREN:** Cindy, did you notice the statement the Society made regarding the members of cults described on page 3 of this issue of *The Watchtower*? They said: "Significantly, most of these people claimed to be Christians and professed belief in the Bible."[7] Since cults often claim that their teachings are from the Bible, how do we know that the Watchtower organization is not a cult when it requires exclusive devotion to the teachings of its leaders who also claim to have been "divinely chosen" by Jehovah God?

**CINDY:** I don't know, Karen, but the Society did bring up a good point when they said: "Cult members often isolate themselves from family, friends, and even society in general. Is that the case with Jehovah's Witnesses?…they do not live in communes, isolating themselves from relatives and others."[8]

**KAREN:** Cindy, didn't you tell me that your mom left the Watchtower organization several years ago? When was the last time she was able to see her grandchildren?

**CINDY:** You're right, Karen. I haven't talked to my mom since she left the organization ten years ago, but the reason Jehovah's Witnesses do not associate with worldly friends and relatives is because the Bible warns that "bad associations spoil useful habits."[9] This is also the reason why new people who come into the organization leave their worldly friends and seek to develop new friendships among Jehovah's Witnesses. It's because Jehovah wants His people to be clean and the way to do that is by being separate from the world.

**KAREN:** So let me sum this up, Cindy. First, the Watchtower Society claims that Jehovah's Witnesses are not a cult because they do not use "manipulative methods to control the minds of their followers," but then we discovered that the Society controls everything

---

[7] *The Watchtower,* February 15, 1994, p. 3
[8] *The Watchtower,* February 15, 1994, p. 6
[9] 1 Corinthians 15:33, *New World Translation*

Jehovah's Witnesses believe on spiritual matters. Next, the Watchtower denies that they are a cult because they do not follow "a human leader" who claims to be "divinely chosen," but when we examined the Society's publications, we found that the Watchtower leadership is made up of a group of men who claim to be exclusively appointed by Jehovah God as His only "channel of communication" to mankind. And last of all, the Society claims that Jehovah's Witnesses are not a cult because they do not "isolate themselves from friends, family," and "society in general," but then you admitted that Jehovah's Witnesses are not allowed to associate or even communicate with friends and family members who have left the organization, and that they are not allowed to have close friendships with people who are not Jehovah's Witnesses. I'm confused! You tell me Jehovah's Witnesses are not a cult, but they control their followers in many of the ways that regular cults do. What is the difference?

**COMMENTS:**

*Friends, the Bible teaches at 1 John 2:27: "As for you, the anointing you received from him remains in you, and you do not need anyone to teach you. But as his anointing teaches you about all things and as that anointing is real, not counterfeit—just as it has taught you, remain in him."*[10]

[10] *New International Version*

## ***DIALOGUE FOUR: How Close Is The End?***

(WDGR LESSON 8: "Family Life that Pleases God")

*Is the end so close that one should not live a "normal" life? Do Jehovah's Witnesses claim to be inspired prophets? What does the record show? Are Watchtower "speculations" false prophecies?*

**CINDY:** Hello, Karen. How is the baby doing today? Did she get over the cold she had last week?

**KAREN:** Yes, Cindy. She is doing a lot better and seems to be getting over her coughing spells. Do you have any kids?

**CINDY:** No, Karen. Steve and I talked about it when we got married and decided instead to put our Kingdom ministry first. Just like we are studying today in the Watchtower brochure *What Does God Require of Us?,* Jehovah expects parents to: "spend time with their children and study the Bible with them, caring for their spiritual and emotional needs."[1] Since Steve and I pioneer full-time, we don't feel that we can devote the time and energy to rearing children in Jehovah's ways and be able to serve in the ministry as much as we are serving Him now.

**KAREN:** Cindy, why is your time in the Kingdom ministry so important to you, that you and Steve would give up the joy of rearing children in order to spend more time serving in the Watchtower organization?

**CINDY:** Well, Karen. I think the Society said it best when they said in the February 15, 2000 issue of *The Watchtower*: "The people of Noah's day 'took no note,' leading a life centered around their regular routine. In a time of **emergency**, one cannot live a 'normal' life."[2] You see, Karen. We're living in the "last days" of this wicked system of things. In an article entitled "Keep on the Watch," *The Watchtower* of January 15, 2000 said: "The destruction of this system of things will come with striking suddenness... Indeed, it has **never been more urgent** for us to keep on the watch."[3] Just as the Society noted in the August 1, 2000 issue of *The Watchtower*: "While this does not imply that it is wrong to have children today, many Christian couples decline to have children so as to become more fully involved in the **urgent** work that Jehovah has given his people to do. Some couples... have decided to remain childless and consider the possibility of bearing children in Jehovah's righteous new world."[4]

---

[1] *What Does God Require of Us?,* 1996, p. 17
[2] *The Watchtower,* February 15, 2000, p. 6
[3] *The Watchtower,* January 15, 2000 p. 14
[4] *The Watchtower,* August 1, 2000 p. 21

**KAREN:** Cindy, are you saying that the reason you and Steve decided not to have children is because you believe the end is so close that you feel it would be better to give your time to the preaching work in hope that after the battle of Armageddon, you may have children in the new world?

**CINDY:** That's right, Karen. One of the reasons we know the end is so close is because the Society said in *The Watchtower* of January 15, 2000: "It seems that by the year 1935, the general ingathering of the anointed was complete… the number of genuine anointed disciples of Christ is dwindling, though some will evidently **still be on earth** when the great tribulation begins."[5] So you see, Karen, because the Society says that some of these anointed brothers will still be on earth when the tribulation begins, we know that the end **must** occur sometime before all of these brothers die. Since we know that the majority of the youngest members of this anointed class of people will be a hundred years old by the year 2035, Armageddon must be only a few years away.

**KAREN:** So, let me get this straight. Cindy, is the Watchtower Society teaching that the generation of people living since 1935 must not pass away before the end comes?

**CINDY:** Well, I guess that is what they're saying, Karen. I hadn't thought of it in those terms before.

**KAREN:** Wasn't it just a few years ago that the Watchtower stopped teaching that Armageddon would come before the generation of the people living in **1914** would pass away?

**CINDY:** Yes, Karen. The Society taught that for nearly thirty years, but in 1995, they received "new light." In the November 1, 1995 issue of *The Watchtower,* the Society announced that the end could come at any time and should not be counted as a generation of people who started living in 1914.[6]

**KAREN:** So, Cindy, what happened to the "new light"? Are they now speculating that the generation should be counted from 1935 instead of their original date of 1914?

**CINDY:** Well, I guess that's what they're saying.

**KAREN:** Cindy, how is this any different from the speculations the Watchtower made regarding the end occurring in 1914, 1915, 1918, 1925, the 1940's, and 1975?[7] Is this the case in which they hope that if they guess enough times, they'll eventually get it right?

**CINDY:** I don't know, Karen. All I know is that the end is very close. Don't you think we're living in the last days?

---

[5] *The Watchtower,* January 15, 2000 pp. 16, 13

[6] *The Watchtower,* November 1, 1995 pp. 17, 19

[7] *The Time Is At Hand,* 1889, p. 101; *The Time Is At Hand,* 1915ed, p. 101; *The Finished Mystery,* 1915, p. 485; *Millions Now Living Will Never Die,* 1920, pp. 89-90, 97; *The Watchtower,* September 15, 1941, p. 288; *Jehovah's Witnesses—Proclaimers of God's Kingdom,* 1993, p. 633

**KAREN:** Yes, Cindy, but didn't Jesus warn that in the last days: "…false prophets will arise, and will mislead many."?[8] Doesn't Deuteronomy 18:20-22 warn that it only takes **one** false prophecy to make a false prophet? How many times does the Watchtower have to be wrong before people will recognize it is a false prophet?

**CINDY:** Karen, in the Watchtower book *Reasoning from the Scriptures,* the Society says: "Jehovah's Witnesses do not claim to be inspired prophets. They have made mistakes. Like the apostles of Jesus Christ, they have at times had some **wrong expectations**."[9]

**KAREN:** Cindy, what is the difference between a "wrong expectation" and a false prophecy? What causes a prediction to be a "wrong expectation" but not a false prophecy?

**CINDY:** Karen, that is a good question. I guess I'd have to say that the difference is when a prophet claims that his prediction is from Jehovah God and it fails, I guess that would make him a false prophet. But Jehovah's Witnesses are not false prophets because in the March 22, 1993 issue of the *Awake!*, the Watchtower Society said: "Jehovah's Witnesses, in their eagerness for Jesus' second coming, have suggested dates that turned out to be incorrect. Because of this, some have called them false prophets. **Never** in these instances, however, did they presume to originate predictions 'in the **name** of Jehovah.' '"[10]

**KAREN:** Cindy, is the Society saying that they have never claimed that their predictions were "in the name of Jehovah"?

**CINDY:** That's right, Karen. This is why our speculations were only "wrong expectations," not false prophecies!

**KAREN:** Cindy, have you read *The Watchtower* article of March 15, 1972? In that article, under the heading, "What is Required of God's Messenger," the Society said: "Therefore, when it came time for the name of Jehovah and his purposes to be declared to the people, along with God's warning that Christendom is in her 'time of the end,' who qualified to be commissioned?…was there any group on whom Jehovah would be willing to bestow the commission to **speak as a 'prophet' in His name**, as was done toward Ezekiel back there in 613 B.C.E.? What were the qualifications?"[11] Then, in subsequent articles, the Society went on to explain that they fulfilled the qualifications to speak as a prophet in Jehovah's name. Why is the Society being dishonest in their *Awake!* article by claiming that they never spoke in Jehovah's name when the facts prove that they did? Do you really want to give your life to an organization that is a false prophet and lies about its history in order to conceal the evidence?

---

[8] Matthew 24:11, *New American Standard Bible*

[9] *Reasoning from the Scriptures,* 1985, 1989ed, p. 136

[10] *AWAKE!,* March 22, 1993, p. 4

[11] *The Watchtower,* March 15, 1972, p. 189

**COMMENTS:**

*Friends, history reveals that not only has the Watchtower Society of Jehovah's Witnesses falsely prophesied the end on a number of occasions, but at various times throughout their history, the Society has encouraged their members to put off marriage, having children, and even obtaining additional education, simply because they said the end was so close.*[12] *Is it any wonder many Jehovah's Witnesses are leaving the Watchtower to find a real relationship with the living Lord Jesus Christ? Are you tired of serving a counterfeit organization? Jesus says: "Come to Me, all who are weary and heavy-laden, and I will give you rest."*[13]

---

[12] *Face The Facts,* 1938, pp. 46-47, 50; *Salvation,* 1939, p. 325; *Kingdom Ministry,* May 1974, p. 3; *The Watchtower,* March 15, 1969, p. 171

[13] Matthew 11:28, *New American Standard Bible*

## *DIALOGUE FIVE: How Honest Is The Watchtower About Its History? —Part I*

(WDGR LESSON 10: "Practices That God Hates")

*What is the Watchtower's definition of a lie? Has the Society used "theocratic war strategy" in covering-up their history? How well has the Watchtower distanced itself from objects inspired by spiritism?*

**CINDY:** Hello, Karen. Have you had a chance to look over our next lesson in the Watchtower brochure *What Does God Require of Us?*

**KAREN:** Oh, yes, Cindy. I've been reading the lesson on "Practices that God Hates" and I have a question. What do Jehovah's Witnesses teach about lying?

**CINDY:** Well, Karen, just as our last lesson discussed: "God's servants must always speak the truth. Liars will not enter God's Kingdom."[1] And just as we are studying today, "Jehovah God cannot lie....Persons who want his approval **must** avoid lying."[2]

**KAREN:** I agree with that, Cindy, but what would you do if you found out that someone you love had lied to you? Would you be able to trust what that person tells you in the future?

**CINDY:** Well, I'm not sure I would Karen, but why are you asking me this?

**KAREN:** Cindy, if you knew that the Watchtower Society has lied to Jehovah's Witnesses by covering-up their history, would you want to know about it?

**CINDY:** Oh, Karen, you've got to be very careful about what you read. Apostates write all kinds of bad things about the Watchtower because they're bitter about some experience they had in the organization. Remember, Satan will use anything he can to try to get you to stop studying about Jehovah. The Watchtower is our "Mother."[3] Apostates write those things to hurt us. How would you feel if someone wrote bad things about your mother? Wouldn't you be hurt too?

**KAREN:** Cindy, if your mother had cancer, would you want her to be honest with you even though you know the truth would hurt, or would you want her to cover it up and make excuses for it?

**CINDY:** Well, I guess I would want to know, but I don't want to read anything from apostates.

**KAREN:** We're not reading anything from apostates. Let's just look at some of your own Watchtower literature and you can be the judge.

---

[1] *What Does God Require of Us?,* 1996, p. 19:6
[2] *What Does God Require of Us?,* p. 20:3
[3] *The Watchtower,* May 1, 1957, p. 274

**CINDY:** OK.

**KAREN:** Cindy, do you remember the history book that the Watchtower Society published in 1959 called, *Jehovah's Witnesses in the Divine Purpose?* Would you read this statement about Charles Russell here on page 63?

**CINDY:** "But, is it true you have **never** published a biography of Pastor Russell? **That's right**. Jehovah's Witnesses admire the qualities he possessed as a man, but were we to give the honor and credit to Pastor Russell, we would be saying that the works and success were his…"

**KAREN:** Is the Society saying that they "**never**" published a biography of Pastor Russell because they didn't want to give "honor and credit" to him?

**CINDY:** Yes, Karen, that is what they're saying.

**KAREN:** Do you remember how Charles Russell, founder of the Watchtower organization, wrote several books which the Society published as a series called, *Studies in the Scriptures*? This book I have here is a 1925 edition of the first book in that series called, *The Divine Plan of the Ages*. As you can see in this 1925 edition, the first thirty pages of this book contain a written "Biography of Pastor Russell."

**CINDY:** That's interesting, but I was reading the Society's **new** history book *Jehovah's Witnesses—Proclaimers of God's Kingdom* published in 1993, and the Society **now** admits on page 64: "A brief biography of Russell along with his will and testament was published in *The Watch Tower* of December 1, 1916, as well as in subsequent editions of the first volume of *Studies in the Scriptures.*" So as you can see, Karen, the Society **now** admits that they did publish a biography of Russell.

**KAREN:** Cindy, why do you think the Society lied about the biography for over thirty years?

**CINDY:** I don't know, but I'm just glad they are honest about it now.

**KAREN:** Cindy, besides the first volume of *Studies in the Scriptures*, where else does the Society say they published the biography?

**CINDY:** Well, they say it was also published in the December 1, 1916 issue of *The Watch Tower.*

**KAREN:** That's right, Cindy. I have here the December 1, 1916 issue of *The Watch Tower* that as you can see contains the biography of Russell. Would you read this statement here on page 377 under "A Personal Tribute to the Pastor"?

**CINDY:** Alright. "Truly these words fittingly apply to our beloved Brother and Pastor! Charles Taze Russell, thou hast, by the Lord, been crowned a king; and through the everlasting ages thy name shall be known amongst the people, and thy enemies shall come and

**worship** at thy feet." **WHAT?** They told the people to "worship" Russell? No way! I can't believe this!

**KAREN:** Cindy, you are holding the article. As you can see, nobody made this up. Even though it was the December 1, 1916 issue of *The Watch Tower* and not the biography that actually told the people to "worship" Russell, it was the biography along with the Watchtower literature at that time, that promoted the false worship of Russell. Is it any wonder that in their history book, the Society lied about the biography for over thirty years? Since God is the God of Truth, how could He be behind an organization that promoted false worship of a man and lied about it in order to cover-up the evidence? Since the Society is still trying to make excuses for the false worship of Russell in their history, how can we trust this organization to teach us the truth?

**CINDY:** I don't know, Karen.

**KAREN:** Cindy, do you know what the Watchtower definition of a lie is?

**CINDY:** No. What is it?

**KAREN:** Under the heading "Lie" in *Insight on the Scriptures,* volume 2, pages 244-245, the Society states: "Lying generally involves saying something false to a person who is **entitled** to know the truth....While malicious lying is definitely condemned in the Bible, this does **not** mean that a person is under obligation to divulge truthful information to people who are not **entitled** to it."

**COMMENTS:**

*Friends, are you "entitled to know the truth"? Jesus said: "I am the way, **the Truth**, and the Life. No one comes to the Father but through Me."[4] Instead of trusting a dishonest organization to tell you the truth, why not place your complete trust in the One who is "**the truth**"—Jesus Himself.*

[4] John 14:6, *New International Version*

## *DIALOGUE FIVE: How Honest Is The Watchtower About Its History? —Part II*

(CONTINUED FROM THE PREVIOUS DIALOGUE)

**KAREN:** Cindy, I've been thinking about the lesson we studied last week in the Watchtower brochure *What Does God Require of Us?*. In that lesson on "Practices That God Hates," we had studied that not only does God hate lying, but He wants us to avoid "spiritism." Since "the power behind all these practices is Satan,"[1] wouldn't you agree that Christians should also stay away from any objects that have been inspired through spiritism?

**CINDY:** Oh, yes, Karen. In the Watchtower book *Knowledge That Leads to Everlasting Life* the Society warns us that: "Even if you have not practiced spiritism, get rid of anything having spiritistic uses or overtones. This includes books, magazines, videos, posters, musical recordings, and objects used for spiritistic purposes."[2]

**KAREN:** Cindy, have you heard of the book called, *Angels and Women*?

**CINDY:** No, Karen, I can't say that I have. Why should I be familiar with it?

**KAREN:** I would think you would want to be familiar with this book because the Watchtower Society gave a "Review of the Book" in one of their articles and encouraged Jehovah's Witnesses to purchase the book. On page 702 of the July 30, 1924 issue of *The Golden Age*, the Society wrote: " 'Angels and Women' is the title of a book just off the press... The book is revised and published by a personal friend of Pastor Russell, and one who was close to him in his work... The publishers advise that the regular price of this book is $2.00; but to all subscribers of The Golden Age, it will be furnished at $1.00 per volume, when ordered in lots of ten or more."

**CINDY:** So, the Society encouraged Jehovah's Witnesses to purchase several copies of this book as they could get it at a discount, but why are you concerned about it?

**KAREN:** Cindy, why don't you read this section of the foreword found on page 5 of *Angels and Women,* and you'll see why.

**CINDY:** "The reviser of this book is of the opinion that the original manuscript was **dictated** to the woman who wrote it **by one of the fallen angels** who desired to return to divine favor."[3]

**KAREN:** Cindy, is this book *Angels and Women* admitting that it was dictated by a demon?

---

[1] *What Does God Require of Us?,* 1996, p. 21:5

[2] *Knowledge That Leads to Everlasting Life,* pp. 114-115

[3] *Angels and Women, A Revision of the Unique Novel Seola,* by Mrs. J.G. Smith, 1924, p. 5

**CINDY:** It sure looks that way, but did the Society know that this book was dictated by a demon when they encouraged Jehovah's Witnesses to purchase it?

**KAREN:** How could they **not** have known, Cindy, when the book had been read by Charles Russell who was the founder of the Watchtower organization and had been revised and re-published by one of his personal friends? After all, even the foreword in the book admits that it had been dictated by a demon.[4]

**CINDY:** That's a good point, Karen. I must admit, this information does concern me. How can an organization that is so concerned about helping people become "servants of God" by loving what is good, justify the promotion of such a book that came from spiritism? Certainly, the Society doesn't do this kind of thing anymore, does it?

**KAREN:** Cindy, I wouldn't be so quick to make that assumption. Under the "Questions from the Readers" section in the April 1, 1983 issue of *The Watchtower,* the question was asked: "Why, in recent years, has *The Watchtower* not made use of the translation by the former Catholic priest, Johannes Greber?" In response, the Society said, "This translation was used occasionally in support of renderings...given in the *New World Translation* and other authoritative Bible versions. But as indicated in a foreword to the 1980 edition of *The New Testament* by Johannes Greber, this translator relied on "God's Spirit world" to clarify for him how he should translate difficult passages... The *Watchtower* has deemed it improper to make use of a translation that has such a close rapport with spiritism."[5] Cindy, is the Society saying that in the past, they used this translation which had been made through the use of spirit-mediums?

**CINDY:** Yes, Karen, but just as they noted in this article, when the 1980 edition of his translation came out with the information that he had relied on the spirit-world to help him, they stopped using it. So, you can see, the Society is **very** careful to avoid spiritism.

**KAREN:** Really, Cindy? Is the Society indicating that that they didn't know about Greber's connection with the spirit-world until the 1980 edition of his translation?

**CINDY:** Well, I don't know, Karen, but it appears that way from this article.

**KAREN:** Cindy, would you read these statements the Society made regarding Johannes Greber found in the February 15, 1956 *Watchtower* article called, "Triumphing Over Wicked Spirit Forces"?

**CINDY:** "Says Johannes Greber in the introduction of his translation of The New Testament, copyrighted in 1937: 'I myself was a Catholic priest, and until I was forty eight years old had never as much as believed in the possibility of communicating with the world of God's spirits. The day came, however, when I involuntarily took my first step toward such communication, and experienced things that shook me to the depths of my

---

[4] See also *The Golden Age,* December 3, 1924, pp. 150-151

[5] *The Watchtower,* April 1, 1983, p. 31

soul… My experiences are related in a book that has appeared in both German and English and bears the title, Communication with the Spirit World: Its Laws and Its Purpose.'…Very plainly **the spirits** in which ex-priest Greber believes **helped him in his translation**."[6] Oh, dear…

**KAREN:** What's wrong, Cindy?

**CINDY:** Well, the Society indicated in their 1983 *Watchtower* that it was the 1980 edition of his translation that contained the information on spiritism, but here we see that as far back as 1956, the Society knew that Greber used the spirit-world to help him.

**KAREN:** That's right, Cindy. I have a copy of the **1937** edition of Greber's translation, and on page 15 of his Introduction, he even said: "In the rare instances in which a text pronounced correct **by the divine spirits** can be found in none of the manuscripts available to-day, I have used the text **as it was given to me by those spirits**." So you can see, the Society **knew** of Greber's use of the spirit-world in his translation **long** before the 1980 edition, and yet they quoted him for over twenty years![7] How could they do this and be God's organization? Would Jehovah really be behind an organization that throughout various periods of its history has knowingly used material from the spirit-world?

**COMMENTS:**

*Friends, at Deuteronomy 18:10-12, God warns: "There should not be found in you anyone who employs divination…or anyone who consults a spirit medium…or anyone who inquires of the dead. For everybody doing these things is something detestable to Jehovah."[8] Instead of putting your trust in an organization of men who at times seek the darkness, why not put your trust in the One who is the "Light." Jesus said: "I have come as light into the world, that everyone who believes in Me may not remain in darkness."[9]*

---

[6] *The Watchtower,* February 15, 1956, pp. 110-111

[7] See *"The Word"—Who Is He? According To John,* 1962, p. 5; *The Watchtower,* September 15, 1962, p 554; *"Make Sure of All Things—Hold Fast To What Is Fine",* 1965, p. 489; *Aid to Bible Understanding,* 1971, pp. 1134, 1669; *The Watchtower,* October 15, 1975, p. 640; *The Watchtower,* April 15, 1976, p. 231

[8] *New World Translation*

[9] John 12:46, *New American Standard Bible*

## *DIALOGUE SIX: How Can You Find The True Religion?*

(WDGR LESSON 13: "How Can You Find the True Religion?")

*How valid is the Watchtower's test for finding the "one" true religion? Are Jehovah's Witnesses the only individuals that fulfill the Watchtower's criteria of being "in the truth"?*[1] *What test does the Bible give for determining "the truth"?*

**CINDY:** Karen, have you ever wondered why there are so many religions that claim to be Christian? Do you believe that all religions please God, or is there just one? What are your thoughts on true religion?

**KAREN:** Well, Cindy, when I think about the religions of the world, I think about Jesus' words at John 14:6 in which He said "I am the way, and **the truth**, and the life; **no one** comes to the Father but **through** Me." Jesus said we have to come to Him in order to get to the Father. So I believe that all religions that teach that a person can go to Jehovah God without first going to Jesus are counterfeit and are leading people astray.

**CINDY:** That's right, Karen. Just as we'll be studying today in the Watchtower brochure *What Does God Require of Us?* "Jesus started one true Christian religion. So today there must be just one body, or group, of true worshipers of Jehovah God."[2] Would you like to find out how you can be in the truth by finding the true religion?

**KAREN:** Yes, Cindy, I would.

**CINDY:** That's great, Karen. At John 13:34-35 Jesus said that his true disciples have love for one another. "The most outstanding mark of true Christians is that they have real *love among themselves.* ...They are not taught...to hate people from other countries. ...So they do not share in wars. ...Another mark of true religion is that its members have a *deep respect for the Bible.* ...They treat God's Word as being more important than human ideas or customs."[3] Because they follow the Bible, they do not accept human ideas such as the Trinity and hell doctrines; nor do they participate in pagan customs such as Christmas and Easter. "The true religion must also *honor God's name.* Who are the people in your community that tell others about God's name?"[4]

**KAREN:** Cindy, are you familiar with the religion called the "Assemblies of Yahweh" located in Bethel, Pennsylvania? The *Encyclopedia of American Religions* notes that: "The Assemblies teaches the necessity of believers' affirming the divine names Yahweh and

---

[1] In this dialogue, Karen does not attempt to refute the false doctrines of the Jehovah's Witnesses belief system that comprise their claim to be the one and only "true religion." Rather, the point of this discussion is to prove that "the truth" claims of the Jehovah's Witness religion are not unique to them. Thus, since other religions claim to adhere to the same "truth" criteria used by the Jehovah's Witnesses, they cannot possibly be "the only true religion" and their "truth" criteria is now open to debate.

[2] *What Does God Require of Us?,* 1996, p. 26:1

[3] *What Does God Require of Us?,* p. 26:3-4

[4] *What Does God Require of Us?,* p. 26:5

Yahshua." So important to this group is the revealing of God's name that: "the Assemblies…publishes its own version of the Sacred Scriptures."[5]

**CINDY:** That's interesting, Karen, but does this group teach the false doctrine of the Trinity and allow its members to go to war?

**KAREN:** Oh, no, Cindy. The *Encyclopedia of American Religions* notes that in the Assemblies of Yahweh, "a non-Trinitarian position is maintained" and "nonviolence and conscientious objection to war are **stressed**."[6]

**CINDY:** Wow! I never knew that, Karen.

**KAREN:** Cindy, this is not the only religion which exalts the name of God. Many other religions such as the Assemblies of the Called out Ones of Ya, House of Yahweh, and the Assembly of YHWHHoshua proclaim God's name.[7] In fact, so important is God's name to people in these groups that many times these religions are **more particular** about God's name than even the Jehovah's Witnesses are! For example, the doctrinal statement that every person in the Assembly of YHWHHoshua is required to believe states: "The true revealed Name of the Almighty is YHWH.…It is quite clear…that His NAME is not to be changed. In the King James (KJV) and other versions of the bible; translators have mistranslated the Divine Name, YHWH, into the word 'LORD'; and 'GOD'.…In their former languages, the title 'LORD' is 'BAAL', which is the supreme idol of heathen Babylon. 'ADONIS', 'ADONAI', or 'ADON' are the Phoenician and Greek idol of beauty from whence comes the name 'JEHOVAH'…."[8] Cindy, do you realize that if a Witness were to use the name "Jehovah" within this religion, he would be condemned for using an erroneous pronunciation of God's name that came from Greek and Phoenician false religion? Since Jehovah's Witnesses exult a name for God that was derived from false religion, how can the Jehovah's Witness religion be the one true religion, when other groups are far more careful about God's Name?

**CINDY:** I'm not sure, Karen. But do these groups celebrate the pagan holidays of Christmas and Easter?

**KAREN:** Oh, no, Cindy, many of them do not. Concerning the House of Yahweh, the *Encyclopedia of American Religions* notes that "holidays such as Christmas, Easter, Halloween…are condemned as **pagan** and un-Biblical. Yahshua was born in the spring (around Passover), not in December."[9] Cindy, doesn't this sound like something the Watchtower Society could have written? Since these groups believe the same things that Jehovah's Witnesses teach about war, holidays, and God's name, does this mean that they are "in the truth"?

---

[5] *Encyclopedia of American Religions,* 5th Edition, by J. Gordon Melton, 1996, p. 529

[6] *Encyclopedia of American Religions,* p. 529

[7] See *Encyclopedia of American Religions,* pp. 528, 531; *Encyclopedia of American Religions: Religious Creeds,* vol. II, (Gale Research Company), p. 398

[8] *Encyclopedia of American Religions: Religious Creeds,* vol. II, p. 398

[9] *Encyclopedia of American Religions,* p. 986

**CINDY:** Well, I'm not sure, Karen, but do they preach about the Kingdom? "True Christians must *preach about God's Kingdom....*that only God's Kingdom will bring true peace and security to this earth."[10] Do those groups you mentioned preach that God's Kingdom on earth is the only hope for mankind?

**KAREN:** Yes, they do, Cindy. Listen to this statement about the Christadelphians found in *The New Schaff-Herzog Encyclopedia of Religious Knowledge.* "Christadelphians **reject** the **Trinity**. They believe in one supreme God....in Jesus Christ...who died for the offenses of sinners. ...in one eternal punishment of the wicked, but not in eternal torment; in hell, **not** as a place of torment, but as the **grave**; in the resurrection of the just and unjust; in the utter **annihilation** of the wicked. ...in a second coming of Christ to establish his **kingdom on earth**, which is to be fitted for the **everlasting** abode of the saints. ...in the millennial reign of Christ on **earth** over the nations..."[11] Since Christadelphians and other religious groups believe in life forever on earth and preach about the Kingdom as the only hope for mankind, does this mean that they are the true religion?

**CINDY:** Well, Karen, maybe they teach the same things about the Kingdom, but do they have an organized preaching work like Jehovah's Witnesses do? I've never seen them go door-to-door.

**KAREN:** Cindy, there are many ways to preach the Kingdom message door-to-door that do not require religious members to knock on the doors of a city. For example, many religious groups take their message door-to-door through radio broadcasts and tracts distributed in public places. Even the Apostle Paul at Acts 17 took the Kingdom message to the people in Thessalonica, Berea, and Athens—not by knocking on the doors of those cities—but by preaching in the temple and public square. If the door-to-door ministry of the Jehovah's Witnesses is the only correct way to preach the Kingdom message, are we to argue that the Apostle Paul was not involved in the preaching work because he failed to knock on the doors of those cities?

**CINDY:** Well, no.

**KAREN:** Then, why do Jehovah's Witnesses argue that other religious groups are not involved in an organized preaching work, simply because they take their message door-to-door in a different way than Jehovah's Witnesses do?

**CINDY:** That's a good point, Karen. But many religions get involved in politics. Jesus said that his: "disciples must be *no part of this wicked world....*They do not get involved in the world's political affairs and social controversies.... Can you identify a religious group in your community that has these marks of true Christianity?"[12]

---

[10] *What Does God Require of Us?,* p. 27:5

[11] *The New Schaff-Herzog Encyclopedia of Religious Knowledge,* vol. III, p. 38; See also *Oxford Dictionary of World Religions,* John Bowker, ed. (Oxford, NY: Oxford University Press, 1997), p. 216

[12] *What Does God Require of Us?,* p. 27:7

**KAREN:** Cindy, the Jehovah's Witness religion isn't the only religion that doesn't get involved in politics. The Christadelphian religion does not take part "in politics, voting, or military service," and the doctrinal statement of the Assembly of YHWHHoshua states that: "The members of the assembly of YHWHHoshua are to be separate from the institutions, customs, traditions, styles and carnal pleasures of... the world. ...YHWHHoshua is our government. ...In no way should we participate in the charities of the world, for these charities are not for YHWH'S people. Thus a servant of YHWH can not vote or contribute to or accept any benefits from the institutions of the United States, such as Social Security, Medicare, unemployment Compensation, etc. ...nor shall he be allowed to be a government official, to be a juror, or to serve in the Armed Forces."[13] Cindy, do Jehovah's Witnesses accept government aid or any benefits from Social Security, Medicare, or Unemployment Compensation?

**CINDY:** Well, yes, Karen they do.

**KAREN:** Since Jesus said His followers are to be separate from the world, why do Jehovah's Witnesses participate in this worldly system by receiving aid from governmental and social institutions? It sure looks like the Assembly of YHWHHoshua is far more neutral and non-political than the Jehovah's Witnesses religion is. Doesn't this prove that the Jehovah's Witnesses cannot possibly be the only true religion? How can Jehovah's Witnesses claim that they are the **only** ones with "the truth" when other groups believe and practice the **exact** same things that Jehovah's Witnesses believe?

**CINDY:** Well, I'm not sure Karen, but if Jehovah's Witnesses aren't "in the truth," then who do you think is?

**KAREN:** Cindy, have you noticed how a person can do all the right things and believe all the right doctrines,[14] but not know God personally? On the outside, that person may appear to be perfectly happy in his religion, but inwardly, there is a gnawing sense of uneasiness that he is not in the truth. Cindy, I believe this is because the Bible reveals that there is only **one** test we should use to determine if we are "in the Truth." 2 Corinthians 13:5 states: "Examine yourselves to see whether you are in the faith; test yourselves. Do you not realize that Christ Jesus is in you—unless, of course, you fail the test?"[15]

---

[13] *Encyclopedia of American Religions: Religious Creeds,* vol. II, p. 399

[14] By talking as if the Jehovah's Witnesses "believe all the right doctrines," Karen is NOT saying that the doctrines of Jehovah's Witnesses are Biblical or that Christians agree with their doctrines. Rather, she is making the point that no matter what a person believes, even if it is all correct, this does not prove that this person is "in the truth."

[15] *New International Version*

**COMMENTS:**

*Friends, when it comes to eternity, the only question Jehovah God will ask you is: "What did you do with My Son Jesus?" Just as Jesus said: "I am...**the truth** and the life" so 1 John 5:11-12 states: "And the witness is this, that God has given us eternal life, and this life is **in** His Son. He who **has the Son** has the life; he **who does not have the Son** of God does not have the life."[16] Have you come into the **truth** by asking Jesus to give you His righteousness in exchange for your sin?*

[16] *New American Standard Bible*

## *DIALOGUE SEVEN: Who Is The "Faithful And Discreet Slave"? —Part I*

(WDGR LESSON 14: "How Jehovah's Witnesses are Organized")

*Does Jehovah God lead His people through an organization? What does history reveal? Does the Watchtower's "Governing Body" arrangement follow first-century Christianity?*

**KAREN:** Cindy, as we've been studying in the Watchtower brochure *What Does God Require of Us?,* I've noticed that often the interpretation that the Watchtower gives for certain Bible verses is different than the interpretation I've heard in other Christian groups. Since there are so many ways to interpret the Bible, how can I determine which interpretation I should trust? How do I know that I should trust the Watchtower's interpretation over what I've heard in other Christian religions?

**CINDY:** Well, Karen, just as this brochure notes: "The Bible foretold that after the death of the apostles, wrong teachings and unchristian practices would slowly come into the Christian congregation. Men would draw away believers to follow them instead of Christ. ...That is why we see so many different religions that claim to be Christian."[1] But the Watchtower book *Knowledge that Leads to Everlasting Life* explains that while: "religion has left multitudes starving for wholesome spiritual food, spiritually speaking, however, Jehovah God is now furnishing food, clothing, and shelter."[2] How do you think Jehovah is doing this, Karen?

**KAREN:** I'm not sure, Cindy. Didn't Jesus say that He would be with Christians forever?[3] And didn't He say at Matthew 16:18, that He would build His church, "and the gates of Hades would not overpower it"?[4] If the Christian congregation has become so apostate that it has stopped giving spiritual food at the proper time, why does the Bible say at Ephesians 3:21: "To Him be the **glory** in the church...to **all** generations forever and ever"?[5]

**CINDY:** You're right, Karen. Even though Christendom as a whole has become apostate, Jehovah has always had His true followers on the earth. For example, the Watchtower *Knowledge* book explains how: "...the Israelites were 'Jehovah's congregation' for some 1,500 years. ...In the first century C.E. Jehovah brought forth the Christian organization. Congregations were formed, and they functioned under the direction of a governing body made up of apostles and older men. ...Likewise today, Jehovah deals with his people through an organized body. ...Jesus said that at the time of his presence in Kingdom power, 'the faithful and discreet slave' would be found providing 'food at

---

[1] *What Does God Require of Us?,* 1996, p. 26:2

[2] *Knowledge That Leads to Eternal Life,* 1995, p. 160:2

[3] Matthew 18:20

[4] Matthew 16:18, *New American Standard Bible*

[5] *New American Standard Bible*

the proper time' for His followers. …When Jesus was installed as heavenly king in 1914, who did this 'slave' prove to be?"[6]

**KAREN:** Cindy, is the Society saying that in 1914, Jesus appointed them to be the faithful slave that would provide spiritual "food at the proper time" to Jehovah's people?

**CINDY:** That's right, Karen. Just as we are studying today in the Watchtower brochure, *What Does God Require of Us?,* "Jehovah's Witnesses had their modern-day start in the 1870's. …From small beginnings the organization has grown to millions of Witnesses, who are busy preaching in more than 230 lands."[7] Don't you think this is evidence that the Watchtower organization is God's organization?

**KAREN:** Cindy, did you know that evangelical Christian ministries network across denominational lines in sending missionaries to literally hundreds of countries throughout the world? If the fact that 6 million Jehovah's Witnesses preach in over 230 countries is to be viewed as evidence that they are God's organization, then wouldn't we also have to admit that Christendom is being used of Jehovah because they are preaching in even more countries than Jehovah's Witnesses are?

**CINDY:** Well, no, Karen, not every religion that claims to be Christian has a form of worship that is acceptable to Jehovah. The June 1, 2001 issue of *The Watchtower* notes that the fact "that Jehovah's Witnesses are stronger and more active now than ever before—and this in the face of worldwide opposition—is proof that Jehovah finds pleasure in what they are doing."[8] You see, Karen, "Jesus forewarned his followers: 'If they have persecuted me, they will persecute you also.' …Ask yourself, 'What religious group is noted for sticking closely to God's Word, even when its teachings differ from the beliefs of most people?…And despite all of these positive things, who are still looked down on, ridiculed, and persecuted?' "[9]

**KAREN:** Cindy, the June 4th, 2001 issue of the *Mission Network News* reported that "local authorities in three Mexican states have told evangelical Christians to **change their religion** or suffer severe consequences. Many of the religious conflicts in Mexico stem from evangelicals' **refusal** to participate in town festivals" because they "usually include activities that evangelicals find unacceptable." The report went on to note that despite religious persecution, "evangelicals in Mexico presently number approximately **4.6 million**" with "some **120,000**" currently undergoing persecution in some form or another. And Mexico isn't the only country where evangelicals are growing despite persecution. *Open Doors International* reports that while in Nigeria: "the Church numbers more than **50 million**. …churches have been the target of the Muslim community with many martyrs over the past 18 years. Between 1982 and 1996 alone some **600 Christians** were **killed** and 200 churches burned." The same is true for Indonesia where: "there are now **25 million** Christians and it is said to be growing at the rate of **5%** per annum. Riots are the order of the day and many **Christians have**

---

[6] *Knowledge That Leads to Eternal Life,* pp. 160-161
[7] *What Does God Require of Us?,* p. 28:1
[8] *The Watchtower,* June 1, 2001, p. 17
[9] *The Watchtower,* June 1, 2001, p. 15-16

**been targeted**." But "the Church is growing despite persecution." Cindy, if the fact that Jehovah's Witnesses are growing in spite of persecution "is proof that Jehovah finds pleasure in what they are doing," then wouldn't we also have to agree that Jehovah finds pleasure in what evangelical Christians are doing, because they continue to grow in many countries in spite of severe opposition to their faith?

**CINDY:** Well, no, Karen. The Watchtower *Knowledge* book notes that at Matthew 24:45-47: "Jesus said that at the time of his presence in Kingdom power, 'the faithful and discreet slave' would be found providing 'food at the proper time' for His followers. ...When Jesus was installed as heavenly King in 1914, who did this 'slave' prove to be? Certainly not the clergy of Christendom. For the most part, they were feeding their flocks propaganda that backed up their own national governments in World War I."[10]

**KAREN:** Cindy, would you read the statement the Watchtower Society made regarding the time period of World War I, found on page 15 of the June 15, 1987 issue of *The Watchtower*?

**CINDY:** OK. "When 'the true Lord' came to the spiritual temple...shortly after the Kingdom was set up in heaven in 1914, what did Jehovah find?...He found the remnant in need of refining and cleansing. For example, *The Watch Tower* had encouraged its readers to set aside May 30, 1918, as a day of prayer for **victory** for the democratic powers. ...This amounted to a **violation** of Christian neutrality."

**KAREN:** Cindy, what did the Society say Jehovah's Witnesses were doing when Jesus inspected them during World War I?

**CINDY:** Well, it says that they were violating "Christian neutrality" by inciting their brothers to pray for the democratic powers to win World War I, but at least, Karen, they weren't participating in the war effort like Christendom was.

**KAREN:** I wouldn't be so sure about that, Cindy. The February 15, 1996 issue of *The Watchtower* notes that "during the World War I period, the remnant of spiritual Israel had not kept entirely clean and aligned with God's will. Some of them were spotted with **doctrinal errors** and **compromised** by not taking a clear stand for Jehovah when put under pressure to **support** the warring nations."[11] In fact, Cindy, the May 15th and June 1st issues of the 1918 *Watch Tower* encouraged Jehovah's Witnesses to purchase "Liberty Bonds" which aided the country in funding World War I. So how can the Watchtower Society claim that when Jesus inspected them in 1914, they fulfilled the qualifications to be the "faithful and discreet slave" when they, like Christendom, supported the war not only with their prayers but with their finances as well? What's the difference between personally killing people in war and paying someone else to go to war and kill people in your place?

---

[10] *Knowledge That Leads to Eternal Life,* p. 161

[11] *The Watchtower,* February 15, 1996, p. 14

**CINDY:** OK, Karen. So maybe Jehovah's Witnesses weren't as neutral as they should have been in 1914, but at least they had a form of worship that was more acceptable to Jehovah God than other religions of Christendom. For example, they didn't believe in the pagan doctrines of the Trinity, hell fire, and the immortality of the human soul, and they preached the Kingdom and taught that God's name is Jehovah.

**KAREN:** Cindy, the religion of the "Christadelphians" was "founded in America in 1848." So they have been around 30 years longer than Jehovah's Witnesses. They reject the doctrine of the Trinity and immortality of the human soul, have no part in politics and war, and like Jehovah's Witnesses, they preach the Kingdom and have no paid ministers.[12] Not only did Christadelphians exist during the time of Jesus' inspection in 1914, but Advent Christians have been around since 1861 and teach many of the doctrines Jehovah's Witnesses teach regarding the unconscious condition of the dead and the hope of the righteous entering "an endless life upon the earth."[13] Since there were other groups that by these standards would have qualified to be appointed as the faithful slave during Christ's inspection in 1914, how do you know that Jesus chose Jehovah's Witnesses over these other groups? Can you show me one thing that proves Jehovah's Witnesses were more acceptable to Jehovah God than these other groups?

**CINDY:** Well, Karen, unlike the Jehovah's Witnesses, Christadelphians don't believe that Satan is a person and they do not recognize that Christ's presence in Kingdom power began in 1914.[14] The Adventist, on the other hand, recognized Christ's presence, but they miscalculated the time of his presence and taught that it occurred in 1844 instead of 1914.[15] So you see, Karen, Jehovah's Witnesses were the only ones that met the test of being the faithful slave.

**KAREN:** Cindy, you bring up a good point regarding Christadelphians rejecting the personality of Satan, and the Adventist's miscalculation of prophetic dates, but if we are going to compare Christadelphians and Adventists to Jehovah's Witnesses during that time period, we have to consider the fact that Jehovah's Witnesses taught many false doctrines as well—including faulty application of certain dates (such as 1914, 1918, and 1925) and strange interpretation of many of the passages of Revelation and Ezekiel.[16] Not only did Jehovah's Witnesses "go beyond the things that are written"[17] in their inaccurate interpretation of Scripture during that time, but the *1975 Yearbook of Jehovah's Witnesses* admits that during that time "the idea adopted by many was that C.T. Russell himself was the 'faithful and wise servant.' This led some into the snare of **creature worship**."[18] "*The Watch Tower* itself set forth this view for a number of

---

[12] *A Dictionary of Comparative Religion,* edited by SGF Brandon MA DD (NW: Charles Scribner's Sons, 1970), p. 190; *The Oxford Dictionary of World Religions,* edited by John Bowker (Oxford, NY: Oxford University Press, 1997), p. 216

[13] *The New Schaff-Herzog Encyclopedia of Religious Knowledge,* vol. I, (Grand Rapids, MI: Baker Book House, 1967), p. 56

[14] *The New Schaff-Herzog Encyclopedia of Religious Knowledge,* vol. III, p. 38

[15] *The New Schaff-Herzog Encyclopedia of Religious Knowledge,* vol. I, p. 56

[16] See *The Finished Mystery,* 1917, pp. 60, 84-85, 103, 128, 188-189, 230, 485

[17] 1 Corinthians 4:6, *New World Translation*

[18] *1975 Yearbook of Jehovah's Witnesses,* p. 88

years."[19] Cindy, which is worse: An inaccurate view of Satan, or creature worship of a man as the "faithful and discreet slave"?

**CINDY:** I'm not sure, Karen.

**KAREN:** Cindy, at Matthew 24 verses 11 and 23-24, Jesus warns that in the last days, "false prophets will arise" and will proclaim that His Kingdom **presence** began when it hadn't. For **50 years**—from 1879 to 1929—Jehovah's Witnesses proclaimed Christ's presence began in **1874**—not in 1914 like they now teach.[20] Since Jesus warned that false prophets would proclaim a false date for His presence, why would He anoint a group of people to represent Jehovah God that were doing the **very thing** He warned His followers about at Matthew 24?

**CINDY:** That's a good question, Karen. I really don't know.

**KAREN:** Cindy, within that period of 50 years, Jehovah's Witnesses died believing that false date for Christ's presence. What are they going to say when they stand before Jehovah God and He asks them, "Why didn't you heed the words of My Son Jesus at Matthew 24 which warned about false prophets that would proclaim a false date for Christ's presence?"

**CINDY:** I don't know, Karen. But if the Watchtower Society isn't the "faithful and discreet slave," then who do you think is?

**KAREN:** That's a good question, Cindy. Can we talk about that next week?

**CINDY:** Sure, Karen, I'll be here.

---

[19] *Jehovah's Witnesses—Proclaimers of God's Kingdom,* 1993, p. 626

[20] See *Jehovah's Witnesses Proclaimers of God's Kingdom,* 1993, pp. 133-134; *Prophecy,* 1929, p. 65

## *DIALOGUE SEVEN: Who Is The "Faithful And Discreet Slave"? —Part II*

(CONTINUED FROM THE PREVIOUS DIALOGUE)

**CINDY:** Karen, last week in our study of the Watchtower brochure *What Does God Require of Us?,* we discussed Jesus' words at Matthew 24:45-47 where he spoke of a "faithful and discreet slave" which in the last days would be appointed over Jehovah's people, "to give them their food at the proper time."[1] We talked about the fact that just as the Watchtower book *Knowledge That Leads To Everlasting Life* notes: "Throughout history, Jehovah has dispensed spiritual food to his people as a group.... the Israelite priests gathered men, women, and children for group instruction of God's Law" and "under the direction of the governing body" made up of apostles and older men, "first-century Christians organized congregations and held meetings for the instruction and encouragement of all. Jehovah's Witnesses follow this pattern."[2] "The world headquarters of Jehovah's Witnesses is in New York. Located there is the Governing Body, a central group of experienced elders who oversee the worldwide congregation." 3

**KAREN:** Yes, Cindy. We talked about that last week, and we also discussed the fact that at Matthew 24 where Jesus speaks of appointing a "faithful and discreet slave" to give spiritual food to God's people, He warns that in the last days, "false prophets will arise" and will proclaim that His Kingdom presence began when it hadn't. While the Watchtower Society claims that its "governing body" of elders is made up of members of this "faithful and discreet slave" class, for **50 years**—from 1879 to 1929—the Watchtower Society proclaimed Christ's presence began in **1874**—not in **1914** like they now teach.[4] Since Jesus warned that in the last days, **false prophets** would proclaim a **false date** for His presence, last week I had asked, why would He appoint the "governing body" of the Watchtower organization to represent Jehovah God when they were doing the **very thing** He warned His followers about at Matthew 24? How could Jehovah's Witnesses have fulfilled the qualifications to be identified as that "faithful and discreet slave" at Christ's presence in 1914 when they were doing **exactly** what Jesus warned **false prophets** would be doing in the last days?

**CINDY:** I don't know, Karen, but if the Watchtower Society isn't the "faithful and discreet slave," then who do you think is? After all, how can any of the churches of Christendom be the faithful slave when they pass the offering plate at their meetings and their ministers get paid for their work. At Matthew 10:8, Jesus told his disciples, "You received free, give free."[5] In keeping with this principle, "admission" at the meetings of Jehovah's Witnesses "is free, and no collections are taken. ...In each congregation, there are elders, or overseers." While "they take the lead in teaching in

---

[1] *New World Translation*

[2] *Knowledge That Leads To Everlasting Life,* 1995, p. 162

[3] *What Does God Require of Us?,* 1996, p. 29:6

[4] See *Jehovah's Witnesses Proclaimers of God's Kingdom,* 1993, pp. 133-134; *Prophecy,* 1929, p. 65

[5] *New World Translation*

the congregation, ...they do not dress differently from others. Neither are they paid for their work."[6]

**KAREN:** Cindy, do members of the Watchtower "Governing Body" get paid for their work, or do they work other jobs in order to make a living?

**CINDY:** Well, yes, Karen. Members the Governing Body do get paid something for their labor, but it's not very much as it only covers basic needs.

**KAREN:** But, Cindy, how can Jehovah's Witnesses point at the fact that some ministers in Christendom make a living from the ministry when members of the Watchtower "Governing Body" do the same thing? If it is wrong for ministers to be paid from the ministry, why did the apostle Paul receive gifts from the congregation at Philippi,[7] and why did he say at 1 Corinthians 9: "Who plants a vineyard, and does not eat the fruit of it?...If we sowed spiritual things in you, is it too much if we should reap **material** things from you?...Do you not know that those who perform sacred services eat the *food* of the temple?...So also the Lord directed those who **proclaim** the gospel to get their **living from** the gospel."[8] Cindy, while it is true that the good news itself is not to be sold for profit, this doesn't change the fact that at 1 Timothy 5:18, the Bible says, "The laborer is worthy of his wages."[9] Since God says at 1 Corinthians 9:14 that those who proclaim the good news should receive their living from the good news, why doesn't the Watchtower pay their full-time employees a decent wage?

**CINDY:** That's a good question. I don't know, Karen, but most ministers in Christendom are given special titles—like "Reverend" and "Father." At Matthew 23:8-10, Jesus told his followers: "But you, do not you be called Rabbi, for **one is your teacher**, whereas all you are brothers. Moreover, do not call anyone your father on earth, for one is your Father, the heavenly One. Neither be called leaders, for your Leader is one, the Christ."[10] Following this example, Jehovah's Witness elders and overseers "are not elevated above the rest of the congregation" and "they are not given special titles."[11]

**KAREN:** Cindy, please correct me if I'm wrong, but aren't Jehovah's Witnesses taught to look to the "Governing Body" of the Watchtower as their "**teacher**" and the **only channel** through whom spiritual instruction is to be given?[12] Since Jesus said not to call anyone "teacher," how is the Jehovah's Witness view of the Watchtower Society as their "teacher" any different from individuals in Christendom who look to their pastors and priests for spiritual instruction?

**CINDY:** Well, Karen, at Acts 15 when the congregation at Antioch was involved in a dispute, they called upon the "Governing Body" of apostles and elders in Jerusalem to settle it.

---

[6] *What Does God Require of Us?,* p. 28:2; 29:4
[7] See Philippians 4:15-18
[8] 1 Corinthians 9:7, 11, 13-14, *New American Standard Bible*
[9] *New American Standard Bible*
[10] *New World Translation*
[11] *What Does God Require of Us?,* p. 29:4
[12] See *The Watchtower,* October 1, 1967, p. 590

You see, Karen, "Jehovah's Witnesses recognize that arrangement. As was true of first-century Christians, they look to the governing body of that" faithful and discreet " 'slave' class to resolve difficult questions," to direct the worldwide preaching-work, and to "provide spiritual food to those making up the household of faith."[13]

**KAREN:** Cindy, if Jehovah God directs His people through a "faithful and discreet slave" "governing body" of elders, why did the Holy Spirit at Acts 13:2 direct the congregation at **Antioch** to send Paul and Barnabas out on their first missionary journey without **any** approval from a "governing body" in Jerusalem? And who did they report to when they returned from their missionary journey at Acts 14:26-28? Wasn't it the congregation at Antioch? Where is the so-called "governing body" of Jerusalem in all of this?[14] At Acts 15, we read of a dispute at Antioch that was **caused** by certain men who had come **from** Judea—the land of Jerusalem. Is it any wonder they went to Jerusalem to settle the dispute that had been **caused** by men from that area? How does this prove that there was a "governing body" of apostles and elders in Jerusalem that directed the preaching-work of first-century Christians?

**CINDY:** Well, Karen, the Bible reports at Acts 16:4, that as the apostles "traveled on through the cities, they would deliver" to the congregations "the decrees that had been decided upon by the apostles and older men who were in Jerusalem."[15] Doesn't this prove that there was a "governing body" in Jerusalem that provided spiritual food for Jehovah's people?

**KAREN:** Cindy, the "decrees" from Jerusalem that the apostles were sharing with the congregations during their second missionary journey at Acts 16, had to do with the dispute that had just been discussed at Acts 15, and had **nothing** to do with an organized distribution of spiritual food. Again I ask, where is the evidence of a "governing body" in Jerusalem which directed the first century Christian congregations? Who commissioned Philip at Acts 8:5 to preach to the city of Samaria? It wasn't until verse 14, that the "apostles in Jerusalem heard that Samaria had received the word of God."[16] And at Acts 8 verses 26, 29, and 40, we read that the Holy Spirit is the one who directed Philip to the territories he should preach in. Since the Bible reports that Jehovah led first-century Christians **individually** through instruction **directly** from the Holy Spirit, with no accountability to a "governing body" in Jerusalem, why do Christians today need a "governing body" of elders to be their spiritual "teacher" and to provide direction for their lives?

**CINDY:** That's a good question, Karen, but if Christians do not need a "governing body" of elders for spiritual instruction, why did Jesus speak of a "faithful and discreet slave" at Matthew 24 who would oversee Jehovah's people in the last days?

---

[13] *Reasoning from the Scriptures,* 1985, 1989ed., p. 205

[14] Note: At Acts 13:2; 15:35-36; 18:22-23, we read that Paul was sent on all **three** of his missionary journeys from the congregation in Antioch, and in none of those journeys did he report directly to a "governing body" of apostles in Jerusalem.

[15] *New World Translation*

[16] *New American Standard Bible*

**KAREN:** Cindy, let's look at that passage at Matthew 24. First of all, at verses 43-44, Jesus warns that Christians should be ready at all times for His coming because He will come quickly as a "thief" in the night. Then, to illustrate this, Jesus gives a parable of a faithful and discreet slave whom his master finds attentively caring for his possessions when he arrives. Jesus says that when He comes, He will put him in charge over all of His possessions. Then He goes on to describe an "evil slave" at verses 48-51 who abuses his position as ruler over the household, and ends up being assigned a place with the hypocrites upon his master's coming. Cindy, if we look at the hypocrites in Christendom who are abusing their power and authority for illicit gain, wouldn't you agree that they collectively qualify as the "evil slave" spoken of in this passage?

**CINDY:** Oh, yes, Karen, I would agree.

**KAREN:** OK, Cindy, since any Christian can become part of the "evil slave" group just by being a hypocrite, why can't any Christian become part of the "faithful and discreet slave" group by being faithfully devoted in his Christian ministry?

**CINDY:** That's a good point, Karen. But Jesus says that he would put the faithful slave in charge over all of Jehovah's possessions. If every loyal Christian qualifies to be in the "faithful and discreet slave" group, what possessions would they rule over?

**KAREN:** Cindy, the Bible speaks of the fact that during the millennial reign of Christ, there will be people on earth who have not made a decision for or against Jehovah God. Don't you think these Christians will rule over them?

**CINDY:** Well, I suppose, Karen. But if the Watchtower organization isn't God's organization, where should I go? What do you have to offer?

**KAREN:** Cindy, what do you want most from Jehovah God? Is it eternal life? Is it His peace and joy? Is it His acceptance, favor, and approval? What do you want most from Him?

**CINDY:** Well, of course I want all these things, Karen, but is that what you have to offer?

**KAREN:** Cindy, it's not what I or an organization has to offer you that counts, but it's what Jesus offers that matters for eternity. At John 10:27, Jesus says: "**My** sheep hear **My** voice, and I know them, and they follow **Me**."[17] They don't follow an organization, Cindy. They follow Jesus, and He goes on at verse 28 to say: "**I** give eternal life to them, and they shall never perish...."[18] Cindy, Jesus gives eternal life. You've got to go to Jesus if you want to have eternal life. At John 6:37, Jesus says: "All that the Father gives Me shall **come to Me**, and the one who **comes to Me** I will certainly not cast out."[19]

---

[17] *New American Standard Bible*
[18] *New American Standard Bible*
[19] *New American Standard Bible*

**COMMENTS:**

*Friends, at John 6:68, Peter said to Jesus, "Lord,* ***whom*** *shall we go away to?* ***You*** *have sayings* ***of everlasting life****."*[20] *Peter recognized that Christians are not to look to anyone or anything but Jesus for everlasting life. At John 5:39-40, Jesus said: "You are searching the Scriptures, because you think that by means of them you will have everlasting life; and these are the very ones that bear witness about* ***me****. And yet you do not want to* ***come to me*** *that you may have life."*[21] *Instead of looking to an organization to lead you into everlasting life, why not look to the One who is* ***the life****. Jesus said: "****I am*** *the way and the truth and* ***the life****. No one comes to the Father except* ***through*** *me."*[22]

[20] *New World Translation*
[21] *New World Translation*
[22] John 14:6, *New World Translation*

# *SECTION TWO:*

# *ANALYZING THE ISSUES RELATING TO ETERNAL LIFE*

*A Christian Householder and*
*One of Jehovah's Witnesses Discuss*
*the Watchtower Publication,*
*"What Does God Require of Us?"*

*"Then you will **call upon Me***
*and **come** and **pray** to Me,*
*and I will listen to you.*
*And you will **seek** Me and **find** Me, when you*
***search** for Me with all your heart."*
*—Jeremiah 29:12-13,*
*New American Standard Bible*

## THE PURPOSE OF SECTION TWO:

## ANALYZING THE ISSUES RELATING TO ETERNAL LIFE:

Jesus said at John 17:3: "This is eternal life, that they may know You, the only true God, and Jesus Christ whom You have sent."[1] Since salvation consists in having a personal relationship with the Father and His Son Jesus Christ through Christ's sacrifice, it is essential to discuss the false views that Jehovah's Witnesses hold concerning the proper use of the name Jehovah, the identity of Jesus Christ and the process by which Christians are to obtain salvation.

The dialogues in this section are designed to focus strictly on these essential doctrines of Biblical Christianity and what is required to gain eternal life. As a result, there are times when non-essential, un-Biblical beliefs of Jehovah's Witnesses are mentioned in the text but left unchallenged in order to keep the focus on the main point being addressed.

The questions asked by Karen, the Christian, in this section are designed to challenge the false presuppositions Jehovah's Witnesses have embraced on the use of the Divine Name in prayer, the nature of the Deity of Christ, His subjection to the Father, the timing of His Kingdom rule, and Jehovah's arrangement for life and the forgiveness of sins. In order to communicate in a more effective way with Cindy, who represents the Jehovah's Witness position, Karen, who represents the Christian, often uses terms in this section that are unique to the Jehovah's Witness religion.

[1] Quoted from the *New American Standard Bible.*

## ***DIALOGUE ONE: Did Jesus Receive His Authority In 1914?***

(WDGR LESSON 6: "What is the Kingdom of God?")

*When did Jesus receive His "authority"? Did Jesus begin ruling as "King of God's Kingdom" in 1914? What does the Bible teach?*

**KAREN:** Hello, Cindy. I've been reading over our next lesson in the Watchtower brochure *What Does God Require of Us?* and I'm confused about when Jesus would be "enthroned as King of God's Kingdom." In this brochure, the Watchtower Society says: "When Jesus was on earth, he proved that he would be a kind, just, and perfect Ruler. When he returned to heaven, he was **not** enthroned as King of God's Kingdom right away." Then the Society said that it wasn't until 1914, that "Jehovah gave Jesus the authority He had promised him."[1] I don't understand why the Watchtower teaches that Jesus did not receive His authority right away when He resurrected from the dead. Didn't Jesus say to His disciples at His resurrection at Matthew 28:18: "**All** authority **has** been given to Me in heaven **and on earth**."?[2]

**CINDY:** Yes, he did say that, Karen, but that doesn't mean that Jesus began his Kingdom rule then. It only means that he was given the authority over the Christian congregation of his followers at that time.

**KAREN:** So, let me get this straight, Cindy. Are you saying that Christ's rulership and authority that was given to Him at His resurrection was limited to the Christian congregation **until** 1914 when He gained rulership over the earth?

**CINDY:** That's right, Karen. The Society says in their book *Knowledge That Leads To Everlasting Life*: "Jesus knew that his rulership over the earth was reserved for the future, **long after his resurrection** and ascension to heaven....The Scriptures had foretold this. How so? Prophetically referring to Jesus as 'Lord,' King David said: 'The utterance of Jehovah to my Lord is: "Sit at my right hand until I place your enemies as a stool for your feet." ' (Psalm 110:1)...This prophecy indicates that Jesus' rulership would not begin immediately after his ascension to heaven. Rather, he would **wait** at God's right hand." Then they reference Hebrews 10:12, 13 and ask the question:s "How long would this waiting go on? When would his rulership begin?"[3] Karen, would you like to read Hebrews 10:12-13?

**KAREN:** Sure. "But He [Christ], having offered one sacrifice for sins for all time, sat down at the right hand of God, waiting from that time onward **until** His enemies be made a footstool for His feet."[4]

---

[1] *What Does God Require of Us?,* 1996, p. 12:2

[2] *New American Standard Bible*

[3] *Knowledge That Leads To Everlasting Life,* 1995, p. 96

[4] *New American Standard Bible*

**CINDY:** So you see, Karen, Jesus had to "wait" at Jehovah's right hand, before Jesus could begin his rulership over the earth.

**KAREN:** But, Cindy, what does the Bible say Jesus was waiting for at God's right hand?

**CINDY:** Why, Karen, it says Jesus was: "awaiting **until** his **enemies** should be placed as a stool for his feet."[5]

**KAREN:** Cindy, what are the enemies Jesus was waiting to be placed under His feet?

**CINDY:** I'm not sure, Karen, but I suppose those enemies have something to do with worldly governments.

**KAREN:** Cindy, would you read 1 Corinthians 15:23-24 in your *New World Translation* Bible?

**CINDY:** OK. "But each one of his own rank: Christ the firstfruits, afterward those who belong to the Christ during his presence. Next, the end, when he hands over the kingdom to his God and Father, when he has brought to nothing all government and all authority and power." There you have it, Karen! These verses show that Jesus will put an end to all worldly governments and then it says Jesus will hand "over the kingdom" to Jehovah God.

**KAREN:** OK, Cindy, now read the next two verses 25 and 26.

**CINDY:** "For he must rule as king **until**" God "has put **all enemies under his feet**. As the **last enemy**, **death** is to be brought to nothing."[6]

**KAREN:** Now, Cindy, according to this passage, what is the last enemy that is going to be put under Jesus' feet?

**CINDY:** Well, it says that the last enemy is death.

**KAREN:** Now, Cindy, we were just reading in Hebrews 10 that Jesus is waiting at the right hand of God **until** His enemies would be put under His feet. Since 1 Corinthians 15 says that the last enemy is death, doesn't this mean that Jesus is still waiting at the right hand of God?

**CINDY:** I never saw that before!

**KAREN:** Cindy, was death destroyed in 1914? Since all of Jesus' enemies have not been put under His feet yet, how can Jesus **not** still be waiting at the right hand of God?

**CINDY:** Well, I guess you're right, Karen. Jesus must be waiting at the right hand of God even today!

---

[5] Hebrews 10:13, *New World Translation*

[6] 1 Corinthians 15:25-26, *New World Translation*

**KAREN:** Now, Cindy, if Christ could not start ruling until God has put all His enemies under His feet, how can Jesus' rule have begun in 1914 "in the midst of his enemies" and why did He have to start His reign with a war against them?

**CINDY:** I don't know, Karen.

**KAREN:** Cindy, would you read verse 28 of 1 Corinthians chapter 15 and tell me what Jesus will do **after** all things have been put under his feet?

**CINDY:** Sure. It says: "But when all things will have been subjected to him, then the Son himself will also subject himself to the One who subjected all things to him, that God may be all things to everyone."[7] What was your question again, Karen?

**KAREN:** My question is, what does this verse say Jesus will do **after** all things are subjected to Him and put under His feet?

**CINDY:** Well, Karen, it says Jesus will turn everything over to God.

**KAREN:** Now, Cindy, let me get this straight. According to the Watchtower Society, Jesus is waiting at the right hand of God and **cannot** start ruling until His enemies are put under His feet, right?

**CINDY:** That's right, Karen.

**KAREN:** Now my question is this: If Jesus cannot start ruling until His enemies are put under his feet and the Bible says at 1 Corinthians 15:24 and 28 that Jesus will turn over the kingdom to God the very moment that His enemies are put under Him, when will Jesus be able to start ruling? What happened to His Kingdom? Because the very moment that it is time for Jesus to start ruling, after all His enemies have been put under His feet, it will be time for Him to hand over the kingdom to God!

**CINDY:** That's a good point, Karen. I don't know.

**KAREN:** Cindy, will you read 1 Corinthians 15:25 again, please?

**CINDY:** "For he" Christ "must rule as king until" God "has put all enemies under his feet."[8]

**KAREN:** Cindy, what does this verse say Jesus is doing while He is at the right hand of God and waiting for all His enemies to be put under His feet?

**CINDY:** Why, Karen, it says: "he must **rule as king until**" God "has put all enemies under his feet."[9]

---

[7] *New World Translation*
[8] *New World Translation*
[9] *New World Translation*

**KAREN:** So, when did Jesus' kingship start? When did Jesus start waiting for God to put all enemies under His feet?

**CINDY:** Well, Karen, He has been waiting since His resurrection. So, He must have begun ruling as king at that time.

**COMMENTS:**

Friends, at *Christ's resurrection, Jesus said that "All authority" both "in heaven" and "on earth" had been given to Him. If "all authority" had been given to Jesus at His resurrection, what authority could be given to Him in 1914 that He didn't already have?*

## *DIALOGUE TWO: Should Christians Use the Divine Name "Jehovah" In Prayer? —Part I*

(WDGR LESSON 7: "Drawing Close to God in Prayer")

*Why do many Christians address Almighty God in prayer by the titles "Lord" or "God" instead of calling Him by His personal name "Jehovah" or "Yahweh"? Is there any evidence for the use of the Divine Name in the original Christian Greek New Testament Scriptures? In what way do true Christians today "sanctify" God's Name?*

**CINDY:** Hi, Karen, what are you reading in your Bible?

**KAREN:** Oh, Cindy, I was reading over the model prayer that Jesus gave us in Matthew 6:9. I was thinking about this in light of the next lesson we'll be studying in the Watchtower brochure *What Does God Require of Us?* I think it's wonderful that God has provided a way for us to be able to approach Him in prayer.

**CINDY:** Oh, yes, I agree Karen, and today we're going to learn more about "Drawing Close to God in Prayer."[1] Why do you think it's important for us to pray regularly?

**KAREN:** Well, Cindy, just as the Society notes in this brochure, prayer enables us to draw closer to God and feel His presence as a dear friend, and just as they discuss here, prayer is a form of worship.[2]

**CINDY:** Yes, Karen, can you see why it is so important that we use Jehovah's name when we pray?[3] After all, Satan is called a "god" too. If you just use the titles "Lord" or "God" when you pray, Satan might think that you're addressing the prayer to him.

**KAREN:** I never thought of it that way before. Cindy, what do you think Satan would do if he thought a prayer belonged to him anyway?

**CINDY:** I don't know, Karen. All I know is that Jehovah doesn't like to be addressed by titles such as "Lord" or "God." You want to pray in a way that pleases Jehovah, don't you?

**KAREN:** That has always confused me, Cindy. If Jehovah wants us to use His personal name when we pray, why didn't Jesus use it when He gave us the model prayer, instead of saying "Our Father"?

**CINDY:** That's a good question, Karen, but one thing we must notice about that prayer is that it says, "Hallowed be thy name," or as the *New World Translation* put it: "Let your name be sanctified."[4] What do you think sanctifying Jehovah's name means?

---

[1] *What Does God Require of Us?,* 1996, p. 14
[2] *What Does God Require of Us?,* p. 14:1, 2
[3] *What Does God Require of Us?,* p. 14:2

**KAREN:** Well, Cindy, the word "sanctify" or "hallowed" means to "set apart as holy." So if we are to "sanctify" God's name as holy, I guess that would mean we are to treat Him with holiness and reverence in all of our acts of worship so that we reveal the person behind the name in all that we do, wouldn't you agree?

**CINDY:** Yes, Karen, but it means much more than that. How can you sanctify a name that you never pronounce in your prayers?

**KAREN:** Well, let me explain, Cindy. I think the Society said it best when they stated in *Insight on the Scriptures:* "...we must keep in mind that names then had **real meaning** and were not just 'labels' to identify an individual as today....Moses' going to the Israelites in the 'name' of the One who sent him meant being the representative of that One, and the greatness of the authority with which Moses would speak would be determined by or be commensurate with that name and what it **represented**....we see at once that to know Jehovah's name is something **very different** from knowing the four letters of which it is composed. It is to know by **experience** that Jehovah really is what his name declares him to be."[5]

**CINDY:** Did the Society really say that "to know Jehovah's name is something very different from knowing the four letters of which it is composed"?

**KAREN:** Yes, Cindy. You can read this on page 12 of volume 2 of the *Insight* books. As you can see, it's not the pronunciation of the name of God that is to be set apart as holy, but the person identified by the name that we are to proclaim throughout the earth. Those four Hebrew characters of the name of God from which we derive the translation "Jehovah" mean absolutely nothing to a person who doesn't know who God really is. Therefore, it is in this way that Christians throughout the centuries have sanctified Jehovah's name—not by promoting a pronunciation— but by proclaiming the person behind it.

**CINDY:** Wow! Is that why Jesus taught his disciples to pray "Our Father. . ." instead of saying "Jehovah"?

**KAREN:** Yes, Cindy, but it goes much deeper than that. Do you remember how we studied how people who are God's sons cry out "Abba! Father!" when they address Him?[6]

**CINDY:** Yes! I remember. "Abba" means Daddy!

**KAREN:** How would your dad like it if you always addressed him as George instead of calling him "Daddy" or "Father"? Wouldn't he wonder what happened to you and why you are being so cold to him?

---

[4] Matthew 6:9

[5] *Insight on the Scriptures,* vol. 2, p. 12

[6] Galatians 4:6

**CINDY:** Well, Karen, I guess he would. I never thought of it that way before. Do you think Jehovah feels the same way when we, His children, address Him in that manner?

**KAREN:** I think He does, Cindy. I know I really struggle with it. Prayer is supposed to bring me closer to God, but whenever I pray using His personal name, I always feel much farther away from Him. Even calling Him "Father Jehovah" feels strange, just like addressing my Father as "Daddy Jim" would sound like I'm trying to keep him straight from other daddies. Since Jehovah God can hear our prayers at any place, time, and can even "hear the silent prayers said in our heart,"[7] don't you think God hears our prayers whether we do or do not use His name?

**CINDY:** I suppose He does, but doesn't the Bible say in Romans 10:13 that: "Everyone who calls on the name of Jehovah will be saved."?[8]

**KAREN:** Cindy, your Bible, the *New World Translation* inserts the divine name "Jehovah" into the text at Romans whereas most Bibles correctly translate it as "Lord." Did you know that there are over 5,000 partial and complete manuscripts of the New Testament in its original Greek language that date back as far as the 2nd century and not a single one of them contains the divine name? Don't you think it's a bit presumptuous for the Watchtower Society to argue that we must use Jehovah's name in prayer based on a verse that doesn't even contain His name in its original language?

**CINDY:** Karen, that's a good question. Could we talk about this next week? I'll bring the Watchtower brochure *The DIVINE NAME That Will Endure Forever* and we can read and discuss it.

**KAREN:** Sounds good, Cindy. I'll see you next week.

**COMMENTS:**

*Friends, just as Cindy discovered, knowing Jehovah God is so much more than knowing His name or even studying hours of literature that describe Him. The Bible teaches us that there is only one name we should call upon for salvation. That name is Jesus—not "Jehovah." Acts 4:10,12 states: "let it be known to all of you, and to all the people of Israel, that by the name of Jesus Christ...whom God raised from the dead—by this name this man stands here before you in good health....And there is salvation in no one else; for there is no other name under heaven that has been given among men, by which we must be saved."*[9]

[7] *What Does God Require of Us?,* p. 14:3

[8] *New World Translation*

[9] *New American Standard Bible*

## *DIALOGUE TWO: Should Christians Use the Divine Name "Jehovah" In Prayer? —Part II*

(CONTINUED FROM THE PREVIOUS DIALOGUE)

**KAREN:** Hello, Cindy. Have you done any research on what we talked about last week? We had discussed how the Watchtower Bible inserts the divine name in their New Testament translation of the Christian Greek Scriptures even though there is not a single Greek manuscript of the Christian Scriptures that contain the name Jehovah. I had asked you why the Watchtower Society argues that we must use Jehovah's name in our prayers based on verses that do not even contain His name in the original language.

**CINDY:** Yes, Karen, the Watchtower brochure *The DIVINE NAME That Will Endure Forever* discusses this very issue. They admit that apart from partial abbreviated forms of Jehovah's name—such as "Jah" in "Hallelujah" that: "...no ancient Greek manuscript that we possess today of the books from Matthew to Revelation contains God's name in full."[1] But since most of the manuscripts of the Christian Greek Scriptures in existence today "were made during or after the fourth century," the Society argues that: "something" happened "to the text of the Christian Greek Scriptures *before* the fourth century that resulted in the omission of God's name."[2]

**KAREN:** Really, Cindy? They believe that by the fourth century, God's name was taken out of the manuscripts? But doesn't the Society say: "Of the Christian Greek Scriptures, there are some 5,000 in Greek, the oldest dating back to the beginning of the **second century** C.E."?[3] And don't they argue that by our ability to compare these manuscripts, we see that the: "small scribal errors and alterations" that have "crept into the text... on the whole...are **insignificant** and have no bearing on the Bible's general integrity"?[4] How can they hold that: "The text we have is substantially the same as the one that the original writers penned"[5] and at the same time argue that something as significant as the divine name was taken out of these manuscripts 237 times?[6]

**CINDY:** I don't know, Karen, but the Society argues that since the Greek *Septuagint* shows evidence that the divine name has been taken out of it, the name must have been taken out of the Christian Greek Scriptures as well.[7]

**KAREN:** But, Cindy, the Septuagint is a Greek translation of the Old Testament Hebrew Scriptures. Of course, the Hebrew Scriptures contain the divine name, but this proves nothing of the New Testament Christian Greek Scriptures. If it is true that the Christian

---

[1] *The DIVINE NAME That Will Endure Forever,* 1984, p. 23
[2] *The DIVINE NAME That Will Endure Forever,* 1984, p. 24
[3] *Reasoning From the Scriptures,* 1989, p. 64
[4] *Insight on the Scriptures,* 1988, vol. 2, p. 313
[5] *The Bible—God's Word or Man's,* 1989, pp. 59-60
[6] *The DIVINE NAME That Will Endure Forever,* p. 27
[7] *The DIVINE NAME That Will Endure Forever,* p. 25

Scriptures were tampered with, like the *Septuagint* was, wouldn't you expect that we would see the same evidence of such tampering in the manuscripts of the Christian Scriptures? If the Society's argument is valid, why is it that in over 5,000 Greek manuscripts that we possess of the Christian Scriptures, we see no evidence whatsoever of the kind of tampering that we see in manuscripts of the Septuagint?

**CINDY:** Are you saying, Karen, that if the Christian Scriptures were tampered with like the Septuagint was, we would see the evidence in those manuscripts?

**KAREN:** That's exactly what I'm saying, Cindy. Not only is such evidence missing in the manuscripts of the Christian Scriptures we possess today, but it is missing in all of the writings of the apostolic and post-apostolic Church Fathers. Did you know that the early church fathers that lived right during the time of the apostles, never used the divine name when they were quoting the Hebrew Scriptures? Don't you think that if the divine name was used by the writers of the Christians Scriptures, we would see this evidence in the writings of the Church Fathers who **quoted** both the Hebrew and Greek Scriptures?

**CINDY:** I suppose we would.

**KAREN:** But, Cindy, such evidence is 100% missing. Out of the 86,000 quotations of the Christian Greek Scriptures that are in the writings of the Church Fathers, **none** of them contain the divine name.[8] Where is the evidence that the Society is talking about?

**CINDY:** Well, Karen, didn't Jesus say in his prayer to Jehovah: "I have made your name known to them and will make it known...."?[9] If the name was not used by the Christian writers, how could Jesus make known a name that he never pronounced?

**KAREN:** Very easily, Cindy. Just like we talked about last week, the Society states: "To know Jehovah's name is something very different from knowing the four letters of which it is composed. It is to know by experience that Jehovah really is what his name declares him to be."[10] Therefore, Cindy, Jesus and the writers of the Christian Scriptures made God's name known—not by promoting a pronunciation—but by revealing Who the person of Jehovah really is. Even the Society admits that there is a good possibility that by the time of Christ, the Jews were not allowed to pronounce God's name as it was only pronounced by the high priest "at religious services at the temple—particularly on the day of Atonement."[11] Although there is insufficient evidence to prove whether or not Jesus pronounced the divine name when He read the Hebrew Scriptures, we can be certain that if the use of Jehovah's name is as important as they say it is, God would have made sure that the name was not removed from His Holy Scriptures, wouldn't you agree?

---

[8] See *Defending Your Faith—How To Answer The Tough Questions,* by Dan Story (Nashville, TN: Thomas Nelson Publishers, 1992), p. 38 and attached documentation of the writings of the Church Fathers Clement, Barnabas, and Irenaeus. Note: In the Greek manuscripts, ΚΥΡΙΟΣ (*Ky'rois*) = "Lord" and ΘΕΟΣ (*The-os'*) = "God."

[9] John 17:26, *New World Translation*

[10] *Insight on the Scriptures,* vol. 2, p. 12

[11] *The DIVINE NAME That Will Endure Forever,* p. 14

**CINDY:** I suppose, He would, Karen. But the translators of the Watchtower Bible were very careful when they inserted the divine name into their Christian Scriptures. The Society states that: "...the *New World Translation of the Christian Greek Scriptures....*has restored God's name **every time** that a portion of the Hebrew Scriptures containing it is **quoted** in the Greek Scriptures."[12] So you see, Karen, this is why the Watchtower Bible inserted the name "Jehovah" instead of "Lord" at Romans 10:13. It is because in this passage, Paul is quoting the Hebrew Scripture passage Joel 2:32 which contains the name.[13]

**KAREN:** So, Cindy, let me make sure I understand what you're saying. The Watchtower Bible contains the divine name in the New Testament Christian Scriptures **every place** the writer is quoting a passage from the Hebrew Old Testament?

**CINDY:** That's right, Karen. So even though there is no Christian Greek manuscript evidence of the divine name being used by the Christian writers, the Watchtower Bible inserts the name every place where the Christian writer is quoting a Hebrew Scripture passage that contains the name.

**KAREN:** That's interesting. Cindy, would you read Isaiah 8:12-13 in your Watchtower Bible?

**CINDY:** Sure. "... 'A conspiracy!' and the object of their fear YOU men must not fear, nor must YOU tremble at it. **Jehovah** of armies—he is the One whom YOU should treat as holy...." [14]

**KAREN:** OK, Cindy. Now, look at the marginal cross-references in your Bible. Does the *New World Translation* cross-reference this passage to 1 Peter 3:14?

**CINDY:** Yes, it does, Karen. I'll read it in my Bible. "...However, the object of their fear do not YOU fear, neither become agitated. But sanctify the **Christ as Lord** in YOUR hearts...." Wait a minute! Why didn't my Bible insert the name Jehovah in this passage since it is quoting Isaiah?

**KAREN:** That's a good question, Cindy. Just as Isaiah says we should sanctify Jehovah as holy, Peter applies this passage to Christ, saying that we should sanctify Christ as Lord Jehovah. If the Society was consistent in their translation, they would have to insert Jehovah's name into this passage, and you know what that would do to their doctrine. Can you see why their doctrine prevents the Society from being consistent in their translation?

---

[12] *The DIVINE NAME That Will Endure Forever,* p. 27

[13] See *The DIVINE NAME That Will Endure Forever,* p. 26

[14] *New World Translation*

**COMMENTS:**

*Friends, the reason the writers of the Christian Greek Scriptures did not promote the divine name in their manuscripts is because there is only* ***one*** *name that we are to call upon for salvation. That name is Jesus. Acts 4:10,12 states: "Let it be known to all of you, and to all the people of Israel, that by the name of Jesus Christ...whom God raised from the dead—by this name this man stands here before you in good health....And there is salvation in no one else; for there is* ***no other name*** *under heaven that has been given among men, by which we must be saved."*[15]

---

[15] *New American Standard Bible;* For an extensive and detailed examination of the *New World Translation's* use of the divine name in the Christian Greek Scriptures, see the 1998 book entitled, *The Tetragrammaton and the Christian Greek Scriptures.* (Word Resources Inc., Portland, OR 97294 - www.tetragrammaton.org)

## *DIALOGUE THREE: Is The "Trinity" Doctrine From Paganism?*

(WDGR LESSON 11: "Beliefs and Customs That Displease God")

*Examining the Watchtower brochure Should You Believe in the Trinity?, Karen asks Cindy why the Watchtower endeavors to substantiate its claims about the Trinity by quoting authors that teach that the Bible is the source of paganism in Christianity.*

**CINDY:** Hello, Karen. What are you reading?

**KAREN:** Oh, Hi, Cindy. I was just reading the Watchtower brochure *Should You Believe in the Trinity?*. In this brochure, the Society quotes a number of sources that say that the doctrine of the Trinity is of pagan origin.

**CINDY:** That's right, Karen. Just as we'll be studying today in the Watchtower brochure *What Does God Require of Us?:* "Not all beliefs and customs are bad. But God does not approve of them if they come from false religion or are against Bible teachings."[1]

**KAREN:** Cindy, until I read this brochure on the Trinity, I never thought of it being pagan. Where did the Society get this information? For example on page 11 of *Should You Believe in the Trinity?,* they say: "Historian Will Durant observed: 'Christianity did not destroy paganism; it adopted it.... From Egypt came the ideas of a divine trinity.'" Who is Will Durant? Are they quoting a book he wrote? If, so, why doesn't the Watchtower give the name of the book and a page number so we can read the quote in context?

**CINDY:** I don't know. Let me look and see if they have an appendix or something in this brochure that tells... hum... I don't see anything at all.

**KAREN:** Cindy, I looked through this whole brochure and not only does the Society fail to reference where they got this quote from Durant, but they do not give page numbers for **any** of the sources they quote. I wonder why.

**CINDY:** Karen, I don't know...but why is this important to you? The Society is **very** careful about their research. They wouldn't put something in their literature if it wasn't true.

**KAREN:** Cindy, as you know, the Bible says to "make sure of all things."[2] What's involved in making sure of all things? Am I supposed to believe everything I read without checking it out?

**CINDY:** Well, no.

---

[1] *What Does God Require of Us?,* 1996, p. 22:1

[2] 1 Thessalonians 5:21, *New World Translation*

**KAREN:** Cindy, because I wanted to obey Jehovah God by making "sure of all things," I wrote the Society about this and they sent me a reference list for their brochure *Should You Believe in the Trinity?*. Looking at their list, I was able to find that this quote from Will Durant came from his book *The Story of Civilization: Part III, Caesar and Christ.* In their brochure, the Society quoted the statement he made on page 595 in which he said: "Christianity did not destroy paganism; it adopted it," but I think you'd be **shocked** at what he said just before he made that statement. Would you read it for me?

**CINDY:** OK. "It seems incredible that the Apocalypse and the Fourth Gospel should have come from the same hand. The Apocalypse is Jewish poetry, the Fourth Gospel is **Greek philosophy**."[3] What? Will Durant says that the gospel of John is "Greek philosophy"?

**KAREN:** That's right, Cindy. Keep reading.

**CINDY:** "Just as Philo, learned in Greek speculation, had felt a need to rephrase Judaism in forms acceptable to the logic-loving Greeks, so **John**...sought to give a **Greek philosophical tinge** to the mystic Jewish doctrine that the Wisdom of God was a living being, and to the Christian doctrine that Jesus was the Messiah. Consciously or not, he continued **Paul's work** of detaching Christianity from Judaism."[4]

**KAREN:** Cindy, is Durant saying that the Biblical writers John and Paul incorporated Greek philosophy in their writings of the New Testament?

**CINDY:** Well, that's what it looks like. "...so John....continued Paul's work of detaching Christianity from Judaism."

**KAREN:** Can you see why the Society doesn't want you to know what kind of historian Will Durant is? After all, isn't Durant saying that the **Bible** is from paganism and that Christianity became pagan because the Biblical writings are pagan?

**CINDY:** Well, I guess that's what he's saying. But, the Watchtower references other sources. You're not going to throw out the Society's argument simply because one historian they quote is wrong, are you?

**KAREN:** That's a good point. Cindy, would you read the next person they quote in this brochure?

**CINDY:** OK. "And in the book *Egyptian Religion,* Siegfried Morenz notes: "The trinity was a major preoccupation of Egyptian theologians...**Three gods** are combined and treated as a **single being**, addressed in the singular. In this way the spiritual force of Egyptian religion shows a direct link with Christian theology."[5]

---

[3] *The Story of Civilization: Part III, Caesar and Christ,* 1944, p. 594

[4] *The Story of Civilization: Part III, Caesar and Christ,* p. 594-595

[5] *Should You Believe in the Trinity,* 1989, p. 11

**KAREN:** So, the Society is quoting Siegfried Morenz as saying that the Trinity doctrine is derived from Egyptian false religion, but would you read some of his other statements found on pages 251-254 of his book *Egyptian Religion*?

**CINDY:** Sure. "...the doctrine of creation through the word ...was one of the **principal** elements in the Egyptian cosmogony....Less important, but more readily comprehensible, is the **influence** of the **Egyptian** court chronicle upon the literary form of the Israelites' chronicle account of **David and Solomon**....**Isaiah's** famous list of appellations for the Prince of Peace....is probably derived from the fivefold titulary of the **Egyptian** king....**Other passages** can, however, be claimed as **Egyptian in inspiration**: for instance, the Egyptian...lists of knowledge, which were the **basis** of the **proverbs** which King Solomon spoke."[6] Oh, my! He's making nearly everything in the Bible pagan.

**KAREN:** That's right, Cindy. And listen to what he says about the New Testament: "...religious forms of the land of the Nile also had an effect upon the New Testament and so upon early Christianity....a concept that figures in the New Testament has been taken to be ultimately of **Egyptian origin**, **Jesus's parable** of Dives and Lazarus....the association between ship and tongue in the **Epistle of St James**, which was **originally Egyptian**. **Romans**: the proverbial 'coals of fire' which were to be heaped upon one's enemy - **derived** from a Late Egyptian penitential rite....the acclamation... '**God is One**'...is **derived** from one employed in the service of Sarapis....and this in turn comes from the early Egyptian theologians' form '**One is Amon**.' "[7] Cindy, do you believe that the Biblical teaching that God is one is from the Egyptian theologian's view that their god Amon is one?

**CINDY:** Absolutely not, Karen!

**KAREN:** Then why do you believe his statements that the doctrine of the Trinity is from paganism? After all, by denying his view that the concept that "God is one" is from Egyptian religion, you are pulling the foundation out from under his argument regarding the Trinity. Either you accept his teaching that these Biblical concepts are from paganism and thus believe that the **Bible** is the **source** of paganism in Christianity, or you deny his arguments altogether. Which is it going to be, Cindy?

**CINDY:** I don't know, Karen.

**KAREN:** Since the Watchtower Society is quoting these sources in support of their arguments, what does this say about their doctrine and literature? When they have to go to books that teach that the Bible is the source of paganism in order to prove their points, how can we trust any of their literature regarding alleged paganism in Christianity?

**CINDY:** I don't know, Karen, but how can the Trinity be from the Bible? Didn't Jesus say "...the Father is greater than I am"?[8]

---

[6] *Egyptian Religion,* 1973, pp. 251-252

[7] *Egyptian Religion,* 1973, pp. 253-254

[8] John 14:28, *New World Translation*

**KAREN:** Yes, He did. Can we talk about that next week?

**CINDY:** Sure, Karen. I'll be here.

**COMMENTS:**

*Friends, have you ever seen a counterfeit $3.00 bill? Obviously, since no U.S. $3.00 bill exists, one will search in vain to find a counterfeit $3.00 bill, for it would be easily recognized. Because the purpose of the counterfeit is to deceive people into substituting the counterfeit for the genuine, counterfeit money is designed to resemble only authentic bills. This same principle applies to the spiritual realm. Simply because one can find numerous similarities between Biblical doctrines and pagan religions does not prove that such doctrines are derived from paganism. Rather, on the contrary, such resemblance actually proves the deceitful tactics of Satan in counterfeiting God's truth.*

## ***DIALOGUE FOUR: Why Is The Father "Greater" Than Jesus —John 14:28?***

(WDGR LESSON 11: "Beliefs and Customs That Displease God")

*If the Trinity is a Biblical doctrine, why does the Bible teach that Jesus is subject to God? Is there a single verse in the Bible that proves the Trinity?*

**CINDY:** Karen, last week in our study of the Watchtower brochure, *What Does God Require of Us?,* we started reading about "Beliefs and Customs that Displease God," [1] and you had mentioned that you believe that the doctrine of the Trinity is from the Bible even though similar concepts are taught in pagan religion.

**KAREN:** Yes, Cindy. In our study we also read from page 11 of the Watchtower brochure *Should You Believe in the Trinity?,* and discovered that **many** of the sources that the Society quotes in order to prove that the Trinity doctrine is from paganism, actually teach that the Biblical writers inserted pagan doctrines into the Bible. Therefore, these sources claim that Christianity adopted paganism because the **Bible** is pagan. I had asked, since the Watchtower has to go to books that teach that the Bible is the source of paganism, in order to prove their point that the Trinity doctrine is pagan, how can we trust any of their literature regarding alleged paganism in Christianity?

**CINDY:** Karen, we had a good discussion on that, but one thing we didn't get to talk about is the fact that the Bible teaches that Jesus is subject to God. If Jehovah really is a Trinity, three persons in one God, why did Jesus say that the Father is greater than he is?[2]

**KAREN:** Cindy, when you were growing up, was there anyone in your family equal in authority to your father?

**CINDY:** No. My father was in charge of leading the family. So, everyone followed the rules and guidelines he setup.

**KAREN:** What about your brother? Did he follow those rules?

**CINDY:** Of course, he did. But what's your point, Karen?

**KAREN:** My point is this. Does the fact that your father was in a greater position of authority than your brother was, prove that your brother (his son) was inferior to him? If so, are we to argue that your brother is less human than your father is because he obeyed your father's rules?

**CINDY:** Of course not, Karen.

---

[1] *What Does God Require of Us?,* 1996, p. 22-23

[2] *What Does God Require of Us?,* p. 22:2

**KAREN:** Then why does the Watchtower Society argue that Jesus as God's Son is inferior to the Father simply because He "is subject to God" and obeys His rules?[3] Being in a greater position of authority doesn't make a person inherently better than someone else, does it? At Luke 2:51, the Bible says that Jesus was subject to Mary and Joseph. Does this mean that He was inferior to them?

**CINDY:** Well, no, Karen. That's a good point. But how can Jesus be God when he said that his Father is the "only true God"? If the Trinity, three persons in one God, is a Bible teaching, why is the **word** "Trinity" not found in the Bible?[4]

**KAREN:** Cindy, do you believe that the new system of things will be a "theocracy" in which Jehovah God will rule the world?

**CINDY:** Yes.

**KAREN:** If the fact that the **word** "Trinity" is not found in the Bible proves that it is not a Biblical teaching, are we to argue that the concept of a theocracy, in which God will rule mankind, is not Biblical simply because the **word** "theocracy" is not found in the Bible?

**CINDY:** Well, no, Karen. But where do we see the **concept** of the Trinity in the Bible? Can you show me even **one** verse that proves the Trinity?

**KAREN:** Yes, Cindy! Would you read John 1:3 in your Bible?

**CINDY:** "All things came into existence through him, and apart from him not even one thing came into existence."[5]

**KAREN:** Who is the "him" that this passage is talking about?

**CINDY:** It's talking about Jesus and how he was "with God" in the beginning creating the world.

**KAREN:** That's right, Cindy. Let's draw this out into a chart. Here on the right side of the column, let's list the things that were created "through" Jesus, and on the left side, let's put the things that were **not** created because they have always existed. Now, what are some things that were created?

**CINDY:** Well, basically everything…the earth, stars, plants, animals, mankind…

**KAREN:** Would angels fit into that category of things that were created through Jesus?

**CINDY:** Oh, yes, Karen! Angels would fit.

---

[3] *What Does God Require of Us?,* p. 22:2

[4] *Knowledge That Leads to Everlasting Life,* 1995, p. 31

[5] *New World Translation*

**KAREN:** OK. Now, let's go to the other side and list things that were never created because they have always existed.

**CINDY:** Jehovah is eternal. He was never created.

**KAREN:** OK. So, let's write down "the Father" in this category of things that have always existed. What about the Holy Spirit? Was God's Spirit created?

**CINDY:** No. God's Spirit is as eternal as Jehovah is.[6]

**KAREN:** So here we have the Father and the Holy Spirit. Now, Cindy, where are we going to put Jesus? John 1:3 says that "All things came into existence" through Christ and that "**nothing**" that has been created was created "**apart"** from Him. So where should we put Jesus? If Jesus is one of those beings that was created, we'd have to put Him in the category of things that were created through Christ. Does that make any sense? How could Jesus have created Himself?

**CINDY:** I guess you're right, Karen. That doesn't make any sense. Jesus could not have created himself.

**KAREN:** So, you can see, Cindy, we must put Jesus in the category of things that were never created because they have always existed, and look at what we have: The Father, the Son, and the Holy Spirit—all sharing the eternal essence of the one true God. Can you see, how even though the **word** "Trinity" is not in the Bible, the **concept** is Biblical? In the Bible, the Father is called "God,"[7] the Son is called "God,"[8] and the Holy Spirit is called "God."[9] Yet, the Bible is very clear that there is only **one** true God. Can you see why Christians throughout history have embraced monotheism in the form of the Trinity doctrine?

**COMMENTS:**

*Friends, just as Cindy discovered, simply because the **word** "Trinity" is not found in the Bible does not prove that it is not a Biblical teaching. At Matthew 28:19, Jesus said: "Go therefore and make disciples... baptizing them in the **name** of **the Father** and **the Son** and **the Holy Spirit**...."[10] Notice that in this verse, plurality within unity is indicated by the fact that the word "name" is in the singular form while the definite article "the" is placed in front of each of the persons: "...**the** Father and **the** Son and **the** Holy Spirit...."*

---

[6] See Hebrews 9:14
[7] See 1 Peter 1:2; Philippians 2:11
[8] See John 1:1 20:28; Hebrews 1:8; 2 Peter 1:1; Titus 2:13
[9] See Acts 5:3-4; 1 Corinthians 3:16-17
[10] *New American Standard Bible*

*The doctrine of the Trinity is not Modalism, the view that the Father, Son, and Holy Spirit are all one Person;* ***nor*** *is it Tritheism, the view that the Father, Son and Holy Spirit are three separate Gods. Each member is distinct in His personhood, yet together, They comprise the one God. Thus, in defining the Trinity doctrine, the Athanasian Creed states: "Neither confounding the Persons,* ***nor*** *dividing the Substance.…and yet they are not three Gods, but one God."*

## *DIALOGUE FIVE: How Can Jesus Be "With" God And At The Same Time Be God —John 1:1?*

(WDGR LESSON 2: "Who Is God?")

*Is Jesus "a god" or is He the one true God? If Jesus is God, why does the Bible say: "No one has ever seen God"? How can Jesus be the Son of God and at the same time be God? Should Jesus be worshipped?*

**CINDY:** Hello, Karen. How was your week?

**KAREN:** Not too good, Cindy. My nephew just returned to the U.S. after spending a year in Japan and evidently he has decided to become a Buddhist. When he was a teenager, he turned his back on God and now he thinks that by following the path of "enlightenment" through his good deeds, he can reach nirvana.

**CINDY:** I'm sorry to hear that, Karen. Can you see why it's important to know who God is? We'll be studying about Him today in the Watchtower brochure, *What Does God Require of Us?* As you are seeing in your nephew, Karen: "People worship many things. But the Bible tells us there is only one TRUE God" and "He is the only One we should worship."[1] Did you know that: "God has many titles but has only one name"?[2]

**KAREN:** I know the Watchtower Society teaches that God's only name is "Jehovah," but doesn't the Bible say that Jesus is God at John 1:1: "In the beginning was the Word, and the Word was with God, and the Word was God."?[3]

**CINDY:** No, Karen! That is what **your** Bible says. Mine says: "the Word was *a* god."[4] How can Jesus be "with God" and at the same time be God? Does this make any sense to you?

**KAREN:** You're right, Cindy. It wouldn't make any sense if I believed that Jesus and the Father are the **same** person. Obviously, Jesus is God's Son, and as such, He is not the Father, but yet, He shares God's nature as the only true God.[5] It's like two distinct persons who are one God.

**CINDY:** But that doesn't make sense, Karen. How can Jesus be the Son of God and at the same time be God?

**KAREN:** Well, it's like this. My father Jim is the son of his father John, but the fact that Jim is called a "son" does not make him any less human than his father is, right?

---

[1] *What Does God Require of Us?,* 1996, p. 4:1
[2] *What Does God Require of Us?,* p. 4:2
[3] *New International Version*
[4] John 1:1, *New World Translation*
[5] Galatians 4:8; c.f. Philippians 2:5

**CINDY:** Yes. . .

**KAREN:** So, just as Jim, as John's son, doesn't make him any less human than his father is, so Jesus as God's Son is not any less God than His Father is. If the Bible says that Jesus is God and there is only **one** true God, then we must conclude that Jesus is either the true God by **nature** or is He a false God. Does this make sense to you?

**CINDY:** I guess it does, Karen, but isn't Satan called "a god"?[6] And what about Moses? Doesn't the Bible say he was "a god" to Pharaoh?[7] Couldn't Jesus be just "a god" in the sense of having "divine" qualities, but not be the true God?

**KAREN:** Cindy, is Satan a true "god"? Did Moses save anyone?

**CINDY:** Well, no.

**KAREN:** Then, wouldn't you agree that they are in reality false "gods"? In other words, don't you think that Satan is called "a god," not because he is one, but because people falsely worship him as such? Just look at 1 Corinthians 8:5-6: "For even though there are those who are **called** 'gods,' whether in heaven or on earth, just as there are many 'gods' and many 'lords,' there is actually to us **one** God the Father...and there is one Lord, Jesus Christ...."[8] Calling Satan a "god" hardly makes him a real "god," does it?

**CINDY:** Well, no, Karen. So, are you saying that Jesus is either a false "god" like Satan or he is the true God?

**KAREN:** That's exactly what I'm saying, Cindy. Either Jesus possesses the attributes of God that make Him the true God by **nature**, or He is some sort of created being, like Satan, that pretends to be "a god" but really isn't. Which category are you going to put Jesus in?

**CINDY:** Well, I guess I'd have to put him in the category of being the "true" God, because a false god cannot save anyone. But I don't understand, how can Jesus be God? Doesn't the Bible say, "God is a Spirit" and "No human has ever seen God"?[9]

**KAREN:** Yes, Cindy, but notice the last part of that verse here in John 1:18: "No one has ever seen God, but God the One and Only, who is at the Father's side, has made him known."[10] As you can see, Cindy, it is "God the One and Only" (Jesus) "who is at the

---

[6] 2 Corinthians 4:4

[7] Exodus 4:16

[8] *New World Translation*

[9] *What Does God Require of Us?,* p. 4:3; John 4:24; John 1:18

[10] *New International Version,* Note: Some Bible translations have the term "only begotten" at John 1:18. However, this does not mean that Jesus was created. When Jesus is called the "only begotten God" at John 1:18, this term is used to refer to Christ's uniqueness as God. Originally, it was thought that the term *monogenese* came from *monos* meaning "only" and *gennao* meaning "begotten." But further research has determined that the term *genese* is derived **not from *gennao*, but rather from *genos*** which means "kind" or "type." Therefore, when certain Bible translations refer to Jesus as the "only begotten God," they are literally saying that Jesus is the "one and only unique God"—hence the

Father's side" and who has revealed God to us. Just as Colossians 1:15 says that Jesus is the "image of the invisible God," Jesus is the visible aspect of God that we can see.

**CINDY:** But, Karen, haven't you heard the saying, "He's the spitting' image of his father"? Don't you think Jehovah gave Jesus all these qualities that make Jesus appear as if he has God's nature; thus, making him "like" Jehovah? But such hardly proves that Jesus is God, does it?

**KAREN:** That's a good point, Cindy, but how do we reconcile that belief with Jehovah's statement that He is the **only** God and there is no God "like" Him. If Jehovah gave His qualities to Jesus and made Jesus a separate and "mighty god," "**like**" Him, how can Jehovah say there is no one like Him. Why don't you read Isaiah 46:9 from your Bible—*The New World Translation.*

**CINDY:** "Remember the first things of a long time ago, that I am the Divine One and there is no other God, nor anyone like me." Are you saying, Karen, that Jehovah could not have made Jesus a "mighty god" "like" Himself or He would be contradicting His statement here in Isaiah?

**KAREN:** Yes, Cindy, and if "Jehovah says that we must worship only him" and that "He will not share his glory with anyone or anything else,"[11] wouldn't you agree that if the Bible says Jesus is worshipped and that He shares Jehovah's glory, this proves Jesus is God by nature?

**CINDY:** Yes, but doesn't Jehovah say in Isaiah 42:8: "I am Jehovah. That is my name, and to no one else shall I give my own glory...."[12] Where in the Bible does it say that Jesus share's Jehovah's glory and is worshipped?

**KAREN:** Cindy, one passage is here in John 17:5 where Jesus states: "So now you, Father, glorify me alongside yourself with the glory that I had alongside you before the world was."[13] Not only do we see the Father sharing His glory with the Son; but in Revelation, we read that Jesus is honored in song and worshipped along with the Father. Would you read Revelation 5:11-14 in your *New World Translation* Bible, Cindy?

**CINDY:** Sure! "And I saw, and I heard a voice of many angels around the throne and the living creatures and the elders...saying with a loud voice: 'The Lamb that was slaughtered is **worthy** to receive the power and riches and wisdom and strength and honor and **glory** and blessing. And every creature that is in heaven and on earth...I heard saying: 'To the One sitting on the throne **and** to the Lamb be the blessing and the honor and the glory and the might forever and ever.' And the four living creatures went saying: 'Amen!' and the elders fell down and **worshipped**."

---

clearer translation "God the one and only" found in the *New International Version* Bible.

[11] *What Does God Require of Us?,* p. 5:5

[12] *New World Translation*

[13] *New World Translation*

**KAREN:** Cindy, you know the Lamb is Jesus and here the Lamb is receiving the same glory and worship that the Father is receiving. Can you see why Christians believe that Jesus possesses the nature of the only true God?

**COMMENTS:**

*Friends, do you give Jesus the same honor and worship that you give the One and only* ***true*** *God? Jesus said that if we do not "honor the Son" we "do not honor the Father" who sent Him.*[14]

[14] John 5:23

## ***DIALOGUE SIX: Was Jesus Created As God's "Firstborn Son" —Colossians 1:15-16?***

(WDGR LESSON 3: "Who Is Jesus Christ?")

*In what way is Jesus the "firstborn over all creation"? Does Proverbs 8:22-23 prove that Jesus was created? If Jesus was not created, why does the Bible say that Jesus is "the beginning of the creation of God" at Revelation 3:14?*

**KAREN:** Hello, Cindy!

**CINDY:** Oh, Hi, Karen! I was thinking about our study last week in the Watchtower brochure, *What Does God Require of Us?* We had talked about how there is only one true God, and you had said that you believe that Jesus is the true God along with the Father. But, I have a question: If Jesus is God, why do you think "Jesus is called God's 'firstborn' Son?"[1]

**KAREN:** That's a good question, Cindy. I'm glad we are studying who Jesus Christ is, for if we do not know who He is, how can we trust Him for our salvation?

**CINDY:** Very well, then. Karen, why don't we start by reading Colossians 1:15-19. Would you like to read this passage in your Bible?

**KAREN:** Sure, Cindy! "He" Jesus "is the image of the invisible God, the firstborn over all creation. For by him **all** things were created: things in heaven and on earth, visible and invisible, whether thrones or powers or rulers or authorities; **all** things were created by him and for him. He is before **all** things, and in him **all** things hold together. And he is the head of the body, the church; he is the beginning and the firstborn from among the dead, so that in **everything** he might have the supremacy. For God was pleased to have all **His** fullness dwell in him."[2]

**CINDY:** Wow, Karen! Your Bible reads differently than mine. My *New World Translation* says that Christ created "all [**other**] things," not that He created "all things," like yours reads. In fact, it puts the word "other" in this passage four times, and I'm also noticing that the word "other" is in brackets. I wonder why.

**KAREN:** Does your Bible have an appendix that might tell us why it adds the word "other" to "all things" in this passage?

**CINDY:** Well, let me see…"Table of the Books of the Bible" … no … that's not it.… Oh, here's something! "Brackets enclose words **inserted** to complete the sense in the English text; [[ ]] suggest interpolations in original text."[3] What do they mean by that?

---

[1] *What Does God Require of Us?,* 1996, p. 6
[2] *New International Version*
[3] *New World Translation,* 1984, p. 1547

**KAREN:** Do you think the Watchtower is saying that their Bible added the word "other" to the text because they believe that this is the best way to translate the passage to fit their doctrine, even though the word "other" is not in the original Greek manuscripts of this passage?

**CINDY:** I guess that's what they're saying, Karen. Here, I have a Greek/English Interlinear Translation of this passage that the Watchtower Society published. Let me look this passage up in it and find out.... Colossians 1:16: "because in him it was created the all (things) in the heavens and upon the earth..." and 17: "and he is before all (things) and the all (things) in him it has stood together."[4]

**KAREN:** Cindy, since this passage is teaching that Jesus created everything, not just all "other" things, but everything that was ever created, wouldn't this prove that Jesus Himself couldn't be created? Otherwise, if he is created and He created **everything**, then he'd have to have created Himself, wouldn't He?

**CINDY:** I wouldn't jump to that conclusion just yet, Karen. Let's look at some other verses. Verse 15 of this passage says that Jesus is the "firstborn." What do you think "firstborn" means?

**KAREN:** Cindy, my *New American Standard Bible* has a footnote on verse 15. Let me read what it says: "Here Jesus Christ is presented as the image of God, the invisible One....The other word to which we must turn our attention and which is used twice in this context is the word *prototokos*... translated as 'first born' or 'first begotten.'...What it means here is that Christ...is **above** all creation. It does **not** mean that He is part of the creation made by God, but that the relation of the whole creation to Him was determined by the fact that He is the **cause** of the creation of all things...and that without Him there could be no creation."[5]

**CINDY:** That's interesting, Karen, but I'd have to disagree with that footnote in your Bible. "Firstborn" **means** "first created" because "Jesus is the only Son that God created by himself."[6]

**KAREN:** But, Cindy, Look! The footnote in my Bible goes on to state that there is a Greek word that the apostle Paul could have used which means "first created." Let me read this: "It is **not** said of Christ that He was *ktistheis,* 'created,' from [the Greek word] *ktizo* 'to create,' ....We **never** find this verb *ktizo* as referring to Jesus Christ as having been created."[7] Cindy, if Jesus was created as the Watchtower Society teaches, and not merely the "firstborn" in the sense of His preeminence **over** the creation, why didn't the apostle Paul use the word that would have clearly communicated this idea of creation?

---

[4] *The Kingdom Interlinear Translation,* 1985ed, p. 880

[5] *New American Standard Bible,* The Hebrew-Greek Key Study Bible, compiled and edited by Spiros Zodhiates, Th.D. (Chattanooga, TN: AMG Publishers, 1990), p. 1579

[6] *What Does God Require of Us?,* p. 6:1

[7] *New American Standard Bible,* The Hebrew-Greek Key Study Bible, p. 1579

**CINDY:** I don't know, Karen, but doesn't the Bible say at Revelation 3:14 that Christ is "the beginning of the creation of God"?

**KAREN:** Yes, it does, Cindy, but this doesn't prove that Jesus is created. The Greek word for "beginning," *Arche,* is often used in Scripture to mean the "cause" or "source" of something.[8] It is in this sense as an originator, that Jesus is called the "beginning of the creation of God," because all of creation began with Christ.

**CINDY:** Well, Karen, if those verses don't prove that Jesus is created, how do you explain Proverbs 8:22-23? Here, we see that as wisdom personified, "Jehovah used the prehuman Jesus as his 'master worker' in creating all other things in heaven and on earth."[9] Let me read it in my Bible, *The New World Translation:* "Jehovah himself **produced** me as the beginning of his way, the earliest of his achievements of long ago. From time indefinite I was installed, from the start, from times earlier than the earth." Can you see, Karen, how Jesus as "wisdom" was "produced" by Jehovah in order to create the earth?

**KAREN:** Cindy, if Jehovah had to "produce" or "create" wisdom, does this mean that there was a point in time that Jehovah had no wisdom, that is, until He created it?

**CINDY:** I never thought of it that way before. You're right, Karen! How could Jehovah have ever been without wisdom? That doesn't make any sense!

**KAREN:** Can you see why my Bible translates Proverbs 8:22 as "The LORD **possessed** me,"[10] rather than your Bible which states that He "produced" wisdom? Which fits the context better? My Bible goes on to translate verse 23 as: "From everlasting I was established." Can you see how wisdom is just as eternal as Jehovah Himself is? And if Jesus is wisdom personified, as the Watchtower argues, wouldn't we have to argue that He is as eternal as wisdom is and therefore could not possibly be created?

**CINDY:** Karen, that's a good question.

**KAREN:** Cindy, we've looked at all of the verses the Society gives in this brochure to try to prove that Jesus is created, and none of them stand up under examination. I'd like to share with you a passage that I believe proves that Jesus could not possibly be created. It's Isaiah 44:24. Would you like to read it in your Bible, Cindy?

**CINDY:** Sure! "This is what Jehovah has said,... 'I, Jehovah, am doing everything, stretching out the heavens by myself, laying out the earth. Who was with me?' "[11]

---

[8] *New American Standard Bible,* The Hebrew-Greek Key Study Bible, p. 1579; *The New Englishman's Greek Concordance and Lexicon,* by Jay P. Green, Sr. (Peabody, MA: Hendrickson Publishers, 1982), p. 94
[9] *What Does God Require of Us?,* p. 6:1
[10] *New American Standard Bible*
[11] *New World Translation*

**KAREN:** Cindy, if Jehovah created Jesus and Jesus created everything else as the Watchtower teaches, how can Jehovah say that He created "everything" by Himself and that no one was "with" Him?

**COMMENTS:**

*Friends, John 1:3 says of Christ: "All things came into existence through him, and apart from him not even one thing came into existence."*[12] *Jesus cannot be part of the creation made by Jehovah, for no one was with Him when Jehovah-Jesus created the universe all alone.*

[12] *New World Translation*

## *DIALOGUE SEVEN: What Is The Proper Balance Between "Faith" And "Works" In Salvation?*

(WDGR LESSON 3: "Who Is Jesus Christ?")

*"If the evidence of our faith is our good works, how many good works are enough so that we know we will be forgiven and accepted by God?" Karen challenges Cindy in regard to the Jehovah's Witness concept that "exercising faith" through the door-to-door preaching activity proves an individual worthy of everlasting life.*[1]

**KAREN:** Hi, Cindy!

**CINDY:** Oh, Hi, Karen. I'm looking forward to our study in the Watchtower brochure *What Does God Require of Us?*. We've talked a lot about who Jesus Christ is, but why do you think Jesus came to earth as a man?[2]

**KAREN:** Well, Cindy, in this brochure, the Society states that one of the reasons Jesus came to earth was "to sacrifice his life to set us free from sin and death,"[3] but I don't understand, why do we need salvation in the first place?

**CINDY:** Karen, we need salvation because the Bible says in Romans 3:23 that: "All have sinned and fall short of the glory of God."[4] "By disobeying God's command, the first man, Adam....passed on sin to all his children....God sentenced him to death." And "That is why we also grow old, get sick, and die."[5]

**KAREN:** But, I don't understand why Jesus had to die to free us from sin. Why isn't it enough to have our good works outweigh the bad? After all, we aren't as bad as Adolph Hitler, are we?

**CINDY:** No, Karen, but it took a "perfect human life to pay for Adam's sin." Jesus is the only perfect human, so it is only through him that: "Adam's children could thus be released from condemnation to death. All who put their faith in Jesus can have their sins forgiven and receive everlasting life."[6]

**KAREN:** Yes, but is it really faith? Doesn't the Bible say that: "...faith without works is dead"?[7]

---

[1] In this dialogue, Karen asks Cindy questions about faith and works not to try to prove that works are necessary for salvation, but rather, to prove that salvation must be based upon faith alone in Christ without any reliance upon human works. Most of the content of this dialogue was taken from the *Free Minds Journal* article entitled: "How to Talk to a Jehovah's Witness About Salvation" by David Englund, Free Minds Journal, July / Sept 2000, vol. 19, no. 3, pages 7-8; (Free Minds, Manhattan Beach, CA 90266 - www.freeminds.org)
[2] *What Does God Require of Us?,* 1996, p. 6
[3] *What Does God Require of Us?,* p. 6:2
[4] *New American Standard Bible*
[5] *What Does God Require of Us?,* p. 6:3
[6] *What Does God Require of Us?,* p. 6:4
[7] See James 2:14-20

**CINDY:** Yes, it does, Karen, but the Bible also says in Ephesians 2:8-9: "By this undeserved kindness, indeed, YOU have been saved through faith; and this not owing to YOU, it is God's gift. No, it is not owing to works, in order that no man should have ground for boasting."[8] Can you see, Karen, why we can't earn our salvation?

**KAREN:** Yes, Cindy, but please don't think I'm being flippant with this question. I don't mean to be, but since faith without works is dead, when it comes to paying off our sin debt, do you think that it would be accurate to say that Christ made the down payment by His sacrifice but that it's up to us to keep up the installments by our good works?

**CINDY:** Yes, Karen. That's a good illustration of the way it works.

**KAREN:** Well, then, Cindy, how much of the debt is really paid off by Christ's sacrifice and how much by our works?

**CINDY:** I'm not sure… I know our works cannot pay off the sin debt. But I think it must be that our salvation comes by faith in Christ's sacrifice, but the evidence of our faith is our good works. When you do good works, Karen, you are showing Jehovah that you are grateful for His gift of salvation, and your works prove that your faith is acceptable.[9] Does this make sense to you?

**KAREN:** Yes, but I'm still not sure. Cindy, if the evidence of our faith is our good works, how many good works are enough so that we know we will be forgiven and accepted by God? For example, I suppose there are Jehovah's Witnesses who do the door-to-door ministry full time and I suppose there are Witnesses who do very little. Most are probably somewhere in the middle. If I were a Witness, how could I know I had enough faith that, if I died in the middle of the night, God would find my faith acceptable?

**CINDY:** I'm not sure, Karen.

**KAREN:** Well, I think of Peter, who had enough faith to walk on the water one minute and who almost drowned the next. Jesus said at that point that he had "little faith."[10] How much is enough? How do we know we are doing enough works to prove our faith?

**CINDY:** Well, Karen, I'm not sure, but I know that Jehovah sees our hearts. I would think that if you are doing the best you can, Jehovah sees this and He will accept you.

**KAREN:** But, Cindy, you've probably learned how to deal with this, but I don't know if I could look at my service as evidence of my faith or whether I do good works out of gratitude to God. I'm afraid I would always be trying to do just a little more to make sure I was in God's favor but never knowing for sure if He accepted me.

---

[8] *New World Translation*

[9] *Commentary on the Letter of James,* 1979, p. 75-77

[10] Matthew 14:28-33

**CINDY:** Karen, that's something I struggle with too.

**KAREN:** Cindy, I look at the many people who do good works without any reference to Christ's sacrifice. How can one know if what he is doing is truly being done from faith in Christ?

**CINDY:** I don't know...

**KAREN:** Sometimes I can con myself into thinking that I'm spiritual when I'm really relying on my performance like the Pharisees did. How can I know if my works really come from faith?

**CINDY:** Well, hum...

**KAREN:** It's difficult, isn't it? The more I try to please God by being spiritual, the less I seem to be trusting in Jesus. Maybe you haven't had that problem, but that's something I struggle with.

**COMMENTS:**

*Friends, the Bible says in Romans 14:23: "...Indeed, everything that is not out of* ***faith*** *is sin."*[11] *Just as James chapter 2 verses 14, 18 and 26 state: "What use is it, my brethren, if a man* **says** *he has faith, but he has not works? Can* ***that faith*** *save him?...But someone may well* ***say****, 'You have faith, and I have works;* ***show*** *me your faith without the works, and I will* ***show*** *you my faith by my works....For just as the body without the spirit is dead, so also faith without works is dead."*[12] *The point that the apostle James is making in this passage, is that a* ***dead*** *faith cannot save a person anymore than a physical body can live without the spirit. Even as fruit on a fruit tree proves that the tree is alive and well, so works* ***follow*** *true Christian faith and* ***proves*** *that the faith which spiritually saves the Christian is alive.*

*While it is true that works* ***prove*** *that a Christian has living faith, works do not make a person worthy of everlasting life. For the apostle Paul states at Romans 5:1, Romans 8:1, and Colossians 3:3: "Therefore having been justified [declared righteous] by* ***faith****, we have peace with God through our Lord Jesus Christ.... There is therefore now* ***no condemnation*** *for those who are in Christ Jesus.... For you have died and your life is* ***hidden*** *with Christ in God."*[13]

[11] *New World Translation*
[12] *New American Standard Bible*
[13] *New American Standard Bible*

## ***DIALOGUE EIGHT: Is Eternal Life In The Watchtower Organization A Reality?***

(WDGR LESSON 5: "What is God's Purpose for the Earth?")

*How realistic is the Watchtower plan of salvation? What does a person have to do in order to be assured of eternal life?*[1]

**KAREN:** Hello, Cindy! I've been reading over our next lesson in the Watchtower brochure, *What Does God Require of Us?,* and I am fascinated by the prospect of eternal life forever in paradise. I can't wait to learn more about how I can have this hope.

**CINDY:** That's great, Karen! Do you know why the earth is not a paradise now?

**KAREN:** Yes, Cindy, the brochure notes that: "Adam and Eve sinned by deliberately breaking God's law. So Jehovah put them out of the garden of Eden. Paradise was lost."[2]

**CINDY:** That's right, Karen, and, "before this earth can become a paradise, wicked people must be removed....This will happen at Armageddon, which is God's war to end wickedness. Next, Satan will be imprisoned for 1,000 years. This means that no wicked ones will be left to spoil the earth. Only God's people will survive."[3] Would you like to be one of those people who survive into this new system of things, Karen?

**KAREN:** Yes, I would, Cindy, but I don't understand. What **exactly** do I need to do in order to be saved and have eternal life?

**CINDY:** Well, the Bible says at John 17:3: "This means everlasting life, their taking in knowledge of you, the only true God, and of the one whom you sent forth, Jesus Christ."[4] So you see, Karen, if: "you would like to share in these future blessings...you need to keep learning about Jehovah and obeying his requirements."[5]

**KAREN:** OK, Cindy. After I do that, then what do I need to do?

**CINDY:** What do you mean, Karen?

**KAREN:** Well, do I need to join your religion?

---

[1] In this dialogue, Karen does not get into a discussion with Cindy about the differences between the Jehovah's Witness view of the afterlife being life on paradise earth instead of heaven and annihilation for the wicked instead of hell because her sole purpose in this dialogue is to demonstrate to Cindy the impossibility of gaining salvation through the Watchtower system of works. Most of the content of this dialogue was taken from the book entitled *The Armageddon Cult—Life in the Watchtower Society Nothing Right!!!,* 2000, by Daniel LeEarl Hall, pp. 140-141, (Reveal Ministries, Walnut Grove, CA)

[2] *What Does God Require of Us?,* 1996, p. 10:3

[3] *What Does God Require of Us?,* p. 10:4

[4] *New World Translation*

[5] *What Does God Require of Us?,* p. 11:7

**CINDY:** Yes! You want to be in the truth so that you won't be destroyed with the wicked of false religion. So, yes, you do need to become one of Jehovah's Witnesses.

**KAREN:** If I do that, then am I saved?

**CINDY:** No, Karen, the Bible says you must endure to the "end" in order to be saved[6]

**KAREN:** What do you mean by "end," Cindy? Do you mean Armageddon?

**CINDY:** Yes.

**KAREN:** OK, so if I endure through Armageddon, then am I saved?

**CINDY:** No.

**KAREN:** I'm in this perfect world, but I'm not saved? Am I perfect?

**CINDY:** Not yet, Karen.

**KAREN:** Well, is **anybody** perfect?

**CINDY:** No, Karen. When Jesus Christ rules as: "King over this earth… He will **gradually** take sin away from our minds and bodies." Then "we will **become** perfect humans just as Adam and Eve were before they sinned."[7]

**KAREN:** So, how long do I have to go without sinning before I can be saved, Cindy?

**CINDY:** A thousand years, Karen. "During Jesus' Thousand Year Reign, faithful humans will work to turn the whole earth into a paradise….If they do what God requires of them, they will continue to live on earth forever. If not, they will be destroyed forever."[8]

**KAREN:** Wait a minute! I'm not perfect and nobody else is perfect and I have to go a **thousand** years without making a major mistake?

**CINDY:** That's right, Karen. This is why it is so important that we learn what Jehovah requires.

**KAREN:** But can you do that, Cindy? Can you go a **thousand** years without making a major mistake even though you are not perfect?

**CINDY:** I don't know if I can, Karen. But I'm sure going to try!

**KAREN:** But, what if I go 999 years without making a major mistake, but in the last year just before the test I mess up. Or what if under the pressure of Satan, I fail the final test?[9] Does this mean I will be destroyed forever?

---

[6] Matthew 24:13

[7] *What Does God Require of Us?,* p. 11:5

[8] *What Does God Require of Us?,* p. 11:6

**CINDY:** Maybe, Karen. In the August 1, 1992 *Watchtower,* the Society said: " 'If anyone wants to come after me,' said Jesus Christ to a gathering of disciples and others, 'let him disown himself…and follow me continually.' (Mark 8:34) When we accept this invitation, we must be prepared to do so 'continually,' not because there is some special merit in self-denial, but because **one moment's indiscretion**, **one lapse in good judgment**, may undo **all** that has been built up, **even jeopardizing our eternal welfare**. Spiritual progress is usually made at a rather slow pace, but how **quickly** it can be **nullified** if we are not on guard constantly!"[10]

**KAREN:** So, is the Society saying that if I make even one major mistake, I will be destroyed forever?

**CINDY:** That is the chance you'll take, Karen.

**KAREN:** But how can anyone pass the test and not make a major mistake if he is not perfect?

**CINDY:** I don't know, Karen. It seems impossible, but this is what Jehovah requires.

**KAREN:** Cindy?

**CINDY:** Yes, Karen?

**KAREN:** Did Jesus pay for **all** of our sins when He died two thousand years ago, or did He just pay for **some** of them?

**CINDY:** Oh, he paid for **all** of them, Karen.

**KAREN:** So, if Jesus paid for **all** of our sins, exactly **what** sin can I commit that He did not pay for and which would cause me to lose my eternal life?

**COMMENTS:**

*Friends, John said at 1 John 5:11-13: "And this is the witness given, that God gave us everlasting life, and this life is in his Son. He that has the Son has this life; he that does not have the Son of God does not have this life. I write YOU these things that YOU may* ***know*** *that You have life everlasting, You who put YOUR faith in the name of the Son of God."*[11]

---

[9] See *Life Does Have A Purpose,* 1977, p. 177
[10] *The Watchtower* August 1, 1992, p. 17
[11] *New World Translation*

### *DIALOGUE NINE: What Must A Person Do In Order To Be Clean In God's Eyes?*

(WDGR LESSON 9: "God's Servants Must Be Clean")

*What did Jesus do for us when He died? Was His death merely a "ransom" sacrifice to release mankind from the "condemnation to death" due to Adam's sin?*[1]

**CINDY:** Karen, are you home?

**KAREN:** Oh, yes, Cindy. Come on in. I'm working on getting grape juice stain out of my blouse. Seems like this is the toughest stain I've ever tried to get out of an outfit.

**CINDY:** That's awful, Karen. I know how hard it is to get grape stain out of clothes. Just like we'll be studying today in the Watchtower brochure *What Does God Require of Us?,* "God's servants must be clean in all respects." Why do you think we must "be clean in every way?"[2]

**KAREN:** Well, Cindy, just as the Society notes in this brochure: "Jehovah God is clean and holy. He expects his worshipers to remain clean—spiritually, morally, mentally, and physically....He sees everything we do, even in secret."[3] But I have a question. What must a person do in order to be clean in God's eyes?

**CINDY:** Well, Karen, this brochure notes that: "It takes real effort to stay clean in God's eyes. We live in an unclean world. We also have a struggle against our own tendencies to do wrong. But we must not give up."[4]

**KAREN:** Cindy, what did Jesus Christ do for us when He died on the torture stake?

**CINDY:** Well, Karen, just as we studied the other day, when the first man Adam sinned by disobeying God's command, he passed sin on to all of his children. Since the penalty of sin is death, Jesus sacrificed: "his perfect human life to pay for Adam's sin" so that "Adam's children could thus be released from condemnation to death." By exercising faith in Jehovah's provision of the ransom sacrifice, we can have our sins forgiven and receive everlasting life.[5]

**KAREN:** OK, Cindy. So, Jesus paid for Adam's sin. What else did He do for us when he died?

---

[1] The false Jehovah's Witness belief that Christ died upon a torture stake instead of a cross is not discussed in this dialogue, because the focus is simply upon presenting the gospel. Since this false Jehovah's Witness belief is not essential to salvation, it remain unchallenged in this dialogue between Karen and Cindy. Most of the content of this dialogue was taken from an audio message entitled, *A Few Effective Methods of Witnessing to Jehovah's Witnesses,* by Arnold Hoffman

[2] *What Does God Require of Us?,* 1996, pp. 18-19

[3] *What Does God Require of Us?,* p. 18:1, 3

[4] *What Does God Require of Us?,* p. 18:1

[5] *What Does God Require of Us?,* pp. 6-7

**CINDY:** Well, by fulfilling the law of Moses that Jehovah gave to the Jews, the ransom sacrifice of Christ released us from the curse of the law of Moses, and set us free from idolatry and superstition of false religion.[6]

**KAREN:** So, Christ's ransom sacrifice sets us free from the curse of the law of Moses, and pays the penalty of Adam's sin. What else did Jesus do for us on the stake?

**CINDY:** What do you mean, Karen?

**KAREN:** Cindy, would you read 1 Peter 2:24 in your Bible?

**CINDY:** "He himself bore our sins in his own body upon the stake, in order that we might be done with sins and live to righteousness."[7]

**KAREN:** What did Jesus bear in His own body on the tree?

**CINDY:** Well, it says he: "bore our sins."

**KAREN:** So, He bore "our sins." What sins are those? Our personal sins?…the times we lied, the times we stole, or thought unclean thoughts? And where did Jesus bear "our sins"?

**CINDY:** It says he bore our sins: "in his own body."

**KAREN:** What does the word "bore" mean?

**CINDY:** It means "to carry."

**KAREN:** So, Jesus carried our personal sins in His body. Let me draw this out for you, Cindy. This here is Jesus hanging on the tree, and these dots over here represent our personal sins—the times we lied, the times we stole, or thought unclean thoughts. Now, the Bible says, Jesus: "bore **our sins** in his own body." So, Jehovah literally transferred our personal sins over here to the body of Jesus, and He died, carrying all of our personal sins **in** His body. Our sins… in Christ's body. Have you ever seen this before?

**CINDY:** What!? Karen, you mean our personal sins? The times we lied or thought bad thoughts? Oh, I don't believe that! Jesus didn't die for my personal sins. "Our sins" is just talking about our sinful tendencies due to Adam's sin.

**KAREN:** Cindy, where do our personal sins come from? They come from Adamic sin, don't they?

**CINDY:** Well, yes… but you're adding the word "personal" here! Where does it say this is talking about our "personal sins"?

---

[6] *The Watchtower,* June 1, 1992, p. 12

[7] *New World Translation*

**KAREN:** What does the word "our" mean? "Our" is **personal**! Right?

**CINDY:** Well, yes.

**KAREN:** Cindy, would you read Ezekiel 18:4.

**CINDY:** "The soul that is sinning—it itself will die."[8]

**KAREN:** According to the Bible, what causes the soul to die?

**CINDY:** Sin...

**KAREN:** What sin? Adam's sin, or our personal sins?

**CINDY:** Well, Karen, I guess it's talking about our personal sins: "the soul that **is** sinning—it **itself** will die." So our personal sins result in death, but what's your point, Karen?

**KAREN:** My point is this, Cindy. Not only are you under the condemnation of death due to Adamic sin, but you are under an additional condemnation of death due to your own personal sins. Now you're either going to have to pay for this, or you're going to have to get someone else to pay for this. It's just like when you get a traffic ticket. You go before the judge and the penalty is $50.00 or one day in jail. Now you can say to the judge: "Oh judge, please forgive me. I've been good. I've been doing the best I can and trying to obey all the laws." But what is the judge going to say? "This must be paid or I cannot forgive you!"

**CINDY:** Humm…

**KAREN:** Now watch this. Say I love you and I go before the judge and I pull out $50.00 and say "I'll pay the penalty." **Now**, the judge can turn to you and say: "Cindy you're free to go." Why? Because you've been good? No! But because the price has been paid. The judge cannot forgive you on the basis of mercy. He can only forgive you because justice has been paid. And that's exactly what Christ did for you. It's as if Jesus walked into Jehovah's courtroom and said: "Father, I love Cindy very much. I know she deserves death and your wrath because of her personal sins. But, Father, you know I haven't done anything wrong, and I don't deserve to die, but if you'll take all of her personal sins—the times she lied, the times she stole or thought unclean thoughts—and transfer them to my body, I'll go down to that torture stake and pay in **full** everything Cindy has coming to her for her personal sins." And you know, Cindy? That's exactly what Jesus Christ did for you.

[8] *New World Translation*

**CINDY:** Wow!

**KAREN:** So, Cindy, what caused the death of Jesus on the torture state? Was it the Jews? Was it the Romans? Or was it your personal sins?

**COMMENTS:**

*Friends, just as Cindy discovered today, spiritual cleanness starts with the realization that Jesus paid the full penalty not only for Adam's sin but for each of our personal sins. At Mark 2:10-11 Jesus said: "...in order that you may know that the Son of Man has* ***authority*** *on earth to forgive sins'—He said to the paralytic—I say to you, rise, take up your pallet and go home."*[9] *Jehovah God has given Jesus the authority to forgive your personal sins. Why not come to Jesus today and ask Him to cleanse you of your personal sins? Jesus said: "I am the bread of life; he who* ***comes to Me*** *shall not hunger....All that the Father gives Me shall* ***come to Me****, and the one who* ***comes to Me*** *I will certainly not cast out."*[10]

[9] *New American Standard Bible*

[10] John 6:35, 37, *New American Standard Bible*

## *DIALOGUE TEN: Doing God's Will—What Does It Mean To "Come To Jesus"?*

(WDGR LESSON 15: "Helping Others to Do God's Will")

*Who did Jesus say we must go to in order to have eternal life? Is it proper to pray to Jesus?*[1]

**CINDY:** Karen, "By now" in our study of the Watchtower brochure *What Does God Require of Us?,* "you have learned many good things from the Bible. This knowledge should lead to your cultivating a Christian personality."[2] Just as John 17:3 states: "This means everlasting life, their taking in knowledge of you, the only true God, and of the one whom you sent forth, Jesus Christ."[3] "Such knowledge is essential in order for you to gain eternal life."[4]

**KAREN:** Cindy, if I take in all the **knowledge** I can about Jehovah God and **believe** in Jesus Christ, it doesn't really matter what church I belong to, does it? As long as I have Jesus, wouldn't I be assured of everlasting life?

**CINDY:** Well, no, Karen. Jehovah requires that we act in harmony with the knowledge we are taking in. While: "belief in Jesus is vital, no doubt you have observed, as I have, that many who say they are Christians really do not live up to what that name represents."[5] "Let us read Matthew 7:21-23 and see if we can isolate a **critical** factor that determines whether all worship is acceptable to God. Jesus said: 'Not everyone saying to me, "Lord, Lord," will enter into the kingdom of the heavens, but the one **doing the will** of my Father who is in the heavens will. Many will say to me in that day, "Lord, Lord, did we not prophesy in your name, and expel demons…in your name, and perform many powerful works in your name?" And yet then I will confess to them: I never knew you! Get away from me, you workers of lawlessness.' Acknowledging Jesus Christ as Lord is essential in true worship. But something would be missing in the worship of many of those claiming to be Jesus' disciples. He said that some would perform 'powerful works,'….However, they would fail to do what Jesus said is vital. They would not be 'doing the will of [his] Father.' If we want to please God, we must **learn** what the will of the Father is and then **do** it."[6]

**KAREN:** Cindy, according to John 5:39-40, what did Jesus say we must do in order to please God and to have everlasting life?

---

[1] The false Jehovah's Witness beliefs that Christ died upon a torture stake instead of a cross and that the wicked are annihilated instead of being tormented in a fiery hell is not discussed in this dialogue because the focus is simply upon presenting the gospel. Since this false Jehovah's Witness belief is not essential to salvation, it remains unchallenged in this dialogue between Karen and Cindy. Most of the content of this dialogue was taken from an audio message entitled, *A Few Effective Methods of Witnessing to Jehovah's Witnesses,* by Arnold Hoffman

[2] *What Does God Require of Us?,* 1996, p. 30:1

[3] *New World Translation*

[4] *What Does God Require of Us?,* p. 30:1

[5] *Reasoning from the Scriptures,* 1985, 1989ed, p. 332

[6] *Knowledge that Leads to Everlasting Life,* 1995, p. 46

**CINDY:** Well, let me see. John 5:39-40: "You are searching the Scriptures, because YOU think that by means of them YOU will have everlasting life; and these are the very ones that bear witness about me. And yet YOU do not want to **come to me** that YOU may have life."

**KAREN:** Cindy, **who** did Jesus say we must go to in order to have eternal life?

**CINDY:** Well, Karen, it says we must "come" to him—to Jesus.

**KAREN:** That's right, Cindy. Have you done that? Have you **come** to Jesus by asking Him to forgive your sins and to give you eternal life?

**CINDY:** What!? Karen, you mean "pray" to Jesus? Oh, no, we don't do that! Who did Jesus tell us to pray to? He told us to pray to Jehovah God—in Jesus' Name—but he did not teach us to pray directly to him. Just as the December 15, 1994 issue of *The Watchtower* notes: "On one occasion Jesus said: 'It is written, "It is Jehovah your God you must worship, and it is to him **alone** you must render sacred service." ' [Since] every prayer is a form of worship....that belongs exclusively to Almighty God, by addressing all our prayers to Jehovah God, we indicate that we have taken to heart Jesus' direction to pray: 'Our Father in the heavens.' "[7]

**KAREN:** Cindy, who did Jesus make that statement to? He made it to His disciples who, according to John 13, were already clean.[8] They already had their sins forgiven, and because of this, they were able to call God their Father. But you haven't gone to Jesus, so you don't have your sins forgiven. You see, Cindy, when Jesus was on earth, people prayed directly to the Father, but once Jesus went to heaven, there was a change in God's arrangement. Now, it's OK to pray to Jesus. Before it wasn't. And you, Witnesses, need to understand the change in God's arrangement. You need to come to Jesus.

**CINDY:** But, Karen, where do you see that in the Bible? Where do you see people praying to Jesus? At John 14:6, Jesus said: "...No one comes to the Father except **through** me.'...Thus, we should present our prayers to God **through** Jesus and not directly to Jesus himself."[9]

**KAREN:** Cindy, one place Jesus told us to pray to Him is here at John 14:14 where Jesus says: "If you **ask Me** anything in My name, **I** will do *it.*"[10]

**CINDY:** Wait a minute, Karen! My Bible doesn't say, "ask **Me** anything...." It says: "...ask anything in My name." Even the Society notes regarding this verse that: "...the asking is addressed to Jehovah God—but in Jesus' name....We petition God that His Son, Jesus, apply his great power and authority in our behalf."[11]

---

[7] *The Watchtower,* December 15, 1994, pp. 24, 23, 25
[8] See John 13:10
[9] *The Watchtower,* December 15, 1994, p. 24
[10] *New American Standard Bible*

**KAREN:** Cindy, what does the Watchtower Society's *Kingdom Interlinear Translation* of the Greek text say regarding the original manuscript of this passage?

**CINDY:** Well, let me look it up, Karen. John 14:14: "If ever anything you should ask **me** in the name of me this I shall do." Oh, my...! The "ask me" is in the Greek text of the verse, but it's left out of the Watchtower's *New World Translation.* I wonder why.

**KAREN:** Cindy, do you think the translators of the *New World Translation,* left the "ask Me" out of their translation of this passage, because this verse contradicts the Watchtower teaching about prayers to Jesus? Notice in this passage, not only does Jesus encourage His followers to pray **directly** to Him, but He is the One who answers the prayers. "If you **ask Me** anything in My name, **I** will do it." You see, Cindy, just as Jesus said: "No one comes to the Father except through Me," He said we must go to Jesus and deal directly with Him before we can go to God. Have you done this? Have you "come" to Jesus—asking Him to give you eternal life? At John 10:27, Jesus says: "...**I give** eternal life" to my sheep. He doesn't say the Father gives eternal life **through** me. He says: "**I** give eternal life...." Don't you want to have eternal life? Don't you want to survive Armageddon into God's new order? Then, you've got to comply with Jehovah's arrangement for life and the forgiveness of sins! You've got to go to Jesus.

**CINDY:** But, Karen, we believe in Jesus and we exercise faith in the ransom sacrifice, but we pray to Jehovah God! We don't pray to Jesus.

**KAREN:** Cindy, Jesus said at John 6:45: "...Everyone who has heard and **learned** from the **Father**, **comes to Me**." Why do you think Jehovah God asks you to do that? Why does He want you to come to Jesus?...It's because Jesus actually forgives your sins. At Mark 2:10-11, Jesus said to those who were questioning Him: " 'But in order that you may know that the **Son of Man** has **authority** on earth **to forgive sins**'—He said to the paralytic—'I say to you, rise, take up your pallet and go home.' " Jesus actually has the **authority** to forgive your sins. He actually has the **authority** to give you eternal life.

**CINDY:** But, Karen, **who** gave Jesus that "authority"?

**KAREN:** Jehovah God did.

**CINDY:** You see then. There He is. You see, Jehovah God is **really** the One with the authority!

**KAREN:** But, Cindy, **why** did Jehovah God do that? Why did He give Jesus that authority? So He could forgive your sins. He gave Jesus the **authority** to forgive your sins, so that **you** could experience the forgiveness of sins. That's the whole point! That's why we go to Jesus, and this is God's arrangement. Cindy, did you know that Jesus never spoke any words except the words that the Father gave Him to speak? He didn't speak out from Himself—but He said only what His Father told Him to say.[12] And in

---

[11] *The Watchtower,* December 15, 1994, p. 25

[12] John 8:28

Matthew 17 when Jesus was on the mountain of transfiguration, what did Jehovah God say? "This is my beloved Son…**listen** to Him!"[13] That is a command! So when Jesus said: "Come to Me," He was expressing the **exact** will of Jehovah God for your life—stating **exactly** what God wants you, Cindy, to do. Why do you think I go to Jesus? Why do you think I pray to Him? Because I want to obey Jehovah God! Don't you? If Jehovah says: "Go to my Son, I have given Him authority to forgive your sins," then I go to Jesus because I want to obey Jehovah God. Otherwise, I wouldn't. If it pleases Jehovah that I deal **directly** with the Son; then that's the way I want it, because I want to comply with God's arrangement. I want to do His will. Have you done that, Cindy? Have you obeyed Jehovah God by complying with His arrangement? Have you come to Jesus? Prayed to Jesus? Asking Him to forgive you of your sins?

**CINDY:** Unh-uh! No, Karen. We honor Jesus, but we don't pray to him.

**KAREN:** Well, then, I'm concerned you don't have eternal life. You don't have your sins forgiven. You're in danger of being wiped out in Armageddon, because you haven't complied with His arrangement. You see, not everyone that says, "Lord, Lord," "Jehovah, Jehovah," will enter the Kingdom of God, but He that does the will of Jehovah God—and you haven't, Cindy. You haven't had your sins forgiven, and when Armageddon comes—why you're going to be annihilated in Armageddon in spite of all your theocratic activity and your theocratic works.

**CINDY:** Karen, who made **you** a judge? How do you know? The Bible says: "Stop judging that you may not be judged."[14]

**KAREN:** Wait a minute, Cindy! Why do you think I said that to you?…Because I want to see you saved—one who's experienced the forgiveness of sins. I love you! I don't want to see you wiped out at Armageddon. That's why I told you these things. That's why I'm concerned about it. And of the words out of your **own** mouth, you have condemned yourself! You have told me you haven't come to Jesus. You haven't complied with God's arrangement. And on the basis of the words out of **your** mouth, I say to you: "You will be annihilated." You see, Cindy, at one time I was religiously active—going about doing street work and preaching about God's Kingdom—but I didn't have peace. I didn't have joy. I didn't have satisfaction in my life. I didn't have a sense of Jehovah's approval on my life. And **then** God showed me the ransom provision. I was under the conviction of sins and God showed me what Jesus did for **me** on the torture stake. I saw my sins being transferred to Him. I saw Him dying for my sins—paying the penalty for my sins and you know, Cindy? I went to Jesus. I asked Him to forgive my sins and do you know what happened to me at that moment when I complied with Jehovah's arrangement?

**CINDY:** No, what happened?

---

[13] Matthew 17:5, *New American Standard Bible*

[14] Matthew 7:1, *New World Translation*

**KAREN:** One moment I was under the conviction of sins. The very next moment, I was free from that, clean, I had a sense of joy, sense of peace, my sins were forgiven. One moment, I was under that feeling that I hadn't done enough for Jehovah God. I hadn't met His approval. The very next moment, I had a God-given sense of Jehovah's approval, and you know what? Jehovah God became a personal Father to me for the very first time in my life. Before He was way up there in heaven — a thousand miles away. I was taking in knowledge of Him, learning about Him, but I didn't **know** Him. I didn't have a close relationship to Him. Something was missing and I didn't know what it was. But the moment I complied with God's arrangement, the moment I obeyed Jehovah God, immediately I had a sense of God's presence, a sense He was a Father to me for the first time. Now, I want you to know I didn't hear voices or see visions. I want you to know it was really a very quiet affair, but I want you to know it was a genuine supernatural, instantaneous event that took place in my heart. And I want you to know it **WASN'T** demonism.

**CINDY:** How do you know it wasn't demonism?! I go door-to-door...I've seen people go down there saying: "I got saved! I got saved!" but boy, you've got to be careful! The: "devil walks about like a roaring lion, seeking to devour someone."[15] How do you know it wasn't demonism?

**KAREN:** I know it wasn't demonism because I did **EXACTLY** what Jehovah God told me to do! He told me to go to Jesus, I went to Jesus. He asked me to pray to Him, to come to Him, and I did it. I obeyed God! And because I obeyed God, my experience was genuine. It is **not** counterfeit.

**COMMENTS:**

*Friends, how well would you know your best friend if all you did was read books and "take in knowledge"* ***about*** *your friend, but never spent time talking to your friend and getting to know Him personally? At Matthew 7:23, Jesus told those individuals who failed to do God's will that He never* ***knew*** *them—not because He didn't know* ***about*** *them—but because they failed to do God's will by getting to* ***know*** *Jesus personally. They failed to come into an intimate relationship with Him by asking Him to forgive their sins, and as a result He cast them away saying: "I never* ***knew*** *you!" This is why Jesus said at John 17:3: "...this is eternal life, that they may* ***know*** *you, the only true God,* ***and*** *Jesus Christ whom you have sent."[16] How can you* ***know*** *Jesus if you do not talk to Him and have never met Him personally? 1 Corinthians 1:9 states: "God is faithful, through whom you were called into* ***fellowship*** *with His Son, Jesus Christ our Lord."[17] How can a person have fellowship with someone he never talks to?*

---

[15] 1 Peter 5:8, *New World Translation*

[16] *New International Version*

[17] *New American Standard Bible*

# SECTION THREE:

# *EVALUATING JEHOVAH'S WITNESS CONSCIENCE ISSUES*

*A Christian Householder and*
*One of Jehovah's Witnesses Discuss*
*the Watchtower Publication,*
*"What Does God Require of Us?"*

*"He has told you, O man, what is good; and* ***what does the LORD require of you*** *but to do justice, to love kindness, and to walk humbly with your God"—Micah 6:8, New American Standard Bible*

## THE PURPOSE OF SECTION THREE:

## EVALUATING JEHOVAH'S WITNESS CONSCIENCE ISSUES

It is not uncommon for a Jehovah's Witness who has been out of the Watchtower organization for many years, to struggle with embracing the cultural customs of Christianity today.

Traditions such as celebrating un-Biblical holidays, Christmas as the birth of Christ, or celebrating *any* birthday for that matter, are strictly forbidden in the Watchtower organization. Likewise, Jehovah's Witnesses are forbidden from receiving life-saving blood transfusions, getting involved in politics or patriotically supporting a country's war effort, and they are taught to shun the Christian symbol of the cross as a pagan symbol, claiming that Jesus died on a single pole or "torture stake" instead.

Trying to find a place to worship in a Christian church can be emotionally exhausting when not only are former Jehovah's Witnesses confronted with these beliefs and so-called "pagan" symbols prominently displayed in Christian churches, but they are asked to believe in a fiery hell reserved for anyone who rejects Jesus Christ as their Savior.

While these issues have more to do with Christian freedom of conscience, than they do salvation, they are, never the less, very important to discuss in helping former Jehovah's Witnesses gain spiritual freedom. My goal in the following dialogues is to provide effective questions and answers that will help former Jehovah's Witnesses get to where they can worship with the rest of the Christian community in freedom of conscience.

## *DIALOGUE ONE: Does God's Law On Blood Require No Blood Transfusions? — Part I*

(WDGR LESSON 12: "Showing Respect for Life and Blood")

*Does God's law to "abstain from...blood" apply to Blood Transfusions? Is a Blood Transfusion the same as "eating blood"? Does God's Law condemn the use of stored blood?*

**KAREN:** Cindy, did you see that article in Friday's paper about the Jehovah's Witness who died after refusing a blood transfusion? According to the article: "...the unborn son of Anthony and Minnie Peoples had a fatal birth defect. And when she delivered Anthony Jr. at a Rock Hill hospital Tuesday night, he was stillborn. But there were complications, and Minnie...needed a blood transfusion....'The doctors really tried to plead with me that without blood, she wasn't going to make it,' said her husband, Anthony Peoples....York County coroner Doug McKnown said.... 'She made a decision to die, basically....I don't fully understand why their God would expect them to die, but I can't question that.'"[1] Cindy, just as McKnown commented, I'm afraid I don't understand either. I thought God's laws were to protect life—not destroy it.

**CINDY:** Karen, this is a tough issue. It's not always easy to understand Jehovah's ways, but we must not try to save our lives by breaking God's laws. Just as we'll be studying today in the Watchtower brochure *What Does God Require of Us?,* "Blood is...sacred in God's eyes. God says that the soul, or life, is in the blood. So...Jehovah requires that we abstain from blood. This means that we must not take into our bodies in any way at all other people's blood or even our own blood that has been stored....True Christians....want to live, but they will not try to save their life by breaking God's laws." 2 If the situation was really that serious, Karen, could the doctors have guaranteed that the patient would not have died if she had been given the blood transfusion?[3]

**KAREN:** Cindy, are you saying that a medical treatment should be rejected if the doctors cannot guarantee that the treatment would save that patient's life?

**CINDY:** Well, no, Karen. But, "don't you agree that, when face to face with death, turning one's back on God by violating his law would be a poor decision?"[4]

**KAREN:** Yes, Cindy, I agree with that, but is a transfusion really the same as eating blood? All of the Bible verses I've read on the blood law have to do with physically **eating** blood—not transfusing it into the veins.[5]

---

[1] *The Charlotte Observer,* Friday, June 25, 1999
[2] *What Does God Require of Us?,* 1996, p. 25:5-6
[3] *Reasoning from the Scriptures,* 1985, 1989ed, p. 76
[4] *Reasoning from the Scriptures,* p. 76
[5] See Leviticus 17:10-14; Deuteronomy 12:16, 23-25; 15:23; 1 Samuel 14:32-34

**CINDY:** Karen, at Acts 15:29, Jehovah tells us to: "abstain from…blood."[6] "In a hospital, when a person cannot eat through his mouth, he is fed intravenously. Now, would a person who never put blood into his mouth but who accepted blood by transfusion really be obeying the command to 'keep abstaining from…blood'?…To use a comparison, consider a man who is told by the doctor that he must abstain from alcohol. Would he be obedient if he quit drinking alcohol but had it put directly into his veins?"[7]

**KAREN:** Cindy, when a substance such as alcohol or a nutritional substance is infused into the veins of the body, what happens to the substance? Does the substance retain its original composition or does it get broken down, and in a sense, digested by the body through the process of metabolism?

**CINDY:** Well, I guess it gets broken down and metabolized by the body.

**KAREN:** That's right, Cindy. But what about blood? When blood is transfused into the veins of the body, does the body feed off of the blood by breaking it down for nourishment?

**CINDY:** Well, no, Karen. Transfused blood is still blood. It does not get digested in the veins of the body.

**KAREN:** Then, how can a blood transfusion be the same as eating blood? Unlike nutritional substances which are broken down and metabolized by the body, blood, on the other hand, when it enters the body through the veins, **retains** its original composition as it mixes with the rest of the blood of the body.[8] Can you see why there is **a big difference** between a blood transfusion which merely replenishes the blood supply, and blood which is physically **eaten** through the mouth and **digested** by the body? After all, doesn't the Watchtower Society admit that: "blood is an organ of the body"[9] and as such a blood transfusion: "is essentially an organ transplant"?[10]

**CINDY:** Where does the Society say that?

**KAREN:** Right here on page 31 of the August 22, 1999 *Awake!*

**CINDY:** "Blood is an organ of the body, and blood transfusion is **nothing less** than an organ transplant."

**KAREN:** Cindy, doesn't the Watchtower Society allow organ transplants? And what about tissue transplants? Don't Jehovah's Witnesses take these?

**CINDY:** Yes, Karen, the 1990 Watchtower brochure *How Can Blood Save Your Life?* notes that: "The Witnesses do not feel that the Bible comments directly on organ transplants;

---

[6] *New World Translation*
[7] *Reasoning from the Scriptures,* 1985, 1989, p. 73
[8] See *Handbook of Infusion Therapy,* (Springhouse, PA: Springhouse Corporation 1999), p. 206
[9] *Awake!,* August 22, 1999, p. 31
[10] *Jehovah's Witnesses and the Question of Blood,* 1977, p. 41

hence, decisions regarding cornea, kidney, or other **tissue transplants** must be made by the individual Witness."[11]

**KAREN:** OK, Cindy. Now, would you look at what they say on page 8 of that **same** brochure?

**CINDY:** Alright. "When doctors transplant a heart, a liver, or another organ, the recipient's immune system may sense the foreign tissue and reject it. *Yet, a transfusion* ***is*** *a* ***tissue transplant.***"[12] Wow! I never noticed that before.

**KAREN:** Cindy, since the Watchtower Society agrees that blood is a tissue of the body, isn't it basically admitting that a blood transfusion is more like a transplant situation, than it is eating blood for nourishment?

**CINDY:** Well, I guess you're right, Karen, but doesn't Jehovah God condemn the use of stored blood? At Leviticus 17:13, Jehovah commands: "...any man...who in hunting catches a wild beast or a fowl that may be eaten, he must... **pour its blood out** and cover it with dust."[13] So you see, Karen, blood transfusions are against God's law because blood must not be stored, but "poured out" on the ground. This is also the reason why Jehovah's Witnesses do not donate blood, nor do they store their own blood in anticipation of transfusion during future surgery.[14]

**KAREN:** Cindy, do hemophiliacs who are Jehovah's Witnesses take hemophiliac preparations of Factor VIII made from blood plasma? And what about other fractions of blood—such as immune globulin, albumin, and fibrinogen? Do Jehovah's Witnesses take these?

**CINDY:** Well, yes, Karen. *The Watchtower* of June 1, 1990 notes that: "Some do, believing that the Scriptures do not clearly rule out accepting an injection of a small fraction, or component, taken from blood."[15]

**KAREN:** But, Cindy, didn't you just tell me that God's law is against the use of stored blood? In the June 15, 1985 *Watchtower,* the Society noted that: "...some 70 million units of concentrated Factor VIII are imported from the United States and are used to treat British haemophiliacs. **Each batch** of Factor VIII is made from plasma that is pooled from as many as **2,500 blood donors**."[16] Do you realize, Cindy, this means that blood from 2,500 donors has to be collected, stored, and processed just for a single hemophiliac treatment that a Jehovah's Witness takes? You just told me that Witnesses don't donate blood because they believe it to be a violation of God's law, and yet, Witnesses freely use small blood fractions taken from thousands of units of stored blood. If the storage of blood is really against God's law, why doesn't the Watchtower Society condemn its use for transfusions and injections of blood components?

---

[11] *How Can Blood Save Your Life?,* 1990, p. 28

[12] Emphasis in the original, *How Can Blood Save Your Life,* p. 8

[13] *New World Translation*

[14] See *The Watchtower,* September 15, 1961, p. 561; *The Watchtower,* March 1, 1989, p. 30

[15] *The Watchtower,* June 1, 1990, pp. 30

[16] *The Watchtower,* June 15, 1985, p. 30

**CINDY:** That's a good point, Karen. I'm not sure why, but one thing you should know is that while some Jehovah's Witnesses accept transfusions of blood plasma fractions, none of the Jehovah's Witnesses will accept a transfusion of any of the primary components of blood such as red cells, white cells, platelets, or blood plasma.[17] So you can see, Karen, it's only a small fraction of stored blood that some Jehovah's Witnesses take.

**KAREN:** Cindy, are you saying that it's OK to break God's law in a little as long as you don't break it in a lot? You know over half of our blood consists of blood plasma. Do you know what blood plasma is made of?

**CINDY:** Yes, Karen. The October 22, 1990 *Awake!* stated that the blood plasma consists of 92% water: "the rest is made up of complex proteins, such as globulins, fibrinogens, and albumin."[18]

**KAREN:** Cindy, we just read how Jehovah's Witnesses are allowed to take the complex proteins which make up 8 % of blood plasma, and of course Witnesses take water which makes up the rest of the substance. So, why doesn't the Society allow Witnesses to take blood plasma when it allows them to take all of the components which make up the plasma? Is this the case where mother won't let you eat the ham sandwich, but if you take it apart and eat the bread, cheese, and meat separately, she'll let you have it?

**CINDY:** That's a good point, Karen. I've never thought of it that way before.

**KAREN:** And what about God's law to "abstain from…blood"? A fraction of the blood is still a blood substance, isn't it? What makes a blood fraction transfusion any different from whole blood?

**CINDY:** I'm not sure, Karen. Let me do some research on this and we can talk about it next week.

**KAREN:** Sounds good, Cindy. I'll be here.

**COMMENTS:**

*Friends, just as Cindy discovered, a blood transfusion is not the same as eating and digesting blood. While the Bible is clear about avoiding the digestive use of blood for nourishment, nowhere does the Bible condemn the medical treatment of transfusion in replenishing the blood supply of a living human. A careful examination of the Biblical passages that stipulate that blood must be "poured out" on the ground, will reveal that these passages deal with blood taken from dead animals used in Jewish sacrifices—not living human donors.*[19]

---

[17] *How Can Blood Save Your Life?*, p. 14

[18] *Awake!* October 22, 1990, p. 4

[19] See Leviticus 17:5-6, 13

*Thus, a blood transfusion made from one human donor to another, does not violate God's law on blood, for it is not the intention of the human donor to become a dead sacrifice poured out to God. Just as the ultimate sacrifice of Jesus' blood bought our redemption for eternity, so animal blood sacrifices of the Levitical law are no longer required to earn Jehovah's approval. Have you been spiritually washed in the precious blood of the Lamb of God?*[20]

[20] See Hebrews 9:14, 22

### *DIALOGUE ONE: Does God's Law On Blood Require No Blood Transfusions? — Part II*

(CONTINUED FROM THE PREVIOUS DIALOGUE)

**CINDY:** Karen, last week we talked about blood transfusions and how God's law commands us to abstain from blood. We discussed the fact that while: "Jehovah's Witnesses do not accept transfusions of whole blood or of its primary components (red cells, white cells, platelets, or plasma)," some "Jehovah's Witnesses accept injections of a blood fraction, such as immune globulin or albumin" made from blood plasma.[1]

**KAREN:** That's right, Cindy. Last week, I had asked if a fraction of blood is still a blood substance, why do Jehovah's Witnesses accept these when the Bible says to abstain from blood? A person is not "abstaining…from blood" if he is taking in fractions of the blood, is he?

**CINDY:** Well, Karen, the "Questions From Readers" portion of the June 15, 2000 *Watchtower* discusses this very issue. The Society notes that: "Some," Jehovah's Witnesses, "refuse anything derived from blood (even fractions intended to provide temporary passive immunity). That is how they understand God's command to 'abstain from blood.'…Their sincere, conscientious stand should be respected." Then, the Society went on to state: "Other Christians decide differently.… 'Questions From Readers' in *The Watchtower* of June 1, 1990, noted that plasma proteins (fractions) move from a pregnant woman's blood to the separate blood system of her fetus. Thus…some Christians may conclude that since blood fractions can pass to another person in this natural setting, they could accept a blood fraction derived from blood plasma or cells."[2]

**KAREN:** Cindy, is the Watchtower Society reasoning that it is not a violation of God's blood law to take small fractions of primary blood components because plasma proteins move naturally from the blood system of the mother to the child?

**CINDY:** Yes, that's right, Karen. But just as the Society noted in the June 1990 *Watchtower:* "The mother does not pass her blood into the fetus. Formed elements (**cells**) from the mother's blood **do not cross** the placental barrier into the fetus' blood."[3] So while Jehovah's Witnesses note that blood fractions "move naturally" from mother to child, primary blood components such as red and white blood cells do not. Therefore, Jehovah's Witnesses consistently reject: "whole blood, red cells, white cells, platelets, or blood plasma."[4]

**KAREN:** Cindy, did you know that white cells are in the human milk that a mother breast-feeds her baby? The book *Breastfeeding—A Guide for the Medical Profession* notes that:

[1] *The Watchtower,* June 1, 1990, p. 30
[2] *The Watchtower,* June 15, 2000, pp. 30-31
[3] *The Watchtower,* June 1, 1990, p. 31
[4] *How Can Blood Save Your Life?,* 1990, p. 14

"Both T- and B-lymphocytes" (white blood cells)[5] "are present in human milk and colostrom and are part of the immunologic system in human milk."[6] Since white blood cells "move naturally" from mother to child, why does the Watchtower Society view white blood cell transfusions as a violation of God's Law? If Jehovah's Witnesses take blood plasma fractions because they "move naturally" from a pregnant mother to her baby, why don't they also take transfusions of white blood cells?

**CINDY:** Karen, that's a good question. I really don't know why.

**KAREN:** Cindy, as you know, the Society stated in the June 1990 *Watchtower* that: "Formed elements (cells) from the mother's blood **do not cross** the placental barrier into the fetus' blood." But did you know that the book *A Pictorial Handbook of Anatomy and Physiology* notes that: "In the last weeks of pregnancy small numbers of the baby's red cells escape through the placenta into the mother's circulation"?[7]

**CINDY:** Wow! I didn't know that.

**KAREN:** Cindy, not only does this transfer of red blood cells from the baby to the mother occur in the last weeks of pregnancy, but Doctors Frank Oski and Lawrence Naiman note in their book *Hematologic Problems In the Newborn* that: "Accumulated evidence indicates that leukocytes [white blood cells], platelets, and erythrocytes [red blood cells] traverse the placental barrier….Fetal red cells can be demonstrated in the maternal circulation in approximately **50 per cent** of all pregnancies."[8]

**CINDY:** That's interesting, Karen. But aren't these doctors admitting that this transfer of red blood cells from the baby to the mother only happen in 50 percent of the pregnancies? Even the Society admits that: "if by some injury the mother's and the fetus' blood mingle, health problems can later develop."[9] This is certainly not God's design, is it?

**KAREN:** Cindy, whether it is God's design or not, I cannot judge. But one thing I do question. If it is strictly against God's law to have a blood transfusion, why does God allow it to occur in 50 percent of the pregnancies? Don't you think that if the transfer of blood from the blood system of one person to another is a serious violation of God's law, He would make certain that such transmission would not occur in any pregnancy at all? While it may be true that this occurred only in 50 percent of the pregnancies spoken of by Doctors Oski and Naiman, this says nothing of what happens in the course of labor. The book *Conception to Birth—Epidemiology of Prenatal Development* notes that it is: "common" for "fetal blood cells [to] gain access to the maternal bloodstream…in the course of labor."[10] Since the entry of fetal red blood cells into the mother's blood

---

[5] See *Awake!* February 8, 2001, p. 14

[6] *Breastfeeding—A Guide for the Medical Profession,* 4th Edition, by Ruth A. Lawrence (Mosby - Year Book, Inc, 1994), p. 154

[7] *A Pictorial Handbook of Anatomy and Physiology,* 1978, by James Brevan, p. 36

[8] *Hematologic Problems In the Newborn,* 3rd Edition, 1982, by Frank A. Oski M.D. and J. Lawrence Naiman M.D., p. 41

[9] *The Watchtower,* June 1, 1990, p. 31

[10] *Conception to Birth—Epidemiology of Prenatal Development,* by Jennie Kline, Zena Stein, Mervyn Susser, (Oxford University Press, 1989), p. 98

stream is common during pregnancy and labor, why does the Society continue to uphold its position that a blood transfusion is a violation of God's law?

**CINDY:** I'm not sure, Karen.

**KAREN:** Cindy, do you remember how last week we talked about the fact that a blood transfusion is not the same as eating blood because it does not get digested when it is transfused into the veins of the body?

**CINDY:** Yes, Karen, and we also discussed how the Watchtower Society admits that blood is a tissue of the body and that a blood transfusion is nothing less than a tissue transplant.[11]

**KAREN:** That's right, Cindy. Did you know that one of the medical ways we know that transfused blood functions as a tissue transplant and not as food for the body, is by the fact that fetal blood cells have been detected in women for several years after giving birth? The book *Williams Obstetrics* notes that: "the failure of the placenta to maintain absolute integrity of the fetal and maternal circulations is documented by **numerous** findings of the passage of cells between mother and fetus **in both directions**....Leukocytes [white blood cells] bearing a Y chromosome have been identified in women for up to 5 years after giving birth to a son."[12] Can you see why God's law only condemns the physical eating of blood and does not apply to the transfer of blood from the blood system of one person to another? Otherwise, why would God allow it to occur naturally in pregnancy and labor?

**CINDY:** Karen, that's a good point, but I don't understand. If Jehovah wanted us to take blood into our bodies through transfusion, why did He command Christians at Acts 15:29 to "keep abstaining...from blood"? Doesn't that rule out **any** form of taking in blood?

**KAREN:** Cindy, let's look at that passage in context. At Acts 15, we read about the congregation at Antioch in which some of the brothers disputed over whether Gentile Christians should be required to comply with the Jewish law of circumcision in order to be saved. A council at Jerusalem was called to discuss this issue and verses 28 and 29 reveal the judicial decision that resulted. Would like to read it, Cindy?

**CINDY:** OK: "For the holy spirit and we ourselves have favored adding no further burden to you, except these necessary things, to keep **abstaining** from things sacrificed to idols and from **blood** and from things strangled and from fornication. If you carefully keep yourselves from these things, you will prosper. Good health to you!"[13]

**KAREN:** Cindy, in addition to abstaining from blood, this passage tells Christians to: "keep abstaining...from things strangled." How does one abstain from things that were strangled? Isn't this talking about abstaining in the sense of not **eating** those things that were strangled because they were not properly bled? And what about the other

---

[11] See *Jehovah's Witnesses and the Question of Blood,* 1977, pp. 40-41; *How Can Blood Save Your Life?,* p. 8; *Awake!,* August 22, 1999, p. 31

[12] *Williams Obstetrics,* 19th Edition (Norwalk, CT: Appleton and Lange, 1993), p. 127

[13] *New World Translation*

command to: "keep abstaining…from things sacrificed to idols"? Isn't this talking about abstaining by not **eating** food that was sacrificed to idols?

**CINDY:** Well, I guess you're right, Karen.

**KAREN:** Then, isn't it logical to conclude from the context of Acts 15, that this passage is talking about "abstaining" in the sense of not **eating** blood, and does not apply to the transfer of blood from the blood system of one person to another?

**CINDY:** I see your point, Karen. But are blood transfusions really that safe? In the October 22, 1990 *Awake,* the Society noted that: "the chances of getting AIDS from a blood transfusion are 1 in 28,000….And AIDS is not the only danger from blood transfusion….Hepatitis infects hundreds of thousands and kills many more transfusion recipients than AIDS does…."[14]

**KAREN:** Cindy, since 1990 when the Society came out with that article, a lot of progress has been made regarding the safety of blood transfusions. While the Society's 1990 article noted that the possibility of contracting AIDS from a blood transfusion was 1 in 28,000, the September 1999 Consumer Reports notes that the chance has significantly decreased to 1 in a million for AIDS and 1 in a hundred thousand for hepatitis C. The 1999 Consumer Reports when on to state that: "…the likelihood of infection from a two-unit blood transfusion is substantially less than the chance of being murdered or of being killed in an auto accident during the year." Then they went on to explain that: "Indeed, for a hospital patient, the greatest risk shown here is dying from an unexpected adverse reaction to some medication….Transfusions save nearly 10,000 lives a day…."[15] So, Cindy, which risk of death is greater—death due to avoiding a blood transfusion or death due to bad blood?

**COMMENTS:**

*Friends, There is a big difference between the respectful manner in which blood is treated as a sacred substance in saving life through transfusion, and the disgraceful manner in which pagan religions of Biblical times drank blood in an attempt to gain strength and victory. While the Bible is clear about avoiding the digestive use of blood for nourishment, nowhere does the Bible condemn the medical treatment of transfusion in replenishing the blood supply of a living human being. Just as donors offer their blood to restore physical life, so Jesus offered His blood to give us life eternally. Would you like to receive the redemption offered in the blood of Christ?*

---

[14] *Awake!* October 22, 1990, pp. 8-9

[15] *Consumer Reports,* September 1999, pp. 61, 63

## *DIALOGUE TWO: Does Christian Love For Brother Demand Abstinence From War?*

(WDGR LESSON 13: "How Can You Find the True Religion?")

*Does the command of Jesus to "love your enemies" require political neutrality during war? Were the Jehovah's Witnesses as politically neutral during World War II in their dealings with Hitler as they claim?*

**CINDY:** Karen, what do you think is the "most outstanding mark" that identifies true Christians and sets them apart from any of the other religions of the world?

**KAREN:** Well, Cindy, our study in the Watchtower brochure *What Does God Require of Us?* notes that: "the most outstanding mark of true Christians is that they have real *love among themselves*."[1] At John 13:35, Jesus told His disciples that: "by this all men will know that you are My disciples, if you have love for one another."[2]

**CINDY:** That's right, Karen. Just as the Watchtower Society explains, true Christians: "are not taught....to hate people from other countries....So they do not share in wars....True Christians treat one another as brothers and sisters."[3] Unlike Christendom whose members fight each other in war, Jehovah's Witnesses have consistently maintained strict neutrality even in the face of fierce persecution and opposition. One example of this occurred in the 1930's, during the Nazis attack upon the Jews. The August 22, 1995 *Awake!* reports that: "Jehovah's Witnesses refused to heil Hitler. They refused because they attribute their salvation to God and have dedicated their lives to him alone....The immovable neutral position of the Witnesses, along with their loyalty to God's Kingdom, was unacceptable to the Hitler government....Jehovah's Witnesses were among the first targets of Nazi abuse....When World War II started in 1939, there were already 6,000 Witnesses confined in camps and prisons....Yes, history reveals that Jehovah's Witnesses have always shown love for their fellowman, even in the face of intense pressure."[4]

**KAREN:** Cindy, at John 15:13, what did Jesus say was the **greatest** love a person could have for another person?

**CINDY:** Well, Karen, John 15:13 says that: "No one has love greater than this, that someone should surrender his soul in behalf of his friends."[5]

**KAREN:** OK, Cindy. Since Jesus said that the greatest love a person could have for another is surrendering one's life for them, why didn't the Jehovah's Witnesses demonstrate this

---

[1] *What Does God Require of Us?,* 1996, p. 26:3

[2] *New American Standard Bible*

[3] *What Does God Require of Us?,* p. 26:3

[4] *Awake!* August 22, 1995, pp. 4, 7, 9-10, 15

[5] *New World Translation*

love by surrendering their lives to defend, protect, and rescue the 6 million persecuted Jews from Hitler's control? According to this principle in the Bible, who showed greater love? The Jehovah's Witnesses who were so neutral that they refused to join in the war-effort of the Allies to deliver the persecuted Jews, or those Christians like Corrie Ten Boom and her family who gave their lives in protecting and rescuing the Jews and other persecuted ones from Hitler's power?

**CINDY:** But, Karen, the Jehovah's Witnesses did take a stand against Hitler! The August 22, 1995 *Awake!* notes that while: "Jehovah's Witnesses….take no part in the wars of the nations," yet "when Hitler waged war throughout Europe, the Witnesses stood firm in the face of the Nazis' brutal attempts to make them join in the orgy of killing."[6] In this article, the Society also explained that: "***even before*** the death camps were set up," Jehovah's Witnesses were: "proclaiming the dangers of Nazism, through *Awake!*"[7] So you see, Karen, "**Love of neighbor** is what compelled the Witnesses to warn the people of Germany not to be fooled by…the Third Reich.…Jehovah's Witnesses were among the first targets of Nazi abuse, but they also loudly decried atrocities against Jews, Poles, the handicapped, and others."[8]

**KAREN:** Cindy, is the Society arguing that even though Jehovah's Witnesses failed to demonstrate greater love by surrendering their lives in **war** to deliver the persecuted Jews, they demonstrated "love for neighbor" by exposing the atrocities of Hitler?

**CINDY:** That's right, Karen. History reveals that while Jehovah's Witnesses: "were not afraid to speak out" and expose the evil of Nazism, "the Catholic church and other churches as well became handmaidens of the evil Hitler government.…Hitler was a baptized Roman Catholic, as were many of the leaders of his government.…True, a few courageous individuals from the Catholic, Protestant, and various other religions stood up against the Nazi State. But even as some of them paid with their lives, their spiritual leaders, who claimed to serve God, were serving as puppets of the Third Reich."[9]

**KAREN:** Cindy, is the Society saying that: "unlike the churches, Jehovah's Witnesses spoke out against Nazism"?[10] That same *Awake!* article of August 22, 1995 states that after the Jehovah's Witness convention in Berlin on June 25, 1933, in which some 7,000 assembled to draft "a declaration of the Facts" to state their case to Hitler, persecution upon the Witnesses began as: "the Nazis did not intend to tolerate any refusal to support their ideology."[11] Yet, this declaration which the Witnesses sent to Hitler is reproduced in the *1934 Year Book of Jehovah's Witnesses.* Would you read what the Jehovah's Witnesses actually said in that declaration?

**CINDY:** OK. "The greatest and the **most oppressive** empire on earth is the Anglo-American empire. By that is meant the British Empire, of which the United States of America

---

[6] *Awake!* August 22, 1995, p. 15
[7] *Awake!* August 22, 1995, p. 3
[8] *Awake!* August 22, 1995, p. 9
[9] *Awake!* August 22, 1995, pp. 3, 14, 12, 14
[10] *Awake!* August 22, 1995, p. 15
[11] *Awake!* August 22, 1995, p. 7

forms a part. It has been the commercial Jews of the British-American empire that have built up and carried on Big Business as a means of exploiting and oppressing the peoples of many nations....The present government of Germany has declared emphatically against Big Business oppressors and in opposition to the wrongful religious influence in the political affairs of the nation. Such is **exactly** our position....Instead of being against the principles advocated by the government of Germany, we stand squarely for such principles."[12]

**KAREN:** Cindy, how can the Society point at certain churches in Christendom which served as puppets for the Nazis, when they supported the socialistic ideals of the government of Germany against "the Anglo-American empire"? How can they claim that they refused "to support the ideology" of the Nazis when they stated in their declaration that: "the greatest and **most oppressive** empire on earth is the Anglo-American empire."?[13] Does this sound like neutrality to you?

**CINDY:** OK, Karen. So maybe the Witnesses weren't as politically neutral as they should have been when they were dealing with Hitler, but at least they did not participate in carnal warfare, and to this day, Jehovah's Witnesses risk imprisonment and death rather than violate Christian neutrality. You see, Karen, at Luke 6:27-28 Jesus said: "...Continue to love your enemies, to do good to those hating you, to bless those cursing you, to pray for those who are insulting you."[14] A Christian is not loving his enemies if he is killing them in war, is he?

**KAREN:** Cindy, since Jesus said to love your enemies, if an intruder were to break into your house and threaten to kill you, does this mean that you should not defend yourself? After all, you're not loving your enemy if you end up killing him in self-defense, are you?

**CINDY:** Oh, Karen, that command to love your enemies doesn't apply to self-defense. Even the Society admits that at Exodus 22:2: "in his Law to Israel, Jehovah God revealed that the individual had the right to self-defense."[15]

**KAREN:** But, Cindy, if the command to love your enemies does not apply to self-defense, why do Jehovah's Witnesses apply it to a nation that is merely attempting to defend itself in war against enemies such as Hitler?

**CINDY:** I never thought of it that way before, Karen, but one thing Jesus made clear is that his: "followers were to make disciples of people of all nations; so worshipers of the true God would in time be found in all those nations....If true Christians in one nation were to go to war against another nation, they would be fighting against fellow believers, against people who prayed for help to the same God that they did."[16] How can Christian brothers have real love for each other if they kill each other in war?

---

[12] *1934 Year Book of Jehovah's Witnesses,* pp. 134-136
[13] *1934 Year Book of Jehovah's Witnesses,* p. 134
[14] *New World Translation;* see also *Reasoning from the Scriptures,* p. 271
[15] *Awake!* September 8, 1975, p. 27
[16] *Reasoning from the Scriptures,* p. 272

**KAREN:** Cindy, suppose your husband, Steve, was in your presence when an intruder broke into your house, threatening your life. Now, he would have three options. He could either come to your aid and protect you, be totally neutral in the conflict and do nothing to protect you, or he could join forces with the intruder and attack you. If he was truly on Jehovah's side, which of these three options would he take: your side, the intruder's side, or neutrality?

**CINDY:** Of course, my husband, Steve, would take my side and attempt to protect me, Karen.

**KAREN:** OK. So why would neutrality in this instance be a violation of God's Law?

**CINDY:** Well, Karen, it's because Jehovah God has given my husband the duty to protect me and those under his jurisdiction. So to take a neutral position in a conflict which threatens the lives of those individuals under his care would be a violation of Jehovah's arrangement for life and order.

**KAREN:** That's right, Cindy. Can you see why this same principle also applies to a nation's responsibility to defend its people against warring nations? After all, wouldn't you agree that in every conflict there is a right side and wrong side? In other words, if Steve were to take any other position—whether your intruder's side or neutrality—he would be on the wrong side by negating his duty before Jehovah God to protect those under his care.

**CINDY:** Yes, I agree, Karen, but how does this change the fact that Christians who get involved in carnal warfare end up killing their Christian brothers in war?

**KAREN:** Cindy, since there is a right side and a wrong side to every conflict, if a true Christian were to evaluate the conflict in light of the principles in God's Word, what is the likelihood of him choosing to join forces with the wrong side of the battle?

**CINDY:** Well, I guess you're right. True Christians wouldn't choose the wrong side of a war, so true Christians would not find themselves fighting on both sides of the battle. But I don't understand, Karen. At Matthew 26:52, Jesus commanded Peter to lay down his sword because: "all those who take the sword will perish by the sword." Why would Jesus command this if taking up the sword to defend one's country is not against God's law?[17]

**KAREN:** Cindy, in the *Awake!* article of September 8, 1975, the Society said regarding this verse that: "Peter's action in this case was **not** a matter of self-defense, but, rather, resistance to authorities and…God's will." Even the Society admitted that at Luke 22:38, Jesus' apostles were known to have had at least two swords.[18] Since Jesus' disciples had several swords for self-defense, how could it be wrong for Christians to take up the sword to defend themselves and their country?

---

[17] *Reasoning from the Scriptures,* p. 271

[18] *Awake!* September 8, 1975, p. 28

**COMMENTS:**

*Friends, just as Jesus said at John 15:13: "Greater love has no one than this, that one lay down his life for his friends."*[19] *So throughout history, true Christians have demonstrated the greatest love for their brothers—not by being neutral in times of conflict—but by surrendering their lives to defend and protect their family, friends, and country from enemy nations. Such sacrificial Christian love for brother is evidenced by the fact that no soldier ever gave up his position after becoming a Christian, and even John the Baptist exhorted the soldiers of his day to "be content" with their "wages."*[20] *How could they be content with their wages, unless, of course, they remained soldiers?*

---

[19] *New American Standard Bible*

[20] See Luke 3:14

## *DIALOGUE THREE: Is Political Neutrality Christian? —Part I*

(WDGR LESSON 13: "How Can You Find the True Religion?")

*What does the Bible mean when it calls Satan "the god of this system of things"? Are human governments under Satan's control? Why did Jesus say that His Kingdom is no part of this world? In what way should Christians be separate from this world?*

**KAREN:** Cindy, I'm confused! Our lesson in the Watchtower brochure *What Does God Require of Us?* says that Jehovah's Witnesses: "do not get involved in the world's political affairs and social controversies."[1] But I was reading the "Questions from Readers" section in the November 1, 1999 *Watchtower* and it stated that: "...during an election...some Witnesses of Jehovah go to the polling booth and others do not."[2] I'm confused! Has the Watchtower Society changed its position on voting and is now allowing Jehovah's Witnesses to vote in political elections?

**CINDY:** No, Karen. Let's look at that article and see what it **really** says. "First," the Watchtower Society notes that: "Jesus Christ said of his followers: 'They are no part of the world, just as I am no part of the world.'...Jehovah's Witnesses take this principle seriously. Being 'no part of the world,' they are neutral in the political affairs of the world."[3]

**KAREN:** Cindy, where in the Bible does it say that "being no part of the world," means that Christians should not take part in governmental affairs of the world? The religious group "Assembly of YHWHHoshua" teaches their people that being "no part of the world" not only means that Christians should remain neutral in political affairs, but they should not: "participate in the charities of the world....or contribute to or accept any benefits from the institutions of the United States, such as Social Security, Medicare, [and] Unemployment Compensation...."[4] If "being no part of the world," means not participating in political aspects of governmental authority, how do you know it does not apply to governmental social institutions as well? Is the Assembly of YHWHHoshua being more consistent in its separation from the world than the Jehovah's Witness' religion is being? How do you know where to draw the line?

**CINDY:** Karen, that's a good point. I'm not sure, but one thing we know is that Christians should have no part in governmental affairs because Satan is in control of worldly governments. The Watchtower book, *Reasoning from the Scriptures* notes that: "1 John 5:19 says, 'the whole world is lying in the power of the wicked one.' At John

---

[1] *What Does God Require of Us?,* 1996, p. 27:7

[2] *The Watchtower,* November 1, 1999, p. 29

[3] *The Watchtower,* November 1, 1999, p. 28

[4] *Encyclopedia of American Religions: Religious Creeds,* vol. II, J. Gordon Melton, Editor (Gale Research Company, 1988), p. 399

14:30, Jesus referred to Satan as being 'the ruler of the world.' So, no matter what worldly fraction a person might support, under whose control would he really come?"[5]

**KAREN:** Cindy, is the Society arguing that if a Christian were to get involved in the political and governmental affairs of the world, he would come under Satan's control?

**CINDY:** That's right, Karen. The Watchtower tract "Who Really Rules the World?" notes that many people often think that God rules the world: "But significantly, nowhere does the Bible say that either Jesus Christ or his Father are the real rulers of this world."[6] At 2 Corinthians 4:4, the Bible calls Satan the "the god of this system of things." "So, then, Satan the Devil really is the unseen ruler of the world!"[7]

**KAREN:** Did I hear you right, Cindy? The Watchtower tract says that: "**nowhere** does the Bible say that either Jesus Christ or his Father are the real rulers of this world"? Would you read Daniel 4:17 in your Bible—*The New World Translation?*

**CINDY:** OK. "…the decree…and…the request is…that people living may know that the Most High is **Ruler** in the kingdom of mankind…."

**KAREN:** Since the "Most High" is Jehovah God,[8] how can the Watchtower Society argue that "**nowhere** does the Bible say that either Jesus Christ or his Father are the real rulers of this world," when the Bible clearly proclaims Jehovah God as: "Ruler over the realm of mankind"?[9]

**CINDY:** Karen, I'm not sure why the Society said what they did in their tract, but in the May 1, 1996 *Watchtower,* the Society noted that: " '…the whole world is lying in the power of the wicked one.'…This does **not** mean that Jehovah has relinquished his sovereignty over the earth.…Satan exercises authority over the kingdoms of the world **only** by God's permission."[10]

**KAREN:** So, let me get this straight. The Society admits that Satan's rulership is limited by Jehovah God's sovereignty, but yet they claim that Satan controls the governments of the world so that anyone who gets involved in governmental affairs comes under the rulership of Satan?

**CINDY:** That's right, Karen. At Matthew 4:8-10: "Satan *tempted* Jesus by offering him 'all the kingdoms of the world.' Yet, would Satan's offer have been a real *temptation* if Satan was not actually the ruler of these kingdoms?… Could Satan have offered Jesus all these world governments if they were not his?"[11]

---

[5] *Reasoning from the Scriptures,* 1985, 1989ed, p. 273
[6] *Who Really Rules The World?,* 1992, p. 2
[7] *Who Really Rules The World?,* pp. 2-3
[8] See *Daniel's Prophecy,* 1999, pp. 92-93
[9] *New American Standard Bible*
[10] *The Watchtower,* May 1, 1996, p. 10
[11] *Who Really Rules the World?,* p. 3-4

**KAREN:** Cindy, is it possible to offer the use of something without actually owning it? For example, suppose a person were to rent a house from a landlord. Even though, for the duration of the lease, that person may call the house his "home," who really owns the house? Is it the tenant, or the landlord? In the same way, does Satan legitimately **own** world governments, or does he merely exercise rulership over the governments through his deceptive influence?

**CINDY:** Well, I guess you're right, Karen. Just as the Society notes: "Satan exercises authority over the kingdoms of the world **only** by God's permission,"[12] so I guess he does not actually own the world governments.

**KAREN:** Can you see why the Bible says at Romans 13:1 that the governing authorities: "...which exist are **established** by God?"[13] Since God is the one who "**established**" human governments, how can it be wrong for Christians to take part in God's arrangement for maintaining law and order?

**CINDY:** Wait a minute, Karen! My Bible doesn't say that God "established" the world governments. It says that: "the existing authorities stand **placed** in their relative positions by God."[14] Just as the Watchtower Society noted in the book *Knowledge that Leads to Everlasting Life,* "Jehovah did not **originate** man's governmental authorities, but they exist by his permission."[15]

**KAREN:** Cindy, would you read Romans 13 verses 2 and 4 in your Bible — *The New World Translation?*

**CINDY:** Alright. "Therefore he who opposes the authority has taken a stand against the **arrangement of God**....for it is **God's minister** to you for good."

**KAREN:** So, the Watchtower would have you believe that the governmental authorities: "stand **placed** in their...positions by God," but God did not **establish** them? They would have you believe that governments are Jehovah God's "**arrangement**," but He did not **originate** them? And the governments are "**God's minister**," but they are ruled and **controlled** by Satan? Does this make any sense to you, Cindy? How can something be Jehovah God's "arrangement" and not truly be **established** and controlled by Jehovah God? Isn't that about as ridiculous as saying that the Christian congregation is God's arrangement, but is controlled by Satan?

**CINDY:** That's a good point, Karen, but if Jehovah God is **truly** in control of human governments, why does the Bible say that Satan rules the world and why did Jesus say that His followers should take no part in the world because His Kingdom is not of this world?

---

[12] *The Watchtower,* May 1, 1996, p. 10
[13] *New American Standard Bible*
[14] *New World Translation*
[15] *Knowledge That Leads To Everlasting Life,* 1995, p. 132

**KAREN:** Cindy, in what way does Satan rule the world? At 1 John 2:15-16, the Bible says: "Do not love the world, nor the things in the world.…For all that is in the world, the lust of the flesh and the lust of the eyes and the boastful pride of life, is not from the Father, but is from the world."[16] Since Satan rules the world through these three lusts: the lust of the eyes, the lust of the flesh, and the pride of life, can you see why Christians are to be Kingdom-focused and be separate from the world, not by isolating themselves from the world, but by taking no part in worldly lusts? Wouldn't you agree there is a big difference between the isolation of oneself from the world and the separation of one's heart from worldly influences? Which attitude do you think Jesus meant for Christians to model? Would you read Daniel 2:20-21 in your Bible?

**CINDY:** OK. "Daniel was answering and saying: 'Let the name of God become blessed.…he is…**removing** kings and **setting** up kings, giving wisdom to the wise ones and knowledge to those knowing discernment.' "[17]

**KAREN:** Cindy, if the governments of the world are owned and controlled by Satan, why is Jehovah God "removing kings and setting up kings" in Satan's governmental system? Doesn't this indicate that Satan does not own or control the governments of the world, but only rules the world through his deceitful influence in the hearts of mankind? At Proverbs 21:1, the Bible says that: "the king's heart is *like* channels of water in the hand of the LORD [Jehovah]; He turns it wherever He wishes."[18] Since Jehovah God is intimately involved in the governmental affairs of the world, even to the point of changing kings' hearts, how can it be wrong for Christians to take part in God's "arrangement" for the present rulership of mankind?

**COMMENTS:**

*Friends, throughout history, in order to fulfill God's purposes, faithful servants of Jehovah have held prominent positions of authority in human government. At Genesis 41, Jehovah God raised Joseph up to the position of prime minister of Egypt (second only to Pharaoh), in order to preserve God's chosen people through an impending seven-year famine. Likewise, during the Babylonian exile, Daniel and his fellow Jewish brothers submitted to State training and became high-ranking governmental officials in the pagan system of Babylon. Even after the fall of the Neo-Babylonian dynasty to the Medo-Persian empire, Daniel maintained his high position of authority[19] as he uncompromisingly held Jehovah's standards in all of his duties. Just as God's faithful servants of old advanced His purposes on the earth by upholding integrity through their governmental duties, so true Christians today endeavor to preserve righteousness in human society by their involvement in the political and social concerns of the culture.*

---

[16] *New American Standard Bible*
[17] *New World Translation*
[18] *New American Standard Bible*
[19] See Daniel 5:30-31

## *DIALOGUE THREE: Is Political Neutrality Christian? —Part II*

(CONTINUED FROM THE PREVIOUS DIALOGUE)

**KAREN:** Cindy, last week in our study of the Watchtower brochure *What Does God Require of Us?,* we discussed the fact that the Bible says that Christians are to be "no part of the world."[1] Jehovah's Witnesses interpret this to mean that Christians are not to: "get involved in the world's political affairs and social controversies."[2] Yet, the Bible says at Romans 13:1-2 that the governmental authorities are: "the arrangement of God," and that they "stand placed in their...positions by God."[3] I had asked, if human governments are God's "arrangement" as the Bible teaches, how can it be wrong for Christians to take part in God's arrangement for maintaining law and order?

**CINDY:** Karen, the "Questions from Readers" section in the November 1, 1999 *Watchtower* notes that: "the apostle Paul referred to himself as an 'ambassador' representing Christ to the people of his day....Jehovah's Witnesses believe that Christ Jesus is now the enthroned King of God's heavenly Kingdom, and they, like ambassadors, must announce this to the nations....Ambassadors are expected to be neutral and not to interfere in the internal affairs of the countries to which they are sent."[4] So, Karen, can you see why: "as representatives of God's heavenly Kingdom, Jehovah's Witnesses feel a similar obligation not to interfere in the politics of the countries where they reside"?

**KAREN:** Cindy, why is a foreign ambassador required not to interfere in the political affairs of the country to which he is sent?

**CINDY:** Well, Karen, I believe it's because he is representing his country to that foreign nation; so to interfere in that country's political system would be a violation of his purpose as an ambassador.

**KAREN:** OK, Cindy. But what if he was to go to that foreign nation as a **visitor**, and **not** as an ambassador for his country. Would he then be allowed to vote in that country's political elections?

**CINDY:** Well, no. He wouldn't be allowed to vote because he is not a citizen of that nation.

**KAREN:** That's right, Cindy. So wouldn't you agree that the **real reason** foreign ambassadors are required to abstain from the political affairs of the countries in which they are serving, is **not** due to their responsibility as foreign representatives, **but rather**, is due

---

[1] John 17:16

[2] *What Does God Require of Us?,* 1996, p. 27:7

[3] *New World Translation*

[4] *The Watchtower,* November 1, 1999, p. 29

to the fact that political involvement is a **privilege** to be granted **only to the citizens** of those nations?

**CINDY:** Well, I guess you're right, Karen.

**KAREN:** But, Cindy, aren't Jehovah's Witnesses **citizens** of the countries in which they reside? Since foreign ambassadors are **not** citizens of the countries in which they serve, but Jehovah's Witnesses are, how can this scenario apply to Jehovah's Witnesses?

**CINDY:** Well, I'm not sure, Karen, but another: "factor to consider is that those who have a part in voting a person into office may become responsible for what he does....Christians have to consider carefully whether they want to shoulder that responsibility."[5]

**KAREN:** Cindy, what would happen to a family if the parents decided not to discipline their children because they don't want to be responsible for how their children grow up? Doesn't God hold parents responsible for their children, regardless of whether they are or are not directly involved in shaping the moral values of their children?

**CINDY:** Well, yes, Karen. Jehovah God does hold parents responsible for their children, but what does this have to do with a Christian's refusal to be responsible for the election of a bad governmental official?

**KAREN:** Cindy, just as God holds parents responsible for instilling Christian moral values in their children, Jesus said that Christians are to be the "salt" and "light" of their world.[6] How can they be "salt" and "light" in **every** aspect of the world if there are **certain levels of society** that Christians **refuse** to influence? For example, what would happen to a nation if all of its citizens who are upright and moral in their viewpoints decided to refrain from politics altogether? By their abstinence from politics, wouldn't they basically be responsible for allowing the wicked, immoral, and unrighteous individuals of that nation to take control of the country? Since God holds Christians **responsible** for influencing **every** aspect of the world, not just the non-political areas of the world, how can "neutrality" in refraining from political elections **not** be a vote for evil?

**CINDY:** That's a good point, Karen, but, "Jehovah's Witnesses greatly value their Christian unity....When religions get involved in politics, the result is often division among their members. In imitation of Jesus Christ, Jehovah's Witnesses avoid becoming involved in politics and thus maintain their Christian unity."[7]

**KAREN:** Cindy, that same November 1, 1999 Watchtower article you are quoting regarding the Jehovah's Witnesses' position on voting states: "There may be people who are stumbled when they observe that **during an election** in their country, **some** Witnesses of Jehovah go to the polling booth and **others do not**. They may say, 'Jehovah's Witnesses are not consistent.' People should recognize, though, that in matters of individual conscience such as this, each Christian has to make his own decision before

---

[5] *The Watchtower,* November 1, 1999, p. 29

[6] Matthew 5:13-16

[7] *The Watchtower,* November 1, 1999, p. 29

Jehovah God."[8] Cindy, since the Watchtower Society admits that Christian unity is **not** violated when "**some**" individual Witnesses: "go to the polling booth and **others** do not," why do they argue that Christian unity is violated when individual Christians participate in the political affairs of their country?

**CINDY:** Karen, the Jehovah's Witnesses who "go to the polling booth" in those countries do so because certain countries require their citizens to vote, but just as the Watchtower Society notes in this article: " 'Where Caesar makes it compulsory for citizens to vote…[Witnesses] can go to the polls and enter the voting booths. It is here that they are called upon to mark the ballot or write in what they stand for.…' "[9] You see, Karen, Jehovah's Witnesses "stand for" Jehovah God and Christ Jesus as the ruler of his heavenly Kingdom. Since they have already voted for King Jesus, when certain countries require them to vote, this is what they write on their ballots. Unlike Christendom whose members look to human political candidates for peace and security, Jehovah's Witnesses are united in their firm position not to break integrity with Jehovah God by pledging their allegiance to human candidates in place of Jehovah God's anointed King Jesus.

**KAREN:** Cindy, when you elected your husband, Steve, to be the spiritual leader in your life, did he take the place of Jehovah God's anointed King Jesus in your life?

**CINDY:** Of course not, Karen, but what's your point?

**KAREN:** My point is this, Cindy. If voting for a human candidate to be the leader of a country is viewed as electing a candidate to take the place of Jehovah God's anointed King Jesus, why isn't the election of a husband as the spiritual leader in the home not also viewed as taking Jehovah's place as well? If the decision to elect a human leader to be the spiritual ruler in the home is **not** a violation of God's rulership over the family, then why is the decision to elect a human leader to be the governmental ruler in the country viewed as a violation of God's rulership by means of Christ Jesus?

**CINDY:** Well, I'm not sure, Karen, but one thing is clear: Jesus said that Christians are to have "no part" in this wicked system of things, so Jehovah's Witnesses refuse to take part in politics in any form. Because Jehovah's Witnesses refuse to compromise on what they stand for, they have been ridiculed, beaten, and even killed in countries where political involvement is required. One example of this persecution is described in the March 22, 1976 *Awake!* where the Society reports that over 36,000 Jehovah's Witnesses were forced to flee the country of Malawi to live in refugee camps in Zambia and Mozambique, because they wouldn't: "violate their conscience and buy membership cards for the dominant political party."[10]

**KAREN:** Cindy, did you know that the English word: "politics has its origin in the Greek words *polis* [meaning] (city) and *polites* [meaning] (citizen)"?[11] And the word "political"

[8] *The Watchtower,* November 1, 1999, p. 29
[9] *The Watchtower,* November 1, 1999, p. 29
[10] *Awake!* March 22, 1976, p. 5
[11] *Morris Dictionary of Words and Phrase Origins,* 2nd Edition, by William and Mary Morris (New York: Harper and

comes from the Greek word "*politikos* having to do with citizens or the State."[12] Since **any** "civil organization" of people is a "polity" or political entity in the strict meaning of the word, to be a **citizen** of a country **is** to be a **member** of that political community, and the taxes or "dues" that every Christian is required to pay to these political communities have to do with their membership status in these entities.

**CINDY:** I never thought of it that way before, Karen.

**KAREN:** Cindy, if it is not a violation of integrity to God for Christians to be citizens of a country, and thus be members of that national political community, how could it have been a violation of integrity for "citizens" of the country of Malawi to purchase a political party card that merely stated their membership in that country's ruling organized entity?

**CINDY:** That's a good point, Karen. I'm not sure why, but one thing Jehovah's Witnesses have found is that: "keeping out of politics gives Jehovah's Witnesses freeness of speech to approach people of all political persuasions with the important message of the Kingdom."[13]

**KAREN:** Cindy, the Bible reports at Acts 8:27, that the Ethiopian eunuch to which Philip preached Christ, held a prominent position in the government of Ethiopia as he served: "under Candace queen of the Ethiopians and ...was over all her treasure."[14] If a Christian's Kingdom work would be hindered by involvement in the political affairs of his country, why didn't the Ethiopian eunuch of Acts 8, abandon his political position after becoming a Christian? If political involvement in God's "arrangement" for governmental authorities[15] is a violation of integrity to Jehovah God, why did Jesus praise the army officer for his "great faith" at Matthew 8:5-13, rather than correct him for his political standing? And what about Cornelius who was: "an army officer of the Italian band"[16] in Caesarea? Why does the Bible report that he was: "a **devout** man and one fearing God....a man of **righteousness**,"[17] when there is no indication whatsoever that he ever gave up his position of authority in the government?

**COMMENTS:**

*Friends, just as Karen and Cindy discussed today, Jesus said at Matthew 5:14-16: "You are the light of the world. A city on a hill cannot be hidden.* ***Neither*** *do people light a lamp and* ***put it under a bowl****. Instead they put it on its stand, and it gives light to* ***everyone*** *in the house. In the same way, let your light shine before men, that they may see your good deeds and praise your Father in heaven."*[18] *If Christians refuse to participate in politics, how can the light of*

---

Row Publishers, 1988), p. 464

[12] *The Barnhart Dictionary of Etymology,* Robert K. Barnhart, editor (The H.W. Wilson Company, 1988), p. 813

[13] *The Watchtower,* November 1, 1999, p. 29

[14] *New World Translation*

[15] See Romans 13:2, *New World Translation*

[16] Acts 10:1, *New World Translation*

[17] Acts 10:2, 22, *New World Translation*

[18] *New International Version*

*Christianity penetrate every aspect of the world if there are certain areas of society which Christians refuse to influence?*

## *DIALOGUE FOUR: Are Holiday And Birthday Celebrations Pagan?*

(WDGR LESSON 11: "Beliefs and Customs That Displease God")

*Why do many individuals in Christendom celebrate birthdays and holidays when these customs originated in paganism? Since Jesus never commanded Christians to celebrate His birth, are Christmas celebrations condemned by God?*

**KAREN:** Cindy, a friend of mine was telling me that Jehovah's Witnesses do not celebrate Christmas, Easter, or birthdays because these: "customs come from ancient false religions." [1]

**CINDY:** That's right, Karen. Just as we'll be studying today in the Watchtower brochure *What Does God Require of Us?,* "Not all beliefs and customs are bad. But God does not approve of them if they come from false religion or are against Bible teachings.…Christmas and its customs come from ancient false religions. The same is true of Easter customs, such as the use of eggs and rabbits. The early Christians did not celebrate Christmas or Easter, nor do true Christians today."[2]

**KAREN:** Cindy, there are many things in our modern culture that are rooted in paganism. The *Encyclopaedia Britannica* notes that names of the days of our week are: "derived from Anglo-Saxon words for the gods of Teutonic mythology."[3] We also see traces of pagan origin in many of the symbols and artwork found in modern stationary, wallpaper, and decorative designs.[4] Does this mean that we should separate ourselves into some kind of community where all traces of paganism have been carefully removed from our presence?

**CINDY:** Of course not, Karen. While it is impossible for us to be able to remove all aspects of paganism around us,[5] the Bible says that Christians are to: "flee from idolatry"[6] and should have "…no part of the world."[7] "Jesus never commanded Christians to celebrate his birth. Rather, he told his disciples to memorialize, or remember, his death.…The custom of celebrating birthdays comes from ancient false religions."[8] You don't want to displease Jehovah by participating in pagan customs do you?

**KAREN:** Cindy, do Jehovah's Witnesses have bridesmaids, wear bridal veils, and exchange wedding rings during their wedding ceremonies?

---

[1] *What Does God Require of Us?,* 1996, pp. 22-23
[2] *What Does God Require of Us?,* p. 22:1, 3
[3] *The New Encyclopaedia Britannica,* vol. 12, 1998, p. 555
[4] *Awake!* December 22, 1976, p. 12
[5] *Awake!* December 22, 1976, p. 15
[6] 1 Corinthians 10:14, *New World Translation*
[7] John 17:16, *New World Translation*
[8] *What Does God Require of Us?,* pp. 22-23:3-4

**CINDY:** Yes.

**KAREN:** Did you know that many of these customs come from pagan beliefs and rituals? For example, the book *Something Old, Something New—Ethnic Weddings in America* notes that: "Although for Americans covering the bride's face with a **veil** has come to represent innocence and purity, the practice was **originally** used in other cultures as **protection** from harm or molestation and was one of many **rituals** adopted out of concern for the happiness, safety, and fertility of the bride and groom....raised chairs, red carpets, special shoes and other forms of insulation or protection have been used to defend against malicious **spirits** on the ground....The current Western practice of having a **bridal party** to attend the couple evolved from a Roman tradition, in which the bridesmaids and ushers dressed exactly like the bride and groom, to **protect** the wedding couple by confusing **evil spirits**."[9] *The World Book Encyclopedia* also notes that: "The custom of giving a **wedding ring** dates back to the ancient Romans....Wearing the wedding ring on the ring finger of the left hand is another old custom. People once thought that a vein or nerve ran directly from this finger to the heart."[10] Also, *The Encyclopedia Americana* reveals that: "The **wedding cake** has its origins far back in time....In Rome the early marriage rite was called *conferreatio* from the cake of wheat...which the couple **first offered to the gods**, then ate together."[11] Thus, the book *A Short History of Marriage* concludes: "There is not a single point connected with marriage which is not shrouded in innumerable superstitions, some of them dating back to hoary antiquity."[12]

**CINDY:** Wow! I didn't know that.

**KAREN:** Cindy, don't you think it's a bit hypocritical for Jehovah's Witnesses to condemn the celebration of birthdays and holidays due to their pagan origin, while at the same time implementing marriage customs in their wedding ceremonies that are rooted in pagan idolatry?

**CINDY:** That's a good point, Karen. But, "Jesus never commanded Christians to celebrate his birth. Rather, he told his disciples to memorialize, or remember, his death....The early Christians did not celebrate Christmas or Easter," nor did they celebrate their birthdays.[13]

**KAREN:** Cindy, did Jesus command us to celebrate our wedding anniversaries? What about the early Christians? Did they celebrate their anniversaries?

**CINDY:** Well, no.

**KAREN:** That's right, Cindy. *The Encyclopedia Americana* notes that: "The family practice of observing wedding anniversaries seems to have grown up in western Europe" around

---

[9] *Something Old, Something New—Ethnic Weddings in America,* (Philadelphia, PA: The Balch Institute for Ethnic Studies, 1987), p. 8

[10] *The World Book Encyclopedia,* vol. 13, 2000, p. 221

[11] *The Encyclopedia Americana,* vol. 28, 1999, p. 565

[12] *A Short History of Marriage,* by Ethel L. Urlin, (Detroit Singing Tree Press, 1969), p. 201

[13] *What Does God Require of Us?,* p. 22:3, 4

"the 17th century."[14] Since Jehovah's Witnesses celebrate their anniversaries even though Jesus never commanded it, why does the Watchtower Society argue that it's wrong to celebrate the birth of Christ simply because Jesus and the early Christians didn't participate in this celebration?

**CINDY:** I don't know, Karen. But, "the only two birthday celebrations spoken of in the Bible were held by persons who did not worship Jehovah"[15] and in both of those cases bad things happened. Since, "Everything that is in the Bible is there for a reason....Jehovah's Witnesses take note that God's Word reports unfavorably about birthday celebrations and so shun these."[16]

**KAREN:** Cindy, do Jehovah's Witnesses celebrate the Jewish Hanukkah?

**CINDY:** Well, no. Why should they?

**KAREN:** If everything that is written in the Bible is written for a purpose, why don't Jehovah's Witnesses celebrate Hanukkah, since the Bible reports that Jesus celebrated it at John 10:22?[17]

**CINDY:** Karen, that's a good point. I don't know why, but one thing the Bible is clear about is the fact that Christians should honor Jehovah God and shun creature worship. Since, "birthday celebrations tend to give excessive importance to an individual,"[18] this is why Jehovah's Witnesses do not to celebrate their birthdays, but choose rather to: "give gifts and have good times together at other times during the year."[19]

**KAREN:** Cindy, there is quite a difference between considering someone special and worshipping or idolizing them. If the celebration of one's birthday is considered giving "excessive importance to an individual," shouldn't the celebration of one's wedding anniversary likewise be considered the giving of "excessive importance" to one's spouse? Don't you think such reasoning is inconsistent?

**CINDY:** Well, I guess you're right, Karen.

**KAREN:** Cindy, I think we would be wise to apply the advice that the Watchtower Society gave in the *Awake!* article of January 8, 2000. In that article, entitled "A Balanced View of Popular Customs," the Society noted: "Customs have been profoundly influenced by religion. Many, in fact, arose from old superstitions and non-Biblical religious ideas....But what about customs that may **once** have been linked to questionable practices but that **today** are primarily viewed as social etiquette?" [20] The Society went

---

[14] *The Encyclopedia Americana,* vol. 28, 1999, p . 564
[15] *What Does God Require of Us?,* p. 22:4
[16] *Reasoning from the Scriptures,* 1985, 1989ed, p. 68-69
[17] See *Illustrated Manners And Customs of the Bible,* J.I. Paker, M.C. Tenney, editors (Nashville, TN: Thomas Nelson Publishers, 1980), p. 409
[18] *School and Jehovah's Witnesses,* 1983, p. 18
[19] *What Does God Require of Us?,* p. 22:4
[20] *Awake!,* January 8, 2000, pp. 26-27

on to say: "...Does this mean that Christians are forbidden to observe such customs? ...Although there may be reason to examine the origin of a particular custom, in some cases it is **more important** to consider *what the custom means to people at the time and in the place where one* ***now*** *lives.*"[21] Cindy, why don't we apply this advice from the Watchtower Society? How many people today even know about the pagan origin of Christmas, Easter, and birthday celebrations, much less believe they are worshipping pagan gods by engaging in such activities? Don't you think these customs have lost their pagan significance and just as this article noted, should be evaluated in light of the time and place where we "now" live?

**COMMENTS:**

*Friends, The Bible reveals that many of the early Christians were allowed to celebrate* ***all*** *of the Jewish religious festivals and national holidays* ***even*** *after the coming of Christ and the abolition of the Law of Moses. Paul at Romans 14:5-6 encouraged individual freedom on this issue by stating: "One man regards one day above another, another regards every day alike. Let each man be fully convinced in his own mind. He who observes the day, observes it for the Lord...."[22] And at Colossians 2:16-17, the Bible states: "Let no man therefore judge you...in respect of an holyday, or of the new moon, or of the sabbath days: which are a shadow of things to come; but the body is of Christ."[23]*

---

[21] Emphasis in the original, *Awake!,* January 8, 2000, pp. 26-27

[22] *New American Standard Bible*

[23] *King James Version*

## *DIALOGUE FIVE: Is Hell Real and the Human Soul Immortal? —Part I*

(WDGR LESSON 11: "Beliefs and Customs That Displease God")

*Are the dead unconscious in the grave or are wicked souls tormented in a fiery hell? When the Bible uses the term "eternal destruction" to refer to the punishment of the wicked, does it mean annihilation? What about the human soul? Does it live on in eternity?*

**KAREN:** Cindy, we've been reading the section on "Beliefs and Customs That Displease God" in the Watchtower brochure *What Does God Require of Us?,* and it says: "The dead cannot do anything or feel anything. ...The soul dies; it does not live on after death."[1] But I don't understand how this can be the case. Doesn't the Bible say at Matthew 25:46: "These will go away into **eternal punishment**, but the righteous into **eternal life**"?[2] If the dead are completely unconscious and cannot feel anything, how can the righteous dead enjoy "eternal life" while the wicked endure "eternal punishment"?

**CINDY:** Well, Karen, Jehovah's Witnesses believe in the resurrection of the righteous dead. So, while we believe they are unconscious in the grave now, they won't stay that way. But as far as eternal punishment for the wicked, your Bible says something different than my Watchtower Bible, *The New World Translation of the Holy Scriptures*. At Matthew 25:46 it states: "And these will depart into **everlasting cutting-off**, but the righteous ones into everlasting life." You see, Karen, many people believe the wicked will suffer eternally in a fiery hell because as the Watchtower Society explains in their book *Reasoning from the Scriptures:* "Translators have allowed their personal beliefs to color their work instead of being consistent in their rendering of the original-language words."[3]

**KAREN:** Cindy, are you saying that my *New American Standard Bible* is biased to teach that wicked people will suffer in hell after they die? If so, why is it that nearly every Bible translation I read on this verse at Matthew 25:46 says "eternal punishment" while yours says "everlasting cutting-off"? Are all the other Bible translations biased? Or is yours the one that is biased?

**CINDY:** Karen, my *New World Translation* is not biased. The Watchtower Society goes on to explain: "For example: ... The *King James Version* rendered *she'ohl'* as 'hell,' 'the grave,' and 'the pit'; *hai'des* is therein rendered both 'hell' and 'grave'; *ge'en·na* is also translated 'hell.' ...Thus the exact meanings of the original-language words have been obscured."[4] So, Karen, since the Greek and Hebrew words translated "hell" in most Bibles mean the grave, this is one of the reasons why we, Jehovah's Witnesses, do not

---

[1] *What Does God Require of Us?,* 1996, p. 23:5

[2] *New American Standard Bible*

[3] *Reasoning from the Scriptures,* 1989, p. 171

[4] *Reasoning from the Scriptures,* 1989, p. 171

believe people will suffer after they die. It is also why my Bible translates the Greek word *Kolasin* as "cutting-off" instead of "eternal punishment." The Watchtower Society explains: "*Kolasin*... is derived from *kolazoo,* which signifies, 1. *To cut off;* as lopping off branches of trees, to prune. 2. *To restrain, to repress....* 3. *To chastise, to punish.* To cut off an individual from life, or society, or even to restrain, is esteemed as *punishment;*—hence has arisen this *third* metaphorical use of the word. ...The righteous go to *life,* the wicked to the *cutting off* from life, or *death.*"[5]

**KAREN:** But, Cindy, I don't agree. How can the simple act of cutting a wicked person off from eternal life be true righteous punishment if that person doesn't want to live in the first place? Just think of how many times you hear on the news about a wicked person **committing suicide in an attempt to avoid judgment**. Isn't that what every vicious criminal wants to do **to escape the consequences of his actions**? How can God be righteous to grant these wicked people their desire of wanting to be eternally annihilated? You call this "eternal punishment"? This seems to be more like eternal escapism of judgment, if you ask me! Just think about Hitler—a man who authorized the torturous murder of 11 million people. Are you going to tell me that God is going to give him the exact same judgment of annihilation that He will give my neighbor Joe who has never murdered a single person but simply refuses to acknowledge Jesus Christ as God's way of salvation?

**CINDY:** Well, Karen, I wouldn't say Hitler and your neighbor Joe are going to have the exact same punishment. If your neighbor is a nice guy, he will likely be, "resurrected with the opportunity to live forever" while "those whose memory was blotted out in Gehenna because of unforgivable sins"[6] will not be resurrected at all. "The Bible does not answer all our questions as to whether certain specific individuals who have died will be resurrected."[7] But, I think it is safe to say that Hitler will be one who will be eternally annihilated.[8]

**KAREN:** But, Cindy, that's my point. If my neighbor still refuses to accept Christ as His Savior and is therefore unworthy to live forever, in the end, if annihilation is the only punishment God has available to give unworthy people, wouldn't my neighbor end up in the exact same annihilated state as Hitler? You call this type of judgment righteous — to give every non-worthy person the **same** treatment?

**CINDY:** I see your point, Karen. I agree that it wouldn't be right for God to give them the same punishment.

---

[5] *Reasoning from the Scriptures,* 1985, 1989ed, p. 171
[6] *Reasoning from the Scriptures,* 1985, 1989ed, p. 339
[7] *Reasoning from the Scriptures,* 1985, 1989ed, p. 340
[8] Here, Cindy correctly describes the Jehovah's Witness teaching that some of the wicked people are so wicked that they will never be resurrected. Space does not allow for a full rebuttal of this false doctrine, but Scripture clearly teaches against it when it claims that the wicked will be resurrected just as the righteous are at Acts 26:15 and Revelation 20:12-15. There is not a single Scripture in the Bible that indicates that some of the wicked will not be resurrected at all.

**KAREN:** Cindy, let's look at Hebrews 10:26-27 and verse 29: "For if we go on sinning willfully...there no longer remains a sacrifice for sins, but a **terrifying expectation of judgment**, and the **fury of a fire** which will **consume the adversaries**. ...How much **severer punishment** do you think he will deserve who has trampled under foot the Son of God."[9] Did you notice how this passage specifically says that there will be a more "severer punishment" for the people who trample under foot the truth about the Son of God than for others who didn't do this? Can you see why "eternal punishment" has to be some form of a measurable degree of torment? Otherwise, it wouldn't make any sense because it is impossible to create a more severer degree of annihilation served to one person over another.

**CINDY:** OK, Karen. I see what you're saying, but what kind of father would torment his children with fire?[10]

**KAREN:** You're right. A good father wouldn't punish his children with fire, but he might torment his enemies with it. Consider this Scripture here at Matthew 25:41. Will you read it for me in your Bible, Cindy?

**CINDY:** OK. It says: "Then he will say, in turn, to those on his left, 'Be on YOUR way from me, YOU who have been cursed, **into the everlasting fire prepared for the Devil and his angels**. '"[11]

**KAREN:** Cindy, God did not prepare "everlasting fire" to torment His children. He prepared it for His enemies—the Devil and his angels. At John 8:44, the Bible calls those people who reject Christ, children of the Devil and says that those people who do Satan's works do so because he is their father. So, we are not all God's children, Cindy. Rather, we are born as children of the Devil destined for "everlasting fire" until we repent and are adopted by Christ's grace out of Satan's family into God's family as Scripture describes here at John 1:12-13: "But as many as received Him, to them **He gave the right to become children of God**, even to those who believe in His name, **who were born**, not of blood nor of the will of the flesh nor of the will of man, but **of God**."[12]

**CINDY:** But, Karen, I don't believe that God's act of throwing His enemies into "everlasting fire" means they will be tormented in a fiery hell forever. There is no way that God would torment people *FOREVER* for deeds they did over a limited period of time here on earth. Does that seem right to you? Even the Bible points out that "hell" has an end when is says in the *King James Bible Version* at Revelation 20:14 that, "death and hell were cast into the lake of fire."

**KAREN:** Cindy, if a human judge were to grant a murderer only five minutes in prison because his dreadful act took only five minutes to complete, would you think that judge is very righteous?

---

[9] *New American Standard Bible*

[10] See *Reasoning from the Scriptures,* 1985, 1989 ed, p. 174

[11] *New World Translation*

[12] *New American Standard Bible*

**CINDY:** No, I wouldn't.

**KAREN:** Of course, you wouldn't. And even after a long period of time in prison, if you could detect that the criminal has not changed, would you want him to be released back into the public where he could commit his crimes again?

**CINDY:** Well, no.

**KAREN:** Cindy, at Revelation 22:11, the Bible says that at the end of time, once everyone has undergone judgment: "Let the one who does wrong, still do wrong; and the one who is filthy, still be filthy..."[13] You can see that by this point, the wicked will be unable to change from their wickedness. That is why God has to make the fires of "eternal punishment" everlasting. Since these people will not change, Revelation 14:11 says: "And the **smoke of their torment goes up forever and ever**; they have no rest day and night..." [14] Can you see why God is righteous to keep these wicked people locked up in a fiery torment "forever"? And just because Revelation 20:14 says that "death" and "hell" or "Hades" as my Bible translates it, are cast into the lake of fire, that doesn't mean that the torments of eternal punishment will stop. As you can see, quite the opposite is the case.

**CINDY:** OK, I understand what you're saying, but I'm still not convinced that God will not simply annihilate the wicked. Doesn't the Bible say the wicked will be destroyed at 2 Thessalonians 1:9? How can they suffer eternally if they will be destroyed?

**KAREN:** Cindy, the word translated "destruction" at 2 Thessalonians 1:9 does not mean annihilation. I can understand why you find it difficult to believe in eternal torment, but the Scriptures have a lot more to say on this topic. Can we discuss this again next week?

**CINDY:** Sure. I'll be here.

---

[13] *New American Standard Bible*

[14] *New American Standard Bible*

## *DIALOGUE FIVE: Is Hell Real and the Human Soul Immortal? —Part II*

(CONTINUED FROM THE PREVIOUS DIALOGUE)

**KAREN:** Cindy, last week in our study of the Watchtower brochure *What Does God Require of Us?,* we discussed "Beliefs and Customs That Displease God" and talked about the Jehovah's Witness belief that God will annihilate the wicked instead of tormenting them in a fiery hell. You asked how I could believe in a loving God who would torment people forever, and I explained that God would neither be loving or righteous to give a viciously wicked person like Hitler the exact same punishment of annihilation that He would give to someone who never murdered a single person but simply rejected Christ's sacrifice for eternal life.

**CINDY:** Yes, Karen, you made a good point that for God to be righteous, He would have to have some type of punishment that could be administered in degrees of torment rather than treat all unworthy people with the exact same judgment of annihilation. However, I still want to know what you think about 2 Thessalonians 1:9 where it says: "These very ones will undergo the **judicial punishment of everlasting destruction** from before the Lord and from the glory of his strength"?[1] Since wicked will undergo "everlasting destruction," doesn't this mean they will be annihilated?

**KAREN:** Cindy, are you sure that the phrase "everlasting destruction" means annihilation? Would you read 1 Corinthians 5:5 in your *New World Translation Bible?*

**CINDY:** OK. 1 Corinthians 5:5 says: "You hand such a man over to Satan for the **destruction of the flesh**, in order that the spirit may be saved in the day of the Lord."

**KAREN:** Cindy, did you notice how this verse specifically says that when this person's flesh undergoes "destruction," his "spirit" is saved? If the Greek word "*olethros*" translated "destruction" in both of these Scriptures means total annihilation, how would it be possible for the person's spirit to be saved? Doesn't it make more sense to interpret this Greek word as indicating a situation of utter "ruin"[2] of the person's flesh, instead of annihilation?

**CINDY:** Well, I guess so. But what about the verses in the Bible that seem to indicate that a person is unconscious when he dies? Don't these Scriptures prove that: "Not even one part of us survives the death of the body. We do not possess an immortal soul or spirit."?[3]

**KAREN:** Cindy, let's look at these verses that the Watchtower uses to try to prove that human souls and spirits do not survive death. The first ones the Watchtower Society lists in this brochure are Psalm 146:4 which says: "His spirit departs, he returns to the earth; In

[1] *New World Translation*

[2] See *The New Englishman's Greek Concordance and Lexicon* by Jay P. Green, Sr., 1982 edition, p. 606

[3] *What Does the Bible Really Teach,* 2005, 2006 edition, p. 58

that very day his **thoughts perish**," and Ecclesiastes 9:5,10 which reads: "For the living know they will die; but the **dead do not know anything, nor have they any longer a reward**, for their memory is forgotten. ... Whatever your hand finds to do, do it with all your might; for **there is no activity or planning** or knowledge or wisdom in Sheol where you are going." Cindy, I thought you said that you believe in a resurrection of the dead, but these verses say that the dead will not have, "any longer a reward." So, do you believe there is no reward after you die?

**CINDY:** No, I believe there is a reward for the righteous at the resurrection, but these verses say that the dead, while they are still dead, do not have any thoughts because they are unconscious. So these verses are not talking about the future resurrection. Remember the other Scripture on this subject that the Watchtower Society references is Ezekiel 18:4 and it says: "...The soul that is sinning—it itself will die."[4] Since the soul dies when the human person dies, it can't survive death.

**KAREN:** Are you sure about that, Cindy? While it is true that sometimes the Bible uses the words "soul" and "spirit" to refer to the physical person, like it does here at Ezekiel 18:4, that is not always the case. Let's look at another Scripture and see what Jesus taught on this subject. Matthew 10:28: "Do not fear those who kill the body but are **unable to kill the soul**; but rather fear Him who is able to destroy both soul and body in hell."[5] Doesn't this seem to indicate that the human soul can survive death?

**CINDY:** No, Karen. Jesus wasn't claiming that the soul can survive the death of the body. The Watchtower Society explains: "By referring to the 'soul' separately, Jesus here emphasizes that God can destroy all of a person's life prospects; thus there is no hope of resurrection for him. So, the references to the 'fiery Gehenna' have the same meaning as the 'lake of fire' of Revelation 21:8, namely, destruction, 'second death.'"[6]

**KAREN:** Cindy, if you were reading these verses without the Watchtower Society's literature, would you come up with the Society's interpretation of these verses or would you get the impression that Jesus was indeed teaching that the soul can survive the death of the body?

**CINDY:** Hum... OK, Karen. I guess, I'd have to admit that if I were reading these verses without Watchtower literature, I would get the impression that the soul can survive death. But I - I can't accept that interpretation. That's the Devil's lie! Didn't Satan say to Eve, "You will not die"?[7] When you claim that the soul or the spirit of a person survives death, aren't you believing Satan's lie that we will not completely die?

**KAREN:** No, I'm not. Cindy, correct me if I'm wrong, but don't Jehovah's Witnesses teach that the people who are destined for eternal life in heaven, will live in heaven without their physical bodies?

---

[4] *New World Translation*

[5] *New American Standard Bible*

[6] *Reasoning from the Scriptures,* 1985, 1989ed, p. 174

[7] See Genesis 3:4 and *What Does the Bible Really Teach,* 2005, 2006 edition, p. 64

**CINDY:** Yes, Karen. We believe the heavenly class of people will not have their fleshly bodies in heaven[8] because, "flesh and blood cannot inherit God's Kingdom."[9] But, what's your point?

**KAREN:** Cindy, my point is that you believe something similar to what I believe. Even you believe that for the people going to heaven, a certain part of them lives on without the body, whether you call it a "soul" or "spirit" or "life-force" or "spirit-creature," the point remains the same. Jehovah's Witnesses believe a certain part of a person that is not connected with their fleshly body will survive to be resurrected to live in heaven. So, even you accept the idea that some type of a life-force or spirit-essence survives outside of the body, even if you do not call it a soul or a spirit.

**CINDY:** Karen, we don't believe that! I think you are misunderstanding what we believe. Regarding the resurrection, the Watchtower Society says: "Is the resurrection a reuniting of an immaterial soul with the physical body? For this to be possible, of course, humans would have to have an immaterial soul that could separate from the physical body. The Bible does not teach such a thing."[10]

**KAREN:** I know the Watchtower Society claims that it does not teach this, but just think about their doctrine a moment. If resurrection means "rising up from death,"[11] what exactly is being raised from death to heavenly life if the person's physical body is not being raised? Wouldn't it have to be some type of spirit-essence or life-force directly from the person that can be raised to survive in heaven, separate from the physical body? Otherwise, how can you call it a resurrection?

**CINDY:** I don't know. I guess I'd have to agree with you that for the people going to heaven, some part of them will exist that can live apart from their fleshly body. I've never thought of it this way before.

**KAREN:** So, since we both agree that it is possible for a part of a person to live in heaven without a fleshly body, the belief in an immaterial soul can't be Satan's lie, now can it? In fact, let's look at more Scripture verses that prove that at the moment when a Christian dies, his soul or spirit is immediately present with Christ. Cindy, will you read 2 Corinthians 5:6-9 in your Bible?

**CINDY:** Sure. "We are therefore always of good courage and know that, **while we have our home in the body, we are absent from the Lord**, for we are walking by faith, not by sight. But we are of good courage and are **well pleased rather to become absent from the body and to make our home with the Lord**. Therefore we are also making it our aim that, **whether having our home with him** or being absent from him, we may be acceptable to him."[12]

---

[8] See *Reasoning from the Scriptures,* 1985, 1989ed, p. 336
[9] 1 Corinthians 15:50
[10] *Reasoning from the Scriptures,* 1985, 1989ed, p. 333
[11] *Reasoning from the Scriptures,* 1985, 1989ed, p. 333
[12] *New World Translation*

**KAREN:** If the Apostle Paul's spirit or soul was to become unconscious in the grave when his physical body died, why would he be "well pleased" to leave his body and be "at home with the Lord"? That doesn't sound like someone who thought he would cease to exist after he died. And consider this Scripture here at 1 Thessalonians 5:23: "Now may the God of peace Himself sanctify you entirely; and may your **spirit** and **soul** and **body** be preserved complete, without blame at the coming of our Lord Jesus Christ..." If the spirit and soul are nothing but terms to describe the physical body of a person, why would Paul utter his wish that each of these parts of a person be "preserved complete, without blame." Don't you think this would be a strange thing to say if he taught that the spirit and soul of a person ceased to exist at death?

**CINDY:** Karen, I agree that these verses do not make a lot of sense with the Jehovah's Witness position that no part of the body exists after death, but I'm sure I can come up with some way to explain them if I research hard enough. For example, John 5:28-29 is another Scripture that seems to indicate that the dead are conscious when Jesus says that those in the "memorial tombs"[13] will "hear" his voice and "come out," but the Watchtower Society explains that this terminology does not prove the dead are conscious, but rather that it: "lays stress on preserving memory of the deceased person."[14]

**KAREN:** Excuse me, Cindy! Are you saying that you actually believe the Watchtower Society's strange interpretation for these verses, instead of accepting what the texts plainly say? In other words, are you saying that Scripture doesn't mean what it says? Again, I have to ask you, if you just read these verses in the Bible without Watchtower literature, would you come up with the Society's conclusions or would you conclude that these verses are indeed teaching what most Christian's believe concerning life after death?

**CINDY:** Yes, you're right. It does sound like the Bible agrees with the popular Christian position on this subject. You certainly have given me something to think about.

**COMMENTS:**

*Friends, the idea that wicked souls will spend eternity in a fiery hell or lake of fire makes many people uncomfortable. It is far easier to believe in the Jehovah's Witness idea of annihilation than to accept what the Scriptures plainly teach on this difficult subject. Yet, Jesus spoke of hell more than He spoke of heaven because this place is as real as heaven is real. If hell is merely the grave where unconscious human souls rest in peace, why would Jesus warn people over and over about the dangers of going to this awful place?*

---

[13] The *New World Translation* is the only translation that adds the word "memorial" to the word "tombs" in this verse to try to justify the Jehovah's Witness belief that the dead are only existing in Jehovah God's memory instead of existing as immaterial souls or spirits.

[14] *Reasoning from the Scriptures,* 1985, 1989ed, p. 339

*At Luke 16, Jesus told a parable about a poor man named Lazarus who went to a blissful place at death while a rich man went to the eternal torments of a fiery hell. Although this story probably did not occur in real life, all of Jesus' other parables resembled real-life situations. There is no reason to think that this story was any different. Revelation 20:15 says: "And if anyone's name was not found written in the book of life, he was thrown into the lake of fire."*[15] *Do you know if your name is written in the Lamb's book of life?*

[15] *New American Standard Bible*

## *DIALOGUE SIX: Is The Cross A Pagan Symbol?*

(WDGR LESSON 11: "Beliefs and Customs That Displease God")

*Was Jesus crucified on a cross or was He impaled on a torture stake? Why does the Greek word translated "cross" in many Bibles mean just one piece of timber? Were crosses used at the time of Christ?*

**KAREN:** Cindy, I noticed that at 1 Corinthians 1:18, your Bible reads differently than mine. My Bible says: "...the word of the **cross** is to those who are perishing foolishness...."[1], but your Bible, *The New World Translation,* says: "...the speech about the **torture stake** is foolishness to those who are perishing."

**CINDY:** That's right, Karen. Just as we'll be studying today in the Watchtower brochure *What Does God Require of Us?,* "Jesus did not die on a cross. He died on a pole, or a stake. The Greek word translated 'cross' in many Bibles meant just one piece of timber."[2]

**KAREN:** Cindy, I was reading the *The Zondervan Pictorial Encyclopedia of the Bible* and while it is true that the Greek word *stauros* which many Bibles translate as "the cross", "**originally** meant an 'upright pointed stake,'" this encyclopedia goes on to explain that "*Stauros* in the NT, however, apparently was a pole sunk into the ground with a cross-bar fastened to it giving it a 'T' shape. Often the word 'cross' referred **only** to the cross-bar...." So you see, Cindy, the Society is right when they say that the Greek word: "meant just one piece of timber," for it referred **only** to the **cross-bar** upon which criminals were nailed and, "hoisted then **with it** up onto the upright stake **already** in place at the execution site."[3]

**CINDY:** But, Karen, were crosses used at the time of Christ? How could a cross-bar have been used to impale Jesus to the torture stake, when the Watchtower notes that it wasn't until "later" that *stauros:* "came to be used for an execution stake having a crosspiece."[4]

**KAREN:** Cindy, is the Society saying that there is no historical evidence for the cross being used at the time of Christ?

**CINDY:** That's right, Karen. In support of this, the Watchtower book *Reasoning from the Scriptures* quotes J.D. Parsons who said in his book *The Non-Christian Cross:* " 'There is not a **single** sentence in any of the numerous writings forming the **New Testament**, which...bears even indirect evidence to the effect that the stauros used in the case of Jesus was other than an ordinary stauros; much less to the effect that it consisted, not of **one piece** of timber, but of **two pieces** nailed together in the form of a cross.'...Thus

---

[1] *New American Standard Bible*

[2] *What Does God Require of Us?,* 1996, p. 23:6

[3] *The Zondervan Pictorial Encyclopedia of the Bible,* Merrill C. Tenney ed, vol. 1, 1976, pp. 1037-1038

[4] *Reasoning from the Scriptures,* 1985, 1989, p. 89

the weight of the evidence indicates that Jesus died on an upright stake and not on the traditional cross."[5]

**KAREN:** Cindy, did you know that the Greek historian Herodotus who lived approximately 400 years prior to the birth of Christ, described a crucifixion in which he stated: "They nailed him to **planks** and hanged him aloft...."[6] How can the Society argue that there is no evidence of more than "one piece of timber" being used in this kind of execution, when Herodotus described the crucifixion of a man upon "planks" long before Jesus' time?

**CINDY:** I don't know, Karen, but just because crosses were used 400 years before Christ, that doesn't mean that they were used at the time of Christ, does it?

**KAREN:** Cindy, I think you'll be surprised at the evidence. The book *The Crucifixion of Jesus* notes that "detailed descriptions" of crucifixion can be found in literature from ancient Roman times. In this literature, "a variety of postures and different kinds of tortures on crosses" are described. "Some victims are thrust head downward... still others have their arms outstretched on a crossbeam."[7] How can the Watchtower Society argue that Jesus' torture stake did not have a crossbeam when historical evidence from literature at that time, describes crossbeams being used in crucifixion?

**CINDY:** I don't know.

**KAREN:** Cindy, not only do we find historical evidence of the cross being described in literature from the time of Christ, but archeologists have recently uncovered the remains of a man who they believe was crucified by the Romans at 7 A.D. According to the *Newsweek* article of January 18, 1971: "What particularly interested the scholars were the marks found on the crucified man's bones....As the scholars see it," this man "was probably held down by soldiers while his outstretched arms were fastened first to the cross bar....Scratches on these two sets of bones are clearly discernible just above the wrist."[8]

**CINDY:** That's interesting Karen, but does the Bible give us any indication that Jesus was impaled on a crossbeam attached to the torture stake?

**KAREN:** Yes, it does, Cindy. Let's look at some of the evidence. If Jesus was impaled on a torture stake with no crosspiece, as the Society argues, how many nails would have been driven through His hands?

**CINDY:** Well, Karen, looking at the picture of Jesus impaled on the stake found on page 7 of the brochure *What Does God Require of Us?,* there was only **one** nail going through his hands.

---

[5] *Reasoning from the Scriptures,* pp. 89-90
[6] *The Crucifixion of Jesus: History, Myth, Faith,* by Gerard S. Sloyan (Minneapolis, MN: Augsburg Fortress Publishers, 1995), p. 15
[7] *The Crucifixion of Jesus: History, Myth, Faith,* p. 15
[8] *Newsweek,* January 18, 1971, p. 53

**KAREN:** That's right, Cindy. Now would you read John 20:25 in your *New World Translation* Bible?

**CINDY:** OK. "...But he [Thomas] said to them: 'Unless I see **in his hands** the print of the **nails** and stick my finger into the print of the **nails** and stick my hand into his side, I will certainly not believe.' "

**KAREN:** Cindy, how many nails does the Bible say were in Jesus' hands?

**CINDY:** Well, Karen, it doesn't say how many nails were used, but it does indicate that there was more than one nail that was driven into his hands.... " 'Unless I see in his **hands** the print of the **nails**....I will certainly not believe." But, Karen, is this the **only** verse you have to prove that Jesus died on a cross?

**KAREN:** Absolutely not, Cindy. Would you read John 21:18-19 in your Bible?

**CINDY:** Alright. " 'Most truly I say to you....when you grow old you will stretch **out** your hands and another [man] will gird you and bear you where you do not wish.' This he said to signify by what sort of death he would glorify God...."[9]

**KAREN:** Cindy, if Jesus died on a torture stake with His hands **up-stretched** over His head as the Watchtower portrays in this picture, how can the Bible say that Peter's hands were **outstretched** when he died, if crosses were not used at the time of Christ? Doesn't this passage indicate that people who died in this way had their hands nailed in an **outstretched** position on a crossbeam? At Matthew 27:37, the Bible says that the sign, giving the charge against Jesus, was posted **above** His **head**, and not above His **hands** as the Watchtower picture depicts. Why does the Society argue that there is no evidence in the Bible for a crosspiece being attached to the torture stake, when the Bible and historical evidence clearly reveal the opposite?

**CINDY:** That's a good point, Karen. I don't know, but isn't it true that: "the symbol of the cross comes from ancient false religions"? In the Watchtower book *Reasoning from the Scriptures,* the Society quotes a number of secular authorities that prove that pagans used crosses in their worship of false gods.[10] Since the Bible says that Christians are to "flee from idolatry,"[11] "do you think it would be right to use a cross in worship?"[12]

**KAREN:** Cindy, do you remember what the Society said in their *Awake!* article of December 22, 1976? In that article, the Society noted: "Snakes, **crosses**, stars, birds, flowers...yes, there is an almost endless number of designs and **symbols** that have at some time or other been linked with idolatrous worship....just because idol worshipers at some time or place might use a certain design, that does not automatically mean that true worshipers must always shun it...."[13]

---

[9] *New World Translation*

[10] *Reasoning from the Scriptures,* pp. 90-91

[11] 1 Corinthians 10:14

[12] *What Does God Require of Us?,* p. 23:6

[13] *Awake!* December 22, 1976, pp. 13-14

**CINDY:** Karen, did the Society really say that?

**KAREN:** Yes, they did, Cindy, and they went on to say: "Many times a design will **change** in significance according to location and time.... *A pagan religious symbol might **lose** its religious connotation*....So the Christian needs to be primarily concerned about what? Not what a certain symbol or design possibly meant thousands of years ago...but what it **means now** to most people where he lives."[14] Cindy don't you think this is good advice from the Watchtower Society?

**CINDY:** Well, I guess, Karen. So maybe the cross has lost its pagan religious connotation, but, "how would you feel if one of your dearest friends was executed on the basis of false charges? Would you make a replica of the instrument of execution? Would you cherish it, or would you rather shun it?"[15]

**KAREN:** Well, no, Cindy, but look at it this way. If one of your best friends died giving birth to a son, you wouldn't shun him because he was the instrument of her death, would you? Rather, you would cherish him because in her death was his life. The same is true for Christians. If it wasn't for Jesus' death on the cross, we would all be spiritually dead. Can you see how, far from being a symbol of death, the cross has become the symbol of life for those who have been cleansed by the blood of Christ?

**COMMENTS:**

*Friends, while it is true that Christians do not worship or venerate the cross, neither do they shun it. Just as Karen noted, far from being a pagan religious symbol of death, for true Christians, the cross has become the symbol of eternal life in Christ. This is why the apostle Paul says: "...may it never be that I should boast, except in the cross of our Lord Jesus Christ....For the word of the **cross** is to those who are perishing foolishness, but to us who are being saved it is the **power** of God."[16] Have you found eternal life in the power of the shed blood of Jesus?*

---

[14] *Awake!* December 22, 1976, p. 14

[15] *Reasoning from the Scriptures,* p. 92

[16] Galatians 6:14; 1 Corinthians 1:18, *New American Standard Bible*

## *DIALOGUE SEVEN: Your Decision To Serve God—Loyalty To Jehovah Or Loyalty To An Organization?*

(WDGR LESSON 16: "Your Decision to Serve God")

*What is involved in "making sure of all things"? Is "doubt" a ploy that Satan uses to break our loyalty to Jehovah God? Is the Watchtower organization the "ark" of safety? Where did you learn the truth? Didn't Jesus say a disciple is not above his teacher? If the Watchtower organization isn't the truth, where else can we go to find accurate knowledge of truth and eternal life?*[1]

**KAREN:** Cindy, I was reading in the Watchtower brochure *What Does God Require of Us?* about what I must do in order to become a "friend of God,"[2] and I have a question.

**CINDY:** Yes, Karen?

**KAREN:** My question is this: If I make my dedication to Jehovah God and decide to be baptized as one of Jehovah's Witnesses, what will be expected of me?

**CINDY:** Well, Karen, just as this brochure notes, "After you have made a dedication, Jehovah will expect you to live up to your promises....The Devil will try to stop you from serving Jehovah....But draw close to God in prayer.... study his Word each day....[and] stick close to the congregation....By doing all of this, you will gain the strength to stay faithful to God."[3]

**KAREN:** Cindy, what are some of the ways the Devil will try to stop me from serving Jehovah?

**CINDY:** Well, Karen, the February 1, 2001 issue of *The Watchtower* had a good article on how to "make the truth your own."[4] In that article, the Society discussed how: "having found the cramped road to life, a Christian's next challenge is to stay on it. Why is that a challenge? It is because our dedication and baptism make us a target of Satan's crafty acts....One ploy that Satan uses is to plant **doubts** in our mind....How does Satan use this tactic today? If we neglect our Bible reading, our personal study, our prayers, and our Christian ministry and meetings, we may leave ourselves open to **doubts** raised by others. For example: 'How do we know that this is the truth as Jesus taught it?'...'Are we on the threshold of Armageddon, or is it a long way off?' If such doubts should arise, what can we do to remove them?...We should 'keep on asking God' in prayer for faith and understanding and bolster our efforts in personal study regarding any questions or doubts."[5]

---

[1] The portion of this discussion that deals with responding to the Jehovah's Witness concept of "doubt" was taken from an audio message entitled *A Few Effective Methods of Witnessing to Jehovah's Witnesses,* by Arnold Hoffman.

[2] *What Does God Require of Us?,* 1996, p. 31:1

[3] *What Does God Require of Us?,* p. 31:3

[4] *The Watchtower,* February 1, 2001, p. 13

[5] *The Watchtower,* February 1, 2001, pp. 9-10

**KAREN:** Cindy, is the Watchtower Society saying that if I become one of Jehovah's Witnesses and I come to the place where I question or doubt something the Watchtower teaches, I would be falling prey to Satan's tactics?

**CINDY:** That's right, Karen. Just as the August 1, 1980 issue of *The Watchtower* noted: "Among the various causes of apostasy, one of the **foremost** is unquestionably a *lack of faith* through **doubt**....one who doubts...sets himself up as a judge. He thinks he knows better than his fellow Christians, better also than the 'faithful and discreet slave,' through whom he has learned the best part, if not **all** that he knows about Jehovah God and his purposes....The apostate makes himself a decider of what is true and what is false, of what is 'good and bad' in the way of spiritual food. He becomes presumptuous."[6]

**KAREN:** Cindy, suppose you had a wrong concept about something you believed and you were reading the Bible and Jehovah decided to give you light. What would be your initial reaction? In other words, if you had a false understanding or an improper view, and you were reading the Scriptures and Jehovah God wanted to show you the truth, what is the first thing that would enter your mind?

**CINDY:** I'm not sure, Karen.

**KAREN:** Cindy, wouldn't it be **doubt**? Wouldn't **doubt** be the first thing that would enter your mind if Jehovah was trying to get your attention and show you the truth?

**CINDY:** Well, I guess you're right. I never thought of it that way before, Karen.

**KAREN:** Can you see, Cindy? **Doubt** is the initial penetration of truth! **Doubt** is not a ploy of Satan, but it's the **Holy Spirit** trying to get you to perform your **personal** responsibility of finding out what is true. You see, to doubt God or to doubt the Word of God is sin, but to doubt whether your **interpretation** is perfectly accurate is **not** wrong. This is God's Spirit trying to get your attention so that you find out what is true. The Bible says: "Make sure of all things; hold fast to what is fine...."[7] That command was given to individuals. It was not given to an organization to "make sure of all things," and then to tell you what they made sure of. Tell me, Cindy, what's involved in making sure of all things?

**CINDY:** Well, Karen, it involves reading the Scriptures, praying, and studying the Watchtower's Bible-based publications.

**KAREN:** OK, Cindy. Now, suppose we were reading the Bible and we ran across a verse that contradicts a Watchtower teaching, and you took it back to the Kingdom Hall, looked it up in the library, asked your brothers about it, and you found out the Society doesn't

---

[6] *The Watchtower,* August 1, 1980, pp. 19-20

[7] 1 Thessalonians 5:21, *New World Translation*

have anything on it. Then, what would you do? Would you go against the Society and believe what you know to be true from the Bible?

**CINDY:** Oh, no, Karen. The Watchtower taught me everything I know about the Bible. I can't go against the Watchtower. That's Jehovah's organization—His channel of communication to mankind.[8] If there's ever a question on anything, the Society will come up with an answer on it eventually.[9]

**KAREN:** OK, Cindy. So, after you've checked the Watchtower's publications and you find they don't have an answer, what do you do with the verse? What does it mean to "make sure of all things"? Doesn't it ultimately lead to you making up your **own** individual, private mind on what that verse means?

**CINDY:** Well, I guess so.

**KAREN:** Cindy, what about those in Berea at Acts 17:11? The apostle Paul, who was no mere presiding overseer of some congregation, came from **headquarters** and visited the congregation at Berea, giving them the latest truth. Do you know what they said to Paul? They whipped out their Scriptures and said: "Thank you brother, Paul. I'll tell you what. Why don't you take that seat way there in the back, and keep your mouth shut. And we're going to take the Word of God and find out whether everything you told us is true or not!" And what did Paul do? Did he say: "Oh that's very un-theocratic. You might be like Christendom—division and confusion"? No, he didn't say that. He said, "Amen! They were more noble-minded than those in Thessalonica, for they received the word with great eagerness, examining the Scriptures daily, *to see* whether these things were so."[10]

**CINDY:** But, Karen, where did we learn the truth? Wasn't it from the Watchtower? Jesus said "a disciple is not above his teacher."[11] You don't think you know better than the Watchtower, do you?[12] The Bible says: "do not lean on your own understanding."[13]

**KAREN:** Cindy, are you saying I am to look to the Watchtower Society to be my spiritual **teacher**? At Matthew 23:8 Jesus told us not to call anyone "teacher" for there is only one teacher—God. Why can't I just personally read the Bible and let God's Holy Spirit be my teacher as Jesus commanded?[14]

**CINDY:** Karen, "it is true that many people can learn a great deal by reading the Bible personally....But, being **honest** with ourselves, are we truly going to grasp the full significance of it all without help?" [15] At Acts 8, when Philip asked the Ethiopian

---

[8] *The Watchtower,* October 1, 1967, p. 590
[9] See *The Watchtower,* May 1, 1957, p. 284
[10] *New World Translation*
[11] Matthew 10:24, *New World Translation*
[12] See *The Watchtower,* February 1, 1952, p. 80; *The Watchtower,* November 15, 1992, p. 20
[13] Proverbs 3:5, *New World Translation*
[14] See John 14:26; 1 John 2:27
[15] *Reasoning from the Scriptures,* 1985, 1989ed, p. 328

eunuch if he understood what he was reading in Scripture, the eunuch replied: "How could I ever do so, unless someone guided me?"[16] Even though the eunuch held a prominent position of authority, he: "was **humble** enough to acknowledge his need for help in understanding Bible prophecy."[17] Karen, if you are going to continue to eat from Jehovah's spiritual table, you need to have the attitude that the eunuch had at Acts 8. You need to be **humble**, **hungry**, and **honest** when you read the Watchtower publications, and "gratitude for the Scriptural things" you "have learned should move" you "to serve Jehovah loyally."[18]

**KAREN:** Cindy, at Acts 8:39, after Philip baptized the Ethiopian eunuch, what happened to his teacher (Philip)?

**CINDY:** Well, it says that: "Jehovah's spirit quickly led Philip away, and the eunuch did not see him anymore,"[19] but that's because the eunuch now had "the truth," so he did not need his teacher any longer. But you are not in the truth yet, Karen, so you still need the Watchtower Society to be your teacher.

**KAREN:** But, Cindy, don't you still have your teacher? Since Philip, the eunuch's teacher, left him after he came into the truth, if Jehovah's Witnesses are in the truth, why do they still need their "teacher," the Watchtower Society? Again I ask, since Jesus told us not to call anyone "teacher," why do Jehovah's Witnesses continue to look to the Watchtower Society as their spiritual "teacher"? If Jehovah God really is a God of love and He wants **everyone** to be saved, why would He write the Bible in such a way that the average person could **not** understand it without the help of a human teacher? If Jehovah is really loving, wouldn't He write it so that **anyone** could read it and be saved, regardless of whether they have help?

**CINDY:** That's a good point, Karen, but where else can we go to find accurate knowledge of truth and eternal life? Christendom certainly doesn't have the truth. Just as *The Watchtower* noted: *"We will be impelled to serve Jehovah loyally with his organization if we remember that there is nowhere else to go for life eternal."*[20] Just as Peter replied to Jesus at John 6:68: "Lord, whom shall we go away to? You have the sayings of everlasting life,"[21] and just as the people of Noah's day had nowhere else to go but to the ark of God, today, "there is nowhere else to go for divine favor and life eternal,"[22] but to the Watchtower organization.

**KAREN:** Cindy, at John 6:68, did Peter say to Jesus, "Lord, **what** shall we go away to?" or did He say: "**whom** shall we go away to?"

**CINDY:** He said to "whom."

---

[16] Acts 8:30-31, *New World Translation*
[17] *Reasoning from the Scriptures,* p. 328
[18] *The Watchtower,* November 15, 1992, p. 19
[19] *New World Translation*
[20] Emphasis in the original, *The Watchtower,* November 15, 1992, p. 21
[21] *New World Translation*
[22] *The Watchtower,* November 15, 1992, p. 21

**KAREN:** That's right, Cindy. So, who are we to go to for eternal life? To a person or to an organization?

**CINDY:** Well, I guess we're to go to a person, to Jesus. But aren't we following Jesus when we submit to Jehovah's organization as the ark of safety?

**KAREN:** Cindy, how do you know the Watchtower is God's organization? Doesn't it take only "one" drop of poison to poison a whole glass of water?[23] Since many of the Watchtower teachings over the years have proved false requiring "new light," how can we have confidence that "new light" down the road won't reveal that there is poison in some of the Society's current teachings? Since the Bible says that Jesus is the only ark of safety we should trust in for eternal life, why not place your complete trust in Jesus alone?[24]

**COMMENTS:**

*Friends, Jehovah God is the God of Truth. Truth does not fear examination. If an organization cannot stand up under examination, then it is not the truth, but is rather a counterfeit and loyalty to a counterfeit is disloyalty to Jehovah God. We would do well to follow the admonition in the March 15, 1998 Watchtower regarding misplaced loyalty. The Society said: "...in today's world the reality is that people often let themselves be manipulated and influenced in so many subtle ways that they end up involuntarily doing what others want them to do....religious organizations get people to support their ideas and goals, not always by means of convincing arguments, but often by appealing to a sense of solidarity or* ***loyalty****....each of us does well to ask himself, 'Of whom am I a slave? Who exercises the greatest influence on my decisions and my way of life?...Whom do I obey—God or men?' "*[25]

[23] See *Reasoning from the Scriptures,* p. 323

[24] See John 14:6

[25] *The Watchtower,* March 15, 1998, pp. 15-16; compare with *The Watchtower,* August 1, 1997, pp. 8-14

## ABOUT THE AUTHOR

For over a year, Christina (Harvey) Darlington was a Christian undercover, studying the mindset of Jehovah's Witnesses at a local Kingdom Hall in Colorado Springs. **During that time, she spent countless hours in conversations, discussing many of the topics covered in this book and learning how Jehovah's Witnesses think on a number of key doctrinal issues**. Originally published under the title, *What Does God Require?,* this book is the direct product of the experiences she has had talking with active and former Jehovah's Witnesses of all levels of leadership in this organization.

She is the director and founder of Witnesses for Jesus Inc, a non-profit ministry to Jehovah's Witnesses and Latter-day Saints (Mormons). As a devoted Christian, her passion is to alert the Christian community to the doctrines of these groups and to train and equip Christians to be effective witnesses to those ensnared by these counterfeit religions. Jehovah God is the God of truth, and truth does not fear examination. If a religious organization or church cannot stand up under examination, it is not "the Truth," but is rather a counterfeit, and LOYALTY to a counterfeit is DISLOYALTY to Jehovah God. The ministry of Witnesses for Jesus was born out of a deep love and concern for Jehovah's Witnesses who have committed their lives to a counterfeit faith.

> "But I am afraid, lest as the serpent deceived Eve by his craftiness, your minds should be **led astray** from the **simplicity** and **purity** of **devotion to Christ**. For if one comes and preaches **another Jesus** whom we have not preached … you bear this beautifully ... Test yourselves to see if you are in the faith; examine yourselves! Or do you not recognize this about yourselves, that **Jesus Christ is in you-unless indeed you fail the test?**" —2 Corinthians 11:3-4; 13:5

Exclusive religions like Jehovah's Witnesses often refer to their religious faiths as being the ultimate "truth." Because the members of these groups are taught that the only way to God is through their particular faith, each person's identity and security is wrapped up in his or her religious faith. Thus, as is the case with Jehovah's Witnesses, when one Jehovah's Witness meets another, he or she will often ask the other person, "How long have you been in THE TRUTH?" Real truth, however, is not found in identifying with a particular religious faith or denomination, but in a personal relationship with Jesus, for He proclaims that He is THE TRUTH: "and you shall **know the truth**, and the truth shall make you free ... If therefore the Son shall make you free, you shall be free indeed ... I am the way, and **the truth**, and the life; no one comes to the Father, but through Me." —John 8:32, 36; 14:6

> "And the witness is this, that God has **given us eternal life**, and this life is in His Son. He who **has the Son has the life**; he who does not have the Son of God does not have the life. These things I have written to you who believe in the name of the Son of God, in order that **you may know** that you have eternal life."
> —1 John 5:11-13

**WITNESSES FOR JESUS INC**
**POBOX 50911**
**COLORADO SPRINGS, CO 80949 USA**
**4witness.org * 4jehovah.org * 4mormon.org**

# DOCUMENTATION FOR SECTION ONE

## *DIALOGUE ONE A: Can You Serve Jehovah Without The Watchtower "New Light"?*

590 The WATCHTOWER. BROOKLYN, N.Y.

Do those associated with your organization seek political positions or reforms? Those in the early congregation had a more permanent hope centered in God's kingdom. (2 Pet. 3:13, 14) Do national or racial barriers exist within your organization? There were none in first-century congregations. (Gal. 3:28; Rev. 7:9) Is discrimination practiced? Early Christians abided by the principle that "there is no partiality with God" but his "will is that all sorts of men should be saved and come to an accurate knowledge of truth." —Rom. 2:11; 1 Tim. 2:4; Jas. 2:1-4.

IDENTIFYING THE THEOCRATIC ORGANIZATION

18 Those in the apostolic organization did not fulfill these requirements for the Christian congregation in just a token way. They viewed their position in Jehovah's chosen visible channel as sacred and would allow nothing to jeopardize their standing with God. They had no fear of this world. (Matt. 10:26-28) Their only concern was to provide for the safety and well-being of the flock of God. Jesus pointed to this mark of the true visible organization in connection with a detailed prophecy relating to this time of the end. He said: "Who really is the faithful and discreet slave whom his master appointed over his domestics, to give them their food at the proper time? Happy is that slave if his master on arriving finds him doing so. Truly I say to you, He will appoint him over all his belongings."—Matt. 24:45-47.

19 Evidences are now conclusive that Jesus Christ was enthroned in heaven in 1914 C.E. and that he accompanied Jehovah to his temple in 1918 C.E., when judgment began with the house of God.* (1 Pet. 4:17) After cleansing those belonging to this house who were alive on earth, Jehovah poured out his spirit upon them and assigned them the responsibility of serving as his sole visible channel, through whom alone spiritual instruction was to come. Those who recognize Jehovah's visible theocratic organization, therefore, must recognize and accept this appointment of the "faithful and discreet slave" and be submissive to it.

20 Today those thus charged with this grand privilege and responsibility are called Jehovah's witnesses, and have been since 1931. As a group they have been separated more and more from the sectarianism of Christendom from the 1870's onward. Since 1879 the *Watch Tower* magazine has been used by this collective group to dispense spiritual food regularly to those of this "little flock" of true Christians. (Luke 12:32) In 1884 they formed a legal servant, a corporation, called Zion's Watch Tower Tract Society, now known as the Watch Tower Bible and Tract Society of Pennsylvania. By 1919, having survived the fiery trials of World War I, this "faithful and discreet slave" class was no novice organization. True, the apostles were no longer in its midst, but they had left behind written instructions as part of Jehovah's great Record Book. Additionally, the modern-day members of this 1900-year-old Christian congregation had received from the days of the apostles onward a rich heritage of Christian loyalty and integrity, long and patient suffering of persecution, abiding faith in Jehovah's precious promises, con-

18. What mark of the true visible organization did Jesus identify, and what reward did he say he would give?
19. What must those who recognize Jehovah's visible organization accept?

* See the book *You May Survive Armageddon into God's New World*, Chapter 6, entitled "A·do·nay' Comes to His Temple." Published by the Watch Tower Bible & Tract Society in 1955.

20, 21. Who today are charged with the responsibility of representing Jehovah's King, and what record provides their recommendation?

OCTOBER

fidence
Lord an
ence to
witnesse
21 In t
they we
tually sl

Fi

JEHOV.
freedo
earth for
under wa
developm
pending d
of things
thousand-
mediately
ceive life
fort. Not
alone. Ja
century
"Faith, if
in itself.
breath is
is dead."
must pro
action, by

1. How and gift of life?

10/1/1967

the evidence, God's will became clear. Those of the nations did not have to get circumcised in order to enjoy Jehovah's approval. The apostles and the older men wasted no time in putting the decision in writing so that fellow Christians could be guided by it. —Acts 15:12-29; 16:4.

[7] Unlike the Jewish religious leaders, who clung to the traditions of their forefathers, most Jewish Christians rejoiced when they received this remarkable new understanding of God's purpose respecting the people of the nations, even though accepting it required a change of viewpoint regarding Gentiles in general. Jehovah blessed their humble spirit, and "the congregations continued to be made firm in the faith and to increase in number from day to day."—Acts 15:31; 16:5.

*Charles Taze Russell knew that light would shine on the book of Revelation in God's due time*

[8] Spiritual light continued to shine throughout the first century. But Jehovah did not reveal every aspect of his purposes to the early Christians. The apostle Paul told first-century fellow believers: "At present we see in hazy outline by means of a metal mirror." (1 Corinthians 13:12) Such a mirror did not have the best reflective surface. At first, then, comprehension of spiritual light would be limited. After the death of the apostles, the light grew dim for a while, but in recent times Scriptural knowledge has become abundant. (Daniel 12:4) How does Jehovah enlighten his people today? And how should we respond when he broadens our understanding of the Scriptures?

### The Light Gets Progressively Brighter

[9] In modern times the first real glimmer of light began to appear in the last quarter of the 19th century as a group of Christian men and women began an earnest study of the Scriptures. They developed a practical method for Bible study. Someone would raise a question; then the group would analyze all related Scripture texts. When one Bible verse seemed to contradict another, these sincere Christians endeavored to harmonize the two. Unlike the religious leaders of the day, the Bible Students

7. In what way were first-century Christians progressive?

8. (a) How do we know that more light could be expected after the first century came to a close? (b) What pertinent questions will we consider?

9. What unique and effective method of Bible study was used by the early Bible Students?

(as Jehovah's W
were determine
not tradition or
guide. After they
tural evidence,
conclusions. In
of many basic Bi

[10] Outstanding
was Charles Taz
of six helpful Bi
*ies in the Script*
to write a seven
plain the Bible
tion. "Whenever
write the Sevent
ed: "If the Lord g
he can write it."

[11] The foregoir
illustrates an im
to understand ce
Brother Russell k
the light to shine
any more than a
sun to rise before

Revealed—B

[12] Just as the
prophecies conce
Jesus' death and
understand Bible
only after it has b
Acts 1:15-21; 4:26
ic book, so we sh
most clearly as th
For example, C. T
rectly understood
ic scarlet-colored
elation 17:9-11,

10. Charles Taze R
study aids?
11. What connecti
our understanding
12. (a) When is B
(b) What example
derstand Bible prop
table? (See footnote

12 THE WATCHTOWER • MARCH 15, 2000

temple relate to the condition of the anointed while they are on the earth. When Ezekiel chapters 40 to 48 were reviewed years later, it was discerned that just as the spiritual temple is operating today, so the temple that Ezekiel saw in vision must also be functioning today. How so?

16 In Ezekiel's vision, priests are seen moving about in the courtyards of the temple as they serve the nonpriestly tribes. These priests clearly represent the "royal priesthood," Jehovah's anointed servants. (1 Peter 2:9) However, they will not be serving in the temple's earthly courtyard throughout the Thousand Year Reign of Christ. (Revelation 20:4) During most of that period, if not all of it, the anointed will be serving God in the spiritual temple's Most Holy, "heaven itself." (Hebrews 9:24) Since priests are seen going to and fro in the courtyards of Ezekiel's temple, that vision must be undergoing fulfillment today, while some of the anointed are still on the earth. Accordingly, the March 1, 1999, issue of this magazine reflected an adjusted view on this subject. Thus, clear down to the end of the 20th century, spiritual light was shed upon Ezekiel's prophecy.

**Be Willing to Adjust Your Viewpoint**

17 Anyone who wishes to come to a knowledge of the truth must be willing to bring "every thought into captivity to make it obedient to the Christ." (2 Corinthians 10:5) That is not always easy, especially when viewpoints are strongly entrenched. For example, before learning God's truth, you may have enjoyed celebrating certain religious holidays with your family. After you began to study the Bible, you realized that these celebrations are actually of pagan origin. At first, you may have been reluctant to apply what you were learning. Finally, however, love for God proved to be stronger than religious sentiment, and you stopped engaging in celebrations that displease God. Has not Jehovah blessed your decision?—Compare Hebrews 11:25.

18 We always benefit by doing things God's way. (Isaiah 48:17, 18) So when our view of a Bible passage is clarified, let us rejoice in advancing truth! Really, our continuing to be enlightened confirms that we are on the right path. It is "the path of the righteous ones," which "is like the bright light that is getting lighter and lighter until the day is firmly established." (Proverbs 4:18) True, at present we see some aspects of God's purpose "in hazy outline." But when God's due time arrives, we will see the truth in all its beauty, provided that our feet have remained firmly planted on "the path." In the meantime, may we exult in the truths that Jehovah has made plain, awaiting enlightenment on those that are not yet clearly understood.

19 How can we demonstrate our love for the light in a practical way? One way is by reading God's Word regularly—daily if possible. Are you following a regular program of Bible reading? The *Watchtower* and *Awake!* magazines also furnish us with an abundance of whole-

17. What adjustments have you made in personal viewpoint since coming to a knowledge of the truth, and how have they benefited you?

18. How should we react when our understanding of Bible truth is clarified?

19. What is one way to show that we love the truth?

**Can You Answer?**

- Why does Jehovah reveal his purposes progressively?
- How did the apostles and older men in Jerusalem settle the issue of circumcision?
- What method of Bible study did the early Bible Students adopt, and why was it unique?
- Illustrate how spiritual light is revealed in God's due time.

14 THE WATCHTOWER • MARCH 15, 2000

some spiritual fo
the books, brochu
that have been p
what about the
Kingdom-preachi
lished in the *Yearl*

20 Yes, Jehovah
swered the prayer

20. What connecti
truth from Jehovah
meetings?

# HOV

JEHOVAH is th
of light and tr
learned in the
article. His Word
way as we travel
path of uprightn
vah leads us by i
us in his ways. (I
105) Like the p
old, we gratefull
to God's leadings
"Instruct me, O
in your way, an
in the path of
ness."—Psalm 27:

2 One way in
struction today
ings. Do we take
provision by (1)
tening carefully
ticipating readily

1, 2. (a) How is Je
(b) What is involve
meetings?

Until his King-
rule of political
:iples follow his
:dience to those
it do not inter-
:rtakings. (Dan-
Jesus left guide-
ting: "Pay back,
to Caesar, but
:hew 22:21) Ear-
e Mount, Jesus
:r authority im-
: a mile, go with
5:41) In the con-
was illustrating
ibmission to le-
: in human rela-
quirements that
s law.—Luke 6:

**:aesar**

were to govern
Christians and
*Rise of Chris-*
Barnes wrote:
) come, a Chris-
s duty towards
rist's authorita-
· taxes: the dues
ıey became in-
se of the West-
stian would en-
wise accept all
:ovided he was
into Caesar the
d."
his that, a lit-

ı, what conscien-
ristians hold with

tians to deal with

***Russell wrote that true Christians "should be found amongst the most law-abiding of the present time"***

tle over 20 years after Christ's death, the apostle Paul told the Christians in Rome: "Let every soul be in subjection to the superior authorities." (Romans 13:1) About ten years later, shortly before his second imprisonment and his execution in Rome, Paul wrote to Titus: "Continue reminding them [Cretan Christians] to be in subjection and be obedient to governments and authorities as rulers, to be ready for every good work, to speak injuriously of no one, not to be belligerent, to be reasonable, exhibiting all mildness toward all men."—Titus 3:1, 2.

**Progressive Understanding of "the Superior Authorities"**

[12] As early as 1886, Charles Taze Russell wrote in the book *The Plan of the Ages:* "Neither Jesus nor the Apostles interfered with earthly rulers in any way. . . . They taught the Church to obey the laws, and to respect those in authority because of their office, . . . to pay their appointed taxes, and except where they conflict with God's laws (Acts 4:19; 5:29) to offer no resistance to any established law. (Rom. 13:1-7; Matt. 22:21) Jesus and the Apostles and the early church were all law-abiding, though they were separate from, and took no share in the governments of this world." This book correctly identified "the higher powers," or "the superior authorities," mentioned by the apostle Paul, as human governmental authorities. (Ro-

mans 13:1, *King James Version*) In 1904 the book *The New Creation* stated that true Christians "should be found amongst the most law-abiding of the present time —not agitators, not quarrelsome, not fault-finders." This was understood by some to mean total submission to the powers that be, even to the point of accepting service in the armed forces during World War I. Others, however, viewed it as contrary to Jesus' statement: "All those who take the sword will perish by the sword." (Matthew 26:52) Obviously, a clearer understanding of Christian submission to the superior authorities was needed.

[13] In 1929, at a time when laws of various governments were beginning to forbid things that God commands or demand things that God's laws forbid, it was felt that the higher powers must be Jehovah

12. (a) What did Charles Taze Russell view as the proper position of a Christian relative to the governmental authorities? (b) Regarding serving in the armed forces, what varied positions did anointed Christians take during World War I?

13. What change in understanding of the identity of the higher powers was presented in 1929, and how did this prove beneficial?

God and Jesus Christ.* This was the understanding Jehovah's servants had during the crucial period before and during World War II and on into the Cold War, with its balance of terror and its military preparedness. Looking back, it must be said that this view of things, exalting as it did the supremacy of Jehovah and his Christ, helped God's people to maintain an uncompromisingly neutral stand throughout this difficult period.

### Relative Submission

14 In 1961 the *New World Translation of the Holy Scriptures* was completed. Its preparation had required an in-depth study of the textual language of the Scriptures. The precise translation of the words used not only in Romans chapter 13 but also in such passages as Titus 3:1, 2 and 1 Peter 2:13, 17 made it evident that the term *"superior* authorities" referred, not to the *Supreme* Authority, Jehovah, and to his Son, Jesus, but to *human governmental authorities.* In late 1962, articles were published in *The Watchtower* that gave an accurate explanation of Romans chapter 13 and also provided a clearer view than that held at the time of C. T. Russell. These articles pointed out that Christian subjection to the authorities cannot be total. It must be *relative,* subject to its not bringing God's servants into conflict with God's laws. Further articles in *The Watchtower* have emphasized this important point.*

* *The Watchtower,* June 1 and 15, 1929.

14. How was increased light shed on Romans 13: 1, 2 and related scriptures in 1962?

**Can You Explain?**

- ☐ Why does subjection to the superior authorities not mean subjection to Satan?
- ☐ What was Jesus' attitude toward the politics of his day?
- ☐ What counsel did Jesus give his followers as to their dealings with Caesar?
- ☐ How did Paul counsel Christians to deal with the rulers of the nations?
- ☐ How has the understanding of the identity of the superior authorities developed over the years?

15 This key to the correct understanding of Romans chapter 13 has enabled Jehovah's people to balance due respect for the political authorities with an uncompromising stand on vital Scriptural principles. (Psalm 97:11; Jeremiah 3:15) It has allowed them to have a proper view of their relationship with God and their dealings with the State. It has ensured that while they pay back Caesar's things to Caesar, they do not neglect to pay back God's things to God.

16 But just what are Caesar's things? What legitimate claims can the State make on a Christian? These questions will be considered in the following article.

* See *The Watchtower,* November 1 and 15, December 1, 1962; November 1, 1990; February 1, 1993; July 1, 1994.

Interestingly, in his commentary on Romans chapter 13, Professor F. F. Bruce writes: "It is plain from the immediate context, as from the general context of the apostolic writings, that the state can rightly command obedience only within the limits of the purposes for which it has been divinely instituted —in particular, the state not only may but must be resisted when it demands the allegiance due to God alone."

15, 16. (a) What better balance did the new understanding of Romans chapter 13 lead to? (b) What questions remain to be answered?

P

ACCORDIN
we owe
Caesar,
back Caesar's
things to God.'
founded his en
the balanced a
relationship w
with the State.
"began to mar
2 Of course, t
servants is tha
to God. (Psalm
ever, they do n
they must rer
sar. Their Bibl
that they cons
tent they can
for. (Romans 1
jurists have re
power has lim
ernments ever
ral law.
3 The apostl
ural law when
the world: "W
is manifest ar
manifest to th

1, 2. (a) Accord
tians balance t
Caesar? (b) Wh
vah's Witnesses
3, 4. What int
made about nat
man law?

14 THE WATCHTOWER—MAY 1, 1996

ffect upon
compared
otally dark
vould take
ljust to the
ıt.
progressive
nge. There
doctrines,
ın conduct
ians, as to
as to prop-
n, and so
. But some
oes it seem
ıs does not
/hat is the
hese ques-
succeeding

vered by the
estion remains

ous

r

is as the
23:3, 4

the world
Lord [Je-
ev. 11:15)
shed forth,
ng without
ore clearly

MBER 1, 1981

the pathway that Jehovah's servants must tread.—2 Sam. 23:3, 4.

2 However, it may have seemed to some as though that path has not always gone straight forward. At times explanations given by Jehovah's visible organization have shown adjustments, seemingly to previous points of view. But this has not actually been the case. This might be compared to what is known in navigational circles as "tacking." By maneuvering the sails the sailors can cause a ship to go from right to left, back and forth, but all the time making progress toward their destination in spite of contrary winds. And that goal in view for Jehovah's servants is the "new heavens and a new earth" of God's promise.—2 Pet. 3:13.

3 There is no question that Jehovah God is continuing to bless the global activity of his witnesses, as directed by the "faithful and discreet slave." This can be seen by the fruits. Remember, Jesus said: "Every good tree produces fine fruit." And such righteous fruits are to be seen internationally today in one people only—the united, global society of Jehovah's Witnesses.—Matt. 7:17.

4 No matter where we may live on earth, God's Word continues to serve as a light to our path and a lamp to our roadway as to our conduct and beliefs. (Ps. 119:105) But Jehovah God has also provided his visible organization, his "faithful and discreet slave," made up of spirit-anointed ones, to help Christians in all nations to understand and apply properly the Bible in their lives. Unless we are in touch with this channel of communication that God is using, we will not progress along the road to life, no matter how much Bible reading we do.—Compare Acts 8:30-40.

2. How may we regard periodic adjustments in viewpoint?
3. What evidence is there that Jehovah is continuing to bless his witnesses?
4, 5. In addition to his inspired Word, what other instrument has Jehovah God used to guide his people?

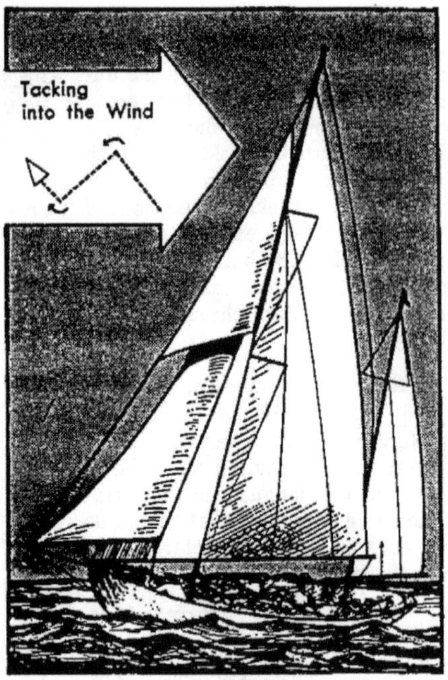


5 Regarding God's channel of communication, Jesus said that the "faithful and discreet slave" would provide spiritual nourishment at the right time for all his followers and that he would set this "slave" over all his belongings. (Matt. 24:45-47) It is also noteworthy that the apostle Paul, at Ephesians 4:11-16, indicated that the Christian congregation needed not only such inspired instruments as apostles and prophets but also evangelizers, shepherds and teachers to help Christians to arrive at the oneness in the faith and the accurate knowledge of the Son of God, and to gain full spiritual maturity.—See also 1 Corinthians 1:10; Philippians 1:9-11.

6 This "faithful and discreet slave,"

6. Because of what factors has it been necessary at times to reevaluate viewpoints?

THE WATCHTOWER — DECEMBER 1, 1981 27

productive land will certainly learn." (Isaiah 26:9) During Judgment Day all the people will learn about Jehovah, and they will be given every opportunity to obey and serve him.

7 It is under such paradise conditions that Jesus Christ and his 144,000 associate kings will judge humankind. People who choose to serve Jehovah will be in a position to receive everlasting life. But, even under these best of circumstances, some will refuse to serve God. As the Scriptures say: "Though the wicked one should be shown favor, he simply will not learn righteousness. In the land of straightforwardness he will act unjustly." (Isaiah 26:10) So after being given full opportunity to change their ways and to learn righteousness, such wicked ones will be destroyed. Some will be put to death even before Judgment Day ends. (Isaiah 65:20) They will not be permitted to remain to corrupt or spoil the paradise earth.

8 Will it be more difficult for some of the resurrected dead to learn and practice righteousness than it will be for others? When Jesus Christ was on earth, he showed that it would be. Most of the persons to whom he and his disciples preached

7. During Judgment Day, what will happen to those who choose to serve God and to those who refuse to do so?
8. How did Jesus show that during Judgment Day it would be more difficult for some to practice righteousness than it would be for others?

For whom will it be harder on Judgment Day?

People who heard Jesus

Those destroyed in Sodom and Gomorrah



did not listen. They rejected Jesus as the Messiah, even after hearing his preaching and seeing him perform miracles. When sending out his disciples to preach, Jesus said of a city that would reject their message: "Truly I say to you, it will be more endurable for the land of Sodom and Gomorrah on Judgment Day than for that city."—Matthew 10:15.

9 By saying this, Jesus showed that at least some of the unrighteous people of ancient Sodom and Gomorrah will be present on earth during Judgment Day. Although they had been very immoral, we can expect that some of them will be resurrected. (Genesis 19:1-26) Jehovah in his mercy will bring them back so that they will have an opportunity to learn about his purposes. But Jesus' words also show that some of the unrighteous ones to whom he and his disciples personally preached will be present during Judgment Day. They, too, will be resurrected and be given further opportunity to learn God's purposes. For whom will it be more difficult to accept Christ as king at that time? For the people of ancient Sodom or for those who had rejected the preaching of Jesus and his disciples?

10 It will be more difficult for those who personally rejected Jesus. Speaking of Capernaum, one of the cities where he performed miracles, Jesus said: "If the powerful works that took place in you had taken place in Sodom, it would have remained until this very day. Consequently I say to you people, It will be more endurable for the land of Sodom on Judgment Day than for you." (Matthew 11:22-24) Yes, during Judgment Day it will be even more difficult for those from Capernaum to admit their mistakes and to accept and serve Christ as king than it will be for the people of ancient Sodom to learn righteousness.

11 So it will be easier for certain "unrighteous" resurrected ones to learn about God and serve him than it will be for certain other "unrighteous" ones. (Matthew 12:41, 42) What, then, about the "righteous" who are resurrected—persons such as Abraham,

9, 10. (a) What unrighteous people will be resurrected during Judgment Day? (b) Why will it be more difficult for some unrighteous ones than for other unrighteous ones?
11. Why will it be easier on Judgment Day for the "righteous" than for any of the "unrighteous"?

productive land will certainly learn." (Isaiah 26:9) During Judgment Day all the people will learn about Jehovah, and they will be given every opportunity to obey and serve him.

[7] It is under such paradise conditions that Jesus Christ and his 144,000 associate kings will judge humankind. People who choose to serve Jehovah will be in a position to receive everlasting life. But, even under these best of circumstances, some will refuse to serve God. As the Scriptures say: "Though the wicked one should be shown favor, he simply will not learn righteousness. In the land of straightforwardness he will act unjustly." (Isaiah 26:10) So after being given full opportunity to change their ways and to learn righteousness, such wicked ones will be destroyed. Some will be put to death even before Judgment Day ends. (Isaiah 65:20) They will not be permitted to remain to corrupt or spoil the paradise earth.

[8] It will truly be a grand privilege to be resurrected on earth during Jehovah's great Judgment Day. However, the Bible indicates that it will be a privilege that not all will enjoy. Consider, for example, the people of ancient Sodom. The Bible says that the men of Sodom sought to have sexual relations with "the men" who were

7. During Judgment Day, what will happen to those who choose to serve God and to those who refuse to do so?

8. What was the moral condition of the men of Sodom?

Why did Jesus say it would be more endurable on Judgment Day for those in Sodom?

visiting Lot. Their immoral behavior was so extreme that even when they were miraculously struck with blindness, "they were wearing themselves out trying to find the entrance" of the house to get inside to have intercourse with Lot's visitors.—Genesis 19: 4-11.

[9] Will such terribly wicked persons be resurrected during Judgment Day? The Scriptures indicate that apparently they will not. For example, one of Jesus' inspired disciples, Jude, wrote first about the angels that forsook their place in heaven to have relations with the daughters of men. Then he added: "So too Sodom and Gomorrah and the cities about them, after they in the same manner as the foregoing ones had committed fornication excessively and gone out after flesh for unnatural use, are placed before us as a warning example by undergoing the judicial punishment of everlasting fire." (Jude 6, 7; Genesis 6:1, 2) Yes, for their excessive immorality the people of Sodom and of the surrounding cities suffered a destruction from which they will apparently never be resurrected.—2 Peter 2:4-6, 9, 10a.

[10] Jesus too indicated that the Sodomites may not be resurrected. When he spoke of Capernaum, one of the cities where he performed miracles, he said: "If the powerful works that took place in you [Capernaum] had taken place in Sodom, it would have remained until this very day. Consequently I say to you people, It will be more endurable for the land of Sodom on Judgment Day than for you." (Matthew 11:22-24) Jesus here was emphasizing the reprehensibility of the people of Capernaum by saying that it would be more endurable for the ancient Sodomites who, in the minds of his Israelite audience, were totally unworthy of a resurrection on Judgment Day.

[11] Surely, then, we should do everything we can to live our lives so as to merit a resurrection. But it may still be asked: Will it be more difficult for some of the resurrected dead to learn and practice righteousness than it will be for others? Well, consider:

9, 10. What do the Scriptures indicate about the prospect of a resurrection for the wicked persons of Sodom?

11. Why will it be easier on Judgment Day for the "righteous" than for any of the "unrighteous"?

discussing restoration of the theocratic organization, not resurrection.

#### JUDGMENT UPON ISRAEL IN JESUS' DAY

15 Another judgment period is brought into view when those championing resurrection for exterminated Sodomites quote Jesus' words on a certain occasion. He had reproached the unrepentant Jewish cities of Chorazin and Bethsaida, which had witnessed many of his powerful works, then said: "And you, Capernaum, will you perhaps be exalted to heaven? Down to Hades you will come; because if the powerful works that took place in you had taken place in Sodom, it would have remained until this very day. Consequently I say to you people, It will be more endurable for the land of Sodom on Judgment Day than for you." (Matt. 10:14, 15; 11:20-24; Luke 10:10-15, *NW*) From this some argue that there is a future judgment, in the millennial reign, for both Sodom and these Jewish cities.

16 If we take this expression to mean that, then it would contradict Jude's statement that Sodom had already undergone the "judicial punishment of everlasting fire". Actually, Jesus was using a form of speech construction common in Biblical times. He used a similar construction when he said: "It is easier, in fact, for a camel to get through the eye of a sewing needle than for a rich man to get into the kingdom of God." (Luke 18:25, *NW*) No sane person would believe a camel could squeeze through a needle's eye. Yet if this obviously impossible thing were said to be easier than something else, would that not powerfully emphasize the utter impossibility of the other thing? So Jesus forcefully made the point that rich ones loath to part with their wealth would not enter the kingdom. Similarly, Sodom did not endure its judgment day, had failed completely, and the Jews knew its fate was sealed. Their opinion of Sodom was the lowest possible. So when Jesus told them that it would be more endurable for utterly depraved Sodom than for these Jewish cities they got the powerful point.

17 These Jewish cities had heard the warning and had seen powerful works; they had had their fair judgment trial and by their decision showed they were worthy of eternal destruction. (Matt. 10:5-15; Luke 10:8-12; John 12:37, *NW*) By witnessing miraculous cures performed by the power of the holy spirit and yet refusing to accept the message, the inhabitants of these cities were sinning against the holy spirit, which is the unforgivable sin meriting second death. They ranged themselves alongside the Pharisees who saw Jesus heal a demon-possessed man, but refused to accept this manifest operation of the holy spirit. Because of this Jesus told them they would never have forgiveness, neither in the present system of things nor in the next, the new world. Being judged adversely, unforgivable in both the old world and the new world, it would be useless to resurrect them in the millennium. Jesus pronounced judgment against them: "Serpents, offspring of vipers, how are you to flee from the judgment of Gehenna?" If the blind religious leaders were to land there, so were their blind Jewish followers. And when the false religious leaders converted some heathen they did not bring him into the true worship that would cleanse him of his past sins against God, but merely added to his past sins the religious sinfulness and hypocrisy which they taught him, doubling his burden of guilt. Thus the proselyte became twice as much a "subject for Gehenna" as the scribes and

15. Why do some argue for a future judgment for both Sodom and the Jews of Jesus' day?
16. What did Jesus mean when he said judgment would be more endurable for Sodom than certain Jewish cities?
17. Why would it be useless to resurrect the Jewish clergy, their Jewish followers, and their Gentile converts?

JUNE 1, 1952

Pharisees.—Ma
33, *NW*.

18 Nor is the
for natural Isr
ago denied by J
veh will rise up
generation and
they repented at
look! something
The queen of th
the judgment wi
condemn it; be
ends of the ear
Solomon, but, lo
Solomon is here
11:31, 32, *NW*)
Ninevites and t
confront the Jew
lennium judgme
to condemn thos
they did in their
millennium pers
basis of what th
did in a previous
are adversely ju
cause nineteen c
lifetime, during
they rejected or
more than Solo
Christ. They ha
second judgment

19 What Jesus
of his day were c
of the repentant
was recorded in t
confronted those
judgment period
record of the qu
to confront the
Gentiles heeded
and Solomon; the
would not heed e
their judgment

18. Why is it illogical
means a resurrection f
19. What do those wo

6/1/1952

## DIALOGUE ONE B: Love Our Brother And Shun Our Mother?

Disfellowshiping, however, implies more than ceasing to have spiritual fellowship. —Titus 3:10, 11.

[18] Paul wrote: "Quit mixing in company . . . , not even eating with such a man." (1 Cor. 5:11) A meal is a time of relaxation and socializing. Hence, the Bible here rules out social fellowship, too, such as joining an expelled person in a picnic or party, ball game, trip to the beach or theater, or sitting down to a meal with him.* (The special problems involving a relative who has been disfellowshiped are considered in the following article.)

[19] Sometimes a Christian might feel under considerable pressure to ignore this Bible advice. His own emotions may create the pressure, or it may be brought to bear on him by acquaintances. For instance, one brother was pressured to officiate at the marriage of two disfellowshiped persons. Could that service be rationalized as a mere kindness? One could feel that way. But why were his services wanted, rather than those of the town mayor or other state marrying agent? Was it not because of his standing as a minister of God and his ability to offer marriage counsel from God's Word? To give in to such pressure would involve him in fellowshiping with the couple, persons who had been expelled from the congregation for their ungodly way.—1 Cor. 5:13.

[20] Other problems arise in connection with business or employment. What if you were employed by a man who now was expelled by the congregation, or you employed a person to whom that happened? What then? If you were contractually or financially obliged to continue the business relationship for the present, you certainly would now have a different attitude toward the disfellowshiped individual. Discussion of business matters with him or contact on the job might be necessary, but spiritual discussions and social fellowship would be things of the past. In that way you could demonstrate your obedience to God and have a protective barrier for yourself. Also, this might impress on him how much his sin has cost him in various ways. —2 Cor. 6:14, 17.

**SPEAK WITH A DISFELLOWSHIPED OR DISASSOCIATED PERSON?**

[21] Would upholding God's righteousness and his disfellowshiping arrangement mean that a Christian should not speak at all with an expelled person, not even saying "Hello"? Some have wondered about that, in view of Jesus' advice to love our enemies and not 'greet our brothers only.'—Matt. 5:43-47.

[22] Actually, in his wisdom God did not try to cover every possible situation. What we need is to get the sense of what Jehovah says about treatment of a disfellowshiped person, for then we can strive to uphold His view. Through the apostle John, God explains:

"Everyone that pushes ahead and does not remain in the teaching of the Christ does not have God. . . . If anyone comes to you and does not bring this teaching, never receive him into your homes or say a greeting to him. For he that says a greeting to him is a sharer in his wicked works."—2 John 9-11.

[23] The apostle who gave that wise warning was close to Jesus and knew well what Christ had said about greeting others. He also knew that the common greeting of

* Our issue of September 1, 1981, discussed 2 Thessalonians 3:14, 15, where the Bible says that it might be necessary to 'mark' a Christian who persists in disorderly conduct. He is still a brother and to be admonished as such, but other Christians are to "stop associating with him." If they should avoid his company on a social basis, much clearer separation should exist in the cases of disfellowshiped or disassociated wrongdoers.

19. Why may it sometimes seem difficult to uphold a disfellowshiping, but why is it important that we do?
20. What should be our reaction if a business associate is disfellowshiped?

21, 22. The Scriptures provide what advice about speaking with a disfellowshiped person?
23, 24. Why is it wise to avoid speaking to expelled individuals?

24

THE WATCHTOWER — SEPTEMBER 15, 1981

that time was "P
some personal "e
in authority who
disfellowshiped o
who is trying to
apostate thinking
ungodly conduct
whom to wish "I
And we all know f
the years that a si
can be the first s
conversation and
Would we want to
a disfellowshiped

[24] 'But what if I
and needs encoura
wonder. There is
such situations. T
gregation serve a
protectors of the
5:2) If a disfello
person inquires, c
ing to come back
ders can speak
explain what he
give him some
They can deal v
facts about his
Others in the c
formation. So if
fellowshiped or
repentant,' migh
on impression
formation? If th
that the person
producing the
would be reinsta
After that occu
gation can war
meetings, displa
and confirm th
urged the Corir
reinstated at C

* For a discussion
of September 1, 19

THE WATCHTOWER -

, or you em-
it happened?
tractually or
the business
you certainly
attitude to-
ividual. Dis-
with him or
ecessary, but
al fellowship
In that way
obedience to
cier for your-
on him how
arious ways.

**VSHIPED**
**ISON?**
ighteousness
arrangement
ld not speak
on, not even
e wondered
dvice to love
our brothers

God did not
uation. What
f what Jeho-
a disfellow-
an strive to
the apostle

and does not
hrist does not
you and does
ceive him into
o him. For he
sharer in his

t wise warn-
w well what
g others. He
greeting of

ice about speak-
ing to expelled



that time was "Peace." As distinct from some personal "enemy" or worldly man in authority who opposed Christians, a disfellowshiped or disassociated person who is trying to promote or justify his apostate thinking or is continuing in his ungodly conduct is certainly not one to whom to wish "Peace." (1 Tim. 2:1, 2) And we all know from our experience over the years that a simple "Hello" to someone can be the first step that develops into a conversation and maybe even a friendship. Would we want to take that first step with a disfellowshiped person?

24 'But what if he seems to be repentant and needs encouragement?' someone might wonder. There is a provision for handling such situations. The overseers in the congregation serve as spiritual shepherds and protectors of the flock. (Heb. 13:17; 1 Pet. 5:2) If a disfellowshiped or disassociated person inquires, or gives evidence of wanting to come back into God's favor, the elders can speak to him. They will kindly explain what he needs to do and might give him some appropriate admonition. They can deal with him on the basis of facts about his past sin and his attitude. Others in the congregation lack such information. So if someone felt that the disfellowshiped or disassociated person 'is repentant,' might that be a judgment based on impression rather than accurate information? If the overseers were convinced that the person was repentant and was producing the fruits of repentance,* he would be reinstated into the congregation. After that occurs, the rest of the congregation can warmly welcome him at the meetings, display forgiveness, comfort him and confirm their love for him, as Paul urged the Corinthians to do with the man reinstated at Corinth.—2 Cor. 2:5-8.

* For a discussion of repentance, see *The Watchtower* of September 1, 1981.

**NOT SHARING IN WICKED WORKS**

25 All faithful Christians need to take to heart the serious truth that God inspired John to write: "He that says a greeting to [an expelled sinner who is promoting an erroneous teaching or carrying on ungodly conduct] is a sharer in his wicked works."—2 John 11.

26 Many of Christendom's commentators take exception to 2 John 11. They claim that it is 'unchristian counsel, contrary to the spirit of our Lord,' or that it encourages intolerance. Yet such sentiments emanate from religious organizations that do not apply God's command to "remove the wicked man from among yourselves," that seldom if ever expel even notorious wrongdoers from their churches. (1 Cor. 5:13) Their "tolerance" is unscriptural, unchristian.—Matt. 7:21-23; 25:24-30; John 8:44.

27 But it is not wrong to be loyal to the righteous and just God of the Bible. He tells us that he will accept 'in his holy mountain' only those who walk faultlessly, practice righteousness and speak truth. (Ps. 15:1-5) If, though, a Christian were to throw in his lot with a wrongdoer who has been rejected by God and disfellowshiped, or has disassociated himself, that would be as much as saying 'I do not want a place in God's holy mountain either.' If the elders saw him heading in that direction by regularly keeping company with a disfellowshiped person, they would lovingly and patiently try to help him to regain God's view. (Matt. 18:18; Gal. 6:1) They would admonish him and, if necessary, 'reprove him with severity.' They want to help him remain 'in God's holy mountain.' But if he will not cease to fellowship with the expelled person, he thus has made himself 'a sharer (supporting or participating) in the wicked works' and must be

25, 26. What does God counsel about becoming a "sharer" with a disfellowshiped person?
27. How might a Christian become such a "sharer," and with what result?

mealtime, he has
'n home. But they
own prayers to
9:145, 146) What
son in the home
ı the family reads
ıs a Bible study?
im be present to
to teach them or

sfellowshiped, the
his physical needs
ng and discipline.
a Bible study di-
h him participat-
an that he would
n on the family
irect attention to
stian publications
needs. (Prov. 1:
1. 6:4) They can
n to and sit with
ngs, hoping that
blical counsel.
elative, such as a
s not live in the
and subsequently
ere? The family
depending on the

ellowshiped par-
ıger able to care
physically. The
a Scriptural and
t. (1 Tim. 5:8)
ary to bring the
nporarily or per-

elders and ministerial
tions from Readers"
1, 1978.

th a disfellowshiped

out a disfellowshiped
ome?

ed to be
n children



manently. Or it may appear advisable to arrange for care where there is medical personnel but where the parent would have to be visited. What is done may depend on factors such as the parent's true needs, his attitude and the regard the head of the household has for the spiritual welfare of the household.

16 This could be true also with regard to a child who had left home but is now disfellowshiped or disassociated. Sometimes Christian parents have accepted back into the home for a time a disfellowshiped child who has become physically or emotionally ill. But in each case the parents can weigh the individual circumstances. Has a disfellowshiped son lived on his own, and is he now unable to do so? Or does he want to move back primarily because it would be an easier life? What about his morals and attitude? Will he bring "leaven" into the home?—Gal. 5:9.

17 In Jesus' parable of the prodigal son, the father ran to meet and then accepted his returning son. The father, seeing the lad's pitiful condition, responded with natural parental concern. We can note, though, that the son did not bring home harlots or come with a disposition to continue his sinful life in his father's home. No, he expressed heartfelt repentance and evidently was determined to return to living a clean life.—Luke 15:11-32.

### DISFELLOWSHIPED RELATIVES NOT LIVING AT HOME

18 The second situation that we need to consider is that involving a disfellowshiped or disassociated relative who is *not* in the immediate family circle or living at one's home. Such a person is still related by blood or marriage, and so there may be some limited need to care for necessary family matters. Nonetheless, it is not as if he were living in the same home where contact and conversation could not be avoided. We should keep clearly in mind the Bible's inspired direction: "Quit mixing in company with *anyone* called a brother that is a fornicator or a greedy person . . . , not even eating with such a man."—1 Cor. 5:11.

19 Consequently, Christians related to such a disfellowshiped person living outside the home should strive to avoid needless association, even keeping business dealings to a minimum. The reasonableness of this course becomes apparent from reports of what has occurred where relatives have taken the mistaken view, 'Though he is disfellowshiped, we are related and so can treat him the same as before.' From one area comes this:

**The prodigal son did not return home to continue his sinful living, but was repentant. His father accepted him back**

16, 17. (a) How might parents react to the possibility of a disfellowshiped child's moving back home? (b) What can we learn on this from the parable of the prodigal son?

18, 19. (a) How should Christians view association with disfellowshiped relatives who are outside the immediate family? (b) Why is this position appropriate? (2 Tim. 2:19)

:o study God's
and to do that

t John makes
ɡht that ema-
ɪth-destroying
reen the life-
ceptive lies of
t pervades the
ıion with the
ıe murderous
went out from
t not all are of
·25; 3:23, 24,
should be our
ld.' And how
faith and by
ans observing

ərfully is this
ɡhout the let-
:ontrast made
he love of the
:ion that "God
al love this is!
ı the Father's
f the world."
an apprecia-
ostle's words:
'st loved us."
ame kind as
ractical, self-
lered his soul
surrender our
ıe door of our
brothers, not
h." (3:16-18)
is this love,
of God, that
ı God in un-
l the Son. (2:
blessed bond
n union with
s Christ. This
–5:20.

'or our benefit,

l as a practical
tian's love be,

**Bible Book Number 63**

# 2 John

*Writer:* **Apostle John**
*Place Written:* **Ephesus, or near**
*Writing Completed:* **c. 98 C.E.**

JOHN'S second letter is short—it could have been written on a single sheet of papyrus—but it is full of meaning. It is addressed "to the chosen lady and to her children." Since "Kyria" (Greek for "lady") did exist as a proper name at the time, some Bible scholars feel that an individual by that name was being addressed. On the other hand, it is thought by some that John was writing to a Christian congregation, referring to it as "the chosen lady." This may have been done in order to confuse persecutors. In that case, the greetings of the "sister" mentioned in the last verse would be those of the members of another congregation. So the second letter was not intended to be as general in scope as the first, for it evidently was written either to an individual or to one particular congregation.—Vs. 1.

² There is no reason to doubt that John wrote this letter. The writer calls himself "the older man." This certainly fits John not only because of his advanced age but also because, as one of the "pillars" (Gal. 2:9) and the last surviving apostle, he was truly an "older man" in the Christian congregation. He was well-known, and no further identification would be required for his readers. His writership is also indicated by the similarity in style to that of the first letter and John's Gospel. Like the first letter, the second letter appears to have been written in or around Ephesus, about 98 C.E. Concerning Second and Third John, McClintock and Strong's *Cyclopedia* comments: "From their general similarity, we may conjecture that the two epistles were written shortly after the 1st Epistle from Ephesus. They both apply to individual cases of conduct the principles which had been laid down in their fullness in the 1st Epistle."* In support of its authenticity, the letter is quoted by Irenaeus, of the second century, and was accepted by Clement of Alexandria, of the same period.* Also, John's letters are listed in the Muratorian Fragment.

³ As was true of First John, the reason for this letter is the onslaught by false teachers against the Christian faith. John wants to warn his readers about such ones so they can recognize them and stay clear of them, while continuing to walk in the truth, in mutual love.

## CONTENTS OF SECOND JOHN

⁴ **Love one another; reject apostates** (Vss. 1-13). After expressing his love in the truth for 'the chosen lady and her children,' John rejoices that he has found some of them walking in the truth, as commanded by the Father. He requests that they show their love for one another by continuing to walk according to God's commandments. For deceivers and antichrists have gone forth into the world, who do not confess Jesus Christ as coming in the flesh. He that pushes ahead beyond the teaching of Christ does not have God, but he that remains in this teaching "has both the Father and the Son." Anyone that does not bring this teaching is not to be received into their homes, nor is he even to be greeted. John has many things to write them, but instead he hopes to come and speak with them face-to-face, that their joy may be "in full measure."—Vss. 9, 12.

## WHY BENEFICIAL

⁵ It appears that in John's day, as in modern times, there were some who were not content to stay with the plain, simple teachings of Christ. They wanted something more, something that would tickle their ego, something that would exalt them and put them in a class with worldly

* 1981 reprint, Vol. IV, page 955.

* *New Bible Dictionary*, second edition, 1986, edited by J. D. Douglas, page 605.

1. To whom may Second John have been written?
2. (a) What evidence points to the apostle John as writer of Second John? (b) What suggests that the letter was written in or near Ephesus, about 98 C.E., and what supports its authenticity?
3. Why did John write the letter?
4. Why particularly does John admonish loving one another, and how must those who push ahead beyond the teaching of Christ be treated?
5. (a) What situation arose in John's day that has also arisen in modern times? (b) Like John, how can we today show appreciation for the unity of the congregation?

259

"ALL SCRIPTURE IS INSPIRED OF GOD AND BENEFICIAL," 1990 ed

## *DIALOGUE TWO: Is Spiritual Adoption Only For 144,000 People?*

ghty God, Jeho-
ı. The very exis-
in the universe
supremely intel-
all. Just as the
qualities, so do
ıat "his invisible
reation onward,
ade." Also, with-
ring the glory of

levision sets and
ınd its creations
ɛlous. The struc-
f cells is beyond
which we think
.ve a purpose in
ıcant inventions,
is awesome cre-
Everything Jeho-

, as he stated to
come many and
ɜ fish of the sea
and every living
Ɉenesis 1:28) Be-
ɜ failed to fill the
lovingly care for
heir failure does
ds of years later,
ırth . . . , did not
it even to be in-
ıe earth endures
*The New English*
be realized: "My

### WHAT JEHOVAH'S WITNESSES BELIEVE

| Belief | Scriptural Reason |
|---|---|
| Bible is God's Word and is truth | 2 Tim. 3:16, 17; 2 Pet. 1:20, 21; John 17:17 |
| Bible is more reliable than tradition | Matt. 15:3; Col. 2:8 |
| God's name is Jehovah | Ps. 83:18; Isa. 26:4; 42: 8, *AS;* Ex. 6:3 |
| Christ is God's Son and is inferior to Him | Matt. 3:17; John 8:42; 14:28; 20:17; 1 Cor. 11:3; 15:28 |
| Christ was first of God's creations | Col. 1:15; Rev. 3:14 |
| Christ died on a stake, not a cross | Gal. 3:13; Acts 5:30 |
| Christ's human life was paid as a ransom for obedient humans | Matt. 20:28; 1 Tim. 2: 5, 6; 1 Pet. 2:24 |
| Christ's one sacrifice was sufficient | Rom. 6:10; Heb. 9:25-28 |
| Christ was raised from the dead as an immortal spirit person | 1 Pet. 3:18; Rom. 6:9; Rev. 1:17, 18 |
| Christ's presence is in spirit | John 14:19; Matt. 24:3; 2 Cor. 5:16; Ps. 110:1, 2 |
| We are now in the 'time of the end' | Matt. 24:3-14; 2 Tim. 3: 1-5; Luke 17:26-30 |
| Kingdom under Christ will rule earth in righteousness and peace | Isa. 9:6, 7; 11:1-5; Dan. 7:13, 14; Matt. 6:10 |
| Kingdom will bring ideal living conditions to earth | Ps. 72:1-4; Rev. 7:9, 10, 13-17; 21:3, 4 |
| Earth will never be destroyed or depopulated | Eccl. 1:4; Isa. 45:18; Ps. 78:69 |
| God will eliminate present system of things in the battle at Har–Magedon | Rev. 16:14, 16; Zeph. 3:8; Dan. 2:44; Isa. 34:2; 55:10, 11 |
| Wicked will be eternally destroyed | Matt. 25:41-46; 2 Thess. 1:6-9 |
| People God approves will receive everlasting life | John 3:16; 10:27, 28; 17:3; Mark 10:29, 30 |
| There is only one road to life | Matt. 7:13, 14; Eph. 4:4, 5 |
| Human death is due to Adam's sin | Rom. 5:12; 6:23 |
| The human soul ceases to exist at death | Ezek. 18:4; Eccl. 9:10; Ps. 6:5; 146:4; John 11: 11-14 |
| Hell is mankind's common grave | Job 14:13, *Dy;* Rev. 20: 13, 14, *AV* (margin) |
| Hope for dead is resurrection | 1 Cor. 15:20-22; John 5: 28, 29; 11:25, 26 |
| Adamic death will cease | 1 Cor. 15:26, 54; Rev. 21:4; Isa. 25:8 |
| Only a little flock of 144,000 go to heaven and rule with Christ | Luke 12:32; Rev. 14: 1, 3; 1 Cor. 15:40-53; Rev. 5:9, 10 |
| The 144,000 are born again as spiritual sons of God | 1 Pet. 1:23; John 3:3; Rev. 7:3, 4 |
| New covenant is made with spiritual Israel | Jer. 31:31; Heb. 8:10-13 |
| Christ's congregation is built upon himself | Eph. 2:20; Isa. 28:16; Matt. 21:42 |
| Prayers are to be directed only to Jehovah through Christ | John 14:6, 13, 14; 1 Tim. 2:5 |
| Images should not be used in worship | Ex. 20:4, 5; Lev. 26:1; 1 Cor. 10:14; Ps. 115:4-8 |
| Spiritism must be shunned | Deut. 18:10-12; Gal. 5: 19-21; Lev. 19:31 |
| Satan is invisible ruler of world | 1 John 5:19; 2 Cor. 4:4; John 12:31 |
| A Christian ought to have no part in interfaith movements | 2 Cor. 6:14-17; 11:13-15; Gal. 5:9; Deut. 7:1-5 |
| A Christian should keep separate from world | Jas. 4:4; 1 John 2:15; John 15:19; 17:16 |
| Obey human laws that do not conflict with God's laws | Matt. 22:20, 21; 1 Pet. 2:12; 4:15 |
| Taking blood into body through mouth or veins violates God's laws | Gen. 9:3, 4; Lev. 17:14; Acts 15:28, 29 |
| Bible's laws on morals must be obeyed | 1 Cor. 6:9, 10; Heb. 13:4; 1 Tim. 3:2; Prov. 5:1-23 |
| Sabbath observance was given only to Israel and ended with Mosaic Law | Deut. 5:15; Ex. 31:13; Rom. 10:4; Gal. 4:9, 10; Col. 2:16, 17 |
| A clergy class and special titles are improper | Matt. 23:8-12; 20:25-27; Job 32:21, 22 |
| Man did not evolve but was created | Isa. 45:12; Gen. 1:27; Matt. 19:4 |
| Christ set example that must be followed in serving God | 1 Pet. 2:21; Heb. 10:7; John 4:34; 6:38 |
| Baptism by complete immersion symbolizes dedication | Mark 1:9, 10; John 3:23; Acts 19:4, 5 |
| Christians gladly give public testimony to Scriptural truth | Rom. 10:10; Heb. 13: 15; Isa. 43:10-12 |

JEHOVAH'S WITNESSES - WHO ARE THEY? WHAT DO THEY BELIEVE?, 2000

Christians, they know Jehovah. (John 17:3) What about circumcision? Some 1,500 years before the making of the new covenant, Moses urged the Israelites: "You must circumcise the foreskin of your hearts." (Deuteronomy 10:16; Jeremiah 4:4) While compulsory fleshly circumcision passed away with the Law, both the anointed and the other sheep must "circumcise" their hearts. (Colossians 2:11) Finally, Jehovah forgives the error of the other sheep on the basis of Jesus' shed "blood of the covenant." (Matthew 26:28; 1 John 1:9; 2:2) God does not adopt them as spiritual sons, as he does the 144,000. But he does declare the other sheep righteous, in the sense that Abraham was declared righteous as God's friend.—Matthew 25:46; Romans 4:2, 3; James 2:23.

7 For the 144,000, being declared righteous opens the way to their having the hope of ruling with Jesus in the heavenly Kingdom. (Romans 8:16, 17; Galatians 2:16) For the other sheep, being declared righteous as God's friends allows them to embrace the hope of everlasting life in a paradise earth—either by surviving Armageddon as part of the great crowd or through the 'resurrection of the righteous.' (Acts 24:15) What a privilege to have such a hope and to be a friend of the Sovereign of the universe, to be "a guest in [his] tent"! (Psalm 15:1, 2) Yes, both anointed and other sheep are blessed in a wonderful way through Jesus, the Seed of Abraham.

### A Greater Atonement Day

8 When discussing the new covenant, Paul reminded his readers of the annual Atonement Day under the Law covenant. On that day, separate sacrifices were offered—one for the priestly tribe of Levi and another for the 12 nonpriestly tribes. This has long been explained as prefiguring Jesus' great sacrifice that would benefit both the 144,000 with a heavenly hope and the millions who have an earthly hope.* Paul showed that in the fulfillment the benefits of Jesus' sacrifice are administered through a greater Atonement Day under the new covenant. As High Priest of this greater day, Jesus gave his perfect life as an atonement sacrifice in order to obtain "an everlasting deliverance" for humans.—Hebrews 9:11-24.

9 Many Hebrew Christians of the first century were still "zealous for the [Mosaic] Law." (Acts 21:20) Fittingly, then, Paul reminded them: "[Jesus] is a mediator of a new covenant, in order that, because a death has occurred for their release by ransom from the transgressions under the former covenant, the ones who have been called might receive the promise of the everlasting inheritance." (Hebrews 9:15) The new covenant freed Hebrew Christians from the old covenant, which exposed their sinfulness. Thanks to the new covenant, they could embrace "the promise of the everlasting [heavenly] inheritance."

10 "Everyone" who "exercises faith in the Son" will benefit from the ransom sacrifice. (John 3:16, 36) Paul said: "The Christ was offered once for all time to bear the sins of many; and the second time that he appears it will be apart from sin and to those earnestly looking for him for their salvation." (Hebrews 9:28) Today, those earnestly looking for Jesus include surviving anointed

7. What prospect opens up for other sheep today, who are declared righteous as Abraham was?
8. What was prefigured by the Atonement Day sacrifices under the Law?

* See *Survival Into a New Earth*, chapter 13, published by the Watchtower Bible and Tract Society of New York, Inc.

9. Being in the new covenant, what could Hebrew anointed Christians embrace?
10. For what do anointed and other sheep thank God?

20 THE WATCHTOWER—FEBRUARY 1, 1998

The gr
Christians
vah's gre
14, 15; 1
that they
tiles. Wh
Court of
ever, in t
mon's an
provision
omon's te
where Isr
women, v
phetic pa

Christians of
lions making
have an everl
es thank Go
the life-givin
including th
the ministry
the heavenly

Bus

11 In his l
stressed the
rifice in the
compared wi
old covenant.
ter sacrifice
sciences from
der sacred s
Hebrew Chri
"the transgr
enant." For (
sins committ
has been tru
has forgiven.

11. With cons
sacrifice, what
happily do?

8 Particularly since 1931 have those with the earthly hope been associating with the Christian congregation. In that year, Jehovah enlightened the remnant of spirit-begotten Christians to see that Ezekiel chapter 9 refers to this earthly class, who are being marked for survival into God's new world. In 1932 it was concluded that such present-day sheeplike ones were prefigured by Jehu's associate Jonadab (Jehonadab). (2 Kings 10:15-17) In 1934 it was made clear that "Jonadabs" should "consecrate," or dedicate, themselves to God. In 1935 the "great multitude," or "great crowd"—formerly thought to be a secondary spiritual class that would be "companions" of the bride of Christ in heaven—was identified as other sheep having an earthly hope. (Revelation 7:4-15; 21:2, 9; Psalm 45:14, 15) And especially since 1935 have anointed ones been spearheading a search for upright people yearning to live forever on a paradise earth.

9 After 1935 some Christians who had been partaking of the bread and wine at the Lord's Evening Meal ceased to partake. Why? Because they realized that their hope was earthly, not heavenly. Said one woman who was baptized in 1930: "Though [partaking] was considered the right thing to do, especially for zealous full-time ministers, I never was convinced that I had a heavenly hope. Then, in 1935, it was made clear to us that there was being gathered a great crowd with the hope of living forever on earth. Many of us rejoiced to understand that we were part of that great crowd, and we ceased partaking of the emblems." Even Christian publications changed in nature. While those of former years had been designed primarily for Jesus' spirit-begotten followers, from 1935 onward *The Watchtower* and other literature of the 'faithful slave' provided spiritual food suited to the needs of both the anointed and their associates having the earthly hope.—Matthew 24:45-47.

10 Suppose an anointed one became unfaithful. Would there be a replacement? Paul indicated as much in his discussion of the symbolic olive tree. (Romans 11:11-32) If a spirit-begotten one needs to be replaced, likely God would give the heavenly calling to someone whose faith had been exemplary in rendering sacred service to him for many years.—Compare Luke 22:28, 29; 1 Peter 1:6, 7.

### Many Reasons for Gratitude

11 Wherever we serve Jehovah in faithfulness, he will satisfy our needs and upright desires. (Psalm 145:16; Luke 1:67-74) Whether we have a genuine heavenly hope or our prospect is earthly, we have many sound reasons for gratitude to God. He always does things that are in the best interests of those who love him. The disciple James said that "every good gift and every perfect present is from above, for it comes down from the Father of the celestial lights," Jehovah God. (James 1:17) Let us take note of a few of these gifts and blessings.

12 *Jehovah has given each of his faithful servants a wonderful hope.* He has called some to heavenly life. To his pre-Christian witnesses, Jehovah gave the splendid hope

8. How did an understanding of the earthly hope develop in the early 1930's?
9. After 1935, why did some Christians cease to partake of the emblems at the Lord's Evening Meal?

10. How might an unfaithful anointed one be replaced?
11. Regardless of the nature of our hope, of what does James 1:17 assure us?
12. Why can we say that Jehovah has given each of his faithful servants a wonderful hope?

of a resurrec
earth. For in
the resurrect
ing real foun
dom under
ed to earthl
Once again, i
granting mil
life on a para
17:3) Surely,
such a grand
ful for it.

13 *Jehovah*
*gift to his pe*
enly hope a
(1 John 2:20;
having earth
help and gui
ses, who had
70 men appo
11:24, 25) Ur
it, Bezalel se
in connection
odus 31:1-11
eon, Jephtha
sha, and oth
of ancient ti
heavenly glor
by holy spir
today. So, th
does not mea
heavenly call
vides guidan
fill other Go
power beyon
in us its fru
suffering, ki
ness, and self
2 Corinthian
Should we no
gift from Go

13. How has
people?

those who would make up spiritual Israel and would be with Christ in heaven; compare Romans 2:28, 29 and Galatians 3:26-29] I saw, and, look! a great crowd, which no man was able to number, out of all nations and tribes and peoples and tongues, standing before the throne and before the Lamb, dressed in white robes; and there were palm branches in their hands. And they keep on crying with a loud voice, saying: 'Salvation we owe to our God, who is seated on the throne, and to the Lamb.' . . . 'The Lamb [Jesus Christ], who is in the midst of the throne, will shepherd them, and will guide them to fountains of waters of life.'"

After listing many pre-Christian persons of faith, Hebrews 11:39, 40 says: "All these, although they had witness borne to them through their faith, did not get the fulfillment of the promise, as God foresaw something better for us, in order that they might not be made perfect apart from us." (Who are here meant by "us"? Hebrews 3:1 shows that they are "partakers of the heavenly calling." The pre-Christian persons who had faith, then, must have a hope for perfect life somewhere other than in heaven.)

Ps. 37:29: "The righteous themselves will possess the earth, and they will reside forever upon it."

Rev. 21:3, 4: "Look! The tent of God is with mankind, and he will reside with them, and they will be his peoples. And God himself will be with them. And he will wipe out every tear from their eyes, and death will be no more, neither will mourning nor outcry nor pain be anymore. The former things have passed away."

**Is it possible for a person to have God's spirit and yet not be "born again"?**

Regarding John the baptizer, Jehovah's angel said: "He will be filled with holy spirit right from his mother's womb." (Luke 1:15) And Jesus later said: "Among those born of women there has not been raised up a greater than John the Baptist; but a person that is a lesser one in the kingdom of the heavens is greater than he is [Why? Because John will not be in the heavens and so there was no need for him to be "born again"]. But from the days of John the Baptist until



now [when Jesus stated this] the kingdom of the heavens is the goal toward which men press."—Matt. 11:11, 12.

The spirit of Jehovah was "operative" upon David and "spoke" by him (1 Sam. 16:13; 2 Sam. 23:2), but nowhere does the Bible say that he was "born again." There was no need for him to be "born again," because, as Acts 2:34 says: "David did not ascend to the heavens."

***What identifies persons today who have God's spirit?***

See pages 381, 382, under the main heading "Spirit."

## If Someone Says—

**'I've been born again'**

**You might reply:** 'That means that you expect someday to be with Christ in heaven, doesn't it? . . . Have you ever wondered what those who go to heaven will do there?' **Then perhaps add:** (1) 'They will be kings and priests, ruling with Christ. (Rev. 20:6; 5:9, 10) Jesus said that these would be just a "little flock." (Luke 12:32)' (2) 'If they are kings, there must also be subjects over whom they will rule. Who will these be? . . . Here are some points that I found to be very interesting when they were drawn to my attention. (Ps. 37: 11, 29; Prov. 2:21, 22)'

**'Have you been born again?'**

**You might reply:** 'I find that what people mean by "born again" is not always the same. Would you tell me what it means to you?'

**Or you could say:** 'You want to know whether I have accepted Jesus as my Savior and have received holy spirit, is that right? May I assure you that the answer is Yes; otherwise I would not be talking to you about Jesus.' **Then perhaps add:** (1) 'But when I think of having the holy spirit, I find that evidence of that spirit is sadly missing in many who claim to be Christians. (Gal. 5:22, 23)' (2) 'Would you enjoy living on this earth if everyone reflected those godly qualities? (Ps. 37:10, 11)'

REASONING FROM THE SCRIPTURES, 1989

## *DIALOGUE THREE: Is The Watchtower Organization A Cult? —Parts 1 and 2*

Vol. 115, No. 4

ign Lord of the
: all peoples with
.owmen and that
ng, Jesus Christ,
*er,* published by
: as its authority.

] by God?

Fear"

o Hell?

**WEEKS OF**

of Your
: used: 98, 177.
ıse Things Be?"
, 189.


**ir publications,**
**ess below.**

280, Ingleburn, N.S.W.
, Bridgetown. ***Canada:***
The Ridgeway, London
**hana:** Box 760, Accra.
IV Rd., Honolulu. ***Hong***
ls., Mah. 410 401. ***Ire-***
gston 10. ***Japan:*** 1271
88, Nairobi. ***Liberia:***
, Manurewa. ***Nigeria:***
ox 2044, 1099 Manila.
**obago, Republic of:**
, Lusaka 10101. ***Zim-***

ild reach us 30 days be-
ve us your old and new
ld address label).

)43-1087) is published
ır Bible and Tract Soci-
25 Columbia Heights,
cond-class postage paid
at additional mailing
ınd address changes
:ill, N.Y. 12589.
Printed in U.S.A.


# Cults—What Are They?

FEBRUARY 28, 1993—more than a hundred law-enforcement agents raided a compound of buildings housing dozens of men, women, and children. The object was to search for illegal weapons and to arrest a suspected criminal. The agents, however, were caught by surprise when a hail of bullets came flying toward them from inside the buildings. They returned the fire.

This confrontation left ten dead and several wounded. During the following 50 days, hundreds of government agents laid siege to the compound with enough guns to wage a small war. The standoff ended in a showdown that left 86 dead, including at least 17 children.

But who was the enemy? An army of drug-dealing mobsters? A guerrilla faction? No. As you may know, the "enemy" was a group of religious devotees, members of a cult. Their tragedy made an inconspicuous community on the plains of central Texas, U.S.A., the focus of international attention. The news media flooded the airwaves and the printed page with a barrage of reports, analyses, and comments on the dangers of fanatical cults.

The public was reminded of previous instances in which cult members were led to death by their leaders: the 1969 Manson murders in California; the 1978 mass suicide of cult members in Jonestown, Guyana; the 1987 murder-suicide pact engineered by cult leader Park Soon-ja of Korea, which resulted in the death of 32 members. Significantly, most of these people claimed to be Christians and professed belief in the Bible.

Jerry Hoefer/Fort Worth Star Telegram/Sipa Press

THE WATCHTOWER—FEBRUARY 15, 1994 3

Understandably, many who respect the Bible as the Word of God are appalled at the brazen misuse of the Scriptures by these cults. As a result, over the years hundreds of organizations have been established for the purpose of monitoring cults and exposing their dangerous practices. Experts on cult behavior predict that the coming of a new millennium in a few years may trigger the proliferation of cults. One news magazine noted that according to anticult groups, there are thousands of cults "out there poised to snatch your body, control your mind, corrupt your soul. . . . Few are armed but most are considered dangerous. They'll seduce you and fleece you, marry and bury you."

### What Is a Cult?

The term "cult" is used loosely by many who may not be fully aware of its connotations. To prevent confusion, some theologians actually avoid using the term.

*The World Book Encyclopedia* explains that "traditionally, the term *cult* referred to any form of worship or ritual observance." By that criterion, all religious organizations could be classified as cults. However, in general usage today, the word "cult" has a different meaning. The same encyclopedia notes that "since the mid-1900's, publicity about cults has altered the meaning of the term. Today, the term is applied to groups that follow a living leader who promotes new and unorthodox doctrines and practices."

Endorsing the popular usage of the term, *Newsweek* magazine explains that cults "are normally small, fringe groups whose members derive their identity and purpose from a single, charismatic individual." Similarly, *Asiaweek* magazine notes that "the term [cult] itself is vague, but it usually denotes a new religious creed built around a charismatic leader, who often proclaims himself to be the personification of God."

The language used in a joint resolution of the 100th Congress of the State of Maryland, U.S.A., also conveys the derogatory connotation of the term cult. The resolution states that "a cult is a group or movement exhibiting excessive devotion to a person or idea and employing unethically manipulative techniques of persuasion and control to advance the goals of its leaders."

Clearly, cults are generally understood to be religious groups with radical views and practices that clash with what is accepted today as normal social behavior. Usually they conduct their religious activities in secrecy. Many of these cultic groups actually isolate themselves in communes. Their devotion to a self-proclaimed human leader is likely to be unconditional and exclusive. Often these leaders boast of having been divinely chosen or even of being themselves divine in nature.

Occasionally, anticult organizations and the media have referred to Jehovah's Witnesses as a cult. A number of recent newspaper articles lump the Witnesses with religious groups known for their questionable practices. But would it be accurate to refer to Jehovah's Witnesses as a small fringe religious group? Cult members often isolate themselves from friends, family, and even society in general. Is that the case with Jehovah's Witnesses? Are the Witnesses using deceptive and unethical techniques to recruit members?

Cult leaders are known to use manipulative methods to control the minds of their followers. Is there any evidence that Jehovah's Witnesses do this? Is their worship cloaked in secrecy? Are they following and venerating a human leader? Pointedly, are Jehovah's Witnesses a cult?



Are

JESUS CH
drunkard
a false w
and a messe
cused of beir
11:19; 12:24;
After Jesu
disciples wer
accusations.
Christians w
by people cry
turned the i
another occa
companion S
ities and ch
the city of P
Paul was
lent fellow a
all the Jew
earth" and
ple." (Acts 2
Jews in Ro
situation of
knowledged:
it is known
ken against.
Evidently
Jesus Christ
a religious
practices th
cepted in t
havior. Un
have consid
tive cult. T
nent and re
nity, and th
to the alleg
sations agai

The "Witnesses have earned the reputation of being honest, courteous, and industrious," adds Corbett in her book *Religion in America*. Many who are not Witnesses readily acknowledge that there is nothing freakish or bizarre about Jehovah's Witnesses. Their conduct does not clash with what is accepted as normal social behavior. *The New Encyclopædia Britannica* accurately states that the Witnesses "insist upon a high moral code in personal conduct."

The director of news and special projects for a television station in the United States wrote to Jehovah's Witnesses in response to a biased report about the Witnesses on the TV news show *60 Minutes*. He said: "If more people lived the way your faith does, this nation wouldn't be in the shape it is in. I am one newsman who knows that your organization is founded on love and a strong faith in the Creator. I want you to know that not all News people are as biased."

### A Well-Known Religion

Is it fair to say that Jehovah's Witnesses are a small fringe religious group? In a sense, Jehovah's Witnesses are few in number compared to some religions. However, recall what Jesus said: "Narrow is the gate and cramped the road leading off into life, and few are the ones finding it."—Matthew 7:13, 14.

At any rate, the Witnesses are far from being a small fringe cult. In the spring of 1993, more than 11 million people attended the Witnesses' Memorial of Christ's death. But more important than their number are their moral character and exemplary behavior, which have brought them worldwide commendation. Undoubtedly this has been a factor in countries that have given them official recognition as a known, bona fide religion.

Outstanding is a recent ruling by the European Court of Human Rights. It declared that the Witnesses should enjoy freedom of thought, conscience, and religion and that they have the right to speak about their faith and teach it to others. This would hardly be the case if Jehovah's Witnesses were known to use deceptive and unethical techniques to recruit members or if they used manipulative methods to control the minds of their followers.

Multitudes around the world are well acquainted with Jehovah's Witnesses. Of the millions of non-Witnesses who are studying the Bible with the Witnesses or who have studied with them at one time or another, we ask, Were there any attempts to brainwash you? Did the Witnesses employ mind-control techniques on you? "No" would doubtless be your frank response. Obviously, if these methods had been used, there would be an overwhelming number of victims in contradiction to any argument in favor of Jehovah's Witnesses.

### "Absorbed in Humanity"

Cult members often isolate themselves from family, friends, and even society in general. Is that the case with Jehovah's Witnesses? "I do not belong to Jehovah's Witnesses," wrote a newsman in the Czech Republic. Yet he added: "It is obvious that they [Jehovah's Witnesses] have tremendous moral strength. . . . They recognize governmental authorities but believe that only God's Kingdom is capable of solving all human problems. But watch it—they are not fanatics. They are people who are absorbed in humanity."

And they do not live in communes, isolating themselves from relatives and others. Jehovah's Witnesses recognize that it is their Scriptural responsibility to love and care for their families. They live and work with people of all races and religions. When disasters strike, they are quick to respond

with relief su
assistance.

More impo
educational p
son. How ma
system to pay
vidual in the
nesses do this
more than 20
Witnesses ar

### Strict

Admittedly
Witnesses ar
by the churc
lieve that Je
that Jesus is
deity. Their
that God's K
to suffering
the imminer
system of th
promise of a
mankind. Th
They do not
lieve that th
is no hellfire
will they ac
abstain fron
participatio
asked yours
vah's Witne

A Massac
*Hampshire* (
Witnesses'
ble forbids
granted . . .
example of f
word of the
*ligion* agree
based on th
is, supply a
most every
granted the

ıld enjoy freedom of
ıd religion and that
speak about their
others. This would
ehovah's Witnesses
ptive and unethical
nembers or if they
hods to control the

e world are well ac-
Witnesses. Of the
es who are studying
nesses or who have
ne time or another,
attempts to brain-
esses employ mind-
you? "No" would
response. Obvious-
d been used, there
ing number of vic-
any argument in
sses.

[umanity"
isolate themselves
d even society in
se with Jehovah's
long to Jehovah's
sman in the Czech
d: "It is obvious
tnesses] have tre-
. . . . They recog-
rities but believe
is capable of solv-
But watch it—they
re people who are

communes, isolat-
tives and others.
ognize that it is
bility to love and
ney live and work
d religions. When
quick to respond

with relief supplies and other humanitarian assistance.

More important, they are engaged in an educational program that has no comparison. How many religions have an organized system to pay personal visits to every individual in their community? Jehovah's Witnesses do this in more than 200 lands and in more than 200 languages! Clearly, Jehovah's Witnesses are "absorbed in humanity."

### Strict Adherence to the Bible

Admittedly, the teachings of Jehovah's Witnesses are different from those provided by the churches. Jehovah's Witnesses believe that Jehovah is the almighty God and that Jesus is his Son, not part of a triune deity. Their faith is anchored in the belief that God's Kingdom alone can bring relief to suffering humanity. They warn people of the imminent destruction of this corrupt system of things. They preach about God's promise of an earthly paradise for obedient mankind. They do not venerate the cross. They do not celebrate Christmas. They believe that the soul is mortal and that there is no hellfire. They will not eat blood, nor will they accept blood transfusions. They abstain from involvement in politics and participation in warfare. Have you ever asked yourself *why* the teachings of Jehovah's Witnesses are so different?

A Massachusetts newspaper, the *Daily Hampshire Gazette,* explains that Jehovah's Witnesses' "strict interpretation of the Bible forbids many activities others take for granted . . . , all in an effort to follow the example of first-century Christians and the word of the Bible." *The Encyclopedia of Religion* agrees that "all that they believe is based on the Bible. They 'proof text' (that is, supply a biblical citation to support) almost every statement of faith, taking for granted the authority of the Bible, which entirely supplants tradition." The book *Religion in America* states: "The group has never wavered from its focus on Bible study, and its teachings are supported by an elaborate system of references to scripture."

### Who Is Their Leader?

It is precisely because of this close adherence to Bible teachings that the veneration and idolization of human leaders so characteristic of cults today is not to be found among Jehovah's Witnesses. They reject the concept of a clergy-laity distinction. *The Encyclopedia of Religion* aptly states about Jehovah's Witnesses: "A clergy class and distinctive titles are prohibited."

They follow Jesus Christ as their Leader and as Head of the Christian congregation. It was Jesus who said: "Do not you be called Rabbi, for one is your teacher, whereas all you are brothers. Moreover, do not call anyone your father on earth, for one is your Father, the heavenly One. Neither be called 'leaders,' for your Leader is one, the Christ."—Matthew 23:8-12.

It is clear that Jehovah's Witnesses are as far from being a cult as Jesus was from being a glutton and a drunkard. Admittedly, not everyone who was influenced by the false reports about Jesus and his disciples fell into the trap of slandering him. Some may simply have been misinformed. If you have questions about Jehovah's Witnesses and their beliefs, why not get to know them better? The doors to their Kingdom Halls are wide open to all who seek truth.

You can also benefit from their careful search for accurate Bible knowledge and learn how to worship God in harmony with Jesus' words: "The hour is coming, and it is now, when the true worshipers will worship the Father with spirit and truth, for, indeed, the Father is looking for suchlike ones to worship him."—John 4:23.

THE WATCHTOWER—FEBRUARY 15, 1994 7

the blood vessels of the human body with blood from another person or other persons that the practitioner of blood transfusion says is necessary for the survival of the recipient.

God's law definitely says that the soul of man is in his blood. Hence the receiver of the blood transfusion is feeding upon a God-given soul as contained in the blood vehicle of a fellow man or of fellow men. This is a violation of God's commands to Christians, the seriousness of which should not be minimized by any passing over of it lightly as being an optional matter for the conscience of any individual to decide upon. The decree of the apostles at Jerusalem declares: "If you carefully keep yourselves from these things, you will prosper." Hence a Christian who deliberately receives a blood transfusion and thus does not keep himself from blood will not prosper spiritually. According to the law of Moses, which set forth shadows of things to come, the receiver of a blood transfusion must be cut off from God's people by excommunication or disfellowshiping.

If the taking of a blood transfusion is the first offense of a dedicated, baptized Christian due to his immaturity or lack of Christian stability and he sees the error of his action and grieves and repents over it and begs divine forgiveness and forgiveness of God's congregation on earth, then mercy should be extended to him and he need not be disfellowshiped. He needs to be put under surveillance and to be instructed thoroughly according to the Scriptures upon this subject, and thereby be helped to acquire strength to make decisions according to the Christian standard in any future cases.

If, however, he refuses to acknowledge his nonconformity to the required Christian standard and makes the matter an issue in the Christian congregation and endeavors to influence others therein to his support; or, if in the future he persists in accepting blood transfusions or in donating blood toward the carrying out of this medical practice upon others, he shows that he has really not repented, but is deliberately opposed to God's requirements. As a rebellious opposer and unfaithful example to fellow members of the Christian congregation he must be cut off therefrom by disfellowshiping. Thereby the Christian congregation vindicates itself from any charge of connivance at the infraction of God's law by a member of the congregation through blood transfusion, and it upholds the proper Christian standard before all the members of the Christian congregation, and keeps itself clean from the blood of all men, even as the apostle Paul did who promulgated to the various Gentile congregations the apostolic decree handed down at Jerusalem.—Acts 20:26.

## ANNOUNCEMENTS

### FIELD MINISTRY

Our hearts must be in harmony with God and his Word to speak good things for salvation. Jehovah's witnesses are pleased to aid others toward salvation by sharing Bible knowledge. During January they will do this by offering a year's subscription for *The Watchtower*, along with three Scriptural booklets, on a $1 contribution.

### BE SPIRITUALLY WELL FED

Is this copy of *The Watchtower* that you hold the first you have ever seen? Whether it is or not, leaf through its pages again. Notice the great variety of Scriptural material, the sound Bible counsel, the interesting and informative experiences, items of prophetic significance. Would you like to receive such instructive and stimulating spiritual fare regularly? Send only $1 for a year's subscription and receive free three booklets on timely Bible subjects. Be spiritually well fed.

### "WATCHTOWER" STUDIES FOR THE WEEKS

February 26: Jehovah's Requirements for Life Seekers. Page 41.

March 5: The Purpose of Our Ministry. Page 47.

1/15/1961

THIS WORLD AND ITS POLITICS DOOMED

The Devil controlled all the kingdoms of the world in Jesus' day; he still does. But soon now the "ruler of this world" will be put out of the way and this present wicked system of things forever come to its end. True Christians, then, demonstrate that they are followers of Christ, not by trying to patch up this world or reform it through politics, but by declaring the good news of the kingdom that will destroy this world. No matter how many votes are cast for the rulers of this system of things it is doomed. No amount of political campaigning, no number of professed Christians in politics and no amount of prayers for this world by the clergy or politicians will save it from certain destruction. "The world is passing away and so is its desire, but he that does the will of God remains forever." —1 John 2:17, *NW.*

When this world comes to its fiery end at the war of Armageddon, all the rulers of the earth and their supporters, no matter of what political ideology or religious belief, will be against Jehovah's King of kings and Lord of lords, Christ Jesus. The Revelation account says: "I saw the wild beast and the kings of the earth and their armies gathered together to wage the war with the one seated on the horse and with his army." The political powers will go down in defeat before Christ Jesus and his heavenly armies and will be hurled into the "fiery lake that burns with sulphur," the Gehenna of everlasting destruction.—Rev. 19:19-21, *NW.*

After this wicked system of things has been destroyed and Satan the Devil put out of the way a new world of righteousness begins under the Kingdom. The Kingdom will give mankind a perfect government and, not only that, but the opportunity for everlasting life. The survivors of Jehovah's "war of the great day of God the Almighty" will enjoy a righteous new world that will be "one world." For there will be but one government, and that government will be heavenly. Politics will be gone, and gone for good. The politics that have divided men of all religions and caused men of the very same religion to kill one another for political systems will be gone for all time.—Rev. 16:14, *NW.*

You can enjoy the everlasting blessings of the righteous government or kingdom that will embrace all this earthly globe in its rule. To do so means changing oneself to harmonize with the requirements of Christianity, paramount of which is the command to be no part of this world.

Today the Christian witnesses of Jehovah, like the witnesses of Jehovah in the early days of Christianity, keep unspotted from the world. They conscientiously refrain from taking part in the politics of this world, yes, even from voting. They know that political participation not only would be futile but would bring God's disapproval. Maintaining the true Christian view of politics will help you keep unspotted from this wicked system of things and gain everlasting life under the perfect government of the post-Armageddon new world.

*Where is the wise man? Where the scribe? Where the debater of this system of things? Did not God make the wisdom of the world foolish? For since, in the wisdom of God, the world through its wisdom did not get to know God, God saw good through the foolishness of what is preached to save those believing. . . . Because a foolish thing of God is wiser than men, and a weak thing of God is stronger than men. . . . and God chose the ignoble things of the world and the things looked down upon, the things that are not, that he might bring to nothing the things that are.*—1 Cor. 1:20-28, *NW.*

HI

MO
w
iently
purse
time w
some pl
of a de
tle. A
wallet,
ceptabl
purpose
lonia ra
worked
as oxe
barley
day so
stipulat
dried fi
lated, tl
It is
form of
"pecuni
consisti
Latin
which
the Ron
or exch
ment, v
Canaan
eightee

Mone
count, l
we kno
related
referenc

11/1/1956

today. More people are disfellowshipped for sexual immorality than for all other reasons combined.

[19] But since Jehovah's servants know that fornication and adultery are against God's laws, why do so many of them become involved in such activity? Well, why did Eve disobey God's law? Because Satan made doing so appear extremely attractive; it was an opportunity she thought that she could not pass up. Similarly today, through his propaganda channels—television, movies, the press, and so forth—fornication and adultery are made to appear not only exciting and pleasurable but also acceptable. So if you bite at the lure offered through the Devil's propaganda channels, what will happen? You, too, may be "hooked"!

**Avoid Independent Thinking**

[20] From the very outset of his rebellion Satan called into question God's way of doing things. He promoted independent thinking. 'You can decide for yourself what is good and bad,' Satan told Eve. 'You don't have to listen to God. He is not really telling you the truth.' (Genesis 3:1-5) To this day, it has been Satan's subtle design to infect God's people with this type of thinking.—2 Timothy 3:1, 13.

[21] How is such independent thinking manifested? A common way is by questioning the counsel that is provided by God's visible organization. For example, God's organization has from time to time given warnings about listening to certain types of immoral and suggestive music, and about frequenting discos and other types of worldly dance halls where such music is played and people are known to engage in immoral conduct. (1 Corinthians 15:33) Yet certain ones have professed to know better. They have rebelled against such counsel and have done what is right in their own eyes. With what result? Very often they have become involved in sexual immorality and have suffered severe spiritual harm. But even if they have not been so affected, are they not reprehensible if others follow their example and suffer bad consequences?—Matthew 18:6.

[22] This fact cannot be overemphasized: We are in a war with superhuman foes, and we constantly need to be aware of this. Satan and his demons are real; they are not mere figments of the imagination. They are "the world rulers of this darkness," and we have a spiritual fight against them. (Ephesians 6:12) It is absolutely vital that we recognize their subtle designs and not allow ourselves to be overreached by them. Very appropriately, then, we will next consider how we can arm ourselves to fight against these wicked spirits.

19. (a) Why do so many of Jehovah's servants become involved in sexual immorality when they know it displeases God? (b) What will help you to avoid becoming involved in sexual immorality?
20. (a) What is another subtle design of the Devil? (b) How has Satan been using this design for some 6,000 years?
21. What are examples of independent thinking in modern times, and what have been the results?

22. (a) Of what must we be constantly aware? (b) What appropriately will be considered in our next study?

**Can You Answer These Questions?**

- ◻ What is the Devil's purpose in subtly approaching Jehovah's people?
- ◻ Why does the Devil use subtle designs?
- ◻ What are various subtle designs Satan uses?
- ◻ What will help us to avoid being overreached by these subtle designs?

22 THE WATCHTOWER—JANUARY 15, 1983

# Ar
# Aga

"We have a wres
the wicked spirit
heavenly places.'

AS LONG as t
the world ur
ist, we must fight
under their influe
wrote: "Put on th
mor from God th
stand firm agains
the Devil; because
not against blood
the governments,
against the world
*against the wick*
*heavenly places."*

[2] Yet it is not on
of wicked spirits
contend; what m
larly hard is our
that resulted fron
and Eve to resist
forts. Thus, as the
nation of the hea
his youth up." (G
12) Even the apo
to do what was r
do what is right,
is bad is present
21-23) "The hea
than anything els
Bible states. (Jer

1. What fight do C
long must it continue
2. (a) As a result of
what additional fight
the Bible show that t
we really need to be

cumb to Satan's
spiritual vision.
ight can be com-
of Elisha's atten-
prayed for him:
'yes, please, that
attendant saw,
nous region was
chariots of fire
Kings 6:15-17) Do
g us? Jehovah is,
ne angels. (Psalm
; Matthew 18:10)
stage, as it were.
4:9.) Having this
ow could a per-
very actions are
oove, engage in

o pursue an im-
the reflection it
ristian congrega-
clude that Jeho-
ot any different
s a result, these
respond to the
Peter 2:2) Think,
n immoral course
members. (Prov-
are married, ask
do such a cruel
it kind of person
everything into
gaging in sexual
y selfish, short-

ys easy to avoid
tle Paul himself
ainst the wrong
once been a slave.

who become involved
have in mind?
considered, will help
al immorality?
ttle did the apostle
able to win? (b) For
vital, and how must

He wrote: "I [beat] my body and lead it as a slave, that, after I have preached to others, I myself should not become disapproved somehow." (1 Corinthians 9:27; Titus 3:3) Paul 'got tough' with himself. He would force himself to do what was right, even when his body desired to do wrong. You must do the same if you are to wage a successful fight.

18 In order to be fully armed you also need regularly to pray to God for help. (Ephesians 6:18) Yet you cannot pray for help and then read immoral literature, go to immoral movies or daydream about or flirt with one of the opposite sex. You must work for what you request in prayer!

→ **Fight Against Independent Thinking**

19 As we study the Bible we learn that Jehovah has always guided his servants in an organized way. And just as in the first century there was only one true Christian organization, so today Jehovah is using only one organization. (Ephesians 4:4, 5; Matthew 24:45-47) Yet there are some who point out that the organization has had to make adjustments before, and so they argue: "This shows that we have to make up our own mind on what to believe." This is independent thinking. Why is it so dangerous?

20 Such thinking is an evidence of pride. And the Bible says: "Pride is before a crash, and a haughty spirit before stumbling." (Proverbs 16:18) If we get to thinking that we know better than the organization, we should ask ourselves: "Where did we learn Bible truth in the first place? Would we know the way of the truth if it had not been for guidance from the organization? Really, can we get along without the direction of God's organization?" No, we cannot!—Compare Acts 15:2, 28, 29; 16:4, 5.

21 When we consider the mighty spirit forces who are fighting against us, we must acknowledge that on our own we could not possibly win. Yet with God's backing, and with the help and support of his organization—our worldwide association of brothers—we cannot lose. (Psalm 118:6-12; 1 Peter 5:9) However, we must never forget that we are in a spiritual war, and that wartime is no time to be relaxing, enjoying only leisure and the pleasures of life. Rather, it is the time for vigorous training, alertness and self-sacrifice. The enemy has been able to get some from among us to relax their guard, and these have become battle casualties. May this never happen to us! It will not if we keep on "the complete suit of armor from God" and "stand firm against the [crafty acts] of the Devil."—Ephesians 6:11, 12.

19. (a) How has Jehovah always guided his people? (b) How is independent thinking manifested by some persons?
20. (a) Of what is independent thinking an evidence? (b) What will help us to avoid placing our own views ahead of the organization's? (c) What first-century example is it well for us to follow?

21. (a) How only can we win in our fight? (b) What must we never forget, and so what kind of life do we now need to lead?

**Can You Answer These Questions?**

- When material things become especially prominent in a Christian's life, what problems can result for that person and for others in the congregation?
- What will help us to combat materialistic inclinations?
- What will help us to avoid succumbing to sexual immorality?
- What is an evidence of independent thinking, and what can help us to avoid it?

N, N.Y.

Further- the laws all men. accord-

believe with the is more telligent organi- ate, non- e. Plants no free- control a result, lerly and an is a desires, an indis- to do so, y would need or- each in- the in- and the has made al needs. free will for or- on, that own.

BOOK izational by God's nts, were the theo- nal gov- Jacob or th. Moses 18) The

needed, and

g with the ation?



children of Israel had been slaves in Egypt. Moses had already freed himself from Egypt's yoke by fleeing to Midian, where he had lived for forty years. But Jehovah directed him to return to Egypt to represent the Israelites as one united body of people. Jehovah then made a common provision for them all, and any who expected to benefit from it had to act upon it in the same identical manner. All must conform in the selection of an animal, a male sheep or goat one year old, and sprinkle its blood on the doorposts of their houses. Then, by families, they must roast and eat its flesh and leave Egypt en masse about midnight as an orderly body, obeying common instructions and receiving a common deliverance. (Ex. 12:1-13, 21-39) When Jehovah brought them all to Mount Sinai in the wilderness, he gave them his Law organizing them as a theocratic nation.

8 All the Law or *Torah* that Jehovah inspired Moses to write was for this theocratic organization of Israel. So were all the other books that now comprise the Hebrew Scriptures, or the "Old Testament" as some persons refer to them. But over fifteen centuries later, Paul, himself an Israelite and an apostle of Jesus Christ, wrote concerning these books that make up three-quarters of our Bible: "For all the things that were written aforetime were written for our instruction, that through our endurance and through the comfort from the Scriptures we might have hope." (Rom. 15:4) By this, Paul meant that the Bible, as an instruction book for the theocratic organization of Israel, had now become a book of instructions for the organization of the Christian congregation.

9 As the canon of books of God's Word was expanded and the Christian Greek Scriptures were added to complete the Bible, each book was written directly to the Christian congregation or to a member of the Christian congregation in its behalf. Thus the Bible is an organizational book and belongs to the Christian congregation as an organization, not to individuals, regardless of how sincerely they may believe that they can interpret the Bible. For this reason the Bible cannot be properly understood without Jehovah's visible organization in mind.

### THE CHRISTIAN CONGREGATION AS AN ORGANIZATION

10 Jesus did not begin the Christian congregation while he was still on earth. He did, however, select twelve apostles at that time, although Judas, who betrayed him, was replaced by another follower after Jesus' ascension to his Father in heaven. These "apostles of the Lamb" began to serve as foundation stones and pillars of the congregation after it was organized. (Rev. 21:14) This came on the day of Pentecost, 33 C.E., when the first Christian congregation was organized at Jerusalem. One hundred and twenty of Jesus' disciples were assembled together with one mind and purpose when Jehovah's spirit was poured out upon them, and the Christian congregation never lost this unity of thought as long as the apostles remained alive.—Acts 1:12-15; 2:1-4.

11 Though separated in person and groups assembling as Christian congregations, those composing the Christian congregation are still one united body, just as Israel was one typical theocratic nation. Paul said: "One body there is, and

8. How did the Hebrew Scriptures become a book of instructions for Christians?
9. How can it be said that the Bible is an organizational book for the Christian congregation?

10. When and how did the Christian congregation have a beginning?
11, 12. (a) What wrong view do some persons take of the Christian congregation? (b) How do Paul and Peter show that the congregation must be one body?

eceived the word with
ness of mind, carefully
criptures daily as to
gs were so."
an that those Beroeans
ws in the message they
hat their attitude was
oes this set a precedent
ically the publications
e "faithful and discreet
to finding fault? Not

us note the setting of
t the noble-minded Be-
mpanied by Silas, was
onary tour. Due to per-
, the brothers at Thes-
on to Beroea. In Beroea
Jews who had strong
l. These were not Chris-
vere simply interested
satisfy themselves that
ling them had the sup-
w Scriptures.
, these devout Jews in
have heard of Jesus
was telling them was
iose noble-minded Jews
the Scriptures daily to
he references that Paul
art of God's Word. And
attitude did they pursue
h a skeptical attitude,
l wrong? No, they were
Paul's critics on Mars
that they heard Paul's
e greatest eagerness of
1, 32.
listened with a readi-
rness, to believe. Thus
open-minded, but they
have this "good news"
ct, for a person to ac-
t have "the will to be-
ermined not to believe,
evidence will convince
son looks for them he



can always find excuses, plausible reasons for not accepting the accountability that belief will bring upon him. As the apostle Paul well said: "Faith is not a possession of all people." (2 Thess. 3:2) But the Beroeans had the will to believe. They considered what they heard with a receptive frame of mind. As a result, "many of them became believers, and so did not a few of the reputable Greek women and of the men."—Acts 17:12.

Jesus' disciples wrote many letters to Christian congregations, to persons who were already in "the way of the truth." (2 Pet. 2:2) But nowhere do we read that those brothers first, in a skeptical frame of mind, checked the Scriptures to make certain that those letters had Scriptural backing, that the writers really knew what they were talking about.

#### OUR VIEW OF THE "SLAVE"

We can benefit from this consideration. If we have once established what instrument God is using as his "slave" to dispense spiritual food to his people, surely Jehovah is not pleased if we receive that food as though it might contain something harmful. We should have confidence in the channel God is using. At the Brooklyn headquarters from which the Bible publications of Jehovah's Witnesses emanate there are more mature Christian elders, both of the "remnant" and of the "other sheep," than anywhere else upon earth.

True, the brothers preparing these publications are not infallible. Their writings are not inspired as are those of Paul and the other Bible writers. (2 Tim. 3:16) And so, at times, it has been necessary, as understanding became clearer, to correct views. (Prov. 4:18) However, this has resulted in a continual refining of the body of Bible-based truth to which Jehovah's Witnesses subscribe. Over the years, as adjustments have been made to that body of truth, it has become ever more wonderful and applicable to our lives in these "last days." Bible commentators of Christendom are not inspired either. Despite their claims to great knowledge, they have failed to highlight even basic Bible truths —such as the coming Paradise earth, the importance of God's name, and the condition of the dead.

Rather, the record that the "faithful and discreet slave" organization has made for the past more than 100 years forces us to the conclusion that Peter expressed when Jesus asked if his apostles also wanted to leave him, namely, "Whom shall we go away to?" (John 6:66-69) No question about it. We all need help to understand the Bible, and we cannot find the Scriptural guidance we need outside the "faithful and discreet slave" organization.

### THE SCYTHIAN

WHEN stressing that fleshly distinctions do not affect a Christian's standing as a member of Christ's body, the apostle Paul wrote: "There is neither Greek nor Jew, circumcision nor uncircumcision, foreigner, Scythian, slave, freeman, but Christ is all things and in all." (Col. 3:11) The inclusion of the Scythians is noteworthy, as these fierce, nomadic people were regarded as the worst of barbarians. However, through the power exerted by God's holy spirit, even they could put on a Christlike personality, discarding their former ways. (Col. 3:9, 10) How powerful is the spirit of God!

Do those associated with your organization seek political positions or reforms? Those in the early congregation had a more permanent hope centered in God's kingdom. (2 Pet. 3:13, 14) Do national or racial barriers exist within your organization? There were none in first-century congregations. (Gal. 3:28; Rev. 7:9) Is discrimination practiced? Early Christians abided by the principle that "there is no partiality with God" but his "will is that all sorts of men should be saved and come to an accurate knowledge of truth." —Rom. 2:11; 1 Tim. 2:4; Jas. 2:1-4.

### IDENTIFYING THE THEOCRATIC ORGANIZATION

18 Those in the apostolic organization did not fulfill these requirements for the Christian congregation in just a token way. They viewed their position in Jehovah's chosen visible channel as sacred and would allow nothing to jeopardize their standing with God. They had no fear of this world. (Matt. 10:26-28) Their only concern was to provide for the safety and well-being of the flock of God. Jesus pointed to this mark of the true visible organization in connection with a detailed prophecy relating to this time of the end. He said: "Who really is the faithful and discreet slave whom his master appointed over his domestics, to give them their food at the proper time? Happy is that slave if his master on arriving finds him doing so. Truly I say to you, He will appoint him over all his belongings."—Matt. 24:45-47.

19 Evidences are now conclusive that Jesus Christ was enthroned in heaven in 1914 C.E. and that he accompanied Jehovah to his temple in 1918 C.E., when judgment began with the house of God.* (1 Pet. 4:17) After cleansing those belonging to this house who were alive on earth, Jehovah poured out his spirit upon them and assigned them the responsibility of serving as his sole visible channel, through whom alone spiritual instruction was to come. Those who recognize Jehovah's visible theocratic organization, therefore, must recognize and accept this appointment of the "faithful and discreet slave" and be submissive to it.

20 Today those thus charged with this grand privilege and responsibility are called Jehovah's witnesses, and have been since 1931. As a group they have been separated more and more from the sectarianism of Christendom from the 1870's onward. Since 1879 the *Watch Tower* magazine has been used by this collective group to dispense spiritual food regularly to those of this "little flock" of true Christians. (Luke 12:32) In 1884 they formed a legal servant, a corporation, called Zion's Watch Tower Tract Society, now known as the Watch Tower Bible and Tract Society of Pennsylvania. By 1919, having survived the fiery trials of World War I, this "faithful and discreet slave" class was no novice organization. True, the apostles were no longer in its midst, but they had left behind written instructions as part of Jehovah's great Record Book. Additionally, the modern-day members of this 1900-year-old Christian congregation had received from the days of the apostles onward a rich heritage of Christian loyalty and integrity, long and patient suffering of persecution, abiding faith in Jehovah's precious promises, con-

18. What mark of the true visible organization did Jesus identify, and what reward did he say he would give?

19. What must those who recognize Jehovah's visible organization accept?

* See the book *You May Survive Armageddon into God's New World*, Chapter 6, entitled "A·do·nay' Comes to His Temple." Published by the Watch Tower Bible & Tract Society in 1955.

20, 21. Who today are charged with the responsibility of representing Jehovah's King, and what record provides their recommendation?

10/1/1967

OCTOBE fidence Lord a ence to witness 21 In they wc tually s

JEHOV freedo earth for under wa developm pending of things thousand mediatel ceive life fort. Not alone. J century "Faith, i in itself. breath is is dead." must pro action, by

1. How and gift of life?

352 The WATCHTOWER BROOKLYN, N. Y.

of voting men into eldership was stopped. This strengthening of theocratic controls continued over a period of twenty years, from 1918 to 1938, and corresponds to the twenty-year building program of Solomon, in which time he completed Jehovah's temple, his own house, the porch of judgment and the House of the Forest of Lebanon or the armory. In 1938 Jehovah revealed this correspondency to his servants and it was published in *The Watchtower* in a two-part article entitled "Organization." This appeared in the issues of June 1 and 15 and proved conclusively that Jehovah's organization must henceforth be guided and directed by Jehovah's spirit through the visible governing body made up of those servants whom Jehovah himself would appoint. The concluding paragraph in this series stated: "Jehovah's theocratic government is now in full control of the people of God."

But this did not mean that the organization would stand still or that new projects or new methods of performing service would not be initiated. On the contrary, in these same articles on "Organization," *The Watchtower* called to our attention that after Solomon completed his twenty-year building he embarked on a nationwide building program. How this was to be done in fulfillment of the type, or what it was to accomplish, was not then known, but *The Watchtower* said: "With full confidence we will wait, and we shall see." Today we are seeing some of the results of the worldwide building program of the Greater Solomon, Jesus Christ, and as we view what has been accomplished we realize that it could be only by God's spirit and through a growth and development of God's people themselves. New features of the work have required new methods, which has meant revisions and changes from time to time in organization instructions, but it is all a part of the advancement of Jehovah's theocratically controlled organization under the immediate direction of Jehovah God himself. Therefore, these revisions and changes are themselves fully theocratic, so they do not alter in any way the fully theocratic structure of the organization.

## ANNOUNCEMENTS

### FIELD MINISTRY

Since Jehovah God loved the world of mankind so much that he gave his only-begotten Son to die on their behalf, those who appreciate that love are likewise under obligation to manifest love. This love moves them to serve God, to expend themselves on behalf of fellow believers, and to carry to others the good news about God's loving provisions for all mankind. For that reason, Jehovah's witnesses will continue to call at the homes of people everywhere to discuss the Bible with them, and during June they will be offering the *New World Translation of the Holy Scriptures* and the book *"All Scripture Is Inspired of God and Beneficial,"* with two booklets, for $2.

### IS PEACE POSSIBLE?

Peace is the desire of all people, yet the nations of this world have not been able to attain it, not even within the borders of individual nations. So commonplace has violence become that many persons view it as an inevitable evil of life. But is it? Will conditions never change? For your peace of mind and assurance of future happiness send for and read the beautifully illustrated hardbound book *From Paradise Lost to Paradise Regained.* It is only 75c.

### EUROPEAN ASSEMBLIES

Conventions featuring instruction in God's Word of Truth are being sponsored by the Watch Tower Society in many parts of the world this year. You are welcome to attend. Admission is free. The dates and locations for the European assemblies are as follows:

June 9-13: Tolka Park, Dublin, Eire; Scottish Rugby Union, Edinburgh, Scotland.
June 17-20: Ullevål Stadion, Oslo, Norway.
June 23-27: Olympic Stadium, Helsinki, Finland.
June 30–July 4: Feyenoord Stadium, Rotterdam, Netherlands.
July 7-11: Palais des Expositions, Charleroi, Belgium; Exhibition Hall, Luxembourg, Luxembourg.
July 14-18: Sportfeld St. Jakob, Basel, Switzerland; Stadhalle, Vienna, Austria.
July 21-25: Deutschlandhalle, Berlin, Germany.

### "WATCHTOWER" STUDIES FOR THE WEEKS

July 4: Joyfulness All the Day Long. Page 328.
July 11: Increase Your Praise of Jehovah! Page 334.

6/1/65

## DIALOGUE FOUR: How Close Is The End?

to take the further step of associating with Jehovah's Witnesses. If we are faced with a disaster, however, is it enough just to hear the warning? As we can see from the case of the Mount Fugen eruption, we need to act on the warning. Remember, at least 15 news reporters and cameramen intent on securing a scoop lost their lives. In fact, one photographer died with his finger on the shutter button of his camera. A volcanologist—who had remarked, "If one day I have to die, I want it to be at the edge of a volcano"—lost his life just as he had wished. They were all dedicated to their work and their pursuits. Yet, they paid with their lives—the price of ignoring the warning.

Many today hear the message about God's decision to destroy this wicked system of things and discern, to a certain extent, the validity of the warning. 'It may eventually come,' they may reason, 'but not today.' They conveniently put off the day of Jehovah to a later time so that they may not be diverted from what seems more important in their eyes at the moment.

Baruch had such a problem. Being the secretary to the ancient prophet Jeremiah, Baruch courageously warned the Israelites of Jerusalem's impending doom. Yet, he once became weary of his commission. At that, Jehovah corrected him: "As for you, you keep seeking great things for yourself. Do not keep on seeking." Be it wealth, prominence, or material security, Baruch was not to 'seek great things for himself.' He was to be interested in one thing, doing God's will to help people to stand on His side. As a result, he would receive 'his soul as a spoil.' (Jeremiah 45:1-5) Comparably, instead of 'seeking great things for ourselves,' we should seek Jehovah, which can lead to the saving of our own lives.

At Mount Fugen, over a dozen policemen and volunteer firemen were on duty when the superheated volcanic flow hit them. They were trying to help and protect endangered people. They were like well-meaning men and women who are immersed in improving this world. Lofty though their motives may be, "that which is made crooked cannot be made straight." (Ecclesiastes 1:15) The crooked system of things cannot be straightened out. Is it reasonable to make oneself "a friend of the world" by trying to save a worldwide system that God is determined to eliminate?

### Once You Have Fled, Stay Away

It is one thing to flee from the endangered system, but it is quite another to remain in the protective care of "the whole association of brothers." (1 Peter 2:17) Let us not forget the farmers who, after being evacuated, went back to check their fields near Mount Fugen. Probably, they were anxious to return to the "normal" life they used to have. But you realize that their decision to go back was unwise. Perhaps that was not their first attempt to cross the line. They might have stepped into the perilous area just for a little while and nothing happened. The next time, they might have stayed a little longer, and still nothing happened. Likely, they soon became accustomed to crossing the protective line and were emboldened to linger in the endangered area.

Jesus Christ referred to a similar situation that would occur during "the conclusion of the system of things." He said: "As they were in those days before the flood, eating and drinking, men marrying and women being given in marriage, until the day that Noah entered into the ark; and they took no note until the flood came and swept them all away, so the presence of the Son of man will be." —Matthew 24:3, 38, 39.

Notice that Jesus mentioned eating, drinking, and getting married. None of those things are in themselves wrong in Jehovah's eyes. What was wrong then? The people of Noah's day "took no note," leading a life centered around their regular routine. In a time of emergency, one cannot live a "normal" life.

*Take refuge alo*
*with Jehoval*
*people and st*
*with the*

Once you have fl
or have separatec
present doomed
urge to go back tc
can be gleaned f
You may be able
ally safe zone an
no one even no
ly will embolden
ing to the world a
ger. Soon the atti
won't come toda

Also, think of t
their lives waitir
cameramen whc
down the slope.
with others whc
the world. What
being coaxed ir
zone is not wort

All the victim
gen crossed th
the danger zon
the mountain v
thought that i

6 THE WATCHTOWER • FEBRUARY 15, 2000

"Jehovah's day is coming exactly as a thief in the night." Referring to men who appear to be worldly-wise, he says: "Whenever it is that they are saying: 'Peace and security!' then sudden destruction is to be instantly upon them." Hence, Paul urges his readers: "Let us not sleep on as the rest do, but let us stay awake and keep our senses." (1 Thessalonians 5:2, 3, 6) Truly, those who look to human institutions to bring peace and security are ignoring reality. Such individuals are fast asleep!

[20] The destruction of this system of things will come with striking suddenness. Therefore, keep in expectation of Jehovah's day. God himself told Habakkuk: "It will not be late"! Indeed, it has never been more urgent for us to keep on the watch.

# "DESIRABLE THINGS" ARE FILLING JEHOVAH'S HOUSE

*"I [Jehovah] will rock all the nations, and the desirable things of all the nations must come in; and I will fill this house with glory."*—HAGGAI 2:7.

WHAT desirable things fill your house? Do you have plush furniture, a state-of-the-art computer, a new car in your garage? Even if you have all these things, would you not agree that the most precious things in your home are the people—the members of your family? Imagine that one night you awake to the smell of smoke. Your house is on fire, and you have just minutes to escape! What is your first concern? Your furniture? Your computer? Your car? Would you not, rather, think of your loved ones? Of course you would, for people are more valuable than things.

[2] Now think about Jehovah God and his Son, Jesus Christ. Jehovah is "the One who made the heaven and the earth and the sea and all the things in them." (Acts 4:24) His Son, the "master worker," was the agent through whom Jehovah made all other things. (Proverbs 8:30, 31; John 1:3; Colossians 1:15-17) Surely both Jehovah and Jesus value all that was created. (Compare Genesis 1:31.) But which aspect of creation do you think means the most to them—things or people? In the role of wisdom personified, Jesus states: "The things I was fond of were with the sons of men," or as William F. Beck's translation renders it, Jesus was "delighted with human beings."

[3] Jehovah unquestionably places high value on people. One indication of this is found in the prophetic words that he spoke in the year 520 B.C.E. through his prophet Haggai. Jehovah declared: "I will rock all the nations, and the desirable things of all the nations must come in; and I will fill this house with glory. . . . Greater will the glory of this later house become than that of the former."—Haggai 2:7, 9.

1. In a time of emergency, why do we think first of our loved ones?
2. What is the extent of Jehovah's creation, and what aspect of it was Jesus most fond of?

3. What prophecy did Jehovah utter through Haggai?



[4] What "desirab
vah's house and t
ry? Lavish furnis
tions? Gold, silv
This would hardly
ber, the former ten
centuries earlier, w
ifice!* Surely, Jehc
temple built by th
repatriated Jews to
in material splend

[5] What, then, a
that would fill Jeh
must be people. A
vah's heart rejoice
people who serve
27:11; 1 Corinthia
sures all the me
who worship him
These are "desirab
more precious to J
that adorned Solo

[6] Despite relentl
was completed in
of Jesus' sacrifice,
mained the center
"desirable things,"
and Gentile prose
sented something

A First-Ce

[7] The temple in

* The amount contrib
omon's temple wou
40 billion dollars in cu
used for the building
treasury.—1 Kings 7:5

4, 5. (a) Why woul
clude that the expres
material splendor? (
sirable things," and v
6. What purpose dic
7. (a) What did Goc
foreshadow? (b) De
priest on Atonement

ıem to have children
' parenthood.

ɔncern
ınderstandable. The
s fundamental and
ıd times. Childbear-
ıgs of joy and hope.
y is a reward," says
to bear children is a
ving Creator.—Psalm

ied couples face im-
ear children. For ex-
· the average wom-
:en, it is common at
ıers say to the newly-
ı now, we expect to
ır house." As a wed-
l groom may receive
w closely watch the
ıot pregnant within
ɔ see if there is any
ɔ to solve.
eason that a couple
ıildren and to carry
mother said to her:
if you are not going
e gave birth to you;
ɔur own children."
ıre practical matters
ın nations, there are
ns to care for the el-
ɛ children who look
ıst as those parents
hey were young. So
ıat unless her chil-
r own, they would,
ıely, unwanted, and
one to bury them

rica, it is considered
ren. In some areas,
o prove their ability
ırriage. Many wom-

en who are not able to conceive will frantically seek medicines and cures to try to reverse their barren condition.

In view of these attitudes, married couples who deliberately refrain from having children are thought to be robbing themselves of something good. They are often viewed as odd, shortsighted, and pitiable.

### Joy and Responsibility

Jehovah's people recognize that while there is joy in rearing children, there is also responsibility. The Bible, at 1 Timothy 5:8, says: "Certainly if anyone does not provide for those who are his own, and especially for those who are members of his household, he has disowned the faith and is worse than a person without faith."

Parents must provide for their families both materially and spiritually, and this takes considerable time and effort. They do not have the attitude that since God provides children, it is left to God to care for them. They realize that rearing children according to Bible principles is a full-time responsibility assigned by God to parents; it is not one that should be delegated to others.—Deuteronomy 6:6, 7.

The task of rearing children is especially difficult in these "last days" of "critical times hard to deal with." (2 Timothy 3:1-5) Apart from worsening economic conditions, the increasing godlessness of society adds to the challenges of child rearing today. Even so, throughout the world, countless Christian couples have taken up this challenge and are successfully rearing godly children "in the discipline and mental-regulating of Jehovah." (Ephesians 6:4) Jehovah loves and blesses these parents for their hard work.

### Why Some Remain Childless

Many Christian couples, on the other hand, do not have children. Some are infertile and yet do not adopt children. Other couples who have the ability to produce offspring decide not to do so. Such couples do not remain childless because they shirk responsibility or are afraid to meet the challenges of parenthood. Rather, they have determined to give their full attention to different avenues of the full-time ministry that the rearing of children would not allow. Some serve as missionaries. Others serve Jehovah in the traveling work or at Bethel.

Like all Christians, they realize that there is an urgent work to do. Jesus said: "This good news of the kingdom will be preached in all the inhabited earth for a witness to all the nations; and then the end will come." This work is being done today. It is a vital work, since "the end" will mean destruction for those who have not heeded the good news.—Matthew 24:14; 2 Thessalonians 1:7, 8.

Ours is a period similar to the time when Noah and his family constructed the gigantic ark that preserved them through the great Flood. (Genesis 6:13-16; Matthew 24:37) Although Noah's three sons were all married, none fathered children until after the Deluge. One reason for that may have been that these couples wanted to devote their full attention and energy to the work at hand. Another may have been reluctance to bring children into a debased and violent world where "the badness of man was abundant . . . and every inclination of the thoughts of his heart was only bad all the time."—Genesis 6:5.

While this does not imply that it is wrong to have children today, many Christian couples decline to have children so as to become more fully involved in the urgent work that Jehovah has given his people to do. Some couples have waited for a time before having children; others have decided to remain childless and consider the possibility of bearing children in Jehovah's righteous new world. Is this shortsighted? Are they missing out on life? Are they to be pitied?

### Secure and Joyful Lives

Dele and Fola, mentioned earlier, have now been married for over ten years, and they

THE WATCHTOWER • AUGUST 1, 2000 21

***Do you know the symbolic significance of Jehovah's ancient temple?***

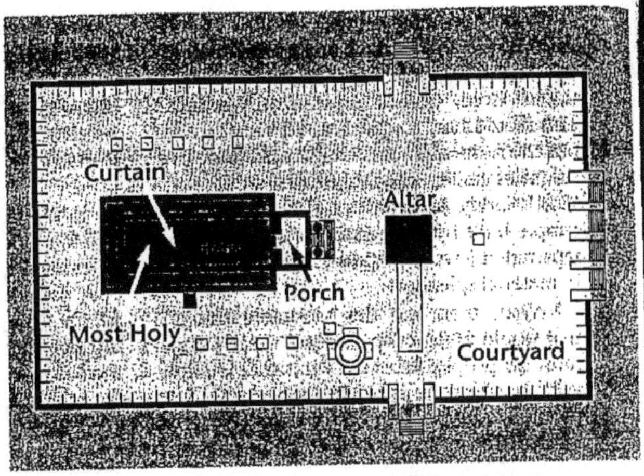


(1 Corinthians 15:44, 50) Since Jesus' human flesh was a barrier, it was well symbolized by the curtain that separated the Holy from the Most Holy in God's ancient temple. (Hebrews 10:20) But three days after his death, Jesus was resurrected by God as a spirit. (1 Peter 3:18) Then he could enter the Most Holy compartment of God's spiritual temple—heaven itself. And this is precisely what happened. Paul writes: "Christ entered, not into a holy place [evidently referring to the Most Holy] made with hands, which is a copy of the reality, but into heaven itself, now to appear before the person of God for us."—Hebrews 9:24.

10 In heaven, Jesus 'spattered the blood' of his sacrifice by presenting the ransoming value of his lifeblood to Jehovah. Yet, Jesus did more. Shortly before his death, he had told his followers: "I am going my way to prepare a place for you. Also, if I go my way and prepare a place for you, I am coming again and will receive you home to myself, that where I am you also may be." (John 14:2, 3) So by gaining entrance into the Most Holy, or heaven, Jesus opened the way for others to follow. (Hebrews 6:19, 20) These individuals, who would number 144,000, would serve as underpriests in God's spiritual temple arrangement. (Revelation 7:4; 14:1; 20:6) Just as the high priest of Israel first took the blood of the bull into the Most Holy to atone for the sins of the priests, the value of Jesus' shed blood was first applied to these 144,000 underpriests.*

10. What did Jesus do upon returning to heaven?

## Modern-Day "Desirable Things"

11 It seems that by the year 1935, the general ingathering of the anointed was complete.# But Jehovah was not finished glorifying his house. No, "desirable things" would yet come into it. Remember that the high priest in Israel offered two animals—a bull for the sins of the priests and a goat for the sins of the nonpriestly tribes. Since the priests pictured the anointed ones who would be with Jesus in the heavenly Kingdom, whom did the nonpriestly tribes represent? The answer is found in Jesus' words recorded at John 10:16: "I have other sheep, which are not of this fold; those also I must bring, and they will listen to my voice, and they will become one flock, one

* Unlike the high priest of Israel, Jesus had no sins for which atonement was needed. However, his associate priests did have sins because they were bought from among sinful mankind.—Revelation 5:9, 10.

\# See *The Watchtower,* February 15, 1998, pages 17-22.

11. In whose behalf did Israel's high priest offer up a goat, and what did this foreshadow?

shepherd." Hence
two groups of pe
whose hope is tc
and second, thos
lasting life on a p
this second grour
sirable things" of
4:1, 2; 1 John 2:1,

12 These "desir
Jehovah's house.
have been lifted i
rica, and other la
of God's establis
hitherto untouc
ones come into
they in turn st
ples, in obedienc
thew 28:19, 20) A

12. How are many
to God's house tod

;ee this prophecy
'nly those who ig-

*:cts of the ouster*
*m heaven, in ful-*
. There, we read:
s hurled, the orig-
. Devil and Satan,
e inhabited earth;
earth, and his an-
him." This has re-
:arth. Truly, there
ınkind, particular-
ıecy in Revelation
; cast down to the
ıas a short period
:) During this pe-
the anointed fol-
ın 12:17) We cer-
of his attack in our
ı will be confined
ht not mislead the
ion 20:1-3.
*ı the time of the*
*mentioned in the*
*tion 17:9-11.* Here
. seven kings, rep-
:rs—Egypt, Assyria,
:ce, Rome, and the
d power. He also
"springs from the
-the last one that

f this prophecy, see
*ge That Leads to Ever-*
Vatchtower Bible and

ges 180-6 of the book
*Hand!,* published by
: Society of New York,

lation 12:9 regarding
; and what will soon

ɔ-11 supply evidence
of the end?

John envisions—now represents the United Nations. John says that this eighth king "goes off into destruction," after which no further earthly kings are mentioned.*

16 *Fourth, we are living in the period symbolized by the feet of Nebuchadnezzar's dream image.* The prophet Daniel interpreted this mysterious dream of an enormous image in human form. (Daniel 2:36-43) The four metallic parts of the image represent various world powers, beginning with the head (the Babylonian Empire) and extending down to the feet and toes (the governments that are ruling today). All the world powers represented in that image have made their appearance. We are living in the period symbolized by the feet of the image. No mention is made of other powers to come.#

17 *Fifth, we see a global preaching work being accomplished, which Jesus said would take place just before the end of this system.* Jesus stated: "This good news of the kingdom will be preached in all the inhabited earth for a witness to all the nations; and then the end will come." (Matthew 24:14) Today, that prophecy is in the course of fulfillment on an unprecedented scale. True, untouched territories still exist, and it may be that in Jehovah's due time, a large door leading to greater activity will open. (1 Corinthians 16:9) Nevertheless, the Bible does not state that Jehovah will wait until every individual on earth has received a personal witness. Rather, the good news must be preached to Jehovah's satisfaction. Then the end will come.—Compare Matthew 10:23.

18 *Sixth, the number of genuine anointed disciples of Christ is dwindling, though some will evidently still be on earth when the great tribulation begins.* Most of the remnant are quite elderly, and over the years the number of those who are truly anointed has been getting smaller. Yet, referring to the great tribulation, Jesus stated: "Unless those days were cut short, no flesh would be saved; but on account of the chosen ones those days will be cut short." (Matthew 24:21, 22) Evidently, then, some of Christ's "chosen ones" will still be on earth when the great tribulation begins.*

### What Lies Ahead?

19 What does the future hold for us? Exciting times are yet to come. Paul warned that

* See *Revelation—Its Grand Climax At Hand!,* pages 251-4.

\# See chapter 4 of the book *Pay Attention to Daniel's Prophecy!,* published by the Watchtower Bible and Tract Society of New York, Inc.

16. How do the facts in fulfillment of Nebuchadnezzar's dream image indicate that we are living in the last days?

17. How does our Kingdom-preaching activity provide further evidence that we are living in the time of the end?

**Do You Recall?**

- What Scriptural examples can help us to keep on the watch?
- How did Jesus illustrate the need for watchfulness?
- What six lines of evidence prove that we are living in the last days?

* In the parable of the sheep and the goats, the Son of man arrives in his glory in the period of the great tribulation and sits in judgment. He judges people on the basis of whether they gave support to Christ's anointed brothers. This standard for judgment would be meaningless if at the time of judgment, all of Christ's brothers had long since left the earthly scene.—Matthew 25:31-46.

18. Evidently, what will be true of some of the anointed when the great tribulation begins, and how may this be determined?

19, 20. Why is it more urgent for us now than ever before to stay awake and keep on the watch?

THE WATCHTOWER • JANUARY 15, 2000 13

*he that*
10, 13.

ıen Babylon
kingdom of
ıf Jesus' en-
ɪind's right-
times of the
But the na-
he incoming
2:1-6, 10-12;

(29-36 C.E.)
e year 1914
ıle were ex-
ıd arrive he
ɜ manner of
the expecta-
ɔomparative-
"generation"
ivine decree.

ve noted how
ı that called
s end. What,
ɪion of man-
ignores him?
faithless gen-

ɪh"!
leading up to

e made of first-
ime? (b) What
1?
we not need to
ay and hour"?
t sound counsel

a time of "great tribulation," Jesus added: "Concerning that day and hour nobody knows, neither the angels of the heavens nor the Son, but only the Father." (Matthew 24:3-36; Mark 13:3-32) We do not need to know the exact timing of events. Rather, our focus must be on being watchful, cultivating strong faith, and keeping busy in Jehovah's service—not on calculating a date. Jesus concluded his great prophecy by saying: "Keep looking, keep awake, for you do not know when the appointed time is. . . . Keep on the watch . . . What I say to you I say to all, Keep on the watch." (Mark 13:33-37) Danger lurks in the shadows of today's world. We must keep awake! —Romans 13:11-13.

6 Not only must we pay attention to the inspired prophecies concerning these final days of a wicked system but we must anchor our faith primarily on the precious sacrifice of Christ Jesus and God's marvelous promises based thereon. (Hebrews 6:17-19; 9:14; 1 Peter 1:18, 19; 2 Peter 1:16-19) Eager to see the end of this evil system, Jehovah's people have at times speculated about the time when the "great tribulation" would break out, even tying this to calculations of what is the lifetime of a generation since 1914. However, we "bring a heart of wisdom in," not by speculating about how many years or days make up a generation, but by thinking about how we "count our days" in bringing joyful praise to Jehovah. (Psalm 90:12) Rather than provide a rule for measuring time, the term "generation" as used by Jesus refers principally to contemporary people of a certain historical period, with their identifying characteristics.*

6. (a) On what should our faith be anchored? (b) How may we "count our days"? (c) What does Jesus basically mean by "generation"?

* See Volume 1, page 918, of *Insight on the Scriptures*, published by the Watchtower Bible and Tract Society of New York, Inc.

Alexandra Boulat/Sipa Press

**Suffering humanity will find relief when this violent, wicked generation passes away**

Left and below: Luc Delahaye/Sipa Press

WATCHTOWER 11/1/95 p.17

ed and
w true
.e mat-
l since
ıges. It
e blood
corism,
. world-
ty have
l: "You
ı these
ıngdom
ıis gen-
ıntil all

[8] Yes, the complete triumph of the Messianic Kingdom is at hand! Is anything to be gained, then, by looking for dates or by speculating about the literal lifetime of a "generation"? Far from it! Habakkuk 2:3 clearly states: "The vision is yet for the appointed time, and it keeps panting on to the end, and it will not tell a lie. Even if it should delay, keep in expectation of it; for it will without fail come true. It will not be late." Jehovah's day of accounting hastens ever closer.—Jeremiah 25:31-33; Malachi 4:1.

[9] When Christ's Kingdom rule began in 1914, Satan was hurled down to earth. This has meant "woe for the earth . . . because the Devil has come down to you, having great anger, knowing he has a *short* period of time." (Revelation 12:12) That time is short, indeed, compared with the thousands of years of Satan's rulership. The Kingdom is at hand, and so is Jehovah's day and hour for executing judgment on this wicked generation!—Proverbs 3:25; 10:24, 25.

**The "Generation" That Passes Away**

[10] Let us examine more closely Jesus' statement at Matthew 24:34, 35: "Truly I say to you that *this generation* will by no means pass away until all these things occur. Heaven and earth will pass away, but my words will by no means pass away." Jesus' words that follow show that 'nobody knows that day and hour.' Far more important, he shows that we must avoid the snares surrounding us in *this generation.* Thus Jesus adds: "For just as the days of Noah were, so the presence of the Son of man will be. For as they were in those days before the flood, eating and drinking, men marrying and women being given in marriage, until the day that Noah entered into the ark; and they took no note until the flood came and swept them all away, so the presence of the Son of man will be." (Matthew 24:36-39) Jesus here compared the generation of his day to that of Noah's day.—Genesis 6:5, 9; footnote.

[11] This was not the first time that the apostles heard Jesus make this comparison of *'generations,'* for some days earlier he had stated concerning himself: "The Son of man . . . must undergo many sufferings and be *rejected by this generation.* Moreover, *just as it occurred in the days of Noah,* so it will be also in the days of the Son of man." (Luke 17:24-26) Thus, Matthew chapter 24 and Luke chapter 17 make the same comparison. In Noah's day "all flesh [that] had ruined its way on the earth" and that was destroyed at the Flood was *"this generation."* In Jesus' day the apostate Jewish people that were rejecting Jesus was *"this generation."*—Genesis 6: 11, 12; 7:1.

[12] Therefore, in the final fulfillment of Jesus' prophecy today, "this generation" apparently refers to the peoples of earth who see the sign of Christ's presence but fail to mend their ways. In contrast, we as Jesus' disciples refuse to be molded by the life-style of "this generation." Though in the world, we must be no part of it, "for the appointed time is near." (Revelation 1:3; John 17:16) The apostle Paul admonishes

8. How do Jehovah's prophets stress the need to keep awake?
9. What developments since 1914 show that the time is short?
10. How is "this generation" like that of Noah's day?
11. What comparison of 'generations' did Jesus make, as reported by Matthew and Luke?
12, 13. (a) What today is "this generation" that must pass away? (b) How are Jehovah's people now coping with this "crooked and twisted generation"?

THE WATCHTOWER—NOVEMBER 1, 1995 19

obtained the dominion (Dan. 2: 37, 38); Medo-Persia existed before it conquered Babylon; and so with all kingdoms: they must first have existed and have received superior power before they could conquer others. So, too, with God's Kingdom: it has existed in an embryo form for eighteen centuries; but it, with the world at large, was made subject to "the powers that be," "ordained of God." Until their "seven times" shall end, the Kingdom of God cannot come into universal dominion. However, like the others, it must obtain power adequate to the overthrow of these kingdoms before it shall break them in pieces.

So, in this "Day of Jehovah," the "Day of Trouble," our Lord takes his great power (hitherto dormant) and reigns, and this it is that will cause the trouble, though the world will not so recognize it for some time. That the saints shall share in this work of breaking to pieces present kingdoms, there can be no doubt. It is written, "This honor have all his saints—to execute the judgments written; to bind their kings with chains, and their nobles with fetters of iron."—of strength. (Psa. 149: 8, 9.) "He that overcometh, and keepeth my works unto the end, to him will I give power over the nations, and he shall rule them with a rod of iron; as the vessels of a potter shall they [the *empires*] be broken to shivers."—Rev. 2: 26, 27; Psa. 2: 8, 9.

But our examination, in the preceding volume, of the great difference in character between the Kingdom of God and the beastly kingdoms of earth, prepares us to see also a difference in modes of warfare. The methods of conquest and breaking will be widely different from any which have ever before overthrown nations. He who now takes his great power to reign is shown in symbol (Rev. 19: 15) as the one whose sword went forth *out of his mouth*, "that with it he should smite the nations; and he shall rule them with a rod of iron." That sword is the TRUTH (Eph. 6: 17);



and the living saints, as well as many of the world, are now being used as the Lord's soldiers in overthrowing errors and evils. But let no one hastily infer a *peaceable conversion* of the nations to be here symbolized; for many scriptures, such as Rev. 11: 17, 18; Dan. 12: 1; 2 Thes. 2: 8; Psalms 149 and 47, teach the very opposite.

Be not surprised, then, when in subsequent chapters we present proofs that the setting up of the Kingdom of God is already begun, that it is pointed out in prophecy as due to begin the exercise of power in A. D. 1878, and that the "battle of the great day of God Almighty" (Rev. 16: 14), which will end in A. D. 1914 with the complete overthrow of earth's present rulership, is already commenced. The gathering of the armies is plainly visible from the standpoint of God's Word.

If our vision be unobstructed by prejudice, when we get the telescope of God's Word rightly adjusted we may see with clearness the character of many of the events due to take place in the "Day of the Lord"—that we are in the very midst of those events, and that "the Great Day of His Wrath is come."

The sword of truth, already sharpened, is to smite every evil system and custom—civil, social and ecclesiastical. Nay, more, we can see that the smiting is commenced: freedom of thought, and human rights, civil and religious, long lost sight of under kings and emperors, popes, synods, councils, traditions and creeds, are being appreciated and asserted as never before. The internal conflict is already fomenting: it will ere long break forth as a consuming fire, and human systems, and errors, which for centuries have fettered truth and oppressed the groaning creation, must melt before it. Yes, truth—and widespread and increasing knowledge of it—is the sword which is perplexing and wounding the heads over many countries. (Psa. 110: 6.)

THE TIME IS AT HAND (Studies In the Scriptures vol. 2) 1889

obtained the dominion (Dan. 2: 37, 38); Medo-Persia existed before it conquered Babylon; and so with all kingdoms: they must first have existed and have received superior power before they could conquer others. So, too, with God's Kingdom: it has existed in an embryo form for eighteen centuries; but it, with the world at large, was made subject to "the powers that be," "ordained of God." Until their "seven times" shall end, the Kingdom of God cannot come into universal dominion. However, like the others, it must obtain power adequate to the overthrow of these kingdoms before it shall break them in pieces.

So, in this "Day of Jehovah," the "Day of Trouble," our Lord takes his great power (hitherto dormant) and reigns, and this it is that will cause the trouble, though the world will not so recognize it for some time. That the saints shall share in this work of breaking to pieces present kingdoms, there can be no doubt. It is written, "This honor have all his saints—to execute the judgments written, to bind their kings with chains, and their nobles with fetters of iron"—of strength. (Psa. 149: 8, 9.) "He that overcometh, and keepeth my works unto the end, to him will I give power over the nations, and he shall rule them with a rod of iron; as the vessels of a potter shall they [the *empires*] be broken to shivers."—Rev. 2: 26, 27; Psa. 2: 8, 9.

But our examination, in the preceding volume, of the great difference in character between the Kingdom of God and the beastly kingdoms of earth, prepares us to see also a difference in modes of warfare. The methods of conquest and breaking will be widely different from any which have ever before overthrown nations. He who now takes his great power to reign is shown in symbol (Rev. 19:15) as the one whose sword went forth *out of his mouth*, "that with it he should smite the nations; and he shall rule them with a rod of iron." That sword is the TRUTH (Eph. 6: 17);



and the living saints, as well as many of the world, are now being used as the Lord's soldiers in overthrowing errors and evils. But let no one hastily infer a *peaceable conversion* of the nations to be here symbolized; for many scriptures, such as Rev. 11: 17, 18; Dan. 12: 1; 2 Thes. 2: 8; Psalms 149 and 47, teach the very opposite.

Be not surprised, then, when in subsequent chapters we present proofs that the setting up of the Kingdom of God is already begun, that it is pointed out in prophecy as due to begin the exercise of power in A. D. 1878, and that the "battle of the great day of God Almighty" (Rev. 16:14.), which will end in A.D. 1915, with the complete overthrow of earth's present rulership, is already commenced. The gathering of the armies is plainly visible from the standpoint of God's Word.

If our vision be unobstructed by prejudice, when we get the telescope of God's Word rightly adjusted we may see with clearness the character of many of the events due to take place in the "Day of the Lord"—that we are in the very midst of those events, and that "the Great Day of His Wrath is come."

The sword of truth, already sharpened, is to smite every evil system and custom—civil, social and ecclesiastical. Nay, more, we can see that the smiting is commenced: freedom of thought, and human rights, civil and religious, long lost sight of under kings and emperors, popes, synods, councils, traditions and creeds, are being appreciated and asserted as never before. The internal conflict is already fomenting: it will ere long break forth as a consuming fire, and human systems, and errors, which for centuries have fettered truth and oppressed the groaning creation, must melt before it. Yes, truth—and widespread and increasing knowledge of it—is the sword which is perplexing and wounding the heads over many countries. (Psa. 110: 6.)

THE TIME IS AT HAND (1889) 1915 edition

24:18. So I spake unto the people in the morning: and at even my wife died; and I did in the morning as I was commanded.—He continued his addresses and writings to the Lord's people; his wife became to him as one dead; and he continued uninterruptedly in the work of the ministry.

24:19. And the people said unto me, Wilt thou not tell us what these things are to us, that thou doest so?—Why was Pastor Russell caused by his Father to endure the fiery trials and ecclesiastical falsehoods in connection with this incident of his life?

THE CHURCHES TO CEASE TO BE

24:20, 21. Then I answered them, The word of the Lord came unto me, saying, Speak unto the house of Israel, Thus saith the Lord God; Behold, I will profane My Sanctuary, the excellency of your strength, the desire of your eyes, and that which your soul pitieth; and your sons and your daughters whom ye have left shall fall by the sword. —God gives the reason. It was as a picture or parable of what is to happen to Christendom. Until 1878 the nominal church had been in a sense God's sanctuary or Temple; but He was from then on, culminating in 1918, to remove it with a stroke or plague of erroneous doctrines and deeds Divinely permitted. The Church was the strength of Christendom, that about which its life centered, and around which its institutions were built. It was the desire of the eyes of the people, that which all Christians loved. Nevertheless, God was to make manifest the profanation which ecclesiasticism had made of the Christian Church, and to cause the church organizations to become to Him as one dead, an unclean thing, not to be touched, or mourned. And the "children of the church" shall perish by the sword of war, revolution and anarchy, and by the Sword of the Spirit be made to see that they have lost their hope of life on the spirit plane—that "the door is shut."

24:22. And ye shall do as I have done: ye shall not cover your lips, nor eat the bread of men.—So universal and dreadful will be the troubles that the dead will literally lie unburied and unwept. There can be no mourning for the dead in a period when the living are overwhelmed by troubles worse than death.

24:23. And your tires shall be upon your heads; and your shoes upon your feet: ye shall not mourn nor weep; but ye shall pine away for your iniquities, and mourn one toward another.—The mourning will be an inner sorrow of a people stupefied by terrible experiences, who pine



away and without outward expression sink together into the fellowship of helpless grief.

24:24. Thus Ezekiel is unto you a sign: according to all that he hath done shall ye do: and when this cometh, ye shall know that I am the Lord God.—Thus the silent sorrow at Pastor Russell's heart was to be a sign to Christendom. The sorrowful experiences of Pastor Russell in this connection shall later on be those of all Christendom; "and when this cometh" they shall know that Jehovah God is supreme, and back of all the judgments of the trouble time.

PASTOR RUSSELL DEAD, BUT SPEAKING AGAIN

24:25, 26. Also, thou son of man, shall it not be in the day when I take from them their strength, the joy of their glory, the desire of their eyes, and that whereupon they set their minds, their sons and their daughters. That he that escapeth in that day shall come unto thee, to cause thee to hear it with thine ears?—Also, in the year 1918, when God destroys the churches wholesale and the church members by millions, it shall be that any that escape shall come to the works of Pastor Russell to learn the meaning of the downfall of "Christianity."

24:27. In that day shall thy mouth be opened to him which is escaped, and thou shalt speak, and be no more dumb: and thou shalt be a sign unto them; and they shall know that I am the Lord.—Pastor Russell's voice has been stilled in death; and his voice is, comparatively speaking, dumb to what it will be. In the time of revolution and anarchy he shall speak, and be no more dumb to those that escape the destruction of that day. Pastor Russell shall "be a sign unto them," shall tell them the truth about the Divine appointment of the trouble, as they consult his books, scattered to the number of ten million throughout Christendom. His words shall be a sign of hope unto them, enabling them to see the bright side of the cloud and to look forward with anticipation to the glorious Kingdom of God to be established. Then "they shall know the Lord."

---

"Build thee more stately mansions, O my soul,
As the swift seasons roll!
Leave thy low vaulted past!
Let each new temple, nobler than the last,
Shut thee from heaven with a dome more vast,
Till thou at length art free,
Leaving thine outgrown shell by life's unresting sea."

THE FINISHED MYSTERY, 1917

seventy jubilees kept. (Jeremiah 25:11; 2 Chronicles 36:17-21) A simple calculation of these jubilees brings us to this important fact: Seventy jubilees of fifty years each would be a total of 3500 years. That period of time beginning 1575 before A. D. 1 of necessity would end in the fall of the year 1925, at which time the type ends and the great antitype must begin. What, then, should we expect to take place? In the type there must be a full restoration; therefore the great antitype must mark the beginning of restoration of all things. The chief thing to be restored is the human race to life; and since other Scriptures definitely fix the fact that there will be a resurrection of Abraham, Isaac, Jacob and other faithful ones of old, and that these will have the first favor, we may expect 1925 to witness the return of these faithful men of Israel from the condition of death, being resurrected and fully restored to perfect humanity and made the visible, legal representatives of the new order of things on earth.

Messiah's kingdom once established, Jesus and his glorified church constituting the great Messiah, shall minister the blessings to the people they have so long desired and hoped for and prayed might come. And when that time comes, there will be peace and not war, as the prophet beautifully states: "In the last days it shall come to pass, that the mountain of the house of the Lord shall be established in the top of the mountains, and it shall be exalted above



the hills; and people shall flow unto it. And many nations shall come, and say, Come, and let us go up to the mountain of the Lord, and to the house of the God of Jacob; and he will teach us of his ways, and we will walk in his paths: for the law shall go forth of Zion, and the word *of the Lord from Jerusalem. And he shall judge* among many people, and rebuke strong nations afar off; and they shall beat their swords into plowshares, and their spears into pruninghooks; nation shall not lift up a sword against nation, neither shall they learn war any more. But they shall sit every man under his vine and under his fig tree; and none shall make them afraid; for the mouth of the Lord of hosts hath spoken it." —Micah 4:1-4.

### EARTHLY RULERS

As we have heretofore stated, the great jubilee cycle is due to begin in 1925. At that time the earthly phase of the kingdom shall be recognized. The Apostle Paul in the eleventh chapter of Hebrews names a long list of faithful men who died before the crucifixion of the Lord and before the beginning of the selection of the church. These can never be a part of the heavenly class; they had no heavenly hopes; but God has in store something good for them. They are to be resurrected as perfect men and constitute the princes or rulers in the earth, according to his promise. (Psalm 45:16; Isaiah 32:1; Matthew 8:11) Therefore we may confidently expect that 1925 will mark the return of Abraham,

Isaac, Jacob and the faithful prophets of old, particularly those named by the Apostle in Hebrews chapter eleven, to the condition of human perfection.

RECONSTRUCTION

All the statesmen of the world, all the political economists, all the thoughtful men and women, recognize the fact that the conditions existing prior to the war have passed away and that a new order of things must be put in vogue. All such recognize that this is a period now marking the beginning of reconstruction. The great difficulty is that these men are exercising only human wisdom and have ignored the divine arrangement. We are indeed at the time of reconstruction, the reconstruction not only of a few things, but of all things. The reconstruction will not consist of patching up old and broken down systems and forms and arrangements, but the establishment of a new and righteous one under the great ruler Christ Jesus, the Prince of Peace. The Apostle Peter at Pentecost, speaking under divine inspiration, and referring to that time, said: "Times of refreshing shall come from the presence of the Lord; and he shall send Jesus Christ, which before was preached unto you: whom the heaven must receive [retain] until the times of restitution of all things, which God hath spoken by the mouth of all his holy prophets since the world began". —Acts 3:19-21.



Examination of the prophecies from Moses to John discloses the fact that every one of the prophets foretold the time coming for restitution blessings. Reconstruction and restitution mean the same thing—i.e., the restoration of mankind to the things which were lost. The reward of the church in heaven is not that which man originally had; but is given as a great reward for faithfulness to the Lord under trying conditions and circumstances. Restitution means the blessings that will be given to mankind in general through the divine arrangement and therefore restoring him to life, liberty and happiness on the earth, once enjoyed by the perfect man Adam and which was included in the promise made to Abraham. This blessing comes to the world through the seed, the exalted, elect class, the Messiah, the Christ.

The Scriptures clearly show that this great time of blessing is immediately preceded by a great time of trouble. This trouble is now on the world. The word Michael used in the following text means "who as God", or representing God—Christ Jesus, the great captain of our salvation. His second coming and the establishment of his kingdom has been the hope and desire of Christians for centuries past. In referring to this time, then, the prophet Daniel under inspiration wrote: "And at that time shall Michael stand up, the great prince which standeth for the children of thy people: and there shall be a time of trouble, such as never

that a plan of redemption exists and that the way is open for him to accept the terms of it and live. Knowledge being essential, it precedes the reception of blessings from the Lord; and knowing this fact, it is easy to be seen why the adversary, the devil, and his agencies so diligently strive to prevent the people from knowing the truth. But when Messiah's kingdom is established we are definitely informed (Revelation 20:1-4) that Satan will be restrained of his power that he might deceive the nations no more; and then the people shall know the truth and nothing shall hinder them from knowing it.

POSITIVE PROMISE

The words of Jesus must be given full force and effect because he spake as never man spake. His speech was with absolute authority. And in God's due time his words must have a fulfillment; and they cannot have a fulfillment until that due time. Jesus plainly said: "Verily, verily, I say unto you, If a man keep my saying, he shall never see death". (John 8:51) As above stated, no one could keep the saying of Jesus until he hears it, until he has a knowledge of God's arrangement. Throughout the Gospel age none but Christians have had this knowledge and all who have kept this saying and keep it faithfully until the end will receive life everlasting on the divine plane. (Revelation 2:10) The remainder of mankind have not heard it; therefore could not keep it. They will hear, however,



in due time after the establishment of the kingdom. Then it shall come to pass that every one who will keep the saying of the Lord shall never see death. This promise would not have been made by Jesus if he did not intend to carry it into full force and effect in due time.

Again he said: "Whosoever liveth and believeth in me shall never die". (John 11:26) Do we believe the Master's statement? If so, when the time comes for the world to know, then they who believe and, of course, render themselves in obedience to the terms have the absolute and positive statement of Jesus that they shall never die.

Based upon the argument heretofore set forth, then, that the old order of things, the old world, is ending and is therefore passing away, and that the new order is coming in, and that 1925 shall mark the resurrection of the faithful worthies of old and the beginning of reconstruction, it is reasonable to conclude that millions of people now on the earth will be still on the earth in 1925. Then, based upon the promises set forth in the divine Word, we must reach the positive and indisputable conclusion that millions now living will never die.

Of course, it does not mean that every one will live; for some will refuse to obey the divine law; but those who have been evil and turn again to righteousness and obey righteousness shall live and not die. Of this we have the positive statement of the Lord's prophet, as follows:

be able to give you girls proper advice, you girls who are looking for a husband. When you see Daniel, David, Moses and all the prophets, listen to what they have to say, and they will properly advise you boys and girls. I am going to have handed to every one of you 15,000 children one of these books as a gracious gift. I ask that you first study it faithfully. Ask someone else to sit with you under the shade of a tree and study that which leads to life and endless blessings. . . . It is your privilege between now and before the day school opens to spend six hours a day in taking the book *Children* to others." The parents should encourage their children to do this very thing, if they would have them live.

Cartons of *Children* that had been deposited in The Arena were now opened, and Judge Rutherford instructed the children how to come and each get a copy thereof, those in the rear half of The Arena marching in two columns out through a side exit, and those in the front half of The Arena marching up over the platform and out through a rear exit. As the march began, the orchestra (minus all its children instrumentalists) struck up and rendered songs, "Children of the Heavenly King," "The Sword of the Lord and of Gideon," and "Who Is on the Lord's Side?" while the vast audience sang. Never was there a more moving sight in these "last days". Many, including strong men, wept at the demonstration. Receiving the gift, the marching children clasped it to them, not a toy or plaything for idle pleasure, but the Lord's provided instrument for most effective work in the remaining months before Armageddon. What a gift! and to so many! The manner of releasing the new book *Children* was an outright surprise to all, but the almighty hand of the All-wise One, Jehovah, was in it, and the maneuver was most blessed indeed. Thereafter *Children*, the author's edition, was disposed of to adult conventioneers, on a contribution.

The blessings of the Assembly were further enhanced by the afternoon session, which provided a delightful anticlimax to "Children's Day". The Arena was again packed out to hear about "Your New Work" and the president's parting words. For weeks the question had been upon many consecrated minds, and at 3 p.m. the first speaker, the factory and office servant at Brooklyn, disclosed the "new work", to wit, the placing of *Children*, and thereafter, over a period of three weeks, sending each obtainer, at no extra cost to him, the "*Children* Study Course", to wit, three attractive, illuminated question-and-answer folders, these to be followed the fourth week by a back-call service by the one placing *Children*. Another speaker, on "Solving the Problem", showed how the new book, together with the "*Children* Study Course", provided the solution for the problem of company publishers to reach their individual quota of twelve back-calls monthly and one model study weekly, as suggested in the recent communication of the president of the Society. Three speakers then spoke, each briefly on "When to Begin", and were in concert as to the answer, that NOW is the time.

When, next, Judge Rutherford came on the platform, he talked extemporaneously, but the unspeakable blessing the Lord bestowed in the morning appeared to have put him in the best of condition and filled his heart and mouth full of words "in season" and "fitly spoken". For forty-five minutes the audience spent a most delightful time listening. Said Judge Rutherford: "It is not exactly a new work, but it is putting on a little more steam for the final roundup." Then concerning the book just released, he added: "We had on the grounds this morning only 40,000 of the autographed edition. . . . But I am glad to tell you that, while that 40,000 are gone, there is another 150,000 copies on the grounds ready for use. [Applause] So you will have 150,000 on the grounds here to start with NOW, and I think it might be well for two or three thousand first-class workers to go into the St. Louis field and get those in the hands of the people here who want to know something about it before you go away." (It developed that more than 3,000 persons of good-will turned in their names at the public meetings, requesting calls by Jehovah's witnesses and further information.)

Then in most interesting fashion he told of his visit to the trailer camp Saturday, and also of the opposition and the difficulties caused by the public service bodies, such as the Chamber of Commerce and the Convention Bureau, all due to their subservience to the religious organization, whom he symbolized under the figure of one distressed "Fayther O'Hooligan". The description of the actions and the bossy orders of this "Fayther O'Hooligan" in his own brogue to local businessmen and Catholic population caused great amusement, and the assembly laughed again and again. (Pss. 2:4; 37:12,13; 52:6) Then he told of the good people of St. Louis and showed how the parable of the "sheep" and "goats" had thus had local fulfillment.—Matthew 25.

The city editor of the *Globe Democrat* sent him a question, "Do you not think it discourteous to criticize another person's religion in his own community?" but, due to "Father O'Hooligan", they refused to publish the answer submitted, though it was of great public interest. The Roman Catholic Hierarchy in America have treated in like manner all proposals, challenges and petitions to public discussion in debate over radio. They have all been warned, and now "we are going to spend our energy and time and strength in going to the people of good-will toward God and his Theocratic kingdom, carrying to them the message". Hope-rousing and stirring was his statement: "I feel absolutely certain that from henceforth . . . those who will form the great multitude will grow by leaps and bounds." The arising of 15,000 children this morning was a decisive answer and reproof to the "evil servant" class who say, "Humph! where's the great multitude?"

For ever to disprove all published false charges and slurs that he is the leader of Jehovah's witnesses, he said: "I want to let any strangers here know what you think about a man being your LEADER, so they won't be forgetting. Every time something rises up and starts to grow, they say there is some man a leader who has a great following. If there is any person in this audience who thinks that I, this man standing here, is the leader of Jehovah's witnesses, say Yes." But there was a unanimous "No"! emphatically. "If you who are here believe that I am just one of the servants of the Lord, and we are working shoulder to shoulder in unity, serving God and serving Christ, say Yes." The unanimous "Yes!" was strong and unequivocal. "Well, you don't have to need me as an earthly leader to get a crowd like that to work." He now asked them to return to their respective parts and "put on more steam . . . put in all the time you can". Then he offered words of benediction.

Briefly referring to the coming convention in Britain in September he asked them to join with him in a cablegram, as follows: "To the Leicester Assembly: Your fellow servants, assembled 115,000 strong at St. Louis, bid our British brethren be very courageous and hold fast your integrity. Theocratic victory is certain. [Signed] Jehovah's witnesses in America." This was adopted with a unanimous "Aye".

His final words were, "Well, my dear brethren, the Lord bless you. Now I won't say Good-bye, because I expect to see you at some time again." By this the brethren were greatly encouraged, and their hearts and minds were turned to the still greater and grander event, "the general assembly" spoken of at Hebrews 12:23. Till then they would keep covenant and maintain integrity toward Jehovah God, and endure hardness as good soldiers of Jesus Christ, and continue on in God's "strange work" as his faithful and true witnesses, till done.

[A more detailed report of the convention will appear in *Consolation*.]

(*Continued from page 274*)

in support of Jehovah's witnesses and in defense of their rights and liberties in His service. The 32 pages of this important documentary matter are enclosed in a neat and strong cover. It is 5c a copy, mailed postage prepaid.

9/15/41

things" had ar-

ıight find paral-
ıs' baptism and
g of an invisible
ın the spring of
en he would as-
would be given
r, they conclud-
ıim in the King-
g in death began
ʼor to natural Is-
n the special op-

e," delivered by
New York City,
it thought to be
), it was pointed
*derstood to be the*
ing after the last
ing to the *begin-*
s could point to
hoped that per-
heir heavenly re-
ons for resurrec-
r to their serving
om. If that really
a in which death
have the hope of
h mistaken, they

, a review of the
ɔor translation of

ace to Jeremiah 16:18
ıad apparently elapsed
ad that the double, or

usalem in 70 C.E. (37
salem) might point to
ıat they thought God
o their end. This date
9-101, 171, 221, 232,
printing of *Millennial*
hed regarding the year



Acts 13:19, 20 in the *King James Version,** along with certain other factors, had thrown off the chronology by over a century.# This later led to the idea—sometimes stated as a possibility, sometimes more firmly—that since the seventh millennium of human history would begin in 1975, events associated with the beginning of Christ's Millennial Reign might start to take place then.

Did the beliefs of Jehovah's Witnesses on these matters prove to be correct? They certainly did not err in believing that God would without fail do what he had promised. But some of their time calculations and the expectations that they associated with these gave rise to serious disappointments.

*Jules Feller*

*When he was a young man, Jules Feller observed severe testings of faith. Some congregations in Switzerland shrank to half their former size or less. But he later wrote: "Those who had set their confidence in Jehovah remained steadfast and continued their preaching activity." Brother Feller determined to do that too, and as a result, down till 1992 he has enjoyed 68 years of Bethel service.*

Following 1925, meeting attendance dropped dramatically in some congregations in France and Switzerland. Again, in 1975, there was disappointment when expectations regarding the start of the Millennium failed to materialize. As a result, some withdrew from the organization. Others, because they sought to subvert the faith of associates, were disfellowshipped. No doubt, disappointment over the date was a factor, but in some instances the roots went deeper. Some individuals also argued against the need to participate in the house-to-house ministry. Certain ones did not simply choose to go their own way; they became aggressive in opposing the organization with which they had been associated, and they made use of the public press and television to air their views. Nevertheless, the number who defected was relatively small.

Although these tests resulted in a sifting and some blew away like chaff when wheat is winnowed, others remained firm. Why? Regarding his own experience and that of others in 1925, Jules Feller explained: "Those who had set their confidence in Jehovah remained steadfast and continued their preaching activity." They recognized that a mistake had been made but that in no respect had God's Word failed, and therefore there was no reason either to let their own hope grow dim or to slow down in the work of pointing people to God's Kingdom as mankind's only hope.

Some expectations had not been fulfilled, but that did not mean that Bible chronology was of no value. The prophecy recorded by Daniel regarding the appearance of the Messiah 69 weeks of years after "the going forth of

* Compare the rendering in *The Emphasised Bible,* translated by J. B. Rotherham; see also the footnote on Acts 13:20 in the *New World Translation of the Holy Scriptures—With References.*

# See *"The Truth Shall Make You Free,"* chapter XI; *"The Kingdom Is at Hand,"* pages 171-5; also *The Golden Age,* March 27, 1935, pages 391, 412. In the light of these corrected tables of Bible chronology, it could be seen that previous use of the dates 1873 and 1878, as well as related dates derived from these on the basis of parallels with first-century events, were based on misunderstandings.

JEHOVAH'S WITNESSES - PROCLAIMERS OF GOD'S KINGDOM, 1993

come because of any craving of his soul to the place that Jehovah will choose,[a] 7 he must also minister in the name of Jehovah* his God the same as all his brothers, the Levites, who are standing there before Jehovah.[b] 8 An equal share he should eat,[c] besides what he gets from things he sells of his ancestral goods.*

9 "When you are entered into the land that Jehovah your God is giving you, you must not learn to do according to the detestable things of those nations.[d] 10 There should not be found in you anyone who makes his son or his daughter pass through the fire,[e] anyone who employs divination,[f] a practicer of magic[g] or anyone who looks for omens[h] or a sorcerer,[i] 11 or one who binds others with a spell[j] or anyone who consults a spirit medium*[k] or a professional foreteller of events[l] or anyone who inquires of the dead.[m] 12 For everybody doing these things is something detestable to Jehovah, and on account of these detestable things Jehovah your God is driving them away from before you.[n] 13 You should prove yourself faultless with Jehovah your God.[o]

14 "For these nations whom you are dispossessing used to listen to those practicing magic[p] and to those who divine;[q] but as for you, Jehovah your God has not given* you anything like this.[r] 15 A prophet from your own midst, from your brothers, like me, is what Jehovah* your God will raise up for you—to him YOU people should listen[s]— 16 in response to all that you asked of Jehovah* your God in Ho'reb on the day of the congregation,[t] saying, 'Do not let me hear again the voice of Jehovah my God, and this great fire do not let me see anymore, that I may not die.'[u] 17 At that Jehovah said to me, 'They have done well in speaking what they did.[v] 18 A prophet I shall raise up for them from the midst of their brothers, like you;[a] and I shall indeed put my words in his mouth,[b] and he will certainly speak to them all that I shall command him.[c] 19 And it must occur that the man who will not listen to my words that he will speak in my name, I shall myself require an account from him.[d]

20 "'However, the prophet who presumes to speak in my name a word that I have not commanded him to speak[e] or who speaks in the name of other gods,[f] that prophet must die.[g] 21 And in case you should say in your heart: "How shall we know the word that Jehovah has not spoken?"[h] 22 when the prophet speaks in the name of Jehovah and the word does not occur or come true, that is the word that Jehovah did not speak. With presumptuousness the prophet spoke it.[i] You must not get frightened at him.'[j]

**19** "When Jehovah your God cuts off the nations[k] whose land Jehovah your God is giving you, and you have dispossessed them and have dwelt in their cities and their houses,[l] 2 you will set apart three cities for yourself in the midst of your land that Jehovah your God is giving you to take possession of it.[m] 3 You will prepare for yourself the way, and you must divide up the territory of your land that Jehovah your God proceeded to give you as a possession into three parts, and it must be for any manslayer to flee there.[n]

4 "Now this is the case of the manslayer who may flee there and has to live: When he strikes his fellowman without knowing it and he was no hater of him formerly;[o] 5 or when he goes with his fellowman into the woods to gather* wood, and his hand has been raised to strike with the ax to cut the tree, and the iron has slipped off from the wooden handle,[p] and it has hit his fellowman and he has died, he himself should flee to one of these cities and must live.[q] 6 Otherwise, the avenger[r]

CHAP. 18
a De 12:5; De 16:2; Ps 26:8
b 2Ch 31:2
c Le 7:10; Lu 10:7; 1Ti 5:18
d Le 18:26; De 12:30
e Le 18:21; De 12:31; 2Ki 16:3; 2Ch 28:3; Ps 106:37; Jer 19:5; Jer 32:35
f 2Ki 17:17; Ac 16:16
g Le 19:26; Ac 19:19
h Eze 21:21
i Ex 22:18
j Isa 47:9
k Le 20:27; 1Ch 10:13
l Le 19:31; 2Ch 33:6
m 1Sa 28:3; 1Sa 28:11; Isa 8:19; Ga 5:20
n Le 18:24; De 9:4
o 2Sa 22:24; Ps 37:18; Mt 5:48; 2Pe 3:14
p Le 19:26; 2Ki 21:2; 2Ki 21:6
q Jos 13:22
r Ps 147:20; Ac 14:16
s Ge 49:10; Nu 24:17; Lu 7:16; Lu 24:19; Joh 1:45; Joh 6:14; Ac 3:22; Ac 7:37
t Ex 19:17; De 9:10
u Ex 20:19
v De 5:28

Second Col.
a Ex 34:28; Nu 12:3; Mal 3:1; Mt 4:2; Mt 11:29; Lu 24:27; Lu 24:44; Joh 5:46
b Joh 8:28; Joh 17:8
c Joh 12:49; Joh 15:15; Heb 1:2
d Ac 3:23
e De 13:1; Jer 14:14; Jer 28:11; Eze 13:6; Mt 7:15
f De 13:2; 1Ki 18:19; Jer 23:13
g De 13:5; Jer 27:15; Zec 13:3
h 1Jo 4:1
i Jer 28:15
j Pr 29:25

CHAP. 19
k Ex 34:24; Jos 24:8
l De 6:10; De 7:1; De 9:1; De 12:29; m Ex 21:13; Nu 35:14; Jos 20:7; n Jos 20:9; o Nu 35:15; De 4:42; p 2Ki 6:5; q Nu 35:25; r Nu 35:12; Nu 35:19; Jos 20:5; 2Sa 14:7.

De 18:7* See App 1c §1. 8* Lit., "besides the things he sells according to the forefathers." 11* See Le 19:31 ftn. 14* Or, "allowed." 15* See App 1c §1. 16* See App 1c §1.

De 19:5* Or, "cut."



of blood* may, becau
chase after the man
overtake him, since
and he may indeed
tally,* whereas ther
death[a] for him, becau
of him formerly. 7
commanding you, s
you will set apart fo
8 "And if Jehoval
out your territory
he swore to your fo
has given you all
promised to give to
9 because you will
mandment that I a
today by doing it, to
God and to walk in
you must then add
for yourself to the
no innocent blood[x] n
midst of your land
God is giving you as
no bloodguilt* has t
11 "But in case t
to be a man hating[i]
he has lain in wait f
en up against him
fatally and he has
has fled to one of th
older men of his ci
and take him from t
deliver him into the
of blood,* and he m
eye should not feel
you must clear awa
cent blood out of Is
have good.
14 "You must n
boundary marks o
when the ancestors
boundaries in your i
will inherit in the
your God is giving
sion of it.
15 "No single wi
against a man resp

De 19:6* "The avenger
go·'el' had·dam'; Vg,
whose blood was shed.
to the soul," M; LXX
8* See App 1c §1. 1
da·mim'. 12* See vs 6
App 1c §1.

What characterizes their way of life? "The works of the flesh are . . . fornication, uncleanness, loose conduct, idolatry, practice of spiritism, enmities, strife, jealousy, fits of anger, contentions, divisions, sects, envies, drunken bouts, revelries, and things like these. . . . Those who practice such things will not inherit God's kingdom. On the other hand, the fruitage of [God's] spirit is love, joy, peace, long-suffering, kindness, goodness, faith, mildness, self-control."—Gal. 5:19-23; see also 2 Peter 2:1-3.

**Have not Jehovah's Witnesses made errors in their teachings?**

Jehovah's Witnesses do not claim to be inspired prophets. They have made mistakes. Like the apostles of Jesus Christ, they have at times had some wrong expectations.—Luke 19:11; Acts 1:6.

The Scriptures provide time elements related to Christ's presence, and Jehovah's Witnesses have studied these with keen interest. (Luke 21:24; Dan. 4:10-17) Jesus also described a many-featured sign that would tie in with the fulfillment of time prophecies to identify the generation that would live to see the end of Satan's wicked system of things. (Luke 21:7-36) Jehovah's Witnesses have pointed to evidence in fulfillment of this sign. It is true that the Witnesses have made mistakes in their understanding of what would occur at the end of certain time periods, but they have not made the mistake of losing faith or ceasing to be watchful as to fulfillment of Jehovah's purposes. They have continued to keep to the fore in their thinking the counsel given by Jesus: "Keep on the watch, therefore, because you do not know on what day your Lord is coming."—Matt. 24:42.

Matters on which corrections of viewpoint have been needed have been relatively minor when compared with the vital Bible truths that they have discerned and publicized. Among these are the following: Jehovah is the only true God. Jesus Christ is not part of a Trinitarian godhead but is the only-begotten Son of God. Redemption from sin is possible only through faith in Christ's ransom sacrifice. The holy spirit is not a person but is Jehovah's active force, and its



fruitage must be evident in the lives of true worshipers. The human soul is not immortal, as the ancient pagans claimed; it dies, and the hope for future life is in the resurrection. God's permission of wickedness has been because of the issue of universal sovereignty. God's Kingdom is the only hope for mankind. Since 1914 we have been living in the last days of the global wicked system of things. Only 144,000 faithful Christians will be kings and priests with Christ in heaven, whereas the rest of obedient mankind will receive eternal life on a paradise earth.

Another factor to consider regarding the teachings of Jehovah's Witnesses is this: Have these truly uplifted people morally? Are those who adhere to these teachings outstanding in their communities because of their honesty? Is their family life beneficially influenced by applying these teachings? Jesus said that his disciples would be readily identified because of having love among themselves. (John 13:35) Is this quality outstanding among Jehovah's Witnesses? We let the facts speak for themselves.

## If Someone Says—

**'My minister said that Jehovah's Witnesses are the false prophets'**

**You might reply:** 'May I ask, Did he show you anything in the Bible that describes what we believe or do and that says people of that sort would be false prophets? . . . May I show you how the Bible describes false prophets? (Then use one or more of the points outlined on pages 132-136.)'

**Or you could say:** 'I'm sure you'll agree that specific evidence should back up such a serious charge. Did your minister mention any specific examples? (If householder refers to some claimed "predictions" that did not come to pass, use material on page 134, and from the bottom of page 135 to the top of 137.)'

**Another possibility:** 'I'm sure that if someone accused you of something similar, you would welcome the opportunity at least to explain your position or point of view, wouldn't you? . . . So may I show you from the Bible . . . ?'

REASONING FROM THE SCRIPTURES, 1985, 1989ed

words do not come true, they should not be viewed as false prophets such as those warned against at Deuteronomy 18:20-22. In their human fallibility, they misinterpreted matters.*

Undeterred by previous failures, some seem to have been spurred on by the approach of the year 2000 and have made further predictions of the end of the world. *The Wall Street Journal* of December 5, 1989, published an article entitled "Millennium Fever: Prophets Proliferate, the End Is Near." With the year 2000 approaching, various evangelicals are predicting that Jesus is coming and that the 1990's will be "a time of troubles that has not been seen before." At the time of this writing, the latest occurrence was in the Republic of Korea, where the Mission for the Coming Days predicted that on October 28, 1992, at midnight, Christ would come and take believers to heaven. Several other doomsday groups made similar predictions.

The flood of false alarms is unfortunate. They are like the wolf-wolf cries of the shepherd boy—people soon dismiss them, and when the true warning comes, it too is ignored.

But why has there been such a tendency through the centuries and down to our day for false alarms to be sounded, as Jesus said they would be? (Matthew 24:23-26) Jesus, after telling his followers about different events that would mark his return, said to them, as we read at Matthew 24:36-42: "Concerning that day and hour nobody knows, neither the angels of the heavens nor the Son, but only the Father. For just as the days of Noah were, so the presence of the Son of man will be. . . . Keep on the watch, therefore, because you do not know on what day your Lord is coming."

They were told not only to be on the watch and to be prepared but also to watch with eagerness. Romans 8:19 says: "For the eager expectation of the creation is waiting for the revealing of the sons of God." Human nature is such that when we fervently hope and yearn for something and wait in eager expectation of it, a powerful temptation arises within us to see it at the door even when the evidence is insufficient. In our eagerness false alarms may be sounded.

What, then, will distinguish the true warning from the false ones? For the answer, please see the following article.

* Jehovah's Witnesses, in their eagerness for Jesus' second coming, have suggested dates that turned out to be incorrect. Because of this, some have called them false prophets. Never in these instances, however, did they presume to originate predictions 'in the name of Jehovah.' Never did they say, 'These are the words of Jehovah.' *The Watchtower*, the official journal of Jehovah's Witnesses, has said: "We have *not* the gift of prophecy." (January 1883, page 425) "Nor would we have our writings reverenced or regarded as infallible." (December 15, 1896, page 306) *The Watchtower* has also said that the fact that some have Jehovah's spirit "does not mean those now serving as Jehovah's witnesses are inspired. It does not mean that the writings in this magazine *The Watchtower* are inspired and infallible and without mistakes." (May 15, 1947, page 157) "*The Watchtower* does not claim to be inspired in its utterances, nor is it dogmatic." (August 15, 1950, page 263) "The brothers preparing these publications are not infallible. Their writings are not inspired as are those of Paul and the other Bible writers. (2 Tim. 3:16) And so, at times, it has been necessary, as understanding became clearer, to correct views. (Prov. 4:18)"—February 15, 1981, page 19.

Awake!

**Why *Awake!* Is Published** *Awake!* is for the enlightenment of the entire family. It shows how to cope with today's problems. It reports the news, tells about people in many lands, examines religion and science. But it does more. It probes beneath the surface and points to the real meaning behind current events, yet it always stays politically neutral and does not exalt one race above another. Most important, this magazine builds confidence in the Creator's promise of a peaceful and secure new world before the generation that saw the events of 1914 passes away.

**Would you welcome more information? Write Watch Tower at the appropriate address on page 5. This is part of a worldwide Bible educational work that is supported by voluntary donations.**

Unless otherwise indicated, *New World Translation of the Holy Scriptures—With References* is used.

*Awake!* (ISSN 0005-237X) is published semimonthly by Watchtower Bible and Tract Society of New York, Inc., 25 Columbia Heights, Brooklyn, N.Y. 11201. Second-class postage paid at Brooklyn, N.Y., and at additional mailing offices. ***Postmaster:*** Send address changes to *Awake!*, c/o Watchtower, ***Wallkill, N.Y. 12589.***
Vol. 74, No. 6 Printed in U.S.A.



A FABLE f
from Ind
phant. Tl
said: "Bless me
wall!" The sec
said: "An ele
The third tou
elephant is ve
reached out a
clear enough t
The fifth touch
vel of an eleph
seized its tail a
very like a rop
long and loud
like, but no one
complete infor
picture.

A similar pr
identifying the
sponse to his

**Semimonthly La**
Afrikaans, Arabic, Ceb
(also cassettes), Finni
an, Iloko, Italian, Japar
Slovak, Spanish, Swa

**Monthly Lang**
Chichewa, Chinese, C
Igbo, Indonesian, Kar
Guinea Pidgin, Polish,
Sesotho, Shona, Sinhal
Tsonga, Tswana,

NDOM?
ight look
sed Jews.
cting as a
Jehovah,
nations of
aim Weiz-
even lent
he chemi-
ent during
Jewish ef-
political,
National
than fur-
h, or the

istendom?
l, compos-
eds of con-
Christen-
but World
s war, and
ed therein.
ovah's sov-
kingdom,
establish-
nent, even
dless Com-
Christen-
nterpart of

ROVE TO
S
hurches of
s qualified
messenger?
ntatives of
e war they
mps. After-
p their dis-
ous friends.
rongly pro-
r it was not
drawing up
of 1919. The



Covenant of the League of Nations was made a part of that peace treaty.

When the League of Nations was proposed as an international organization for world peace and security, the bloodstained religious organizations backed it, seizing upon this circumstance as an opportunity to "save face." The Church of England and the churches of Canada supported the League, since Great Britain was the League's proposer and chief backer. In the United States of America there was the Federal Council of the Churches of Christ in America (superseded in 1950 by the National Council of the Churches of Christ in the U.S.A., a federation of 33 Protestant and Orthodox churches). On December 18, 1918, this Council sent its adopted Declaration to the American president and urged him to work for the League. The Declaration said, in part:

> "Such a League is not a mere political expedient; it is rather the political expression of the Kingdom of God on earth. . . . The Church can give a spirit of good-will, without which no League of Nations can endure. . . . The League of Nations is rooted in the Gospel. Like the Gospel, its objective is 'peace on earth, good-will toward men.'"

By accepting the League of Nations as "the political expression of the Kingdom of God on earth," the members of the Federal Council of churches were really accepting a counterfeit "Kingdom of God on earth." Why? Because Jesus Christ, the Head of the church, when on trial for his life before the Roman governor Pontius Pilate, in 33 C.E., said: "My kingdom does not belong to this world. If it did, my followers would be fighting to save me from arrest by the Jews. My kingly authority comes from elsewhere." (John 18:36, *New English Bible*) The fact that they were not, as a body, a commissioned messenger of God was made clear and their hypocrisy exposed when, twenty years later, the League of Nations was knocked out of business by the outbreak of World War II. The churches again entered into this war with all their might, encouraging their members to take part.

**WHAT IS REQUIRED OF GOD'S MESSENGER**

Therefore, when it came time for the name of Jehovah and his purposes to be declared to the people, along with God's warning that Christendom is in her "time of the end," who qualified to be commissioned? Who was willing to undertake this monumental task as Jehovah's "servant"? Was there anyone to whom Jehovah's heavenly "chariot" could roll up and whom it could confront? More accurately, was there any group on whom Jehovah would be willing to bestow the commission to speak as a "prophet" in His name, as was done toward Ezekiel back there in 613 B.C.E.? What were the qualifications?

Certainly such a messenger or "servant" group would have to be made up of persons who had not been defiled with bloodguilt as had Christendom and the rest of Babylon the Great, the world empire of false religion, by sharing in carnal warfare. In fact, they would be a group that had come out from the religious organizations of Babylon the Great. More than that, they would be persons who not only saw the hypocrisy and God-defaming action of these religions, but in addition actually rejected them and turned to Jehovah God in true worship of him as set forth in the Bible. Who would they be?

In identifying the group that is truly commissioned as God's messenger, these are points for us to consider seriously. God does not deal with persons who ignore his Word and go according to their own independent ideas. Nor does he recognize those who make a profession of serving him and at the same time associate with religions that teach God-dishonoring doc-

Only eight persons survived the flood, and now, after a few brief centuries, the earth is filled with human creatures numbering many millions and almost all of whom are wicked by reason of the Devil's influence. If only a few millions survive Armageddon, what may those few millions do under the direction of Christ Jesus during the period of the thousand-year reign? It is absolutely certain that God's mandate to fill the earth must be carried out, because he has given his word, and his word shall not return unto him void. It therefore follows that it will be fulfilled within the thousand-year period with the creatures appointed to that work.

### MARRY

If this conclusion is Scripturally correct, then it would mean that those men and women forming the "great multitude" will marry and bring forth children in righteousness and unto life. There are now on earth Jonadabs devoted to the Lord and who doubtless will prove faithful. Would it be Scripturally proper for them to now marry and to begin to rear children? No, is the answer, which is supported by the Scriptures. Referring to the prophetic picture: Noah's sons and their wives had no children before or during the flood, and none were born of them until after the flood was dried up, and the record is that it was two years after the flood before children born are mentioned. (Genesis 11:10, 11) There is no Scriptural evidence that any children were taken into the ark, but only eight persons were



taken therein: "And the Lord said unto Noah, Come thou and all thy house into the ark; for thee have I seen righteous before me in this generation." (Genesis 7:1) This is proof that the class pictured by those taken into the ark will be counted righteous by reason of their faith and obedience, and which is evidenced by their being carried over Armageddon. The Scriptures fully support the conclusion that the filling of the earth is not due to begin before, but after Armageddon. The words of Jesus further support this conclusion, to wit: "And woe unto them that are with child, and to them that give suck in those days!"—Matthew 24:19.

It is the great privilege of the Jonadabs to now see that the kingdom is here and that it is their bounden duty, if they would live, to fully support the kingdom and do what the Lord has commanded them to do, which is to seek righteousness and meekness, and to join forces with the remnant and give testimony to the world of and concerning the kingdom of God under Christ. It will be far better to be unhampered and without burdens, that they may do the Lord's will now, as the Lord commands, and also be without hindrance during Armageddon.

There are Jonadabs who are fully devoted to the Lord and his kingdom many of whom have children and may have more. What must be expected of them? The obligation is laid upon the parents to teach their children the truth of and concerning the kingdom and to thus lead them in right paths that they too may seek righteous-

forth children in righteousness to the glory of God.

Those Jonadabs who now contemplate marriage, it would seem, would do better if they wait a few years, until the fiery storm of Armageddon is gone, and to then enter the marital relationship and enjoy the blessings of participating in filling the earth with righteous and perfect children.

Let the Jonadabs now view with calmness and sobriety and with keen joy the marvelous prospect set before them. Jehovah's unchangeable mandate is that the earth shall be filled with a righteous people who, continuing in righteousness, shall receive everlasting life through Jesus Christ; furthermore, that the survivors of Armageddon, who form the great multitude, will be righteous in God's sight and will be granted the marvelous privilege of carrying out his mandate first given to Adam, and that such will be done under the supervision of the righteous ruler, Christ Jesus, who will administer life to all who receive life; that the great multitude and their children shall live for ever in peace and joy, and need never have any fear of death, but such faithful ones, together with the princes of the earth, shall fully realize the righteous government on earth wherein God's will shall be done as in heaven; all of which was made possible by the full obedience of Christ Jesus unto death and by his resurrection and his kingdom.

What should the Jonadabs do now? They should devote themselves wholly to the kingdom



interests of Christ, they should see to it that their substance is now used to the glory of God and his kingdom, and therefore should do all within their power to advance the kingdom interest. As companions of the remnant of the body of Christ now on earth the Jonadabs should join with them in actively bearing witness to the people, giving them warning and telling them of the kingdom blessings that will come to those who obey. The faithful from Abel to John looked for the coming of God's righteous government and sacrificed everything that they might have a place to live thereunder. Now the glorious kingdom is here in full sight and will soon be in full operation, and those who love God will delight now to do all within their power to make known to others the blessings of that kingdom. It is the kingdom of God under Christ now pitted against everything of Satan's organization, and the Jonadabs must align themselves uncompromisingly on the Lord's side, faithfully serving him and his kingdom at all times.

### REDEMPTION

Children born to the Jonadabs before Armageddon must come under the redemptive provision made through Christ Jesus. The parents being imperfect, such children are born with imperfections and must be taught by the parents and must be obedient to the Lord if they receive life. Children born after Armageddon likewise must belong to Christ Jesus, because he has paid the redemptive price for all, including them.

more than three primary branches, to wit, Shemitic, Japhetic and Hamitic. The Bible record shows only these three branches of the human race. (Genesis 10:1-32) Concerning all the patriarchs from Adam to Noah's father, Lamech, the Bible record is that, after each had begotten the next in line of descent, 'he begot sons and daughters.' (Genesis 5:3-30) The Bible record concerning Noah and his sons is: "And Noah was five hundred years old; and Noah begat Shem, Ham, and Japheth." (Genesis 5:32) There is no Bible record that Noah had other sons than those three sons above named, either before or after the flood and after the giving of the divine mandate to "fill the earth". As to Noah's three sons, the names of their children and grandchildren, born after the flood and after the restating the divine mandate, are set forth in the record to the number of seventy persons. (Genesis 10:1-32) There is a complete absence of anything in the record of any children's being born to these three sons before the flood, and a complete absence in the record that Noah had any children after the flood. For this reason it appears that the divine mandate to "multiply and fill the earth" does not apply to the spirit-begotten ones, that is, to the remnant, but that such as were pictured by Noah, the faithful ones who inherit the kingdom with Christ Jesus, are included in and associated with Christ Jesus, "the Everlasting Father," who administers life to all who receive life after Armageddon, including those who shall be raised from the dead.

Seeing that the divine mandate was given only to righteous men or those counted righteous by



the Lord, and that the great multitude who survive the battle of Armageddon will be the only ones of the human race to abide on the earth, and that those of the great multitude will be counted righteous by the Lord by reason of their faith and obedience, is it not reasonable and Scriptural to conclude that the members of the great multitude will carry out the divine mandate according to the will of Jehovah God under the immediate command and direction of Christ? The question then arises, Since the Lord is now gathering his "other sheep", who will form the great multitude, should those begin now to marry and bring forth children in fulfillment of the divine mandate? No, is the answer; which the Scriptures fully support. The sons of Noah and their wives had no children during the flood. There is no evidence that any children were taken into the ark. Only eight persons came forth from the ark, and that is conclusive proof that no children were born to Noah's sons either before the flood or during the flood. (Genesis 7:13; 8:16) In the prophetic picture it is shown that no children were born to Noah's sons and their wives until after the flood, and the first one mentioned was born two years after the flood. (Genesis 11:10) The apostle Peter, under inspiration of the holy spirit, corroborates this when he says: "The ark . . . wherein few, that is, eight souls were saved by water." The conclusion, therefore, seems inevitable that the beginning of the fulfillment of the divine mandate is after Armageddon. In support of this conclusion the words of Jesus relating to Armageddon are here set forth, to wit: "And woe unto them

# HOW ARE YOU USING YOUR LIFE?

IS IT not apparent that most of mankind are living their lives for themselves? They are using their lives as *they* see fit, without concern for others. But what about us? The apostle Paul wrote to fellow servants of Jehovah, saying: "None of us, in fact, lives with regard to himself only, and no one dies with regard to himself only; for both if we live, we live to Jehovah, and if we die, we die to Jehovah. Therefore both if we live and if we die, we belong to Jehovah."—Rom. 14:7, 8.

This is something for all of us to give serious thought to: It would be entirely inappropriate for us, while professing to be Jehovah's people, to try to live our lives with regard to ourselves only. As the apostle Paul wrote: "You do not belong to yourselves, for you were bought with a price. By all means, glorify God."—1 Cor. 6:19, 20.

Are we not thankful that Jehovah God has purchased us and that we now belong to Him? He has bought us with the life of his own dear Son so that eternal death does not have to be our lot, but we have before us the opportunity to enjoy everlasting life. (John 3:16, 36) How are you affected by this loving provision of God? Does it not cause you to want to show Jehovah your deep appreciation? The apostle Peter noted that if we have the proper mental disposition we will be moved to "live the remainder of [our] time in the flesh, no more for the desires of men, *but for God's will*."—1 Pet. 4:2.

Is that what you are doing? Are you living no longer simply to satisfy personal ambitions or desires, but to do God's will? Are there ways in which you could share more fully in doing the will of God?

### *God's Will for Us*

Jehovah makes clear in his Word that his will for us today includes accomplishing a great work of Kingdom-preaching before the end of this system comes. (Matt. 24:14) Jesus Christ did a similar work. He said: "Also to other cities I must declare the good news of the kingdom of God, *because for this I was sent forth*."—Luke 4:43.

Jesus did not hold back, but was whole-souled in his service to God. When we read the historical accounts of his ministry in the Gospels, how impressed we are with his energy and zeal in doing the Kingdom-preaching! Jesus knew that he had only a short time, and he did not spare himself in finishing his assignment. Should we not today be imitating his example, especially since we have such a short time left now in which to complete the Kingdom-preaching?

Yes, the end of this system is so very near! Is that not reason to increase our activity? In this regard we can learn something from a runner who puts on a final burst of speed near the finish of a race. Look at Jesus, who apparently stepped up his activity during his final days on earth. In fact, over 27 percent of the material in the Gospels is devoted to just the last week of Jesus' earthly ministry!—Matt. 21:1–27:50; Mark 11:1–15:37; Luke 19:29–23:46; John 11:55–19:30.

By carefully and prayerfully examining our own circumstances, we also may find that we can spend more time and energy in preaching during this final period before the present system ends. Many of our brothers and sisters are doing just that. This is evident from the rapidly increasing number of pioneers.

Yes, since the summer of 1973 there have been new peaks in pioneers every month. Now there are 20,394 regular and special pioneers in the United States, an all-time peak. That is 5,190 more than there were in February 1973! A 34-percent increase! Does that not warm our hearts? Reports are heard of brothers selling their homes and property and planning to finish out the rest of their days in this old system in the pioneer service. Certainly this is a fine way to spend the short time remaining before the wicked world's end.—1 John 2:17.

Circumstances such as poor health or responsibilities in connection with your family may limit what you can do in the field ministry. And yet, the pioneer ranks include many who have health limitations, as well as some persons with families. But these broth-

going in the way
istians cannot af
it in its mad race
and finally death
hey cannot slow
own, take time out
travel side roads,
r follow others
ho do not know
here they are go-
ig. Yet, this is ex-
ctly what Chris-
ians would be
oing if they partic-
pated in office par-
ies and company
onventions or out-
igs where, because
f their association,
to let down their
ace of employment
d by fellow work-
ve sporting groups
of our time for Bi-
hing the good news
his is unnecessary
t can influence us
ons and can easily
rality. The Watch
Society has in its
h cases.

e of us are exempt
e influence of this
age are surrounded
is by no means an
s immorality among
on exams, stealing,
e and rebelliousness
ther authority. The
h is to be accepted
be accepted as one
ould mean lowering

l have what influence
Christian school student
Standing firm for wha
ction from other youths?



your standards, being influenced to think and act without regard for Bible principles. When you stand up for what is right and conduct yourself as a Christian, fellow students will often be cutting and at times vicious in voicing their disapproval. They may call you a "square," a "religious bug," and many other even more unkind things. Because you will not let the barrier down, you are not invited to various functions in school and in the neighborhood and are more or less left alone. Be thankful for this, for it is actually a protection for you. Wisely continue to stick to what is right. Keep in mind Exodus 23:2, which says, "You must not follow after the crowd for evil ends." You know the evil that is being practiced. Do not let it or those who practice it influence your decisions. Do you want to be a minister of God's Word? Then take the right course!

[12] The influence and spirit of this world is to get ahead, to make a name for oneself. Many schools now have student counselors who encourage one to pursue higher education after high school, to pursue a career with a future in this system of things. Do not be influenced by them. Do not let them "brainwash" you with the Devil's propaganda to get ahead, to make something of yourself in this world. This world has very little time left! Any "future" this world offers is no future! Wisely, then, let God's Word influence you in selecting a course that will result in your protection and blessing. Make pioneer service, the full-time ministry, with the possibility of Bethel or missionary service your goal. This is a life that offers an everlasting future!

12. How does the world view higher education, and how should we reason on this?

DECISIONS CHRISTIANS FACE

[13] Now that we have discussed the influences that we must guard against in making decisions, let us turn our attention to some of the decisions we must make and to those things that will influence our decisions for good. It is vital that we build a pattern of making right decisions in our everyday life. Some of the decisions we face each day may seem small and unimportant, having little to do with our receiving everlasting life. But does not God's Word counsel, "The person faithful in what is least is faithful also in much"? (Luke 16:10) If we can be influenced to disregard Bible principles in making small, everyday decisions, then what assurance do we have that, when we are faced with the necessity of making a decision affecting our everlasting welfare, we will suddenly reverse the trend and decide in harmony with Bible principles?

[14] Then there are vital decisions that may arise very unexpectedly. Suppose we were involved in an accident and were faced with the decision of whether to submit to blood transfusion either for ourself or for one of our family. Are we convinced in our heart that we could undergo and withstand the pressure from doctors and unbelieving friends and relatives? Are we prepared to take a firm, unshakable stand because of our knowing what God's Word says, although death may face us? Many of our Christian brothers and sisters have already been faced with this sobering decision.

[15] There is also the matter of neutrality. More and more the emotional tide of nationalism is increasing its demands toward

13. Why should we never be careless in making small decisions?
14. (a) What issue could arise that would demand an on-the-spot decision? (b) What should we consider now?
15. The influence of nationalism poses what question to us all, and how real is this issue?

## DIALOGUE FIVE: How Honest Is The Watchtower About Its History? —Parts 1 and 2



picture of the old world's children in Christendom.—2 Cor. 3:15; 4:4, 6.

² What a contrast when we look at the children of the New World society of Jehovah's witnesses! They carry a lamp too, the same lamp in fact, God's written Word. But as it is written in Psalm 119:105 (*AS*): "Thy word is a lamp unto my feet, and light unto my path." Why is it they have light whereas the children of Christendom do not? Both have the same lamp, God's Word, the Bible. Where is the difference? The answer is that they looked with unveiled faces at the gleaming Word of the heavenly Father and they also accepted enlightening instruction through his motherly organization. As it is written at Proverbs 6:20, 23 (*RS*): "My son, keep your father's commandment, and forsake not your mother's teaching. For the commandment is a lamp and the teaching a light, and the reproofs of discipline are the way of life."

³ Consider that for a moment. Two things are mentioned: the commandment of the father and the teaching or law of the mother. Then the proverb explains that the commandment of the father is a burning lamp but that there is light also from the teaching or law of the mother. The world is full of Bibles, which Book contains the commandments of God. Why, then, do the people not know which way to go? Because they do not also have the teaching or law of the mother, which is light. Jehovah God has provided his holy written Word for all mankind and it contains all the information that is needed for men in taking a course leading to life. But God has not arranged for that Word to speak independently or to shine forth life-giving truths by itself. His Word says: "Light is sown for the righteous." (Ps. 97:11) It is through his organization that God provides this light that the proverb says is the teaching or law of the mother. If we are to walk in the light of truth we must recognize not only Jehovah God as our Father but his organization as our mother.

⁴ Some who call themselves Christians and who claim God as their Father boast that they walk with God alone, that he directs their steps personally. Such persons not only forsake the teaching or law of the mother, but they literally throw God's woman out into the streets. The light of God's truth is not for them. In the nation of Israel Jehovah made obedience to parents mandatory. "Honor your father and your mother" was the fifth commandment of the Ten. (Ex. 20:2-17; Deut. 5:16, *NW*) The reward for obedience was long life; for disobedience, death. "In case a man should happen to have a son who is stubborn and rebellious, he not listening to the voice of his father or the voice of his mother, and they have corrected him but he will not listen to them, then . . . all the men of his city must stone him with stones and he must die." (Deut. 21:18-21, *NW*) Such honor and obedience was required not only as due the immediate parents in the flesh but also as rightfully belonging to the older men of influence in Israel. Failure to render such proper respect to Elisha, the prophet of Jehovah, brought upon a gang of juvenile delinquents the just sentence of speedy execution. (2 Ki. 2:24) Today, also, God requires and exacts from his children obedience, honor and respect. These must be rendered not only to the living God himself, but to his wifely organization as well.

### IDENTIFYING THE MOTHER ORGANIZATION

⁵ The real mother of Christians is not

2. In what significant way do the New World society's children differ from Christendom's?
3. What is required of those who would have light from the Bible?
4. To what extent were the Israelites required to honor father and mother? and to what extent are Christians today?
5. How does Paul identify the true mother of Christians?

MAY 1, [...]

and can [...] show thi[...] of fleshly [...] or Christ[...] lem abov[...] (Gal. 4:[...] a proph[...] prophecy [...] Isaiah w[...] tity of th[...] five and [...] husband; [...] the Holy [...] . . . For [...] forsaken [...] way Pau[...] invisible [...] er of Chr[...]

⁶ Then [...] between [...] ible the[...] World s[...] spect du[...] of Isaiah [...] six, vers[...] the man[...] Christ J[...] children, [...] curred i[...] (*AS*) it [...] day? sh[...] once? fo[...] brought [...] tells the [...] time on [...] land tha[...] on earth [...] in a Ne[...] for Jeho[...] service t[...] the rem[...] from Ba[...] lished ne[...]

6. (a) Wha[...] salem above [...] in Isaiah 6[...] they to be [...]

5/1/1957

ssue: 8,000,000

nguages

an Swahili
inese Swedish
ean Tagalog
igasy Thai
wegian Xhosa
uguese Yoruba
tho Zulu
ish

pango Slovenian
gasinan Tamil
amento Tshiluba
sh Tswana
lan Turkish
ar-Leyte Twi
oan Ukrainian
o Urdu
di Vietnamese
lan
i
alese

subscription rates for semi-
y editions in local currency
. 11201 $1.50
.W. 2135 $1.50
rio M6A 1Z5 $1.50
London NW7 1RN 75p
£1.90
and S $1.50
gos State N1.05
P8
ein, Transvaal R1,10
above rates.)

the office in your country.

s before subscription expires.
and at additional mailing

rty days before your moving
ossible, your old address la-
yn, New York 11201, U.S.A.

ver" is the modern-language
," unless otherwise indicated.
Printed in U.S.A.

# Can You Be True to God, YET HIDE THE FACTS?

WHAT results when a lie is let go unchallenged? Does not silence help the lie to pass as truth, to have freer sway to influence many, perhaps to their serious harm?

What happens when misconduct and immorality are allowed to go unexposed and uncondemned? Is this not like covering over an infection without any effort to cure it and keep it from spreading?

When persons are in great danger from a source that they do not suspect or are being misled by those they consider their friends, is it an unkindness to warn them? They may prefer not to believe the warning. They may even resent it. But does that free one from the moral responsibility to give that warning?

If you are among those seeking to be faithful to God, the issues these questions raise are vital for you today. Why? Because God's servants in every period of history have had to face up to the challenge these issues present. They have had to expose falsehood and wrongdoing and warn people of dangers and deception—not just in a general way, but in a specific way, in the interest of pure worship. It would have been far easier to keep silent or say only what people wanted to hear. But faithfulness to God and love of neighbor moved them to speak. They realized that "better is a revealed reproof than a concealed love."—Prov. 27:5.

**WOULD YOU RATHER HAVE THE TRUTH COVERED OVER . . . ?**

### THE CONTINUING PATTERN

Consider the situation in ancient Israel and the example that God's prophets then set. Wrongdoing became rampant in that nation. Dishonesty, violence, immorality and hypocrisy disgraced the name of the God whom the Israelites claimed to worship. Did the people welcome divine correction? To the contrary, the Bible shows that they said this to God's prophets:

> "'You must not see,' and to the ones having [inspired] visions, 'You must not envision for us any straightforward things. Speak to us smooth things; envision deceptive things. Turn aside from the way; deviate from the path.'"—Isa. 30:9-11.

The majority of the religious leaders sought popularity by doing just that, condoning and "whitewashing" the wrongdoing and violation of God's righteous standards and ways. But God's instructions to his true prophets are exemplified by what he said to the prophet Ezekiel:

> "Now as regards you, O son of man, a watchman is what I have made you to

**. . . OR DO YOU WANT TO KNOW THE FACTS?**

dictated a thou-
ınaged every de-
evangelistic cam-
kers and person-
amazing Biblical

ı amazing record
blisher. One can
e practically wore
ous work that he
nired. I can imag-
the organization

sed for some time.
ımber of his close
oke of their great
funeral talk, deliv-
d, this tribute was

a fertile brain, and
oted to the Lord, he
f his power to teach
Messiah's Kingdom
it will bring to the

BSERVATION

r Russell was not
istendom. Some of
d him in death al-
ı he was alive; and
ir attacks that prej-
ne still lingers. In
he facts speak for
strated in this im-
vritten over forty

g that no Pittsburgh
o much as contained
aze Russell, since his
the widest of any man
ty, not even excepting

major religious move-
in the Pittsburgh dis-
rs, a movement which
scope and is still one

, Press, Aug. 23, 1953, Mag-
p. 356-359. k Ibid., p. 373;
83, 384, for reproduction of
burgh, Pa., January 6, 1917.



of the fastest growing religious organizations in many countries. . . .

Pastor Russell, . . . a name as sincerely loved and as bitterly hated as almost any in American history.

Around that name for years raged some of the bitterest controversies which ever divided the Christian world, and the controversies still rage, although his name is not so much heard in the discussions. . . .

All through his life, he had told his followers not to revere him as more than just a fellow man with divine guidance. And he taught them this so well that his work passed into the hands of others with hardly a moment's halt and the publishing house which he founded has never published a biography of Pastor Russell.[1]

LOIS: Perhaps the fact that his name has been ignored by the world is in his favor. It would seem that all of God's servants in times past were considered of little importance in the eyes of the world, yet their works continue. That pattern certainly seems to have been the same in Pastor Russell's life, doesn't it? But, is it true you have never published a biography of Pastor Russell?

JOHN: That's right. Jehovah's witnesses admire the qualities he possessed as a man, but were we to give the honor and credit to Pastor Russell, we would be saying that the works and success were his; but Jehovah's witnesses believe it is God's spirit that guides and directs his people.

Some have stumbled over that point; and these qualities that he possessed and that were so admired by many in the organization at that time were to provide a real test that caused them to fail in their endurance and seek an occasion against Russell's successor as president of the Watch Tower Society, J. F. Rutherford, and against the Society itself.

1 *Where Else but Pittsburgh!* by George Swetnam (Pittsburgh, Pa., 1958: Davis & Warde, Inc.), pp. 110, 116.

CHARLES T. RUSSELL IN 1906

JOSEPH F. RUTHERFORD IN 1915

JEHOVAH'S WITNESSES IN THE DIVINE PURPOSE, 1959

To the King of Kings and Lord of Lords

IN THE INTEREST OF

HIS CONSECRATED SAINTS,

WAITING FOR THE ADOPTION.

—AND OF—

"ALL THAT IN EVERY PLACE CALL UPON THE LORD"

"THE HOUSEHOLD OF FAITH"

—AND OF—

THE GROANING CREATION, TRAVAILING AND WAITING FOR THE

MANIFESTATION OF THE SONS OF GOD

THIS WORK IS DEDICATED.

"To make all see what is the fellowship of the mystery which from the beginning of the world hath been hid in God." "Wherein He hath abounded toward us in all wisdom and prudence, having made known unto us the mystery of His will, according to His good pleasure which He hath purposed in Himself; that in the dispensation of the fulness of the times He might gather together in one all things, under Christ."

Ephesians 3:4, 5, 9; 1:8-10.



WATCH TOWER BIBLE & TRACT SOCIETY
BROOKLYN, N. Y., U. S. A.
Written in 1886 by Pastor Russell
Made in U. S. A.

N. B.—This volume can also be supplied in the Arabic, Armenian, Dano-Norwegian, Finnish, French, German, Greek, Hollandish, Hungarian, Italian, Polish, Roumanian, Slovak, Spanish, Swedish, and Ukrainian languages.

1925

## Biography of Pastor Russell

CHARLES TAZE RUSSELL, known the world over as Pastor Russell, author, lecturer and minister of the Gospel, was born at Pittsburgh, Pa., February 16, 1852; died October 31, 1916. He was the son of Joseph L. and Eliza Birney Russell, both of Scotch-Irish lineage. He was educated in the common schools and under private tutors. Author of "OBJECT AND MANNER OF OUR LORD'S RETURN," "FOOD FOR THINKING CHRISTIANS," "TABERNACLE SHADOWS," "THE DIVINE PLAN OF THE AGES," "THE TIME IS AT HAND," "THY KINGDOM COME," "BATTLE OF ARMAGEDDON," "THE ATONEMENT," "THE NEW CREATION," "WHAT SAY THE SCRIPTURES ABOUT HELL," "SPIRITISM," "OLD THEOLOGY TRACTS," "THE PHOTO-DRAMA OF CREATION," et cetera, et cetera.

Pastor Russell was married in 1879 to Maria Frances Ackley. No children blessed this union. Seventeen years later they disagreed about the management of his journal; and a separation followed.

Reared under the influence of Christian parents, at an early age he became interested in theology, united himself with the Congregational church, and became active in local mission work. The doctrine of eternal torment of all mankind except the few elect became so abhorrent to him that at the age af seventeen he was a skeptic. He said: "A God that would use his power to create human beings whom he foreknew and predestinated should be eternally tormented, could be neither wise, just nor loving. His standard would be lower than that of many men." He continued to believe, however,

1

THE DIVINE PLAN OF THE AGES, 1886, 1925 edition

*On October 31, 1916, 64-year-old Charles Taze Russell died on a train at Pampa, Texas; many newspapers reported on the funeral*

After funeral services at The Temple in New York and at Carnegie Hall in Pittsburgh, Brother Russell was buried at Allegheny, in the Bethel family plot, according to his request. A brief biography of Russell along with his will and testament was published in *The Watch Tower* of December 1, 1916, as well as in subsequent editions of the first volume of *Studies in the Scriptures*.

What would happen now? It was difficult for the Bible Students to imagine someone else in Brother Russell's place. Would their understanding of the Scriptures continue to be progressive, or would it stop where it was? Would they become a sect centered around him? Russell himself had made it quite clear that he expected the work to go on. So following his death, some obvious questions soon arose: Who will supervise the contents of *The Watch Tower* and other publications? Who should succeed Russell as president?

## A Change in Administration

In his will Brother Russell outlined an arrangement for an Editorial Committee of five to determine the contents of *The Watch Tower*.* In ad-

* The five members of the Editorial Committee as named in Russell's will were William E. Page, William E. Van Amburgh, Henry Clay Rockwell, E. W. Brenneisen, and F. H. Robison. In addition, to fill any vacancies, others were named—A. E. Burgess, Robert Hirsh, Isaac Hoskins, G. H. Fisher, J. F. Rutherford, and John Edgar. Page and Brenneisen, however, promptly resigned—Page because he could not take up residence in Brooklyn, and Brenneisen (later the spelling was changed to Brenisen) because he had to take up secular work to support his family. Rutherford and Hirsh, whose names were listed in the December 1, 1916, *Watch Tower*, replaced them as members of the Editorial Committee.

A TIME OF T

dition, the
made arra
W. E. Van
of all the
rectors.* V
would be
months lat

At firs
encouragin
*Watch Tow*
written bef
began to m
of their ch
respect for
his qualitie
dents, how
which Russ

As the
would succ
reported th
son, with v
love for Brc
from friend
er J. F. Rutl
sympathy w
and seconde
the ballot as
choice of th

With th
*Watch Towe.*
prayed earne
election; anc
lieving that
prayers. Perf

That "p
president wa

* According t
posed of seven n
tors to fill a vaca
A. N. Pierson to
W. E. Van Ambu
erford. The sever

JEHOVAH'S WITNESSES - PROCLAIMERS OF GOD'S KINGDOM, 1993

But persecutions only stirred him to greater efforts in the cause of the King of kings, knowing, as he did, that such persecutions are evidences that the night is drawing on when no man can work. Without murmur or complaint, early and late, in winter and in summer, in heat and in cold, in season and out of season, amidst storms and in sunshine, as a mighty giant he fought on to the goal, never faltering or looking back. Truly, he died a hero, and died in the harness! "Precious in the sight of the Lord is the death of His saints." Truly at the close of his earthly career, as such a hero, he could say:

"I have fought my way through;
I have finished the work
Thou didst give me to do."

Silently listening we hear the response from the Throne of the Lord and Master:

"Well and faithfully done;
Enter into My joy and sit
Down on My Throne!"

Is his work finished? Ah, no indeed! Of such faithful ones who die during the presence of the Lord the Great Master said, "Blessed are the dead which die in the Lord from henceforth; yea, saith the Spirit, that they may rest from their labors; and their works do follow them."—Revelation 14:13.

THE PRESENCE OF THE LORD

The work that Pastor Russell did was not his work alone, but it was and is the Lord's work. It was Jesus who said that at His coming He would gird Himself and cause His servants to sit down at meat; and that He would come forth and serve them.—Luke 12:37.

For forty years the Lord has been present, feeding those who have been hungering and thirsting for righteousness. For forty years Pastor Russell—that faithful servant of the Lord—has set forth clear and unmistakable evidence of the presence of the Master. He nailed the banner of Christ's presence on the title page of THE WATCH TOWER; and it shall never come down until the Kingdom is known in the earth. The flood of Present Truth has been rising for more than forty years, and it is rising higher and higher. As well might the enemies of the Truth seek with a common broom to sweep back the waves of the mighty Atlantic as to try to suppress the flood of Truth that is rising now. In spite of all the opposition that can be brought to bear, it will continue to rise until, as the Prophet declares, "the knowledge of the glory of the Lord shall fill the whole earth as the waters fill the deep"; until such time as it will not be necessary for any man to teach his neighbor, saying, Know ye the Lord: for all shall know Him, from the least unto the greatest."—Isa. 11:9; Jer. 31:34.

The thousands of Christian men and women in the earth today who have fought by the side of Pastor Russell have not been blindly following him. They have followed the Lord; they have followed Pastor Russell only as he followed the Lord. Recognizing him as the special servant of the Lord, they have fought by his side as his brethren, looking to Jesus, the Captain of their salvation: and having thus started in the fight, they will fight on until every one of the Kingdom class has gained the victory.

A PERSONAL TRIBUTE TO THE PASTOR

I cannot pass this moment without paying a personal tribute to Pastor Russell. He was my friend, and a true friend indeed. It is written, "A true friend loves you all the time." I loved him; I know he loved me. Long before I knew Pastor Russell, he had done much for me. While I was engaged in the law practice in the Middle West, there came into my office one day a lady, bearing some books in her arms. She was modest, gentle and kind. I thought she was poor, and that it was my privilege and duty to help her. I found that she was rich in faith in God. I bought the books and afterwards read them. Up to that time I knew nothing about the Bible; I had never heard of Pastor Russell. I did not even know that he was the author of the books at the time I read them; but I know that the wonderfully sweet, harmonious explanation of the Plan of God thrilled my heart and changed the course of my life from doubt to joy.

Why should not I love him? I know that he loved me. A little incident illustrates this: Several years ago he requested me to go on a mission of importance. After talking with him I said, "Brother Russell, I feel that I cannot do it." He answered, "Yes you can, by the Lord's grace." I said, "I am willing to try." "Go on," he replied, "and I will pray God to give you the wisdom." "I went"; and having succeeded far beyond my expectations I returned and gave him a report. Seated in his study, as I went over the report in detail, his face lighted up with joy; and like a loving father he rose and put his arms around me, drew me to him and kissed me, saying, "Brother, I love you very much." I have walked with him; I have talked with him; I have eaten with him; I have slept with him; I have been with him through trials and triumphs; I have seen him in storm and in sunshine. Amidst all of these I have marked his complete joy in the Lord, his magnanimous heart, and his absolute loyalty and devotion to the Lord and to His cause. Gentle, kind, fearless and affectionate, magnanimous, sincere and filled with the spirit of the Lord, he was a giant of power in the world. I count it the greatest honor that I have known to have had Pastor Russell for my true and loyal friend, and that I have been privileged to be associated with him.

I will relate to you an incident that throws some light on his sweet relationship with the Lord. For more than a year prior to his death he suffered a great deal of physical pain, yet never did he murmur. His great desire was to have the approval of the Lord and Master. He spoke the Master's name in loving terms, and his face lighted when he mentioned the Lord. A few weeks prior to this last illness, speaking to one whom he loved very dearly and in whom he had great confidence, he said, "I have had such a longing desire to be embraced by the Lord Jesus, to think of myself as the woman, or bride, and to have the Master press me to His bosom. I have prayed earnestly to the Lord that I might experience this sweet relationship, and He has given me this assurance that I do enjoy that sweet relationship." Truly the Lord loved him m[illegible]! Truly for him to live was for Christ to live!

God's Book is written for those who are loyal to Him. His promises are to such. Among these sweet promises are the words of the Master: "Be thou faithful unto death, and I will give thee the Crown of Life." "These shall be kings and priests unto God and unto Christ and shall reign with Him." Long ago God caused the Sweet Singer to record in His holy Book, concerning the faithful and loyal followers of Christ Jesus, these sweet words:

"The king shall joy in Thy strength, O Lord: and in Thy salvation how greatly shall he rejoice. Thou hast given him his heart's desire, and hast not withholden the request of his lips. Selah. For Thou preventest him with the blessings of goodness; Thou settest a crown of pure gold on his head. He asked life of Thee, and Thou gavest it him, even length of days forever and ever. His glory is great in Thy salvation: honour and majesty hast thou laid upon him, for Thou hast made him most blessed forever: Thou hast made him exceeding glad with Thy countenance."—Psalm 21:1-6.

Truly these words fittingly apply to our beloved Brother and Pastor!

Charles Taze Russell, thou hast, by the Lord, been crowned a king; and through the everlasting ages thy name shall be known amongst the people, and thy enemies shall come and worship at thy feet.

We take the last view of this piece of clay that so faithfully bore the banner of the King. He has been a true, loyal, faithful ambassador of Christ. Thanks be to God, he has entered into his everlasting reward. The greatest desire of our lives is that we, together with him, may soon be forever with the Lord and participate in blessing all the families of the earth. God help us, as we here renew our consecration, to keep it faithfully to the end.

We sorrow not for him who has gone, because we know he has entered into his everlasting joy. For him we rejoice; but we sorrow for ourselves. Yet trusting in the Lord we will continue to fight the good fight of faith.

Scriptures, the Christian can be helped to avoid what displeases God and to do what pleases him.

**LIBERTY.** See FREEDOM; JUBILEE.

**LIBNAH** (Lib'nah) [from a root meaning "white"; or, possibly, "storax tree"].

1. An Israelite wilderness encampment. Its location is unknown.—Nu 33:20, 21.

2. A royal Canaanite city taken by Joshua before the conquest of Lachish. (Jos 10:29-32, 39; 12:15) Libnah was one of the cities in the territory of Judah given to "the sons of Aaron." (Jos 15:21, 42; 21:13; 1Ch 6:57) Centuries later King Josiah's father-in-law lived there.—2Ki 23:31; 24:18; Jer 52:1.

At the time of the Edomite revolt in the tenth century B.C.E., Libnah also rebelled against Judean King Jehoram. (2Ki 8:22; 2Ch 21:10) In 732 B.C.E., Assyrian King Sennacherib's army moved from Lachish to Libnah. He had sent a military detachment from Lachish to threaten Jerusalem. While at Libnah, the Assyrians received reports that Tirhakah the king of Ethiopia intended to fight them. Therefore, Sennacherib, to encourage Jerusalem's surrender, sent messengers a second time with intimidating letters to Hezekiah the king of Judah. Subsequently Jehovah's angel slew 185,000 of the Assyrian host, apparently still encamped near Libnah.—2Ki 19:8-35; Isa 37:8-36.

Tell es-Safi has been suggested as a possible identification of ancient Libnah. However, since the weight of evidence points to identifying Tell es-Safi with Gath, contemporary scholars tend to identify Libnah with Tell Bornat (Tel Burena), about 8 km (5 mi) NNE of Lachish.

**LIBNI** (Lib'ni) [from a root meaning "white"].

1. A grandson of Levi and the son of Gershon (Gershom). (Ex 6:17; 1Ch 6:17) He was the founder of a Levitical family (Nu 3:18, 21; 1Ch 6:19, 20) and was evidently also called Ladan.—1Ch 23:6, 7; 26:21.

2. A Levite who descended from Merari through Mahli.—1Ch 6:29.

**LIBNITES** [Of (Belonging to) Libni]. A family of Levites who descended from Gershon (Gershom) through his son Libni.—Nu 3:21; 26:58.

**LIBYA** (Lib'y·a), **LIBYANS** (Lib'y·ans). Ancient Libya occupied an area of northern Africa W of Egypt. Its inhabitants are generally thought to have been designated by the Hebrew term *Lu·vim'*. (2Ch 12:3; "Libyans," *LXX, NW, RS*) If *Lu·vim'* is a variant of *Leha·vim'* (Lehabim), this may indicate that at least some of the Libyans descended from Ham through Mizraim. (Ge 10:13) The traditional Jewish view found in the writings of Josephus (*Jewish Antiquities*, I, 130-132 [vi, 2]) makes the Libyans descendants of Ham through Put. (Ge 10:6) Also, the Greek *Septuagint* and the Latin *Vulgate* read "Libyans" in Jeremiah 46:9, Ezekiel 27:10, and 38:5 where the Hebrew text says "Put." It is possible, of course, that descendants of both Put and Mizraim settled in the geographic region of northern Africa that came to be called Libya. This would mean that the designation "Libyans" is more comprehensive than the Hebrew term *Lu·vim'*.

Egypt's King Shishak, regarded as the founder of the "Libyan dynasty," captured numerous cities when he invaded Judah in the fifth year of King Rehoboam (993 B.C.E.). His powerful force of chariots and horsemen included Libyans. Although Jerusalem itself was spared, Shishak stripped the city of its treasures. (1Ki 14:25, 26; 2Ch 12:2-9) About 26 years later (967 B.C.E.), the Libyans were represented among the troops of Zerah the Ethiopian, which penetrated Judah but suffered humiliating defeat. (2Ch 14:9-13; 16:8) In the seventh century B.C.E., the assistance of the Libyans and others was seemingly of no avail in saving the Egyptian city of No-amon from calamity at the hands of the Assyrians. (Na 3:7-10) It was foretold that the Libyans and Ethiopians would be at the "steps" of the "king of the north," implying that these former supporters of Egypt would come under his control.—Da 11:43.

In the year 33 C.E., among the Jews and proselytes at Jerusalem for the Festival of Pentecost were persons from "the parts of Libya, which is toward Cyrene," that is, the western part of Libya. Likely some of these were baptized in response to Peter's discourse and later carried the message of Christianity back to the land of their residence. —Ac 2:10.

**LIE.** The opposite of truth. Lying generally involves saying something false to a person who is entitled to know the truth and doing so with the intent to deceive or to injure him or another person. A lie need not always be verbal. It can also be expressed in action, that is, a person may be living a lie. The Hebrew verb that conveys the idea of speaking that which is untrue is *ka·zav'*. (Pr 14:5) Another Hebrew verb *sha·qar'* means "deal or act falsely," and the noun form is rendered "lie; deception; falsehood." (Le 19:11; Ps 44:17; Le 19:12; Ps 33:17; Isa 57:4) Hebrew *shaw'*, at times rendered "untruth; falsehood," basically refers to

something worthless, v
5:20; Ps 60:11; 89:47; Z
*ka·chash'* (deceive) evid
ing "prove disappointin
Greek term *pseu'dos* an
with lying and falsehoo

The father, or origin
Devil. (Joh 8:44) His lie
serpent to the first wom
death to her and to her
16-19) That first lie was
wrong desire. It was de
and obedience of the fir
who had presented him
benefactor. (Compare 2
cious lies uttered since
been a reflection of selfi
People have told lies to
ment, to profit at the e
gain or maintain certain
wards, or the praise of r

Especially serious hav
as they have endangered
deceived by them. Said
scribes and Pharisees,
traverse sea and dry lar
and when he becomes or
for Gehenna twice as m
23:15) The exchange of
the falsehood of idolatr
become a practicer of wl
—Ro 1:24-32.

The case of the religic
the time of Jesus' eart
can happen when one a
schemed to have Jesus p
he was resurrected, they
had guarded the tomb s
truth and spread a lie ab
Jesus' body.—Mt 12:14;
Mr 14:1; Lu 20:19.

Jehovah God cannot lie
and he hates "a false tong
to the Israelites required
resulting from deception
6:2-7; 19:11, 12) And a
testimony was to receive
desired to inflict upon a
lies. (De 19:15-21) God's
as reflected in the Law,
desiring to gain his appro
practice of lying. (Ps 5:6;
3:11; Re 21:8, 27; 22:15)
lie, claiming to love God
er. (1Jo 4:20, 21) For p

INSIGHT ON THE SCRIPTURES, vol. 2, 1988

m′ (Lehabim), this may
of the Libyans descend-
zraim. (Ge 10:13) The
und in the writings of
ties, I, 130-132 [vi, 2])
dants of Ham through
eek *Septuagint* and the
ins" in Jeremiah 46:9,
here the Hebrew text
of course, that descen-
Mizraim settled in the
ern Africa that came to
d mean that the desig-
omprehensive than the

egarded as the founder
ptured numerous cities
n the fifth year of King
His powerful force of
included Libyans. Al-
was spared, Shishak
easures. (1Ki 14:25, 26;
rs later (967 B.C.E.), the
d among the troops of
h penetrated Judah but
t. (2Ch 14:9-13; 16:8) In
E., the assistance of the
seemingly of no avail in
of No-amon from calam-
Assyrians. (Na 3:7-10)
Libyans and Ethiopians
the "king of the north,"
er supporters of Egypt
ntrol.—Da 11:43.
ong the Jews and prose-
e Festival of Pentecost
parts of Libya, which is
e western part of Libya.
e baptized in response to
r carried the message of
land of their residence.

uth. Lying generally in-
false to a person who is
h and doing so with the
jure him or another per-
s be verbal. It can also be
s, a person may be living
that conveys the idea of
ntrue is *ka·zav′*. (Pr 14:5)
a·qar′ means "deal or act
rm is rendered "lie; de-
9:11; Ps 44:17; Le 19:12;
ew *shaw′*, at times ren-
od," basically refers to



something worthless, vain, valueless. (Ps 12:2; De 5:20; Ps 60:11; 89:47; Zec 10:2) The Hebrew verb *ka·chash′* (deceive) evidently has the basic meaning "prove disappointing." (Le 19:11; Ho 9:2) The Greek term *pseu′dos* and related words have to do with lying and falsehood.

The father, or originator, of lying is Satan the Devil. (Joh 8:44) His lie conveyed by means of a serpent to the first woman Eve ultimately brought death to her and to her husband Adam. (Ge 3:1-5, 16-19) That first lie was rooted in selfishness and wrong desire. It was designed to divert the love and obedience of the first human pair to the liar, who had presented himself as an angel of light, a benefactor. (Compare 2Co 11:14.) All other malicious lies uttered since that time have likewise been a reflection of selfishness and wrong desire. People have told lies to escape deserved punishment, to profit at the expense of others, and to gain or maintain certain advantages, material rewards, or the praise of men.

Especially serious have been the religious lies, as they have endangered the future life of persons deceived by them. Said Jesus Christ: "Woe to you, scribes and Pharisees, hypocrites! because you traverse sea and dry land to make one proselyte, and when he becomes one you make him a subject for Gehenna twice as much so as yourselves." (Mt 23:15) The exchange of God's truth for "the lie," the falsehood of idolatry, can cause a person to become a practicer of what is degrading and vile. —Ro 1:24-32.

The case of the religious leaders of Judaism in the time of Jesus' earthly ministry shows what can happen when one abandons the truth. They schemed to have Jesus put to death. Then, when he was resurrected, they bribed the soldiers who had guarded the tomb so they would conceal the truth and spread a lie about the disappearance of Jesus' body.—Mt 12:14; 27:1, 2, 62-65; 28:11-15; Mr 14:1; Lu 20:19.

Jehovah God cannot lie (Nu 23:19; Heb 6:13-18), and he hates "a false tongue." (Pr 6:16-19) His law to the Israelites required compensation for injuries resulting from deception or malicious lying. (Le 6:2-7; 19:11, 12) And a person presenting false testimony was to receive the punishment that he desired to inflict upon another by means of his lies. (De 19:15-21) God's view of malicious lying, as reflected in the Law, has not changed. Those desiring to gain his approval cannot engage in the practice of lying. (Ps 5:6; Pr 20:19; Col 3:9, 10; 1Ti 3:11; Re 21:8, 27; 22:15) They cannot be living a lie, claiming to love God while hating their brother. (1Jo 4:20, 21) For playing false to the holy spirit by lying, Ananias and his wife lost their lives.—Ac 5:1-11.

However, persons who are momentarily overreached in telling a lie do not automatically become guilty of an unforgivable sin. The case of Peter, in denying Jesus three times, illustrates that if a person is truly repentant, God will forgive him. —Mt 26:69-75.

While malicious lying is definitely condemned in the Bible, this does not mean that a person is under obligation to divulge truthful information to people who are not entitled to it. Jesus Christ counseled: "Do not give what is holy to dogs, neither throw your pearls before swine, that they may never trample them under their feet and turn around and rip you open." (Mt 7:6) That is why Jesus on certain occasions refrained from giving full information or direct answers to certain questions when doing so could have brought unnecessary harm. (Mt 15:1-6; 21:23-27; Joh 7:3-10) Evidently the course of Abraham, Isaac, Rahab, and Elisha in misdirecting or in withholding full facts from nonworshipers of Jehovah must be viewed in the same light.—Ge 12:10-19; chap 20; 26:1-10; Jos 2:1-6; Jas 2:25; 2Ki 6:11-23.

Jehovah God allows "an operation of error" to go to persons who prefer falsehood "that they may get to believing the lie" rather than the good news about Jesus Christ. (2Th 2:9-12) This principle is illustrated by what happened centuries earlier in the case of Israelite King Ahab. Lying prophets assured Ahab of success in war against Ramoth-gilead, while Jehovah's prophet Micaiah foretold disaster. As revealed in vision to Micaiah, Jehovah allowed a spirit creature to become "a deceptive spirit" in the mouth of Ahab's prophets. That is to say, this spirit creature exercised his power upon them so that they spoke, not truth, but what they themselves wanted to say and what Ahab wanted to hear from them. Though forewarned, Ahab preferred to be fooled by their lies and paid for it with his life.—1Ki 22:1-38; 2Ch 18.

**LIFE.** The principle of life or living; the animate existence, or term of animate existence, of an individual. As to earthly, physical life, things possessing life generally have the capabilities of growth, metabolism, response to external stimuli, and reproduction. The Hebrew word used in the Scriptures is *chai·yim′*, and the Greek word is *zo·e′*. The Hebrew word *ne′phesh* and the Greek word *psy·khe′*, both meaning "soul," are also employed to refer to life, not in the abstract sense, but to life as a person or an animal. (Compare the words "soul" and "life," as used at Job 10:1; Ps 66:9; Pr 3:22.) Vegetation has life, the life principle

mean that wicked spirits will stop trying to capture you? By no means! After tempting Jesus three times, Satan "retired from him until another convenient time." (Luke 4:13) Similarly, obstinate spirits not only attract people but also attack them.

[13] Recall our earlier consideration of Satan's attack on God's servant Job. The Devil caused the loss of his livestock and the death of most of his servants. Satan even killed Job's children. Next, he struck Job himself with a painful disease. But Job kept his integrity to God and was greatly blessed. (Job 1:7-19; 2:7, 8; 42:12) Since then, the demons have made some people speechless or blind and have continued to revel in the suffering of humans. (Matthew 9:32, 33; 12:22; Mark 5:2-5) Today, reports show that demons sexually harass some and drive others to insanity. They incite still others to murder and suicide, which are sins against God. (Deuteronomy 5:17; 1 John 3:15) Nonetheless, thousands of people once ensnared by these wicked spirits have been able to break free. How has this been possible for them? They have done so by taking vital steps.

## HOW TO RESIST WICKED SPIRITS

[14] What is one way that you can resist wicked spirits and protect yourself and your family from their snares? First-century Christians in Ephesus who had practiced spiritism before becoming believers took positive steps. We read that "quite a number of those who practiced magical arts brought their books together and burned them up before everybody." (Acts 19:19) Even if you have not practiced spiritism, get rid of anything having spiritistic uses or overtones. This includes books, mag-

14. In harmony with the example of first-century Ephesian Christians, how can you resist wicked spirits?



azines, videos, posters, musical recordings, and objects used for spiritistic purposes. Also included are idols, amulets and other items worn for protection, and gifts received from practicers of spiritism. (Deuteronomy 7:25, 26; 1 Corinthians 10:21) To illustrate: A married couple in Thailand had long been harassed by demons. Then they got rid of objects associated with spiritism. What was the result? They were relieved of the demonic attacks and thereafter made real spiritual progress.

[15] In order to resist wicked spirits, another necessary step is to apply the apostle Paul's counsel to put on the complete suit of God-given spiritual armor. (Ephesians 6:11-17) Christians must fortify their defenses against wicked spirits. What does this step include? "Above all things," said Paul, "take up the large shield of faith, with which you will be able to quench all the wicked one's burning missiles." Indeed, the stronger your faith, the greater will be your ability to resist wicked spirit forces. —Matthew 17:14-20.

[16] How can you strengthen your faith? By continuing to study the Bible and apply its counsel in your life. The strength of one's faith depends largely on the firmness of its base—the knowledge of God. Do you not agree that the accurate knowledge you have gained and taken to heart as you have studied the Bible has built up your faith? (Romans 10:10, 17) No doubt, therefore, as you continue this study and make it your custom to attend the meetings of Jehovah's Witnesses, your faith will be fortified even more. (Romans 1:11, 12; Colossians 2:6, 7) It will be a mighty bulwark against demon attacks. —1 John 5:5.

15. In resisting wicked spirit forces, what is another necessary step?
16. How can you strengthen your faith?

KNOWLEDGE THAT LEADS TO EVERLASTING LIFE, 1995

and he bringeth them out of their distresses. He maketh the storm a calm, so that the waves thereof are still. Then are they glad because they be quiet; so he bringeth them unto their desired haven."—Psalm 107:27-30.

***Remedy for Earth's Turmoil***

THERE is but one remedy for this distressing condition of humanity, and that remedy is the kingdom of the Lord. God, through His prophet, said that he would shake all nations and then the desire of all nations would come. Again, through the prophet Zephaniah He said: "For then will I turn to the people a pure language, that they may all call upon the name of the Lord, to serve him with one consent."—Zephaniah 3:9.

When the peoples of earth turn their hearts and minds to the Lord He will bring them out of their distressed condition and will establish amongst them a government of righteousness that shall fulfil the desire of every honest heart.

The kingdom of heaven is at hand. The evidence of this fact is conclusive. Soon the earth shall have established in it a righteous government.

## Illustrated Lectures

WE ARE pleased to announce that Mr. W. A. Russell is exhibiting some motion pictures of Palestine, made when Judge Rutherford was there; and that he has had successful meetings in the vincinity of Philadelphia. He will be glad to serve any one within a radius of twenty miles of Philadelphia. Address him at 1410 Mayfield Street, Philadelphia.

## An Aid to the Blind

A BLIND friend at Lowell, Mass., Mr. H. G. Burke, writes us that he earns his living by making certain articles in a workshop for the blind at 159 Moody St., in that city. Among other things he has to sell are self-threading needles, brooms and whiskbrooms. THE GOLDEN AGE calls attention to this matter not as an advertisement, but for the purpose of helping this blind man. We quote one paragraph from his letter:

"Many do not know that there is such a thing as a self-threading needle. You will be surprised how easy it is to thread these needles. They are made especially for the blind and for people with imperfect sight. Ten cents a package, postpaid to any address."

## Review of Book

"ANGELS AND WOMEN" is the title of a book just off the press. It is a reproduction and revision off the novel, "Seola" which was written in 1878, and which deals with conditions prior to the flood.

Pastor Russell read this book with keen interest, and requested some of his friends to read it because of its striking harmony with the Scriptural account of the sons of God described in the sixth chapter of Genesis. Those sons of God became evil, and debauched the human family prior to, and up to, the time of the great deluge. We call attention to this book because we believe it will be of interest to Bible Students, who are familiar with the machinations of the devil and the demons and with the influence exercised by them prior to the flood and also now in this evil day. The book throws light on the subject and it is believed, will aid those who carefully consider it to avoid the baneful effects of spiritism, now so prevalent in the world.

The book is revised and published by a personal friend of Pastor Russell, and one who was close to him in his work. It is published by the A. B. Abac Company, New York city.

The publishers advise that the regular price of this book is $2:00; but to all subscribers of THE GOLDEN AGE, it will be furnished at $1.00 per volume, when ordered in lots of ten or more. This is not an advertisement, but a voluntary comment.

7/30/1924

# ANGELS
AND
# WOMEN

A Revision of the Unique Novel
*Seola* by Mrs. J. G. Smith

Published by
A. B. ABAC COMPANY
NEW YORK

started good human beings on the downward road. Evil angels and bad women have made countless millions mourn.

The Bible story of fallen angels or evil spirits is briefly told as follows:

Lucifer, once a good spirit being, of great knowledge and authority, in order to satisfy his ambitious desire for greater authority, deceived Eve, the first woman, causing her to sin. Adam, the first man, joined her in the transgression. The sentence of death and expulsion from Eden resulted. Nine hundred and thirty years were employed in executing that death sentence. During that time there was born to Adam and Eve a number of children. Sixteen hundred years later, among these descendants of Adam and Eve, were Noah and his family.

Lucifer, now degraded, was named by Jehovah the Dragon, that old Serpent, Satan the Devil. God had permitted the angels, prior to the flood, to have supervision of the peoples of earth. (Hebrews 2:3.) These angels had power to materialize in human form and mingle amongst the human race. Satan seduced many of these angels and caused them to become wicked or fallen ones. They in turn debauched the women descendants of Adam. The materialized angels, called "sons of God saw the daughters of men that they were fair; and they took them wives of all which they chose." (Genesis 6:2.) A mongrel race resulted from these fallen angels with the offspring of Adam. These filled the earth with wickedness and violence. Their wickedness became so great that the Lord Jehovah brought upon the world the great deluge that destroyed all of this mongrel race.

The sons of God who succumbed to the temptations and thus became the fallen angels are alluded to as "Devas" in this book; their offspring as "Darvands."



The fallen angels or evil spirits were not destroyed in the flood, but imprisoned in the darkness of the atmosphere near the earth. Upon this point the inspired words of holy writ are: "For God spared not the angels that sinned, but cast them down to hell, and delivered them into chains of darkness, to be reserved unto judgment." (2 Peter 2:4.) "And the angels which kept not their first estate, but left their own habitation, he hath reserved in everlasting chains under darkness unto the judgment of the great day." (Jude 6.)

Since the flood these evil angels have had no power to materialize, yet they have had the power and exercised it, of communicating with human beings through willing dupes known as spirit mediums. Thus have been deceived hundreds of thousands of honest people into believing that their dead friends are alive and that the living can talk with the dead.

All students, familiar with the Bible teaching concerning spiritism, will read this book with the keenest interest because it shows the method employed by Satan and the wicked angels to debauch and overthrow the human race. <u>The reviser of this book is of the opinion that the original manuscript was dictated to the woman who wrote it by one of the fallen angels who desired to return to divine favor.</u> It is believed that reverential persons now examining the revised edition of this book will have a better understanding of the evil influence about us and be better fortified in the Lord's word and grace to shield and protect themselves from these evil influences.

Spiritism, otherwise named demonism, is working great evil amongst men. It should be studiously avoided. To be forewarned is to be forearmed. Hence this publication.

ANGELS AND WOMEN, A Revision of the Unique Novel Seola by Mrs. J. G. Smith

Jewish jubilee system which foreshadows the "restitution of all things". Therefore where the type ends, the thing forshadowed begins. The Fifth Universal Empire of Earth will be ushered in with power and great glory. He "whose right it is" will speak peace to the peoples, and then they shall not learn war any more.

The abortive efforts of the Inter-Church World Movement; the Paris, Washington, Geneva, Hague, and other conferences to create a counterfeit of Christ's kingdom, have all failed, and were but the dying gasps of a Satanic order upon whose tomb is being indelibly engraved and written in anguish and blood, "Gone, But Not Forgotten."

Hail the glad day when Christ's kingdom has actually come; for it will be the "desire of all nations."—Haggai 2:7.

We are coming to the "new earth", to the new order of things, to Paradise, which means "Garden of God". It will take a thousand years to restore all the race to Paradisaic conditions after the kingdom is established. And this is the only panacea for the ills of humankind. Its arrival is inevitable, its benefits are world-wide, its results eternal.

## Angels and Women

WE PRESENT some letters regarding this book (a review of which recently appeared in our columns) which we feel sure will be of interest to many of our readers:

To THE GOLDEN AGE:

Pardon me for taking this much of your time on what may be so simple a matter; but I was approached about going into a club to get a certain book called, "Angels and Women". I made some inquiries, and was told that it was a book that a fallen angel dictated to a woman, showing a desire to come back into harmony with God; and that Pastor Russell approved of the book. I had never heard of the book before; and as we are to shun anything akin to spiritism I should like to know positively whether the book has your approval before buying one; so if it is not asking too much would like a reply.

(Mrs.) W. S. Davis, *Los Angeles, Cal.*

To THE GOLDEN AGE:

With much pleasure and profit has the book, "Angels and Women" been read by many Truth friends. It contains so much to encourage one to loyalty and faith in God.

Do you think that it would be a real service to purchase these books in quantities of ten or more copies at a time so as to get the special $1 per copy rate, which you have so kindly secured for us, and thus to have them on hand as Christmas and birthday presents or for other gift occasions to give to our relatives and friends, whom we may have been unable to otherwise interest in Present Truth or only slightly so?

Would not some be disposed to read a fascinating novel of this kind, who might not be able to get first interested in "The Harp" or STUDIES?

Would this not be considered one way of instructing the people about matters concerning which there is so much ignorance, and direct them to the real Bible Keys, the WATCH TOWER publications?

Should we send such orders to THE GOLDEN AGE?

If not, will you kindly give us the complete address of the A. B. Abac Company? There are many who would like to get a little more information regarding these items.

An Appreciative Reader

### Reply

TO BOTH above letters we reply as follows:

When Pastor Russell was here, he read a book dealing with conditions that obtained prior to the Flood. He requested some other brethren to read it. It was so much in harmony with the Bible account of the fallen angels that he regarded the book as remarkable. Under his supervision it was revised, and later published by one who was formerly his confidential associate. The new book is published under the title "Angels and Women". Scriptural citations are given. An appendix is added. Pastor Russell remarked that at some opportune time the book, revised, should be published.

As to its being a violation of the Vow to read this book, such idea is not worthy of consideration. It would be no more wrong to read it than to read "What Say the Scriptures about Spiritism" or "Talking with the Dead"; for both these books quote much as to what the evil spirits do. Many have derived much benefit from reading "Angels and Women" because it aids in getting a clearer vision of how Satan

12/3/1924

overreached the angels and overreached the human race, and caused all the havoc amongst men and the angels. It helps one to a better understanding of the devil's organization.

The book is published by the A. B. Abac Company, Madison Square, P. O. Box 101, New York City, N. Y.

THE GOLDEN AGE does not handle the publication; but all who desire it should write directly to the publisher at the above address.

## A Remarkable Fulfilment of Prophecy

*"And it shall be, that whoso will not come up of all the families of the earth unto Jerusalem to worship the King, the Lord of hosts, even upon them shall be no rain."—Zechariah 14:17.*

ON MAY 6th the Spanish Government refused permission to Judge Rutherford to speak in Madrid in support of his belief, and our belief, that we have come to the time of the establishment of the Lord's kingdom in the earth—an event described in the Revelation of St. John as "the new Jerusalem, coming down from God out of heaven".

Now whether or not others can see in it what we see in it, nevertheless a most unusual item of information comes to us in a report from our correspondent in Switzerland. The gentleman in question knew of the Spanish Government's action in refusing permission to have the truth regarding the Lord's kingdom presented to the Spanish people, and in a report to us dated August 23rd says:

"We herewith beg to enclose a copy of the *Zurichsee Zeitung* of August 21 in which you will find a report, marked in blue pencil, that while the whole of Central Europe is complaining about a miserable summer, no rain has fallen in Madrid, the capital of Spain, since May 6. As this was the date upon which Judge Rutherford was refused permission to lecture in that city, we feel that the matter will be of interest to you. May we assume that there is a connection between the two things?"

## Blessing Automobiles *By Joseph Greig*

THE latest superstition of Greater Papacy now is the blessing of automobiles, said to have begun at Pittsburgh. Labels are placed on the machine head, and holy water applied with a pronouncement of Latin to the God of Rome. This insures from accident and the jam of Protestant aggression.

We remember in 1799 how the Pope himself blessed Napoleon. But at that time the Most High saw fit to visit judgment on the system, which had reached a crisis in its abominations. Instead, therefore, of the Pope's receiving worship, Napoleon exacted a lump sum from the "Vicar of Christ" and he too went along as prisoner of France. Indeed, "his highness" died in solitude after this blessing. Likewise, we remember, how a later pontiff blessed the Spanish navy at the instant when the United States entered into war with Spain. Evidently at that time the infallibility invoked failed of operation on account of certain other forces blocking the spiritual headship.

Soon, thank God! a further blessing is to be enjoyed when this symbolical "beast" passes away with its earthly pomp and mouthiness. Then the peoples will taste of the liberty with which Christ makes free. History tells of the long train of Jesuit priestcraft in the way of life, liberty, and happiness, not the least of which can be read off during the war on slavery while Lincoln was in office. Conspiracy among Lincoln's Catholic generals more than once threatened the disruption of the Lincolnian forces. Therefore, this boastful tyrant must go down in ignominy and chaos, as the prophet of the Lord of hosts has foretold. True religion will then spring from the efforts of the New Zionism, now bestirring itself toward the promised land of Abraham.

All hail such a prospect and token from the true Lord of lords and Decider of sovereignty rights, in behalf of a restored race, from the deceptions of Satan, forced on mankind in the name of truth! The bandages must all be torn loose ere this sunlight reaches the eyes of human understanding.

ng

ls to Gaius
he love ex-
:ers in the

ɔu, yet I do
vith ink and
directly, and
ɣ you have
ir greetings.
s by name."

› Gaius, but
ıll in writ-
"hoping to
mediately."
ıtion) Then
:," enjoying
Phillips.
ırnestly de-
peace—the
ın intimate
ıe tranquil-
ty and puts
Philippians
ıpostle sent
ends," thus
ɔelievers in

ıus, what did

ı desired that
:luding Third
beloved fel-

Gaius
ievers?
phes
serve

a way that Jehovah's Witnesses often do today. (Compare John 15:13, 14.) And how appropriate that John should know members of the local congregation so well that he could ask Gaius to convey his greetings to them *"by name"!*

**Keep on Serving Loyally as Fellow Workers**

24 Surely, the second and third inspired letters of John impress modern-day Christians with the need to love one another, reject apostasy, cling to the truth and promote the interests of true worship. Hence, we, as Jehovah's Witnesses, are determined to remain loyal to Scriptural truth as we sing our Father's praises, declare the good news of the Kingdom and point to Jesus Christ's vital role in God's arrangement for blessing mankind.

25 As Jehovah's Witnesses, we face many tests of faith in these critical "last days." (2 Timothy 3:1-5) But the apostle John's sound counsel will help us to continue "walking in the truth" as our way of life. May we, therefore, imitate what is good, do all we can to promote Kingdom interests and go on serving together loyally as "fellow workers in the truth"—all to the praise of the marvelous God of truth, Jehovah.

24, 25. Second and Third John should impress Jehovah's Witnesses with what need, and how should these letters motivate us?

# Questions from Readers

**■ Why, in recent years, has *The Watchtower* not made use of the translation by the former Catholic priest, Johannes Greber?**

This translation was used occasionally in support of renderings of Matthew 27:52, 53 and John 1:1, as given in the *New World Translation* and other authoritative Bible versions. But as indicated in a foreword to the 1980 edition of *The New Testament* by Johannes Greber, this translator relied on "God's Spirit World" to clarify for him how he should translate difficult passages. It is stated: "His wife, a medium of God's Spiritworld was often instrumental in conveying the correct answers from God's Messengers to Pastor Greber." *The Watchtower* has deemed it improper to make use of a translation that has such a close rapport with spiritism. (Deuteronomy 18:10-12) The scholarship that forms the basis for the rendering of the above-cited texts in the *New World Translation* is sound and for this reason does not depend at all on Greber's translation for authority. Nothing is lost, therefore, by ceasing to use his *New Testament.*

**■ What does Hebrews 1:7 mean when it says that God "makes his angels spirits, and his public servants a flame of fire"?**

The apostle Paul, contrasting the angels with God's Son, made this statement in Hebrews 1:7. He was quoting Psalm 104:4.

Since all angels are spirit creatures without fleshly bodies, it seems that when the verses say that God "makes his angels spirits" they are not referring to the type of organism that angels have. Rather, the understanding involves the underlying meaning of "spirit." The original words rendered "spirit" (Hebrew, *ruahh;* Greek, *pneuma*) have the basic meaning of "to breathe or blow." Depending on the context, they can be rendered "wind" or "active force." Hence, the point of Hebrews 1:7 and Psalm 104:4 evidently is that God makes his invisible angels to be spirit forces or powerful forces in his service. He also can use them as "a flame of fire," or, "a devouring fire," when employing them to carry out his fiery judgments.

THE WATCHTOWER—APRIL 1, 1983 31

ing spiritualism *The Encyclopedia Americana* (volume 25, 1929 ed.) says:

8 "The conclusions of the higher intelligences who have expressed themselves as being convinced of the reality of Spiritualism may be summed up as follows: Through mediumship is proved the continuity of life beyond the grave; it is no longer a religious dogma but a living fact. Spiritual intelligences are as anxious to communicate with us as we with them, but the lower and grosser intelligence seem to be the nearest to us, and most likely to be heard from in communication, and they like to impersonate great individuals and personal deceased friends of those present. This is held to account for much of the 'information' that comes through, and is valueless. For many years the *Banner of Light*, published in Boston, was the leading organ of this cult. In common with other Spiritualist papers it has disappeared. They have apparently given way to Psychological publications and New Thought periodicals. While the great public includes a vast number who are virtually Spiritualists, they are less and less known by that name, but are affiliated with New Thought, Mental Science, Theosophy, Oriental cults, Psychical Research and other modern movements. Spiritualistic teaching is largely in accord with the writings in the Bible."

9 In harmony with this last statement of the *Americana*, it is the claim of many spiritualists that this psychic religion is based on the Bible or that the Bible supports and agrees with spiritualism. Especially is this true of Catholic and Protestant clergymen who have become spiritualists. They claim that the Bible teaches survival after death or the immortality of the human soul, which is the teaching upon which spiritualism rests. For this reason it is also called Immortalism, and was first called so by a Protestant clergyman. In 1909 the New York *World* published an interview with this clergyman, namely, Bishop Samuel Fallows of the Reformed Episcopal church, Chicago, Illinois, in which he said: "There are great truths in Spiritualism. Many Spiritualistic phenomena we cannot understand, but we have to admit them. I have called the new science 'Immortalism' because it depends for its existence upon the immortality of the soul, in which we all believe, and the preservation of identity beyond the grave. Immortalism is simply Spiritualism with all the fraud and trickery eliminated. On account of these frauds Spiritualism has been shunned by many right thinking people, but immortalism will claim their most earnest attention." Four years earlier he said: "As a Christian and a believer in the Bible, I must believe in communication between the two worlds—that in which we live and that to which our friends have gone. . . . I believe in apparitions, however, and think it possible that there are persons possessed of a certain mysterious psychic power which enables them to make of their spirits a channel, as it were, through which the earth-bound spirit can communicate with the friend from the other side."—*The Watch Tower*, June 1, 1905; December 1, 1909.

10 Says Johannes Greber in the introduction of his translation of The New Testament, copyrighted in 1937: "I myself was a Catholic priest, and until I was forty-eight years old had never as much as believed in the possibility of communicating with the world of God's spirits. The day came, however, when I involuntarily took my first step toward such communication, and experienced things that shook me to the depths of my soul. . . . My experiences are related in a book that has appeared in both German and English and bears the

9, 10. (a) How is the widely held doctrine of the 'immortality of the human soul' related to spiritualism? (b) Clergymen of Christendom have chosen what attitude toward spiritualism?

FEBRUAR

title, Co
World: I
15, ¶ 2,
Catholic
bound w
front cov
mentione
"The mc
is the Bit
endeavor
translati
11 Spiri
good spir
not want
bad spiri
with the
Bible sa
spirit, bu
of God:
gone out
the Spiri
fesseth t
flesh is c
fesseth n
flesh is r
of antich
it should
in the wc
verses re
lieve eve
learn wh
many fa
abyss an
speaking
how you
comes f
fesses th
as a ma
spirit wh
as our L
God, but
You hav
come, an
the wor

11, 12. (a)
4:1-3? (b)
derived fro

Feb. 15, 1956

:LYN, N. Y.
talism, and
:ant clergy-
*World* pub-
clergyman,
; of the Re-
igo, Illinois,
;reat truths
alistic phe-
but we have
he new sci-
depends for
ality of the
ıd the pres-
: grave. Im-
sm with all
.ted. On ac-
sm has been
ing people,
their most
; earlier he
iever in the
nication be-
ı which we
:iends have
tions, how-
.t there are
mysterious
em to make
ıs it were,
d spirit can
om the oth-
ıne 1, 1905;

ıe introduc-
New Testa-
myself was
was forty-
nuch as be-
municating
:s. The day
ıtarily took
munication,
hook me to
experiences
appeared in
d bears the

FEBRUARY 15, 1956 — The WATCHTOWER — 111

title, Communication with the Spirit-World: Its Laws and Its Purpose." (Page 15, ¶ 2, 3) In keeping with his Roman Catholic extraction Greber's translation is bound with a gold-leaf cross on its stiff front cover. In the Foreword of his aforementioned book ex-priest Greber says: "The most significant spiritualistic book is the Bible." Under this impression Greber endeavors to make his New Testament translation read very spiritualistic.

11 Spiritualism claims that there are good spirits and bad spirits and that it does not want to have anything to do with the bad spirits but tries to communicate only with the good spirits. At 1 John 4:1-3 the Bible says: "Beloved, believe not every spirit, but try the spirits whether they are of God: because many false prophets are gone out into the world. Hereby know ye the Spirit of God: Every spirit that confesseth that Jesus Christ is come in the flesh is of God. And every spirit that confesseth not that Jesus Christ is come in the flesh is not of God: and this is that spirit of antichrist, whereof ye have heard that it should come; and even now already is it in the world." Greber's translation of these verses reads: "My dear friends, do not believe every spirit, but test the spirits to learn whether they come from God. For many false spirits have emerged from the abyss and gone out into the world, and are speaking through human mediums. This is how you can find out whether a spirit comes from God: every spirit who confesses that Jesus Christ appeared on earth as a man, comes from God. While every spirit who seeks to destroy belief in Jesus as our Lord incarnated does not come from God, but is sent by the adversary of Christ. You have been told that such spirits would come, and they are already appearing in the world." Very plainly the spirits in which ex-priest Greber believes helped him in his translation.

11, 12. (a) What is a questionable translation of 1 John 4:1-3? (b) What right understanding of this passage is derived from its accurate translation?

### "TRY THE SPIRITS"

12 However, when the apostle John says, "Try the spirits," or, "Test the spirits," he does not mean for us to dabble in spiritualism and get in touch with the spirits by means of spirit mediums, ouija boards or planchettes or other spiritistic paraphernalia and try out which is a good spirit and which is a bad one. By "spirits" here John is referring, not to invisible spirit creatures, but to the purpose, the intent or the motivation of the prophesying or public declaration made by men respecting God and Christ. Hence *An American Translation* reads: "Do not believe every inspired utterance, but test the utterances to see whether they come from God, for many false prophets have come out into the world." And the *New World Translation* reads: "Do not believe every inspired expression, but test the inspired expressions to see whether they originate with God." To test these inspired utterances or inspired expressions of the prophets or mouthpieces of various religions to see whether they are inspired by God's spirit or not, we do not have to go to spiritualist séances or mediums. Long ago Jehovah God inspired his prophet Isaiah to say: "Bind up the testimony, seal the teaching among my disciples. And when they say to you, 'Consult the mediums and the wizards who chirp and mutter,' should not a people consult their God? Should they consult the dead on behalf of the living? To the teaching and to the testimony! Surely for this word which they speak there is no dawn. They will . . . be thrust into thick darkness." (Isa. 8:16, 19-22, *RS*) Obediently those who seek true, reliable information concerning the human dead and future events go to Jehovah's teaching and testimony as found in the Bible.

# The
# New Testament

## A New Translation and Explanation

**Based on the Oldest Manuscripts**

by

**Johannes Greber**

PART I

**Translation**

1937
JOHN FELSBERG, Inc.
80 Fourth Avenue
New York, N. Y.

*Published and distributed by*
Johannes Greber Memorial Foundation
139 Hillside Avenue
Teaneck, N. J. 07666

The Catholic Church tries to explain the division into sects on the ground that all of the other Christian creeds seceded from her, whose faith alone was the true one. But it was precisely that church which drove God's spirit-world from the Christian faith. It was that church which, leagued with the temporal powers, destroyed all who believed otherwise than was prescribed by the authority of the pope. In the name of Catholic Christianity, the blood of hundreds of thousands has flowed.

It is true that the Catholic Church has succeeded in creating a human substitute for the divine spirits which were active in the early days of the Christian era. It has instituted an office vested with infallibility. That was the simplest way of solving the problem of providing an authentic source of the truth. Now Christ was spared the task of sending spirits of truth to groping humanity, as he had promised to do. Moreover, there was no longer any need of the fulfillment of his promise to be with the faithful always, "even to the end of the world." Was there not a pope, a "vicar of Christ" on earth? Where there is a vicar, he whom that vicar represents surely need not appear.

Thanks to the doctrine of an "infallible vicar of Christ on earth," the dispensation of the truth was placed wholly in the hands of erring, sinful men, to the exclusion of God's messengers of truth. Thus the gates were thrown open to human caprice and worldly ambition. True, the Catholic Church maintains that the "Holy Spirit" also acts through the papal office, but if we study the procedure of selecting the pope, and the history of the papacy, we shall soon realize that God's spirits can have little voice in the matter. Were not some of the popes instruments of hell rather than vicars of Christ in their deeds and in their whole manner of living?

To surmount this objection, however, a curious explanation has been devised. A distinction is drawn between the pope as a man and the pope as a vicar of Christ. It is maintained that even the worst of men, as soon as he becomes pope, may represent Christ and acquire infallibility. In other words, he might be an instrument of Satan and at the same time the vicar of Christ. Could man utter a greater blasphemy? Are we to believe that God entrusts His precious gifts, such as those on which salvation depends, to a servant of the evil one? Ordinary common sense should teach any one that this is unthinkable. God's spirits are sent only to the God-fearing, and remain with them only so long as they keep their faith. This is illustrated by the story of King Saul. As long as that king obeyed God, he was in daily communion with the world of God's spirits and could inquire of God whenever he wished to be enlightened on any matter. God always answered him through His spirits. But when Saul broke faith with God, further access to the world of God's spirits was denied him. Answers were no longer returned to the questions which he addressed to God, and instead of divine messengers, evil spirits took possession of Saul. The gifts with which he had been endowed were taken from him.

No man who is evil, not even if he is the pope, can ever be the bearer of God's sacred gifts. Consequently, the evil popes, at least, never possessed the gift of infallibility; and so the whole dogma of papal infallibility collapses of its own weight.

Only God chooses those to whom He sends the spirits of truth. No human choice can make any man the channel through which the truth is conveyed. Not even Christ chose his apostles at his own discretion, for the *Acts of the Apostles* expressly states that he made his choice through a holy spirit. It follows that God would certainly not invest a human office, such as the papacy, with infallibility. God alone is infallible; even His spirits are not. They are infallible only when they bring a message from God.





Whoever, then, seeks to know what is true and what is untrue in the Bible as we have it to-day, can find out only in the way in which all God-fearing people in the past have sought the truth, namely by communicating with God's spirit-world. He must accept the invitation which God extends to each one of us through the prophet Jeremiah: "Ask Me and I will answer you and show you great and mighty things, which you did not know before." God's answer will come through His spirits, for "God's spirits are His servants, sent to serve all who earnestly desire salvation." The assurance that God will send us His messengers in answer to our prayers was given to us by Christ when he said: "If you, then, being evil, know how to give good gifts to your children, how much more will your Father in heaven *give a holy spirit to those who ask Him for it.*"

I myself was a Catholic priest, and until I was forty-eight years old had never so much as believed in the possibility of communicating with the world of God's spirits. The day came, however, when I involuntarily took my first step toward such communication, and experienced things that shook me to the depths of my soul. After I had taken the first step, I could not stop. I must go forward, I must have enlightenment. On I went, treading carefully, and bearing in mind the words of the apostle Paul: "Test all things, keep that which is good." It was only the good that I sought. I wanted the truth. I was ready to accept it, come what might. I knew that God does not desert an earnest, disinterested seeker, and that, in the words of Christ, He will not offer a humble suppliant a stone instead of bread. I also realized the grave consequences of my step. My position as a clergyman, my entire material existence, my whole future in the worldly sense were threatened with ruin if I proceeded further. I knew that I was bound to undergo abuse, ridicule, persecution, and suffering to excess. But the truth meant more to me. And on the path that I followed I found the truth.

My experiences are related in a book that has appeared in both German and English and bears the title, *Communication with the Spirit-World: Its Laws and Its Purpose.* (*Der Verkehr mit der Geisterwelt, seine Gesetze und sein Zweck*). Many of the readers of this book who have sought to communicate with God's spirit-world have had experiences similar to my own and found the same truths that I found.

I availed myself of this contact with the source of truth to seek enlightenment above all in regard to the text of the Bible as we know it to-day; for on the occasion of my first experience with the world of divine spirits my attention had been called to the fact that the books of both the Old and the New Testament contained a great deal of spurious matter which had given rise to the many erroneous ideas prevailing in the Christian churches of our day. Subsequently I learned about these falsifications in detail.

This led me to a close study of the manuscripts of the New Testament. I found that the text of *Codex D* (*Codex Bezae Cantabrigiensis*), which unfortunately has several gaps, most nearly approaches the truth. It was consequently the one that I used as the basis for my translation.

In the rare instances in which a text pronounced correct by the divine spirits can be found in none of the manuscripts available to-day, I have used the text as it was given to me by those spirits. But in my Explanation I have always been careful to indicate which passages are derived from this source.

In my German translation I made it my chief concern to reproduce the exact meaning of the Greek text in good but simple German, so that people of limited education may be able to understand every sentence without difficulty. The translation of the German original into English was made by a professional translator,



THE NEW TESTAMENT, 1937, by Johannes Greber

corrected by a committee of American clergymen who are perfectly versed in both languages, and thoroughly revised by a teacher, so that not only the exact meaning of the German text is found in the English translation but also the same simplicity of language.

The *Explanation* of the New Testament, appended as Part II of the book, is not so much intended to make the translation clearer as it is to offer reasons for the several truths contained therein, to correlate them, and to build them into a compact edifice of truth. In this way the reader should be enabled to find the right answer to the great questions of our life here and in the hereafter.

May this book of truth deliver many from the burden of error and guide them to the road that leads to God. Christ says, "The truth will make you free." It delivers us from everything in the way of man-made ordinances and human error that has crept into religion; it frees us from a man-made Christianity and takes us back to the true Christianity of Christ.

May God's spirits of truth enlighten the hearts of my readers and bestow on them the spiritual gifts promised by Christ to all who believe in him.

I dedicate this book with heartfelt love to the One who said, "I am the way, the truth, and the life."

Good Friday, 1937 JOHANNES GREBER.



# The Gospel according to MATTHEW

## CHAPTER 1.

1 THE following are the ancestors of Jesus, the Messiah, the proof
of his descent from David and Abraham:
2 Abraham was the father of Isaac, Isaac was the father of Jacob,
3 Jacob was the father of Judah and his brothers. Judah was the
father of Phares and Zerah, by their mother Tamar. Phares was
4 the father of Esrom, and Esrom the father of Aram. Aram was the
father of Aminadab, Aminadab the father of Naason, and Naason
5 the father of Salmon. Salmon was the father of Boaz by Rahab;
6 Boaz was the father of Obed, by Ruth. Obed was the father of Jesse;
Jesse was the father of King David. David was the father of Sol-
7 omon, whose mother had been Uriah's wife. Solomon was the father
of Rehoboam, Rehoboam the father of Abijah, and Abijah the father
8 of Asa. Asa was the father of Jehoshaphat, Jehoshaphat the father
9 of Joram, Joram the father of Uzziah. Uzziah was the father of
Jotham, Jotham the father of Ahaz, and Ahaz the father of Hezekiah.
10 Hezekiah was the father of Manasseh, Manasseh the father of Amon,
11 and Amon the father of Josiah. Josiah was the father of Jechoniah
12 and his brothers in the time of the Babylonian captivity. After the
Babylonian captivity Jechoniah had a son called Shealthiel, the
13 father of Zerubbabel. Zerubbabel was the father of Abiud, Abiud
14 the father of Eliakim, and Eliakim the father of Azor. Azor was the
father of Zadok, Zadok the father of Achim, Achim the father of
15 Eliud, Eliud the father of Eleazar. Eleazar was the father of
16 Matthan, Matthan the father of Jacob. Jacob was the father of
Joseph, the husband of Mary, who bore of his seed Jesus, the
Messiah.

17 Thus the generations from Abraham to David are fourteen, from
David to the Babylonian captivity fourteen, and from the Babylonian
captivity to the Messiah, fourteen.

18 The human birth of the Messiah came about as follows: His
mother, Mary, was betrothed to Joseph, but before they lived together it was found that she was with child through the intervention
19 of a holy spirit. Joseph, being a God-fearing man and unwilling to

in translating them right in order to bring out the exact meaning.

4 Of course, the Bible reader who uses the generally accepted versions or translations will at once say: "Why, there should be no difficulty about knowing who the Word is. It plainly says that the Word is God; and God is God." But, in answer, we must say that not all our newer modern translations by Greek scholars read that way, to say just that. For instance, take the following examples: *The New English Bible,* issued in March of 1961, says: "And what God was, the Word was." The Greek word translated "Word" is *lógos;* and so Dr. James Moffatt's *New Translation of the Bible* (1922) reads: "The Logos was divine." *The Complete Bible—An American Translation* (Smith-Goodspeed) reads: "The Word was divine." So does Hugh J. Schonfield's *The Authentic New Testament.* Other readings (by Germans) are: By Boehmer: "It was tightly bound up with God, yes, itself of divine being."* By Stage: "The Word was itself of divine being."† By Menge: "And God (=of divine being) the Word was."‡ By Pfaefflin: "And was of divine weightiness."□ And by Thimme: "And God of a sort the Word was."○

5 But most controversial of all is the following reading of John 1:1, 2: "The Word was in the beginning, and the Word was with God, and the Word was a god. This *Word* was in the beginning with God." This reading is found in *The New Testament in An Improved*

* "Es war fest mit Gott verbunden, ja selbst goettlichen Wesens," *The New Testament,* by Rudolf Boehmer, 1910.

† "Das Wort war selbst goettlichen Wesens," *The New Testament,* by Curt Stage, 1907.

‡ "Und Gott (= goettlichen Wesens) war das Wort," *The Holy Scriptures,* by D. Dr. Hermann Menge, twelfth edition, 1951.

□ "Und war von goettlicher Wucht," *The New Testament,* by Friedrich Pfaefflin, 1949.

○ "Und Gott von Art war das Wort," *The New Testament,* by Ludwig Thimme, 1919.

4. Do all modern translations read like the old accepted versions of the Bible, and what examples do we have to illustrate whether?

5. What is the most controversial translation of all, as shown by two examples, and why may the translation by Professor Torrey be placed alongside the above?



*Version,* published in London, England, in 1808.* Similar is the reading by a former Roman Catholic priest: "In the beginning was the Word, and the Word was with God, and the Word was a god. This was with God in the beginning. Everything came into being through the Word, and without it nothing created sprang into existence." (John 1:1-3)† Alongside that reading with its much-debated expression "a god" may be placed the reading found in *The Four Gospels—A New Translation,* by Professor Charles Cutler Torrey, second edition of 1947, namely: "In the beginning was the Word, and the Word was with God, and the Word was god. When he was in the beginning with God all things were created through him; without him came no created thing into being." (John 1:1-3) Note that what the Word is said to be is spelled without a capital initial letter, namely, "god."

6 So in the above-quoted Bible translations we are confronted with the expressions "God," "divine," "God of a sort," "god," and "a god." Men who teach a triune God, a Trinity, strongly object to the translation "a god." They say, among other things, that it means to believe in polytheism. Or they call it Unitarianism or Arianism. The Trinity is taught throughout those parts of Christendom found in Europe, the Americas and Australia, where the great majority of the 4,000,000 readers of *The Watchtower* live. Readers in the other parts, in Asia and Africa, come in contact with the teaching of the Trinity through the missionaries of Christendom. It becomes plain, in view of this, that we have to make sure of not only who the Word or Logos is but also who God himself is.

* The title page reads: "The New Testament in An Improved Version, upon the basis of Archbishop Newcome's New Translation: with a Corrected Text, and Notes Critical and Explanatory. Published by a Society for Promoting Christian Knowledge and the Practice of Virtue, by the Distribution of Books."—Unitarian.

† *The New Testament—A New Translation and Explanation Based on the Oldest Manuscripts,* by Johannes Greber (a translation from German into English), edition of 1937, the front cover of this bound translation being stamped with a golden cross.

6. With what differing expressions are we confronted in the above-quoted translations, and so now whose identity do we have to find out?

God, yes, itself of divine being."[*] By Stage: "The Word was itself of divine being."[†] By Menge: "And God (=of divine being) the Word was."[‡] By Pfaefflin: "And was of divine weightiness."[□] And by Thimme: "And God of a sort the Word was."[°]

5 But most controversial of all is the following reading of John 1:1, 2: "The Word was in the beginning, and the Word was with God, and the Word was a god. This *Word* was in the beginning with God." This reading is found in *The New Testament in An Improved Version,* published in London, England, in 1808.[⊕] Similar is the reading by a former Roman Catholic priest: "In the beginning was the Word, and the Word was with God, and the Word was a god. This was with God in the beginning. Everything came into being through the Word, and without it nothing created sprang into existence." (John 1:1-3)[◊] Alongside that reading with its much-debated expression "a god" may be placed the reading found in *The Four Gospels—A New Translation,* by Professor Charles Cutler Torrey, second edition of 1947, namely: "In the beginning was the Word, and the Word was with God, and the Word was god. When he was in the beginning with God all things were created through him; without him came no created thing into being." (John 1:1-3) Note that what the Word is said to be is spelled without a capital initial letter, namely, "god."

6 So in the above-quoted Bible translations we are confronted with the expressions "God," "divine," "God of a sort," "god," and "a god." Men who teach a triune God, a Trinity, strongly object to the translation "a god." They say, among other things, that it means to believe in polytheism. Or they call it Unitarianism or Arianism. The Trinity is taught throughout those parts of Christendom found in Europe, the Americas and Australia, where the great majority of the 4,000,000 readers of *The Watchtower* live. Readers in the other parts, in Asia and Africa, come in contact with the teaching of the Trinity through the missionaries of Christendom. It becomes plain, in view of this, that we have to make sure of not only who the Word or Logos is but also who God himself is.

7 Christendom believes that the fundamental doctrine of her teachings is the Trinity. By Trinity she means a triune or three-in-one God. That means a God in three Persons, namely, "God the Father, God the Son, and God the Holy Ghost." Since this is said to be, not three Gods, but merely "one God in three Persons," then the term God must mean the Trinity; and the Trinity and God must be interchangeable terms. On this basis let us quote John 1:1, 2 and use the equivalent term for God, and let us see how it reads:

8 "In the beginning was the Word, and the Word was with the Trinity, and the Word was the Trinity. The same was in the beginning with the Trinity." But how

[*] "Es war fest mit Gott verbunden, ja selbst goettlichen Wesens," *The New Testament,* by Rudolf Boehmer, 1910.

[†] "Das Wort war selbst goettlichen Wesens," *The New Testament,* by Curt Stage, 1907.

[‡] "Und Gott (= goettlichen Wesens) war das Wort," *The Holy Scriptures,* by D. Dr. Hermann Menge, twelfth edition, 1951.

[□] "Und war von goettlicher Wucht," *The New Testament,* by Friedrich Pfaefflin, 1949.

[°] "Und Gott von Art war das Wort," *The New Testament,* by Ludwig Thimme, 1919.

[⊕] The title page reads: "The New Testament in An Improved Version, upon the basis of Archbishop Newcome's New Translation: with a Corrected Text, and Notes Critical and Explanatory. Published by a Society for Promoting Christian Knowledge and the Practice of Virtue, by the Distribution of Books."—Unitarian.

[◊] *The New Testament—A New Translation and Explanation* Based on the Oldest Manuscripts, by Johannes Greber (a translation from German into English), edition of 1937, the front cover of this bound translation being stamped with a golden cross.

5. What is the most controversial translation of all, as shown by two examples, and why may the translation by Professor Torrey be placed alongside the above?

6. With what differing expressions are we confronted in the above-quoted translations, and so now whose identity do we have to find out?

7, 8. What does Christendom say that God is, but by applying this equivalent term to John 1:1, 2 what tangle do we get into?



could such a thin
himself a Person
Trinity, then ther
But the Word is s
be the Second Per
ly, "God the Son.
could John say th
Son, was the Tri
Persons? How cou

9 However, let t
in John 1:1 *God*
Person of the Tri
Father," and so t
the Father in the
of this definition
said that the Wor
the Son," is "God
does their "God th
the picture? If G
the Word with "C
well as with "G
beginning?

10 Suppose, now,
1:1, 2, *God* means
the Trinity, so th
Word was with G
the Holy Ghost. I
this difficulty, nam
the Word was God
Holy Ghost, the o
Trinity. Thus the
the Second Person
to be also the Firs

[*] Says *La Sainte Bible*
original texts by the M
Maredsous, 1949, in a f
*The Word:* the Word
Father, constituting th
Trinity." (1:1. *Le Ver*
eternelle du Pere, consti
sainte Trinité.)
BÍBLIA SAGRADA, a
Hebrew, Aramaic and G
version of the Benedict
gium) by the Catholic E
edition, 1960, says the
reads: "Cap. 1:—1. *O V*
eterna do Pai, que co
Santissima Trindade."

9. If it is claimed that
then into what difficulty d
10. What if it is said th
Persons of the Trinity, a
does not explain it?

September 15, 1962

Trinity 488

at the right hand of God; and he said, 'Behold, I see the heavens opened, and the Son of man standing at the right hand of God.'"

**Dan. 7:9, 13,** ***RS*** "As I looked, thrones were placed and one that was ancient of days took his seat; his raiment was white as snow. . . . I saw in the night visions, and behold, with the clouds of heaven there came one like a son of man, and he came to the Ancient of Days and was presented before him." (Compare Matt. 26:64.)

***Masculine pronoun in some texts does not prove personality; the antecedent, "Comforter" or "Helper," is masculine in Greek text, thus pronoun is masculine to agree grammatically***

**John 15:26,** ***AV*** "When the Comforter is come, whom I will send unto you from the Father, even the Spirit of truth, *which* proceedeth from the Father, he shall testify of me."

**Rom. 8:26,** ***AV*** "The Spirit also helpeth our infirmities: for we know not what we should pray for as we ought: but the Spirit *itself* maketh intercession for us."

"SPIRIT. PNEUMA primarily denotes the wind (akin to *pneō*, to breathe, blow); also breath; then, especially the spirit, which, like the wind, is invisible, immaterial and powerful. . . . 'Spirit' and 'Ghost' are renderings of the same word *pneuma*; . . . the noun *pneuma* is neuter in Greek, while the corresponding word in Aramaic . . . is feminine (*rûchâ*, cf. Heb. *rûach*)."—*An Expository Dictionary of New Testament Words* (London; 1962), by W. E. Vine, Vol. IV, pp. 62-64.

**Scriptures Mentioning Father, Son and Holy Spirit Together Do Not Say They Are Equal, Coeternal or One God**

**Matt. 28:19,** ***RS*** "Go therefore and make disciples of all nations, baptizing them in the name of the Father and of the Son and of the Holy Spirit."

**Matt. 3:16, 17,** ***AV*** "Jesus, when he was baptized, went up straightway out of the water: and, lo, the heavens were opened unto him, and he saw the Spirit of God descending like a dove, and lighting upon him: and lo a voice from heaven, saying, This is my beloved Son, in whom I am well pleased."

***Trinitarian statement in 1 John 5:7, found in some Bibles, is spurious***

**1 John 5:7,** ***AV*** "For there are three that bear record in heaven, the Father, the Word, and the Holy Ghost: and these three are one."

"5:7 This verse has not been found in Greek in any manuscript in or out of the New Testament earlier than the thirteenth century. It does not appear in any Greek manuscript of I John before the fifteenth century, when one cursive has it; one from the sixteenth also contains the reading. These are the only Greek manuscripts of the New Testament in which it has ever been found. But it occurs in no ancient Greek manuscript or Greek Christian writer or in any of the oriental versions. Its chief support is in two Old Latin manuscripts of the sixth and eighth centuries and in some manuscripts of the Latin Vulgate, but not the oldest ones. Erasmus did not include it in his first edition of the New Testament in Greek (1516) nor in his second (1519). When criticized for the omission, he rashly said that if anyone could show him a Greek manuscript containing the passage he would insert it, and the sixteenth-century Codex Montfortianus containing it was brought to his attention. He felt obliged to include the reading in his third edition (1522), and it was this edition that Tyndale used in making his translation of the Greek Testament (1525). From Tyndale the verse found its way into the King James Version. It is universally discredited by Greek scholars and editors of the Greek text of the New Testament."—*The Goodspeed Parallel New Testament* (Chicago; 1943), Edgar J. Goodspeed, p. 557.

"The words, 'in heaven, the Father . . . bear witness on earth', constitute what is often called the *Comma Ioanneum*, or text of the Heavenly Witnesses. Without it the translation would run, 'For there are three that bear witness, the Spirit and the water and the blood'. In the opinion of nearly all critics and of most Catholic writers of the present day the words were not contained in the original text; at the same time, until further action be taken by the Holy See it is not open to Catholic editors to eliminate the words from a version made for the use of the faithful."—*The Westminster Version of the Sacred Scriptures* (London; 1931), Cuthbert Lattey, S. J., and Joseph Keating, S. J., general editors, Vol. IV, pp. 145, 146.

489 War

**John 1:1, 2 Mentions Only Two Persons, Not Three**

**John 1:1, 2,** ***AV*** "In the beginning was the Word, and the Word was with God, and the Word was God. The same was in the beginning with God."

***Modern translations and Greek grammar make meaning clear***

**John 1:1,** ***AT*** "In the beginning the Word existed. The Word was with God, and the Word was divine."

"In the beginning was the Word, and the Word was with God; and the Word was a god."—*The New Testament—A New Translation and Explanation* Based on the Oldest Manuscripts (a translation from German into English; 1937), by Johannes Greber.

"In the beginning the Word was, and the Word was with God, and the Word was a god."—*New World Translation* (New York; 1961).

# War

**War in Our Day Part of Sign of Conclusion of Wicked System of Things**

**Matt. 24:3, 4, 7, 8** "While he was sitting upon the Mount of Olives, the disciples approached him privately, saying: 'Tell us, When will these things be, and what will be the sign of your presence and of the conclusion of the system of things?' And in answer Jesus said to them: '. . . nation will rise against nation and kingdom against kingdom, and there will be food shortages and earthquakes in one place after another. All these things are a beginning of pangs of distress.'"

**Dan. 11:40** "In the time of the end the king of the south will engage with him in a pushing, and against him the king of the north will storm with chariots and with horsemen and with many ships; and he will certainly enter into the lands and flood over and pass through."

See also Rev. 6:4.

**War to Be Brought to an End by God Through His Prince of Peace**

**Ps. 46:9** "He is making wars to cease to the extremity of the earth. The bow he breaks apart and does cut the spear in pieces; the wagons he burns in the fire."

"MAKE SURE OF ALL THINGS – Hold Fast to What Is Fine" 1965

a memorial (sepulchre as a monument)." Related to *mne·mei'on* is the word *mne'ma*, which appears to have a corresponding meaning, referring also to "a memorial or record of a thing or a dead person, then a sepulchral monument, and hence a tomb."—*An Expository Dictionary of New Testament Words*, Vol. II, by W. E. Vine, pp. 172, 173.

Such tomb might be an excavated grave in the ground or, as was often the case among the Hebrews, might be a natural cave or a rock-cut vault. (Compare Acts 7:16 and Genesis 23:19, 20.) As has been seen above, whereas the word *ta'phos* or "grave" gives emphasis to the idea of *burial*, the words *mne'ma* and *mne·mei'on* lay stress on the thought of preserving the memory of the deceased person. These latter words, therefore, appear to carry a greater idea of permanence than *ta'phos;* they are related to the Latin word *monimentum*.

It seems evident that Jewish burial tombs were customarily built outside the cities, a major exception being those of the kings. The references to such tombs in the Christian Greek Scriptures would all appear to place them outside the cities, except the reference to David's tomb at Acts 2:29. Being thus withdrawn and also being avoided by the Jews, due to the ceremonial uncleanness connected with them, the areas in which such tombs were located were at times the haunt of crazed or demonized persons.—Matt. 8:28; Mark 5:5.

NOT ORNATE

While serving as a remembrance of the deceased person, the Jewish memorial tombs in general do not appear to have been ornate or ostentatious. Some were so unpretentious and inconspicuous that men might walk upon them without being aware of it. (Luke 11:44) Although it was the custom of the pagan peoples around them to make their tombs as lavish as their circumstances allowed, the early Jewish tombs that have been found are notable for their simplicity. This was due mainly to their worship being based on the Hebrew Scriptures and which allowed no veneration of the dead nor fostered any ideas of a conscious existence after death in a spirit world, ideas such as those held by the Egyptians, Canaanites, Babylonians and others. Thus, while many critics make the claim that the worship of the nation of Israel was, from early times, "syncretistic," that is, resulting from the union of conflicting beliefs and having developed by the addition of tenets and practices from earlier religions, the fundamental resistance to such religious corruption is evidenced once again in the plainness of these tombs. Apostasy, of course, did occur among the Israelites and would account for any deviations from the usual attitude toward the dead. Likewise, Jesus shows that in his day it was the practice of the scribes and Pharisees to decorate the memorial tombs of the prophets and others. (Matt. 23:29, 30) Under Greek and Roman influence, the tendency among the wealthy at this time was toward more pretentious tombs.

Aside from the tomb of John the Baptist (Mark 6:29), the principal tombs considered in the Greek Scriptures are those of Lazarus and of Jesus. Lazarus' tomb was typically Jewish, being a cave with a stone lying against the opening, which opening may have been relatively small, as has been true of similar tombs found in Palestine. The context would indicate it was outside the village.—John 11:30-34, 38-44.

JESUS' TOMB

The tomb used for Jesus' burial was a new one belonging to Joseph of Arimathea, and was not a cave but had been carved in a rock of a garden not far from the site of Jesus' impalement. The tomb had a door requiring a big stone to close it and this stone apparently was of the circular type sometimes used. (Matt. 27:57-60; Mark 16:3, 4; John 19:41, 42). Like other tombs found, it seems to have had within a benchlike shelf or shelves cut into the walls on which bodies could be placed.—Compare Mark 16:5.

Claims are made for two principal sites as being the original location of Jesus' tomb. One is the traditional site over which the Church of the Holy Sepulchre has been erected. The other site is that known as the Garden Tomb, which is cut out of a huge stone protruding from the side of a hill and is outside even the present city walls. Inside it gives evidence of being a "new" tomb, since, of the several places for bodies, only one seems to have been completed. No definite proof exists, however, that either of these places authentically represents the memorial tomb in which Jesus was laid.

'TOMBS OPENED' AT JESUS' DEATH

The text at Matthew 27:52, 53 concerning the "memorial tombs [that] were opened" as the result of an earthquake occurring at the time of Jesus' death has caused considerable discussion, some holding that a resurrection occurred. However, a comparison with the texts concerning the resurrection makes clear that these verses do not describe a resurrection but merely a throwing of bodies out of their tombs, similar to incidents that have taken place in recent times, as in Ecuador in 1949, and again in Bogotá, Colombia, in 1962, when two hundred corpses in the cemetery were thrown out of their tombs by a violent earth tremor.—*El Tiempo*, Bogotá, Colombia, July 31, 1962.

→ The translation by Johannes Greber (1937) of these verses reads as follows: "Tombs were laid open, and many bodies of those buried were tossed upright. In this posture they projected from the graves and were seen by many who passed by the place on their way back to the city."

REMEMBRANCE BY GOD

In view of the thought of remembrance underlying the word *mne·mei'on*, Jesus' use of this word (rather than *ta'phos*) at John 5:28 with regard to the resurrection of "all those in the memorial tombs" seems particularly appropriate and contrasts sharply with the thought of complete repudiation and effacement from all memory represented by Gehenna. (Matt. 10:28; 23:33; Mark 9:43) The importance attached to burial by the Hebrews (see BURIAL, BURIAL PLACES) is indicative of their concern that they be remembered, primarily by Jehovah God in whom they had faith as "the rewarder of those earnestly seeking him." (Heb. 11:1, 2, 6) Inscriptions of the tombs of Israelite origin are very rare and, when found, usually consist of only the name. The outstanding kings of Judah left no magnificent monuments with their praises and exploits engraved thereon, as did the kings of other nations. Thus it seems evident that the concern of faithful men of ancient times was that their name be in the "book of remembrance" described at Malachi 3:16 and not be as the "name of the wicked one [which] will rot."—Prov. 10:7; compare Ecclesiastes 7:1; see NAME.

The basic idea of remembrance involved in the original Greek words for "tomb" or "memorial tomb" also gives added meaning to the plea of the thief impaled alongside Jesus to "remember me when you get into your kingdom."—Luke 23:42.

**MEMPHIS** (Mem'phis). One of the capitals of ancient Egypt, identified with the ruins near Mit Rahiney, about fourteen miles (22.5 kilometers) S of Cairo, on the W side of the Nile River. Memphis was for long the most important city in "Lower Egypt" (that is, the Delta region and a small section to the S thereof).

At Hosea 9:6 the city is called *Moph* in the Hebrew text (rendered "Memphis" in most English translations). Elsewhere it is referred to by the Hebrew *Noph*. (Isa. 19:13; Jer. 2:16; 44:1; 46:14, 19; Ezek. 30:13, 16) This Hebrew name is believed to come from Egyptian *Mn-nfr* (the vowels not being written), the name

AID TO BIBLE UNDERSTANDING, 1971

ohn 8:31,
ssue with
ngs made
att. 15:6;

d of God
obedience
1; 11:28;
e ministry
the word
hemselves.
19:10) As
, and the
-Acts 6:7;

o peddlers
were. What
ed message
Paul told
ourself ap-
oe ashamed
." Further-
ne word, be
lesome sea-
eled Chris-
at the word
—Titus 2:5.
at God had
been many
persons who
ives for do-
history can
ry that per-
ion of God's

) SPIRIT
r upon its
to Israel in
e does man
mouth does
"the word of
of God, and
have spoken
63.
[or message,
nd is sharper
even to the
its and their
nd intentions
he heart and
according to

can sanctify
make a per-
lish whatever
sa. 55:10, 11)
ry good work,
wicked one.

anointed him
at through the
oppressed by
" (Acts 10:38)
rsions of per-
sive words of
ation of spirit
that he spoke
Scriptures, the
make the con-
Thessalonica:
urn up among
power and with
Thess. 1:5.
ah's spirit and
irive and force.
that he spoke
strong power:
back the hearts
bedient ones to





the practical wisdom of righteous ones, to get ready for Jehovah a prepared people."—Luke 1:17.

The message of the good news from God's Word the Bible should therefore not be underrated. These words are more powerful than any words men can devise or speak. The ancient Beroeans were commended for "carefully examining the Scriptures" to see whether what an apostle taught was correct. (Acts 17:11) God's ministers, speaking God's powerful Word, are energized and backed up by "power of holy spirit."—Rom. 15:13, 19.

### "THE WORD" AS A TITLE

In the Christian Greek Scriptures "the Word" (Gr., *ho Lo'gos*) also appears as a title. (John 1:1, 14; Rev. 19:13) The apostle John identified the one to whom this title belongs, namely, to Jesus, he being so designated not only during his ministry on earth as a perfect man, but also during his prehuman spirit existence as well as after his exaltation to heaven.

Regarding the Son's prehuman existence, John says: "In the beginning *the Word* was, and *the Word* was with God, and *the Word* was a god." (John 1:1, *NW*) The *Authorized Version* and the *Douay Version* read: "In the beginning was the Word, and the Word was with God, and the Word was God." This would make it appear that the Word was identical with Almighty God, while the former reading, in the *New World Translation*, indicates that the Word is not *the* God, Almighty God, but is a "mighty one," a god. (Even the judges of ancient Israel, who wielded great power in the nation, were called "gods." [Ps. 82:6; John 10:34, 35]) Actually, in the Greek text, the definite article *ho*, "the," appears before the first "God," but there is no article before the second.

Other modern translations aid in getting the proper view. The interlinear word-for-word reading of the Greek translation in the *Emphatic Diaglott* reads: "In a beginning was the Word, and the Word was with the God, and a god was the Word." The accompanying text of the *Diaglott* uses capital and small capital letters for *the* God, and initial capital and lowercase letters for the second appearance of "god" in the sentence: "In the Beginning was the Logos, and the Logos was with God, and the Logos was God."

These renderings would support the fact that Jesus, being the Son of God and the one used by God in creating all other things (Col. 1:15-20), is indeed a "god," a "mighty one," and has the quality of mightiness, but is not the Almighty God. Other translations reflect this view. *The New English Bible* (1961) says: "And what God was, the Word was." The Greek word translated "Word" is *Lo'gos;* and so Dr. James Moffatt's *New Translation of the Bible* (1922) reads: "The Logos was divine." *The Complete Bible—An American Translation* (Smith-Goodspeed) reads: "The Word was divine." Other readings (by German translators) are: By Boehmer: "It was tightly bound up with God, yes, itself of divine being." By Stage: "The Word was itself of divine being." By Menge: "And God (= of divine being) the Word was." By Pfaefflin: "And was of divine weightiness." And by Thimme: "And God of a sort the Word was." All these renderings highlight the *quality* of the Word, not his identity with his Father, the Almighty God. Being the Son of God (Jehovah), he would have the divine quality, for divine means 'godlike.'—Col. 2:9; compare 2 Peter 1:4, where "divine nature" is promised to Christ's joint heirs.

A translation by a former Roman Catholic priest, Johannes Greber (1937 ed.) renders the second appearance of the word "god" in the sentence as "a god." And *The Four Gospels—A New Translation*, by Professor Charles Cutler Torrey (second ed., 1947), says: "In the beginning was the Word, and the Word was with God, and the Word was god. When he was in the beginning with God all things were created through him; without him came no created thing into being." (John 1:1-3) Note that what the Word is said to be is spelled without a capital initial letter, namely, "god."

#### *How "in the beginning with God"*

This Word or *Lo'gos* was God's only direct creation, the only-begotten son of God, and evidently the close associate of God to whom God was speaking when he said: "Let *us* make man in *our* image, according to *our* likeness." (Gen. 1:26) Hence John continued, saying: "This one was in the beginning with God. All things came into existence through him, and apart from him not even one thing came into existence." —John 1:2, 3.

Other scriptures plainly show that the Word was God's agent through whom all other things came into existence. There is "one God the Father, out of whom all things are, . . . and there is one Lord, Jesus Christ, through whom all things are." (1 Cor. 8:6) The Word, God's Son, was "the beginning of the creation by God," otherwise described as "the first-born of all creation; because by means of him all other things were created in the heavens and upon the earth." —Rev. 3:14; Col. 1:15, 16.

#### *Earthly ministry and heavenly glorification*

In due time a change came about. John explains: "So *the Word* became flesh and resided among us [as the Lord Jesus Christ], and we had a view of his glory, a glory such as belongs to an only-begotten son from a father." (John 1:14) By becoming flesh the Word became visible, hearable, feelable to eyewitnesses on earth. In this way men of flesh could have direct contact and association with *"the word* of life," which, John says, "was from the beginning, which we have heard, which we have seen with our eyes, which we have viewed attentively and our hands felt."—1 John 1:1-3.

The glorified Lord Jesus Christ continues to carry the title "the Word," as noted in Revelation 19:11-16. There in a vision of heaven John says he saw a white horse whose rider was called "Faithful and True," "The Word of God," and "upon his outer garment, even upon his thigh, he has a name written, King of kings and Lord of lords."

#### *Why God's Son is entitled "the Word"*

A title often describes the function served or the duty performed by the bearer. So it was with the title *Kal Hatze*, meaning "the voice or word of the king," that was given an Abyssinian officer. Based on his travels from 1768 to 1773, James Bruce describes the duties of the *Kal Hatze* as follows. He stood by a window covered with a curtain through which, unseen inside, the king spoke to this officer. He then conveyed the message to the persons or party concerned. Thus the *Kal Hatze* acted as the word or voice of the Abyssinian king.

Recall, too, that God made Aaron the word or "mouth" of Moses, saying: "He must speak for you to the people; and it must occur that he will serve as a mouth to you, and you will serve as God to him." —Ex. 4:16.

In a similar way God's firstborn Son doubtless served as the Mouth or Spokesman for his Father, the great King of Eternity. He was God's Word of communication for conveying information and instructions to the Creator's other spirit and human sons. Prior to Jesus' coming to earth, on many of the occasions when God communicated with humans it is reasonable to think he used the Word as his angelic mouthpiece. (Gen. 16:7-11; 22:11; 31:11; Ex. 3:2-5; Judg. 2:1-4; 6:11, 12; 13:3) Since the angel that guided the Israelites through the wilderness had 'Jehovah's name within him,' he may have been God's Son, the Word. —Ex. 23:20-23; see JESUS CHRIST (Prehuman Existence; Why called "the Word"; Jesus' Godship).

Showing that Jesus continued to serve as his Father's Spokesman or Word during his earthly ministry, he told his listeners: "I have not spoken out of my own impulse, but the Father himself who sent me has given me a commandment as to what to tell and what to speak. . . . Therefore the things I speak, just as the

AID TO BIBLE UNDERSTANDING, 1971

after Jesus' own resurrection, on the third day after this, before leaving their tombs? Why would God resurrect such "saints" or "holy ones" at this time, since Jesus was to be "the firstborn from the dead"? (Col. 1:18; 1 Cor. 15:20) Also, it was during Christ's future presence that anointed Christians or "holy ones" were to share in the first resurrection. —1 Thess. 3:13; 4:14-17; Rev. 20:5, 6.

Observe that, strictly speaking, the account does not say that the "bodies" came to life. It merely says that they were raised up or thrown out of the tombs by the earthquake. A similar thing happened in the town of Sonson in Colombia in 1962. *El Tiempo* (July 31, 1962) reported: "Two hundred corpses in the cemetery of this town were thrown out of their tombs by the violent earth tremor." Persons passing by or through that cemetery saw the corpses, and, as a result, many of the people in Sonson had to go out and rebury their dead relatives.

Without wresting the Greek grammar, a translator can render Matthew 27:52, 53 in a way that suggests that a similar exposing of corpses resulted from the earthquake occurring at Jesus' death. Thus the translation by Johannes Greber (1937) renders these verses: "Tombs were laid open, and many bodies of those buried there were tossed upright. In this posture they projected from the graves and were seen by many who passed by the place on their way back to the city."—Compare the *New World Translation*.

Along with the rending of the temple curtain separating the Holy from the Most Holy, this violent earthquake, which exposed corpses that were soon seen by travelers who brought the news into Jerusalem, served as additional proof that Jesus was no mere criminal executed for wrongdoing. He was the Messiah and the one who would shortly be the firstborn from the dead destined for heavenly life.

---

**"WATCHTOWER" STUDIES FOR THE WEEKS**

November 23: One World, One Government, Under God's Sovereignty. Page 611. Songs to Be Used: 2, 27.

November 30: The One Government for One World Under God's Sovereignty. Page 617. Songs to Be Used: 46, 51.

l conscience and
vhat is pleasing
keeping himself
:an prevent vio-
; 15:18 states:
contention, but
r quiets down

: remaining pa-
? The disciple
stion and then
"Is there any-
you? Let him
13.
God for help,
n him.' As to
lm 55:22 says:
ou. Never will
ne to totter."
d with prayer,
reason things
is present sys-
d needless up-
ot be changed.
his spirit, Je-
r minds points
: Word, giving
need to exer-
y. Should the
int where the
Jehovah may
hers to come
ly upon him,
ll never allow
in and to lose
it endurance.
le to exercise
Thereby we
e before God
ing, maintain
tuations and
cause of our
bout matters
, too, we can
: prospect of
s conditions.
ine reward.

·APRIL 15, 1976

# Insight on the News

**Pontiff's Protection**

● The Vatican's Swiss Guards have now added tear gas to their arsenal, according to a recent Associated Press report. The ninety-man force was said to want some protective weapon "less harmful" than their submachine guns and bayoneted rifles, or the combination spear and battle-ax with which they stand guard. But why should Vatican City have such armed guards in the first place? "Their principal function is the protection of the person of the pontiff," says the "New Catholic Encyclopedia." However, what of the one whom this pontiff as the "vicar of Christ" claims to represent? Jesus Christ said to Roman Governor Pilate: "Mine is not a kingdom of this world; if my kingdom were of this world, my men would have fought to prevent my being surrendered to the Jews"—for execution. For this reason, Christ's "men" did not need an arsenal. But the pope apparently feels that his "men" do. It seems that neither his faith, courage nor "kingdom" matches that of Christ.—John 18:36, Catholic "Jerusalem Bible."

**Blood Tells All**

● Forensic (criminal) medicine may soon 'make it possible to reconstruct the personality image of every person who leaves behind a bloodstain,' according to English criminologists who spoke at a meeting of the International Juridic Scientists in Zürich, Switzerland. As reported in the German newspaper "Die Welt," researchers have found that each person's blood carries a great variety of disease antibodies accumulated throughout life that mark the blood of that person as distinct from all others. "It is today accepted that every person has his own specific type of blood with which no other blood can compare exactly," notes the paper. Information about where a person has lived, his approximate age, his allergies, even something about his occupation and sexual habits, is coming within the scope of blood analysis. "In short there seem to be no limits to the possibilities of reconstructing a 'recognizable' person together with his life's history and his environment," the article concludes. Truly it can be said that, in more ways than one, "the life of every living creature is the blood."—Lev. 17:11, 14, "New English Bible."

**Event Clarifies Bible**

● The recent Guatemalan earthquake affected even some of those already dead. "Time" magazine reports that "several mourners who went to bury their dead in family plots found that the coffins of long-dead relatives had been uncovered by the quake." Something similar occurred during an earthquake in the Jerusalem area at Jesus' death. At that time, dead bodies were customarily placed in vaults or chambers cut from Palestine's soft limestone rock, often in hillsides. A report in the Bible, as translated by Johannes Greber, says that when Jesus died, "the earth quaked, and the rocks were shattered. Tombs were laid open, and many bodies of those buried there were tossed upright. In this posture they projected from the graves and were seen by many who passed by the place on their way back to the city." Hence, rather than a resurrection, as some Bible translations imply, there appears to have been merely an exposure of the dead to observers, as in Guatemala.—Matt. 27:51-53.

**Bad Precedent**

● India's Cardinal Joseph Parecattil, president of the Catholic Bishops Conference, has urged that Catholicism in that country strive to develop into "an Indian Church." At a general meeting of the conference, he emphasized the need, as reported in the Indian "Express," of 'drawing on the vast resources of Indian religions, thought and systems of philosophy' for this purpose. As a precedent, he referred the bishops to 'the first four centuries [after Christ, when] Christian theologians were open to constructive dialogue with other faiths.' Of course, the only 'other faiths' were non-Christian, but that did not hinder the cardinal from pleading that, as in the first four centuries, 'this absorption of terms and thought patterns from local cultures should be an ongoing process in the church.' Thus Cardinal Parecattil confirms the accuracy of the Bible's warning about "the apostasy," and that its beginnings were "already at work" from the first century onward.—2 Thess. 2:3, 7.

THE WATCHTOWER—APRIL 15, 1976 231

## DIALOGUE SIX: How Can You Find The True Religion?



High; and to foster growth of the Assemblies throughout the world. During the 1960s, it published a periodical, *The Word.*

**★978★**
**Assemblies of Yahweh**
Bethel, PA 19507

Jacob O. Meyer, a former member of the Church of the Brethren, left the church of his childhood and began a spiritual pilgrimage that led him to a small independent Sacred Name assembly meeting in Hamburg, Pennsylvania. In 1964 he moved to Idaho to become assistant editor of the *Sacred Name Herald.* In 1965 at a Feast of Tabernacles meeting in Nevada, Missouri, he was consecrated for the ministry. Then in 1966, after having previously moved to Bethel, Pennsylvania, near to his birthplace, he began his radio ministry. The Sacred Name Broadcast first aired over a station in Baltimore, Maryland. A magazine, *The Sacred Name Broadcaster,* was begun in 1968. In 1969, to facilitate the preaching of the Sacred Name message, he founded the Assemblies of Yahweh. Ten elders were ordained. As the membership grew, a second periodical for members only, *The Narrow Way,* was added. Under Meyer's leadership the Assemblies has grown into the largest Sacred Name organization in the world. The Assemblies also publishes its own version of the Sacred Scriptures.

Doctrinally, the Assemblies of Yahweh has concepts at variance with Christianity. Members affirm "that in order to interpret correctly the Inspired Scriptures, we must use the Old Testament as a basis of our faith." This hermeneutical position toward the dominance of the Old Testament in biblical interpretation is related to the basic Israelite faith and Judaism. The Assemblies teaches the necessity of believers' affirming the divine names Yahweh and Yahshua, the marks of the Divine Father that stand in contrast to the mark of the beast (Rev. 13: 16-17). A non-Trinitarian position is maintained. All the Old Testament commandments, including the feast days and excepting only the ritual and annual sacrifice laws, must be kept. Tithing is stressed. Women cover their heads for worship and wear modest dress. Nonviolence and conscientious objection to war are stressed.

The Assemblies of Yahweh is headed by the directing elder as the earthly shepherd under the Savior, Yahshua the Messiah. Under his direction are the ordained preaching elders who serve in spiritual matters and the deacons who handle temporal affairs. Under these members (who are always males) are the senior missionaries and missionaries (who may be either male or female). Affiliated assemblies are located in 50 countries around the world. The missionary thrust, both foreign and domestic, is concentrated through the Sacred Name Broadcast, heard over 24 stations across the United States (as of 1995) and in 75 foreign countries, over shortwave radio station WMLK owned and operated by the Assemblies of Yahweh. The Sacred Name Telecast, a half-hour program, is aired weekly over several networks. Listeners may receive a wide variety of literature and enroll in a correspondence course. Foreign offices are maintained in England, the Philippines, and Trinidad. Affiliated members are found in 115 countries.

**Membership:** The Assemblies does not count members but (as of 1992) estimates the number to be several thousand. There are 75 congregations and six elders (ministers).

**Educational Facilities:** Obadiah School of the Bible, Bethel, Pennsylvania.

**Periodicals:** *The Sacred Name Broadcaster.* • *The Narrow Way.*

**Sources:**


Meyer, Jacob O. *Exploding the Inspired Greek New Testament Myth.* Bethel, PA: Assemblies of Yahweh, 1978.

Meyer, Jacob O. *The Memorial Name—Yahweh.* Bethel, PA: Assemblies of Yahweh, 1978.

*Psalms, Anthems, Spiritual Songs for the Assemblies of Yahweh.* Bethel, PA: Assemblies of Yahweh, n.d.

*The Sacred Scriptures, Bethel Edition.* Bethel, PA: Assemblies of Yahweh, 1981.

*Statement of Doctrine.* Bethel, PA: Assemblies of Yahweh, 1981.


**★979★**
**Assemblies of Yahweh (Eaton Rapids, Michigan)**
Box 102
Holt, MI 48842

The Sacred Name movement began among members of the Seventh Day Church of God during the 1930s. Possibly the oldest surviving assembly is the Assembly of Yahweh, of Eaton Rapids, Michigan, originally chartered as the Assembly of Y.H.W.H. in 1939. Among its charter members were Joseph Owsinski, John Bigelow Briggs, Squire LaRue Cessna, Harlan Van Camp, George Reiss, Daniel Morris, William L. Bodine, John M. Cardona, Edmond P. Roche, and Marvin Gay. The original charter allowed some variation in the spelling of the Sacred Name, but Yahweh came to be accepted. It associated with other independent assemblies, in large part through the efforts of C. O. Dodd, an early Sacred Name advocate.

Dodd founded a magazine, *The Faith,* at Salem, West Virginia, in 1937, originally to promote the observance of Yaweh's feasts (as described in the Old Testament) among the members of the Seventh Day Church of God. In 1938 he organized the Faith Bible and Tract Society. Within a few years Dodd had become convinced of the Sacred Name position and began using it on the pages of *The Faith.* The magazine tied together the growing movement and became a major instrument in its spread. After Dodd's death it was passed to several assemblies until 1969 when the assembly at Eaton Rapids took responsibility for publishing it. The Faith Bible and Tract Society was continued by Dodd's family in Amherst, Ohio.

A lengthy statement of faith asserts the Assemblies' aim to remove the names substituted by man for the true names: Yahweh, the Father, and his son, Yahshua the Messiah. The Assemblies uphold the Ten Commandments, including the seventh-day Sabbath, and practice footwashing, baptism by immersion, and the festivals according to Leviticus 23. The Old Testament food laws are advocated, as are tithing and divine healing. The assembly is non-Trinitarian. The Assembly of Yahweh at Eaton Rapids is autonomous, but has fellowship and communication with like assemblies across the United States and in some 30 countries around the world.

**Membership:** Not known. The assembly is in fellowship with other assemblies across the country and around the world.

**Periodicals:** *The Faith.*

**Sources:**


Snow, E. D. "A Brief History of the Name Movement in America." *The Faith* 45 (January-February 1982).


**★980★**
**Assembly of Yahvah**
Box 89
Winfield, AL 35594

*History.* Among the first to accept the idea of the Sacred Name movement were Elder Lorenzo Snow (b. 1913) and his wife, Icie Lela Paris Snow (b. 1912), members of the Seventh Day Church of God at Fort Smith, Arkansas. They affiliated with the original Assembly of Yahweh led by C. O. Dodd, and L. D. Snow was licensed to preach by the church in the early 1940s. In 1945, he began publishing *The Yahwist Field Reporter.* Four years later, he moved to Emory, Texas, where he and other sacred name believers attending a camp meeting formed the Assembly of Yahvah. They used the spelling of the Creator's name that Snow had come to believe was

529

ENCYCLOPEDIA OF AMERICAN RELIGIONS, 5th Edition

five-member editorial committee are elected. Affiliated ecclesias are found in 30 countries. Active correspondence and interchange with the British Bible Students of the Bible Fellowship Union are promoted.

**Membership:** Not reported. In 1992 the institute's periodical circulated sightly more than 3,000 copies in the United States and Canada, and slightly less than 1,000 overseas. The church had affiliate congregations (ecclesias) in England, and continued in fellowship with the Berean Bible Institute in Australia.

**Periodicals:** *The Herald of Christ's Kingdom.*

**Sources:**


Streeter, R. E. *Daniel the Beloved of Jehovah.* Brooklyn, NY: Pastoral Bible Institute, 1928.

———. *The Revelation of Jesus Christ.* 2 vols. Brooklyn, NY: Pastoral Bible Institute, 1923-1924.


**★974★**
**Philanthropic Assembly**
709 74th St.
North Bergen, NJ 07047

F. L. Alexander Freytag (1870-1947) was in charge of the Swiss Bureau of the International Bible Students Association. Though an able leader, he was never an exponent of founder Charles Taze Russell's theology, and in 1917 he began to criticize Russell's main teaching books, the six-volume *Studies in the Scripture.* Then in 1920 he published the *Message of Laodicea* as an attack on the society, and Judge J. R. Rutherford, who succeeded Russell, took up the debate in *The Harp of God,* his first major book, before the year was out. In 1921, Freytag withdrew and set up the Church of the Kingdom of God, also known as the Philanthropic Assembly of the Friends of Man, taking with him many Swiss, German, and French Bible Students.

Freytag concentrated on the religious problem of death. He believed that he had found the answer in his intimate relationship with the person of Christ. One overcomes death by conforming to the form of Jesus. By eschewing sin and following Jesus, one escapes the wages of sin. Freytag's message of death conquered was set within a framework of Russell's theology. He added an important point: eternal happiness is God's goal for all mankind, without exception. The replacement of death with hell's torment was not good enough for Freytag, who demanded the conquering of death itself. The idea is further supported by allegiance to the Universal Law-"God is love." This characteristic is the supreme fact of creation.

Freytag's movement main strength was in central Europe (Switzerland, Germany, France, Spain, Austria, Belgium and Italy), but it found some adherents among Bible Students in the eastern United States. The American headquarters circulates English-language editions of Freytag's books and two periodicals.

**Membership:** Not reported. American adherents are estimated to be in the hundreds. Internationally, the *Monitor,* the main periodical, circulates 120,000 copies in several languages.

**Periodicals:** *The Monitor of the Reign of Justice.* • *Paper for All.* Available from L'Ange de l'Eternal, Le Chateau, 1236 Cartigny, Switzerland.

**Sources:**


Freytag, F. L. Alexander. *The Divine Revelation.* Geneva, Switz.: Disciples of Christ, 1922.

———. *Eternal Life.* Geneva, Switz.: Messenger of the Lord, 1933.

———. *The New Earth.* Geneva, Switz.: Bible and Tract House, 1922.


**★975★**
**Western Bible Students Association**
Current address not obtained for this edition.

The Western Bible Students Association centered in Seattle, Washington, is at one in doctrine with the Christian Believers Conference but administratively separate. It holds an annual conference at Mission Springs, Santa Cruz, California.

**Membership:** Not reported.

## Sacred Name Groups

**★976★**
**Assemblies of the Called Out Ones of Yah**
Current address not obtained for this edition.

The Assemblies of the Called Out Ones of Yah began in 1974 when Sam Surratt, a believer who had previously been convinced that "Yah" was the correct name of the Creator and "Yeshuah" that of His son, the Messiah, felt compelled to create a unity of the truly Called Out Ones of Yah. Surratt felt that the true church would be guided by Yah through Yeshuah and the Holy Spirit, rather than by one leader, and that leaders would be chosen by casting lots. Following a Biblical pattern, the Called Out Ones are led by twelve apostles, the seven, and the seventy. The seven, which constitute the officers for the assemblies, are elected for two-year terms and, together with the seventy (directors at large), comprise the board of directors for the assemblies.

The assemblies follow the main ideas of the Sacred Name Movement and are very clear in their rejection of both the Trinitarian position and the "Oneness" or "Jesus Only" position of some Pentecostals. The assemblies teach the importance of the baptism of the Holy Spirit and the reception of the gifts of the Spirit (1 Corinthians 12). Members of the assemblies refrain from military duty but will accept alternative humanitarian government service. Members tithe ten percent of their increase (net income) annually. A second tithe is given at the annual feast days (Deuteronomy 14: 22-26), and every third year there is a poor fund tithe. Baptism is by immersion. Weekly worship is on the Sabbath.

In the early 1970s Surratt began to send literature to Sacred Name and Sabbatarian believers across the United States and into foreign fields. He built a mailing list of many thousands that has produced some new members who have begun local assemblies. Branch chapters were designated wherever two or more of the Called Out Ones gathered. Surratt died in 1990 and the present status of the church is unknown.

**Membership:** Not reported. According to the assemblies, the Called Out Ones of Yah consists of the great multitude (which no one can number) from all nations being called out by Yah from all Babylonish religions to serve with Yeshuah in the coming kingdom. It numbers more than 144,000.

**Periodicals:** *Called Out Ones Bible Thought Provoker Messenger.*

**Sources:**


Surratt, Sam. *"Judge" or "Be Judged," That's the Question.* Jackson, TN: Assemblies of the Called Out Ones of Yah, n.d.

———. *The Point of No Return.* Jackson, TN: Assemblies of the Called Out Ones of Yah, n.d.

———. *Virgin Lamps.* Jackson, TN: Assemblies of the Called Out Ones of Yah, 1977.


**★977★**
**Assemblies of Yah**
(Defunct)

The Assemblies of Yah was a small Sacred Name group headquartered in Albany, Oregon. Its aims were to present Yah's name to the world; to teach the laws, statutes and judgments of the

...at that point, the Hegira. From that time, there would be 1290 days (or years) until the consummation. In 1912, World War began in the Balkans. After this began, there could be only one generation (45 years) until the end. Thus, the end is imminent.

In Jerusalem, Dugger began a Hebrew-Christian ministry and publishing concern which prints books, numerous booklets and tracts, church school material, a correspondence course, and several periodicals. Members are scattered around the world. Following Dugger's death in 1975, the work of the church passed into the hands of his wife, Effie Dugger, his daughter Naomi Dugger Fauth, and his son-in-law, Gordon Fauth. They keep in touch with members and assemblies around the world and in the United States through their regular mailing and voluminous correspondence. A. N. Dugger's son Charles Andy Dugger broke with the family and began another group, Workers Together with Elohim.

**Membership:** In 1986 the church reported more than 40,000 members and 300 congregations worldwide.

**Periodicals:** *The Mount Zion Reporter.*

**Sources:**

Dugger, A. N. *A Bible Reading for the Home Fireside.* Jerusalem: "Mt. Zion" Press. Reprint. Decatur, MI: Johnson Graphics, 1982.

Dugger, A. N., and C. O. Dodd. *A History of the True Religion.* Jerusalem: Mt. Zion Reporter, 1968.

**★984★**
**House of Yahweh (Abilene, Texas)**
Box 242
Abilene, TX 79604

Among the people with whom Jacob Hawkins, founder of the House of Yahweh (Odessa, Texas), communicated during his inspired discovery of the Name of the true organization of the Called out One of Yahweh was his brother Yisrayl B. Hawkins in Abilene, Texas. Yisrayl joined Jacob in building the sanctuary of the House of Yahweh even while Jacob was in Israel. However, in 1980, Yisrayl Hawkins began to hold Sabbath services in a mobile home refurbished as a sanctuary outside Abilene, Texas, when he became convinced of the necessity of establishing the House of Yahweh according to the prophecies of Micah 4:1-2 and Isaiah 2:2. He asserted that the chartering of the House of Yahweh in Abilene by the State of Texas (and its subsequent recognition by the Internal Revenue Service) was the fulfillment of prophecy of the establishment of Yahweh's House in the last days, with the coming of Yahshua Messiah. It would fulfill the prophecies in Micah 4:2 and Isaiah 2:2 that the House of Yahweh would be exalted above every other form of government and religion.

Yahweh himself is the head of the House of Yahweh. Yahshua Messiah is second in command under His Father, and is the High Priest over the House of Yahweh. The overseer of the international headquarters of the House of Yahweh, Abilene, is Yisrayl B. Hawkins, who is assisted by the elders, deacons, and deaconesses. Weekly worship is held in the sanctuary building in Abilene each Saturday morning. Holy days, including those commanded in Leviticus 23 are celebrated: Yahshua's Memorial, Yahweh's Passover, the Feast of Unleavened Bread, the the Day of Pentecost, the Feast of Tabernacles, and the Last Great Day. Adjacent to the sanctuary is a campground for those attending the feasts from out of town.

The House of Yahweh carries on an active publishing program that includes a monthly magazine, a number of booklets on various doctrinal subjects, and a new holy name version of the Holy Scriptures, *The Book of Yahweh.*

**Membership:** In 1992 the House of Yahweh reported seven congregations served by 35 ministers. The subscription list of *The Prophetic Word* now reaches several thousand, and the magazine is sent to most foreign countries outside of the former Soviet bloc.

**Periodicals:** *The Prophetic Word.*

**Sources:**

*The Book of Yahweh.* Abilene, TX: House of Yahweh, 1987.

Hawkins, Yisrayl B. *True Stories About Christmas.* Abilene, TX: House of Yahweh, n.d.

*The House of Yahweh Established.* Abilene, TX: House of Yahweh, n.d.

*Who Do You Worship?* Abilene, TX: House of Yahweh, n.d.

*Yahweh's Passover and Yahshua's Memorial.* Abilene, TX: House of Yahweh, n.d

**★985★**
**House of Yahweh (Odessa, Texas)**
℅ Jacob Hawkins
Box 4938
Odessa, TX 79760

The House of Yahweh was founded in 1973 in Nazareth, Israel, by Jacob Hawkins, an American who had gone to Israel in 1967 to work on a kibbutz in the Negev. Hawkins learned of the discovery in 1973 of an ancient sanctuary dating to the first century that had "House of Yahweh" engraved over its entrance in Hebrew. In his own study of Scripture, he had determined that the name of the people called out by Yahweh was the "House of Yahweh." Thus he was led to found Yahweh's House anew. He began to correspond with people about his discovery and his subsequent actions. In 1975 he returned to the United States and built a sanctuary of the House of Yahweh in Odessa, Texas.

Members of the House of Yahweh direct their worship to Yahweh the Father, whose title is Elohim, and His son Yeshua, whose title is Messiah. Yahshua's shed blood cleanses believers from sin if they keep the Ten Commandments, Yahweh's law. Members tithe one-tenth of their income to the support of the ministry. They are sabbatarians.

The House of Yahweh observes the Old Testament feast days as mentioned in Leviticus 23. Further, it teaches that all believers must come together for the feasts of Passover, Pentecost, and Tabernacles, and members travel from around the United States and the world for these events. In like measure, holidays such as Christmas, Easter, Halloween, and Sunday as a day of worship are condemned as pagan and un-Biblical. Yahshua was born in the spring (around Passover), not in December.

The House of Yahweh is organized on a Biblical pattern with twelve apostles and seventy elders. They meet to conduct business each new moon.

**Membership:** The House of Yahweh does not keep membership records. In 1980 the House of Yahweh reported congregations in the United States, Israel, India, South Africa, West Africa, Burma, Australia, and Belgium.

**Educational Facilities:** Ministers Training School, Odessa, Texas.

**Periodicals:** *The Prophetic Watchman.*

**Sources:**

*Directory of Sabbath-Observing Groups.* Fairview, OK: Bible Sabbath Association, 1980.

**★986★**
**Missionary Dispensary Bible Research**
Box 5296
Buena Park, CA 90622

Associated with the Assembly of Yahvah is the Missionary Dispensary Bible Research, headquartered in Buena Park, California. The group is responsible for the production of *The Restoration of Original Sacred Name Bible* which used Yahvah, Elohim, and Yahshua for the Sacred Names. It is based on Joseph B. Rotherham's translation but uses the King James Version's form of paragraphing. Rotherham included a paragraph entitled "The Name Suggested"



ENCYCLOPEDIA OF AMERICAN RELIGIONS, 5th Edition

**STATEMENT OF FAITH (WORLDWIDE CHURCH OF GOD) (continued)**

(Leviticus 27:30, Numbers 18:20-21, Matthew 23:23, Hebrews 7:4-14)

THE SECOND COMING

Jesus Christ, as he promised, will return to earth to judge and reign over all nations, in the kingdom of God. His second coming will be visible, and in power and glory. This event is the hope of the Church, because it inaugurates the resurrection of the dead and the reward of the righteous.

(John 14:3, Revelation 17:14, Acts 1: 11, Revelation 1:7, Matthew 24:30, I Thessalonians 4:16-17)

THE MILLENNIUM

The Millennium is the one-thousand-year period during which Jesus Christ and the resurrected saints rule the world in peace, justice, and equity. It begins when Christ returns as King of kings and Lord of lords to establish the kingdom of God over all nations. At the beginning of the Millennium, Satan is bound and the prophesied "times of refreshing" begin. After the Millennium, when all enemies will have been put under his feet and all things made subject to him, Christ will deliver the kingdom to God the Father.

(Revelation 20:1-4, 6, Acts 3:19-21, Revelation 11:15, I Corinthians 15:24)

THE INHERITANCE OF THE BELIEVER

The inheritance of the believer is eternal life in the kingdom of God. This inheritance is reserved in heaven and will be bestowed at the second coming of Christ. The resurrected saints will then rule the nations with Christ in the kingdom of God.

(I John 2:25, Romans 8:16-19, Daniel 7:27, I Peter 1:3-5, Revelation 5:10)

THE FATE OF THE UNREPENTANT

Unrepentant sinners are those who, after coming to a full knowledge of God, deliberately and ultimately reject him. Their fate is to perish in the lake of fire. This death is eternal, and the Scriptures refer to it as the second death.

(Matthew 10:28, 3:12, 25:41, Revelation 20:14-15)

THE KINGDOM OF GOD

The kingdom of God in the broadest sense is God's supreme sovereignty. God reigns in the Church and in the life of each believer who is submissive to his will. The kingdom of God will be established over the whole world after the return of Jesus Christ and will increase to encompass all things.

(Luke 17:20-21, Daniel 2:44, Mark 1:14-15, I Corinthians 15:24-28, Revelation 11:15, 21:3, 22-27, 22:1-5)

**Notes:** *The Worldwide Church of God is the most successful of the several sabbatarian Church of God groups. These groups dissent from orthodox Christianity on the doctrine of the Trinity. Though non-Trinitarian, the Church affirms much of the substance of the traditional trinitarian doctrine. The Bible is considered the infallible Word of God. The Church worships on Saturday, and keeps the Sabbath of the Ten Commandments and Jewish festivals. It advocates tithing as the biblical form of giving.*

* * *

## Sacred Name Groups

**THE DOCTRINES AND TEACHINGS (ASSEMBLY OF YHWHHOSHUA)**

1. DENOMINATIONS AND AFFILIATIONS

The Assembly of YHWHHOSHUA is not affiliated or in accord with any other of the denominational or non-denominational churches or sects, and its members of the Assembly of YHWHHOSHUA are not simultaneously members of any other assembly, sect or church unless that sect, assembly or church, is preaching the true unadulterated Word of YHWHHOSHUA. The various churches in the United States in one form or another are in, the state of disobedience to the laws of YHWH. So we can not partake in these unrighteous churches.

2. THE NAME OF THE ALMIGHTY AND HIS MESSIAH

The true revealed Name of the Almighty is YHWH, and His Messiah, the Savior, is YHWHHOSHUA. The name YHWH, meaning, I AM or HE WHO IS, was declared by the Almighty, Himself, to Mosheh (Moses) on Mt. Horeb (Ex. 3:13-15), in which He declares, "This is My Name forever, and My Memorial unto all generations." It is quite clear from these passages that His NAME is not to be changed. In the King James (KJV) and other versions of the bible; translators have mistranslated the Divine Name, YHWH, into the word 'LORD'; and 'GOD' instead of 'ELOHIM', the Hebrew title for the Supreme Being. In their former languages, the title 'LORD' is 'BAAL', which is the supreme idol of heathen Babylon. 'ADONIS', 'ADONAI', or 'ADON' are the Phoenician and Greek idol of beauty from whence comes the name 'JEHOVAH'. 'GOD' is the Assyrian deity of fortune. The NAME of the Son—"I am come in My Father's Name" (John 5:43)—is the Name YHWH, together with the Name HOSHUA (SAVIOR). In full, it is YHWHHOSHUA, meaning, I AM THE SAVIOR, or YHWH has become SALVATION. "I, even I, am YHWH, and beside ME there is no Savior." (Isaiah 43:11) This uncompromising statement leaves no room for any savior named Jesus, Zeus, or any other name but YHWHHOSHUA. Jesus is the English form of the Greek name for their savior, which in Greek mythology is Zeus (Ie-Zeus or Ea-Zeus—healing Zeus). These facts can be documented. It is also disrespectful to call our Father and Savior by a shortened name or nickname, thus disallowing the terms 'YAH', 'Yahshua', or 'Yahoshua', and others in reference to our Father and Savior.

398

THE ENCYCLOPEDIA OF AMERICAN RELIGIONS: RELIGIOUS CREEDS, Vol. 2
J. Gordon Melton, Editor (Gale Research Company, 1988)

Portugal in 1317, like the Spanish orders of Alcantara and Calatrava (qq.v.) under Cistercian rule and to fight against the Moors. It was endowed with property of the Templars, who had been suppressed in 1312. Papal confirmation was received from John XXII. in 1319, the grand master being made subordinate to the abbot of the Cistercian monastery of Alcobaça. The knights gained important victories and became rich and powerful. At their chief seat, Thomar (75 m. n.e. of Lisbon) in Estremadura, and at Batalha, twenty miles farther west, they erected magnificent buildings in pointed style, imitating the churches of the Templars in Cyprus and the Mosque of Omar in Jerusalem (cf. the Viscount de Condeixa, *O mosteiro da Batalha*, with French transl., Lisbon and Paris, 1892; J. Dernjac, *Thomar und Batalha*, in the *Zeitschrift für bildende Kunst*, new series, vi [1895], 98–106). About 1500 Pope Alexander VI. released the order from the vow of poverty. It had then 450 commanderies and an enormous income. A reform was effected in 1550 by the Hieronymite abbot Anton of Lisbon, and confirmed by Pope Julius III. At the same time the grand-mastership was formally attached to the crown, as it had been actually from the time of King Emmanuel (1495–1521). Pius V. in 1567 removed the jurisdiction of the abbot of Alcobaça, and Gregory XIII. in 1576 granted the king supreme power over both knights and monks. The order was secularized in 1797 and its property confiscated in 1834. It is now merely an order of merit. A less important Italian *Ordine di Christo* was founded by Pope John XXII. about 1320. It also became an order of merit. (O. Zöckler†.)

Bibliography: Helyot, *Ordres monastiques*, vi. 72–76, Paris, 1718; G. Giucci, *Iconografia storica degli ordini religiosi e cavallereschi*, i. 34–36, Rome, 1836; G. Moroni, *Dizionario di erudizione storico-ecclesiastica*, xviii. 210–219, Venice, 1843; Heimbucher, *Orden und Kongregationen*, i. 227; Currier, *Religious Orders*, p. 217.

**CHRIST**, crist, **PAUL**: Swiss Protestant; b. at Zurich Oct. 25, 1836; d. there Jan. 14, 1908. He was educated at the universities of Tübingen and Basel, and after being a pastor successively in the canton of Grisons (1858–62) and at Chur, the capital of the same canton (1862–65), he was a professor in the cantonal school of Chur from 1865 to 1870. He was then pastor at Lichtensteig (1871–75) and Rheineck (1875–80), both in the canton of St. Gall, and after four years of retirement on account of impaired health (1880–84) was municipal archivist at Chur (1884–87) and again professor in the cantonal school of the same city (1887–89). Since 1889 he has been professor of systematic and practical theology at the University of Zurich. In theology he represents the speculative and liberal school. He has written *Christliche Religionslehre* (Zurich, 1875); *Bilder aus der Geschichte der christlichen Kirche und Sitte* (St. Gall, 1876); *Religiöse Betrachtungen* (1881); *Der Pessimismus und die Sittenlehre* (Haarlem, 1882); *Die Lehre vom Gebet nach dem Neuen Testament* (Leyden, 1886); *Die sittliche Weltordnung* (1894); and *Grundriss der Ethik* (Berlin, 1905).

**CHRISTADELPHIANS**: A small sect which originated in the United States about 1850. They call themselves Christadelphians because of the belief that all that are in Christ are his brethren, and designate their congregations as "ecclesias" to "distinguish them from the so-called churches of the apostasy." John Thomas, the founder, a physician, born in England, came to America in 1844 and joined the Disciples of Christ. In a short time, however, he established a separate denomination, because he believed that, though the Disciples were the most "apostolic and spiritually enlightened religious organization in America," the religious teaching of the day was contrary to the teaching of the Bible.

Christadelphians reject the Trinity. They believe in one supreme God, who dwells in unapproachable light; in Jesus Christ, in whom was manifest the eternal spirit of God, and who died for the offenses of sinners, and rose for the justification of believing men and women; in one baptism only—immersion, the "burial with Christ in water into death to sin," which is essential to salvation; in immortality only in Christ; in eternal punishment of the wicked, but not in eternal torment; in hell, not as a place of torment, but as the grave; in the resurrection of the just and unjust; in the utter annihilation of the wicked, and in the non-resurrection of those who have never heard the Gospel, lack in intelligence (as infants), or are sunk in ignorance or brutality; in a second coming of Christ to establish his kingdom on earth, which is to be fitted for the everlasting abode of the saints; in the proximity of this second coming; in Satan as a Scriptural personification of sin; in the millennial reign of Christ on earth over the nations, during which sin and death will continue in a milder degree, and after which Christ will surrender his position of supremacy, and God will reveal himself, and become Father and Governor of a complete family; in salvation only for those who can understand the faith as taught by the Christadelphians, and become obedient to it. They have no ordained ministers. There are about sixty "ecclesias" in the United States, and a few in England, where most of their literature is published. H. K. Carroll.

Bibliography: Sources of doctrine are the works of the founder, generally published in pamphlet form in Birmingham and London. The principal are: *Eureka*, 1869; *The Revealed Mystery*, 1869; *Who are the Christadelphians?* 1869; *The Book Unsealed*, 1870; *Phanerosis*, 1870; *Anastasis*, 1871; *Clerical Theology Unscriptural*, 1877, and *Elpis Israel*, West Hoboken, 1871. Also the following works by Robert Roberts: *A Defence of the Faith Proclaimed in Ancient Times, . . . Revived in the Christadelphians*, Birmingham, 1868; *Everlasting Punishment not "Eternal Torments,"* ib. 1871; *Meaning of the Christadelphian Movement*, London, 1872; *Thirteen Lectures on the Things Revealed in . . . "Revelation,"* Birmingham, 1880; *The Good Confession*, ib. 1881; *Dr. Thomas, his Life and Work*, ib. 1884. Their organ is *The Christadelphian*, published at Birmingham, Eng. Consult H. K. Carroll, *Religious Forces of the U. S.*, pp. 89–90, 454, New York, 1896.

**CHRISTENTUMSGESELLSCHAFT, DIE DEUTSCHE** ("The German Society for Christendom"): A society which had a wide influence at the end of the eighteenth and beginning of the nineteenth centuries. In that period of deep depression and discouragement for the Evangelical



Church of Germany, it broug
Christians together by persona
correspondence, and helped
cooperation. Its special objec
bold depreciation and mockery
then so common, as well as
sented by Nikolai's *Zeitschrif*
*Gothaer Zeitung*. Its founde
August Urlsperger (q.v.), of
longed to the old school of si
and piety. He thought that
Gospel should stand together
another as did its enemies. I
number of German, Dutch, I
theologians without getting
in 1779 and 1780 traveled wi
effecting more by personal con
was still the same, and he ca
couraged. In Basel, the last p
to visit, he found a response.
stirred up by D'Annone, the ze
tens, a number of like-minde
been organized, who listened
sperger's ideas; and the society
first formal meeting on Aug. 30
ning once made, the thing sp
formed at Nuremberg the next
gart, Frankfort, Berlin, Magd
numbers grew, and correspon
from America, a more forma
required. Basel was made the
end of 1782, and a manifold ac
it, embracing all that is meant
and foreign missions. Selecti
mass of correspondence were sen
in printed form after 1783.
inally wished to write and circu
treatises, but the central body
a more practical direction, wi
hold the true faith, but not to
troversies. The name, too, w
original *Deutsche Gesellschaf*
*christlicher Wahrheit und Got*
Society for the Promotion of
Piety") to the present title.
who had been the general secr
the Savoy Chapel in London,
between Germany and Englan
revival of spiritual life set a sta
The Basel Bible Society was fo
first result; and the second wa
also at Basel, planned as earl
Spittler on the model of the
(founded in 1800 by Jänicke, a
ciety), and realized in 1815
C. G. Blumhardt (q.v.). A nu
dations and special organizatio
ceeding years. Among them
school and orphanage at Be
Society of the Friends of Israel
for the Spread of Christian
the deaf and dumb asylum at
the deaconess home in the
The original association fulfille
the impulse to so many and
it still exists, however, under

THE NEW SCHAFF-HERZOG ENCYCLOPEDIA OF RELIGIOUS KNOWLEDGE (Baker Book House, Grand Rapids, MI, 1950, 1967) VOL. III

which elects its own officers. Christadelphians take no part in politics, voting, or military service.

**Christian Fellowship Church** or **Etoism.** The main independent church in Melanesia, founded on New Georgia in the Solomon Islands in 1959 by Silas Eto (b. 1905). As a *catechist-teacher in the *Methodist mission, he developed deviationist practices from the 1930s, and, in disillusionment with staid mission forms, began his own true church. He remained an admirer of J. F. Goldie, founder of the mission, and claimed authority from both God and Goldie as revealed to him in a dream. Ecstatic worship was combined with healing, successful economic activities, and development of a model village, Paradise, as a 'holy city'. Despite incipient *messianism concerning Eto himself, relations with Methodists, now in the United Church, were being re-established in the 1970s.

**Christianity.** The origins of Christianity lie, historically, in the life and ministry of *Jesus, extended through his death, *resurrection, and *ascension. In its own estimate, its origins lie further back in the former *covenants (hence, from a Christian point of view, the Old Testament) made with Israel.

Christianity exists in a vast diversity of different styles and forms of organization, but all are agreed that the figure of Jesus is the disclosure of God and the means of human reconciliation with him. The life and ministry of Jesus seemed (to at least some of those who witnessed or experienced them at the time) to be a restoration in word and action of the power (Gk., *dunamis*) not of himself but of God, leading to the conclusion that 'he who has seen me has seen the Father'; 'I and the Father are one' (John 14. 9, 10. 30). The once fashionable argument is no longer tenable that Jesus was a simple Jewish teacher who was gradually promoted (see EUHEMERUS) into being the Son of God, as a result of *Paul transforming the teaching of Jesus into a *hellenized new religion. From the earliest writings in the New Testament, Jesus was closely associated with God, with extremely high titles and status in relation to God. The extraordinary way in which Jesus acted as one who was mediating the consequence of God through his own person produced 'the phenomenon of the New Testament': the ways in which these documents speak of Jesus, and which relate him uniquely to God, have clear connections with both Jewish and Hellenistic categories, and yet they are always distinctive and idiosyncratic.

In the early years, 'Christianity' was one interpretation, among many at that time, of what God's covenant with Israel and his purpose in creation should be; but in this interpretation, it was believed that Jesus was the promised *messiah (Heb., *ha-Mashiach* = messiah = Gk., *ho Christos*, hence the name 'Christianity', which was first used, according to Acts 2. 26, in *c.*40 CE). Since for other Jews, many of the marks of a messiah did not accompany Jesus, and since claims (impossible to them) were being made about Jesus in relation to God, the two religions separated, although for centuries a small number of Christians continued to believe that Jewish *Torah should still be observed. On the majority Christian side, the keeping of Torah was no longer regarded as a necessary condition of being in a covenant relation with God. The separation from Judaism was made by universalizing the consequences of Christ to all people. That process was accelerated by the fall of Jerusalem in 70 CE, after which an increasing hostility to Judaism led to a long (and still unended, though moderated) history of *anti-Semitism.

Characteristic Christian doctrines emerged from the demand of the New Testament evidence (and from the experience which brought it into being). Jesus mediated the consequence and effect of God, so that on the one hand it was evidently God who was acting and speaking in and through him, and yet on the other it was clear that Jesus addressed God (e.g. in prayer) as apart from himself, as Father (see ABBA): this produced a quest in the early centuries to find ways of speaking of these two natures in one person (*Christology; the willingness and obedience of *Mary in accepting the conception and birth of Jesus produced a widespread, though not universal, devotion to Mary, and a close association of her with the work of *redemption). At the same time, God was clearly present to the life of Jesus (e.g. at his birth and his baptism, and in the directing of his mission), in the ways traditionally spoken of as the *Holy Spirit. This led to a further quest to find ways of speaking of the interior nature of God, as being in itself, not an abstract unity, but social and relational (i.e. as *Trinity).

It was also recognized that what Jesus had done during his life for some particular people, in reconciling them to God when they had become estranged from him and from each other, was, as a consequence of his death, resurrection, and ascension, extended to others, and indeed made universal, at least as an opportunity for those who respond in faith. This led to doctrines of *atonement.

This extension of the consequence of Christ was made immediately realistic, and thus realizable, through the enacted signs of *baptism (taking believers into the death of Christ and raising them to a new life already here on earth) and of the *last supper (*eucharist). From the earliest days (*Pentecost), the followers of Christ felt that they had been empowered by the Holy Spirit conferring on them special gifts. Initially, they looked for an early return of Christ (Second Coming or *parousia), and although that expectation faded, it has remained as an important *eschatological component of Christian belief. The sense of being, in the meantime, the continuing Body of Christ led to the mystical interpretation of the *Church, which lies apart from the many divisions of Christians into separated Churches.

Diverse writings evoked by the ev
life and ministry, and their conseque
of believers) were gathered eventuall
Testament. During the New Testam
*kelal of Jesus (the context-indepen
of love) was made context-depen
applications to particular circumsta
general command to love God and
was applied to the circumstances i
found themselves, as they asked wh
of that love should be in practice. C
relation between the context-indepe
and the context-dependent applica
tension between liberty and law in
ics.

During the New Testament p
nature of Christian community
changed dramatically: the original
Church as the Body of Christ, with
equal importance under the headsh
Colossians 1. 17 f.; 1 Corinthians
changed into a metaphor derived f
army, with a hierarchical organiza
levels of authority of *bishops, *p
cons: the clericalization of the C
subordination of the *laity has rem
istic of most parts of Christianit
present. However, the two model
hood of all believers, 1 Peter 2
controlling authority of ordained
remained in tension throughout C
although the authoritarian model
nant (e.g. in *Roman or Vatican C
the *pope assuming the title fr
Empire of Pontifex Maximus).

Initially Christianity was a small
ment, though confident in itself
resurrection and the experience o
from the Holy Spirit. In the early
held in suspicion by some because i
noxious superstition' (Tacitus), by c
its exclusive monotheism which co
prevailing Graeco-Roman syncretic
sive emphasis occasionally brough
with imperial authorities. Wh
occurred, Christianity in fact gain
(see TERTULLIAN), and the witness a
tyrs gained an importance which
the present: on the basis of the n
the 20th cent. has been called
martyrs'. After the support of *Co
recognition of Christianity as the
Empire under Theodosius I (e
Christianity became the major
Roman world.

Sometimes in conflict with exis
philosophies (e.g. *gnosticism), it
ing this period, drew on many suc
ing gnosticism and Greek philoso
its faith. Equally, it reworked vario
in the artistic sphere (e.g. Orpheus

THE OXFORD DICTIONARY OF WORLD RELIGIONS, John Bowker, ed
(Oxford, NY: Oxford University Press, 1997)

"I am YHWH, that is My Name, and My glory will I not five to another. . ." (Isaiah 42:8)

3. THE LAW OF YHWH AND THE GRACE OF YHWHHOSHUA

We believe that we are saved by the grace of YHWHHOSHUA, in that He shed his blood for the remission of our sins; and that we accept this grace by faith in what He did and taught as well as what He teaches today. We do not misconstrue this grace as a license to continue in our sin by disobeying YHWH's laws, but rather the strength to repent from our former lives of sin. It is by repentance and the keeping of YHWH's laws that we have access to His Holy Spirit.

4. IMMERSION (BAPTISM)

Once an individual decides that he or she is willing to dedicate their life of obedience to YHWH, it is required that one be baptized by full immersion in a natural body of water (lake, river or sea), by a minister of YHWHHOSHUA, as a token of the covenant that he is going to cleanse his life. We believe that YHWHHOSHUA honors this token of faith by applying the redeeming value of the blood that He shed to the individual's soul; cleansing him from all the sins that were committed previous to baptism. "He that believeth and is immersed shall be saved; but he that believeth not shall be damned." (Mark 16:16) "Repent and be immersed every one of you in the Name of YHWHHOSHUA the Messiah, for the remission of sins, and ye shall receive the gift of the Holy Spirit." (Acts 2:38) "Except a man be born of water and of the Spirit, he can not enter into the kingdom of YHWH". (John 3:5)

5. THE GIFT OF THE HOLY SPIRIT

Once a believer totally yields his heart, mind, body and soul to the perfect will of YHWH, he will receive the gift of the Holy Spirit, the Power of the Almighty, which will be initially evidenced by a marked improvement in the individual's life in the way of love, joy, peace, longsuffering, gentleness, faith, meekness, temperance, and a willingness to obey the laws of YHWH. When one receives the fullness and infilling of the Holy Spirit, he will speak in a heavenly tongue as the Spirit moves in him. "For with stammering lips and another tongue will He speak to this people." To whom He said, "This is the rest wherewith ye may cause the weary to rest; and this is the refreshing: yet they should not hear." (Isaiah 28:11-12) "And these signs shall follow them that believe; in My Name shall they cast out demons; they shall speak with new tongues:" (Mark 16:17)

6. MINISTERS

A minister or pastor of YHWHHOSHUA is a man (not a woman) who is in obedience to the doctrine of YHWHHOSHUA. ". . . ordain elders in every city. . ., If any be blame less, the husband of one wife. . ." (Titus 5:6) "That the man of YHWH may be perfect, thoroughly furnished unto all good works." (Timothy 3:17) "Let your women keep silence in the assemblies: for it is not permitted unto them to speak; but they are commanded to be under obedience, as also saith the law." (I Corinthians 14:34) "But I do not allow a woman to preach, nor to usurp authority over the man, but to be quiet. " (I Timothy 2:12)

7. SANCTIFICATION

The members of the assembly of YHWHHOSHUA are to be separate from the institutions, customs, traditions, styles and carnal pleasures of the United States as well as the world. A member in no way should participate into the affairs and practices of the world.

8. GOVERNMENT

YHWHHOSHUA is our government. He is our counselor, our welfare, medicare. He is our social security and old age care, our employment. Through YHWHHOSHUA all things are provided. The widows and orphans, the elderly and sick, those who are unable to work are to be supported by the assembly as a whole; the men working and giving out of the generosity of their hearts. It is the duty of every member of the assembly to help all those members of the assembly of YHWHHOSHUA who are in need. In no way should we participate in the charities of the world, for these charities are not for YHWH'S people. Thus a servant of YHWH can not vote or contribute to or accept any benefits from the institutions of the United States, such as Social Security, Medicare, Unemployment Compensation, etc. . . . nor shall he be allowed to be a government official, to be a juror, or to serve in the Armed Forces.

9. INCOME TAX

Members of the assembly of YHWHHOSHUA are not to pay the Federal Income Tax. The income tax of the United States is used to pay for such things that are contrary to the law of YHWH. Such as, the armed forces of America, "Thou shalt not kill." (Exodus 20) Numerous government medical benefits are provided by the income tax (abortion clinics, birth control research grants, experimental animal killing, etc . . .) These things are contrary to the law of YHWH. The lists seems endless, these are just a few of the atrocities the income tax encourages. "Render therefore unto Caesar (United States) the things which are Caesar's; and unto YHWH the things that are YHWH's." (Matthew 22:21) The money that the servants of YHWH earn belongs to YHWH and is to be used to supply the needs of YHWH's people, not those of the world. "And the multitude of them that believed were of one heart and of one soul; neither was there any among them that lacked; for as many as were possessors of lands or houses sold them and brought the prices of the things that were sold, and laid them down at the apostles' feet; and distribution was made unto every man according as he had need." (Acts 4:32, 34, 35) "Come out of her, My people, that ye be not partakers of her sins, and that ye received not of her plagues." (Rev. 18:4) "YHWHHOSHUA spoke to him, saying, What thinkest thou, Simon? of whom do the kings of the earth take custom or tribute? of their own children, or of strangers? Peter saith unto Him, Of strangers. YHWHHOSHUA saith unto him, Then are the children free." (Matthew 17:25-26)

10. HOLIDAYS

Christmas (Saturnalia), Easter (Ishtar), New Years, Independence Day, Thanksgiving, and any other heathen holiday are



THE ENCYCLOPEDIA OF AMERICAN RELIGIONS: RELIGIOUS CREEDS, vol. 2
J. Gordon Melton, Editor (Gale Research Company, 1988)

## *DIALOGUE* SEVEN: Who Is The "Faithful And Discreet Slave"? —Parts 1 and 2

CHAPTER 17

# FIND SECURITY AMONG GOD'S PEOPLE

IMAGINE that a violent storm has ravaged the area where you live. Your home is destroyed, and all your possessions are lost. Food is scarce. The situation seems hopeless. Then, unexpected relief supplies arrive. Food and clothing are provided in abundance. A new house is built for you. Surely you would be grateful to the person who made these provisions available.

2 Something comparable is occurring today. Like that storm, the rebellion of Adam and Eve caused great damage to the human race. Mankind's Paradise home was lost. Since then, human governments have failed to shelter people from war, crime, and injustice. Religion has left multitudes starving for wholesome spiritual food. Spiritually speaking, however, Jehovah God is now furnishing food, clothing, and shelter. How is he doing that?

### "THE FAITHFUL AND DISCREET SLAVE"

3 Relief supplies are generally dispensed through an organized channel, and Jehovah has similarly made spiritual provision for his people. For example, the Israelites were "Jehovah's congregation" for some 1,500 years. Among them were those who served as God's channel to

1, 2. How is mankind's situation like that of people in a storm-ravaged area?
3. How does Jehovah supply provisions for mankind, as shown by what examples?

FIND SECURITY 161

teach his Law. (1 Chronicles 28:8; 2 Chronicles 17:7-9) In the first century C.E., Jehovah brought forth the Christian organization. Congregations were formed, and they functioned under the direction of a governing body made up of apostles and older men. (Acts 15:22-31) Likewise today, Jehovah deals with his people through an organized body. How do we know this?

4 Jesus said that at the time of his presence in Kingdom power, "the faithful and discreet slave" would be found providing "food at the proper time" for His followers. (Matthew 24:45-47) When Jesus was installed as heavenly King in 1914, who did this "slave" prove to be? Certainly not the clergy of Christendom. For the most part, they were feeding their flocks propaganda that backed up their own national governments in World War I. But proper and timely spiritual food was being dispensed by the group of true Christians who were anointed by God's holy spirit and were a part of what Jesus called the "little flock." (Luke 12:32) These anointed Christians preached God's Kingdom rather than man's governments. As a result, over the years millions of righteously disposed "other sheep" have joined the anointed "slave" in practicing true religion. (John 10:16) Using the 'faithful slave' and its present-day Governing Body, God directs his organized people to make spiritual food, clothing, and shelter available to all who wish to have these provisions.

### "FOOD AT THE PROPER TIME"

5 Jesus said: "Man must live, not on bread alone, but on every utterance coming forth through Jehovah's

4. Who has "the faithful and discreet slave" proved to be in modern times, and how are God's spiritual provisions made available?
5. What spiritual condition exists in the world today, but what is Jehovah doing about this?

KNOWLEDGE THAT LEADS TO EVERLASTING LIFE, 1995

mouth." (Matthew 4:4) Sadly, though, the vast majority of people are not paying attention to God's utterances. As foretold by Jehovah's prophet Amos, there is "a famine, not for bread, and a thirst, not for water, but for hearing the words of Jehovah." (Amos 8:11) Even very religious people are spiritually famished. Nevertheless, Jehovah's will is that "all sorts of men should be saved and come to an accurate knowledge of truth." (1 Timothy 2:3, 4) Accordingly, he is providing spiritual food in abundance. But where can it be obtained?

6 Throughout history, Jehovah has dispensed spiritual food to his people as a group. (Isaiah 65:13) For instance, the Israelite priests gathered men, women, and children for group instruction in God's Law. (Deuteronomy 31:9, 12) Under the direction of the governing body, first-century Christians organized congregations and held meetings for the instruction and encouragement of all. (Romans 16:5; Philemon 1, 2) Jehovah's Witnesses follow this pattern. You are cordially invited to attend all their meetings.

7 Of course, you may already have learned much in your personal study of the Bible. Perhaps someone has assisted you. (Acts 8:30-35) But your faith might be likened to a plant that will wither and die if it is not given suitable care. Hence, you must receive proper spiritual nourishment. (1 Timothy 4:6) Christian meetings provide a continuous program of instruction designed to nourish you spiritually and help you to keep on growing in faith as you increase in the knowledge of God.—Colossians 1:9, 10.

6. How has Jehovah fed his people spiritually in times past?
7. How is regular attendance at Christian meetings related to knowledge and faith?



8 Meetings serve another vital purpose. Paul wrote: "Let us consider one another to incite to love and fine works, not forsaking the gathering of ourselves together." (Hebrews 10:24, 25) The Greek word translated "to incite" can also mean "to sharpen." A Bible proverb states: "By iron, iron itself is sharpened. So one man sharpens the face of another." (Proverbs 27:17) All of us need continual 'sharpening.' Daily pressures from the world can dull our faith. When we attend Christian meetings, there is an interchange of encouragement. (Romans 1:11, 12) Members of the congregation follow the apostle Paul's admonition to "keep comforting one another and building one another up," and such things sharpen our faith. (1 Thessalonians 5:11) Regular presence at Christian meetings also indicates that we love God and affords us opportunities to praise him. —Psalm 35:18.

### "CLOTHE YOURSELVES WITH LOVE"

9 Paul wrote: "Clothe yourselves with love, for it is a perfect bond of union." (Colossians 3:14) Jehovah has graciously provided this clothing for us. In what way? Christians can display love because it is one of the God-given fruits of Jehovah's holy spirit. (Galatians 5:22, 23) Jehovah himself has displayed the greatest love by sending his only-begotten Son so that we might have everlasting life. (John 3:16) This supreme demonstration of love provided a model for us in expressing this quality. "If this is how God loved us," wrote the apostle John, "then we are ourselves under obligation to love one another." —1 John 4:11.

8. Why are we encouraged to attend the meetings of Jehovah's Witnesses?
9. How has Jehovah set the example in displaying love?

KNOWLEDGE THAT LEADS TO EVERLASTING LIFE, 1995

God is with you

ıovah's Witness-
lone have God's
: so than when
ed to have God's
ptians' belief, or
; claimed to have
on of Jewish reli-
: themselves. In
es are doing the
s true followers
of the end: "This
will be preached
r a witness to all
end will come."

of Jehovah's Wit-
e the true religion?

[18] Jehovah's Witnesses will continue to carry out this commission, never allowing persecution or opposition to impede their activity. Jehovah's work must and will be done. Every attempt others have made during the past century to hinder the Witnesses from accomplishing God's work has ended in ultimate failure, for Jehovah promised: "Any weapon whatever that will be formed against you will have no success, and any tongue at all that will rise up against you in the judgment you will condemn. This is the hereditary possession of the servants of Jehovah, and their righteousness is from me."—Isaiah 54:17.

[19] That Jehovah's Witnesses are stronger and more active now than ever before—and this in the face of worldwide opposition—is proof that Jehovah finds pleasure in what they are doing. King David said: "By this I do know that you have found delight in me, because my enemy does not shout in triumph over me." (Psalm 41:11; 56:9, 11) Never will God's enemies be able to shout in triumph over Jehovah's people, for their Leader, Jesus Christ, is moving ahead to final victory!

18, 19. (a) Why is there no reason for Jehovah's Witnesses to desist from doing their preaching work, even though they are opposed? (b) How does Psalm 41:11 support the fact that the Witnesses have God's backing?

# MOVING AHEAD TO FINAL VICTORY!

*"Look! a white horse; and the one seated upon it had a bow; and a crown was given him, and he went forth conquering and to complete his conquest."*
—REVELATION 6:2.

BY DIVINE inspiration the apostle John was able to look some 1,800 years into the future and describe the enthronement of Christ as King. John needed faith to believe what he saw in vision. We today have clear evidence that this foretold enthronement took place in 1914. With eyes of faith, we see Jesus Christ going "forth conquering and to complete his conquest."

[2] Following the birth of the Kingdom, Satan was evicted from heaven, causing him to fight

1. What future events did John see in vision?
2. How did the Devil react to the Kingdom's birth, and of what is this an evidence?

THE WATCHTOWER 6/1/2001,
p. 17

ully because of the
eart, but you your-
because of the pain
wl because of sheer
aiah 65:13, 14.
*duct and their de-*
. "Trust in Jehovah
do not lean upon
" the writer of Prov-
ur ways take notice
ill make your paths
i) God backs those
ection rather than
ies of humans who
) the extent that a
ı his life after God's
ng to learn by trial
; 1 Corinthians 1:

*the manner of the*
*ıgregation.* Jesus set
: you be called Rab-
whereas all you are
ɔt call anyone your
is your Father, the
called 'leaders,' for
hrist. But the great-
be your minister."
gregation of broth-
ud clergy class that
ounding titles and
ty. (Job 32:21, 22)
ɔck of God are told
ulsion, but willing-
ıonest gain, but ea-
over those who are
ecoming examples
3) Genuine Chris-

:e true religion avoid
ror?
the true religion not
laity class? (b) What
e lead among God's

tian shepherds refrain from trying to make themselves masters over the faith of others. As fellow workers in God's service, they simply strive to set a fine example.—2 Corinthians 1:24.

12 *They are submissive to human governments and yet remain neutral.* He who fails to be "in subjection to the superior authorities" cannot expect to have God's backing. Why? Because "the existing authorities stand placed in their relative positions by God. Therefore he who opposes the authority has taken a stand against the arrangement of God." (Romans 13:1, 2) However, Jesus recognized the possibility of a conflict of interests when he said: "Pay back Caesar's things to Caesar, but God's things to God." (Mark 12:17) Those desiring to have God's backing must "keep on . . . seeking first the kingdom [of God] and his righteousness," while at the same time obeying the laws of the land that are compatible with their higher responsibilities to God. (Matthew 6:33; Acts 5:29) Jesus stressed neutrality when he said of his disciples: "They are no part of the world, just as I am no part of the world." He later added: "My kingdom is no part of this world."—John 17:16; 18:36.

12. What balanced position regarding human governments does God require of those desiring to have his backing?

*Christian elders serve as examples for the flock*

13 *They are impartial in working "what is good toward all."* (Galatians 6:10) Christian love knows no partiality, accepting all people regardless of their skin color, economic or educational status, nationality, or language. The working of what is good toward all and especially toward those related to them in the faith helps to identify those having God's backing. Jesus said: "By this all will know that you are my disciples, if you have love among yourselves."—John 13:35; Acts 10:34, 35.

14 *They are willing to suffer persecution for doing God's will.* Jesus forewarned his followers: "If they have persecuted me, they will persecute you also; if they have observed my word, they will observe yours also." (John 15:20; Matthew 5:11, 12; 2 Timothy 3:12) Those having God's backing have always been unpopular, as was Noah, who condemned the world through his faith. (Hebrews 11:7) Today, those desiring God's backing dare not water down God's word or compromise godly principles so as to avoid persecution. As long as they faithfully serve God, they know that people will be "puzzled and go on speaking abusively" of them.—1 Peter 2:12; 3:16; 4:4.

13. What part does love play in identifying God's people?
14. Do people having God's approval necessarily find universal acceptance? Explain.

### Time to Evaluate the Facts

15 Ask yourself, 'What religious group is noted for sticking closely to God's Word, even when its teachings differ from the beliefs of most people? Who stress the importance of God's personal name, even using it to identify themselves? Who optimistically point to God's Kingdom as the only solution to all human problems? Who uphold Bible standards of conduct, at the risk of being considered old-fashioned? What group is noted for having no paid clergy, all of its members being preachers? Who are praised for being law-abiding citizens, even though they refrain from taking part in politics? Who lovingly spend time and money in helping others to learn about God and his purposes? And despite all of these positive things, who are still looked down on, ridiculed, and persecuted?'

16 Millions of people throughout the world have evaluated the facts and have become convinced that Jehovah's Witnesses alone are practicing the true religion. They have reached this conclusion on the basis of what Jehovah's Witnesses teach and how they conduct themselves, as well as on the basis of the benefits their religion has brought. (Isaiah 48:17) Millions are, in effect, saying, as foretold at Zechariah 8:23: "We will go with you people, for we have heard that God is with you people."

15, 16. (a) What questions will help us identify the religious group that enjoys God's backing? (b) What conclusion have millions of people reached, and why?

**Can You Answer?**

- What are some ancient examples of people having God's backing?
- What are some identifying marks of the true religion?
- Why are you personally convinced that Jehovah's Witnesses have God's backing?

17 Is it presumptuous of Jehovah's Witnesses to point out that they alone have God's backing? Actually, no more so than when the Israelites in Egypt claimed to have God's backing in spite of the Egyptians' belief, or when first-century Christians claimed to have God's backing to the exclusion of Jewish religionists. The facts speak for themselves. In 235 lands Jehovah's Witnesses are doing the work Jesus foretold that his true followers would be doing in the time of the end: "This good news of the kingdom will be preached in all the inhabited earth for a witness to all the nations; and then the end will come." —Matthew 24:14.

17. Why is it not presumptuous of Jehovah's Witnesses to point out that they have the true religion?



18 Jehovah's
ry out this cor
cution or opp
Jehovah's wor
attempt other
century to hin
plishing God'
failure, for Jel
whatever that
have no succe

18, 19. (a) Wh
Witnesses to d
work, even thou
Psalm 41:11 su
have God's back

# MO
# FI

*"Look! a w*
*had a bow; a*
*forth conq*

BY DIVINE
able to lo
ture and descri
King. John nee
in vision. We t
foretold enthr
eyes of faith,
conquering an

2 Following
was evicted fr

1. What future e
2. How did the I
of what is this an

June 4th 2001

4.5 Min MP3 Go

**(Nigeria)--Topping the news, as the second anniversary of the restoration of Nigeria's civilian rule has come and gone, few are celebrating.** President Olusegun Obasanjo ended corrupt military rule, but too late, for some. Nigeria's health sector infrastructure is in a shambles after 15 years of neglect. That has led to a doctor strike and the shutdown of the public hospitals. **SIM's** Jonathan Shea explains the impact on their medical mission work. "This is the second one this year for the non-mission hospitals. The mission hospitals are staying open. They've had a lot of extra people coming in. It's just an ongoing thing. Anybody who comes in has to have light, they can walk in it if they'd like." Shea asks believers to pray for Christian medical workers. "During this time, all of the folks in the mission hospitals, as few as they might be, would be overworked. So that would be a really welcome thing, if folks would support them during the extra busy time."

**(Mexico)--Elsewhere, Open Doors reports that local authorities in three Mexican states have told evangelical Christians to change their religion or suffer severe consequences.** Many of the religious conflicts in Mexico stem from evangelicals' refusal to participate in town festivals -- an important source of income for local authorities. The festivals usually include activities that evangelicals find unacceptable. Please pray for Christians there as they struggle to maintain their testimony.

Subscribe

Add Tab to Netscape 6

**(USA)--A new radio program in the United States is targeting Spanish Speaking people. Back to the Bible** began airing their Spanish broadcast today on selected radio stations across the country. Back to the Bible's Dave Hansen says La Biblia Dice (lah BEEB-lee-ah DEE-say), or 'The Bible Says', will be a home missions project. "In the last 10 years there's been an increase of 58-percent, as far as the Hispanic population in the United States (is concerned). So, obviously the growth in the United State, particularly in the southern states, is in the area of Hispanics and we're wanting to take advantage of that opportunity." Hansen is asking people to pray for this new outreach. "Pray for the group in Houston, Texas. We're in partnership with KHCB and they will be answering the phones. And, pray for the staff that will be preparing the radio programs that they will be able to know how to deal with a North American audience, because historically they've dealt with a Latin American audience in South America."

**(International)--Next, this September, Food for the Hungry marks of 30 years of helping transform nations, one person at a time.** What started out as one man's dream to help desperate and hungry refugees in Bangladesh, is now a worldwide ministry helping churches, families and leaders in 30 countries overcome obstacles. Programs are developed to meet spiritual and physical needs, and include child sponsorship, agriculture, clean water projects, education, health and nutrition, and disaster relief.

**(International)--And, the safety of missionaries traveling while on the field is the concern of JAARS water safety director Glenn Smith.** "A lot

Natural resources: Petroleum, silver, copper, gold, lead, zinc, natural gas, timber.

Agriculture: Products--corn, beans, oilseeds, feedgrains, fruit, cotton, coffee, sugarcane, winter vegetables.

Industry: Manufacturing (19.1%), petroleum and mining. Unprecedented high-level political assassinations and several kidnappings of prominent businessmen caused foreign investors to withdraw, leading to the worst recession in 60 years. Unemployment and inflation rose sharply, deteriorating social conditions, which in turn escalated the crime rate dramatically, resulting in a severe devaluation of the Mexican peso in 1994. By 1998 the country had recuperated somewhat, reaching a 4% growth rate.

Return to top.

## Religion

Mexico has a current population of 98 million people, of whom 87% are estimated adherents to the Roman Catholic religion. Although predominantly Roman Catholic, the church in Mexico lost much of its political and economic power in the Revolution of 1910.

Vicente Fox, Mexico's new President, has made known his desired intention to sign the San Andres Agreement, thus agreeing to the demands of the Zapatista insurgency movement. This would mean that the pagan/Catholic synchretistic, traditionalist religion would be officially recognized and institutionalized, and persecution of "other religions" would be legal and unpunishable. Evangelical believers would be at much greater risk than they are at present which, as the informed reader knows, is more than substantial.

Evangelicals in Mexico presently number approximately 4.6 million, some 120,000 belonging to the Suffering Church.

Chiapas, frequent arena for Zapatista rebellion and severe persecution of the Evangelical community, has elected a new governor who, it is reported, is a member of the Church of the Nazarene, which may signal some relief and potentially fairer treatment in the future for those on whose behalf legal recourse is sought by fellow-Evangelical lawyers in that state.

Return to top

## Major Sources of Persecution

**Caciques:** The most evident Evangelical persecution in Chiapas arises from the wealthy mafia-like local landlords and business owners known as Caciques. Self-proclaimed defenders of ancient indigenous pagan traditions, they have established their own laws by which to judge and sentence their own people for the "crimes" of:

- ***Embracing Christianity as their religion***
- Meeting with other believers, even in private homes
- Building evangelical churches
- Refusing to drink the addictive native alcoholic drink "posh" after coming to Christ.
- No longer participating in the pagan rituals (seen as harmless folklore by the outside world), which demand offerings of candles, flowers, animals (usually chickens) and "posh", all of which are sold profitably by the caciques.

**ii. Zapatistas:** Calling themselves the National Liberation Army, they espouse a "Join, leave the area, or die" philosophy.

**iii. Religious Extremists:** Includes all groups fomenting violence..

Return to top.

OPEN DOORS

Welcome

Vision Statement

Our Work

OD History

Our Offices

Country Info

Persecution List

Links

# OPEN DOORS

INTERNATIONAL

## Country Info

### Country Profiles

Bangladesh
China
Colombia
Cuba
Iran
Laos
Mexico
Peru
Saudi Arabia
Sri Lanka
Uzbekistan
Vietnam

### More Profiles

**Afghanistan:** The Taliban has declared a new theocratic government, which is based on a strict interpretation of the Sharia Law. Freedom of religion is severely restricted. Non-Muslims in the country may practice their faith but not to evanglise. All Muslim men must attend daily prayers at the Mosque but women are not permitted to enter and must pray at home. The church in Afghanistan is currently in decline due to persecution and warfare.

**Azerbaijan:** Islamic revival has caused many Azerbaijanis to be less open to Christianity. Few countries have experienced deterioration of freedom of religion as Azerbaijan did in 1996 and 1997. Through direct and indirect means the government has warred against Christians. Some have lost their jobs, a street library threatened with closure and a Baptist Pastor shot. In January 2000 two Christians were detained and threatened.

**Djibouti:** Islam is the state religion of Djibouti and virtually the entire population is Sunni Muslim. The inhabitants are mainly Somalis of the Isa clan and Afars. Various Christian churches operate for the benefit of expatriates, but the government discourages proselytising. The only registered churches are Catholic, Orthodox and Eglise Protestante (the only Protestant church). It is against the law to preach to the local people on the streets, or to convert them. All church based activities must be held within the church compounds or the believers' homes without disturbing the population. No missionaries are allowed. They only go there as tentmakers, social developers, etc.

**Nigeria:** Nigeria is home to around 111million people making it one of the most populous countries in all of Africa. The Church numbers more than 50 million and growing. While there is freedom to evangelise, evangelists and churches have been the target of the Muslim community with many martyrs over the past 18 years. Between 1982 and 1996 alone some 600 Christians were killed and 200 churches burned. The Church will continue to grow. Many of the countries animist population (some 6%) are converting to Christianity.

**Ethiopia:** There are some 62 million people in Ethiopia with more the one hundred ethnic groups. Ethiopia is the oldest independent country in Africa and one of the world's oldest nations. It is mentioned over sixty times in the Bible. Fifty-four percent of the population is Orthodox and Protestant and some forty percent is Muslim. The pressure from Muslims and the Orthodox Church continues to affect evangelical believers in different places. This movement coming out of the traditional church may in some ways find it less difficult than when they first started because of the great increase in numbers. The traditional Church and Muslims work in an alliance against evangelical Christians in the north.

**North Korea:** Twenty-Four million people live in this communist state ruled by a one-man dictatorship. The country is slowly opening up to the outside world but

there remain economic pressures and widespread famine. About two-thirds of the population would profess to be non- religious. Less than 2% are said to be Christian. Today there are 3 'show' churches in the capital Pyongyang and it is estimated a number of believers worship in secret house churches.

**Indonesia:** Indonesia consists of some 17,000 islands of which 6,000 are inhabited. Having more than 212 million people Indonesia is home to the largest number of Muslims of any country in the world today (77% if the population). There are now 25 million Christians and it is said to be growing at the rate of 5% per annum. Riots are the order of the day and many Christians have been targeted. The Church is growing despite persecution.

**Guatemala:** As in the case of Colombia and Mexico we received (more) reports on violence in Guatemala. There are troubles enough to consider Guatemala a country for active research.

| | | | |
|---|---|---|---|
| **Open Doors International** | welcome<br>vision statement<br>persecution list | what we do<br>our offices<br>links | OD history<br>country information |

ward to a
this time
.ew 24:3;
3:10-13.
i's people
in a time
Malachi's
ptember 1
looks be-
our Lord's
the time
glory and
uld judge
nce again,
; again his
y fire, and
are being

1, a special
time. This
lual, but a
tizer. Since
is now the
Society in a
work. This
ic truths to
me of these
t possess an
; there is no
ould not re-
is one God,
a work that
ovah' for his

"the true
ual temple.
in the first-
there Jesus
three and a

le made aware
ent?
, in what way
time?
hovah come to
oes this raise?

half years after he was *anointed* as King at the Jordan. True to that pattern, since Jesus was *enthroned* as King in the autumn of 1914, it seems reasonable that three and a half years later he would be expected to accompany "the true Lord" Jehovah to the spiritual temple. According to the prophecy, what was to happen from that time onward? Testing and sifting. But this raises some important questions: What evidences are there of this cleansing? Does it continue down to the present time? And how does all of this affect you personally? Let us see.

# TESTING AND SIFTING in Modern Times

"Who will be putting up with the day of his coming, and who will be the one standing when he appears?"—Malachi 3:2

WHEN "the true Lord" came to the spiritual temple accompanied by his "messenger of the covenant," shortly after the Kingdom was set up in heaven in 1914, what did Jehovah find? His people were in need of refining and cleansing. Would they subject themselves to this and endure any needed cleaning of their organization, activity, doctrine, and conduct? As Malachi put it: "Who will be putting up with the day of his coming, and who will be the one standing when he appears?"—Malachi 3:1, 2.

[2] Jehovah accepts responsibility for cleansing and refining "the sons of Levi." (Malachi 3:3) In ancient Israel, the tribe of Levi furnished the priests and temple assistants. Such "sons of Levi" correspond to the collective body of anointed ones today serving as priests under Jesus, the High Priest. (1 Peter 2:7-9; Hebrews 3:1) They are the ones who first underwent testing when Jehovah came to the spiritual temple with his "messenger of the covenant." Now, what evidence is there that this refinement took place from the closing days of World War I onward?

### A Time of Fiery Trials

[3] When Jehovah accompanied his "messenger of the covenant" to the spiritual temple, He found the remnant in need of refining and cleansing. For example, *The Watch Tower* had encouraged its readers to set aside May 30, 1918, as a day of prayer for victory for the democratic powers, as requested by the U.S. congress and by President Wilson. This amounted to a violation of Christian neutrality.—John 17:14, 16.

[4] The clergy and the governments brought great pressure to bear on

1. When Jehovah came to the spiritual temple in modern times, what did he find, raising what question?
2. In modern times, who are "the sons of Levi" of Malachi 3:3?

3. By the spring of 1918, what was the condition of God's witnesses?
4. What developed as to persecution of Jehovah's servants?

they were in considerable darkness. When was that? And what did Jehovah God do about it?

[4] It was in the World War I period, soon after God's Messianic Kingdom was set up in heaven in 1914. The nations, with the backing of the clergy of the churches in various lands, were wrathful with one another. (Revelation 11:17, 18) God, of course, was as opposed to apostate Christendom with its elevated clergy class as he had been to the high-minded nation of Edom. Hence, Christendom, the antitypical Edom, is in line to feel the modern-day fulfillment of Isaiah chapter 34. This fulfillment by means of permanent extermination is just as certain as was the first fulfillment against ancient Edom.—Revelation 18:4-8, 19-21.

[5] What of chapter 35 of Isaiah's prophecy, with its emphasis on joy? That has also undergone fulfillment in our time. How is that? It has been fulfilled in a restoration of spiritual Israel from a type of captivity. Let us examine the facts in what really is recent theocratic history, falling within the lifetime of many still alive.

[6] For a relatively brief span during the World War I period, the remnant of spiritual Israel had not kept entirely clean and aligned with God's will. Some of them were spotted with doctrinal errors and compromised by not taking a clear stand for Jehovah when put under pressure to support the warring nations. During those war years, they suffered all manner of persecution, their Bible literature even being banned in many places. Finally, some of the more prominent brothers were convicted and imprisoned on false charges. In retrospect it is not difficult to see that, in a sense, God's people, rather than being free, were in a captive condition. (Compare John 8:31, 32.) They were seriously lacking in spiritual vision. (Ephesians 1:16-18) They showed a relative muteness as to praising God, with the result that they were unfruitful spiritually. (Isaiah 32:3, 4; Romans 14:11; Philippians 2:11) Do you see how this parallels the situation of the ancient Jews in captivity in Babylon?

[7] But would God leave his modern-day servants in that state? No, he was determined to restore them, in line with what was foretold through Isaiah. Thus this same prophecy in chapter 35 finds a distinct fulfillment in our time, with the restoration of the remnant of spiritual Israel to prosperity and health in a spiritual paradise. At Hebrews 12:12, Paul applied Isaiah 35:3 in a figurative sense, bearing out the validity of our making a spiritual application of this portion of Isaiah's prophecy.

[8] In the post-war period, the remaining anointed ones of spiritual Israel came out of captivity, as it were. Jehovah God used Jesus Christ, the Greater Cyrus, to liberate them. Thus, this remnant could do a rebuilding work, comparable to the work of the remnant of ancient Jews, who went back to their land to rebuild the literal temple in Jerusalem. Furthermore, these spiritual Israelites in modern times could set about cultivating and producing a verdant spiritual paradise, a figurative garden of Eden.

[9] With the above in mind, let us consider once again Isaiah chapter 35, and look first at verses 1 and 2. What had seemed to be a waterless region truly began to blossom and be productive like the ancient plains of Sharon. Then, look at verses 5 to 7. The rem-

5. What sort of fulfillment has Isaiah chapter 35 had in our time?
6. Why can it be said that the remnant of spiritual Israel came into a captive condition?

7, 8. What type of restoration did the modern-day remnant experience?
9. How did something like that described at Isaiah 35:1, 2, 5-7 develop in our time?

nant, a
active i
underst
ter the
1914 an
fluence
"great
remnan

Are

[10] Tak
came i
es, did
you did
have? Y
about t
you cou
matter
ter 2, I
chapter
Yes, yo
teaches
put, th
can ex
undoub

[11] We
'How di
Before
I locate
Had I n
right c
frank
ably no
a state
cally yc
their m
there i
them o
were yo
what J
35:5 up

10, 11.
outwork
sonally f

# The WATCH TOWER
## AND HERALD OF CHRIST'S PRESENCE

VOL. XL MARCH 1, 1919 No. 5


## STAND FAST—STRIVING TOGETHER

*"Stand fast in one spirit, with one mind, striving together for the faith of the Gospel; and in nothing terrified by your adversaries; which is to them an evident token of perdition, but to you of salvation, and that of God. For unto you it is given in the behalf of Christ, not only to believe on him, but also to suffer for his sake."—Philippians 1:27-29.*

NO TEXT of Scripture is more applicable to the time in which we are now living than are the above words of St. Paul to the Philippian church. Perhaps also no other passage has been more comforting to the feet members of the body of Christ during their experiences of the past year than has this one. Surely all have been called upon to suffer much, and we may have further privileges along this line. Yet it is not the suffering that especially concerns the Lord's people, it being a "light affliction" compared with "the glory that shall follow," if we prove faithful. When we realize the great favor that has been bestowed upon us in our being appointed ambassadors of the great Messianic Kingdom, now being established upon the ruins of the old order, we count it indeed a privilege to endure hardship and trial in connection with this glorious message. Such was the spirit of St. Paul, in the words of our text. He had been held up to ridicule and scorn, beaten almost to death, thrown into prison and his feet made fast in the stocks. Yet in it all he was able to sing praises to God for the privilege of suffering for Christ's sake, for the truth and for the brethren.

### THE MESSAGE OF THE HOUR

The first statement in our text is especially important now. Not merely the admonition to "stand fast," but the *manner* in which we should stand is the thing of essential value. The admonition must be taken in its entirety. The Apostle would have us understand that to be pleasing to the Lord we must "stand fast in *one spirit*, with *one mind, striving together* for the faith of the Gospel." We find some today who claim and probably think that they are standing fast; but instead they are turning aside and not striving together with their brethren in proclaiming the full message of the Gospel. Because of some difference of opinion respecting secular matters, they apparently feel it their duty to raise questions that cause division in the ranks of the Lord's people, and then start independent movements that tend to confuse the minds of the saints and to give rise to roots of bitterness. Let us, dear brethren, avoid any and every spirit that would hinder our striving together in the dissemination of the truth now due. Nothing would please the adversary more than to have the ambassadors of Christ's kingdom contend one with another on non-essentials, thereby to have their minds distracted and their efforts slackened regarding the real work to which they have devoted their lives; namely, the proclaiming of the message regarding the utter downfall of Babylon and the overthrow of Satan's empire.

The commission of the Christ, Head and body, is found in Isaiah 61:1-3; and the special message of the feet members is the proclamation of "the day of vengeance of our God." The evidence that this particular message would be given by the last members of the body of Christ on earth is emphasized by the fact that our Lord omitted this portion of the prophecy when he read from the book of Isaiah in the synagogue at Nazareth (Luke 4:16-22), and then declared: "This day is this Scripture fulfilled in your ears." His thought manifestly was that only the portion of the prophecy which he had read to them was fulfilled at that time, and that the portion which he had failed to read would be fulfilled at a later time by his body members. It is therefore the *duty*, as well as the privilege, of the Lord's people at this time to "proclaim the day of vengeance of our God"; and if they fail to do so, the very stones would cry out; for the prophet's words are inspired of God and must be fulfilled.—Luke 19:40; Zechariah 9:9.

### "ONWARD, CHRISTIAN SOLDIERS!"

It is with sorrow that we see some retreating from the front ranks of the battle. It is not surprising to find some such excusing their action by claims of steadfastness and special courage. The faithful and triumphant in battle do not desert in the hour of need, however, but strive together with one spirit and one mind, as the Apostle enjoins. Those who are looking for pretexts to turn aside will surely find a motive satisfactory to themselves for their course, while those who are anxious to do the Lord's work *will be looking* for opportunities through which they may vigorously co-operate in the closing work of the church in the flesh.—Isaiah 52:7.

A few in certain localities, under the influence of leading minds, have felt obliged to withdraw their support of the Society on most trivial and unbelievable grounds. Some have magnified and distorted certain statements in THE WATCH TOWER, and under the misconception thus developed have withdrawn from classes and have sought to draw away others after them. The more influential in the service any such has been, the more disturbance his course causes among the dear sheep when he thus deflects. Some have even found fault with the statement in the TOWER of May 15, 1918, which said: "When the government asks to borrow his money, and gives its promise to pay in the nature of a bond, if he can consistently do so he should buy the bond." Reference to the article in question will disclose the fact that this is part of a statement given to the public press, and properly showed that our Society was not opposed to the methods used by the government in carrying on the war, and that its work is strictly a religious one. All such questions are matters of individual conscience; and nobody can or should assume to regulate the conscience of another in such matters. This

etc., has been misunderstood by many people. Few persons do much thinking in war time and what little they do is mostly in line with their natural emotions. We cannot therefore expect much calm and dispassionate thinking now from the worldly. Therefore in our honest effort to render our proper dues to the Government under which we are privileged to live we should be doubly careful not to "speak evil of dignitaries" nor to do anything which would avoidably embarrass them in the solution of their weighty problems. See Matthew 17:25-27; Luke 20:22-25; Romans 13:7; 1 Peter 2:13-17.

### OUR STATEMENT TO THE PRESS

Statements have been recently made to several newspapers which requested an expression from us. But the statements, if printed at all, have been so garbled as to be well nigh incoherent. We therefore print below in full a statement prepared by the President of our Association for the *Brooklyn Eagle* at its request:

"On my return to Brooklyn I learned of the unpleasant occurrence at the Brooklyn Tabernacle last Sunday, April 28th. Mr. W. T. Baker was in the pulpit and at the conclusion of his discourse a request was brought to the platform that the congregation hear a speech by some one on the Liberty Bonds. Mr. Baker put the matter to a vote and the majority voted in the negative.

"I am sure this action was not intended as any reflection on the Government, nor to be taken as against the Liberty Loan. Those who worship at the Tabernacle believe in worshipping the Lord in spirit and in truth. To them a religious service is the most sacred; and while at religious service they always refrain from discussing temporal matters. This congregation at no time ever held a social tea, a grab-bag party, a bazaar, or anything of that kind in the church. The Tabernacle auditorium is used exclusively for religious matters, especially on Sunday. No previous request had been made to use the Tabernacle by any one in the interest of the Liberty Loan campaign. The worshippers had just listened to a helpful spiritual lesson on the Bible. They desired to withdraw from the building with these sacred thoughts in mind and therefore deemed it inappropriate to discuss any temporal matters whatsoever, or to hear them discussed by any one else. We are pleased to grant the use of the Tabernacle for a meeting in the interest of the public when the same does not interfere with our religious services.

"The people of our Association are not against the Government, nor against the Liberty Loan. Our thought is that the Liberty Loan is not a religious question, but purely one pertaining to the affairs of the Government; and that each person should be left to the free exercise of his individual conscience as to whether he will or will not purchase Liberty Bonds. Our views are very well expressed in a statement given to the public press some weeks ago, as follows:

"'The International Bible Students Association is not against the Liberty Loan. Many of its members have bought and hold Liberty Bonds. Some have not money with which to buy.

"'The Liberty Loan is not a religious question. It has solely to do with the Government. Every person who mails a letter supports the Government to that extent by paying the additional postage on account of the war.

"'The International Bible Students Association is composed of Christians. Every Christian gladly obeys the law. The United States has always stood for religious liberty and freedom of speech. Every Christian appreciates the privilege of living in such a country and gladly meets his obligations in the payment of taxes. When the Government asks to borrow his money and gives its promise to pay in the nature of a bond, if he can do so he should buy the bond.

"'The Association has no power to direct members thereof with reference to buying Liberty Bonds. It certainly will not and has not advised any one to refuse to buy bonds. That is an individual matter which each person must determine for himself according to his ability. The Association believes in supporting the Government in every way it can and each one should do so according to his ability and his conscience.'

"Some members of the Brooklyn Tabernacle congregation had previously purchased Liberty Bonds. Doubtless all had been personally solicited before that time. They are surrounded on all hands by opportunities to purchase, and to them it seemed inappropriate to transact business in the church on Sunday. There are six days in the week for the transaction of business and Sunday is regarded by them as a day for sacred worship of the Lord.

"It is to be regretted that one representing the public press should so disgrace himself as publicly to encourage mob violence against inoffensive people. It seems that any one wearing the uniform of the United States Army would have more respect for that uniform and for law and order than to disturb the peace by loud and uncouth language and in encouraging mob violence. We cannot believe that any responsible person in the Government would approve of such action.

"As to the members of the Bethel Home, it is well known that those who labor there receive merely their food and lodging and a small allowance for incidental expenses. This was thoroughly aired in the *Brooklyn Eagle* libel case, as the record shows. At that time the amount received was only $10.00 per month, which since, on account of increased cost of necessities, is now $15.00 per month. At the opening of the Third Liberty Loan campaign, a very elegant gentleman of the Borough of Brooklyn called on me with reference to soliciting the members of the Bethel Home to buy bonds. I invited him to see each one of them personally. He questioned me as to their ability to buy; and when I told him of the amount they received monthly he said, 'Then they cannot buy on that amount and it is useless for me to see them. I am sure you must be doing much good here in your own way when men and women sacrifice their time for such a small allowance.' It is a well known fact that there are other institutions that are not asked or even expected to buy Liberty Bonds because of their financial inability.

"Members of our Association who have some personal means have bought Liberty Bonds, including Tabernacle workers who are paying 25% of their monthly allowance to purchase a bond. We do not believe the Government would expect any one to purchase bonds who receives barely enough for his daily expenses.

"The picketing of the Bethel Home on last Sunday morning and accosting every one who passed out and demanding that they buy Liberty Bonds seems to be a very uncalled-for and unusual thing, when any one authorized to solicit for bonds can have free access to the Bethel Home to interview any person there at any reasonable hour during the day or evening. As above stated, a gentleman had called for that purpose some days ago. The action of the men on Sunday morning seemed not only wholly uncalled for, but was taken designedly for the purpose of placing the members of the Bethel Home at a disadvantage. We cannot believe that order-loving, law-abiding people of Brooklyn at all approve such action or conduct."

## CHRIST IS ALL

Though all thy life seem full of care
And trials seem too hard to bear,
Upon thy Father call.
He'll from his Word send message meet
And grace sufficient, promise sweet;
For Christ is all in all.

If little tests thy walk harrass
And troubles small thy way compass,
In these thou must not fall.
Thy Father lets thee have them, so
Thy character may stronger grow
And Christ be all in all.

If for a while thy life be bright
Nor foes assail nor storms affright
Nor darkened hours appall,
In heaven above still find thy joy,
Earth's good is but a transient toy;
Let Christ be all in all.

5/15/1918

June 1, 1918



not lawful for him to eat, but only for the priests." (Matthew 12:3, 4) It is vital, according to Paul, for brothers in Christ to "avoid contentions" (Titus 3:9); but "Paul thought not good to take him [John Mark] with them, who departed from them from Pamphylia, and went not with them to the work. And the contention was so sharp between them, that they [Barnabas and Paul, who had 'lived in all good conscience before God'—Acts 23:1] departed asunder one from the other." —Acts 15:38, 39.

In apostolic times some Christians made it a matter of principle to "observe the days, months, times and years" (Galatians 4:10) of the Hebrew ritual; others did not. "One believed that he might eat all things; another who was weak [in the faith] eateth herbs." (Romans 14:2) "And," says Paul, "he that doubteth is damned [judged] if he eat, because he eateth not of faith [with confidence that it is proper]; for whatsoever is not of faith, is sin." (Romans 14:23) In modern times one Christian can eat pork, another can not; one can observe Sunday, another Saturday, and still another can keep all days holy to God; one can engage in temperance work, another cannot; one can own an automobile, another cannot. At one time a Christian feels unable to do certain things; later, with additional knowledge or thought, he can do them with a good conscience.

A Christian might not have been able conscientiously to engage in the military activities of a country offering only combatant service; later, when the opportunity is enlarged so that he may choose some good work such as the hospital or ambulance service, he may with a free conscience take such service. A Christian to whom may have been presented the perverted viewpoint that the Red Cross work is only the aiding of that killing which is against his conscience, cannot help the Red Cross; then he gains the broader viewpoint that the Red Cross is the embodiment of helping the helpless, and he finds himself able and willing to help the Red Cross according to ability and opportunity. A Christian, unwilling to kill, may have been conscientiously unable to buy government bonds; later he considers what great blessings he has received under his government, and realizes that the nation is in trouble and facing dangers to its liberty, and he feels himself conscientiously able to lend some money to the country, just as he would lend to a friend in distress.

The Christian with the broadest mind is the one who is best informed Scripturally. That Christian who is able to see from but one viewpoint is in danger of being what St. Paul calls "weak," in the sense that his inability to see all around a question limits his sphere of action. Narrow-mindedness invites troubles and persecutions for causes not even indirectly connected with true Christianity. Such trouble may usually well be avoided, and should be avoided in order that such trials or persecutions which are our portion may come upon the clear-cut issue of faithfulness in the consecrated life and not for other causes. The true footstep follower of Christ will have enough to suffer as a Christian. He will do his best to study all sides of every question and remove from himself causes for offense, other than his truly Christian and religious beliefs and principles which are vital.

"If ye be reproached for the name of Christ, happy are ye; for the spirit of glory and of God resteth upon you; on their part he [Christ in you] is evil spoken of, but on your part [in you as a new creature] he is glorified; but let none of you suffer as a murderer, or as a thief, or as an evil doer, or as a busybody in other men's affairs. Yet if any man suffer as a Christian, let him not be ashamed, but let him glorify God on this behalf."—1 Peter 4:14-16.

## FAITH

[This poem was a reprint of that which appeared in issue of June 15, 1917, which please see.]

## PRAYING TO GOD

[Paragraphs 1, 2 and 23 of this article, as it originally appeared in issue of June 1, 1918, were reprinted from article entitled, "Lord Teach Us to Pray," published in issue of July 1, 1906, which please see.]

JULY 21.—LUKE 11:1-13; PSA. 145:18, 19.

WHO ARE PRIVILEGED TO PRAY—HOW WE MAY "PRAY WITHOUT CEASING"—A MODEL PRAYER—ITS ASCRIPTIONS OF PRAISE—EXPRESSIONS OF CONFIDENCE IN GOD'S PROMISED KINGDOM—ACKNOWLEDGMENT OF OUR DEPENDENCE UPON HIM—CONFIDENCE IN HIS POWER TO PROTECT US AND FINALLY TO DELIVER US—PROPER ATTITUDE TOWARD THE EXPERIENCES OF LIFE—PURPOSE OF PRAYER—REQUEST FOR THE HOLY SPIRIT THE ESSENCE OF OUR PETITIONS.

*"Let us therefore draw near with boldness unto the throne of grace, that we may receive mercy, and may find grace to help in time of need."*—Hebrews 4:16.

The advanced Christian should be so fully in accord with the Father, the Son and the divine program that his entire life will be a prayer and a song of praise. He will have in his mind primarily the thought, 'What is God's will in this matter?' The heart that is thus ever looking for divine direction in all of life's affairs is thus continuously in an attitude of prayer; and no other condition is proper to the Christian.—Prov. 3:6; Psalm 37:4.

### WHO IS PRIVILEGED TO SAY, "OUR FATHER"

Only those who have become children of God by forsaking sin and laying hold upon Christ as their Savior are accorded the privilege of approaching the throne of grace to obtain mercy and to find grace sufficient for their time of need. Only those who are accepted in the Beloved are privileged to call Jehovah God by the endearing name, "Our Father who art in heaven." The attempt thus to approach God implies (1) faith in him; (2) realization of dependence upon him; (3) faith that a way of reconciliation with him has been effected through our Redeemer; (4) realization that God no longer condemns the suppliant, but accepts him as a son. Moreover, it implies that the suppliant recognizes the fact that there are other sons of God who, like himself, have fled from sin and been adopted into God's family; for the petition begins, "our Father," not "my Father."

Therefore whoever thus addresses God must have concern for all the interests of the family of God. Whatever selfishness he might formerly have had he must divest himself of when he comes to the Father, and must realize himself as merely one of the favored class of sons thus privileged. It is in harmony with this thought that all of the Lord's consecrated people have special pleasure when permitted to approach the throne of grace together, whether but two or three or in larger numbers.

The more clearly we recognize that the privilege of prayer is an exclusive one, the more we shall be inclined to use it in a most reverent manner. The kings of earth make regulations respecting times, seasons, dress, etc., to be observed by those who wish to enter their presence; and all who have a proper appreciation of the majesty of the King Eternal, the only true God, will approach in a worshipful, reverent spirit, implied in the expression: "Hallowed be thy name." Our holy God is to be revered. His sacred name stands for everything that is just, wise and loving.

### THE KINGDOM FOR WHICH WE PRAY

In the older manuscripts the words, "Thy will be done, as in heaven so in earth," are not found in Luke's Gospel, but in Matthew's. They are therefore properly to be considered a part of the petition. Be it noted, however, that while this petition as it stands is appropriate enough as a prayer, it evidently was not our Lord's intention that these words should continually be used as the only petition at the throne of grace, but rather he gave it as a sample. The various items of this prayer should therefore be to the Lord's people a suggestion of the general character of their petitions, and not understood as binding their terms, their expressions, their words.

The thoughts of true disciples are directed to the fact that the present condition of sin and death is not to be everlasting; that God has provided for a glorious kingdom through his Son and the church, his bride, under which all evil will be conquered and brought under complete subjugation to righteousness. Those in proper heart relationship to the Lord must recognize this fact, and be so separated from the spirit of this world that they will long for the installation of the reign of righteousnees, even though they know that this will imply the overthrow of the present order. Their hearts are so in accord with the Lord that they are out of accord with every form, institution and vine not of the Father's right hand planting. (Isaiah 60:21) Longing for the Kingdom that will bless the world, they also long for the promised privilege of being joint-heirs with their Redeemer as members of that kingdom class which shall bless the world and uplift mankind out of sin and death.

influence in every major aspect of Chi. social life. The permeation of Chi. society by the popular relig. is everywhere evidenced: by the number and variety of temples and wide range of functions which they serve; by festivals, → pilgrimages, ceremonies etc. of a relig. character; by the spirit-tablets, images and pictures of deities to be found in every traditional Chi. home; and by the rituals of relig. brought to bear on every major event of social or family life. Belief in the supernatural is an outstanding mark of Chi. popular relig., but its main concern is to seek the help of these supernatural agencies, whether they be gods, Buddhas, immortals or mere tutelary and nature spirits, to avoid or overcome the ills of life, and guarantee a happier existence in the future. Yet, through a combination of Confucian ethics, Taoist mysticism, Buddhist discipline and techniques of meditation, relig. has proved to be a most potent factor in the development of Chi. civilisation. D.H.S.

W. E. Soothill, *The Three Religions of China* (1923); E. R.-K. Hughes, *Religion in China* (1950); K. L. Reichelt, *Religion in Chinese Garment* (1951); C. K. Yang, *Religion in Chinese Society* (1961); D. H. Smith, *Chinese Religions* (1968).

**Ching** Chinese character used for classic books; e.g. *Wu Ching*—the five books which make up the Confucian Canon; *Hsin Ching*—the *Heart Sūtra* (Buddhist); *Shêng Ching*—the Holy Bible (Chr.). D.H.S.

**Ch'ing Ming** Chinese spring festival (lit.—'Pure and Bright') falls usually in 3rd month of lunar year. Now an → All Souls' Festival, when the ancestral graves are visited, repaired and decorated, and offerings of food etc. are made to spirits of dead. Its origins go back to an orgiastic life-renewing and spring-mating festival. It is preceded by eating of cold food (*han shih*), when no fires are lighted for twenty-four hours. As late as T'ang dynasty, new fire was produced by rubbing two willow sticks together. An alternative name, Chih-shu-chieh (Tree-planting festival), also indicates its primitive origin. D.H.S.

**Ching T'u** → Pure Land School (Buddhist). D.H.S.

**Chinvat Bridge** → Bridges. S.G.F.B.

**Chou I** → I Ching. D.H.S.

**Christ** *Ex.* Grk. *Christos*, 'anointed', which trans. Heb. *māshīah*, i.e. → Messiah, the divinely appointed deliverer of Israel, acc. to Jew. apocalyptic hope. As Mk. 8:27ff. shows, the disciples of → Jesus of Nazareth recognised him as the C., and there can be little doubt that he was popularly so regarded, and that he was executed as a Messianic pretender, as were many others, by the Romans. The Gospels give no certain evidence that Jesus claimed himself to be C., though many of his actions (e.g. Triumphal Entry into Jerusalem) imply such a claim. In Apostolic Age, the title C. quickly became so closely assoc. with Jesus as to be used as personal designation, without article, i.e. 'Jesus Christ' or 'Christ Jesus'. Paul's use of both together in letters to Gentiles reveals basic premise of his theology that the → Old Testament or Covenant with Israel was completed in incarnation of C. in person of Jesus. This view led to re-interpretation of orig. Jewish idea of Messiah (→→ Christianity; Christology, Jesus Christ). S.G.F.B.

*H.D.B.*[2], pp. 646, 653ff.; *P.C.*[2], pp. 739ff.; *R.A.C.*, I, 1250–62; *R.G.G.*[3], I, 1745–62; *B.C.*, I, pp. 345ff.; J. Klausner, *Jesus of Nazareth* (E.T. 1929), pp. 293; S. G. F. Brandon, *Jesus and the Zealots* (1967), pp. 175–82.

**Christadelphians** Chr. sect founded in America in 1848 by John Thomas. C. accept Bible as infallible revelation, reject doc. of → Trinity, and expect return of Christ to estab. → theocracy for 1,000 yrs. They teach → baptism by immersion only, annihiliation of wicked, exclusion of those ignorant of Divine Will from → resurrection. They have no ministers. (→ Chiliasm). S.G.F.B.

*E.R.E.*, III, *s.v.*; *D.C.C.*, *s.v.*

**Christian Ethics** *Basis*: Chr. Ethics derives from belief that God has revealed his nature and purpose for men in → Jesus Christ; it is the way of life appropriate to that disclosure. The → Bible is regarded as the authoritative witness to that disclosure: the O.T. by way of preparation, the N.T. to Jesus himself and early years of community which resulted from his mission and message. Jesus Christ is thus the key to the Scriptures: he fulfils and in part negates O.T.; the N.T. derives from him. The Gospels are, therefore, of key importance for faith and ethics. The whole weight of Scripture is profoundly ethical, growing out of deepening ethical understanding of God in O.T., and involving a moral renewal of those who follow Christ. This renewal is at once personal and corporate: the Christian is a member of a new community in Christ, i.e. the Church, intended to be moral leaven in the world. Christians were orig. known as followers of a 'Way (of life)'.

*Characteristics*: the word most used to summarise C.-E. is *love*. This one word in Eng. has to cover wide range of meanings (1) *Libido* or fundamental instinctive drives (2) *philia* or brotherly affection (3) *eros* or yearning for satisfaction, from the coarse level (which adjective 'erotic' now suggests) to desire for beauty, truth and goodness; (4) *agape*, the distinctively Chr. word (though C.-E. allows for other three). → *Agape* is a noun coined from a rather colourless Grk. verb to describe new quality of life brought into world by Jesus. St. → Paul describes it in *I Cor.* 13; it is taught in 'farewell discourses' of

John's Gospel (14–7), and 1
→ Synoptic Gospels, Jesus
and neighbour constitute
his parables and actions b
close radical goodness of t
loved. This is done largely
or Rule of God which Jesus
in his ministry, as an earne
pose for world. God's pov
to be highly paradoxical
thinking: Jesus seeks out
wrongdoers, not by punish
ness and bearing consequ
doing; he calls into quest
'good' people and finds the
as the 'good' think them;
trictions on the neighbour
(Lk. 10:29ff). In Matthe
section of Jesus' ethical teac
gether in chs. 5–7, form
Mount'. It begins with tl
strike a radical note comp
goes on to demand absolute
sincerity as the ethic of Kin
ground of what God is like
A moral goodness is disclos
Jesus, which is inexhaustibl
of it, the more we find there
be noted that ethical criti
made of certain words a
(usually on ground that tl
own best). There can be no
who do not find Jesus mo
criticisms arise from misun
ground of Gospels, whic
modern commentary would
*Motive*: the key motive i
response to love of God rev
it involves any outgoing lov
in fact, the way by which
fulfilment. But negation o
C.-E.: rather, 'Freely ye
give', or 'Love as I have
another motive in the G
rewards (in heaven) or fear
motive is frequently said by
to be mainspring of C.-E.;
however, a secondary motiv
misunderstood by those wh
do what is right without
Rewards in the Chr. life a
those who live by the first
direct object. If God is as Je
pure in heart must in the
Christ-like conduct must bri
the reward is no reward to
pure in heart, nor could th
only come to those who fol
sake, not the reward's sake.



A DICTIONARY OF COMPARATIVE RELIGION
SGF Brandon MA DD eD (NY: Charles Scribner's Sons 1970)

which elects its own officers. Christadelphians take no part in politics, voting, or military service.

**Christian Fellowship Church** or **Etoism.** The main independent church in Melanesia, founded on New Georgia in the Solomon Islands in 1959 by Silas Eto (b. 1905). As a *catechist-teacher in the *Methodist mission, he developed deviationist practices from the 1930s, and, in disillusionment with staid mission forms, began his own true church. He remained an admirer of J. F. Goldie, founder of the mission, and claimed authority from both God and Goldie as revealed to him in a dream. Ecstatic worship was combined with healing, successful economic activities, and development of a model village, Paradise, as a 'holy city'. Despite incipient *messianism concerning Eto himself, relations with Methodists, now in the United Church, were being re-established in the 1970s.

**Christianity.** The origins of Christianity lie, historically, in the life and ministry of *Jesus, extended through his death, *resurrection, and *ascension. In its own estimate, its origins lie further back in the former *covenants (hence, from a Christian point of view, the Old Testament) made with Israel.

Christianity exists in a vast diversity of different styles and forms of organization, but all are agreed that the figure of Jesus is the disclosure of God and the means of human reconciliation with him. The life and ministry of Jesus seemed (to at least some of those who witnessed or experienced them at the time) to be a restoration in word and action of the power (Gk., *dunamis*) not of himself but of God, leading to the conclusion that 'he who has seen me has seen the Father'; 'I and the Father are one' (John 14. 9, 10. 30). The once fashionable argument is no longer tenable that Jesus was a simple Jewish teacher who was gradually promoted (see EUHEMERUS) into being the Son of God, as a result of *Paul transforming the teaching of Jesus into a *hellenized new religion. From the earliest writings in the New Testament, Jesus was closely associated with God, with extremely high titles and status in relation to God. The extraordinary way in which Jesus acted as one who was mediating the consequence of God through his own person produced 'the phenomenon of the New Testament': the ways in which these documents speak of Jesus, and which relate him uniquely to God, have clear connections with both Jewish and Hellenistic categories, and yet they are always distinctive and idiosyncratic.

In the early years, 'Christianity' was one interpretation, among many at that time, of what God's covenant with Israel and his purpose in creation should be; but in this interpretation, it was believed that Jesus was the promised *messiah (Heb., *ha-Mashiach* = messiah = Gk., *ho Christos*, hence the name 'Christianity', which was first used, according to Acts 2. 26, in *c.*40 CE). Since for other Jews, many of the marks of a messiah did not accompany Jesus, and since claims (impossible to them) were being made about Jesus in relation to God, the two religions separated, although for centuries a small number of Christians continued to believe that Jewish *Torah should still be observed. On the majority Christian side, the keeping of Torah was no longer regarded as a necessary condition of being in a covenant relation with God. The separation from Judaism was made by universalizing the consequences of Christ to all people. That process was accelerated by the fall of Jerusalem in 70 CE, after which an increasing hostility to Judaism led to a long (and still unended, though moderated) history of *anti-Semitism.

Characteristic Christian doctrines emerged from the demand of the New Testament evidence (and from the experience which brought it into being). Jesus mediated the consequence and effect of God, so that on the one hand it was evidently God who was acting and speaking in and through him, and yet on the other it was clear that Jesus addressed God (e.g. in prayer) as apart from himself, as Father (see ABBA): this produced a quest in the early centuries to find ways of speaking of these two natures in one person (*Christology; the willingness and obedience of *Mary in accepting the conception and birth of Jesus produced a widespread, though not universal, devotion to Mary, and a close association of her with the work of *redemption). At the same time, God was clearly present to the life of Jesus (e.g. at his birth and his baptism, and in the directing of his mission), in the ways traditionally spoken of as the *Holy Spirit. This led to a further quest to find ways of speaking of the interior nature of God, as being in itself, not an abstract unity, but social and relational (i.e. as *Trinity).

It was also recognized that what Jesus had done during his life for some particular people, in reconciling them to God when they had become estranged from him and from each other, was, as a consequence of his death, resurrection, and ascension, extended to others, and indeed made universal, at least as an opportunity for those who respond in faith. This led to doctrines of *atonement.

This extension of the consequence of Christ was made immediately realistic, and thus realizable, through the enacted signs of *baptism (taking believers into the death of Christ and raising them to a new life already here on earth) and of the *last supper (*eucharist). From the earliest days (*Pentecost), the followers of Christ felt that they had been empowered by the Holy Spirit conferring on them special gifts. Initially, they looked for an early return of Christ (Second Coming or *parousia), and although that expectation faded, it has remained as an important *eschatological component of Christian belief. The sense of being, in the meantime, the continuing Body of Christ led to the mystical interpretation of the *Church, which lies apart from the many divisions of Christians into separated Churches.

Diverse writings evoked by the ev
life and ministry, and their conseque
of believers) were gathered eventual
Testament. During the New Testam
*kelal of Jesus (the context-indepen
of love) was made context-depen
applications to particular circumstar
general command to love God and
was applied to the circumstances i
found themselves, as they asked wh
of that love should be in practice. C
relation between the context-indepe
and the context-dependent applica
tension between liberty and law in
ics.

During the New Testament p
nature of Christian community
changed dramatically: the original
Church as the Body of Christ, with
equal importance under the headsh
Colossians 1. 17 f.; 1 Corinthians
changed into a metaphor derived f
army, with a hierarchical organizat
levels of authority of *bishops, *p
cons: the clericalization of the C
subordination of the *laity has rem
istic of most parts of Christianit
present. However, the two model
hood of all believers, 1 Peter 2
controlling authority of ordained
remained in tension throughout C
although the authoritarian model
nant (e.g. in *Roman or Vatican C
the *pope assuming the title fr
Empire of Pontifex Maximus).

Initially Christianity was a small
ment, though confident in itself
resurrection and the experience o
from the Holy Spirit. In the early
held in suspicion by some because i
noxious superstition' (Tacitus), by c
its exclusive monotheism which co
prevailing Graeco-Roman syncretic
sive emphasis occasionally brough
with imperial authorities. Wh
occurred, Christianity in fact gaine
(see TERTULLIAN), and the witness a
tyrs gained an importance which
the present: on the basis of the n
the 20th cent. has been called
martyrs'. After the support of *Co
recognition of Christianity as the
Empire under Theodosius I (e
Christianity became the major
Roman world.

Sometimes in conflict with exist
philosophies (e.g. *gnosticism), it r
ing this period, drew on many such
ing gnosticism and Greek philosop
its faith. Equally, it reworked vario
in the artistic sphere (e.g. Orpheus

THE OXFORD DICTIONARY OF WORLD RELIGIONS, John Bowker, ed (Oxford, NY: Oxford University Press, 1997)

full sense, but the relations referred to lift it and the succeeding Sundays above ordinary Sundays. See CHURCH YEAR. W. CASPARI.

In the present usage of the West, the season begins on the nearest Sunday to St. Andrew's day (Nov. 30), whether before or after. In the Anglican prayer-book the service for the first Sunday emphasizes the second coming; that for the second, the Holy Scriptures; that for the third, the Christian ministry; while only the fourth relates specifically to the first coming. Advent in the Eastern Church begins on Nov. 14, thus making a season of forty days analogous to Lent.

BIBLIOGRAPHY: The lectionaries in *Liber comicus*, i., Oxford, 1893, and in *Sacramentarium Gelasianum* published in L. A. Muratori, *Liturgia romanum vetus*, vol. i., Venice, 1748, and in *MPL*, lxxiv.; Smaragdus, in *MPL*, cii.; Amalarius Metensis, *De ecclesiasticis officiis*, ib. cv.; Berno of Reichenau, *De celebratione adventus*, *MPL*, cxlii.; Isidore of Seville, *De officiis*, ed. Cochlæus, Leipsic, 1534, and in M. de la Bigne, *Magna bibliotheca veterum patrum*, x., Paris, 1654; E. Martène, *De antiquis ecclesiæ ritibus*, Rouen, 1700.

ADVENT CHRISTIANS. See ADVENTISTS, 3.

ADVENTISTS: The general name of a body embracing several branches, whose members look for the proximate personal coming of Christ. William Miller (q.v.), their founder, was a converted deist, who in 1816 joined the Baptist Church in Low Hampton, N. Y. He became a close student of the Bible, especially of the prophecies, and soon satisfied himself that the Advent was to be personal and premillennial, and that it was near at hand. He began these studies in 1818, but did not enter upon the work of the ministry until 1831. The year 1843 was the date agreed upon for the Advent; then, more specifically, Oct. 22, 1844, the failure of which divided a body of followers that had become quite numerous. In the year of his death (1849) they were estimated at 50,000. Many who had been drawn into the movement by the prevalent excitement left it, and returned to the churches from which they had withdrawn. After the second failure, Miller and some other leaders discouraged attempts to fix exact dates. On this question and on the doctrine of the immortality of the soul there have been divisions. There are now at least six distinct branches of Adventists, all of which agree that the second coming of Christ is to be personal and premillennial, and that it is near at hand. The Seventh-day Adventists and the Church of God are presbyterial, the others congregational in their polity. All practise immersion as the mode of baptism.

1. Evangelical Adventists: This is the oldest branch, indeed the original body. The members adopted their *Declaration of Principles* in conference in Albany, N. Y., in 1845, and in 1858 formed the American Millennial Association to print and circulate literature on eschatology from their point of view. Their organ was the weekly paper *The Signs of the Times*, which had been established in Boston in 1840; subsequently its name was changed to *The Advent Herald*, and later still to *Messiah's Herald*, its present (1906) title. The paper has always been published in Boston. The Evangelical Adventists differ from all the other branches in maintaining the consciousness of the dead in Hades and the eternal sufferings of the lost.

BIBLIOGRAPHY: H. F. Hill, *The Saint's Inheritance*, Boston, 1852; D. T. Taylor, *The Reign of Christ*, Peacedale, R. I., 1855, and Boston, 1889.

2. Seventh-day Adventists: This branch dates from 1845, in which year, at Washington, N. H., a body of Adventists adopted the belief that the seventh day of the week is the Sabbath for Christians and is obligatory upon them. In 1850 their chief organ, *The Advent Review and Sabbath Herald*, was first issued at Battle Creek, Mich., which was made the headquarters of the body: and there in 1860 a publishing association, in 1862 a general annual conference, in 1866 a health institute, and in 1874 an educational society and a foreign mission board were established. In 1903 the publishing business and the general headquarters were removed to Washington, D. C. Their organ is now styled *The Review and Herald*. Besides the tenet which gives them their name they hold that man is not immortal, that the dead sleep in unconsciousness, and that the unsaved never awake. They practise foot-washing and accept the charismata, maintain a tithing system, and pay great attention to health and total abstinence. They accept Mrs. Ellen G. White as an inspired prophetess.

BIBLIOGRAPHY: J. N. Andrews, *History of the Sabbath and First Day*, Battle Creek, 1873 (3d ed., 1887); *Life Sketches of Elder James White and his wife Mrs. Ellen G. White*, 1880; J. N. Loughborough, *Rise and Progress of the Seventh-Day Adventists*, ib. 1892.

3. Advent Christians: The organization under this name dates from 1861, when a general association was formed. The organ of these Adventists is *The World's Crisis and Second Advent Messenger*, published in Boston. Their creed is given in the *Declaration of Principles*, approved by the general conference of 1900. They believe that through sin man forfeited immortality and that only through faith in Christ can any live forever; that death is a condition of unconsciousness for all persons until the resurrection at Christ's second coming, when the righteous will enter an endless life upon this earth, and the rest will suffer complete extinction of being; that this coming is near; that church government should be congregational; that immersion is the only true baptism; and that Sunday is the Christian Sabbath.

BIBLIOGRAPHY: I. C. Wellcome, *History of the Second Advent Message*, Yarmouth, Me., 1874.

4. Life and Advent Union: This may be said to have existed since 1848, but it was not until 1862 that it was organized, at Wilbraham, Mass., under the leadership of Elder George Stores. Its organ is *The Herald of Life and of the Coming Kingdom*, published at Springfield, Mass., weekly since 1862. It holds that all hope of another life is through Jesus Christ, and that only believers in him, who have manifested in their daily lives the fruits of the Spirit, attain to the resurrection of the dead, which will take place at Christ's coming, and that such coming will be personal, visible, and literal, and is impending. The Union holds four camp-meetings annually: two in Maine, one in Connecticut, which is the principal one, and one in Virginia.



BIBLIOGRAPHY: O. S. Halsted, *The Theology of*
Newark, 1860; *Discussion between Miles Grant*
*Curry*, Boston, 1863.

5. Church of God: This is a branc
Seventh-day Adventists, which seceded
because its members denied that Mrs. Ell
White was an inspired prophetess. The
is *The Bible Advocate and Herald of the*
*Kingdom*, published at Stanberry, Mo.,
their center. Like the parent body, the C
God has tithes, sanatoriums, and a publishi

BIBLIOGRAPHY: A. F. Dugger, *Points of Differen*
*the Church of God and Seventh-Day Adventists*,
Mo.; J. Brinkerhoff, *Mrs. White's Visions*. C
*of the early Writings of Mrs. E. G. White with la*
*tions, showing the Suppressions made in them to*
*erroneous Teaching*; D. Nield, *The Good Fri*
*lem, showing from Scripture, Astronomy and H*
*the Crucifixion of Christ took Place on Wednesd*
*Resurrection on Saturday*.

6. Churches of God in Christ Jesus,
known as the Age-to-come Adventists: T
existed since 1851, when their organ, *The*
*tion* (Plymouth, Ind.), was established,
were not organized till 1888, when th
conference was formed. They believe in
toration of Israel, the literal resurrectio
dead, the immortalization of the right
the final destruction of the wicked, et
being through Christ alone.

BIBLIOGRAPHY: J. P. Weethee, *The Coming Ag*
1884.

The statistics of the Adventists are t
by H. K. Carroll in *The Christian Adv*
Jan. 25, 1906:

| Name. | Ministers. | Churche |
|---|---|---|
| Evangelical | 34 | 30 |
| Seventh-day | 486 | 1,707 |
| Advent Christians | 912 | 610 |
| Life and Advent Union | 60 | 28 |
| Church of God | 19 | 29 |
| Churches of God in Christ Jesus | 54 | 95 |
| Total Adventists | 1,565 | 2,499 |

ADVERTISEMENTS OF ELIZABETH
commonly applied to the regulations pro
in 1566 by Matthew Parker, archbishop o
bury, for the purpose, as alleged, of sec
formity and decency in public worshi
the tendencies of the extreme Protesta
(see PURITANS, PURITANISM, § 6). It
generally admitted that, though they re
Elizabeth's policy in ritual matters, th
received her formal sanction. They assu
importance in the ritual controversies of
teenth century, the High-church party c
that they were merely an archiepiscopal
enforcing an irreducible minimum of rit
their opponents attempted to show that
a legal prescription of a positive kind, wh
the surplice the only lawful vestment of
in parish churches.

BIBLIOGRAPHY: The text of the Advertisement
Gee and Hardy, *Documents*, pp. 467-475. Consu
*Life and Acts of Matthew Parker*, London, 1
*Quarterly Review*, xvii. (1881) 54-60.

ADVOCATE OF THE CHURCH (Lat.
or *Defensor Ecclesiæ*): An officer cha
the secular affairs of an ecclesiastical esta

THE NEW SCHAFF-HERZOG ENCYCLOPEDIA OF RELIGIOUS KNOWLEDGE Vol. I
(Baker Book House, Grand Rapids, MI, 1950, 1967)

Portugal in 1317, like the Spanish orders of Alcantara and Calatrava (qq.v.) under Cistercian rule and to fight against the Moors. It was endowed with property of the Templars, who had been suppressed in 1312. Papal confirmation was received from John XXII. in 1319, the grand master being made subordinate to the abbot of the Cistercian monastery of Alcobaça. The knights gained important victories and became rich and powerful. At their chief seat, Thomar (75 m. n.e. of Lisbon) in Estremadura, and at Batalha, twenty miles farther west, they erected magnificent buildings in pointed style, imitating the churches of the Templars in Cyprus and the Mosque of Omar in Jerusalem (cf. the Viscount de Condeixa, *O mosteiro da Batalha*, with French transl., Lisbon and Paris, 1892; J. Dernjac, *Thomar und Batalha*, in the *Zeitschrift für bildende Kunst*, new series, vi [1895], 98–106). About 1500 Pope Alexander VI. released the order from the vow of poverty. It had then 450 commanderies and an enormous income. A reform was effected in 1550 by the Hieronymite abbot Anton of Lisbon, and confirmed by Pope Julius III. At the same time the grand-mastership was formally attached to the crown, as it had been actually from the time of King Emmanuel (1495–1521). Pius V. in 1567 removed the jurisdiction of the abbot of Alcobaça, and Gregory XIII. in 1576 granted the king supreme power over both knights and monks. The order was secularized in 1797 and its property confiscated in 1834. It is now merely an order of merit. A less important Italian *Ordine di Christo* was founded by Pope John XXII. about 1320. It also became an order of merit. (O. ZÖCKLER†.)

BIBLIOGRAPHY: Helyot, *Ordres monastiques*, vi. 72–76, Paris, 1718; G. Giucci, *Iconografia storica degli ordini religiosi e cavallereschi*, i. 34–36, Rome, 1836; G. Moroni, *Dizionario di erudizione storico-ecclesiastica*, xviii. 210–219, Venice, 1843; Heimbucher, *Orden und Kongregationen*, i. 227; Currier, *Religious Orders*, p. 217.

CHRIST, crist, PAUL: Swiss Protestant; b. at Zurich Oct. 25, 1836; d. there Jan. 14, 1908. He was educated at the universities of Tübingen and Basel, and after being a pastor successively in the canton of Grisons (1858–62) and at Chur, the capital of the same canton (1862–65), he was a professor in the cantonal school of Chur from 1865 to 1870. He was then pastor at Lichtensteig (1871–75) and Rheineck (1875–80), both in the canton of St. Gall, and after four years of retirement on account of impaired health (1880–84) was municipal archivist at Chur (1884–87) and again professor in the cantonal school of the same city (1887–89). Since 1889 he has been professor of systematic and practical theology at the University of Zurich. In theology he represents the speculative and liberal school. He has written *Christliche Religionslehre* (Zurich, 1875); *Bilder aus der Geschichte der christlichen Kirche und Sitte* (St. Gall, 1876); *Religiöse Betrachtungen* (1881); *Der Pessimismus und die Sittenlehre* (Haarlem, 1882); *Die Lehre vom Gebet nach dem Neuen Testament* (Leyden, 1886); *Die sittliche Weltordnung* (1894); and *Grundriss der Ethik* (Berlin, 1905).

CHRISTADELPHIANS: A small sect which originated in the United States about 1850. They call themselves Christadelphians because of the belief that all that are in Christ are his brethren, and designate their congregations as "ecclesias" to "distinguish them from the so-called churches of the apostasy." John Thomas, the founder, a physician, born in England, came to America in 1844 and joined the Disciples of Christ. In a short time, however, he established a separate denomination, because he believed that, though the Disciples were the most "apostolic and spiritually enlightened religious organization in America," the religious teaching of the day was contrary to the teaching of the Bible.

Christadelphians reject the Trinity. They believe in one supreme God, who dwells in unapproachable light; in Jesus Christ, in whom was manifest the eternal spirit of God, and who died for the offenses of sinners, and rose for the justification of believing men and women; in one baptism only—immersion, the "burial with Christ in water into death to sin," which is essential to salvation; in immortality only in Christ; in eternal punishment of the wicked, but not in eternal torment; in hell, not as a place of torment, but as the grave; in the resurrection of the just and unjust; in the utter annihilation of the wicked, and in the non-resurrection of those who have never heard the Gospel, lack in intelligence (as infants), or are sunk in ignorance or brutality; in a second coming of Christ to establish his kingdom on earth, which is to be fitted for the everlasting abode of the saints; in the proximity of this second coming; in Satan as a Scriptural personification of sin; in the millennial reign of Christ on earth over the nations, during which sin and death will continue in a milder degree, and after which Christ will surrender his position of supremacy, and God will reveal himself, and become Father and Governor of a complete family; in salvation only for those who can understand the faith as taught by the Christadelphians, and become obedient to it. They have no ordained ministers. There are about sixty "ecclesias" in the United States, and a few in England, where most of their literature is published. H. K. CARROLL.

BIBLIOGRAPHY: Sources of doctrine are the works of the founder, generally published in pamphlet form in Birmingham and London. The principal are: *Eureka*, 1869; *The Revealed Mystery*, 1869; *Who are the Christadelphians?* 1869; *The Book Unsealed*, 1870; *Phanerosis*, 1870; *Anastasis*, 1871; *Clerical Theology Unscriptural*, 1877, and *Elpis Israel*, West Hoboken, 1871. Also the following works by Robert Roberts: *A Defence of the Faith Proclaimed in Ancient Times, . . . Revived in the Christadelphians*, Birmingham, 1868; *Everlasting Punishment not "Eternal Torments,"* ib. 1871; *Meaning of the Christadelphian Movement*, London, 1872; *Thirteen Lectures on the Things Revealed in . . . "Revelation,"* Birmingham, 1880; *The Good Confession*, ib. 1881; *Dr. Thomas, his Life and Work*, ib. 1884. Their organ is *The Christadelphian*, published at Birmingham, Eng. Consult H. K. Carroll, *Religious Forces of the U. S.*, pp. 89–90, 454, New York, 1896.

CHRISTENTUMSGESELLSCHAFT, DIE DEUTSCHE ("The German Society for Christendom"): A society which had a wide influence at the end of the eighteenth and beginning of the nineteenth centuries. In that period of deep depression and discouragement for the Evangelical



Church of Germany, it brough
Christians together by personal
correspondence, and helped
cooperation. Its special object
bold depreciation and mockery
then so common, as well as
sented by Nikolai's *Zeitschrift*
*Gothaer Zeitung*. Its founder
August Urlsperger (q.v.), of
longed to the old school of sir
and piety. He thought that
Gospel should stand together
another as did its enemies. In
number of German, Dutch, D
theologians without getting
in 1779 and 1780 traveled wic
effecting more by personal cont
was still the same, and he ca
couraged. In Basel, the last pl
to visit, he found a response.
stirred up by D'Annone, the ze
tenz, a number of like-mindec
been organized, who listened
sperger's ideas; and the society
first formal meeting on Aug. 30
ning once made, the thing spr
formed at Nuremberg the next
gart, Frankfort, Berlin, Magde
numbers grew, and correspond
from America, a more forma
required. Basel was made the
end of 1782, and a manifold act
it, embracing all that is meant
and foreign missions. Selectic
mass of correspondence were sen
in printed form after 1783. U
inally wished to write and circul
treatises, but the central body
a more practical direction, wis
hold the true faith, but not to
troversies. The name, too, wa
original *Deutsche Gesellschaft*
*christlicher Wahrheit und Gott*
Society for the Promotion of C
Piety") to the present title.
who had been the general secr
the Savoy Chapel in London,
between Germany and England
revival of spiritual life set a star
The Basel Bible Society was fou
first result; and the second was
also at Basel, planned as early
Spittler on the model of the B
(founded in 1800 by Jänicke, a
ciety), and realized in 1815
C. G. Blumhardt (q.v.). A nu
dations and special organizatio
ceeding years. Among them
school and orphanage at Be
Society of the Friends of Israel
for the Spread of Christian
the deaf and dumb asylum at
the deaconess home in the
The original association fulfille
the impulse to so many and
it still exists, however, under

THE NEW SCHAFF-HERZOG ENCYCLOPEDIA OF RELIGIOUS KNOWLEDGE
(Baker Book House, Grand Rapids, MI, 1950, 1967) Vol. III

Joachim heretics." His application of the correct principle, "a year for a day," made in the very depths of the Dark Ages, is one of the most pathetic incidents in the history of mankind; but his study of time-prophecy brought him peace and joy of heart. He was an opponent of the prevailing "doctrine of the Trinity." William Miller, in the year 1829, was privileged to see (approximately) the correct date for the setting up of the abomination of desolation (539 A. D.), and for the beginning of the Time of the End (1799 A. D.) Morton Edgar, author of *Pyramid Passages*, has found foreshown in the Great Pyramid of Egypt abundant evidence of the accuracy of the Bible chronology of Pastor Russell and the supplements thereto supplied by Dr. John Edgar, deceased. These findings are set forth in his work, *Pyramid Passages*, Vol. II, of which we recommend sections numbered in the following table. For convenience we give the citations to Pastor Russell's works in which the same items are discussed. The Pyramid is still there, and the measurements can be made by anybody. Pastor Russell's chronology was written before he ever saw the Pyramid.

| Date Foreshown | | Event | Pastor Russell's Works | Sections of Pyramid Passages |
|---|---|---|---|---|
| Fall | 4127 B. C. | Fall of Adam. | Z 04-343 | 25-30-58 |
| Fall | 3127 B. C. | End of Adam's 1000-year day. | Z 04-343 | 25-28 |
| Fall | 2473 B. C. | Flood. | B 42 | 24-30 |
| Fall | 2021 B. C. | Birth of Isaac. | R 231 | 45 |
| Spring | 1813 B. C. | Death of Jacob. | B 218-232 | 16-17 |
| Spring | 1615 B. C. | Exodus and giving of the Law. | B 42 | 11 |
| Spring | 1575 B. C. | Entrance into Canaan. | B 42 | 43-46 |
| Fall | 626 B. C. | Last Jubilee. | B 185 | 50 |
| Fall | 607 B. C. | Desolation of the Land. | B 51 | 19-46-48 |
| Fall | 455 B. C. | Nehemiah's Commission. | B 67 | 51-52-53 |
| Fall | 2 B. C. | Birth of Christ. | B 54 | 10-43 |
| Fall | 29 A. D. | Baptism of Christ. | B 60 | 10-24-43-58 |
| Spring | 33 A. D. | Death of Christ. | B 61 | 10-11-14-32-45 |
| Fall | 36 A. D. | Conversion of Cornelius. | B 71 | 51 |
| Spring | 1378 A. D. | Wycliffe. | Z 05-185 | 37 |
| Spring | 1521 A. D. | Diet of Worms. | Z 05-180 | 38 |
| Fall | 1846 A. D. | Evangelical Alliance. | C 95-119 | 14-52 |
| Fall | 1874 A. D. | Second Advent of the Lord. | B 173-247 | 16-32-50 |
| Spring | 1878 A. D. | Favor to Jews and sleeping Saints. | C 233 | 17-28 |
| Fall | 1914 A. D. | End of Times of the Gentiles. | B 73 | 19-48 |
| Fall | 2875 A. D. | Restitution completed. | Z 04-344 | 37 |
| Fall | 2914 A. D. | Dominion restored to mankind. | Z 04-343 | 58 |



The chronology as it appears in the STUDIES IN THE SCRIPTURES is accurate. The year 1914 brought the end of the Times of the Gentiles, but not the end of the Harvest work. Have the teachings of the Parallels lost their value? Not at all. The point not previously noticed is that the Jewish polity was not to be destroyed in Jerusalem only, but throughout all Judea. Nor does *Judea* mean all of Palestine. The actual depopulation of the whole of Palestine did not occur until the year 135 A. D. (corresponding to our year 1980), on the ninth day of the month of Ab, the anniversary of the burning of the Temple under Titus. On that day came to an end the insurrection of Bar-Cocheba, the false Messiah, who wrought his own destruction and that of 580,000 of his followers, when he attempted to regain control of Judea and Jerusalem. The struggle was of five years' duration having begun in 130 A. D. "It was the effort, under the leadership of Bar-Cocheba, to regain their independence, that brought about a repetition of scenes enacted under Titus, and resulted actually in the depopulation of Palestine. The whole of Judea was turned into a desert; about 985 towns and villages were laid in ashes; fifty of their fortresses were razed to the ground; even the name of their capital was changed to Ælia Capitolina, and they were forbidden to approach it on pain of death; thousands of those who had escaped death were reduced to slavery, and such as could not be thus disposed of were transported into Egypt."—McC.

When the Lord gave His wonderful prophecy in which the destinies of nominal Fleshly Israel, nominal Spiritual Israel, and the Israel of God, are set forth, it was in answer to three definite questions: "*When* shall these things be? and what shall be the sign of Thy Parousia, and of the *end* of the Age?" (Matt. 24:3.) The Lord did not ignore their question. He answered it with a reply that sweeps the history of twenty centuries. He showed that the *end* of Fleshly Israel foreshadowed the *end* of Spiritual Israel. Fleshly Israel had three ends; the destruction of Jerusalem in A. D. 70, the complete subjugation of Judea in A. D. 73, and the actual depopulation of the whole of Palestine in A. D. 135. Which did He mean should be the end that would be a guide to His followers? Not the end in A. D. 70, foreshadowing 1915; for the Harvest of the Gospel Age is still in progress. Not the end in A. D. 135, foreshadowing 1980; for the *Harvest is the end.* He must have meant the end in Judea, even as He said, "Then let them which be in *Judea* flee into the mountains." (Matt. 24:16.) See also Matt. 2:22; 3:5;

THE FINISHED MYSTERY, 1917

among the people? And all the people shouted and said, God save the king." (1 Sam. 10:17-24.) Saul was God's choice for king; his name means "desired," and in this he typified Christ, the "desire of all nations." This incident looks forward to the time when all the people of the world will say of Christ, "Oh! who is like unto our God? Lo! This is our God; this is our King; this is the One we have waited for; He is head and shoulders, as a ruler, above all kings and rulers we have had."

(5) *Job*, after the Sabeans had made off with his oxen and asses, after a bolt of lightning had burned up his sheep, after the Chaldeans had stolen his camels and murdered his servants, after a whirlwind had blown down his house and killed all his children, after he was covered with boils from head to foot, after his wife had gone back on him, and after his three remaining friends tried to prove to him that he was a hypocrite, prayed that he might go to hell and stay there until God's wrath should be past, and that then God would remember him in resurrection. (Job 14:13-15.) Job records Elihu's prophetic statement that when the Messenger of the Covenant has returned, death will cease and men not need to go into the tomb. (Job 33:19-30.) Job also describes the steam engine—stationary, railway and marine.

The following is a corrected translation of Job 40:15 to 41:34, with comments thereon from the pen of one of Pastor Russell's followers: "Behold now one with great heat [the stationary steam engine], which I have made to be with thee; he will consume fodder [peat, wood, coal] as do cattle. Behold now his strength is in his loins [boiler plates], and his power is within the parts bent in a circle [boiler shell] of his belly. His tail [smoke stack—opposite the feeding end] will set upright like a cedar; the couplings of his leaping parts [connecting rods, pitmans] will be clamped together. His bones are tubes of copper; his solid bones [grate bars] are as hammered-out bars of iron. He is the greatest of the ways of power. He that made him [the Lord] can make His sword [Word] to approach unto [reveal] him. [Isa. 27:1, 2.] He shall rest under thin shelter [steam jackets] within a covering of fibrous reeds [jute] and clay [mortar]. The willows of the valley [the trees overhead] will enclose him around about. Behold [as a pumping engine] he will drink up an overflowing river without much exertion; he will cause the people to trust [that their cellars will keep dry], though a Jordan should rush forth over its border. He will gather it up in his fountains by means of traps and with a perforated nozzle.



"Thou wilt lengthen out leviathan [the locomotive] with a hook [automatic coupler] or with a snare [coupling-pin] which thou wilt cause his tongue [coupling-link] to drop down. Wilt thou not place a ring [piston] in his nostrils [cylinders] or pierce through his cheeks [piston-ends] with a staff [piston-rod]? Will he make repeated supplication unto thee [to get off the track]? Or will he utter soft tones unto thee [when he screeches with the whistle]? Will he make a covenant with thee, that thou mayest take him for a servant forever [without repairs]? Wilt thou play with him as with a bird [make him whistle at will]? Or wilt thou bind [enslave] him for thy maidens [so that you can take them to a picnic or convention]? Companies [of stockholders] will feast upon him [his earnings]; they will share him among speculators. [Psa. 74:14.] Thou wilt fill his skin with pointed irons [bolts], and his head with a cabin of fishermen [a cab similar to the cabins on fishing vessels]. Place thy hand upon him, be mindful of the conflict [raging within the boiler] and thou wilt add no further questions. Behold, his confidence [boiler] being deceived [not properly supplied with water], shall not at once his mighty form be spread asunder [by an explosion]? There is none so bold that he will stir him up [to run at his very highest possible speed], and none who will then place himself before him [to be run over]. Who will compete with this one and endure [pass him on the track]? Under the whole heaven, none, unless [one like] himself.

"I will not pass in silence his members, nor the cause of his mighty forces, nor the beauty of his equipment. Who can strip off the facings of his jacket? Who can penetrate between the double lap of his shield [the overlapping sections of the boiler plates]? Who can force open the doors of his shield [the boiler ends]? The circuits of his teeth [rows of rivets] are formidable. His strength depends on courses of shields [sections of plates] closed up tightly with a seal [calked]. They shall join one upon another so that a hiss of air [steam] shall not escape from between them. One to the other shall adhere. They will be welded together that they cannot be sundered. In his sneezing [when he puffs from the cylinders] light will shine, a flood of light prevading the mass of vapors: and his eyes [headlights] will be as the eyelashes of the morning [as rays of light from the rising sun]. Out of his mouth [fire-door] will leap forth flaming torches, and [from the smoke stack] glowing sparks will slip themselves away. From his nostrils [cylinders] will issue forth vapor as from a boiling pot or caldron. His inhaling

THE FINISHED MYSTERY, 1917

**By Thy blood.**—"If the blood of bulls and of goats . . . sanctifieth to the purifying of the flesh, how much more shall the blood of Christ, who, through the eternal spirit, offered Himself without spot to God."—Heb. 9:13-15.

**Out of every kindred.**—"In thy Seed shall all the kindreds of the earth be blessed."—Acts 3:25.

**And tongue.**—"Every knee shall bow, every tongue shall swear."—Isa. 45:23.

**And people.**—"The heavens declare His righteousness, and all the people see His glory."—Psa. 97:6.

**And nation.**—"And in thy Seed shall all the nations of the earth be blessed."—Gen. 26:4, 22:18; Rev. 14:6.

5:10. **And hast made** [us] THEM unto our God [**Kings**] A KINGDOM.—"It will be the Kingdom of the saints, in that they shall reign and judge and bless the world in conjunction with their Lord, Jesus. (Rom. 8:17, 18.) The Kingdom class proper will consist only of our Lord and His 'elect' Little Flock."—D618.

**And** [**priests**] PRIESTHOOD.—"The Divine provision for a 'Royal Priesthood' implies weakness, imperfection, on the part of some whom the priests are to help, and instruct, and from whom they are to accept sacrifice and offerings for sin, and to whom they are to extend mercy and forgiveness."—E486, 476; 1 Pet. 2:5, 9; Rev. 1:6; 20:6.

**And** [**we**] THEY **shall reign.**—"But before the Royal Priesthood begin their reign, they must 'suffer with Him,' sharing in the antitypical sacrifices. (2 Tim. 2:12.)"—T 26.

**On.**—*Ept.* over.—Rev. 6:16.

**The earth.**—"The Kingdom and dominion, even the majesty of the Kingdom *under* the whole heaven shall be given to the people of the saints of the Most High, whose kingdom is an everlasting Kingdom, and all rulers shall serve and obey Him. (Dan 7:27.)"—D618.

5:11. **And I beheld.**—John beheld this in vision and will behold it in reality.

**And I heard.**—John heard in the vision, and will hear in the reality.

**As it were the voice of many angels.**—Besides the angels, the Great Company are in this happy throng. The events to the end of the chapter have their fulfilment in the future.

**Round about the Throne.**—"In the circuit of Heaven" (Job 22:14), the circle of the Universe.

**And the beasts.**—Justice, Power, Love and Wisdom.—Rev. 4:6, 7.

**And the elders.**—The prophecies.—Rev. 4:10.

**And the number of them.**—"Whose number no man knoweth."—Rev. 7:9.



**Was ten thousand times ten thousand, and thousands of thousands.**—The number of the Great Company will apparently exceed one hundred millions. Num. 4:46-48 and Ex. 28:1 indicate but one priest to each 2,860 Levites, which would make the number of the Great Company approximate 411,840,000.—T118, 119; Dan. 7:10.

5:12. **Saying with a loud voice.**—The Great Company will be very enthusiastic workers on the other side of the veil, for they really love the Lord with all their heart, soul, mind and strength (Mark 12:30); and need only to be liberated to give full expression to that love.

**Worthy is the Lamb that was slain.**—"Our Lord Jesus demonstrated before the Father, before angels, and before His 'brethren,' His fidelity to the Father and to the Father's Law, demonstrating that it was not beyond the ability of a perfect being, even under the most adverse conditions."—E134, 120.

**To receive power.**—The Great Company class humbly realize that their faithfulness and zeal was not sufficient to warrant their own exaltation to power.

**And riches.**—They realize they did not lay up all the Heavenly treasures they might have done, but hid their talents in earthly pursuits.

**And wisdom.**—They realize their own unwisdom in seeking the praise of men and that the Christ Company, though apparently fools for Christ's sake, were really the wisest of the wise.

**And strength.**—They know that they used their own strength for the support and maintenance of institutions which really hindered rather than helped the Bride to make herself ready.

**And honor.**—They know that, as a class, they sought and obtained the honor that cometh from men, but failed to properly seek the honor that cometh from God only.

**And glory.**—They know that they failed to meet the high conditions of self-sacrifice, and were therefore unworthy of the high reward.

**And blessing.**—They feel that the blessings which the Lord gave to them were thoughtlessly appropriated to themselves and their families, with hardly a serious thought about the needs of the Lord's dear family; and that appropriately, the chiefest of all blessings, the privilege of extending God's blessings to the needy world, should go to those who most earnestly "by patient perseverance in well doing (did) seek for glory, honor and immortality." (Rom. 2:7.) Thus they reverence the Lamb, and His Bride, for they are one.—Rev. 19:7.

5:13. **And every creature.**—After the destruction of the

THE FINISHED MYSTERY, 1917

**Have sealed the servants of our God.**—See Rev. 19:20; 14:1. Satan is a diligent student of time prophecy (Luke 12:39); but not having the Holy Spirit he is unable to reach accurate conclusions. Seeing a definite Plan, and a definite time for every important feature of that Plan, his aim has ever been to thwart the purposes of the Almighty. This attempt to destroy the Seed began with the death of Abel and still continues. No doubt Satan *believed* the Millennial Kingdom was due to be set up in 1915; and no doubt, also, he knew that seven years prior to the time of the setting up of that kingdom the restraints upon the evil spirits would be lifted. Be that as it may, there is evidence that the establishment of the Kingdom in Palestine will probably be in 1925, ten years later than we once calculated. The 70 jubilees, reckoned as 50 years each, expire October, 1925. (B186.) Gen. 15:1-16:3, read connectedly, indicates that Abraham's vision as to when he would receive the Kingdom was not granted until ten years after the Covenant was made, or 2035 B. C. The ages of the animals offered aggregated eleven years, which, applied prophetically, on the scale of a year for a day, equal 3960 years, the length of time from the date of the visions to A. D. 1925 (Z.'07-79). It seems conclusive that the hour of Nominal Zion's travail is fixed for the Passover of 1918. (See Rev. 3:14.) That will be 7 years prior to 1925. At that time there is every reason to believe the fallen angels will invade the minds of many of the Nominal Church people, driving them to exceedingly unwise conduct and leading to their destruction at the hands of the enraged masses, who will later be dragged to the same fate. The great war now raging is most certainly the work of evil spirits, and the Kaiser is not the only clever ruler who has been deceived by evil spirits, as history will sometime show.—*Lu. 12:56*.

If our reasoning is correct, we inquire whether there was any indication of a move on Satan's part 7 years prior to 1915, showing that he expected the restraints to be removed from the evil spirits at that time; and we answer that there was something very definite indicated at that time. In the Vow, advised by Pastor Russell in that year, and in the experiences of many, for and against it, it is plain that the Enemy *then* attempted to come in like a flood, but was held back—restrained until the sealing work is done. (Matt. 10:25; Luke 22:42-44; Heb. 12:4; Isa. 63:3.) After the demons have been turned loose on the *swine* class, we shall see what happens. (Matt. 7:6; 8:31-34.) Those now fearful that they might learn something will be terror-stricken then for a different reason.



**In their foreheads.**—"The storm is held in check until the faithful servants of God are 'sealed in their foreheads' (Ex. 13:9; 28:36, 38; Deut. 6:8; Ezek. 9:4-6; Rev. 14:1), i. e., until such are given an intellectual appreciation which will not only comfort them, and shield them, but also be a mark, seal or evidence of their sonship, as indicated by our Lord when He promised that the Holy Spirit should show to the faithful 'things to come.' (John 16:13.") (B169.) When the demon test comes, those who have the mark of sonship (Ezek. 9:2-4) will know it and will stand the test, while all others will surely fall. A letter from one of the Bethel workers, written shortly after Pastor Russell's death, says: "About three months ago I asked several questions at the table, the last one being as follows, 'Since I now see that the Jewish Time of Trouble did not end until the year 73 A. D., as I fully proved to myself by consulting the historians, what then are we to expect in the parallel year 1918?' Brother Russell put the question to three prominent brethren, all of whom replied that they did not know, but were willing to wait and see. When he called upon me I said, 'Since the year 73 A. D. saw the complete overthrow of nominal Natural Israel in Palestine, so in the parallel year 1918, I infer we should look for the complete overthrow of nominal Spiritual Israel; i. e., the fall of Babylon. (Rev. 18.) Brother Russell replied: 'Exactly. That is exactly the inference to draw.'" The conclusion of the Church's career comes first. (Rev. 3:14.)

"If you see the 'door' of opportunity for sacrifice and service open before you, enter in. But enter quickly; for the night of darkness and of intense opposition to the truth will ere long be upon us and will hinder you from engaging in the service. 'The morning cometh, and also the night.' 'The night cometh in which no man can work.' When that is true, you may know that 'the door is shut,' that all the wise virgins have entered in, that all have been proved, and that all vacancies have been acceptably filled. All the special 'servants of God' having by that time been 'sealed in their foreheads' (given an intellectual appreciation of God's Plan), the four winds will be loosed and will produce the great 'whirlwind' of trouble in the midst of which the remnant of the Elijah class will be 'changed,' and exalted to Kingdom glory."—C225.

**7:4. And I heard the number of them which were sealed.**—"We have every reason to believe that the definite, fixed number of the Elect is that several times stated in Revelation, namely, 144,000 'redeemed from amongst men.'" (F179; Rev. 14:1.) This is the equivalent of one saint fully developed for each five days of the Age.

9

THE FINISHED MYSTERY, 1917

Pope Martin stated the matter in his own behalf as follows: "All the earth is my diocese, and I am the ordinary of all men, having the authority of the King of all kings upon subjects. I am all in all, and above all, so that God Himself, and I, the vicar of God, have both one consistory, and I am able to do almost all that God can do. In all things that I list my will is to stand for reason, for I am able by the law to dispense above the law, and of wrong to make justice in correcting laws and changing them. Wherefore, if those things that I do be said not to be done of man, but of God—What can you make me but God? Again, if prelates of the church be called and counted of Constance for Gods, I then, being above all prelates, seem by this reason to be above all Gods. Wherefore, no marvel if it be in my power to change time and times, to alter and abrogate laws, to dispense with all things, yea, with the precepts of Christ."—B314; Dan. 7:25.

12:6. **And the woman.**—The true Church of God.

**Fled into the wilderness.**—"Error, always more popular than truth, when exalted to influence and power, hunted down, proscribed and made disreputable the truth, and all who held it. This was the time when the true Church (woman) fled into the wilderness—into solitude—an outcast because of her fidelity to the truth, and to the true Lord and Head of the Church."—B329.

**Where she hath a place prepared of God.**—"The secret place of the Most High."—Psa. 91:1.

**That they.**—The antitypical ravens that fed the Elijah class, the unknown, "faithful men" who, in secret, broke the bread of life to those that hungered for righteousness.

**Should feed her there.**—As Elijah was fed in the wilderness.—Rev. 2:20.

**A thousand two hundred and threescore days.**—1260 years, from A. D. 539 to 1799.—Rev. 11:2, 3.

12:7. **And there was war in heaven.**—Between the two ecclesiastical powers, Pagan Rome and Papal Rome.

**Michael.**—"Who as God," the Pope.—B275; C62.

**And his angels.**—The Bishops. The following is the reply given in the Catholic catechism to the question, "Who are the successors of the Apostles?" Ans. "The bishops who are rightly consecrated, and are in communion with the head of the Church, the Pope."

**[Fought against] TO WAR WITH the dragon.**—Attempted to get the temporal power away from the civil rulers.—Rev. 2:12.

**And the dragon.**—Imperial Rome.—B288; Rev. 12:3; 20:2.



**Fought and his angels.**—Did everything possible to circumscribe the growing power of the papacy, but all in vain.—Rev. 2:12.

12:8. **And THEY prevailed not AGAINST HIM, neither was [their place] HE THEN found any more in heaven.**—The Papacy came out of the contest victorious. "Paganism, defeated, relinquished all things pertaining to religious affairs and contented itself with social, civic and political affairs," so stated one of Pastor Russell's coworkers.

12:9. **And the great dragon was cast out.**—Verses 9 to 12 contain the rejoicings of the Papacy over their triumph.

**That old serpent, called the Devil, [and] Satan.**—"To this fourth beast, representing Rome, Daniel gives no descriptive name. While the others are described as lion-like, bear-like and leopard-like, the fourth was so ferocious and hideous that none of the beasts of earth could be compared with it. John the Revelator, seeing in vision the same symbolic beast (government), was also at a loss for a name by which to describe it, and finally gives it several. Among others, he called it 'the Devil.' He certainly chose an appropriate name; for Rome, when viewed in the light of its bloody persecutions, certainly has been the most devilish of all earthly governments. Even in its change from Rome Pagan to Rome Papal it illustrated one of Satan's chief characteristics; for he also transforms himself to appear as an angel of light (2 Cor. 11:14), as Rome transformed itself from heathenism and claimed to be Christian—the Kingdom of Christ."—A258.

**Which deceiveth the whole world.**—By intimating that anybody in it except the pope has any right to say anything about how it should be run.

**He was cast out into the earth.**—We, the Papacy, are in control!

**And his angels were cast out with him.**—We, the cardinals, etc., have the positions of power once held by the priests of Pagan Rome!

12:10. **And I heard a loud voice saying in heaven.**—In the Roman Catholic Church.

**Now is come salvation, and strength.**—"Cardinal Manning, Papacy's chief representative in England, endorses and draws public attention to the following clause of the Catholic faith: 'We declare, affirm, define, and pronounce it necessary to salvation, for every human creature to be subject to the Roman Pontiff.' And in a published discourse he represents the pope as saying, 'I claim to be the Supreme Judge and Director of the consciences of men; of the peasant that tills the field, and the prince that sits on the throne; of the household that lives in the

THE FINISHED MYSTERY, 1917

cometh; when your fear cometh as desolation, and your destruction cometh as a whirlwind; when distress and anguish cometh upon you. Then shall they call upon Me, but I will not answer; they shall seek Me early, but they shall not find Me; for that they hated knowledge, and did not choose the fear of the Lord. They would none of my counsel: they despised all my reproof. Therefore shall they eat of the fruit of their own way."—Prov. 1:24-31.

By the space of a thousand and [six] TWO hundred furlongs.—This can not be interpreted to refer to the 2100 mile battle line of the world war. A furlong or stadium is not a mile and this is without the city whereas the battle line is within the city. See Rotherham's translation.

A stadium is 606¾ English ft.; 1200 stadii are, mi., 137.9

The work on this volume was done in Scranton, Pa. As fast as it was completed it was sent to the Bethel. Half of the work was done at an average distance of 5 blocks from the Lackawanna station, and the other half at a distance of 25 blocks. Blocks in Scranton are 10 to the mile. Hence the average distance to the station is 15 blocks, or........... 1.5 mi.

The mileage from Scranton to Hoboken Terminal is shown in time tables as 143.8 and this is the mileage charged to passengers, but in 1911, at an expense of $12,000,000, the Lackawanna Railroad completed its famous cut-off, saving 11 miles of the distance. From the day the cut-off was completed the trainmen have been allowed 11 miles less than the time table shows, or a net distance of........ 132.8 "

Hoboken Ferry to Barclay Street Ferry, New York, is.......................... 2.0 "

Barclay Street Ferry to Fulton Ferry, New York, is 4,800 feet or................ 0.9 "

Fulton Ferry, New York, to Fulton Ferry, Brooklyn, is 2,000 feet or......... 0.4 "

Fulton Ferry, Brooklyn, to Bethel, is 1,485 feet or .......................... 0.3 "

Shortest distance from place where the winepress was trodden by the Feet Members of the Lord, Whose guidance and help alone made this volume possible. (John 6:60, 61; Matt. 20:11.)...................mi., 137.9

## REVELATION 15

## THE SONG OF THE SAINTS

15:1. And I saw another sign.—*Seemion*, the same word used by our Lord when He said, "Then shall appear the *sign* of the Son of Man." The proofs of the Lord's Second Advent are here referred to.

In heaven.—Among God's professed people.

Great and marvelous.—Very different in tone and contents from other Bible "helps."

Seven angels.—The seven volumes of *Studies in the Scriptures*.

Having the seven last plagues.—The seven volumes of *Studies in the Scriptures* together constitute the third and last woe poured out upon papacy.—Rev. 16:1-21; 22:18.

For in them is filled up the wrath of God.—Their united testimony is that the Times of the Gentiles have expired, the Reign of Christ has begun, all earthly potentates—Civil, Social, Ecclesiastical and Financial—must give way to the New Order of things, and will not give way peaceably, but must be ejected.

15:2. And I saw as it were a sea of glass.—The Time of Trouble made transparent. We can see why the Lord permits it, and see the Golden Age of glory, peace and Divine blessing that lies just beyond.

Mingled with fire.—The coming anarchy. "They are the waves of the Red Sea, which appears on fire as the Sun of righteousness arises upon them, on the margin of which the true Israelites sing the song of Moses and the saving Lamb. Standing on its shore are seen those who are delivered from the beasts' sway as the Israelites were in their exodus from the land of Pharaoh. The song of Moses is sung by delivered Israel after the Egyptian plagues: here the hymn of praise is sung by the redeemed before the plagues are renewed and the Church gains its last victory over the antichristian world."—Cook.

And them that had gotten the victory over the beast, and [over] his image.—Who understand and live in harmony with the knowledge that both Papacy and Protestantism, and the governments under their influence, are of Satanic spirit.—Rev. 13:11, 13, 14, 15; 14:11; 16:2, 13; 19:20; 20:10; Matt. 24:24.



THE FINISHED MYSTERY, 1917

24:18. So I spake unto the people in the morning: and at even my wife died; and I did in the morning as I was commanded.—He continued his addresses and writings to the Lord's people; his wife became to him as one dead; and he continued uninterruptedly in the work of the ministry.

24:19. And the people said unto me, Wilt thou not tell us what these things are to us, that thou doest so?—Why was Pastor Russell caused by his Father to endure the fiery trials and ecclesiastical falsehoods in connection with this incident of his life?

### THE CHURCHES TO CEASE TO BE

24:20, 21. Then I answered them, The word of the Lord came unto me, saying, Speak unto the house of Israel, Thus saith the Lord God; Behold, I will profane My Sanctuary, the excellency of your strength, the desire of your eyes, and that which your soul pitieth; and your sons and your daughters whom ye have left shall fall by the sword. —God gives the reason. It was as a picture or parable of what is to happen to Christendom. Until 1878 the nominal church had been in a sense God's sanctuary or Temple: but He was from then on, culminating in 1918, to remove it with a stroke or plague of erroneous doctrines and deeds Divinely permitted. The Church was the strength of Christendom, that about which its life centered, and around which its institutions were built. It was the desire of the eyes of the people, that which all Christians loved. Nevertheless, God was to make manifest the profanation which ecclesiasticism had made of the Christian Church, and to cause the church organizations to become to Him as one dead, an unclean thing, not to be touched, or mourned. And the "children of the church" shall perish by the sword of war, revolution and anarchy, and by the Sword of the Spirit be made to see that they have lost their hope of life on the spirit plane—that "the door is shut."

24:22. And ye shall do as I have done: ye shall not cover your lips, nor eat the bread of men.—So universal and dreadful will be the troubles that the dead will literally lie unburied and unwept. There can be no mourning for the dead in a period when the living are overwhelmed by troubles worse than death.

24:23. And your tires shall be upon your heads; and your shoes upon your feet: ye shall not mourn nor weep; but ye shall pine away for your iniquities, and mourn one toward another.—The mourning will be an inner sorrow of a people stupefied by terrible experiences, who pine



away and without outward expression sink together into the fellowship of helpless grief.

24:24. Thus Ezekiel is unto you a sign: according to all that he hath done shall ye do: and when this cometh, ye shall know that I am the Lord God.—Thus the silent sorrow at Pastor Russell's heart was to be a sign to Christendom. The sorrowful experiences of Pastor Russell in this connection shall later on be those of all Christendom; "and when this cometh" they shall know that Jehovah God is supreme, and back of all the judgments of the trouble time.

### PASTOR RUSSELL DEAD, BUT SPEAKING AGAIN

24:25, 26. Also, thou son of man, shall it not be in the day when I take from them their strength, the joy of their glory, the desire of their eyes, and that whereupon they set their minds, their sons and their daughters. That he that escapeth in that day shall come unto thee, to cause thee to hear it with thine ears?—Also, in the year 1918, when God destroys the churches wholesale and the church members by millions, it shall be that any that escape shall come to the works of Pastor Russell to learn the meaning of the downfall of "Christianity."

24:27. In that day shall thy mouth be opened to him which is escaped, and thou shalt speak, and be no more dumb: and thou shalt be a sign unto them; and they shall know that I am the Lord.—Pastor Russell's voice has been stilled in death; and his voice is, comparatively speaking, dumb to what it will be. In the time of revolution and anarchy he shall speak, and be no more dumb to those that escape the destruction of that day. Pastor Russell shall "be a sign unto them," shall tell them the truth about the Divine appointment of the trouble, as they consult his books, scattered to the number of ten million throughout Christendom. His words shall be a sign of hope unto them, enabling them to see the bright side of the cloud and to look forward with anticipation to the glorious Kingdom of God to be established. Then "they shall know the Lord."

---

"Build thee more stately mansions, O my soul,
As the swift seasons roll!
Leave thy low vaulted past!
Let each new temple, nobler than the last,
Shut thee from heaven with a dome more vast,
Till thou at length art free,
Leaving thine outgrown shell by life's unresting sea."

THE FINISHED MYSTERY, 1917

hardships can be borne. Peter told fellow believers: "Beloved ones, do not be puzzled at the burning among you, which is happening to you for a trial, as though a strange thing were befalling you. On the contrary, go on rejoicing forasmuch as you are sharers in the sufferings of the Christ."—1 Pet. 4:12, 13.

Jehovah and his "messenger of the covenant," Jesus Christ, came to inspect the spiritual temple in 1918 C.E. Judgment then began with the "house of God" and a period of refining and cleansing commenced. (Mal. 3:1-3; 1 Pet. 4:17) Something else also occurred. Men manifesting the marks of an "evil slave" came forward and figuratively began 'beating' their fellow slaves. Jesus Christ had foretold how such ones would be dealt with. At the same time he showed that a "faithful and discreet slave" class would be in evidence, dispensing spiritual food.—Matt. 24:45-51.

The identity of the "faithful and discreet slave," or "faithful and wise servant" (*King James Version*), was a matter of quite some concern back in those years. Much earlier, in 1881, C. T. Russell wrote: "We believe that every member of this body of Christ is engaged in the blessed work, either directly or indirectly, of giving meat in due season to the household of faith. 'Who then is that *faithful* and *wise servant* whom his Lord hath made ruler over his household,' to give them meat in due season? Is it not that 'little flock' of consecrated servants who are *faithfully* carrying out their consecration vows—the body of Christ—and is not the whole body individually and collectively, giving the meat in due season to the household of faith—the great company of believers?"

So it was understood that the "servant" God used to dispense spiritual food was a class. With the passing of time, however, the idea adopted by many was that C. T. Russell himself was the "faithful and wise servant." This led some into the snare of creature worship. They felt that all the truth God saw fit to reveal to his people had been presented through Brother Russell, that nothing more could be brought forth. Annie Poggensee writes: "This caused a great sifting out of those who chose to stay back with Russell's works." In February 1927 this erroneous thought that Russell himself was the "faithful and wise servant" was cleared up.

Shortly after Brother Rutherford became president of the Watch Tower Society, a real conspiracy developed. The seed of rebellion was planted and then the trouble spread, as explained below.

C. T. Russell had seen the need to send someone from headquarters to Britain to strengthen the Bible Students there after the outbreak of World War I.



He intended to send Paul S. L. Johnson, a Jew who forsook Judaism and became a Lutheran minister before coming to a knowledge of God's truth. Johnson had served as one of the Society's traveling speakers and was well known for his ability. Out of respect for Russell's wish, the executive committee that served for a short time before Rutherford's election as president sent Johnson to England, giving him certain papers that would facilitate entry into that country. He was to learn all he could about the work in England and then make a full report to the Society, but he was to make no personnel changes at the British headquarters. However, his reception in England during November 1916 seemed to warp his judgment and finally his reason, "until," as A. H. Macmillan stated, "he came to the ridiculous conclusion that he was the 'steward' of Jesus' parable of the penny. He later thought he was the world's high priest." In discourses to Bible Students throughout England, Johnson characterized himself as Russell's successor, contending that the mantle of Pastor Russell had fallen upon him just as Elijah's cloak ("official garment") fell upon Elisha.—2 Ki. 2:11-14.

Evidently, Johnson's aspirations had developed even earlier, for Edythe Kessler recalls: "In 1915 I left Bethel and, before starting for Arizona, I visited a couple of old friends I had known for years, and while I was there they entertained a pilgrim, P. S. L. Johnson by name. Satan was already showing his ugly underhanded methods to gain control, no matter how. Johnson said, 'I'd like to talk with you. Let's sit in the living room,' which we did. He commenced by saying: 'Sister, we know that it is possible for Brother Russell to pass on most any time, but the friends need not be fearful when that happens. I can step into his place and take right over without any stopping of the work.'"

While in England, Johnson endeavored to take complete control of the British field of activity, even trying, without authority, to dismiss certain members of the London headquarters staff. So much confusion resulted that the branch overseer complained to Brother Rutherford. In turn, Rutherford appointed a commission of several brothers in London who were not members of the headquarters staff. They met, heard and weighed the facts and recommended that Johnson be recalled. Rutherford told Johnson to return. Instead of doing so, Johnson sent letters and cablegrams charging the committee with bias, and also trying to justify his course. Seeking to make his position indispensable in Britain, he improperly used the documents furnished him by the Society and impounded its funds in the

1975 YEARBOOK OF JEHOVAH'S WITNESSES

at the head of affairs? He surely did. In the past we were all prone to worship the creature more than the Creator. The Lord knew that. So he placed a creature with a different disposition at the head of affairs, or I should say in charge of the work, the harvest work. You desire nobody to worship you. I know that, but you *do* desire that all of like precious faith should enjoy the light that is now shining on the pathway of the just, as the Lord sees fit for it to shine. And that is what the Lord wants done."

## Clearing Up the Identity of the "Faithful and Wise Servant"

Many who were sifted out at that time clung to the view that a single individual, Charles Taze Russell, was the "faithful and wise servant" foretold by Jesus at Matthew 24:45-47 (*KJ*), which servant would distribute spiritual food to the household of faith. Particularly following his death, *The Watch Tower* itself set forth this view for a number of years. In view of the prominent role that Brother Russell had played, it appeared to the Bible Students of that time that this was the case. He did not personally promote the idea, but he did acknowledge the apparent reasonableness of the arguments of those who favored it.* He also emphasized, however, that whoever the Lord might use in such a role must be humble as well as zealous to bring glory to the Master, and that if the one chosen by the Lord failed, he would be replaced by another.

***The "faithful and wise servant" had not passed off the scene when Brother Russell died***

However, as the light of truth progressively shone even more brightly after Brother Russell's death, and as the preaching that Jesus had foretold became even more extensive, it became evident that the "faithful and wise servant" (*KJ*), or "faithful and discreet slave" (*NW*), had not passed off the scene when Brother Russell died. In 1881, Brother Russell himself had expressed the view that that "servant" was made up of the entire body of faithful spirit-anointed Christians. He saw it as being a collective servant, a class of persons who were united in doing God's will. (Compare Isaiah 43:10.) This understanding was reaffirmed by the Bible Students in 1927. Jehovah's Witnesses today recognize the *Watchtower* magazine and kindred publications to be the ones used by the faithful and discreet slave to dispense spiritual food. They do not claim that this slave class is infallible, but they do view it as the *one channel* that the Lord is using during the last days of this system of things.

## When Pride Got in the Way

There have been times, however, when individuals in responsible positions came to view themselves as the channel of spiritual light, so that they

* According to Brother Russell, his wife, who later left him, was the first one to apply Matthew 24:45-47 to him. See the *Watch Tower* issues of July 15, 1906, page 215; March 1, 1896, page 47; and June 15, 1896, pages 139-40.



resisted what w
the desire to exe
to follow them,
after themselves
spiritual stabilit
examples:
Special letter
them to a meeti
invited and did
signed by E. Bry
that the meeting
It turned out to
poison the mind
Brother Russell's
by arguing that B
ed for themselve
printed page to sp
giving discourses
views). The cong
many were stumb
come more spiritu
Over 20 years
intention to send
strengthen the Bib
wish, the Society c
ever, once he was
Seeing himself as a
spondence that wh
Ezra, Nehemiah, a
charge) referred to
control of the Soci
of London to achie
Thwarted in his
to elicit support fro
of directors. Those
achieve their aims b
ciety that authorize
thority for all decisi
er Rutherford to safe
seeking to disrupt its
nual meeting of the
the board of directo

al Bible teaching had

Witnesses have con-
ınsom. The very first
l that "merit toward
onvention sponsored
dar Point, Ohio, the
elcome! All Believers
er of *The Watchtower*
ıcerning the purpose
reigning King, Jesus
. to gain eternal life."

: all at once. In many
tern of truth but did
vere willing to learn.
. What they learned
;s they taught; they
hey came to appreci-
the details of his pur-
9; compare John 16:

point. If mistakes are
nility is needed. This
ch a course strongly
iculed by those who
ny centuries, though

those who were dil-
erned that when the
John 14:3, 19.
ıt the error of Second
nd teaching that the
ɔurned up in 1873 or
ude ideas generally as
ɔr less reproach upon
ing Kingdom. These
nanner of the Lord's
*Manner of Our Lord's*



*Return.*'" This pamphlet was published in 1877. Brother Russell had some 50,000 copies of it printed and distributed.

In that pamphlet, he wrote: "We believe the scriptures to teach, that, at His coming and for a time after He has come, He will remain invisible; afterward manifesting or showing Himself in judgments and various forms, so that 'every eye shall see Him.'" In support of this, he discussed such texts as Acts 1:11 ('he will come in the same *manner* as you have beheld him go'—that is, unobserved by the world) and John 14:19 ("a little longer and the world will behold me no more"). Brother Russell also referred to the fact that *The Emphatic Diaglott,* which had first been published in complete form in 1864 with an interlinear word-for-word English translation, gave evidence that the Greek expression *pa·rou·si'a* meant "presence." In analyzing the Bible's use of that term, Russell explained in this pamphlet: "The Greek word generally used in referring to the second advent—*Parousia,* frequently translated *coming*—invariably signifies *personal presence,* as having come, arrived and never signifies to *be on the way,* as we use the word *coming.*"

> **Progressive Truth**
>
> *In 1882, C. T. Russell wrote: "The Bible is our only standard, and its teachings our only creed, and recognizing the progressive character of the unfolding of Scriptural truths, we are ready and prepared to add to or modify our creed (faith—belief) as we get increase of light from our Standard." —"Watch Tower," April 1882, p. 7.*

When discussing the purpose of Christ's presence, Russell made it clear that this was not something that would be accomplished in a single world-shattering moment. "The second advent, like the first," he wrote, "covers a period of time, and is not the event of a moment." During that time, he wrote, the "little flock" would be given their reward with the Lord as joint heirs in his Kingdom; others, perhaps billions, would be given opportunity for perfect life on an earth restored to Edenic beauty.—Luke 12:32.

Within just a few years, on the basis of further study of the Scriptures, Russell realized that Christ would not only *return* invisibly but also *remain* invisible, even when manifesting his presence by judgment upon the wicked.

In 1876, when Russell had first read a copy of *Herald of the Morning,* he had learned that there was another group who then believed that Christ's return would be invisible and who associated that return with blessings for all families of the earth. From Mr. Barbour, editor of that publication, Russell also came to be persuaded that Christ's invisible presence had begun in 1874.* Attention was later drawn to this by the

* This was influenced by the belief that the seventh millennium of human history had begun in 1873 and that a period of divine disfavor (of equal length to a former period considered to be one of favor) upon natural Israel would end in 1878. The chronology was flawed because of relying on an inaccurate rendering of Acts 13:20 in the *King James Version,* belief that there was a transcription error at 1 Kings 6:1, and failure to take into account Biblical synchronisms in the dating of reigns of the kings of Judah and of Israel. A clearer understanding of Biblical chronology was published in 1943, in the book *"The Truth Shall Make You Free,"* and it was then refined the following year in the book *"The Kingdom Is at Hand,"* as well as in later publications.

JEHOVAH'S WITNESSES - PROCLAIMERS OF GOD'S KINGDOM, 1993

1993

134 JEHOVAH'S WITNESSES—PROCLAIMERS OF GOD'S KINGDOM

subtitle "Herald of Christ's Presence," which appeared on the cover of *Zion's Watch Tower.*

Recognition of Christ's presence as being invisible became an important foundation on which an understanding of many Bible prophecies would be built. Those early Bible Students realized that the presence of the Lord should be of primary concern to all true Christians. (Mark 13:33-37) They were keenly interested in the Master's return and were alert to the fact that they had a responsibility to publicize it, but they did not yet clearly discern all the details. Yet, what God's spirit did enable them to understand at a very early time was truly remarkable. One of these truths involved a highly significant date marked by Bible prophecy.

**End of the Gentile Times**

The matter of Bible chronology had long been of great interest to Bible students. Commentators had set out a variety of views on Jesus' prophecy about "the times of the Gentiles" and the prophet Daniel's record of Nebuchadnezzar's dream regarding the tree stump that was banded for "seven times."—Luke 21:24, *KJ;* Dan. 4:10-17.

***They could see that 1914 was clearly marked by Bible prophecy***

As early as 1823, John A. Brown, whose work was published in London, England, calculated *the "seven times" of Daniel chapter 4 to be 2,520 years in length.* But he did not clearly discern the date with which the prophetic time period began or when it would end. He did, however, *connect these "seven times" with the Gentile Times of Luke 21:24.* In 1844, E. B. Elliott, a British clergyman, drew attention to *1914 as a possible date* for the end of the "seven times" of Daniel, but he also set out an alternate view that pointed to the time of the French Revolution. Robert Seeley, of London, in 1849, handled the matter in a similar manner. At least by 1870, a publication edited by Joseph Seiss and associates and printed in Philadelphia, Pennsylvania, was setting out calculations that *pointed to 1914 as a significant date,* even though the reasoning it contained was based on chronology that C. T. Russell later rejected.

Then, in the August, September, and October 1875 issues of *Herald of the Morning,* N. H. Barbour helped to harmonize details that had been pointed out by others. Using chronology compiled by Christopher Bowen, a clergyman in England, and published by E. B. Elliott, Barbour identified *the start of the Gentile Times with King Zedekiah's removal from kingship as foretold at Ezekiel 21:25, 26,* and he pointed to *1914 as marking the end of the Gentile Times.*

Early in 1876, C. T. Russell received a copy of *Herald of the Morning.* He promptly wrote to Barbour and then spent time with him in Philadelphia during the summer, discussing, among other things, prophetic time periods. Shortly thereafter, in an article entitled "Gentile Times: When Do

GROWING IN /

They End?·
and stated t
A.D. 1914."
*Examiner.**
duced in 187
to the same
as the ones
1914 C.E. a:
prophecy. I
*Dawn* (later
"The Times (
mean?

The Bib
They were c(
and a blottin
nificant poir
that date the
trol. When t
that marked
had marked (

Similarly
anarchy (whi
great day of
But then, ten
turmoil that
come right *a*
to mark a sig
said that 'Jeru
fulfilled. Wh
humans and t
with earlier e
take place at t

As the ye
their faith in
from stating v
they endeavo
in the Scriptu

**Did the "Al**

Great tur
outbreak of \

* A magazine p

parable as the "wheat" and the "tares" growing in the same field. He declared they must continue thus to grow together until the end of the world. (Matt. 13:24, 30, 39) Thus growing together, the true followers of Christ were greatly hindered by the false. The teachers in the churches were selfish men interested in political influence and personal flattery. Under the influence and control of the enemy Satan, they caused the truth to become obscure and to be seen very dimly.

Again attention is called to the words of Jesus, the great Prophet, who with authority from Jehovah said to his disciples: "I go to prepare a place for you. And if I go . . . I will come again and receive you unto myself." It should therefore be expected that the coming again of the Lord would mark the beginning of a better understanding of God's Word. In harmony with this, Peter at Pentecost uttered a prophecy saying: "Times of refreshing shall come from the presence [face] of the Lord [Jehovah]; and he shall send Jesus Christ, which before was preached unto you; whom the heaven must receive [retain] until the times of restitution of all things, which God hath spoken by the mouth of all his holy prophets since the world began." (Acts 3:19-21) In this the apostle clearly foretells a time of refreshing to the people of the Lord, and that the time would be at the second coming of the Lord Jesus.

That would not mean that Jesus must be bodily present again on the earth, because with him distance is no barrier. He is a spirit being of the divine nature, and his power is without limitation, regardless of his actual bodily position. Being clothed with all power in heaven and in earth, he could administer the affairs of the church from one point as well as from another.



The apostle's words mean that, at a stated time and acting in accord with Jehovah's orders, Christ Jesus would begin to minister to those consecrated to God and give them refreshing. What would be the nature of that refreshing?

Peter mentions "restitution", which would mean a restoring of that which had been taken away or hidden, and would necessarily include the truth that was hidden during the "dark ages". On another occasion Jesus said that 'Elijah must first come and restore all things'. (Matt. 17:11) Elijah was a prophet of God who did a restitution work in his time, in that he restored to the Israelites an understanding of the truth concerning God and their covenant relationship with God. (1 Ki. 18:39) His work was prophetic and foretold that the Lord would restore his truth to his own people. After Elijah was dead, Malachi prophesied that God would send Elijah the prophet before the great and dreadful day of the Lord. (Mal. 4:5, 6) That prophecy is proof that another should do a work similar to that done by Elijah, but on a far greater scale and of much more importance.

The restitution or restoring of all things, of which Jesus spoke, and also that mentioned by the Apostle Peter, must begin with the restoring to the people of God the truths that had been hidden during the dark ages. That restitution work would progress during the manifestation of the second presence of Jesus Christ. It would be expected that the days of understanding of the prophecies would begin sometime after the manifestation of the Lord's second presence, and the understanding would continue to increase thereafter.

The Scriptural proof is that the second presence of the Lord Jesus Christ began in 1874 A.D. This proof

Do those associated with your organization seek political positions or reforms? Those in the early congregation had a more permanent hope centered in God's kingdom. (2 Pet. 3:13, 14) Do national or racial barriers exist within your organization? There were none in first-century congregations. (Gal. 3:28; Rev. 7:9) Is discrimination practiced? Early Christians abided by the principle that "there is no partiality with God" but his "will is that all sorts of men should be saved and come to an accurate knowledge of truth." —Rom. 2:11; 1 Tim. 2:4; Jas. 2:1-4.

#### IDENTIFYING THE THEOCRATIC ORGANIZATION

18 Those in the apostolic organization did not fulfill these requirements for the Christian congregation in just a token way. They viewed their position in Jehovah's chosen visible channel as sacred and would allow nothing to jeopardize their standing with God. They had no fear of this world. (Matt. 10:26-28) Their only concern was to provide for the safety and well-being of the flock of God. Jesus pointed to this mark of the true visible organization in connection with a detailed prophecy relating to this time of the end. He said: "Who really is the faithful and discreet slave whom his master appointed over his domestics, to give them their food at the proper time? Happy is that slave if his master on arriving finds him doing so. Truly I say to you, He will appoint him over all his belongings."—Matt. 24:45-47.

19 Evidences are now conclusive that Jesus Christ was enthroned in heaven in 1914 C.E. and that he accompanied Jehovah to his temple in 1918 C.E., when judgment began with the house of God.* (1 Pet. 4:17) After cleansing those belonging to this house who were alive on earth, Jehovah poured out his spirit upon them and assigned them the responsibility of serving as his sole visible channel, through whom alone spiritual instruction was to come. Those who recognize Jehovah's visible theocratic organization, therefore, must recognize and accept this appointment of the "faithful and discreet slave" and be submissive to it.

20 Today those thus charged with this grand privilege and responsibility are called Jehovah's witnesses, and have been since 1931. As a group they have been separated more and more from the sectarianism of Christendom from the 1870's onward. Since 1879 the *Watch Tower* magazine has been used by this collective group to dispense spiritual food regularly to those of this "little flock" of true Christians. (Luke 12:32) In 1884 they formed a legal servant, a corporation, called Zion's Watch Tower Tract Society, now known as the Watch Tower Bible and Tract Society of Pennsylvania. By 1919, having survived the fiery trials of World War I, this "faithful and discreet slave" class was no novice organization. True, the apostles were no longer in its midst, but they had left behind written instructions as part of Jehovah's great Record Book. Additionally, the modern-day members of this 1900-year-old Christian congregation had received from the days of the apostles onward a rich heritage of Christian loyalty and integrity, long and patient suffering of persecution, abiding faith in Jehovah's precious promises, con-

18. What mark of the true visible organization did Jesus identify, and what reward did he say he would give?
19. What must those who recognize Jehovah's visible organization accept?

* See the book *You May Survive Armageddon into God's New World*, Chapter 6, entitled "A·do·nay' Comes to His Temple." Published by the Watch Tower Bible & Tract Society in 1955.

20, 21. Who today are charged with the responsibility of representing Jehovah's King, and what record provides their recommendation?

OCTOBER

fidence
Lord an
ence to
witnesse
21 In t
they we
tually sl

F

JEHOV
freedo
earth for
under wa
developm
pending d
of things
thousand-
mediately
ceive life
fort. Not
alone. Ja
century
"Faith, if
in itself.
breath is
is dead."
must pro
action, by

1. How and
gift of life?

10/1/1967

Bible, their faith in the Bible itself as God's Word gives them the conviction that what they have is indeed the truth. So their position is not egotistical but demonstrates their confidence that the Bible is the right standard against which to measure one's religion. They are not self-centered but are eager to share their beliefs with others.

***Do not other religions also follow the Bible?***

Many use it to some extent. But do they really teach and practice what it contains? Consider: (1) From most of their Bible translations they have removed the name of the true God thousands of times. (2) The Trinity doctrine, their concept of God himself, is borrowed from pagan sources and was developed in its present form centuries after Bible writing was completed. (3) Their belief in immortality of the human soul as the basis for continued life is not taken from the Bible; it has roots in ancient Babylon. (4) The theme of Jesus' preaching was the Kingdom of God, and he sent his disciples out to talk personally to others about it; but the churches today seldom mention that Kingdom and their members are not doing the work of preaching "this good news of the kingdom." (Matt. 24:14) (5) Jesus said that his true followers could be readily identified by their self-sacrificing love for one another. Is that true of the religions of Christendom when the nations go to war? (6) The Bible says that Christ's disciples would be no part of the world, and it warns that whoever wants to be a friend of the world makes himself an enemy of God; but the churches of Christendom and their members are deeply involved in the political affairs of the nations. (Jas. 4:4) In view of such a record, can it honestly be said that they really adhere to the Bible?

**How do Jehovah's Witnesses arrive at their explanation of the Bible?**

A key factor is that the Witnesses really believe that the Bible is God's Word and that what it contains is there for our instruction. (2 Tim. 3:16, 17; Rom. 15:4; 1 Cor. 10:11) So they do not resort to philosophical arguments to evade its clear statements of truth or to justify the way of life of people who have abandoned its moral standards.



In pointing out the meaning of symbolic language in the Bible, they let the Bible provide its own explanation, instead of giving their theories as to its significance. (1 Cor. 2:13) Indications as to the meaning of symbolic terms are usually found in other parts of the Bible. (As an example, see Revelation 21:1; then, regarding the meaning of "sea," read Isaiah 57:20. To identify "the Lamb" referred to in Revelation 14:1, see John 1:29 and 1 Peter 1:19.)

As for fulfillment of prophecy, they apply what Jesus said about being alert to events that correspond to what was foretold. (Luke 21:29-31; compare 2 Peter 1:16-19.) Conscientiously they point out those events and draw attention to what the Bible indicates they mean.

Jesus said that he would have on earth a "faithful and discreet slave" (his anointed followers viewed as a group), through which agency he would provide spiritual food to those making up the household of faith. (Matt. 24:45-47) Jehovah's Witnesses recognize that arrangement. As was true of first-century Christians, they look to the governing body of that "slave" class to resolve difficult questions—not on the basis of human wisdom, but by drawing on their knowledge of God's Word and his dealings with his servants, and with the help of God's spirit, for which they earnestly pray.—Acts 15:1-29; 16:4, 5.

**Why have there been changes over the years in the teachings of Jehovah's Witnesses?**

The Bible shows that Jehovah enables his servants to understand his purpose in a progressive manner. (Prov. 4:18; John 16:12) Thus, the prophets who were divinely inspired to write portions of the Bible did not understand the meaning of everything that they wrote. (Dan. 12:8, 9; 1 Pet. 1:10-12) The apostles of Jesus Christ realized that there was much they did not understand in their time. (Acts 1:6, 7; 1 Cor. 13:9-12) The Bible shows that there would be a great increase in knowledge of the truth during "the time of the end." (Dan. 12:4) Increased knowledge often requires adjustments in one's thinking. Jehovah's Witnesses are willing humbly to make such adjustments.

REASONING FROM THE SCRIPTURES, 1985, 1989ed

# DOCUMENTATION FOR SECTION TWO

## DIALOGUE ONE: Did Jesus Receive His Authority In 1914?



Warning them not to speculate about the matter, Jesus said: "It does not belong to you to get knowledge of the times or seasons which the Father has placed in his own jurisdiction." Jesus knew that his rulership over the earth was reserved for the future, long after his resurrection and ascension to heaven. (Acts 1:6-11; Luke 19:11, 12, 15) The Scriptures had foretold this. How so?

15 Prophetically referring to Jesus as "Lord," King David said: "The utterance of Jehovah to my Lord is: 'Sit at my right hand until I place your enemies as a stool for your feet.'" (Psalm 110:1; compare Acts 2:34-36.) This prophecy indicates that Jesus' rulership would not begin immediately after his ascension to heaven. Rather, he would wait at God's right hand. (Hebrews 10:12, 13) How long would this waiting go on? When would his rulership begin? The Bible helps us to find the answers.

16 The only city in all the earth upon which Jehovah placed his name was Jerusalem. (1 Kings 11:36) It was also the capital of a God-approved earthly kingdom typical of God's heavenly Kingdom. Therefore, the destruction of Jerusalem by the Babylonians in 607 B.C.E. was very significant. This event marked the beginning of a lengthy interruption of God's direct rule over his people on earth. Some six centuries later, Jesus indicated that this period of interrupted rule was still in effect, for he said: "Jerusalem will be trampled on by the nations, until the appointed times of the nations are fulfilled."—Luke 21:24.

17 During "the appointed times of the nations," worldly governments would be allowed to interrupt rulership ap-

15. How does Psalm 110:1 shed light on the timing of Jesus' rulership?
16. What happened in 607 B.C.E., and how was this related to God's Kingdom?
17. (a) What are "the appointed times of the nations," and how long were they to last? (b) When did "the appointed times of the nations" begin and end?



proved by God. That period began with the destruction of Jerusalem in 607 B.C.E., and Daniel indicated that it would go on for "seven times." (Daniel 4:23-25) How long is that? The Bible shows that three and a half "times" equal 1,260 days. (Revelation 12:6, 14) Twice that period, or seven times, would be 2,520 days. But nothing noteworthy happened at the end of that short period of time. By applying "a day for a year" to Daniel's prophecy and counting 2,520 years from 607 B.C.E., however, we arrive at the year 1914 C.E.—Numbers 14:34; Ezekiel 4:6.

18 Did Jesus begin to reign in heaven at that time? Scriptural reasons for saying that he did will be discussed in the next chapter. Of course, the beginning of Jesus' rule would not be marked by immediate peace on the earth. Revelation 12:7-12 shows that just after receiving the Kingdom, Jesus would oust Satan and the demon angels from heaven. This would mean woe for the earth, but it is heartening to read that the Devil has only "a short period of time" left. Soon, we will be able to rejoice not only because God's Kingdom rules but also because it will bring blessings to the earth and obedient mankind. (Psalm 72:7, 8) How do we know that this will happen soon?

18. What did Jesus do shortly after receiving Kingdom power, and how did this affect the earth?

### TEST YOUR KNOWLEDGE

What is God's Kingdom, and from where does it rule?

•

Who rules in the Kingdom, and who are its subjects?

•

How has Jehovah assured us that his Kingdom is a reality?

•

When did "the appointed times of the nations" begin and end?

**HEBREWS 9:25—10:19** **Law a shadow. Ransom foretold** **1446**

entered, not into a holy place made with
hands,[a] which is a copy of the reality,*[b] but into heaven itself,[c] now to appear before the person of God for us.[d]
25 Neither is it in order that he should
offer himself often, as indeed the high
priest enters into the holy place*[e] from
year to year[f] with blood not his own.
26 Otherwise, he would have to suffer
often from the founding*[g] of the world.
But now he has manifested himself[h]
once[i] for all time at the conclusion*
of the systems of things^[j] to put sin
away through the sacrifice of himself.[k]
27 And as it is reserved for men[l] to
die once for all time, but after this a
judgment,[m] 28 so also the Christ was
offered once[n] for all time to bear the
sins of many;[o] and the second time[p]
that he appears[q] it will be apart from
sin*[r] and to those earnestly looking for
him for [their] salvation.[s]

**10** For since the Law has a shadow[t]
of the good things to come, but
not the very substance of the things,
[men] can never with the same sacrifices from year to year which they
offer continually make those who approach perfect.[u] 2 Otherwise, would
the [sacrifices] not have stopped being
offered, because those rendering sacred
service* who had been cleansed once for
all time would have no consciousness
of sins anymore?[v] 3 To the contrary,
by these sacrifices there is a reminding
of sins from year to year,[w] 4 for it is
not possible for the blood of bulls and
of goats to take sins away.[x]
5 Hence when he comes into the
world he says: "'Sacrifice and offering
you did not want,[y] but you prepared a
body for me.[z] 6 You did not approve

**Heb 9:24*** Or, "into holy places . . . which are copies of the realities." **25*** Or, "the holy places." **26*** Lit., "throwing down [of seed]." Gr., *ka·ta·bo·les'*. **26*** Or, "joint end; consummation; ending together." Gr., *syn·te·lei'ai*, dative, sing. **26^** Or, "of the **orders of things**." Gr., *ton ai·o'non;* Lat., *sae·cu·lo'rum;* J[22](Heb.), ***ha·'oh·la·mim'***. **28*** Or, "be without a sin offering." **10:2*** "Rendering sacred service." Gr., *la·treu'on·tas;* J[18](Heb.), ***ha·'o·vedhim'***, "the ones **serving (worshiping)**." See Ex 3:12 ftn.

**CHAP. 9**
a Heb 8:2
b Col 2:17
c Heb 6:20, Heb 9:12, Heb 10:19
d Le 16:15, Joh 16:28, Ro 8:34
e Le 16:2
f Le 16:34
g Eph 1:4
h Ga 4:4, 1Pe 1:20
i Heb 7:27, 1Pe 3:18
j Mt 24:3, 1Co 10:11, Heb 1:2
k Isa 53:12, Da 9:24, 1Co 5:7
l Ex 29:9, Le 16:11, Heb 7:27, Heb 7:28, Heb 9:7
m Joh 17:1
n Ro 6:10
o Isa 53:12, 1Pe 2:24
p Mt 24:3, Tit 2:13
q 2Th 1:7
r Mt 24:30
s Mt 25:34, 2Ti 4:8

**CHAP. 10**
t Col 2:17, Heb 8:5
u Heb 7:19, Heb 9:9
v Ga 3:21
w Le 16:30, Le 16:34
x Isa 1:11, Mic 6:7
y Ps 50:8, Am 5:22
z Ps 40:6 ftn, LXX

**Second Col.**
a Ps 40:6
b Ps 40:7
c Ps 40:8
d Ps 40:6
e Le 17:5
f Ps 40:8, Joh 6:38
g Col 2:14, Heb 8:13
h Ps 40:8, Ga 1:4
i Joh 17:19, 1Co 6:11, Heb 13:12
j Eph 5:2
k Ro 6:10, Heb 9:28
l 1Sa 2:28, 1Ch 24:19, 2Ch 29:11
m Ex 29:38, Nu 28:3
n Heb 7:18, Heb 7:27, Heb 10:1
o Heb 9:28
p Ro 8:34, Col 3:1
q Ps 110:1, Ac 2:35, 1Co 15:25
r Heb 9:28
s Heb 7:11, Heb 7:19
t Jer 1:4

of whole burnt offerings* and sin [of-
fering].'[a] 7 Then I said, 'Look! I am
come (in the roll of the book* it is written about me)[b] to do your will, O God.'"[c]
8 After first saying: "You did not want
nor did you approve of sacrifices and
offerings and whole burnt offerings and
sin [offering]"[d]—[sacrifices] that are offered according to the Law[e]— 9 then
he actually says: "Look! I am come
to do your will."*[f] He does away with
what is first that he may establish what
is second.[g] 10 By the said "will"[h] we
have been sanctified[i] through the offering[j] of the body of Jesus Christ once[k]
for all time.
11 Also, every priest takes his station[l] from day to day[m] to render public
service and to offer the same sacrifices
often, as these are at no time able to
take sins away completely.[n] 12 But
this [man] offered one sacrifice for sins
perpetually[o] and sat down at the right
hand of God,[p] 13 from then on awaiting until his enemies should be placed
as a stool for his feet.[q] 14 For it is
by one [sacrificial] offering[r] that he
has made those who are being sanctified perfect[s] perpetually. 15 Moreover, the holy spirit[t] also bears witness
to us, for after it has said: 16 "'This
is the covenant that I shall covenant toward them after those days,' says Jehovah.* 'I will put my laws in their hearts,
and in their minds I shall write them,'"[u]
17 [it says afterwards:]* "And I shall
by no means call their sins and their law-
less deeds to mind anymore."[v] 18 Now
where there is forgiveness[w] of these,
there is no longer an offering for sin.[x]
19 Therefore, brothers, since we have
boldness* for the way of entry[y] into

u Jer 31:33; Heb 8:10; v Jer 31:34; Heb 8:12; w Joh 8:36; x Joh 20:23; y Joh 14:6; Ro 5:2.

**Heb 10:6*** "Whole burnt offerings." Gr., *ho·lo·kau·to'ma·ta;* Lat., *ho·lo·cau·sto'ma·ta*. These holocausts are sacrifices completely consumed by fire. **7*** "Roll of the book." Or, "scroll." **9*** "Your will." Gr., *the'le·ma' sou;* Lat., *vo·lun·ta'tem tu'am;* J[17,18,22](Heb.), ***retsoh·nekha'***. **16*** See App 1D. **17*** "It says afterwards," Vg[mss]Sy[h(margin)] and Minuscule mss 104, 323, 945, 1739, 1881, etc. **19*** Or, "freeness of speech." Lit., "outspokenness."

**1447** **Assemble.**

the holy place*[a] by th
20 which he inaugur
new and living way
tain,[b] that is, his flesh
we have a great pries
of God,[d] 22 let us ap
hearts in the full as
having had our heart
a wicked conscience[e]
bathed with clean wa
hold fast the public
our hope[g] without w
is faithful[i] that promis
us consider one anot
love and fine works,[k]
ing the gathering of ou
as some have the cus
aging[m] one another, an
as YOU behold the day
26 For if we prac
ly[o] after having recei
knowledge of the truth
ger any sacrifice for si
[there is] a certain fea
of judgment[r] and [ther
ousy that is going to
in opposition.[s] 28 An
disregarded the law of
out compassion, upon
two or three.[t] 29 Of
severe a punishment,[u]
will the man be count
has trampled[v] upon the
who has esteemed as o
the blood[w] of the coven
was sanctified, and wh
the spirit[x] of undeserve
contempt? 30 For we
said: "Vengeance is m
ompense";*[y] and again:
judge his people."[z] 31
thing to fall into the
living God.[a]
32 However, keep o
the former days in which
enlightened,[b] YOU endur
test under sufferings,[c]
while YOU were being

**Heb 10:19*** See 9:8 ftn. 2
tion." Lit., "confession."
pense," P[46]ℵ*D*ItSy[p]; ℵ[c]AD[c]S
pense,' says [the] Lord"; J
recompense,' says Jehovah."

NEW WORLD TRANSLATION

**position** **1384**

the whole congrega-
er to one place and
ongues,[a] but ordinary
ers come in, will they
ire mad? **24** But if
sying and any unbe-
person comes in, he
m all,[b] he is closely
**25** the secrets of his
ifest,[c] so that he will
e* and worship God,
really among YOU."[d]
e done, then, broth-
me together, one has
has a teaching, an-
ation, another has a
s an interpretation.[e]
e place for upbuild-
omeone speaks in a
nited to two or three
turns; and let some-
**8** But if there be no
n keep silent in the
peak to himself[h] and
er, let two or three
d let the others dis-
[i] **30** But if there is
other[k] one while sit-
first one keep silent.
ll prophesy[l] one by
learn and all be en-
nd [gifts of] the spir-
are to be controlled
**33** For God is [a
ler,[n] but of peace.[o]
ongregations of the
the women keep si-
gations, for it is not
m to speak, but let
on,[q] even as the Law[r]
, they want to learn
n question their own
for it is disgraceful[s]
ak in a congregation.
it from YOU that the
forth,[t] or was it only
it reached?
inks he is a prophet
spirit,* let him ac-

rate [himself]." 26* Or,
32* Lit., "And spirits."
spirit." Lit., "spiritual

**1385** **Resurrection proof, basis. The end**

knowledge the things I am writing to
YOU, because* they are the Lord's commandment.[a] **38** But if anyone is ignorant, he continues ignorant. **39** Consequently, my brothers, keep zealously
seeking the prophesying,[b] and yet do
not forbid the speaking in tongues.[c]
**40** But let all things take place decent-
ly and by arrangement.*[d]

**15** Now I make known to YOU,
brothers, the good news[e] which
I declared to YOU,[f] which YOU also
received, in which YOU also stand,[g]
**2** through which YOU are also being
saved,[h] with the speech with which I
declared the good news to YOU, if YOU
are holding it fast, unless, in fact, YOU
became believers to no purpose.[i]
**3** For I handed on to YOU, among
the first things, that which I also received,[j] that Christ died for our sins
according to the Scriptures;[k] **4** and
that he was buried,[l] yes, that he has
been raised[m] up the third day[n] according
to the Scriptures;[o] **5** and that he appeared to Ce'phas,[p] then to the twelve.[q]
**6** After that he appeared to upward of
five hundred brothers at one time, the
most of whom remain to the present,[r]
but some have fallen asleep [in death].
**7** After that he appeared to James,[s]
then to all the apostles;[t] **8** but last of
all he appeared also to me[u] as if to one
born prematurely.*
**9** For I am the least[v] of the apostles,
and I am not fit to be called an apostle,
because I persecuted[w] the congregation
of God. **10** But by God's undeserved
kindness[x] I am what I am. And his undeserved kindness that was toward me
did not prove to be in vain,[y] but I la-
bored in excess of them all,[z] yet not
I but the undeserved kindness of God
that is with me.[a] **11** However, whether it is I or they, so we are preaching
and so YOU have believed.[b]
**12** Now if Christ is being preached
that he has been raised up from the

1Co 14:37* Or, "that." 40* Or, "according to order." Gr., *ka·ta' ta'xin*. See Nu 1:52 ftn, "Camp." 15:8* Or, "to an abortive." Lat., *abor·ti'vo*.

**CHAP. 14**
a 1Jo 4:6
b 1Co 12:31
1Th 5:20
c 1Co 14:27
d 1Co 14:33
Col 2:5

**CHAP. 15**
e Ga 1:11
f Ac 18:11
g Ro 5:2
h Ro 1:16
i Ga 3:4
j Ga 1:12
k Ps 22:15
Isa 53:8
Isa 53:12
Da 9:26
1Pe 2:24
l Isa 53:9
Mt 27:60
m Mt 28:7
n Lu 24:46
o Ps 16:10
Isa 53:10
Jon 2:10
p Lu 24:34
q Joh 20:26
r Mt 28:17
s Ac 12:17
t Ac 1:2
Ac 1:6
u Ac 9:4
1Co 9:1
v Eph 3:8
w Ac 8:3
Ga 1:13
1Ti 1:13
x Eph 4:7
y 2Co 6:1
z 2Co 11:23
a Php 2:13
b Ac 18:10

**Second Col.**
a Ac 4:2
Ac 17:31
b Mt 22:23
Ac 26:8
c Ro 10:7
d 1Th 4:14
e Ac 3:15
f Ac 1:22
g Ac 2:24
Ac 4:10
Ac 13:30
h Ac 17:31
1Co 6:14
i Ro 4:25
Heb 7:25
j Ac 7:59
k 1Co 15:14
l Joh 1:12
m 1Pe 1:3
n Le 23:10
Col 1:18
o Ac 26:23
p Ge 3:19
q Joh 11:25
r Ro 5:12
s Ro 5:17
Ro 6:23
t Re 1:5
u Mt 24:3
Mt 25:31
1Th 4:16
v Ps 110:2
Da 2:44
w Ps 110:1
x Re 20:14
y Ps 8:6
Eph 1:22
z Heb 2:8
a 1Pe 3:22

**1 CORINTHIANS 14:38—15:27**

dead,[a] how is it some among YOU say
there is no resurrection* of the dead?[b]
**13** If, indeed, there is no resurrection
of the dead, neither has Christ been
raised up.[c] **14** But if Christ has not
been raised up, our preaching is certainly in vain, and our faith is in vain.[d]
**15** Moreover, we are also found false
witnesses of God,[e] because we have
borne witness[f] against God that he
raised up the Christ,[g] but whom he did
not raise up if the dead are really not
to be raised up.[h] **16** For if the dead
are not to be raised up, neither has
Christ been raised up. **17** Further, if
Christ has not been raised up, YOUR
faith is useless; YOU are yet in YOUR
sins.[i] **18** In fact, also, those who fell
asleep [in death] in union[j] with Christ
perished.[k] **19** If in this life only we
have hoped in Christ,[l] we are of all men
most to be pitied.
**20** However, now Christ has been
raised up from the dead,[m] the firstfruits[n] of those who have fallen asleep
[in death].[o] **21** For since death[p] is
through a man, resurrection[q] of the
dead is also through a man. **22** For
just as in Adam all are dying,[r] so also
in the Christ all will be made alive.[s]
**23** But each one in his own rank:
Christ the firstfruits,[t] afterward those
who belong to the Christ during his
presence.*[u] **24** Next, the end,* when
he hands over the kingdom to his God
and Father, when he has brought to
nothing all government and all authority and power.[v] **25** For he must rule
as king until [God]* has put all enemies
under his feet.[w] **26** As the last enemy, death is to be brought to nothing.*[x]
**27** For [God] "subjected all things under his feet."[y] But when he says that
'all things have been subjected,'[z] it is
evident that it is with the exception of
the one who subjected all things to him.[a]

1Co 15:12* "Resurrection." Gr., *a·na'sta·sis*, "raising up; standing up" (from *a·na'*, "up" and *sta'sis*, "standing"); Lat., *re·sur·rec'ti·o*. 23* See App 5B. 24* Or, "accomplished (completed) end." Gr., *te'los*. 25* Lit., "he." 26* Or, "is to be destroyed." Lit., "is being made ineffective." Gr., *ka·tar·gei'tai*.

NEW WORLD TRANSLATION

# DIALOGUE TWO: Should Christians Use the Divine Name "Jehovah" In Prayer? —Parts 1 and 2

JEHOVAH 12

Then, too, we must keep in mind that names then had real meaning and were not just "labels" to identify an individual as today. Moses knew that Abram's name (meaning "Father Is High (Exalted)") was changed to Abraham (meaning "Father of a Crowd (Multitude)"), the change being made because of God's purpose concerning Abraham. So, too, the name of Sarai was changed to Sarah and that of Jacob to Israel; in each case the change revealed something fundamental and prophetic about God's purpose concerning them. Moses may well have wondered if Jehovah would now reveal himself under some new name to throw light on his purpose toward Israel. Moses' going to the Israelites in the "name" of the One who sent him meant being the representative of that One, and the greatness of the authority with which Moses would speak would be determined by or be commensurate with that name and what it represented. (Compare Ex 23:20, 21; 1Sa 17:45.) So, Moses' question was a meaningful one.

God's reply in Hebrew was: *'Eh·yeh' 'Asher' 'Eh·yeh'*. Some translations render this as "I AM THAT I AM." However, it is to be noted that the Hebrew verb *ha·yah'*, from which the word *'Eh·yeh'* is drawn, does not mean simply "be." Rather, it means "become," or "prove to be." The reference here is not to God's self-existence but to what he has in mind to become toward others. Therefore, the *New World Translation* properly renders the above Hebrew expression as "I SHALL PROVE TO BE WHAT I SHALL PROVE TO BE." Jehovah thereafter added: "This is what you are to say to the sons of Israel, 'I SHALL PROVE TO BE has sent me to you.'" —Ex 3:14, ftn.

That this meant no change in God's name, but only an additional insight into God's personality, is seen from his further words: "This is what you are to say to the sons of Israel, 'Jehovah the God of your forefathers, the God of Abraham, the God of Isaac and the God of Jacob, has sent me to you.' This is my name to time indefinite, and this is the memorial of me to generation after generation." (Ex 3:15; compare Ps 135:13; Ho 12:5.) The name Jehovah comes from the Hebrew verb *ha·wah'*, "become," and actually means "He Causes to Become." This reveals Jehovah as the One who, with progressive action, causes himself to become the Fulfiller of promises. Thus he always brings his purposes to realization. Only the true God could rightly and authentically bear such a name.

This aids one in understanding the sense of Jehovah's later statement to Moses: "I am Jehovah. And I used to appear to Abraham, Isaac and Jacob as God Almighty, but as respects my name Jehovah I did not make myself known to them." (Ex 6:2, 3) Since the name Jehovah was used many times by those patriarchal ancestors of Moses, it is evident that God meant that he manifested himself to them in the capacity of Jehovah only in a limited way. To illustrate this, those who had known the man Abram could hardly be said to have really *known* him as *Abraham* (meaning "Father of a Crowd (Multitude)") while he had but one son, Ishmael. When Isaac and other sons were born and began producing offspring, the name Abraham took on greater meaning or import. So, too, the name Jehovah would now take on expanded meaning for the Israelites.

To "know," therefore, does not necessarily mean merely to be acquainted with or cognizant of something or someone. The foolish Nabal knew David's name but still asked, "Who is David?" in the sense of asking, "What does he amount to?" (1Sa 25:9-11; compare 2Sa 8:13.) So, too, Pharaoh had said to Moses: "Who is Jehovah, so that I should obey his voice to send Israel away? I do not know Jehovah at all and, what is more, I am not going to send Israel away." (Ex 5:1, 2) By that, Pharaoh evidently meant that he did not know Jehovah as the true God or as having any authority over Egypt's king and his affairs, nor as having any might to enforce His will as announced by Moses and Aaron. But now Pharaoh and all Egypt, along with the Israelites, would come to know the real meaning of that name, the person it represented. As Jehovah showed Moses, this would result from God's carrying out His purpose toward Israel, liberating them, giving them the Promised Land, and thereby fulfilling His covenant with their forefathers. In this way, as God said, "You will certainly know that I am Jehovah your God." —Ex 6:4-8; see ALMIGHTY.

Professor of Hebrew D. H. Weir therefore rightly says that those who claim Exodus 6:2, 3 marks the first time the name Jehovah was revealed, "have not studied [these verses] in the light of other scriptures; otherwise they would have perceived that by *name* must be meant here not the two syllables which make up the word Jehovah, but the idea which it expresses. When we read in Isaiah, ch. lii. 6, *'Therefore my people shall know my name;'* or in Jeremiah, ch. xvi. 21, *'They shall know that my name is Jehovah;'* or in the Psalms, Ps. ix. [10, 16], *'They that know thy name shall put their trust in thee;'* we see at once that to know Jehovah's name is something very different from knowing the four letters of which it is composed. It is to know by experience that Jehovah really is what his name declares him to be. (Compare also Is. xix. 20, 21; Eze. xx. 5, 9; xxxix. 6, 7; Ps. lxxxiii.

[18]; lxxxi
Bible-Dicti
**Known** J
Jehovah w
certainly k
tially appe
after the
there it id
earth as "J
that Jehov
of creation
his doing s
Jehovah r
Adam. Ye
show he
had produ
2:21-23) N
place betw
not includ
Eve is t
have used
learned th
Adam, fr
command
good and
directly re
to her).—
As is sh
was made
the day o
not done i
ner. For h
Enoch (n
with the t
Heb 11:4-
edge of t
Flood per
peoples a
ted to th
dants.—(
**The Pe**
vah is th
Cause; he
(Re 4:11)
ing." (Job
upon him
which to
called "th
stretches
also with
ible, und
eternity"
but as a
Jer 10:10
Despite

INSIGHT ON THE SCRIPTURES, 1988, vol. 2

Vhat is highly im-
clear that this is a
re are several texts
erly understood if
me by a common
much worse, by a
tive [for example,

ner translation, by
is interesting. He
his translation but
'ahweh. However,
*dies in the Psalms,*
ne returned to the
ny? He explains:
nployment of this
: Memorial name
present version of
t arise from any
more correct pro-
ng Yahwéh; but
. evidence person-
e desirability of
ith the public ear
· of this kind, in
thing is the easy
Divine name in-

orshipers of Jeho-
O magnify Jeho-
people, and let us
ether." How can
slations that omit
fully to that ex-
s are happy that
ors have had the
God's name in
he Hebrew Scrip-
erve what Smith
the "flavor of the

ranslations, even
God's name in the
omit it from the
ptures, the "New
s the reason for
stification for in-
in this last por-

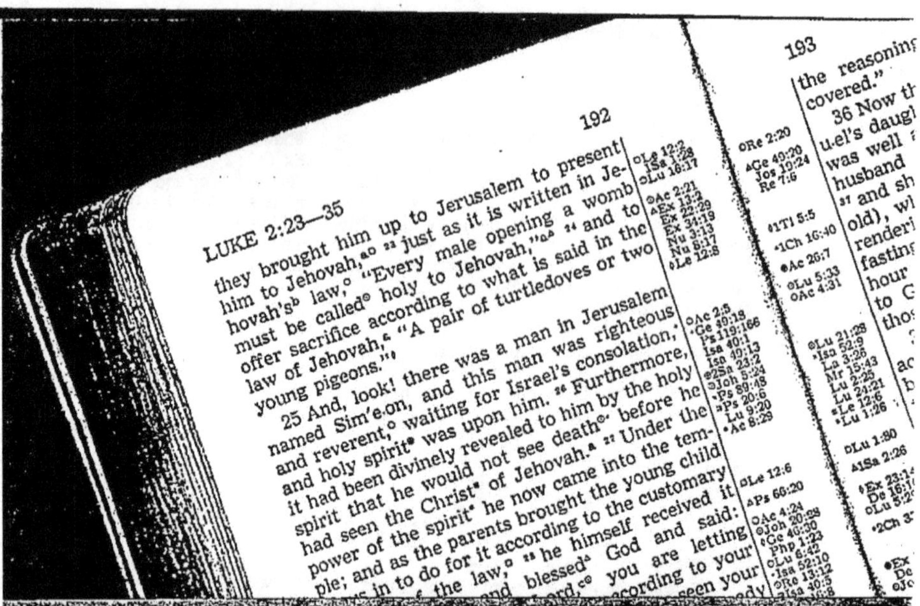


# God's Name and the "New Testament"

THE position of God's name is unshakable in the Hebrew Scriptures, the "Old Testament." Although the Jews eventually stopped pronouncing it, their religious beliefs prevented them from removing the name when they made copies of older manuscripts of the Bible. Hence, the Hebrew Scriptures contain God's name more often than any other name.

With the Christian Greek Scriptures, the "New Testament," the situation is different. Manuscripts of the book of Revelation (the last book of the Bible) have God's name in its abbreviated form, "Jah," (in the word "Hallelujah"). But apart from that, no ancient Greek manuscript that we possess today of the books from Matthew to Revelation contains God's name in full. Does that mean that the name should not be there? That would be surprising in view of the fact that Jesus' followers recognized the importance of God's name, and Jesus taught us to pray for God's name to be sanctified. So what happened?

**The *New World Translation of the Christian Greek Scriptures* properly uses God's name 237 times**

To understand this, remember that the manuscripts of the Christian Greek Scriptures that we possess today are not the originals. The actual books written by Matthew, Luke and the other Bible writers were well used and quickly wore out. Hence, copies were made, and when those wore out, further copies were made of those copies. This is what we would expect,

The Name 23

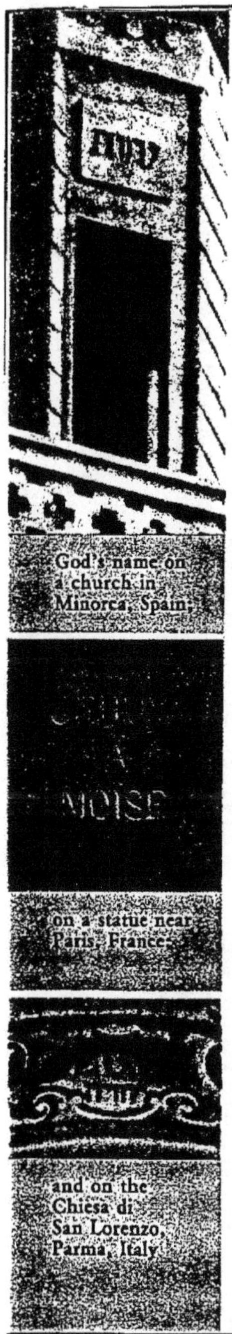

God's name on a church in Minorca, Spain; on a statue near Paris, France; and on the Chiesa di San Lorenzo, Parma, Italy.

since the copies were usually made to be used, not preserved.

There are thousands of copies of the Christian Greek Scriptures in existence today, but most of them were made during or after the fourth century of our Common Era. This suggests a possibility: Did something happen to the text of the Christian Greek Scriptures *before* the fourth century that resulted in the omission of God's name? The facts prove that something did.

### The Name *Was* There

We can be sure that the apostle Matthew included God's name in his Gospel. Why? Because he wrote it originally in Hebrew. In the fourth century, Jerome, who translated the Latin *Vulgate,* reported: "Matthew, who is also Levi, and who from a publican came to be an apostle, first of all composed a Gospel of Christ in Judaea in the Hebrew language . . . Who translated it after that in Greek is not sufficiently ascertained. Moreover, the Hebrew itself is preserved to this day in the library at Caesarea."

Since Matthew wrote in Hebrew, it is inconceivable that he did not use God's name, especially when quoting from parts of the "Old Testament" that contained the name. However, other writers of the second part of the Bible wrote for a worldwide audience in the international language of that time, Greek. Hence, they did not quote from the original Hebrew writings but from the *Septuagint* Greek version. And even Matthew's Gospel was eventually translated into Greek. Would God's name have appeared in these Greek writings?

Well, some very old fragments of the *Septuagint Version* that actually existed in Jesus' day have survived down to our day, and it is noteworthy that the personal name of God appeared in them. *The New International Dictionary of New Testament Theology* (Volume 2, page 512) says: "Recent textual discoveries cast doubt on the idea that the compilers of the LXX [*Septuagint*] translated the tetragrammaton *YHWH* by *kyrios.* The oldest LXX MSS (fragments) now available to us have the tetragrammaton written in Heb[rew] characters in the G[ree]k text. This custom was retained by later Jewish translators of the O[ld] T[estament] in the first centuries A.D." Therefore, whether Jesus and his disciples read the Scriptures in Hebrew or Greek, they would come across the divine name.

Thus, Professor George Howard, of the University of Georgia, U.S.A., made this comment: "When the Septuagint which the New Testament church used and quoted contained the Hebrew form of the divine name, the New Testament writers no doubt included the Tetragrammaton in their quotations." (*Biblical Archaeology Review,* March 1978, page 14) What authority would they have had to do otherwise?

God's name remained in Greek translations of the "Old Testament" for a while longer. In the first half of the second century C.E., the Jewish proselyte Aquila made a new translation of the Hebrew Scriptures into Greek, and in this he represented God's name by the Tetragrammaton in ancient Hebrew characters. In the third century, Origen wrote: "And in the most accurate manuscripts THE NAME occurs in Hebrew characters, yet not in today's Hebrew [characters], but in the most ancient ones."

Even in the fourth century, Jerome writes in his prologue to the books of Samuel and Kings: "And we find the name of God, the Tetragrammaton [יהוה], in certain Greek volumes even

to this day expre
ters."

### The Remova

By this time, hc
foretold by Jesus l
the name, althc
manuscripts, was
(Matthew 13:24-
Eventually, many
recognize what
reports that in hi
rant ones, becaus
the characters, wl
[the Tetragramma
were accustomed

In later copie
God's name was
like "God" (*T*
(*Ky'ri·os*) were s
that this happen
early fragments
where God's nar
later copies of th
*Septuagint* where
removed.

The same thi
"New Testament
Scriptures. Profe
goes on to say:
form for the di
nated in favor o
the Septuagint,
from the New
of the Septuagin
divine name wa
church except ir
ed in the con
remembered by

Hence, while
nounce God's
Christian churc
it completely
manuscripts of t
as well as fron
sions.

### The Nee

Eventually,
name was restc
tions of the H

THE DIVINE NAME THAT WILL ENDURE FOREVER, 1984, p. 24

A report published in 1971 shows that there are possibly 6,000 handwritten copies containing all or part of the Hebrew Scriptures; the oldest dates back to the third century B.C.E. Of the Christian Greek Scriptures, there are some 5,000 in Greek, the oldest dating back to the beginning of the second century C.E. There are also many copies of early translations into other languages.'

In the introduction to his seven volumes on *The Chester Beatty Biblical Papyri*, Sir Frederic Kenyon wrote: "The first and most important conclusion derived from the examination of them [the papyri] is the satisfactory one that they confirm the essential soundness of the existing texts. No striking or fundamental variation is shown either in the Old or the New Testament. There are no important omissions or additions of passages, and no variations which affect vital facts or doctrines. The variations of text affect minor matters, such as the order of words or the precise words used . . . But their essential importance is their confirmation, by evidence of an earlier date than was hitherto available, of the integrity of our existing texts."—(London, 1933), p. 15.

It is true that some translations of the Bible adhere more closely to what is in the original languages than others do. Modern paraphrase Bibles have taken liberties that at times alter the original meaning. Some translators have allowed personal beliefs to color their renderings. But these weaknesses can be identified by comparison of a variety of translations.

## If Someone Says—

**'I don't believe in the Bible'**

**You might reply:** 'But you do believe there is a God, don't you? . . . May I ask what there is in the Bible that you find hard to accept?'

**Or you could say:** 'May I ask, Have you always felt that way? . . . I've heard others say that, even though they have not made a thorough study of the Bible. But since the Bible clearly says that it is a message from God himself and that he offers us eternal life if we believe and live by what it says,



don't you agree that it would be worthwhile at least to examine it to find out whether its claims are true or not? (Use material on pages 60-63.)'

**'The Bible contradicts itself'**

**You might reply:** 'I've had other people tell me that, but no one has ever been able to show me what is actually a contradiction. And in my own personal reading of the Bible I've never seen one. Could you give me an example?' **Then perhaps add:** 'What I *have* found is that many persons simply never found answers to questions that the Bible made them think about. For example, Where did Cain get his wife? (Use material on pages 301, 302.)'

**'Men wrote the Bible'**

**You might reply:** 'That's true. About 40 of them had a part in it. But it was *inspired* by God.' **Then perhaps add:** (1) 'What does that mean? That God directed the writing, much as a businessman uses a secretary to write letters for him.' (2) 'The idea of receiving messages from someone out in space should not surprise us. Even humans have sent messages and pictures from the moon. How did they do it? By using laws that originated long ago with God himself.' (3) 'But how can we be sure that what the Bible contains is really from God? It contains information that could not possibly have come from a human source. What kind? Details about the future; and these have always proved to be completely accurate. (For examples, see pages 60-62, also pages 234-239, under the heading "Last Days.")'

**'Everyone has his own interpretation of the Bible'**

**You might reply:** 'And obviously not all of them are right.' **Then perhaps add:** (1) 'Twisting the Scriptures to fit our own ideas can result in lasting harm. (2 Pet. 3:15, 16)' (2) 'Two things can help us to understand the Bible correctly. First, consider the context (surrounding verses) of any statement. Next, compare texts with other statements in

REASONING FROM THE SCRIPTURES, 1985, 1989ed

synagogues where the
reading of God's Word.
nong Christ's followers,
ored to reproduce the
nefit of the multiplying
that there might be an
culation of these.—Col

novable type became
ntury C.E. onward), the
d also copies of them
they are called manu-
us, "written by hand").
ndwritten copy of the
part, as distinguished
ible manuscripts were
form of rolls and co-

leather, papyrus, and
Scriptures. The noted
r instance, is a leather
r made from the fibers
or Bible manuscripts in
or translations thereof
ry C.E. At that time its
egan to be superseded
e grade of parchment
lamb, or goat skins, a
earlier use of animal
ich manuscripts as the
(Sinaitic Manuscript)
(Vatican Manuscript
ntury C.E. are parch-

*limpsestus;* Gr., *pa-*
ed again") is a manu-
riting was removed or
for later writing. A
Codex Ephraemi Syri
ury C.E. If the earlier
d off) is the important
ars can often read this
g technical means that
reagents and photog-
f the Christian Greek
elected Bible readings

e manuscripts written
tions of the Hebrew
Christian Greek Scrip-
ed, or classified, as to
an aid in dating them.
specially down to the
ncial manuscript, writ-
al letters. In it there is



generally no word separation, and punctuation and accent marks are lacking. The Codex Sinaiticus is such an uncial manuscript. Changes in writing style began to develop in the sixth century, eventually leading (in the ninth century C.E.) to the cursive, or minuscule, manuscript, written in smaller letters, many of which were joined in a running or flowing writing style. The majority of extant manuscripts of the Christian Greek Scriptures have a cursive script. Cursive manuscripts remained in vogue until the inception of printing.

**Copyists.** As far as is known today, no handwritten original, or autograph, manuscripts of the Bible are in existence. Yet the Bible has been preserved in accurate, reliable form because Biblical copyists in general, accepting the Scriptures as being divinely inspired, sought perfection in their arduous labor of producing manuscript copies of God's Word.

The men who copied the Hebrew Scriptures in the days of Jesus Christ's ministry on earth and for centuries before that time were called scribes (Heb., *soh·pherim'*). Among the early scribes was Ezra, spoken of in the Scriptures as "a skilled copyist." (Ezr 7:6) Later scribes made some deliberate alterations of the Hebrew text. But their scribal successors, the Masoretes, detected these and recorded them in the Masora, or notes appearing in the margins of the Hebrew Masoretic text they produced.

Copyists of the Christian Greek Scriptures also made earnest efforts to reproduce faithfully the text of the Scriptures.

***What assurance is there that the Bible has not been changed?***

Despite the care exercised by copyists of Bible manuscripts, a number of small scribal errors and alterations crept into the text. On the whole, these are insignificant and have no bearing on the Bible's general integrity. They have been detected and corrected by means of careful scholastic collation or critical comparison of the many extant manuscripts and ancient versions. Critical study of the Hebrew text of the Scriptures commenced toward the end of the 18th century. Benjamin Kennicott published at Oxford (in 1776-1780) the readings of over 600 Masoretic Hebrew manuscripts, and the Italian scholar Giambernardo de Rossi published at Parma comparisons of 731 manuscripts in 1784 to 1798. Master texts of the Hebrew Scriptures were also produced by the German scholar Baer and, more recently, by C. D. Ginsburg. Hebrew scholar Rudolf Kittel released in 1906 the first edition of his *Biblia Hebraica* (The Hebrew Bible), providing therein a textual study through a footnote service, comparing many Hebrew manuscripts of the Masoretic text. The basic text he used was the Ben Hayim text. But, when the older and superior Ben Asher Masoretic texts became available, Kittel undertook the production of an entirely new third edition, which was completed by his colleagues after his death.

The 7th, 8th, and 9th editions of the *Biblia Hebraica* (1951-1955) furnished the basic text used to render the Hebrew Scriptures into English in the *New World Translation of the Holy Scriptures* originally published in 1950-1960. A new edition of the Hebrew text, namely *Biblia Hebraica Stuttgartensia,* is dated 1977. This edition was used for updating the information presented in the footnotes of the *New World Translation* published in 1984.

The first printed edition of the Christian Greek Scriptures was that appearing in the Complutensian Polyglott (in Greek and Latin), of 1514-1517. Then in 1516 the Dutch scholar Desiderius Erasmus published his first edition of a master Greek text of the Christian Greek Scriptures. It contained many errors, but an improved text thereof was made available through four succeeding editions from 1519 to 1535. Later, Paris printer and editor Robert Estienne, or Stephanus, issued several editions of the Greek "New Testament," based principally on Erasmus' text, but having corrections according to the Complutensian Polyglott (edition of 1522) and 15 late manuscripts. The third edition of Stephanus' Greek text (issued in 1550) became, in effect, the "Received Text" (called *textus receptus* in Latin), which was used for many early English versions, including the *King James Version* of 1611.

Quite noteworthy in more recent times is the master Greek text prepared by J. J. Griesbach, who availed himself of materials gathered by others but who also gave attention to Biblical quotations made by early writers such as Origen. Further, Griesbach studied the readings of various versions, such as the Armenian, Gothic, and Philoxenian. He viewed extant manuscripts as comprising three families, or recensions, the Byzantine, the Western, and the Alexandrian, giving preference to readings in the latter. Editions of his master Greek text were issued between 1774 and 1806, his principal edition of the entire Greek text being published in 1796-1806. Griesbach's text was used for Sharpe's English translation of 1840 and is the Greek text printed in *The Emphatic Diaglott,* by Benjamin Wilson, in 1864.

INSIGHT ON THE SCRIPTURES, 1988

place centuries earlier. Yet, modern historians are able to successfully derive the events even from these ancient periods of time."[6]

[6] In other words, the historical parts of the Christian Greek Scriptures are worthy of at least as much credence as secular histories. Certainly, in the few decades between the events of early Christianity and their being recorded in writing, there was no time for myths and legends to develop and be universally accepted.

**Eyewitness Testimony**

[7] This is especially true in view of the fact that many of the accounts speak of eyewitness testimony. The writer of the Gospel of John said: "This is the disciple [the disciple that Jesus loved] that bears witness about these things and that wrote these things." (John 21:24) The writer of the book of Luke says: "Those who from the beginning became eyewitnesses and attendants of the message delivered these to us." (Luke 1:2) The apostle Paul, speaking of those who witnessed the resurrection of Jesus, said: "Most of [them] remain to the present, but some have fallen asleep in death."—1 Corinthians 15:6.

[8] In this connection, Professor F. F. Bruce makes a keen observation: "It can have been by no means so easy as some writers seem to think to invent words and deeds of Jesus in those early years, when so many of His disciples were about, who could remember what had and had not hap-

7, 8. (a) Who were still alive while the Christian Greek Scriptures were being written and circulated? (b) What must we conclude in line with the comment of Professor F. F. Bruce?



1989

pened. . . . The disciples could not afford to risk inaccuracies (not to speak of willful manipulation of the facts), which would at once be exposed by those who would be only too glad to do so. On the contrary, one of the strong points in the original apostolic preaching is the confident appeal to the knowledge of the hearers; they not only said, 'We are witnesses of these things,' but also, 'As you yourselves also know' (Acts 2:22)."[7]

**Is the Text Trustworthy?**

[9] Is it possible that these eyewitness testimonies were accurately recorded but later corrupted? In other words, were myths and legends introduced after the original writing was completed? We have already seen that the text of the Christian Greek Scriptures is in better condition than any other ancient literature. Kurt and Barbara Aland, scholars of the Greek text of the Bible, list almost 5,000 manuscripts that have survived from antiquity down to today, some from as early as the second century C.E.[8] The general testimony of this mass of evidence is that the text is essentially sound. Additionally, there are many ancient translations—the earliest dating to about the year 180 C.E.—that help to prove that the text is accurate.[9]

[10] Hence, by any reckoning, we can be sure that legends and myths did not infiltrate into the Christian Greek Scriptures after the original writers finished their work. The text we have is substantially the same as the one that the original writers

9, 10. As far as the Christian Greek Scriptures are concerned, of what can we be certain?

penned, and its accuracy is confirmed by the fact that contemporaneous Christians accepted it. Can we, then, check the historicity of the Bible by comparing it with other ancient histories? To some extent, yes.

**The Documentary Evidence**

11 In fact, for events in the lives of Jesus and his apostles, documentary evidence apart from the Bible is quite limited. This is only to be expected, since in the first century, Christians were a relatively small group that did not get involved in politics. But the evidence that secular history does provide agrees with what we read in the Bible.

12 For example, after Herod Antipas suffered a resounding military defeat, the Jewish historian Josephus, writing in 93 C.E., said: "To some of the Jews the destruction of Herod's army seemed to be divine vengeance, and certainly a just vengeance, for his treatment of John, surnamed the Baptist. For Herod had put him to death, though he was a good man and had exhorted the Jews to lead righteous lives, to practise justice towards their fellows and piety towards God."[10] Thus Josephus confirms the Bible account that John the Baptizer was a righteous man who preached repentance and who was executed by Herod.—Matthew 3:1-12; 14:11.

13 Josephus also mentions James, the half brother of Jesus, who, the Bible tells us, did not initially follow Jesus but later became a prominent elder in Jerusalem. (John 7:3-5; Galatians 1:18, 19) He documents James' arrest in these words: "[The high priest Ananus] convened the judges of the Sanhedrin and brought before them a man named James, the brother of Jesus who was called the Christ, and certain others."[11] In writing these words, Josephus additionally confirms that "Jesus, who was called the Christ" was a real, historical person.

11. To what extent does external documentary evidence support the historical accounts in the Christian Greek Scriptures?
12. What does Josephus tell us about John the Baptizer?
13. How does Josephus support the historicity of James and of Jesus himself?



14 Other early writers too refer to things mentioned in the Greek Scriptures. For example, the Gospels tell us that Jesus' preaching around Palestine met with a wide response. When he was sentenced to death by Pontius Pilate, his followers were confused and disheartened. Soon afterward, these same disciples boldly filled Jerusalem with the message that their Lord had been resurrected. In a few years, Christianity had spread throughout the Roman Empire.—Matthew 4:25; 26:31; 27:24-26; Acts 2:23, 24, 36; 5:28; 17:6.

15 Witness to the truth of this comes from the Roman historian Tacitus, who was no friend of Christianity. Writing soon after 100 C.E., he tells of Nero's cruel persecution of the Christians and adds: "Christus, the founder of the name, had undergone the death penalty in the reign of Tiberius, by sentence of the procurator Pontius Pilatus, and the pernicious superstition was checked for a moment, only to break out once more, not merely in Judaea, the home of the disease, but in the capital [Rome] itself."[12]

14, 15. What support does Tacitus give to the Bible record?

*New International*
*'estament Theology*
12) says: "Recent
:ast doubt on the
ilers of the LXX
ed the tetragram-
*kyrios*. The oldest
its) now available
rammaton written
ers in the G[ree]k
is retained by later
the O[ld] T[esta-
centuries A.D."
Jesus and his disci-
ires in Hebrew or
come across the

eorge Howard, of
Georgia, U.S.A.,
: "When the Sep-
New Testament
oted contained the
divine name, the
ters no doubt in-
mmaton in their
*il Archaeology Re-*
page 14) What
y have had to do

tained in Greek
"Old Testament"
n the first half of
C.E., the Jewish
de a new transla-
v Scriptures into
s he represented
Tetragrammaton
characters. In the
n wrote: "And in
manuscripts THE
Hebrew characters,
Hebrew [charac-
it ancient ones."
a century, Jerome
ie to the books of
"And we find the
Tetragrammaton
eek volumes even

to this day expressed in ancient letters."

### The Removal of the Name

By this time, however, the apostasy foretold by Jesus had taken shape, and the name, although appearing in manuscripts, was used less and less. (Matthew 13:24-30; Acts 20:29, 30) Eventually, many readers did not even recognize what it was and Jerome reports that in his time "certain ignorant ones, because of the similarity of the characters, when they would find [the Tetragrammaton] in Greek books, were accustomed to read ΠΙΠΙ."

In later copies of the *Septuagint*, God's name was removed and words like "God" (*The·os'*) and "Lord" (*Ky'ri·os*) were substituted. We know that this happened because we have early fragments of the *Septuagint* where God's name was included and later copies of those same parts of the *Septuagint* where God's name has been removed.

The same thing occurred in the "New Testament," or Christian Greek Scriptures. Professor George Howard goes on to say: "When the Hebrew form for the divine name was eliminated in favor of Greek substitutes in the Septuagint, it was eliminated also from the New Testament quotations of the Septuagint. . . . Before long the divine name was lost to the Gentile church except insofar as it was reflected in the contracted surrogates or remembered by scholars."

Hence, while Jews refused to pronounce God's name, the apostate Christian church managed to remove it completely from Greek language manuscripts of both parts of the Bible, as well as from other language versions.

### The Need for the Name

Eventually, as we saw earlier, the name was restored to many translations of the Hebrew Scriptures. But

## "The LORD" —Equivalent of "Jehovah"?

To remove God's distinctive personal name from the Bible and substitute a title such as "Lord" or "God" makes the text weak and inadequate in many ways. For example, it can lead to meaningless combinations of words. In its foreword, *The Jerusalem Bible* says: "To say, 'The Lord is God' is surely a tautology [a needless, or meaningless, repetition], as to say 'Yahweh is God' is not."

Such substitutions can also lead to awkward phrases. Thus in the *Authorized Version*, Psalm 8:9 reads: "O LORD our Lord, how excellent is thy name in all the earth!" What an improvement when the name Jehovah is restored to such a text! Thus, *Young's Literal Translation of the Holy Bible* reads here: "Jehovah, our Lord, how honourable Thy name in all the earth!"

Removing the name can also lead to confusion. Psalm 110:1 says: "THE LORD said unto my Lord, Sit thou at my right hand, until I make thine enemies thy footstool." (*Authorized Version*) Who is talking to whom? How much better the rendering: "The utterance of Jehovah to my Lord is: 'Sit at my right hand until I place your enemies as a stool for your feet.'"—*New World Translation*.

Additionally, substituting "Lord" for "Jehovah" removes something of pivotal importance from the Bible: the personal name of God. *The Illustrated Bible Dictionary* (Volume 1, page 572) states: "Strictly speaking, Yahweh is the only 'name' of God."

*The Imperial Bible-Dictionary* (Volume 1, page 856) describes the difference between "God" (*Elohim*) and "Jehovah," stating: "[Jehovah] is everywhere a *proper* name, denoting the personal God and him only; whereas Elohim partakes more of the character of a *common* noun, denoting usually, indeed, but not necessarily nor uniformly, the Supreme."

J. A. Motyer, principal of Trinity College, England, adds: "Much is lost in Bible reading if we forget to look beyond the substitute word [Lord or God] to the personal, intimate name of God himself. By telling his people his name, God intended to reveal to them his inmost character."—*Eerdmans' Handbook to the Bible*, page 157.

No, one cannot render a distinctive proper name by a mere title. A title can never convey the full, rich meaning of the original name of God.

The Name 25

words, we will consider evidence that establishes the historicity of Jesus as well as the historical reliability of the New Testament. The first grouping of evidence is bibliographical.

## BIBLIOGRAPHICAL EVIDENCE

We do not possess any of the autographs of the New Testament. Like the Old Testament, the New Testament books were originally written on materials that quickly wore out and therefore had to be copied and recopied by hand for centuries before the invention of the printing press. So we need to determine how closely the extant copies represent the autographs. That is, how do we know that the New Testament we have today is close enough to the original writings as to be equally reliable? The bibliographical evidence is concerned with answering this question. And here we find three primary areas of evidence that demonstrate our present New Testament documents are virtually identical to their original writings.

### Copies Galore

The first area of evidence has to do with the available number of New Testament manuscripts. What we discover is that there are more extant New Testament manuscripts than any other document from antiquity. More than 24,000 partial and complete copies of the New Testament are in existence today. By comparison, the ancient document second in number of available copies is the *Iliad,* which has only 643 surviving manuscripts. And this number is extremely high compared to other ancient documents. For example, the *History of Thucydides,* the *History of Herodotus,* Caesar's *Gallic War,* Tacitus' *Histories* and *Annals,* and many other ancient documents have fewer than two dozen surviving copies.[4]

In addition to New Testament manuscripts, there are over 86,000 early patristic (church fathers') quotations from the New Testament and several thousand Lectionaries (early church-service books containing selected Scripture readings) dating to the early centuries of the church. In fact, there are enough quotations from the early church fathers that even if we did not have a single copy of the Bible, scholars could still reconstruct all but 11 verses of the entire New



Testament from material written within 150 to 200 years from the time of Christ.[5]

| AUTHOR | When Written | Earliest Copy | Time Span | No. of Copies |
|---|---|---|---|---|
| Caesar | 100–44 B.C. | A.D. 900 | 1,000 yrs. | 10 |
| Livy | 59 B.C.–A.D. 17 | | | 20 |
| Plato *(Tetralogies)* | 427–347 B.C. | A.D. 900 | 1,200 yrs. | 7 |
| Tacitus *(Annals)* | A.D. 100 | A.D. 1100 | 1,000 yrs. | 20 (–) |
| also minor works | A.D. 100 | A.D. 1000 | 900 yrs. | 1 |
| Pliny the Younger *(History)* | A.D. 61–113 | A.D. 850 | 750 yrs. | 7 |
| Thucydides *(History)* | 460–400 B.C. | A.D. 900 | 1,300 yrs. | 8 |
| Suetonius *(De Vita Caesarum)* | A.D. 75–169 | A.D. 950 | 800 yrs. | 8 |
| Herodotus *(History)* | 480–425 B.C. | A.D. 900 | 1,300 yrs. | 8 |
| Horace | | | 900 yrs. | |
| Sophocles | 496–406 B.C. | A.D. 1000 | 1,400 yrs. | 193 |
| Lucretius | Died 55 or 53 B.C. | | 1,100 yrs. | 2 |
| Catullus | 54 B.C. | A.D. 1550 | 1,600 yrs. | 3 |
| Euripides | 480–406 B.C. | A.D. 1100 | 1,500 yrs. | 9 |
| Demosthenes | 383–322 B.C. | A.D. 1100 | 1,300 yrs. | 200* |
| Aristotle | 384–322 B.C. | A.D. 1100 | 1,400 yrs. | 49† |
| Aristophanes | 450–385 B.C. | A.D. 900 | 1,200 yrs. | 10 |

*All from one copy.
†Of any one work.
From Josh McDowell, *Evidence That Demands a Verdict,* rev. ed. (San Bernardino, CA: Here's Life, 1979), 42.

### Shorter Is Best

The second area of bibliographical evidence concerns the short time span between when events recorded in the New Testament actually happened and when they were first written down. The time span is shorter for the New Testament than for any other document from antiquity. There is strong evidence that the gospels of Matthew, Mark, and Luke were written within thirty years of Jesus' death, and the gospel of John before the end of the first century. A. T. Robinson, a scholar who once assumed that all the New Testament books were written between the late first century and second century, later

DEFENDING YOUR FAITH - HOW TO ANSWER THE TOUGH QUESTIONS
by Dan Story (Nashville, TN: Thomas Nelson Publishers, 1992)

70-132 AD



what saith He; *And whosoever shall set his hope on Him, shall live for ever.* Is our hope then set upon a stone? Far be it. But it is because the Lord hath set His flesh in strength. For He saith; *And He set Me as a hard rock.* And the prophet saith again; *The stone which the builders rejected, this became the head of the corner.* And again He saith; *This is the great and wonderful day, which the Lord made.* I write to you the more simply, that ye may understand, I who am the offscouring of your love. What then saith the prophet again? *The assembly of evil-doers gathered about Me, they surrounded Me as bees surround a comb*; and; *For My garment they cast a lot.* Forasmuch then as He was about to be manifested in the flesh and to suffer, His suffering was manifested beforehand. For the prophet saith concerning Israel; *Woe unto their soul, for they have counselled evil counsel against themselves saying, Let us bind the righteous one, for he is unprofitable for us.* What saith the other prophet Moses unto them? *Behold, these things saith the Lord God; enter into the good land which the Lord sware unto Abraham, Isaac and Jacob, and inherit it, a land flowing with milk and honey.* But what saith knowledge? Understand ye. Set your hope on Him who is about to be manifested to you in the flesh, even Jesus. For man is earth suffering; for from the face of the earth came the creation of Adam. What then saith He? *Into the good land, a land flowing with milk and honey.* Blessed is our Lord, brethren, who established among us wisdom and understanding of His secret things. For the prophet speaketh a parable concerning the Lord. Who shall comprehend, save he that is wise and prudent and that loveth his Lord? Forasmuch then as He renewed us in the remission of sins, He made us to be a new type, so that we should have the soul of children, as if He were re-creating us. For the scripture saith concerning us, how He saith to the Son; *Let us make man after our image and after our likeness, and let them rule over the beasts of the earth and the fowls of the heaven and the fishes of the sea.* And the Lord said when He saw the fair creation of us men; *Increase and multiply and fill the earth.* These words refer to the Son. Again I will shew thee how the Lord speaketh concerning us. He made a second creation at the last; and the Lord saith; *Behold I make the last things as the first.* In reference to this then the prophet preached; *Enter into a land flowing with milk and honey, and be lords over it.* Behold then we have been created anew, as He saith again in another prophet; *Behold, saith the Lord, I will take out from these,* that is to say, from those whom the Spirit of the



Lord foresaw, *their stony hearts, and will put into them hearts of flesh;* for He Himself was to be manifested in the flesh and to dwell in us. For a holy temple unto the Lord, my brethren, is the abode of our heart. For the Lord saith again; *For wherein shall I appear unto the Lord my God and be glorified? I will make confession unto Thee in the assembly of my brethren, and I will sing unto Thee in the midst of the assembly of the saints.* We therefore are they whom He brought into the good land. What then is the milk and the honey? Because the child is first kept alive by honey, and then by milk. So in like manner we also, being kept alive by our faith in the promise and by the word, shall live and be lords of the earth. Now we have already said above; *And let them increase and multiply and rule over the fishes.* But who is he that is able [now] to rule over beasts and fishes and fowls of the heaven; for we ought to perceive that to rule implieth power, so that one should give orders and have dominion. If then this cometh not to pass now, assuredly He spake to us for the hereafter, when we ourselves shall be made perfect so that we may become heirs of the covenant of the Lord.

7. Understand therefore, children of gladness, that the good Lord manifested all things to us beforehand, that we might know to whom we ought in all things to render thanksgiving and praise. If then the Son of God, being Lord and future Judge of quick and dead, suffered that His wound might give us life, let us believe that the Son of God could not suffer except for our sakes. But moreover when crucified He had vinegar and gall given Him to drink. Hear how on this matter the priests of the temple have revealed. Seeing that there is a commandment in scripture, *Whosoever shall not observe the fast shall surely die,* the Lord commanded, because He was in His own person about to offer the vessel of His Spirit a sacrifice for our sins, that the type also which was given in Isaac who was offered upon the altar should be fulfilled. What then saith He in the prophet? *And let them eat of the goat that is offered at the fast for all their sins.* Attend carefully; *And let all the priests alone eat the entrails unwashed with vinegar.* Wherefore? Since ye are to give Me, who am to offer My flesh for the sins of My new people, gall with vinegar to drink, eat ye alone, while the people fasteth and waileth in sackcloth and ashes; that He might shew that He must suffer at their hands. Attend ye to the commandments which He gave. *Take two goats, fair and alike, and offer them, and let the priest take the one for a whole burnt-offering for sins.* But the

THE APOSTOLIC FATHERS (1891), 1984, by J.B. Lightfoot and J.R. Harmer

70-132AD



ὁμοίωσιν ἡμετέραν· πῶς οὖν ὑπέμεινεν ὑπὸ χειρὸς ἀνθρώπων
παθεῖν; μάθετε. 6. οἱ προφῆται, ἀπ' αὐτοῦ ἔχοντες τὴν
χάριν, εἰς αὐτὸν ἐπροφήτευσαν. αὐτὸς δὲ ἵνα καταργήσῃ
τὸν θάνατον καὶ τὴν ἐκ νεκρῶν ἀνάστασιν δείξῃ, ὅτι ἐν
σαρκὶ ἔδει αὐτὸν φανερωθῆναι, ὑπέμεινεν, 7. ἵνα καὶ τοῖς
πατράσιν τὴν ἐπαγγελίαν ἀποδῷ καὶ αὐτὸς ἑαυτῷ τὸν λαὸν
τὸν καινὸν ἑτοιμάζων ἐπιδείξῃ, ἐπὶ τῆς γῆς ὤν, ὅτι τὴν
ἀνάστασιν αὐτὸς ποιήσας κρινεῖ. 8. πέρας γέ τοι διδάσκων
τὸν Ἰσραὴλ καὶ τηλικαῦτα τέρατα καὶ σημεῖα ποιῶν ἐκήρυσ-
σεν, καὶ ὑπερηγάπησεν αὐτόν. 9. ὅτε δὲ τοὺς ἰδίους ἀποστό-
λους τοὺς μέλλοντας κηρύσσειν τὸ εὐαγγέλιον αὐτοῦ ἐξελέξατο,
S. Matt. ix. 13. ὄντας ὑπὲρ πᾶσαν ἁμαρτίαν ἀνομωτέρους, ἵνα δείξῃ ὅτι οὐκ
ἦλθεν καλέσαι δικαίους ἀλλὰ ἁμαρτωλούς, τότε ἐφανέρωσεν
ἑαυτὸν εἶναι υἱὸν Θεοῦ. 10. Εἰ γὰρ μὴ ἦλθεν ἐν σαρκί, οὐδ'
ἂν πως οἱ ἄνθρωποι ἐσώθησαν βλέποντες αὐτόν· ὅτε τὸν
μέλλοντα μὴ εἶναι ἥλιον, ἔργον τῶν χειρῶν αὐτοῦ ὑπάρχοντα,
ἐμβλέποντες οὐκ ἰσχύουσιν εἰς τὰς ἀκτῖνας αὐτοῦ ἀντοφθαλ-
μῆσαι. 11. οὐκοῦν ὁ υἱὸς τοῦ Θεοῦ εἰς τοῦτο ἐν σαρκὶ
ἦλθεν, ἵνα τὸ τέλειον τῶν ἁμαρτιῶν ἀνακεφαλαιώσῃ τοῖς
διώξασιν ἐν θανάτῳ τοὺς προφήτας αὐτοῦ. 12. οὐκοῦν εἰς
τοῦτο ὑπέμεινεν. λέγει γὰρ ὁ Θεὸς τὴν πληγὴν τῆς σαρκὸς
Zech. xiii. 7. αὐτοῦ ὅτι ἐξ αὐτῶν· Ὅταν πατάξωσιν τὸν ποιμένα ἑαυτῶν,
S. Matt. xxvi. 31. τότε ἀπολεῖται τὰ πρόβατα τῆς ποίμνης. 13. Αὐτὸς δὲ ἠθέλησεν
οὕτω παθεῖν. ἔδει γὰρ ἵνα ἐπὶ ξύλου πάθῃ. λέγει γὰρ ὁ
Ps. xxii. 21, cxix. 120, xxii. 17. προφητεύων ἐπ' αὐτῷ· Φεῖσαί μου τῆς ψυχῆς ἀπὸ ῥομφαίας· καί·
Καθήλωσόν μου τὰς σάρκας, ὅτι πονηρευομένων συναγωγαὶ
Is. l. 6, 7. ἐπανέστησάν μοι. 14. καὶ πάλιν λέγει· Ἰδοὺ τέθεικά μου τὸν
νῶτον εἰς μάστιγας, τὰς δὲ σιαγόνας μου εἰς ῥαπίσματα, τὸ δὲ
πρόσωπόν μου ἔθηκα ὡς στερεὰν πέτραν.
Is. l. 8, 9. VI. Ὅτε οὖν ἐποίησεν τὴν ἐντολήν, τί λέγει; Τίς ὁ κρι-
νόμενός μοι; ἀντιστήτω μοι· ἢ τίς ὁ δικαιούμενός μοι; ἐγγισάτω
τῷ παιδὶ Κυρίου. 2. οὐαὶ ὑμῖν, ὅτι ὑμεῖς πάντες ὡς ἱμάτιον
παλαιωθήσεσθε, καὶ σὴς καταφάγεται ὑμᾶς. καὶ πάλιν λέγει ὁ
Is. xxviii. 16. προφήτης, ἐπεὶ ὡς λίθος ἰσχυρὸς ἐτέθη εἰς συντριβήν· Ἰδοὺ

THE APOSTOLIC FATHERS (1891)



ἐμβαλῶ εἰς τὰ θεμέλια Σιὼν λίθον πολυτελῆ, ἐκλεκτόν, ἀκρογω-
νιαῖον, ἔντιμον. 3. εἶτα τί λέγει; Καὶ ὃς ἐλπίσει ἐπ' αὐτὸν
ζήσεται εἰς τὸν αἰῶνα. ἐπὶ λίθον οὖν ἡμῶν ἡ ἐλπίς; μὴ γέ-
νοιτο. ἀλλ' ἐπεὶ ἐν ἰσχύϊ τέθεικεν τὴν σάρκα αὐτοῦ Κύριος.
λέγει γάρ· Καὶ ἔθηκέν με ὡς στερεὰν πέτραν. 4. λέγει δὲ Is. l. 7.
πάλιν ὁ προφήτης· Λίθον ὃν ἀπεδοκίμασαν οἱ οἰκοδομοῦντες, Ps. cxviii. 22.
οὗτος ἐγενήθη εἰς κεφαλὴν γωνίας. καὶ πάλιν λέγει· Αὕτη Ps. cxviii. 24. ←
ἐστὶν ἡ ἡμέρα ἡ μεγάλη καὶ θαυμαστή, ἣν ἐποίησεν ὁ Κύριος.
5. Ἁπλούστερον ὑμῖν γράφω, ἵνα συνίητε, ἐγὼ περίψημα
τῆς ἀγάπης ὑμῶν. 6. τί οὖν λέγει πάλιν ὁ προφήτης; Περι- Ps. xxii. 17, cxviii. 12.
έσχεν με συναγωγὴ πονηρευομένων, ἐκύκλωσάν με ὡσεὶ μέλισ-
σαι κηρίον· καί· Ἐπὶ τὸν ἱματισμόν μου ἔβαλον κλῆρον. 7. ἐν Ps. xxii. 19.
σαρκὶ οὖν αὐτοῦ μέλλοντος φανεροῦσθαι καὶ πάσχειν, προε-
φανερώθη τὸ πάθος. λέγει γὰρ ὁ προφήτης ἐπὶ τὸν Ἰσραήλ·
Οὐαὶ τῇ ψυχῇ αὐτῶν, ὅτι βεβούλευνται βουλὴν πονηρὰν καθ' ἑαυ- Is. iii. 9, 10.
τῶν, εἰπόντες· Δήσωμεν τὸν δίκαιον, ὅτι δύσχρηστος ἡμῖν ἐστίν.
8. τί λέγει ὁ ἄλλος προφήτης Μωϋσῆς αὐτοῖς; Ἰδοὺ τάδε Ex. xxxiii. 1, 3. ←
λέγει Κύριος ὁ Θεός· Εἰσέλθατε εἰς τὴν γῆν τὴν ἀγαθήν, ἣν
ὤμοσεν Κύριος τῷ Ἀβραὰμ καὶ Ἰσαὰκ καὶ Ἰακώβ, καὶ κατακληρο-
νομήσατε αὐτήν, γῆν ῥέουσαν γάλα καὶ μέλι. 9. τί δὲ λέγει ἡ
γνῶσις; μάθετε. ἐλπίσατε ἐπὶ τὸν ἐν σαρκὶ μέλλοντα φανεροῦσθαι ὑμῖν Ἰησοῦν. ἄνθρωπος γὰρ γῆ ἐστὶν πάσχουσα·
ἀπὸ προσώπου γὰρ τῆς γῆς ἡ πλάσις τοῦ Ἀδὰμ ἐγένετο.
10. τί οὖν λέγει· Εἰς τὴν γῆν τὴν ἀγαθήν, γῆν ῥέουσαν γάλα Ex. xxxiii. 3.
καὶ μέλι; εὐλογητὸς ὁ Κύριος ἡμῶν, ἀδελφοί, ὁ σοφίαν καὶ
νοῦν θέμενος ἐν ἡμῖν τῶν κρυφίων αὐτοῦ. λέγει γὰρ ὁ
προφήτης παραβολὴν Κυρίου· τίς νοήσει, εἰ μὴ σοφὸς καὶ
ἐπιστήμων καὶ ἀγαπῶν τὸν Κύριον αὐτοῦ; 11. Ἐπεὶ οὖν
ἐκαίνισεν ἡμᾶς ἐν τῇ ἀφέσει τῶν ἁμαρτιῶν, ἐποίησεν ἡμᾶς
ἄλλον τύπον, ὡς παιδίων ἔχειν τὴν ψυχήν, ὡς ἂν δὴ ἀνα-
πλάσσοντος αὐτοῦ ἡμᾶς. 12. λέγει γὰρ ἡ γραφὴ περὶ ἡμῶν,
ὡς λέγει τῷ υἱῷ· Ποιήσωμεν κατ' εἰκόνα καὶ καθ' ὁμοίωσιν Gen. i. 26.
ἡμῶν τὸν ἄνθρωπον, καὶ ἀρχέτωσαν τῶν θηρίων τῆς γῆς καὶ
τῶν πετεινῶν τοῦ οὐρανοῦ καὶ τῶν ἰχθύων τῆς θαλάσσης. καὶ

1984, by J.B. Lightfoot and J.R. Harmer

 95 A.D.

known unto all men that they which are double-minded and they which doubt concerning the power of God are set for a judgment and for a token unto all the generations.

12. For her faith and hospitality Rahab the harlot was saved. For when the spies were sent forth unto Jericho by Joshua the son of Nun, the king of the land perceived that they were come to spy out his country, and sent forth men to seize them, that being seized they might be put to death. So the hospitable Rahab received them and hid them in the upper chamber under the flax-stalks. And when the messengers of the king came near and said, *The spies of our land entered in unto thee: bring them forth, for the king so ordereth:* then she answered, *The men truly, whom ye seek, entered in unto me, but they departed forthwith and are journeying on the way;* and she pointed out to them the opposite road. And she said unto the men, *Of a surety I perceive that the Lord your God delivereth this city unto you; for the fear and the dread of you is fallen upon the inhabitants thereof. When therefore it shall come to pass that ye take it, save me and the house of my father.* And they said unto her, *It shall be even so as thou hast spoken unto us. Whensoever therefore thou perceivest that we are coming, thou shalt gather all thy folk beneath thy roof, and they shall be saved; for as many as shall be found without the house shall perish.* And moreover they gave her a sign, that she should hang out from her house a scarlet thread, thereby showing beforehand that through the blood of the Lord there shall be redemption unto all them that believe and hope on God. Ye see, dearly beloved, not only faith, but prophecy, is found in the woman.

13. Let us therefore be lowly-minded, brethren, laying aside all arrogance and conceit and folly and anger, and let us do that which is written. For the Holy Ghost saith, *Let not the wise man boast in his wisdom, nor the strong in his strength, neither the rich in his riches; but he that boasteth let him boast in the Lord, that he may seek Him out, and do judgment and righteousness;* most of all remembering the words of the Lord Jesus which He spake, teaching forbearance and long-suffering: for thus He spake; *Have mercy, that ye may receive mercy: forgive, that it may be forgiven to you. As ye do, so shall it be done to you. As ye give, so shall it be given unto you. As ye judge, so shall ye be judged. As ye show kindness, so shall kindness be showed unto you. With what measure ye mete, it shall be measured withal to you.* With this commandment and these precepts let us confirm ourselves, that we may walk in obedience to His hallowed words, with lowliness of mind. For



the holy word saith, *Upon whom shall I look, save upon him that is gentle and quiet and feareth Mine oracles?*

14. Therefore it is right and proper, brethren, that we should be obedient unto God, rather than follow those who in arrogance and unruliness have set themselves up as leaders in abominable jealousy. For we shall bring upon us no common harm, but rather great peril, if we surrender ourselves recklessly to the purposes of men who launch out into strife and seditions, so as to estrange us from that which is right. Let us be good one towards another according to the compassion and sweetness of Him that made us. For it is written: *The good shall be dwellers in the land, and the innocent shall be left on it; but they that transgress shall be destroyed utterly from it.* And again He saith; *I saw the ungodly lifted up on high and exalted as the cedars of Lebanon. And I passed by, and behold he was not; and I sought out his place, and I found it not. Keep innocence and behold uprightness; for there is a remnant for the peaceful man.*

15. Therefore let us cleave unto them that practise peace with godliness, and not unto them that desire peace with dissimulation. For He saith in a certain place; *This people honoureth Me with their lips, but their heart is far from Me;* and again, *They blessed with their mouth, but they cursed with their heart.* And again He saith, *They loved Him with their mouth, and with their tongue they lied unto Him; and their heart was not upright with Him, neither were they stedfast in His covenant. For this cause let the deceitful lips be made dumb which speak iniquity against the righteous.* And again; *May the Lord utterly destroy all the deceitful lips, the tongue that speaketh proud things, even them that say, Let us magnify our tongue; our lips are our own; who is lord over us? For the misery of the needy and for the groaning of the poor I will now arise, saith the Lord. I will set him in safety; I will deal boldly by him.*

16. For Christ is with them that are lowly of mind, not with them that exalt themselves over the flock. The sceptre [of the majesty] of God, even our Lord Jesus Christ, came not in the pomp of arrogance or of pride, though He might have done so, but in lowliness of mind, according as the Holy Spirit spake concerning Him. For He saith; *Lord, who believed our report? and to whom was the arm of the Lord revealed? We announced Him in His presence. As a child was He, as a root in a thirsty ground. There is no form in Him, neither glory. And we beheld Him, and He had no form nor comeliness, but His form was*

THE APOSTOLIC FATHERS (1891) 1984, by J. B. Lightfoot and J. R. Harmer

95 A.D.

τελείως λειτουργήσαντας τῇ μεγαλοπρεπεῖ δόξῃ αὐτοῦ. 3. λά-
βωμεν Ἐνώχ, ὃς ἐν ὑπακοῇ δίκαιος εὑρεθεὶς μετετέθη, καὶ
οὐχ εὑρέθη αὐτοῦ θάνατος. 4. Νῶε πιστὸς εὑρεθεὶς διὰ τῆς
λειτουργίας αὐτοῦ παλιγγενεσίαν κόσμῳ ἐκήρυξεν, καὶ διέσω-
σεν δι᾽ αὐτοῦ ὁ δεσπότης τὰ εἰσελθόντα ἐν ὁμονοίᾳ ζῶα εἰς
τὴν κιβωτόν.

X. Ἀβραάμ, ὁ φίλος προσαγορευθείς, πιστὸς εὑρέθη ἐν
τῷ αὐτὸν ὑπήκοον γενέσθαι τοῖς ῥήμασιν τοῦ Θεοῦ. 2. οὗτος
δι᾽ ὑπακοῆς ἐξῆλθεν ἐκ τῆς γῆς αὐτοῦ καὶ ἐκ τῆς συγγενείας
αὐτοῦ καὶ ἐκ τοῦ οἴκου τοῦ πατρὸς αὐτοῦ, ὅπως γῆν ὀλίγην
καὶ συγγένειαν ἀσθενῆ καὶ οἶκον μικρὸν καταλιπὼν κληρονο-
Gen. xii. 1—3. μήσῃ τὰς ἐπαγγελίας τοῦ Θεοῦ. λέγει γὰρ αὐτῷ· 3. Ἄπελθε
ἐκ τῆς γῆς σου καὶ ἐκ τῆς συγγενείας σου καὶ ἐκ τοῦ οἴκου τοῦ
πατρός σου εἰς τὴν γῆν ἣν ἄν σοι δείξω, καὶ ποιήσω σε εἰς ἔθνος
μέγα καὶ εὐλογήσω σε καὶ μεγαλυνῶ τὸ ὄνομά σου, καὶ ἔσῃ εὐλο-
γημένος· καὶ εὐλογήσω τοὺς εὐλογοῦντάς σε καὶ καταράσομαι τοὺς
καταρωμένους σε, καὶ εὐλογηθήσονται ἐν σοὶ πᾶσαι αἱ φυλαὶ τῆς
γῆς. 4. καὶ πάλιν ἐν τῷ διαχωρισθῆναι αὐτὸν ἀπὸ Λὼτ
Gen. xiii. 14—16. εἶπεν αὐτῷ ὁ Θεός· Ἀναβλέψας τοῖς ὀφθαλμοῖς σου, ἴδε ἀπὸ τοῦ
τόπου, οὗ νῦν σὺ εἶ, πρὸς βορρᾶν καὶ λίβα καὶ ἀνατολὰς καὶ
θάλασσαν· ὅτι πᾶσαν τὴν γῆν, ἣν σὺ ὁρᾷς, σοὶ δώσω αὐτὴν καὶ
τῷ σπέρματί σου ἕως αἰῶνος· 5. καὶ ποιήσω τὸ σπέρμα σου ὡς
τὴν ἄμμον τῆς γῆς· εἰ δύναταί τις ἐξαριθμῆσαι τὴν ἄμμον τῆς
γῆς, καὶ τὸ σπέρμα σου ἐξαριθμηθήσεται. 6. καὶ πάλιν λέγει·
Gen. xv. 5, 6. Ἐξήγαγεν ὁ Θεὸς τὸν Ἀβραὰμ καὶ εἶπεν αὐτῷ· Ἀνάβλεψον εἰς
τὸν οὐρανὸν καὶ ἀρίθμησον τοὺς ἀστέρας, εἰ δυνήσῃ ἐξαριθμῆσαι
αὐτούς· οὕτως ἔσται τὸ σπέρμα σου· ἐπίστευσεν δὲ Ἀβραὰμ τῷ
Θεῷ, καὶ ἐλογίσθη αὐτῷ εἰς δικαιοσύνην. 7. Διὰ πίστιν καὶ
φιλοξενίαν ἐδόθη αὐτῷ υἱὸς ἐν γήρᾳ, καὶ δι᾽ ὑπακοῆς προσή-
νεγκεν αὐτὸν θυσίαν τῷ Θεῷ πρὸς ἓν τῶν ὀρέων ὧν ἔδειξεν
αὐτῷ.

XI. Διὰ φιλοξενίαν καὶ εὐσέβειαν Λὼτ ἐσώθη ἐκ Σοδό-
μων, τῆς περιχώρου πάσης κριθείσης διὰ πυρὸς καὶ θείου·
πρόδηλον ποιήσας ὁ δεσπότης, ὅτι τοὺς ἐλπίζοντας ἐπ᾽ αὐτὸν



οὐκ ἐγκαταλείπει, τοὺς δὲ ἑτεροκλινεῖς ὑπάρχοντας εἰς κόλα-
σιν καὶ αἰκισμὸν τίθησιν· 2. συνεξελθούσης γὰρ αὐτῷ τῆς
γυναικός, ἑτερογνώμονος ὑπαρχούσης καὶ οὐκ ἐν ὁμονοίᾳ, εἰς
τοῦτο σημεῖον ἐτέθη ὥστε γενέσθαι αὐτὴν στήλην ἁλὸς ἕως
τῆς ἡμέρας ταύτης, εἰς τὸ γνωστὸν εἶναι πᾶσιν ὅτι οἱ δίψυχοι
καὶ οἱ διστάζοντες περὶ τῆς τοῦ Θεοῦ δυνάμεως εἰς κρίμα
καὶ εἰς σημείωσιν πάσαις ταῖς γενεαῖς γίνονται.

XII. Διὰ πίστιν καὶ φιλοξενίαν ἐσώθη Ῥαὰβ ἡ πόρνη·
2. ἐκπεμφθέντων γὰρ ὑπὸ Ἰησοῦ τοῦ τοῦ Ναυὴ κατασκόπων
εἰς τὴν Ἱεριχώ, ἔγνω ὁ βασιλεὺς τῆς γῆς ὅτι ἥκασιν κατα-
σκοπεῦσαι τὴν χώραν αὐτῶν, καὶ ἐξέπεμψεν ἄνδρας τοὺς
συλλημψομένους αὐτούς, ὅπως συλλημφθέντες θανατωθῶσιν.
3. ἡ οὖν φιλόξενος Ῥαὰβ εἰσδεξαμένη αὐτοὺς ἔκρυψεν εἰς τὸ
ὑπερῷον ὑπὸ τὴν λινοκαλάμην. 4. ἐπισταθέντων δὲ τῶν
παρὰ τοῦ βασιλέως καὶ λεγόντων· Πρὸς σὲ εἰσῆλθον οἱ κατά- Josh. ii. 6 sq. ←
σκοποι τῆς γῆς ἡμῶν· ἐξάγαγε αὐτούς, ὁ γὰρ βασιλεὺς οὕτως
κελεύει· ἡ δὲ ἀπεκρίθη· Εἰσῆλθον μὲν οἱ ἄνδρες, οὓς ζητεῖτε,
πρός με, ἀλλὰ εὐθέως ἀπῆλθον καὶ πορεύονται τῇ ὁδῷ· ὑποδεικ-
νύουσα αὐτοῖς ἐναλλάξ. 5. Καὶ εἶπεν πρὸς τοὺς ἄνδρας·
Γινώσκουσα γινώσκω ἐγὼ ὅτι Κύριος ὁ Θεὸς ὑμῶν παραδίδωσιν
ὑμῖν τὴν πόλιν ταύτην, ὁ γὰρ φόβος καὶ ὁ τρόμος ὑμῶν ἐπέπεσεν
τοῖς κατοικοῦσιν αὐτήν. ὡς ἐὰν οὖν γένηται λαβεῖν αὐτὴν ὑμᾶς,
διασώσατέ με καὶ τὸν οἶκον τοῦ πατρός μου. 6. καὶ εἶπαν
αὐτῇ· Ἔσται οὕτως ὡς ἐλάλησας ἡμῖν. ὡς ἐὰν οὖν γνῷς παρα-
γινομένους ἡμᾶς, συνάξεις πάντας τοὺς σοὺς ὑπὸ τὸ τέγος σου,
καὶ διασωθήσονται· ὅσοι γὰρ ἐὰν εὑρεθῶσιν ἔξω τῆς οἰκίας, ἀπο-
λοῦνται. 7. καὶ προσέθεντο αὐτῇ δοῦναι σημεῖον, ὅπως
κρεμάσῃ ἐκ τοῦ οἴκου αὐτῆς κόκκινον, πρόδηλον ποιοῦντες
ὅτι διὰ τοῦ αἵματος τοῦ Κυρίου λύτρωσις ἔσται πᾶσιν τοῖς
πιστεύουσιν καὶ ἐλπίζουσιν ἐπὶ τὸν Θεόν. 8. Ὁρᾶτε, ἀγα-
πητοί, οὐ μόνον πίστις ἀλλὰ προφητεία ἐν τῇ γυναικὶ
γέγονεν.

XIII. Ταπεινοφρονήσωμεν οὖν, ἀδελφοί, ἀποθέμενοι πᾶσαν ἀλαζονείαν καὶ τύφος καὶ ἀφροσύνην καὶ ὀργάς, καὶ

THE APOSTOLIC FATHERS (1891), 1984, by J. B. Lightfoot and J. R. Harmer

ποιήσωμεν τὸ γεγραμμένον· λέγει γὰρ τὸ πνεῦμα τὸ ἅγιον·
1 Sam. ii. 10. Jer. ix. 23, 24. Μὴ καυχάσθω ὁ σοφὸς ἐν τῇ σοφίᾳ αὐτοῦ, μηδὲ ὁ ἰσχυρὸς ἐν τῇ
ἰσχύϊ αὐτοῦ, μηδὲ ὁ πλούσιος ἐν τῷ πλούτῳ αὐτοῦ, ἀλλ' ἢ ὁ καυ-
χώμενος ἐν Κυρίῳ καυχάσθω, τοῦ ἐκζητεῖν αὐτὸν καὶ ποιεῖν
κρίμα καὶ δικαιοσύνην· μάλιστα μεμνημένοι τῶν λόγων τοῦ
Κυρίου Ἰησοῦ, οὓς ἐλάλησεν διδάσκων ἐπιείκειαν καὶ μακρο-
S. Matt. v. 7, vi. 14, vii. 1, 2. S. Luke vi. 31, 36—38. θυμίαν· 2. οὕτως γὰρ εἶπεν· Ἐλεᾶτε ἵνα ἐλεηθῆτε, ἀφίετε
ἵνα ἀφεθῇ ὑμῖν· ὡς ποιεῖτε, οὕτω ποιηθήσεται ὑμῖν· ὡς δίδοτε,
οὕτως δοθήσεται ὑμῖν· ὡς κρίνετε, οὕτως κριθήσεσθε· ὡς χρη-
στεύεσθε, οὕτως χρηστευθήσεται ὑμῖν· ᾧ μέτρῳ μετρεῖτε, ἐν
αὐτῷ μετρηθήσεται ὑμῖν. 3. Ταύτῃ τῇ ἐντολῇ καὶ τοῖς παρ-
αγγέλμασιν τούτοις στηρίξωμεν ἑαυτοὺς εἰς τὸ πορεύεσθαι
ὑπηκόους ὄντας τοῖς ἁγιοπρεπέσι λόγοις αὐτοῦ, ταπεινοφρο-
Is. lxvi. 2. νοῦντες. φησὶν γὰρ ὁ ἅγιος λόγος· 4. Ἐπὶ τίνα ἐπιβλέψω,
ἀλλ' ἢ ἐπὶ τὸν πραῢν καὶ ἡσύχιον καὶ τρέμοντά μου τὰ λόγια;

XIV. Δίκαιον οὖν καὶ ὅσιον, ἄνδρες ἀδελφοί, ὑπηκόους
ἡμᾶς μᾶλλον γενέσθαι τῷ Θεῷ ἢ τοῖς ἐν ἀλαζονείᾳ καὶ ἀκα-
ταστασίᾳ μυσεροῦ ζήλους ἀρχηγοῖς ἐξακολουθεῖν. 2. βλά-
βην γὰρ οὐ τὴν τυχοῦσαν, μᾶλλον δὲ κίνδυνον ὑποίσομεν
μέγαν, ἐὰν ῥιψοκινδύνως ἐπιδῶμεν ἑαυτοὺς τοῖς θελήμασιν
τῶν ἀνθρώπων, οἵτινες ἐξακοντίζουσιν εἰς ἔριν καὶ στάσεις
εἰς τὸ ἀπαλλοτριῶσαι ἡμᾶς τοῦ καλῶς ἔχοντος. 3. χρη-
στευσώμεθα αὐτοῖς κατὰ τὴν εὐσπλαγχνίαν καὶ γλυκύτητα
Prov. ii. 21, 22. Ps. xxxvii. 9, 38. τοῦ ποιήσαντος ἡμᾶς. 4. γέγραπται γάρ· Χρηστοὶ ἔσονται
οἰκήτορες γῆς, ἄκακοι δὲ ὑπολειφθήσονται ἐπ' αὐτῆς· οἱ δὲ παρα-
νομοῦντες ἐξολεθρευθήσονται ἀπ' αὐτῆς· 5. καὶ πάλιν λέγει·
Ps. xxxvii. 35—37. Εἶδον ἀσεβῆ ὑπερυψούμενον καὶ ἐπαιρόμενον ὡς τὰς κέδρους
τοῦ Λιβάνου, καὶ παρῆλθον καὶ ἰδοὺ οὐκ ἦν, καὶ ἐξεζήτησα τὸν
τόπον αὐτοῦ καὶ οὐχ εὗρον. φύλασσε ἀκακίαν καὶ ἴδε εὐθύτητα, ὅτι
ἐστὶν ἐγκατάλειμμα ἀνθρώπῳ εἰρηνικῷ.

XV. Τοίνυν κολληθῶμεν τοῖς μετ' εὐσεβείας εἰρηνεύ-
ουσιν, καὶ μὴ τοῖς μεθ' ὑποκρίσεως βουλομένοις εἰρήνην.
Is. xxix. 13. 2. λέγει γάρ που· Οὗτος ὁ λαὸς τοῖς χείλεσίν με τιμᾷ, ἡ δὲ
Ps. lxii. 5. καρδία αὐτῶν πόρρω ἄπεστιν ἀπ' ἐμοῦ. 3. καὶ πάλιν· Τῷ



στόματι αὐτῶν εὐλογοῦσαν, τῇ δὲ καρδίᾳ αὐτῶν κατηρῶντο.
4. καὶ πάλιν λέγει· Ἠγάπησαν αὐτὸν τῷ στόματι αὐτῶν καὶ τῇ Ps. lxxviii. 36, 37.
γλώσσῃ αὐτῶν ἐψεύσαντο αὐτόν, ἡ δὲ καρδία αὐτῶν οὐκ εὐθεῖα
μετ' αὐτοῦ, οὐδὲ ἐπιστώθησαν ἐν τῇ διαθήκῃ αὐτοῦ. 5. διὰ Ps. xxxi. 19.
τοῦτο ἄλαλα γενηθήτω τὰ χείλη τὰ δόλια τὰ λαλοῦντα κατὰ τοῦ
δικαίου ἀνομίαν· καὶ πάλιν· Ἐξολεθρεύσαι Κύριος πάντα τὰ χείλη Ps. xii. 4—6. ←
τὰ δόλια, γλῶσσαν μεγαλορήμονα, τοὺς εἰπόντας· Τὴν γλῶσσαν
ἡμῶν μεγαλύνωμεν, τὰ χείλη ἡμῶν παρ' ἡμῖν ἐστιν· τίς ἡμῶν
κύριός ἐστιν; 6. ἀπὸ τῆς ταλαιπωρίας τῶν πτωχῶν καὶ ἀπὸ
τοῦ στεναγμοῦ τῶν πενήτων νῦν ἀναστήσομαι, λέγει Κύριος·
θήσομαι ἐν σωτηρίῳ, 7. παρρησιάσομαι ἐν αὐτῷ.

XVI. Ταπεινοφρονούντων γάρ ἐστιν ὁ Χριστός, οὐκ
ἐπαιρομένων ἐπὶ τὸ ποίμνιον αὐτοῦ. 2. τὸ σκῆπτρον [τῆς
μεγαλωσύνης] τοῦ Θεοῦ, ὁ Κύριος [ἡμῶν] Χριστὸς Ἰησοῦς,
οὐκ ἦλθεν ἐν κόμπῳ ἀλαζονείας οὐδὲ ὑπερηφανίας, καίπερ
δυνάμενος, ἀλλὰ ταπεινοφρονῶν, καθὼς τὸ πνεῦμα τὸ ἅγιον
περὶ αὐτοῦ ἐλάλησεν· φησὶν γάρ· 3. Κύριε, τίς ἐπίστευσεν Is. liii. 1—12. ←
τῇ ἀκοῇ ἡμῶν; καὶ ὁ βραχίων Κυρίου τίνι ἀπεκαλύφθη; ἀνηγ-
γείλαμεν ἐναντίον αὐτοῦ, ὡς παιδίον, ὡς ῥίζα ἐν γῇ διψώσῃ· οὐκ
ἔστιν εἶδος αὐτῷ, οὐδὲ δόξα· καὶ εἴδομεν αὐτόν, καὶ οὐκ εἶχεν
εἶδος οὐδὲ κάλλος, ἀλλὰ τὸ εἶδος αὐτοῦ ἄτιμον, ἐκλεῖπον παρὰ
τὸ εἶδος τῶν ἀνθρώπων· ἄνθρωπος ἐν πληγῇ ὢν καὶ πόνῳ καὶ
εἰδὼς φέρειν μαλακίαν, ὅτι ἀπέστραπται τὸ πρόσωπον αὐτοῦ, ἠτι-
μάσθη καὶ οὐκ ἐλογίσθη. 4. οὗτος τὰς ἁμαρτίας ἡμῶν φέρει καὶ
περὶ ἡμῶν ὀδυνᾶται, καὶ ἡμεῖς ἐλογισάμεθα αὐτὸν εἶναι ἐν πόνῳ
καὶ ἐν πληγῇ καὶ ἐν κακώσει. 5. αὐτὸς δὲ ἐτραυματίσθη διὰ τὰς
ἁμαρτίας ἡμῶν καὶ μεμαλάκισται διὰ τὰς ἀνομίας ἡμῶν. παιδεία
εἰρήνης ἡμῶν ἐπ' αὐτόν· τῷ μώλωπι αὐτοῦ ἡμεῖς ἰάθημεν.
6. πάντες ὡς πρόβατα ἐπλανήθημεν, ἄνθρωπος τῇ ὁδῷ αὐτοῦ
ἐπλανήθη· 7. καὶ Κύριος παρέδωκεν αὐτὸν ὑπὲρ τῶν ἁμαρτιῶν
ἡμῶν, καὶ αὐτὸς διὰ τὸ κεκακῶσθαι οὐκ ἀνοίγει τὸ στόμα· ὡς
πρόβατον ἐπὶ σφαγὴν ἤχθη, καὶ ὡς ἀμνὸς ἐναντίον τοῦ κείραντος
ἄφωνος, οὕτως οὐκ ἀνοίγει τὸ στόμα αὐτοῦ. ἐν τῇ ταπεινώσει
ἡ κρίσις αὐτοῦ ἤρθη· 8. τὴν γενεὰν αὐτοῦ τίς διηγήσεται; ὅτι

THE APOSTOLIC FATHERS (1891). 1984, by J.B. Lightfoot and J.R. Harmer

self make all things freely, and as He pleased, again David says, "But our God is in the heavens above, and in the earth; He hath made all things whatsoever He pleased."[1] But the things established are distinct from Him who has established them, and what have been made from Him who has made them. For He is Himself uncreated, both without beginning and end, and lacking nothing. He is Himself sufficient for Himself; and still further, He grants to all others this very thing, existence; but the things which have been made by Him have received a beginning. But whatever things had a beginning, and are liable to dissolution, and are subject to and stand in need of Him who made them, must necessarily in all respects have a different term [applied to them], even by those who have but a moderate capacity for discerning such things; so that He indeed who made all things can alone, together with His Word, properly be termed God and Lord: but the things which have been made cannot have this term applied to them, neither should they justly assume that appellation which belongs to the Creator.

CHAP. IX.—ONE AND THE SAME GOD, THE CREATOR OF HEAVEN AND EARTH, IS HE WHOM THE PROPHETS FORETOLD, AND WHO WAS DECLARED BY THE GOSPEL. PROOF OF THIS, AT THE OUTSET, FROM ST. MATTHEW'S GOSPEL.

1. This, therefore, having been clearly demonstrated here (and it shall yet be so still more clearly), that neither the prophets, nor the apostles, nor the Lord Christ in His own person, did acknowledge any other Lord or God, but the God and Lord supreme: the prophets and the apostles confessing the Father and the Son; but naming no other as God, and confessing no other as Lord: and the Lord Himself handing down to His disciples, that He, the Father, is the only God and Lord, who alone is God and ruler of all;—it is incumbent on us to follow, if we are their disciples indeed, their testimonies to this effect. For Matthew the apostle—knowing, as one and the same God, Him who had given promise to Abraham, that He would make his seed as the stars of heaven,[2] and Him who, by His Son Christ Jesus, has called us to the knowledge of Himself, from the worship of stones, so that those who were not a people were made a people, and she beloved who was not beloved[3]—declares that John, when preparing the way for Christ, said to those who were boasting of their relationship [to Abraham] according to the flesh, but who had their mind tinged and stuffed with all manner of evil, preaching that repentance which should call them back from their evil doings, said, "O generation of vipers, who hath shown you to flee from the wrath to come? Bring forth therefore fruit meet for repentance. And think not to say within yourselves, We have Abraham [to our] father: for I say unto you, that God is able of these stones to raise up children unto Abraham."[4] He preached to them, therefore, the repentance from wickedness, but he did not declare to them another God, besides Him who made the promise to Abraham; he, the forerunner of Christ, of whom Matthew again says, and Luke likewise, "For this is he that was spoken of from the Lord by the prophet, The voice of one crying in the wilderness, Prepare ye the way of the Lord, make straight the paths of our God. Every valley shall be filled, and every mountain and hill brought low; and the crooked shall be made straight, and the rough into smooth ways; and all flesh shall see the salvation of God."[5] There is therefore one and the same God, the Father of our Lord, who also promised, through the prophets, that He would send His forerunner; and His salvation—that is, His Word—He caused to be made visible to all flesh, [the Word] Himself being made incarnate, that in all things their King might become manifest. For it is necessary that those [beings] which are judged do see the judge, and know Him from whom they receive judgment; and it is also proper, that those which follow on to glory should know Him who bestows upon them the gift of glory.

2. Then again Matthew, when speaking of the angel, says, "The angel of the Lord appeared ← to Joseph in sleep."[6] Of what Lord he does himself interpret: "That it may be fulfilled which was spoken of the Lord by the prophet, Out of Egypt have I called my son."[7] "Behold, a virgin shall conceive, and shall bring forth a son, and they shall call his name Emmanuel; which is, being interpreted, God with us."[8] David likewise speaks of Him who, from the virgin, is Emmanuel: "Turn not away the face of Thine anointed. The LORD hath sworn a truth to David, and will not turn from him. Of the fruit of thy body will I set upon thy seat."[9] And again: "In Judea is God known; His place has been made in peace, and His dwelling in Zion."[10] Therefore there is one and the same God, who was proclaimed by the prophets and announced by the Gospel; and His Son, who was of the fruit of David's body, that is, of the virgin of [the house of] David, and Emmanuel; whose star also Balaam thus prophesied: "There shall come a star out of Jacob, and a

1 Ps. cxv. 3.
2 Gen. xv. 5.
3 Rom. ix. 25.
4 Matt. iii. 7.
5 Matt. iii. 3.
→ 6 Matt. i. 20.
7 Matt. ii. 15.
8 Matt. i. 23.
9 Ps. cxxxii. 11.
10 Ps. lxxvi. 1.

I

leader shall rise in Israel."[1]
that the Magi, coming from
"For we have seen His sta
come to worship Him;"[2]
led by the star into the
Emmanuel, they showed,
they offered, who it was t
*myrrh*, because it was He w
buried for the mortal huma
He was a King, "of whose
and *frankincense*, because
"was made known in Jud
clared to those who sought
3. And then, [speaking
Matthew says, "The heave
He saw the Spirit of God
upon Him: and lo a voice
This is my beloved Son,
pleased."[6] For Christ did
scend upon Jesus, neither
Jesus another: but the Wor
Saviour of all, and the ruler
who is Jesus, as I have alre
did also take upon Him fle
by the Spirit from the Fath
Christ, as Esaias also says,
forth a rod from the root o
shall rise from his root; a
shall rest upon Him: the
understanding, the spirit o
the spirit of knowledge and
of the fear of God, shall fill
judge according to glory,[7]
manner of speech; but H
ment to the humble man, an
ones of the earth."[8] And
ing out beforehand His un
why he was anointed, doe
Spirit of God is upon M
anointed Me: He hath se
Gospel to the lowly, to h
heart, to proclaim liberty
sight to the blind; to ann
year of the Lord, and the
comfort all that mourn."[9]
Word of God was man fro
and son of Abraham, in
Spirit of God rest upon H
to preach the Gospel to the
as He was God, He did no

1 Num xxiv. 17.
2 Matt. ii. 2.
3 Luke i. 33.
4 Ps. lxxvi. 1.
5 Isa. lxv. 1. [A beautiful idea for
be pressed dogmatically.]
6 Matt. iii. 16.
7 This is after the version of the S
but the word δόξα may have the mea
If this be admitted here, the passag
sense as it does in the authorized vers
the sight of His eyes."
8 Isa. xi. 1, etc.
9 Isa. lxi. 1.

THE ANTE-NICENE FATHERS, vol. I

ACCORDING TO

# MATTHEW

1 The book of the history[a] of Jesus Christ, son of David,[b] son of Abraham:[c]
2 Abraham became father to Isaac;[d]
Isaac became father to Jacob;[e]
Jacob became father to Judah[f] and his brothers;
3 Judah became father to Pe'rez[g] and to Ze'rah by Ta'mar;
Pe'rez became father to Hez'ron;[h]
Hez'ron became father to Ram;[i]
4 Ram became father to Am-min'a-dab;
Am-min'a-dab became father to Nah'shon;[j]
Nah'shon became father to Sal'mon;[k]
5 Sal'mon became father to Bo'az by Ra'hab;[l]
Bo'az became father to O'bed by Ruth;[m]
O'bed became father to Jes'se;[n]
6 Jes'se became father to David[o] the king.[p]
David became father to Sol'o-mon[q] by the wife of U-ri'ah;
7 Sol'o-mon became father to Re-ho-bo'am;[r]
Re-ho-bo'am became father to A-bi'jah;
A-bi'jah[s] became father to A'sa;[t]
8 A'sa became father to Je-hosh'a-phat;[u]
Je-hosh'a-phat became father to Je-ho'ram;[v]
Je-ho'ram became father to Uz-zi'ah;
9 Uz-zi'ah became father to Jo'tham;
Jo'tham[w] became father to A'haz;[x]
A'haz became father to Hez-e-ki'ah;[y]

CHAP. 1 a Ge 5:1 b 1Ch 17:11 Mt 9:27 Lu 1:32 c Ge 22:18 d Ge 21:3 1Ch 1:28 Lu 3:34 e Ge 25:26 1Ch 1:34 f Ge 29:35 g Ge 38:29 1Ch 2:4 h Ru 4:18 Lu 3:33 i 1Ch 2:9 j Nu 2:3 Ru 4:20 1Ch 2:10 Lu 3:32 k 1Ch 2:11 l Jos 2:1 m Ru 4:13 n 1Ch 2:12 o Ru 4:17 1Ch 2:15 p 2Sa 5:4 q 2Sa 12:24 1Ch 3:5 Lu 3:31 r 1Ki 11:43 s 1Ch 3:10 t 2Ch 14:1 u 1Ki 15:24 v 1Ch 3:11 2Ch 21:1 w 2Ki 15:32 x 2Ki 15:38 y 2Ki 16:1 1Ch 3:13

Second Col. a 2Ki 20:21 b 2Ki 21:18 c 2Ch 33:20 d 2Ki 21:24 1Ch 3:14 e 2Ki 23:34 f 1Ch 3:15 1Ch 3:16 Jer 28:4 g 2Ki 24:15 2Ch 36:10 Jer 27:20 Jer 29:2 h 1Ch 3:17 Lu 3:27 i 1Ch 3:19 Ezr 3:2 Ne 12:1 Lu 3:27 j Mt 13:55 Mr 6:3 k Mt 27:17

10 Hez-e-ki'ah became father to Ma-nas'seh;[a]
Ma-nas'seh[b] became father to A'mon;[c]
A'mon[d] became father to Jo-si'ah;
11 Jo-si'ah[e] became father to Jec-o-ni'ah[f] and to his brothers at the time of the deportation to Babylon.[g]
12 After the deportation to Babylon Jec-o-ni'ah became father to She-al'ti-el;[h]
She-al'ti-el became father to Ze-rub'ba-bel;[i]
13 Ze-rub'ba-bel became father to A-bi'ud;
A-bi'ud became father to E-li'a-kim;
E-li'a-kim became father to A'zor;
14 A'zor became father to Za'dok;
Za'dok became father to A'chim;
A'chim became father to E-li'ud;
15 E-li'ud became father to El-e-a'zar;
El-e-a'zar became father to Mat'than;
Mat'than became father to Jacob;
16 Jacob became father to Joseph the husband of Mary, of whom Jesus was born,[j] who is called Christ.[k]
17 All the generations, then,
from Abraham until David were
fourteen generations, and from
David until the deportation to
Babylon fourteen generations,
and from the deportation to
Babylon until the Christ fourteen generations.
18 But the birth of Jesus
Christ was in this way. During the time his mother Mary

1216

1217 Jesus born. Astrologers. Flee to Egypt **MATTHEW 1:19—2:15**

was promised[a] in marriage to
Joseph, she was found to be
pregnant by holy spirit[b] before
they were united. 19 How-
ever, Joseph her husband, because he was righteous and did
not want to make her a public spectacle,[c] intended to di-
vorce[d] her secretly. 20 But after he had thought these things
→ over, look! Jehovah's angel appeared to him in a dream, saying: "Joseph, son of David, do
not be afraid to take Mary
your wife home, for that which
has been begotten in her is
by holy spirit.[e] 21 She will
give birth to a son, and you
must call his name Jesus,[f] for
he will save[g] his people[h] from
their sins."[i] 22 All this actually came about for that to be
fulfilled which was spoken by
Jehovah[j] through his prophet,[k]
saying: 23 "Look! The virgin[l]
will become pregnant and will
give birth to a son, and they
will call his name Im-man'u-
el,"[m] which means, when translated, "With Us Is God."[n]
24 Then Joseph woke up
from his sleep and did as the
angel of Jehovah had directed
him, and he took his wife home.
25 But he had no intercourse[o]
with her until she gave birth to
a son;[p] and he called his name
Jesus.[q]
2 After Jesus had been born
in Beth'le-hem[r] of Ju-de'a in
the days of Herod[s] the king,
look! astrologers[t] from eastern parts came to Jerusalem,
2 saying: "Where is the one
born king[u] of the Jews? For we
saw his star[v] [when we were] in
the east, and we have come to do
him obeisance." 3 At hearing
this King Herod was agitated,
and all Jerusalem along with
him; 4 and on gathering together all the chief priests and
scribes of the people he began
to inquire of them where the
Christ was to be born. 5 They
said to him: "In Beth'le-hem[w]
of Ju-de'a; for this is how it

CHAP. 1 a Lu 1:27 b Lu 1:35 c De 22:23 d De 24:1 e Lu 1:35 f Mt 1:25 Lu 1:31 Lu 2:21 g Lu 2:30 Heb 7:25 h Ac 5:31 i Joh 1:29 Ac 4:12 Eph 1:7 1Pe 2:24 j Isa 55:11 k Jas 5:10 1Pe 1:21 l Isa 7:14 m Isa 8:8 n Isa 8:10 o Lu 1:34 p Lu 2:7 q Lu 1:31 Lu 2:21

CHAP. 2 r Mic 5:2 Lu 2:4 s Lu 1:5 t Da 1:20 u Ge 49:10 Mt 27:37 v Isa 47:13 Mt 2:9 w Joh 7:42

Second Col. a Mic 5:2 b Isa 44:28 c 2Sa 5:2 d Ps 37:12 Pr 19:11 e Mt 2:2 f Mt 2:22 g Mt 1:20 Mt 2:19 h Mt 5:17

has been written through the
prophet, 6 'And you, O Beth'-
le-hem[a] of the land of Judah, are
by no means the most insignificant [city] among the governors
of Judah; for out of you will
come forth a governing one,[b]
who will shepherd[c] my people,
Israel.'"
7 Then Herod secretly sum-
moned the astrologers and carefully ascertained from them the
time of the star's appearing;
8 and, when sending them to
Beth'le-hem, he said: "Go make
a careful search for the young
child, and when YOU have found
it report back to me, that I too
may go and do it obeisance."[d]
9 When they had heard the
king, they went their way; and,
look! the star they had seen
[when they were] in the east[e]
went ahead of them, until it
came to a stop above where
the young child was. 10 On
seeing the star they rejoiced
very much indeed. 11 And
when they went into the house
they saw the young child with
Mary its mother, and, falling
down, they did obeisance to it.
They also opened their treasures and presented it with
gifts, gold and frankincense and
myrrh. 12 However, because
they were given divine warning[f] in a dream not to return to
Herod, they withdrew to their
country by another way.
13 After they had with-
drawn, look! Jehovah's angel[g]
appeared in a dream to Joseph, saying: "Get up, take the
young child and its mother
and flee into Egypt, and stay
there until I give you word;
for Herod is about to search
for the young child to destroy
it." 14 So he got up and took
along the young child and its
mother by night and withdrew
into Egypt, 15 and he stayed
there until the decease of Herod, for that to be fulfilled[h]
which was spoken by Jeho-
vah through his prophet, say-

NEW WORLD TRANSLATION OF THE HOLY SCRIPTURES, 1984

every Scripture of
.t with an uplifted
liscord. For these
ve themselves the
and they set their
ie God who made
pinions on what is
standing. For this
3e not wise beyond
but be wise pru-
forth by eating of
:n (that knowledge
ould do) from the
:adise the Lord has
Iis call, "summing
are in heaven, and
e things in heaven
arth constitute the
: (*secundum homi-*
iings, therefore, He
uniting man to the
t to dwell in man,
i of the Spirit, and
iead of man: for
see, and hear, and

(EAD OF ALL THINGS
'AS FITTING THAT HE
THER, THE CREATOR
HUMAN NATURE, AND
:AN, THAT HE MIGHT
CARRY OFF A GLORI-

is work of recapitu-
;s, both waging war
shing him who had
y captives in Adam,
. as thou canst per-
said to the serpent,
:ween thee and the
eed and her seed;
or (*observabit*[9]) thy
ch for His heel."[10]
should be born of
he Virgin, after the
ied as keeping watch
This is the seed of
: Epistle to the Gala-
was established until
om the promise was
)ited in a still clearer
iere he thus speaks:
:ime was come, God

*r been confounded.*



sent forth His Son, made of a woman."[1] For indeed the enemy would not have been fairly vanquished, unless it had been a man [born] of a woman who conquered him. For it was by means of a woman that he got the advantage over man at first, setting himself up as man's opponent. And therefore does the Lord profess Himself to be the Son of man, comprising in Himself that original man out of whom the woman was fashioned (*ex quo ea quæ secundum mulierem est plasmatio facta est*), in order that, as our species went down to death through a vanquished man, so we may ascend to life again through a victorious one; and as through a man death received the palm [of victory] against us, so again by a man we may receive the palm against death.

2. Now the Lord would not have recapitulated in Himself that ancient and primary enmity against the serpent, fulfilling the promise of the Creator (*Demiurgi*), and performing His command, if He had come from another Father. But as He is one and the same, who formed us at the beginning, and sent His Son at the end, the Lord did perform His command, being made of a woman, by both destroying our adversary, and perfecting man after the image and likeness of God. And for this reason He did not draw the means of confounding him from any other source than from the words of the law, and made use of the Father's commandment as a help towards the destruction and confusion of the apostate angel. Fasting forty days, like Moses and Elias, He afterwards hungered, first, in order that we may perceive that He was a real and substantial man—for it belongs to a man to suffer hunger when fasting; and secondly, that His opponent might have an opportunity of attacking Him. For as at the beginning it was by means of food that [the enemy] persuaded man, although not suffering hunger, to transgress God's commandments, so in the end he did not succeed in persuading Him that was an hungered to take that food which proceeded from God. For, when tempting Him, he said, "If thou be the Son of God, command that these stones be made bread."[2] But the Lord repulsed him by the commandment of the law, saying, "It is written, Man doth not live by bread alone."[3] As to those words [of His enemy,] "If thou be the Son of God," [the Lord] made no remark; but by thus acknowledging His human nature He baffled His adversary, and exhausted the force of his first attack by means of His Father's word. The corruption of man, therefore, which occurred in paradise by both [of our first parents] eating, was done away with by [the Lord's] want of food in this world.[4] But he, being thus vanquished by the law, endeavoured again to make an assault by himself quoting a commandment of the law. For, bringing Him to the highest pinnacle of the temple, he said to Him, "If thou art the Son of God, cast thyself down. For it is written, That God shall give His angels charge concerning thee, and in their hands they shall bear thee up, lest perchance thou dash thy foot against a stone;"[5] thus concealing a falsehood under the guise of Scripture, as is done by all the heretics. For that was indeed written, [namely], "That He hath given His angels charge concerning Him;" but "cast thyself down from hence" no Scripture said in reference to Him: this kind of persuasion the devil produced from himself. The Lord therefore confuted him out of the law, when He said, "It is written again, Thou shalt not tempt the LORD thy God;"[6] pointing out by the word contained in the law that which is the duty of man, that he should not tempt God; and in regard to Himself, since He appeared in human form, [declaring] that He would not tempt the LORD his God.[7] The pride of reason, therefore, which was in the serpent, was put to nought by the humility found in the man [Christ], and now twice was the devil conquered from Scripture, when he was detected as advising things contrary to God's commandment, and was shown to be the enemy of God by [the expression of] his thoughts. He then, having been thus signally defeated, and then, as it were, concentrating his forces, drawing up in order all his available power for falsehood, in the third place "showed Him all the kingdoms of the world, and the glory of them,"[8] saying, as Luke relates, "All these will I give thee,—for they are delivered to me; and to whom I will, I give them,—if thou wilt fall down and worship me." The Lord then, exposing him in his true character, says, "Depart, Satan; for it is written, Thou shalt worship the Lord thy God, and Him only shalt thou serve."[9] He both revealed him by this name, and showed [at the same time] who He Himself was. For the Hebrew word "Satan" signifies an apostate. And thus, vanquishing him for the third time, He spurned him from Him finally as being conquered out of the law; and there was done away with that infringement of God's commandment which had occurred in Adam, by means of the precept of the law, which the Son of man ob-

[1] Gal. iv. 4.
[2] Matt. iv. 3.
[3] Deut. viii. 3.

[4] The Latin of this obscure sentence is: Quæ ergo fuit in Paradiso repletio hominis per duplicem gustationem, dissoluta est per eam, quæ fuit in hoc mundo, indigentiam. Harvey thinks that *repletio* is an error of the translation reading ἀναπλήρωσις for ἀναπήρωσις. This conjecture is adopted above.
[5] Ps. lxxxix. 11.
[6] Deut. vi. 16.
[7] This sentence is one of great obscurity.
[8] Luke iv. 6, 7.
[9] Matt. iv. 10.

THE ANTE-NICENE FATHERS, Vol. I

MATTHEW 2:16—3:15 Herod kills young boys. John preaches 1218

ing: "Out of Egypt[a] I called my
son."
16 Then Herod, seeing he
had been outwitted by the
astrologers, fell into a great
rage, and he sent out and had
all the boys in Beth'le-hem
and in all its districts done
away with, from two years of
age and under, according to
the time that he had carefully ascertained from the astrologers.[b] 17 Then that was
fulfilled which was spoken
through Jeremiah the prophet,
saying: 18 "A voice was heard
in Ra'mah,[c] weeping and much
wailing; it was Rachel[d] weeping for her children, and she
was unwilling to take comfort,
because they are no more."
19 When Herod had de-
ceased, look! Jehovah's angel
appeared in a dream[e] to Joseph in Egypt 20 and said:
"Get up, take the young child
and its mother and be on your
way into the land of Israel, for
those who were seeking the soul
of the young child are dead."
21 So he got up and took the
young child and its mother and
entered into the land of Israel.
22 But hearing that Ar-che-la'-
us ruled as king of Ju-de'a instead of his father Herod, he became afraid to depart for there.
Moreover, being given divine
warning in a dream,[f] he withdrew into the territory of Gal'-
i-lee,[g] 23 and came and dwelt
in a city named Naz'a-reth,[h]
that there might be fulfilled
what was spoken through the
prophets: "He will be called a
Naz-a-rene'."[i]

3 In those days John the Baptist[j] came preaching in the
wilderness[k] of Ju-de'a, 2 saying: "REPENT,[l] for the kingdom of the heavens has drawn
near."[m] 3 This, in fact, is the
one spoken of through Isaiah
the prophet[n] in these words:
"Listen! Someone is crying out
in the wilderness, 'Prepare[o]
the way of Jehovah, YOU people! Make his roads straight.'"
4 But this very John had his
clothing of camel's hair[a] and a
leather girdle[b] around his loins;
his food too was insect locusts[c]
and wild honey.[d] 5 Then Jerusalem and all Ju-de'a and all
the country around the Jordan
made their way out to him,
6 and people were baptized by
him in the Jordan River,[e] openly confessing their sins.
7 When he caught sight of
many of the Pharisees and Sadducees[f] coming to the baptism,
he said to them: "YOU offspring
of vipers,[g] who has intimated
to YOU to flee from the coming wrath?[h] 8 So then produce fruit that befits repentance;[i] 9 and do not presume
to say to yourselves, 'As a father we have Abraham.'[j] For I
say to YOU that God is able to
raise up children to Abraham[k]
from these stones. 10 Already
the ax[l] is lying at the root of
the trees; every tree, then, that
does not produce fine fruit is
to be cut down[m] and thrown
into the fire.[n] 11 I, for my
part, baptize YOU with water[o]
because of YOUR repentance;[p]
but the one coming[q] after me is
stronger than I am, whose san-
dals I am not fit to take off.[r]
That one will baptize YOU people with holy spirit[s] and with
fire.[t] 12 His winnowing shov-
el is in his hand, and he will
completely clean up his thresh-
ing floor, and will gather his
wheat into the storehouse,[u] but
the chaff he will burn[v] up with
fire that cannot be put out."
13 Then Jesus came from
Gal'i-lee[w] to the Jordan to John,
in order to be baptized[x] by him.
14 But the latter tried to prevent him, saying: "I am the one
needing to be baptized by you,
and are you coming to me?"
15 In reply Jesus said to him:
"Let it be, this time, for in that
way it is suitable for us to carry out all that is righteous."[y]
Then he quit preventing him.

1219 Jesus baptized. 3 tests. John arrested MATTHEW 3:16—4:24

16 After being baptized Jesus
immediately came up from the
water; and, look! the heavens were opened up,[a] and he
saw descending like a dove[b]
God's spirit coming upon him.[c]
17 Look! Also, there was a
voice[d] from the heavens that
said: "This is my Son,[e] the beloved,[f] whom I have approved."[g]

4 Then Jesus was led by the
spirit up into the wilderness[h] to be tempted[i] by the
Devil. 2 After he had fasted
forty days and forty nights,[j]
then he felt hungry. 3 Also,
the Tempter[k] came and said
to him: "If you are a son of
God,[l] tell these stones to become loaves of bread." 4 But
in reply he said: "It is written,
'Man must live, not on bread
alone, but on every utterance
coming forth through Jehovah's
mouth.'"[m]
5 Then the Devil took him
along into the holy city,[n] and
he stationed him upon the bat-
tlement of the temple 6 and
said to him: "If you are a son
of God, hurl yourself down;[o]
for it is written, 'He will give
his angels a charge concerning
you, and they will carry you on
their hands, that you may at no
time strike your foot against a
stone.'"[p] 7 Jesus said to him:
"Again it is written, 'You must
not put Jehovah your God to
the test.'"[q]
8 Again the Devil took him
along to an unusually high
mountain, and showed him all
the kingdoms of the world[r] and
their glory, 9 and he said to
him: "All these things I will
give you[s] if you fall down and
do an act of worship to me."[t]
10 Then Jesus said to him: "Go
away, Satan! For it is written,
→ 'It is Jehovah your God you
must worship,[u] and it is to him
alone[v] you must render sacred
service.'"[w] 11 Then the Devil
left him,[x] and, look! angels came
and began to minister to him.[y]
12 Now when he heard
that John had been arrest-
ed,[a] he withdrew into Gal'i-lee.[b]
13 Further, after leaving Naz'-
a-reth, he came and took up residence in Ca-per'na-um[c] beside
the sea in the districts of Zeb'-
u-lun and Naph'ta-li,[d] 14 that
there might be fulfilled what
was spoken through Isaiah the
prophet, saying: 15 "O land of
Zeb'u-lun and land of Naph'ta-li,
along the road of the sea, on the
other side of the Jordan, Gal'-
i-lee[e] of the nations! 16 the
people sitting in darkness[f] saw a
great light,[g] and as for those sitting in a region of deathly shadow, light[h] rose[i] upon them."
17 From that time on Jesus
commenced preaching and saying: "Repent,[j] YOU people, for
the kingdom[k] of the heavens
has drawn near."
18 Walking alongside the sea
of Gal'i-lee he saw two brothers, Simon[l] who is called Peter[m] and Andrew his brother,
letting down a fishing net into
the sea, for they were fishers.
19 And he said to them: "Come
after me, and I will make YOU
fishers of men."[n] 20 At once
abandoning the nets,[o] they followed him. 21 Going on also
from there he saw two others[p] [who were] brothers, James
[the son] of Zeb'e-dee[q] and John
his brother, in the boat with
Zeb'e-dee their father, mending
their nets, and he called them.
22 At once leaving the boat and
their father, they followed him.
23 Then he went around[r]
throughout the whole of Gal'-
i-lee,[s] teaching in their synagogues[t] and preaching the
good news of the kingdom
and curing every sort of disease[u] and every sort of infirmity among the people. 24 And
the report about him went
out into all Syria;[v] and they
brought him all those faring

NEW WORLD TRANSLATION OF THE HOLY SCRIPTURES, 1984

# Christians and the Name

NO ONE can say for sure exactly when orthodox Jews ceased to pronounce God's name out loud and instead substituted the Hebrew words for God and Sovereign Lord. Some believe that God's name passed out of everyday use well before Jesus' time. But there is strong evidence that the high priest continued to pronounce it at religious services at the temple—particularly on the day of Atonement—right up until the temple was destroyed in 70 C.E. Hence, when Jesus was on earth, the pronunciation of the name was known, although perhaps it was not widely used.

Why did the Jews cease to pronounce God's name? Probably, at least in part, because of misapplying the words of the third commandment: "You must not take up the name of Jehovah your God in a worthless way." (Exodus 20:7) Of course, this commandment did not prohibit the *use* of God's name. Otherwise, why did God's ancient servants such as David use it so freely and still enjoy Jehovah's blessing? And why did God pronounce it to Moses and tell Moses to explain to the Israelites who it was that had sent him?—Psalm 18:1-3, 6, 13; Exodus 6:2-8.

**This picture of a Jewish high priest, with the sign on his turban in Hebrew meaning "Holiness Belongs to Jehovah," is found in the Vatican**

Nevertheless, by Jesus' time there was a strong tendency to take the reasonable commands of God and interpret them in a highly unreasonable way. For example, the fourth of the Ten Commandments obligated the Jews to observe the seventh day of each week as a day of rest, a Sabbath. (Exodus 20:8-11) Orthodox Jews took that command to ridiculous lengths, making innumerable rules to govern even the smallest act that could or could not be done on the Sabbath. It was doubtless in the same spirit that they took a reasonable command, that God's name must not be dishonored, to a most unreasonable extreme, saying that the name should not even be pronounced.*

### Jesus and the Name

Would Jesus have followed such an unscriptural tradition? Hardly! He certainly did not hold back from doing works of healing on the Sabbath, even though this meant breaking the man-made rules of the Jews and even risking his life. (Matthew 12:9-14) In fact, Jesus condemned the Pharisees as hypocrites because their traditions went beyond God's inspired Word.

* Some suggest another reason: The Jews may have been influenced by Greek philosophy. For example, Philo, a Jewish philosopher of Alexandria who was approximately contemporary with Jesus, was greatly influenced by the Greek philosopher Plato, who he thought was divinely inspired. The *Lexikon des Judentums* (Lexicon of Judaism), under "Philo," states that Philo "united the language and ideas of Greek philosophy (Plato) with the revealed faith of the Jews" and that to begin with he "had a visible effect upon the Christian church fathers." Philo taught that God was indefinable and, hence, unnameable.



16 nem Bey
Nazareth
kam, de
Gewohnh
die Syn
17 er auf,
reichte ih
ten Jsaia
18 fiel er a
werde vo
getrieben
um den i
richt zu
19 trübten
genen die
die Oeffn

**As this 1805 G**
**translation of t**
**indicates, when**
**read in the syn**
**from the scroll**
**he pronounced**
**out loud.—Luk**

(Matthew 15:1
ly that he wou
pronouncing (
in view of the
Jesus, meant "J

On one occ
a synagogue ar
scroll of Isaial
was what we t
where God's n
once. (Luke 4
refused to pro
there, substitu
Of course, n
meant followi
dition of the
Rather, we r
them as a pe
and *not* as th
7:29.

In fact, as
taught his fol

**ad containing**
**ns God's name**
**pt (left), a copy**
**iose same verses**
**.ord")**

: that we should
*Jehovah*. Hence,
.eve in Jesus, our
ıked with a prop-
ɔd's name.
ınstrates how the
of God from the
tributed to con-
vah in the minds
!y, it contributed
lopment of the
:y!

**Be Restored?**

· have any right
in view of the
nuscripts do not
l have that right.
: recognize that
'd" in the Bible
r example, in its
:ek word *Ky'ri·os*
s *A Greek and*
: *New Testament*
's that it means
*Lord* and sover-
:sually in Sept[u-
יְהוָה *Jehovah*."
re the Christian
rs quote the ear-
s, the translator
nder the word
" wherever the

divine name appeared in the Hebrew original.

Many translators have done this. Starting at least from the 14th century, numerous Hebrew translations were made of the Christian Greek Scriptures. What did the translators do when they came to quotations from the "Old Testament" where God's name appeared? Often, they felt forced to restore God's name to the text. Many translations of parts or all of the Christian Greek Scriptures into Hebrew contain God's name.

Translations into modern languages, particularly those used by missionaries, have followed this example. Thus many African, Asian, American and Pacific-island language versions of the Greek Scriptures use the name Jehovah liberally, so that readers can clearly see the difference between the true God and the false ones. The name has appeared, too, in versions in European languages.

One translation that boldly restores God's name with good authority is the *New World Translation of the Christian Greek Scriptures*. This version, currently available in 11 modern languages, including English, has restored God's name every time that a portion of the Hebrew Scriptures containing it is quoted in the Greek Scriptures. Altogether, the name appears with a sound basis 237 times in that translation of the Greek Scriptures.

### Opposition to the Name

In spite of the efforts of many translators to restore God's name in the Bible, there has always been religious pressure to eliminate it. The Jews, while leaving it in their Bibles, refused to pronounce it. Apostate Christians of the second and third centuries removed it when they made copies of Greek Bible manuscripts and left it out when they made translations of the Bible. Translators in modern times have removed it, even when they based their translations on the original Hebrew, where it appears almost 7,000 times. (It appears 6,973 times in the Hebrew text of the *New World Translation of the Holy Scriptures*, 1984 edition.)

How does Jehovah view those who remove his name from the Bible? If you were an author, how would you feel about someone who went to great lengths to remove your name from the book you authored? Translators who object to the name, doing so on account of problems of pronunciation or because of Jewish tradition, might be compared to those who Jesus said "strain out the gnat but gulp down the camel!" (Matthew 23:24) They stumble over these smaller problems but end up creating a major problem—by removing the name of the greatest personage in the universe from the book that he inspired.

**John W. Davis, a missionary in China during the 19th century, explained why he believed that God's name should be in the Bible: "If the Holy Ghost says Jehovah in any given place in the Hebrew, why does the translator not say Jehovah in English or Chinese? What right has he to say, I will use Jehovah in this place and a substitute for it in that? . . . If any one should say that there are cases in which the use of Jehovah would be wrong, let him show the reason why; the *onus probandi* [burden of proof] rests upon him. He will find the task a hard one; for he must answer this simple question,—If in any given case it is wrong to use Jehovah in the translation then why did the inspired writer use it in the original?"—*The Chinese Recorder and Missionary Journal*, Volume VII, Shanghai, 1876.**

The psalmist wrote: "How long, O God, will the adversary keep reproaching? Will the enemy keep treating your name with disrespect forever?"—Psalm 74:10.

The Name 27

This fragment of the *Septuagint* (right) dated to the first century C.E. and containing Zechariah 8:19-21 and 8:23–9:4 is in Jerusalem's Israel Museum. It contains God's name four times, three of which are indicated here. In the Alexandrine Manuscript (left), a copy of the *Septuagint* made 400 years later, God's name has been replaced in those same verses by KY and KC, abbreviated forms of the Greek word *Ky'ri·os* ("Lord").

what about the Greek Scriptures? Well, Bible translators and students came to realize that without God's name, some parts of the Christian Greek Scriptures are very difficult to understand properly. Restoring the name is a big help in increasing the clarity and comprehensibility of this portion of the inspired Bible.

For example, consider the words of Paul to the Romans, as they appear in the *Authorized Version:* "For whosoever shall call upon the name of the Lord shall be saved." (Romans 10:13) Whose name do we have to call on to be saved? Since Jesus is often spoken of as "Lord," and one scripture even says: "Believe on the Lord Jesus Christ, and thou shalt be saved," should we conclude that Paul was here speaking about Jesus?—Acts 16:31, *Authorized Version.*

No, we should not. A marginal reference to Romans 10:13 in the *Authorized Version* points us to Joel 2:32 in the Hebrew Scriptures. If you check that reference, you will find that Paul was actually quoting the words of Joel in his letter to the Romans; and what Joel said in the original Hebrew was: "Everyone who calls on the name of *Jehovah* will get away safe." (*New World Translation*) Yes, Paul meant here that we should call on the name of *Jehovah.* Hence, while we have to believe in Jesus, our salvation is closely linked with a proper appreciation of God's name.

This example demonstrates how the removal of the name of God from the Greek Scriptures contributed to confusing Jesus and Jehovah in the minds of many. Undoubtedly, it contributed greatly to the development of the doctrine of the Trinity!

**Should the Name Be Restored?**

Would a translator have any right to restore the name, in view of the fact that existing manuscripts do not have it? Yes, he would have that right. Most Greek lexicons recognize that often the word "Lord" in the Bible refers to Jehovah. For example, in its section under the Greek word *Ky'ri·os* ("Lord"), Robinson's *A Greek and English Lexicon of the New Testament* (printed in 1859) says that it means "God as *the Supreme Lord* and sovereign of the universe, usually in Sept[uagint] for Heb[rew] יְהוָה *Jehovah.*" Hence, in places where the Christian Greek Scripture writers quote the earlier Hebrew Scriptures, the translator has the right to render the word *Ky'ri·os* as "Jehovah" wherever the



divine name app
original.
Many translat
Starting at least
ry, numerous
were made of
Scriptures. What
when they came
the "Old Testa
name appeared
forced to restor
text. Many trans
of the Christian
Hebrew contain
Translations i
particularly tho
ies, have follow
many African,
Pacific-island la
Greek Scripture
vah liberally, so
ly see the differ
God and the fal
appeared, too, i
languages.
One translati
God's name wit
*New World Tra*
*Greek Scriptures.*
ly available in
including Engli
name every tim
Hebrew Script
quoted in the
gether, the nam
basis 237 time
the Greek Scri

**Oppositi**

In spite of
translators to
the Bible, ther
gious pressure
Jews, while le
refused to p
Christians of
centuries remo
copies of Gree
left it out whe

gions." 12 But A'haz said: "I shall not ask, neither shall I put Jehovah to the test."

13 And he proceeded to say: "Listen, please, O house of David. Is it such a little thing for YOU to tire out men, that YOU should also tire out my God?[a] 14 Therefore Jehovah himself will give YOU men a sign: Look! The maiden[b] herself will actually become pregnant,[c] and she is giving birth to a son,[d] and she will certainly call his name Im·man'u·el. 15 Butter and honey he will eat by the time that he knows how to reject the bad and choose the good.[e] 16 For before the boy will know how to reject the bad and choose the good,[f] the ground of whose two kings you are feeling a sickening dread will be left entirely.[g] 17 Jehovah will bring against you[h] and against your people and against the house of your father days such as have not come since the day of E'phra·im's turning away from alongside Judah,[i] namely, the king of As·syr'i·a.[j]

18 "And it must occur in that day that Jehovah will whistle for the flies that are at the extremity of the Nile canals of Egypt and for the bees[k] that are in the land of As·syr'i·a,[l] 19 and they will certainly come in and settle down, all of them, upon the precipitous torrent valleys and upon the clefts of the crags and upon all the thorn thickets and upon all the watering places.[m]

20 "In that day, by means of a hired razor in the region of the River,[n] even by means of the king of As·syr'i·a,[o] Jehovah will shave the head and the hair of the feet, and it will sweep away even the beard itself.[p]

21 "And it must occur in that day that an individual will preserve alive a young cow of the herd and two sheep.[q] 22 And it must occur that, due to the abundance of the producing of milk, he will eat butter; because butter and honey[a] are what everyone left remaining in the midst of the land will eat.

23 "And it must occur in that day that every place where there used to be a thousand vines, worth a thousand pieces of silver,[b] will come to be—for the thornbushes and for the weeds it will come to be.[c] 24 With arrows and the bow he will come there,[d] because all the land will become mere thornbushes and weeds. 25 And all the mountains that used to be cleared of troublesome plants with a hoe—you will not come there for fear of thornbushes and weeds; and it will certainly become a place for letting bulls loose and a trampling ground of sheep."[e]

8 And Jehovah proceeded to say to me: "Take for yourself a large tablet[f] and write upon it with the stylus of mortal man, 'Ma'her-shal'al-hash-baz.' 2 And let me have attestation[g] for myself by faithful witnesses,[h] U·ri'ah the priest[i] and Zech·a·ri'ah the son of Je·ber·e·chi'ah."

3 Then I went near to the prophetess, and she came to be pregnant and in time gave birth to a son.[j] Jehovah now said to me: "Call his name Ma'her-shal'al-hash-baz, 4 for before the boy will know how to call out,[k] 'My father!' and 'My mother!' one will carry away the resources of Damascus and the spoil of Sa·mar'i·a before the king of As·syr'i·a."[l]

5 And Jehovah proceeded to speak yet further to me, saying: 6 "For the reason that this people has rejected[m] the waters of the Shi·lo'ah[n] that are going gently, and there is exultation[o] over Re'zin and the son of Rem·a·li'ah;[p] 7 even therefore, look! Jehovah is bringing up against them[q] the mighty



and the many waters of the River,[a] the king of As·syr'i·a[b] and all his glory.[c] And he will certainly come up over all his streambeds and go over all his banks 8 and move on through Judah. He will actually flood and pass over.[d] Up to the neck he will reach.[e] And the outspreading of his wings[f] must occur to fill the breadth of your land, O Im·man'u·el!"[g]

9 Be injurious, O YOU peoples, and be shattered to pieces; and give ear, all YOU in distant parts of the earth![h] Gird yourselves,[i] and be shattered to pieces![j] Gird yourselves, and be shattered to pieces! 10 Plan out a scheme, and it will be broken up![k] Speak any word, and it will not stand, for God is with us![l] 11 For this is what Jehovah has said to me with strongness of the hand, that he may make me turn aside from walking in the way of this people, saying: 12 "YOU men must not say, 'A conspiracy!' respecting all that of which this people keep saying, 'A conspiracy!'[m] and the object of their fear YOU men must not fear, nor must YOU tremble at it.[n] 13 Jehovah of armies—he is the One whom YOU should treat as holy,[o] and he should be the object of YOUR fear,[p] and he should be the One causing YOU to tremble."[q]

14 And he must become as a sacred place;[r] but as a stone to strike against and as a rock over which to stumble[s] to both the houses of Israel, as a trap and as a snare to the inhabitants of Jerusalem.[t] 15 And many among them will be certain to stumble and to fall and be broken, and to be snared and caught.[u]

16 Wrap up the attestation,[v] put a seal about the law among my disciples![w] 17 And I will keep in expectation of Jehovah,[x] who is concealing his face from the house of Jacob,[a] and I will hope in him.[b]

18 Look! I and the children whom Jehovah has given me[c] are as signs[d] and as miracles in Israel from Jehovah of armies, who is residing in Mount Zion.[e]

19 And in case they should say to YOU people: "Apply to the spiritistic mediums[f] or to those having a spirit of prediction who are chirping[g] and making utterances in low tones," is it not to its God that any people should apply?[h] [Should there be application] to dead persons in behalf of living persons?[i] 20 To the law and to the attestation![j]

Surely they will keep saying what is according to this statement[k] that will have no light of dawn.[l] 21 And each one will certainly pass through the land hard pressed and hungry;[m] and it must occur that because he is hungry and has made himself feel indignant, he will actually call down evil upon his king and upon his God[n] and will certainly peer upward. 22 And to the earth he will look, and, lo! distress and darkness,[o] obscurity, hard times and gloominess with no brightness.[p]

9 However, the obscureness will not be as when the land had stress, as at the former time when one treated with contempt the land of Zeb'u·lun and the land of Naph'ta·li[q] and when at the later time one caused [it] to be honored[r]—the way by the sea, in the region of the Jordan, Gal'i·lee of the nations.[s] 2 The people that were walking in the darkness have seen a great light.[t] As for those dwelling in the land of deep shadow,[u] light itself

NEW WORLD TRANSLATION

**1 PETER 2:10—3:7** Subjections. Christ a model. Chaste conduct 1510

that called YOU out of darkness into his wonderful light.[a] 10 For YOU were once not a people, but are now God's people;[b] YOU were those who had not been shown mercy, but are now those who have been shown mercy.[c]

11 Beloved, I exhort YOU as aliens and temporary residents[d] to keep abstaining from fleshly desires,[e] which are the very ones that carry on a conflict against the soul.[f] 12 Maintain YOUR conduct fine among the nations,[g] that, in the thing in which they are speaking against YOU as evildoers, they may as a result of YOUR fine works[h] of which they are eyewitnesses glorify God in the day for [his] inspection.[i]

13 For the Lord's sake subject[j] yourselves to every human creation:[k] whether to a king[l] as being superior 14 or to governors as being sent by him to inflict punishment on evildoers but to praise doers of good.[m] 15 For so the will of God is, that by doing good YOU may muzzle the ignorant talk of the unreasonable men.[n] 16 Be as free people,[o] and yet holding YOUR freedom, not as a blind for badness,[p] but as slaves of God.[q] 17 Honor [men] of all sorts,[r] have love for the whole association of brothers,[s] be in fear of God,[t] have honor for the king.[u]

18 Let house servants be in subjection[v] to [their] owners with all [due] fear,[w] not only to the good and reasonable, but also to those hard to please. 19 For if someone, because of conscience toward God, bears up under grievous things and suffers unjustly, this is an agreeable thing.[x] 20 For what merit is there in it if, when YOU are sinning and being slapped, YOU endure it?[y] But if, when YOU are doing good and YOU suffer,[z] YOU endure it, this is a thing agreeable with God.[a]

21 In fact, to this [course] YOU were called, because even Christ suffered for YOU,[a] leaving YOU a model for YOU to follow his steps closely.[b] 22 He committed no sin,[c] nor was deception found in his mouth.[d] 23 When he was being reviled,[e] he did not go reviling in return.[f] When he was suffering,[g] he did not go threatening, but kept on committing himself to the one[h] who judges righteously. 24 He himself bore our sins[i] in his own body upon the stake,[j] in order that we might be done with sins[k] and live to righteousness. And "by his stripes YOU were healed."[l] 25 For YOU were like sheep, going astray;[m] but now YOU have returned to the shepherd[n] and overseer of YOUR souls.

3 In like manner,[o] YOU wives, be in subjection[p] to YOUR own husbands, in order that, if any are not obedient[q] to the word, they may be won[r] without a word through the conduct of [their] wives,[s] 2 because of having been eyewitnesses of YOUR chaste conduct[t] together with deep respect. 3 And do not let YOUR adornment be that of the external braiding of the hair[u] and of the putting on of gold ornaments[v] or the wearing of outer garments, 4 but let it be the secret person[w] of the heart in the incorruptible [apparel][x] of the quiet and mild spirit,[y] which is of great value in the eyes of God. 5 For so, too, formerly the holy women who were hoping in God used to adorn themselves, subjecting themselves to their own husbands, 6 as Sarah used to obey Abraham, calling him "lord."[z] And YOU have become her children, provided YOU keep on doing good and not fearing any cause for terror.[a]

7 YOU husbands, continue dwelling in like manner[b] with

1511 Weaker vessel. Defense of hope. Baptism **1 PETER 3:8—4:5**

them according to knowledge,[a] assigning them honor[b] as to a weaker vessel, the feminine one, since YOU are also heirs[c] with them of the undeserved favor of life, in order for YOUR prayers not to be hindered.[d]

8 Finally, all of YOU be like-minded,[e] showing fellow feeling, having brotherly affection, tenderly compassionate,[f] humble in mind,[g] 9 not paying back injury for injury[h] or reviling for reviling,[i] but, to the contrary, bestowing a blessing,[j] because YOU were called to this [course], so that YOU might inherit a blessing.

10 For, "he that would love life and see good days,[k] let him restrain his tongue[l] from what is bad and [his] lips from speaking deception,[m] 11 but let him turn away from what is bad[n] and do what is good; let him seek peace and pursue it.[o] 12 For [the] eyes[p] of Jehovah are upon the righteous ones, and his ears are toward their supplication;[q] but [the] face of Jehovah is against those doing bad things."[r]

13 Indeed, who is the man that will harm YOU if YOU become zealous for what is good?[s] 14 But even if YOU should suffer for the sake of righteousness, YOU are happy.[t] However, the object of their fear do not YOU fear,[u] neither become agitated.[v] 15 But sanctify the Christ as Lord in YOUR hearts,[w] always ready to make a defense[x] before everyone that demands of YOU a reason for the hope in YOU, but doing so together with a mild temper[y] and deep respect.

16 Hold a good conscience,[z] so that in the particular in which YOU are spoken against they may get ashamed[a] who are speaking slightingly of YOUR good conduct in connection with Christ.[b] 17 For it is better to suffer because YOU are doing good,[c] if the will of God wishes it, than because YOU are doing evil.[d] 18 Why, even Christ died once for all time concerning sins,[a] a righteous [person] for unrighteous ones,[b] that he might lead YOU to God,[c] he being put to death in the flesh,[d] but being made alive in the spirit.[e] 19 In this [state] also he went his way and preached to the spirits in prison,[f] 20 who had once been disobedient[g] when the patience of God[h] was waiting in Noah's days, while the ark was being constructed,[i] in which a few people, that is, eight souls, were carried safely through the water.[j]

21 That which corresponds to this is also now saving YOU,[k] namely, baptism, (not the putting away of the filth of the flesh, but the request made to God for a good conscience,)[l] through the resurrection of Jesus Christ.[m] 22 He is at God's right hand,[n] for he went his way to heaven; and angels[o] and authorities and powers were made subject to him.[p]

4 Therefore since Christ suffered in the flesh,[q] YOU too arm yourselves with the same mental disposition;[r] because the person that has suffered in the flesh has desisted from sins,[s] 2 to the end that he may live the remainder of [his] time in the flesh,[t] no more for the desires of men, but for God's will.[u] 3 For the time[v] that has passed by is sufficient for YOU to have worked out the will of the nations[w] when YOU proceeded in deeds of loose conduct,[x] lusts, excesses with wine,[y] revelries, drinking matches, and illegal idolatries.[z] 4 Because YOU do not continue running with them in this course to the same low sink of debauchery,[a] they are puzzled and go on speaking abusively of YOU.[b] 5 But these people

NEW WORLD TRANSLATION

## DIALOGUE THREE: Is The "Trinity" Doctrine From Paganism?

▲ 3. Palmyra. Triad of moon god, Lord of Heavens, sun god, c. 1st century C.E.

▲ 5. Kampuchea. Triune Buddhist godhead, c. 12th century C.E.

c. 14th C.E.

▲ 10. Germany Trinity, 20th century C.E.

### *What Influenced It*

THROUGHOUT the ancient world, as far back as Babylonia, the worship of pagan gods grouped in threes, or triads, was common. That influence was also prevalent in Egypt, Greece, and Rome in the centuries before, during, and after Christ. And after the death of the apostles, such pagan beliefs began to invade Christianity.

Historian Will Durant observed: "Christianity did not destroy paganism; it adopted it. . . . From Egypt came the ideas of a divine trinity." And in the book *Egyptian Religion*, Siegfried Morenz notes: "The trinity was a major preoccupation of Egyptian theologians . . . Three gods are combined and treated as a single being, addressed in the singular. In this way the spiritual force of Egyptian religion shows a direct link with Christian theology."

Thus, in Alexandria, Egypt, churchmen of the late third and early fourth centuries, such as Athanasius, reflected this influence as they formulated ideas that led to the Trinity. Their own influence spread, so that Morenz considers "Alexandrian theology as the intermediary between the Egyptian religious heritage and Christianity."

In the preface to Edward Gibbon's *History of Christianity*, we read: "If Paganism was conquered by Christianity, it is equally true that Christianity was corrupted by Paganism. The pure Deism of the first Christians . . . was changed, by the Church of Rome, into the incomprehensible dogma of the trinity. Many of the pagan tenets, invented by the Egyptians and idealized by Plato, were retained as being worthy of belief."

*A Dictionary of Religious Knowledge* notes that many say that the Trinity "is a corruption borrowed from the heathen religions, and ingrafted on the Christian faith." And *The Paganism in Our Christianity* declares: "The origin of the [Trinity] is entirely pagan."

That is why, in the *Encyclopædia of Religion and Ethics*, James Hastings wrote: "In Indian religion, *e.g.*, we meet with the trinitarian group of Brahmā, Siva, and Viṣṇu; and in Egyptian religion with the trinitarian group of Osiris, Isis, and Horus . . . Nor is it only in historical religions that we find God viewed as a Trinity. One recalls in particular the Neo-Platonic view of the Supreme or Ultimate Reality," which is "triadically represented." What does the Greek philosopher Plato have to do with the Trinity?

### *Platonism*

PLATO, it is thought, lived from 428 to 347 before Christ. While he did not teach the Trinity in its present form, his philosophies paved the way for it. Later, philosophical movements that included triadic beliefs sprang up, and these were influenced by Plato's ideas of God and nature.

The French *Nouveau Dictionnaire Universel* (New Universal Dictionary) says of Plato's influence: "The Platonic *trinity*, itself merely a rearrangement of older *trinities* dating back to earlier peoples, appears to be the rational philosophic *trinity* of attributes that gave birth to the three hypostases or divine persons taught by the Christian churches. . . . This Greek philosopher's conception of the divine *trinity* . . . can be found in all the ancient [pagan] religions."

*The New Schaff-Herzog Encyclopedia of Religious Knowledge* shows the influence of this Greek philosophy: "The doctrines of the Logos and the Trinity received their shape from Greek Fathers, who . . . were much influenced, directly or indirectly, by the Platonic philosophy . . . That errors and corruptions crept into the Church from this source can not be denied."

*The Church of the First Three Centuries* says: "The doctrine of the Trinity was of gradual and comparatively late formation; . . . it had its origin in a source entirely foreign from that of the Jewish and Christian Scriptures; . . . it grew up, and was ingrafted on Christianity, through the hands of the Platonizing Fathers."

By the end of the third century C.E., "Christianity" and the new Platonic philosophies became inseparably united. As Adolf Harnack states in *Outlines of the History of Dogma*, church doctrine became "firmly rooted in the soil of Hellenism [pagan Greek thought]. Thereby it became a mystery to the great majority of Christians."

The church claimed that its new doctrines were based on the Bible. But Harnack says: "In reality it legitimized in its midst the Hellenic speculation, the superstitious views and customs of pagan mystery-worship."

In the book *A Statement of Reasons*, Andrews Norton says of the Trinity: "We can

*SHOULD YOU BELIEVE IN THE TRINITY?* 11

Bibliography to the *Trinity* brochure Page 2

27. *The New Encyclopædia Britannica*, 1985, Vol. 11, Micropædia, (Encyclopædia Britannica, Inc., Chicago, IL) p. 928.
28. *A Short History of Christian Doctrine*, by Bernhard Lohse, 1966, (Fortress Press, Philadelphia, PA) p. 38.
29. *The New International Dictionary of New Testament Theology*, Colin Brown, general editor, 1976, Vol. 2, (Zondervan Publishing House, Grand Rapids, MI) p. 84.
30. *Origin and Evolution of Religion*, by E. Washburn Hopkins, 1923, (Yale University Press, New Haven, CT) p. 336.
31. *The Paganism in Our Christianity*, p. 197.
32. *The New International Dictionary of New Testament Theology*, Vol. 2, p. 84.
33. *The Paganism in Our Christianity*, p. 198.
34. *Encyclopædia of Religion and Ethics*, edited by James Hastings, 1922, Vol. XII, (Charles Scribners' Sons, NY) p. 461.
35. *New Catholic Encyclopedia*, 1967, Vol. XIV, p. 299.
36. *The Church of the First Three Centuries*, by Alvan Lamson, 1869 edition, (Horace B. Fuller, Boston, MA) pp. 124, 125.
37. Ibid., pp. 70, 71.
38. Ibid., p. 103.
39. Ibid., pp. 106, 107, 108.
40. Ibid., p. 180.
41. Ibid., pp. 182, 183.
42. Ibid., pp. 56, 57.

How Did the Trinity Doctrine Develop?

43. *Babylon the Great Has Fallen!*, by Watchtower Society, 1963, p. 477.
44. *The Early Church*, by Henry Chadwick, 1967, (Penguin Books Ltd., Harmondsworth, Middlesex, England) pp. 122, 124.
45. *Encyclopædia Britannica*, 1971, Vol. 6, (Encyclopædia Britannica, Inc., Chicago, IL) p. 386.
46. *A Short History of Christian Doctrine*, by Bernhard Lohse, 1966, p. 51.
47. *The New Encyclopædia Britannica*, 1985, Micropædia, Vol. 11, p. 689.
48. *The Encyclopedia Americana*, 1977, Vol. 27, p. 117.
49. *Catholicism*, edited by George Brantl, 1962, pp. 69, 70.
50. *The New Encyclopædia Britannica*, 1985, Micropædia, Vol. 1, pp. 664, 665; *History of Dogma*, by Adolph Harnack, Vol. 4, 1958 edition, (Russell and Russell, NY) p. 136.
51. *Origin and Evolution of Religion*, by E. Washburn Hopkins, 1923, p. 339.
52. *The Encyclopedia Americana*, 1956, p. 294L.
→ 53. *The Story of Civilization: Part III*, Caesar and Christ, by Will Durant, 1944, (Simon and Schuster, NY) p. 595.
→ 54. *Egyptian Religion*, by Siegfried Morenz, 1973, (Cornell University Press, Ithaca, NY) p. 255.
55. Ibid., p. 257.
56. *History of Christianity*, by Edward Gibbon, 1891, (Peter Eckler, No. 35, NY) p. xvi.
57. *A Dictionary of Religious Knowledge*, by Lyman Abbott, 1875, p. 944.
58. *The Paganism in Our Christianity*, p. 197.

from their graves, and the drowned will be drawn up out of the seas. On that dread day all "whose names are not found in the Book of Life" will be "flung into . . . a burning lake of fire and brimstone." [80] The faithful will "gather for God's great banquet, and will eat the bodies of kings, commanders, mighty men . . . the bodies of all men, slaves or freemen, high or low," [81] who have not heeded the call of Christ. A new heaven and earth will be formed, and a New Jerusalem will come down from the hand of God to be a paradise on earth. It will have a foundation of precious stones, buildings of translucent silver or gold, walls of jasper, and each gate a single pearl; through it will run a "river of living water," on whose bank will grow the "tree of life." The reign of evil will be ended for all time; the faithful of Christ will inherit the earth; "there will be no death any longer, nor night, nor any grief or pain." [82]

The influence of the Book of Revelation was immediate, enduring, and profound. Its prophecies of salvation for loyal believers, and of punishment for their enemies, became the sustenance of a persecuted Church. Its theory of the millennium solaced those who mourned the long delay in the second coming of Christ. Its vivid images and brilliant phrases entered into both the popular and the literary speech of Christendom. For nineteen centuries men have interpreted the events of history as fulfillments of its visions; and in some recesses of the white man's world it still gives its dark colors and bitter flavor to the creed of Christ.

It seems incredible that the Apocalypse and the Fourth Gospel should have come from the same hand. The Apocalypse is Jewish poetry, the Fourth Gospel is Greek philosophy. Perhaps the apostle wrote Revelation in justifiable wrath after Nero's persecution, and the Gospel in the mellow metaphysics of his old age (A.D. 90?). His memories of the Master may by this time have faded a bit, so far as one could ever forget Jesus; and doubtless in the isles and cities of Ionia he had heard many an echo of Greek mysticism and philosophy. Plato had set a theme by picturing the Ideas of God as the patterns on which all things were formed; the Stoics had combined these Ideas into the *Logos Spermatikos* or fertilizing wisdom of God; the Neo-Pythagoreans had made the Ideas a divine person; and Philo had turned them into the Logos or Reason of God, a second divine principle, through which God created, and communicated with, the world. If we reread the famous exordium of the Fourth Gospel with all this in mind, and retain the *Logos* of the Greek original in place of the translation *Word*, we perceive at once that John has joined the philosophers:

> In the beginning was the Logos; the Logos was with God, and the Logos was God. . . . All things were made by the Logos; without

CHAP. XXVII

him nc
came i
dwelt

Just as P
Judaism in
lived for tv
Greek philo
of God wa
the Messiah
Christianity
more or les
"you," and
save the los
the future j
this perspec
ground, fad
to the relig
the pagan w
Christian
dying, came
the Greek l
the vehicle
down into
tributed to
trinity, the
ishment; fro
theosophy t
tian creed;
its source.
Syria the re
Dionysus, t
"ages of the
of Darkness
shining in th
ritual so clo
fathers cha
minds.[85] Ch

The Story of Civilization: Part III, Caesar and Christ
by Will Durant, 1944. p 594

him nothing was made that was made. It was by him that all things came into existence. . . . So the Logos became flesh and blood, and dwelt amongst us.

Just as Philo, learned in Greek speculation, had felt a need to rephrase Judaism in forms acceptable to the logic-loving Greeks, so John, having lived for two generations in a Hellenistic environment, sought to give a Greek philosophical tinge to the mystic Jewish doctrine that the Wisdom of God was a living being,[83] and to the Christian doctrine that Jesus was the Messiah. Consciously or not, he continued Paul's work of detaching Christianity from Judaism. Christ was no longer presented as a Jew, living more or less under the Jewish Law; he was made to address the Jews as "you," and to speak of their Law as "yours"; he was not a Messiah sent "to save the lost sheep of Israel," he was the coeternal Son of God; not merely the future judge of mankind, but the primeval creator of the universe. In this perspective the Jewish life of the man Jesus could be put into the background, faded almost as in Gnostic heresy; and the god Christ was assimilated to the religious and philosophical traditions of the Hellenistic mind. Now the pagan world—even the anti-Semitic world—could accept him as its own.

Christianity did not destroy paganism; it adopted it. The Greek mind, dying, came to a transmigrated life in the theology and liturgy of the Church; the Greek language, having reigned for centuries over philosophy, became the vehicle of Christian literature and ritual; the Greek mysteries passed down into the impressive mystery of the Mass. Other pagan cultures contributed to the syncretist result. From Egypt came the ideas of a divine trinity, the Last Judgment, and a personal immortality of reward and punishment; from Egypt the adoration of the Mother and Child, and the mystic theosophy that made Neoplatonism and Gnosticism, and obscured the Christian creed; there, too, Christian monasticism would find its exemplars and its source. From Phrygia came the worship of the Great Mother; from Syria the resurrection drama of Adonis; from Thrace, perhaps, the cult of Dionysus, the dying and saving god. From Persia came millennarianism, the "ages of the world," the "final conflagration," the dualism of Satan and God, of Darkness and Light; already in the Fourth Gospel Christ is the "Light shining in the darkness, and the darkness has never put it out."[84] The Mithraic ritual so closely resembled the eucharistic sacrifice of the Mass that Christian fathers charged the Devil with inventing these similarities to mislead frail minds.[85] Christianity was the last great creation of the ancient pagan world.

The Story of Civilization: Part III, Caesar and Christ
by Will Durant, 1944, p. 595

about the Egyptian saviour hero Imhotep was translated into Greek. The account of this culminates in the characteristic words: 'The entire Greek language will relate thy tale and every Greek will worship Imouthes [Imhotep], son of Ptah.'[93]

In conclusion we may single out from the overwhelming material at least one other point which in its way also demonstrates the main lines of religious development: Grecianizing influence, dissemination abroad, and the bond with the individual in need of salvation. In this case we are thinking not of a deity but of an institution: the mysteries associated with Isis and Osiris, or to be more precise their form and function in the Hellenistic world. These afford impressive proof of the radical transformation which took place in Egyptian custom, despite the many formal parallels between the ancient Egyptian burial ceremonies (in which the deceased becomes Osiris and enters into God by the performance of the funerary rites) and the Hellenistic mysteries (which sought to elevate the mystic to the divine plane by associating him with Isis and Osiris). This transformation consists in the following: in Egypt it was the *dead*, whereas in the Hellenistic world it was the *living* who were so consecrated and thereby saved from their state of worldly terror.[94] Admittedly, it will probably be no coincidence, but rather the effect of Egyptian tradition, that even in the hellenized Isis mysteries the person to be initiated has to traverse the realm of the dead symbolically.[95] As regards the dissemination of the Isis–Osiris mysteries, our chief witness Apuleius suggests that such celebrations took place in Rome as well as Corinth (Kenchreai);[96] indeed, the worship of Egyptian gods is corroborated by many other sources. Finally, the bond with the individual in distress becomes evident from the rite itself, which endeavours to bring the person to be initiated into communion with the deity through acts of a most personal kind.[97] The peculiar charm of the history of these Egypto-Hellenistic mysteries lies in the curious fact of their revival at the time of classical freemasonry – as will be familiar to those who are well acquainted with Mozart's *Magic Flute*. It has remained alive up to the present time, so that one can draw a line connecting Egypt, through Antiquity, with the modern West.



### *Contribution to Old and New Testaments*

The impact of a historical phenomenon may thus be temporal as well as spatial, as our last example shows. The influence of Egyptian religion on posterity is mainly felt through Christianity and its antecedents. Egypt's contribution to the Old Testament is actually a product of that country's relations with Syria; its contribution to the New Testament, indeed even to early Christian theology, must be seen as a special instance of that general influence exerted by Egypt upon the Hellenistic world. It was only when these two religions became established that the Egyptian influences contained within them could be transmitted to later generations. We know that there were major differences between Egyptian religion on the one hand and Judaism and Christianity on the other, since both the latter were scriptural religions, deemed by their adherents to have been revealed by God (see pp. 31 ff., 214 ff.); we therefore cannot expect the Egyptian influence to be very marked. It is rather a matter of certain details which were taken over ready-made by the younger and less developed neighbours of the land on the Nile. Yet such details are not to be despised; the transmission and adoption of minor details accounts for much of the historical continuity between different peoples and ages. In expounding this principle it is to be hoped that we have left no room for any suspicion on the reader's part that in what follows we are either depreciating the role of Judaism or Christianity in the history of religion or overestimating the importance of trivia.

Let us begin with the Old Testament. In the first place we may refer once again to the possibility that a sentence in the Instruction of Ptah-hotep was conceived in a later period of Egyptian history in the following way: 'Take no word away, and add nothing thereto, and put not one thing in the place of another',[98] and that this sentence found its way to Palestine together with Egyptian wisdom literature. There it may have led to the formulation, in an admittedly most effective way, of the central concern of a scriptural religion: the safeguarding of the text against omissions, additions or alterations.[99] Keeping to such rigorous interpretation of the evidence, we may go on to recall the doctrine of creation through the word, which as we know (see pp. 163–6) was one of the principal

by Siegfried Morenz.

elements in the Egyptian cosmogony; this was not published again until the eighth century, and so became relevant for the Late period. It had an effect upon the account of the creation contained in the priestly writing, and thus upon one of the chief elements in the concept of God entertained by the Jews – and passed on by them to the Christians.

Less important, but more readily comprehensible, is the influence of the Egyptian court chronicle upon the literary form of the Israelites' chronicle account of David and Solomon.[100] Here we may mention the traces left by Egyptian royal ritual upon the courts of Israelite rulers,[101] which affected even Isaiah's famous list of appellations for the Prince of Peace. For this, although mutilated, is probably derived from the fivefold titulary of the Egyptian king.[102] The similarity of genres in this case extends even to Mesopotamia. It is also found in the familiar parallels between Egyptian and Israelite wisdom literature, which in general may be regarded as a gift of Egypt. From the standpoint of subject-matter, i.e. judged with an eye to specific points of Old Testament religion, we have here another instance of texts losing some of their significance in transmission. For the Chokma literature, which has a supranational character because it is located in the general area between the Nile and Tigris, does not take us to the heart of Old Testament prophecy. The best known links of this character are those between the Instruction of Amenemope and the Biblical Book of Proverbs. However, in this one case we may not be dealing with an original Egyptian work; the sentences attributed to Amenemope may have been composed in Hebrew or Aramaic, in which case the verses in the Book of Proverbs would be derived in the last instance from Semitic tradition.[103] Other passages can, however, be claimed as Egyptian in inspiration: for instance, the Egyptian (and Mesopotamian) lists of knowledge, which were the basis of the proverbs which King Solomon spoke on all manner of things, ranging from the cedar to the hyssop,[104] or the various Egyptian influences upon the mood, concepts and diction of the so-called 'preacher of Solomon' (Koheleth). We may recall here only the *carpe diem*, recommended on the Nile from the time of the Songs of the Harpers onward (see p. 195), and the concept of καιρός, which we now know to have been common currency in Egypt (see pp. 76 ff.).[105] Finally, examples may be



mentioned which show that Biblical texts had 'local colour' from Egypt, without this involving any borrowings from Egyptian religion. These passages are naturally to be found most frequently where the Old Testament story takes place upon Egyptian soil and where it relates to Egyptian conditions: most notably in the narratives about Joseph.[106]

Here wo can do no more than point out the range of influences transmitted, from major religious values down to minor matters of merely cultural interest. Unfortunately the degree to which this influence is perceptible stands in indirect proportion to the significance of the facts.[107] A few words may be added on the Greek translation of the Old Testament made at Alexandria and known as the Septuagint on account of the seventy translators employed on it. This eventually became almost a kind of holy writ for Christians. It can be demonstrated that the place of translation left its mark on many passages. Certainly these were not of crucial importance; nevertheless it is in the Septuagint that we find an invocation unknown to Israelite or Judaic theology: 'Lord, lord, king of the gods.'[108] In my view this may be explained without difficulty if one assumes that the translators had in mind a designation of God which combined two proper names (κύριος also renders the proper name of Yahveh) with the title 'king of the gods'. This is precisely the case with Amon-Rasonther, i.e. 'Amon-Re, king of the gods', who at that time was still important.[109]

Egypt's links with the religion of the Old Testament have been known and studied for a long time. But hardly any consideration has been given to the fact that the religious forms of the land of the Nile also had an effect upon the New Testament and so upon early Christianity. Such lack of interest can scarcely be due to dogmatic reservations, for if this were so such a ban would also have affected investigations into the contributions of Greek philosophy and the Hellenistic mystery religions, which have long since been recognized. It is rather the case that scholars have failed to appreciate the influence which Egypt had exerted upon the entire Hellenistic world in which Christianity was destined to take shape. By putting matters in this way we wish to make it clear that the contributions which Egypt made to Christianity in its formative stage of evolution should not be seen simply as direct contacts between a particular form developed in Egypt and some-

by Siegfried Morenz

thing morphologically akin in Christianity. It is most important that this point should be properly understood and appreciated. In one of the few cases where a concept that figures in the New Testament has been taken to be ultimately of Egyptian origin, Jesus's parable of Dives and Lazarus, it has quite correctly been assumed that this transmission took place by way of Jewish material.[110] How complex the process may be within the Egyptian tradition itself, and how large a part was played by Greek elements (Stoic diatribes), emerged some years ago from an analysis of the association between ship and tongue in the Epistle of St James, which was originally Egyptian.[111] The way in which Egyptian influence made itself felt is fairly clear in those cases where it first affected images in the Old Testament (including the Apocrypha) which were later taken over by New Testament writers. This seems to me to be the case with two passages in the Epistle to the Romans: the proverbial 'coals of fire' which were to be heaped upon one's enemy – derived from a Late Egyptian penitential rite[112] – and, much more significantly, the Apostle's words on the absolute power of the Creator to confer honour and dishonour, so making a quite arbitrary distinction between his creatures; here St Paul is giving universal currency to a formula that we first hear of with Amenemope.[113]

Finally, the path taken by Egyptian influence can also be followed where the Christian form can be traced back first to an Egypto-Hellenistic one, and this in turn traced back to Egypt itself. This is the case with the acclamation εἷς θεός ('God is One'), used by the earliest Christian communities: this is derived from one employed in the service of Sarapis ('One is Zeus-Sarapis'), and this in turn comes from the early Egyptian theologians' form ('One is Amon', etc.).[114] In most cases, however, intermediary stages cannot as yet be identified. Attempts to establish the lines of transmission must be based upon the fundamental principle which we have formulated above: namely, that Egyptian religion passed on its forms to the Hellenistic world and so enlarged the range of expression available to the latter. In our view this influence makes itself felt, for example, in the much-cited 'second death' in the Revelation of St John, which may owe something to the widely disseminated Egyptian concept of a second mortality.[115] It is also present in the notion of a 'crown of life', or in those of



righteousness and glory; in elucidating these concepts one must draw not only upon Greek material but also upon the 'crown of righteousness' to which there were so many references during the last centuries of Egyptian paganism.[116]

*Egypt's significance for early Christian theology*

These few examples must suffice.[117] The remainder of this chapter will be devoted to a cursory examination of Egypt's significance for early Christian theology. When considering Egyptian religious thought we learned of the phenomenon whereby three gods were combined to form one. Various motives led to the evolution of this concept, which allowed for many shades of interpretation between the two poles of monism and triadism; as we have seen, the trinity was a major preoccupation of Egyptian theologians (see pp. 142 ff.). The evidence quoted above extended down to the Late period; here we may add that we also find such evidence in Greek only one generation before the beginnings of Christian theological speculation on such matters. An amulet dating from the period around A.D. 100, now in the British Museum, bears a distich which forms the accompanying text to a rendering, on the reverse side, of three Egyptian deities: a falcon-headed Bait,[118] a frog-headed Hathor and a winged serpent by the name of Akori.[119] It runs, in prose translation: 'One is Bait, one is Hathor, one is Akori – to these belongs *one* power. Be greeted, father of the world, be greeted, God in three forms (τρίμορφος θεός).'[120] This distich contains the εἷς θεός acclamation just mentioned, which goes back at least to the Amon theology of the Ramesside period; the one God (father of the cosmos) has as his attributes (to use the Egyptian terminology) three *ḫprw* or *bꜣw*, 'forms' or 'appearances'; thus three gods are combined and treated as a single being, addressed in the singular. In this way the spiritual force of Egyptian religion shows a direct link with Christian theology.

In order to avoid any gross misunderstanding, we must at once emphasize that the substance of the Christian Trinity is of course Biblical: Father, Son and Holy Ghost. The three are mentioned alongside one another in the New Testament, probably for liturgical reasons.[121] But one essential point is still lacking for the Trinity in the proper sense: the concept or notion of such a combination. Indeed, there is no sign as yet of an awareness of

by Siegfried Morenz

## DIALOGUE FOUR: Why Is The Father "Greater" Than Jesus —John 14:28?

Scriptures 1280

ined to deliver Israel;[a]
all these things, this
day since these things
ːoreover, certain wom-
us also astonished us,
. been early to the me-
ı but did not find his
ːame saying they had
ːrnatural sight of an-
is alive. 24 Further,
ith us went off to the
and they found it so,
en had said, but they

. to them: "O sense-
ıw in heart to believe
the prophets spoke![d]
cessary for the Christ
things and to enter
27 And commencing
! the Prophets[h] he in-
ı things pertaining to
Scriptures.
y got close to the vil-
were journeying, and
vas journeying on far-
ːy used pressure upon
y with us, because it
; and the day has al-
Vith that he went in
ı. 30 And as he was
m at the meal he took
t, broke it and began
n.[i] 31 At that their
ɔpened and they rec-
he disappeared from
hey said to each oth-
hearts burning* as he
ıs on the road, as he
up the Scriptures to
that very hour they
d to Jerusalem, and
even and those with
ogether, 34 saying:
Lord* was raised up
o Simon!"[k] 35 Now
ːlated the [events] on
he became known to
ːing of the loaf.[l]
ːere speaking of these

ʼ ĸAB; D, "veiled"; Sy[p,h], It[ms c], "blinded." 34* Or,

1281 **Christ ascends to heaven. The "Word"** **LUKE 24:37—JOHN 1:7**

things he himself stood in their midst
[[and said to them: "May YOU have
peace."]]* 37 But because they were
terrified, and had become frightened,[a]
they were imagining they beheld a spirit. 38 So he said to them: "Why are
YOU troubled, and why is it doubts come
up in YOUR hearts? 39 See my hands
and my feet, that it is I myself; feel[b] me
and see, because a spirit does not have
flesh and bones[c] just as YOU behold that
I have." 40 [[And as he said this he
showed them his hands and his feet.]]*
41 But while they were still not believing[d] for sheer joy and were wondering,
he said to them: "Do YOU have something
there to eat?"[e] 42 And they handed
him a piece of broiled fish;*[f] 43 and
he took it and ate it[g] before their eyes.
44 He now said to them: "These are
my words which I spoke to YOU while I
was yet with YOU,[h] that all the things
written in the law of Moses and in the
Prophets[i] and Psalms[j] about me must be
fulfilled." 45 Then he opened up their
minds fully to grasp the meaning of the
Scriptures,[a] 46 and he said to them:
"In this way it is written that the Christ
would suffer and rise from among the
dead on the third day,[b] 47 and on the
basis of his name repentance for forgiveness of sins[c] would be preached in
all the nations[d]—starting out from Jerusalem,[e] 48 YOU are to be witnesses[f]
of these things. 49 And, look! I am
sending forth upon YOU that which is
promised by my Father. YOU, though,
abide in the city until YOU become
clothed with power from on high."[g]
50 But he led them out as far as
Beth'a·ny, and he lifted up his hands and
blessed them.[h] 51 As he was blessing them he was parted from them
and began to be borne up to heaven.*[i]
52 And they did obeisance to him and*
returned to Jerusalem with great joy.[j]
53 And they were continually in the
temple blessing God.[k]

CHAP. 24
a Mt 14:26
b 1Jo 1:1
c 1Co 15:50
d Ge 45:26
e Joh 21:5
f Joh 21:13
g Ac 10:41
h Mt 16:21 Lu 9:22 Joh 5:39
i Lu 24:27
j Ps 2:2 Ps 16:10 Ps 27:12 Ps 69:9 Ps 78:2 Ps 118:22 Ps 132:11

Second Col.
a Joh 12:16
b Isa 53:5 Ho 6:2 Jon 1:17 Mr 9:31
c Ac 5:31 Ac 13:38
d Ge 22:18 1Co 15:12 Ga 3:14 1Ti 3:16
e Ac 4:2 Ac 5:28
f Joh 15:27 Ac 1:8
g Joe 2:28 Joh 14:16 Ac 1:4 Ac 2:4
h De 33:1
i Ac 1:9
j Joh 14:28 Joh 16:22 Ac 1:10 Ac 1:12
k Ac 2:46

Lu 24:36* "And said . . . peace," P[75]ĸAB; DIt omit. 40* According to P[75]ĸABWVgSy[h,p]Arm (compare Joh 20:20); DItSy[c,s] omit vs 40. 42* VgSy[c,p] and mss ENXΔΘ (sixth to tenth cent.) add, "and a honeycomb"; P[75]ĸABDSy[s] omit.

Lu 24:51* "And began to be borne up to heaven," P[75]ĸ[c]ABCWVgSy[p]Arm; ĸ'DSy[s] omit. 52* "Did obeisance to him and," P[75]ĸABCWSy[h,p]; DIt[mss]Sy[s] omit. Compare Heb 1:6.

ACCORDING TO

# JOHN*

1 In [the] beginning[a] the Word*[b] was,
and the Word was with God,*[c] and
the Word was a god.*[d] 2 This one was
in [the] beginning[e] with God.[f] 3 All
things came into existence through
him,[a] and apart from him not even one
thing came into existence.
What has come into existence 4 by
means of him was life,[b] and the life was
the light[c] of men.* 5 And the light is
shining in the darkness,[d] but the darkness has not overpowered it.
6 There arose a man that was sent
forth as a representative of God:[e] his
name was John.*[f] 7 This [man] came

CHAP. 1
a Pr 8:22 Col 1:15 Re 3:14
b Joh 12:50 Re 19:13
c Pr 8:30 Joh 17:5
d Isa 9:6 Joh 1:18 Joh 10:35 Php 2:6
e Ge 1:1 Mic 5:2
f Ge 1:26 Ge 3:22

Second Col.
a Joh 1:10 1Co 8:6 Col 1:16 Heb 1:2

b Joh 5:26; Ac 3:15; 1Jo 1:2; 1Jo 5:11; c Joh 8:12; d Joh 3:19; Joh 12:35; e Lu 3:2; f Mt 3:1; Lu 1:13.

Joh Title* "John." Gr., *I·o·a'nen*, contracted form of the Heb. name *Yoh·cha·nan'*, meaning "Jehovah Has Shown Favor; Jehovah Has Been Gracious." Compare 1Ch 26:3 ftn. 1:1* Or, "the Logos." Gr., *ho lo'gos;* Lat., *Ver'bum;* J[17,18,22](Heb.), *had·Da·var'*. 1* Lit., "was toward the God." Gr., *en pros ton The·on';* J[17,18](Heb.), *ha·yah' 'eth ha·'Elo·him'*. 1* "A god." Gr., *the·os'*, in contrast with *ton The·on'*, "the God," in the same sentence; J[17,18](Heb.), *we'lo·him'*, "and god." For a discussion of "a god," see App 6A.

Joh 1:4* The punctuation of vss 3 and 4 is according to WH, Vg[ww] and *The Greek New Testament* by the United Bible Societies. 6* See Mt 3:1 ftn, "John."

NEW WORLD TRANSLATION - WITH REFERENCES, 1984

THE NICENE CREED (continued)

*process, a variety of creeds were developed. The most important, because of its gaining almost universal acceptance among the major Christian groupings, was the Nicene Creed. It was first promulgated by the Council of Nicea in 325 C.E. and later expanded by the Council at Constantinople in 381. It became the standard creed of both the Eastern and Western Churches during the early middle ages and is integral to their liturgies. The creed is considered the unitive statement of faith by the organizationally separate Eastern Orthodox bodies. Like the Apostles' Creed, the Nicene Creed is formally recognized as a doctrinal standard by some Protestant bodies and informally recognized by most others. For example, it is printed as an optional confession of faith to be used in worship services in both the* Hymnal *and the* Book of Worship *of the United Methodist Church.*

*There is only one major variation in the text of the Nicene Creed. A theological difference between the Eastern and Western Churches at the time of the Great Schism of 1054 underlies the Roman Catholic Church's addition of the so-called "filioque clause," which affirmed that, within the mystery of the Godhead, the Holy Spirit proceeded from both the Father and the Son, not just the Father. Generally, churches deriving from the Roman Catholic Church have kept the clause in their reprinting of the creed. During the nineteenth century, the filioque (i.e., Latin for "and the Son") clause became a major item of discussion for the Old Catholics.*

* * *

## THE CHALCEDONIAN FORMULA

Following the holy fathers, we all unanimously teach that one and same Son, our Lord Jesus Christ, is to be confessed:

Perfect in Deity and perfect in Humanity,
Truly God and truly Man,
Of a *rational soul* and body,
Consubstantial with the Father according to his Deity,
Consubstantial with us according to his Humanity,
Like us in all respects, apart from sin;
Before the ages begotten of the Father according to his Deity,
And in these last days for us and for our salvation was born of the Virgin Mary, *the Mother of God [Theotokos]* according to his Humanity,
One and the same Christ, Son, Lord, only-begotten,
To be acknowledged in Two Natures
*without confusion or change*
*without division or separation;*
The difference of the Natures being by no means removed by the union,
but rather the property of each Nature being preserved and concurring in one Person and one Subsistence,
Not parted or divided into two Persons,
but one and the same Son and Only-begotten, God the Word, the Lord Jesus Christ;
According as at first the prophets, then the Lord Jesus Christ himself, taught us concerning him,
And as the Creed of the fathers has handed down to us.

Notes: *Largely confined to theological textbooks today, the Chalcedonian Formula promulgated in 451 C.E. represents the culmination of the major controversies that occupied the Christian Church leaders during the early centuries. It defined the orthodox solution to the problems of the Trinity, the dual nature of Jesus Christ, and the role of the Holy Spirit. The importance of its determinative theological role cannot be underestimated, though its popularity for liturgical use has never approached that of the Nicene Creed.*

*Because the Chalcedonian Formula has not been utilized as a liturgical confession and the Greek words used in it continue to provoke theological discussions, no standard accepted English text exists, such as exist for the Apostles' and the Nicene Creeds. The formula's several translations vary from extremely literal to free flowing and interpretive. The text presented here tends toward the literal. Notice should be taken of the formula's affirmation of Mary as "theotokos" [mother of God], an implication of Jesus's divinity that had significant influence on the latter development of understanding the Virgin Mary in the life of the Church.*

*The Apostles' Creed, the Nicene Creed, and the Chalcedonian Formula were by no means the only creeds of the early church. They are the ones that continue to have the most direct effect upon contemporary church bodies by their use and theological impact.*

* * *

## THE CREED OF ATHANASIUS (*SYMBOLUM QUICUNQUE*)

1. Whosoever will be saved, before all things it is necessary that he hold the Catholic [true Christian] faith,
2. Which Faith except every one do keep whole and undefiled, without doubt he shall perish everlastingly.
3. And the Catholic [true Christian] faith is this: that we worship one God in Trinity, and Trinity in Unity;
4. <u>Neither confounding the Persons; nor dividing the Substance.</u>
5. For there is <u>one Person</u> of the <u>Father</u>, <u>another</u> of the <u>Son</u>, and <u>another</u> of the <u>Holy Ghost</u>.
6. But the Godhead of the Father, of the Son, and of the Holy Ghost, is all one: the Glory Equal, the Majesty Coeternal.
7. Such as the Father is, such is the Son: and such is the Holy Ghost.
8. The Father uncreate, the Son uncreate: and the Holy Ghost uncreate.
9. The Father incomprehensible, the Son incomprehensible and the Holy Ghost incomprehensible.
10. <u>The Father eternal, the Son eternal: and the Holy Ghost eternal.</u>
11. <u>And yet they are not three Eternals: but one Eternal.</u>

2

THE ENCYCLOPEDIA OF AMERICAN RELIGIONS: RELIGIOUS CREEDS, First Edition vol. 1, by J. Gordon Melton, Editor (Gale Research Company, 1988)

**Ancient Creeds of the Christian Church**

12. As there are not three uncreated, nor three incomprehensibles: but one uncreated and one incomprehensible.
13. So likewise the Father is Almighty, the Son Almighty: and the Holy Ghost Almighty.
14. And yet they are not three Almighties: but one Almighty.
15. So the Father is God, the Son is God: and the Holy Ghost is God.
16. And yet they are not three Gods: but one God.
17. So likewise the Father is Lord, the Son Lord: and the Holy Ghost Lord.
18. And yet not three Lords: but one Lord.
19. For like as we are compelled by the Christian verity: to acknowledge every Person by himself to be God and Lord; So are we forbidden by the Catholic [Christian] Religion: to say, There be three Gods, or three Lords.
20. The Father is made of none: neither created nor begotten.
21. The Son is of the Father alone: not made, nor created, but begotten.
22. The Holy Ghost is of the Father, and of the Son; neither made, nor created, nor begotten, but proceeding.
23. So there is one Father, not three Fathers; one Son, not three Sons; one Holy Ghost, not three Holy Ghosts.
24. And in this Trinity none is before, or after other: none is greater, or less than another;
25. But the whole three Persons are coeternal together, and coequal: So that in all things, as is aforesaid: the Unity in Trinity, and the Trinity in Unity is to be worshipped.
26. He therefore that will be saved must thus think of the Trinity.
27. Furthermore, it is necessary to Everlasting Salvation; that he also believe rightly the Incarnation of our Lord Jesus Christ.
28. For the right Faith is, that we believe and confess: that our Lord Jesus Christ, the Son of God, is God and Man;
29. God, of the Substance of the Father begotten before the worlds: and Man of the Substance of his mother, born in the world;
30. Perfect God, and perfect Man: of a reasonable soul and human flesh subsisting.
31. Equal to the Father, as touching his Godhead: and inferior to the Father, as touching his Manhood.
32. Who although he be God and Man: yet he is not two, but one Christ;
33. One; not by conversion of the Godhead into flesh: but by taking the Manhood into God;
34. One altogether; not by confusion of Substance: but by Unity of Person.
35. For as the reasonable soul and flesh is one man: so God and Man is one Christ;
36. Who suffered for our salvation: descended into hell, rose again the third day from the dead.
37. He ascended into heaven; he sitteth on the right hand of the Father, God Almighty: from whence he shall come to judge the quick and the dead.
38. At whose coming all men shall rise again with their bodies: and shall give account for their own works.
39. And they that have done good shall go into life everlasting: and they that have done evil into everlasting fire.
40. This is the Catholic [true Christian] faith: which except a man believe faithfully, he cannot be saved.

Notes: *Although now thought to have been written sometime between the fourth and eighth centuries, this creed was for centuries ascribed to Athanasius (299?-373 C.E.), the fourth-century bishop who championed what became the orthodox Christian position on the nature of Christ. Even though the creed was never officially accepted by a church council (resulting in a variety of texts with different renderings, rather than one standard text), it became a widely accepted church document. Rendered into liturgical form, it was chanted in both the Roman Catholic Church and Church of England several times per year.*

*The creed has lost popularity in the contemporary era, although it is still accepted and used in the Roman Catholic Church. The Lutherans included the creed in their doctrinal material as part of their broader case for catholic orthodoxy. The text reproduced here is taken from the Lutheran* Book of Concord. *The creed is also found in the official materials of other churches, such as the* Psalter Hymnal *of the Christian Reformed Church. The Protestant Episcopal Church deleted the creed from its prayer book in 1785.*

*The words in brackets have been inserted into the text by the Lutheran translators to explain their understanding of the word "catholic," which differs considerably from the common meaning of Roman Catholic.*

3

THE ENCYCLOPEDIA OF AMERICAN RELIGIONS: RELIGIOUS CREEDS, First Edition Vol. I, by J. Gordon Melton, Editor (Gale Research Company, 1988)

## DIALOGUE FIVE: How Can Jesus Be "With" God And At The Same Time Be God —John 1:1?

3431 μοιχεύω

| Strong's number | Arndt-Gingr. | Greek word | Kittel vol.,pg. | Thayer pg., col. |
|---|---|---|---|---|

ev.10:11. And he said unto *me*, Thou must
11: 1. And there was given *me* a reed
14:13. saying unto *me*, Write, Blessed
17: 1. saying unto *me*, Come hither;
7. And the angel said unto *me*,
15. And he saith unto *me*, The waters
19: 9. And he saith unto *me*, Write,
— And he saith unto *me*, These are
10. And he said unto *me*, See
21: 5. And he said unto *me*, Write:
6. And he said unto *me*, It is done.
7. and he shall be *my* son.
10. and shewed *me* that great city,
22: 1. And he shewed *me* a pure river
6. And he said unto *me*, These sayings
8. which shewed *me* these things.
9. Then saith he unto *me*, See
10. And he saith unto *me*, Seal not

428 527 μοιχαλίς 4:729 416b
*f. adulteress*, Rm 7:3; Js 4:4; 2 P 2:14; as adj., *dulterous*, Mt 12:39; 16:4; Mk 8:38* ✓3432
lat.12:39. An evil and *adulterous* generation
16: 4. A wicked and *adulterous* generation
lar 8:38. in this *adulterous* and sinful generation;
.o. 7: 3. she shall be called an *adulteress*:
— so that she is no *adulteress*,
as. 4: 4. Ye adulterers and *adulteresses*,
Pet. 2:14. Having eyes full of *adultery*,

429 528 μοιχάω 4:729 417a
*v.* mid., *to commit adultery*, Mt 5:32; 19:9; Mk 0:11,12* ✓3432
at. 5:32. causeth her *to commit adultery*:
— her that is divorced *committeth adultery*.
19: 9. marry another, *committeth adultery*:
— is put away *doth commit adultery*.
ar 10:11. *committeth adultery* against her.
12. to another, she *committeth adultery*.

430 528 μοιχεία 4:729 417a
*f. adultery*, Mt 15:19; Mk 7:21; Jn 8:3 ✓3431
at.15:19. murders, *adulteries*, fornications,
ar 7:21. evil thoughts, *adulteries*, fornications,
oh. 8: 3. unto him a woman taken in *adultery*;
al. 5:19. *Adultery*, fornication, uncleanness,

431 528 μοιχεύω 4:729 417a
*v. to commit adultery*, Mt 5:27; fig., Rv 2:22. ✓3432
at. 5:27. Thou *shalt not commit adultery*:
28. *hath committed adultery* with her
19:18. Thou *shalt* not *commit adultery*,
ar 10:19. *Do* not *commit adultery*,
u. 16:18. marrieth another, *committeth adultery*:
— from (her) husband *committeth adultery*.
18:20. *Do* not *commit adultery*,
oh. 8: 4. was taken *in adultery*,
o. 2:22. a man should not *commit adultery*, *dost* thou *commit adultery*?
13: 9. Thou *shalt* not *commit adultery*,
s. 2:11. *Do* not *commit adultery*,
— Now if thou *commit* no *adultery*,
ev. 2:22. and them *that commit adultery* with her

3432 μοιχός — 579 — 3441 μόνος

| Strong's number | Arndt-Gingr. | Greek word | Kittel vol.,pg. | Thayer pg., col. |
|---|---|---|---|---|

3432 528 μοιχός 4:729 417a
*n.m. adulterer*, Lk 18:11; fig., *apostate*, Js 4:4.
Lu. 18:11. extortioners, unjust, *adulterers*,
1Co. 6: 9. nor idolaters, nor *adulterers*,
Heb 13: 4. whoremongers and *adulterers* God will
Jas. 4: 4. Ye *adulterers* and adulteresses,

3433 528 μόλις 4:735 417a
*adv. with difficulty, hardly*, Ac 14:18. ✓3425
Acts 14:18. *scarce* restrained they the people,
27: 7. and *scarce* were come over against
8. And, *hardly* passing it, came unto
16. we had much work to come by (lit. we were able *with difficulty* to get) the boat:
Ro. 5: 7. *scarcely* for a righteous man will one die:
1Pet. 4:18. if the righteous *scarcely* be saved,

3434 528 Μολόχ 417b
*n.pr.m.* indecl. *Moloch, Molech*, a god to whom the Ammonites sacrificed children, Ac 7:43*
Ac 7:43. ye took up the tabernacle of *Moloch*

3435 528 μολύνω 4:736 417b
*vb. to defile, pollute, morally contaminate*, Rv 3:4; pass., 1 Co 8:7; Rv 14:4*
1Co. 8: 7. their conscience being weak *is defiled*.
Rev. 3: 4. which *have* not *defiled* their garments;
14: 4. which *were* not *defiled* with women;

3436 528 μολυσμός 4:736 417b
*n.m. defilement, moral contamination*, 2 Co 7:1
2 Co 7:1. from all *filthiness* of the flesh

3437 528 μομφή 4:571 417b
*n.f. blame, fault, complaint*, Co 3:13* ✓3201
Co 3:13. if any man have a *quarrel* against any

3438 529 μονή 44:574 417b
*n.f. an abode, dwelling*, Jn 14:2,23* ✓3306
Jn 14:2. In my Father's house are many *mansions*
Jn 14:23. and make our *abode* with him

3439 529 μονογενής 4:737 417b
*adj. only-begotten, unique, one of its special kind*, Lk 7:12; Jn 1:14,18; 3:16,18; 1 Jn 4:9. ✓3441/1096
Lu. 7:12. the *only* son of his mother,
8:42. For he had one *only* daughter,
9:38. for he is mine *only child*.
Joh. 1:14. as of the *only begotten* of the Father,
18. the *only begotten* Son, which is
3:16. his *only begotten* Son, that whosoever
18. of the *only begotten* Son of God.
Heb 11:17. offered up his *only begotten* (son),
1Joh. 4: 9. God sent his *only begotten* Son

3440 529 μόνον 418a
*adv. nt* of 3441, *only, alone, but*, Mt 5:47; 9:21
Mat. 5:47. if ye salute your brethren *only*,
8: 8. but speak the word *only*,
9:21. If I may *but* touch his garment,
10:42. a cup of cold (water) *only*

Mat. 14:36. that they might *only* touch the
21:19. nothing thereon, but leaves *only*,
21. not *only* do this (which is done) to the
Mar 5:36. Be not afraid, *only* believe.
6: 8. for (their) journey, save a staff *only*;
Lu. 8:50. Fear not: believe *only*,
Joh. 5:18. not *only* had broken the sabbath,
11:52. not for that nation *only*, but that also
12: 9. not for Jesus' sake *only*, but
13: 9. not my feet *only*, but also
17:20. pray I for these *alone*, but for them
Acts 8:16. *only* they were baptized in the
11:19. but unto the Jews *only*.
18:25. knowing *only* the baptism of John.
19:26. not *alone* at Ephesus, but almost
27. So that not *only* this our craft
21:13. not to be bound *only*, but also to die
26:29. not *only* thou, but also all that
27:10. not *only* of the lading and ship,
Ro. 1:32. not *only* do the same, but have pleasure
3:29. the God of the Jews *only*?
4:12. not of the circumcision *only*, but who also
16. not to that *only* which is of the law,
23. for his sake *alone*,
5: 3. And not *only* (so), but we glory ...
11. And not *only* (so), but we also joy
8:23. And not *only* (they), but ourselves
9:10. And not *only* (this); but when
24. not of the Jews *only*, but also
13: 5. not *only* for wrath, but also for
1Co. 7:39. to whom she will; *only* in the Lord.
15:19. If in this life *only* we have hope
2Co. 7: 7. And not by his coming *only*, but by
8:10. not *only* to do, but also to be forward
19. And not (that) *only*, but who was also
21. not *only* in the sight of the Lord,
9:12. not *only* supplieth the want of
Gal. 1:23. But they had heard *only*,
2:10. *Only* (they would) that we should
3: 2. This *only* would I learn of you,
4:18. not *only* when I am present with you.
5:13. *only* (use) not liberty for an occasion
6:12. *only* lest they should suffer persecution
Eph. 1:21. not *only* in this world, but also
Phi. 1:27. *Only* let your conversation be
29. not *only* to believe on him, but also
2:12. not as in my presence *only*, but
27. and not on him *only*, but on me also,
1Th. 1: 5. not unto you in word *only*, but also in
8. not *only* in Macedonia and Achaia, but
2: 8. not the gospel of God *only*, but also
2Th. 2: 7. *only* he who now letteth (will let),
1Ti. 5:13. not *only* idle, but tattlers also
2Ti. 2:20. there are not *only* vessels of gold
4: 8. and not to me *only*, but unto all them
Heb 9:10. *only* in meats and drinks, and divers
12:26. I shake not the earth *only*, but also
Jas. 1:22. and not hearers *only*, deceiving
2:24. and not by faith *only*.
1Pet. 2:18. not *only* to the good and gentle,
1Joh. 2: 2. and not for our's *only*, but also for
5: 6. not by water *only*, but by water and blood.

3441 529 μόνος 418a
*adj. only, alone, by oneself*, Mt 14:23; Rm 11:3.
Mat. 4: 4. shall not live by bread *alone*,

THE NEW ENGLISHMAN'S GREEK CONCORDANCE AND LEXICON, 1982
by Jay P. Green, Sr.

## JOHN 1:18 AND μονογενὴς θεός

A key passage that goes directly to the textual choices made by scholars is found in the prologue of the Gospel of John. The KJV reads at John 1:18:

> No man hath seen God at any time; the only begotten Son, which is in the bosom of the Father, he hath declared him.

The NASB, however, has:

> No man has seen God at any time; the only begotten God, who is in the bosom of the Father, He has explained Him.

Even more interpretive is the rendering of the NIV:

> No one has ever seen God, but God the One and Only, who is at the Father's side, has made him known.

One might well think that KJV Only advocates would welcome the modern renderings, concerned as they claim to be about the deity of Christ. Yet, this is surely not the case. One critic of most modern versions, Jay P. Green, has written under the topical heading, "EXAMPLES OF HOW THE 'BEST' MSS. ROB CHRIST OF GLORY,"

> 1. ℵ in John 1:18 refers to Christ as the "only-begotten God." How can anyone claim that one that is begotten is at the same time essential God, equal in every respect to God the Father, and to God the Holy Spirit? This makes Christ to be a created Being. And it is a Gnostic twist given to the Bible by the heretic Valentinus and his followers, who did not regard the Word and Christ as one and the same; who thought of the Son of God and the Father as being one and the same Person. Therefore, they determined to do away with *"the only-begotten Son"* in order to accommodate their religion.[4]

We note that Mr. Green's reaction is based upon his understanding of theology, not upon the external evidence of the text. And while it is true that heretics down through the ages have appealed to this text or that, we must not allow the *misuse* of biblical texts to determine the readings we choose for the text of Scripture.

In reality we find five variant readings in the manuscript tradition at this point, two of which have obviously given rise to the others. Here is the textual evidence as given by the UBS 4th edition text:

[4] *Unholy Hands on the Bible, An Introduction to Textual Criticism*, edited by Jay P. Green, Sr. (Lafayette, Indiana : Sovereign Grace Trust Fund, 1990), p. 12.



| μονογενὴς θεός | ὁ μονογενὴς θεός |
| --- | --- |
| 𝔓66 ℵ* B C* L syr^{p,h(mg)} geo^2 Origen^{gr2/4} Didymus Cyril^{1/4} | 𝔓75 ℵ2 33 cop^{bo} Clement^{2/3} Clement^{from Theodotus 1/2} Origen^{gr2/4} Eusebius^{3/7} Gregory-Nyssa Epiphanius Serapion Cyril^{2/4} |

We note that when the definite article is passed over, the reading "only-begotten God" or more properly, "unique God,"[5] is found in the two oldest manuscripts, 𝔓66 and 𝔓75, as well as in both ℵ and B. Given the great antiquity of these manuscripts and the correlation with the great uncials, this reading bears great weight. We also note that the Syrian, Georgian, and Coptic translations support this rendering. The survey of the Fathers also shows the wide-spread nature of the reading, and the fact that such notably orthodox men as Gregory, the bishop of Nyssa, a staunch defender of the doctrine of the Trinity, knew this reading and found no objection to it; rather he utilized it often in his writings as evidence of the glory of Christ.[6]

The evidence for the reading ὁ μονογενὴς υἱός is very great indeed. It is, obviously, the majority reading of both the manuscripts, the translations, and the Fathers (though some Fathers show familiarity with more than one reading). The last two variants, μονογενὴς υἱὸς θεοῦ and ὁ μονογενής obviously arose from the preceding variants. They command little manuscript support.

The question that immediately faces the person desiring to know John's original wording is plain: given that both readings have ancient attestation, one commanding the earliest papyri (𝔓66 and 𝔓75) and the other the majority of the manuscript tradition, how can we account for the rise of a variant at this point? Which reading gives us the most logical reason for the existence of the other?

It is difficult to see how the reading θεός could arise from υἱός. The terms are simply too far removed from one another in form to account for scribal error based upon morphology. However, it is easily understood how θεός could give way to υἱός, given the appearance of "the only-begotten Son" at John 3:16 and 18. "Only-begotten Son" is Johannine in character, and hence

[5] The translation "only-begotten" is inferior to "unique." It was thought that the term came from μόνος (*monos*), meaning "only" and γεννάω (*gennao*), meaning "begotten." However, further research has determined that the term is derived not from γεννάω but from γένος (*genos*), meaning "kind" or "type." Hence the better translation, "unique" or "one of a kind." See Louw and Nida, *A Greek-English Lexicon of the New Testament Based on Semantic Domains* (1988) p. 591; Newman and Nida, *A Translator's Handbook on the Gospel of John*, 1980, p. 24; and Moulton and Milligan, *The Vocabulary of the Greek Testament*, 1930, pp. 416-417.

[6] See relevant passages in *Nicene and Post-Nicene Fathers*, Second Series (Grand Rapids: Wm. B. Eerdmans Publishing Company, 1954), V:102, 104, 125, 140, 198, 240.

THE KING JAMES ONLY CONTROVERSY, by JamesR.White

# DIALOGUE SIX: Was Jesus Created As God's "Firstborn Son" —Colossians 1:15-16?



Christ. [22]But you know that Timothy has proved himself, because as a son with his father he has served with me in the work of the gospel. [23]I hope, therefore, to send him as soon as I see how things go with me. [24]And I am confident in the Lord that I myself will come soon.

[25]But I think it is necessary to send back to you Epaphroditus, my brother, fellow worker and fellow soldier, who is also your messenger, whom you sent to take care of my needs. [26]For he longs for all of you and is distressed because you heard he was ill. [27]Indeed he was ill, and almost died. But God had mercy on him, and not on him only but also on me, to spare me sorrow upon sorrow. [28]Therefore I am all the more eager to send him, so that when you see him again you may be glad and I may have less anxiety. [29]Welcome him in the Lord with great joy, and honor men like him, [30]because he almost died for the work of Christ, risking his life to make up for the help you could not give me.

*No Confidence in the Flesh*

3 Finally, my brothers, rejoice in the Lord! It is no trouble for me to write the same things to you again, and it is a safeguard for you.

[2]Watch out for those dogs, those men who do evil, those mutilators of the flesh. [3]For it is we who are the circumcision, we who worship by the Spirit of God, who glory in Christ Jesus, and who put no confidence in the flesh— [4]though I myself have reasons for such confidence.

If anyone else thinks he has reasons to put confidence in the flesh, I have more: [5]circumcised on the eighth day, of the people of Israel, of the tribe of Benjamin, a Hebrew of Hebrews; in regard to the law, a Pharisee; [6]as for zeal, persecuting the church; as for legalistic righteousness, faultless.

[7]But whatever was to my profit I now consider loss for the sake of Christ. [8]What is more, I consider everything a loss compared to the surpassing greatness of knowing Christ Jesus my Lord, for whose sake I have lost all things. I consider them rubbish, that I may gain Christ [9]and be found in him, not having a righteousness of my own that comes from the law, but that which is through faith in Christ—the righteousness that comes from God and is by faith. [10]I want to know Christ and the power of his resurrection and the fellowship of sharing in his sufferings, becoming like him in his death, [11]and so, somehow, to attain to the resurrection from the dead.

*Pressing on Toward the Goal*

[12]Not that I have already obtained all this, or have already been made perfect, but I press on to take hold of that for which Christ Jesus took hold of me. [13]Brothers, I do not consider myself yet to have taken hold of it. But one thing I do: Forgetting what is behind and straining toward what is ahead, [14]I press on toward the goal to win the prize for which God has called me heavenward in Christ Jesus.

[15]All of us who are mature should take such a view of things. And if on some point you think differently, that too God will make clear to you. [16]Only let us live up to what we have already attained.

[17]Join with others in following my example, brothers, and take note of those who live according to the pattern we gave you. [18]For, as I have often told you before and now say again even with tears, many live as enemies of the cross of Christ. [19]Their destiny is destruction, their god is their stomach, and their glory is in their shame. Their mind is on earthly things. [20]But our citizenship is in heaven. And we eagerly await a Savior from there, the Lord Jesus Christ, [21]who, by the power that enables him to bring everything under his control, will transform our lowly bodies so that they will be like his glorious body.

4 Therefore, my brothers, you whom I love and long for, my joy and crown, that is how you should stand firm in the Lord, dear friends!

*Exhortations*

[2]I plead with Euodia and I plead with Syntyche to agree with each other in the Lord. [3]Yes, and I ask you, loyal yokefellow,[a] help these women who have contended at my side in the cause of the gospel, along with Clement and the rest of my fellow workers, whose names are in the book of life.

[4]Rejoice in the Lord always. I will say it again: Rejoice! [5]Let your gentleness be evident to all. The Lord is near. [6]Do not be anxious about anything, but in everything, by prayer and petition, with thanksgiving, present your requests to God. [7]And the peace of God, which transcends all understanding, will guard your hearts and your minds in Christ Jesus.

[8]Finally, brothers, whatever is true, whatever is noble, whatever is right, whatever is pure, whatever is lovely, whatever is admirable—if anything is excellent or praiseworthy—think about such things. [9]Whatever you have learned or received or heard from me, or seen in me—put it into practice. And the God of peace will be with you.

*Thanks for Their Gifts*

[10]I rejoice greatly in the Lord that at last you have renewed your concern for me. Indeed, you have been concerned, but you had no opportunity to show it. [11]I am not saying this because I am in need, for I have

[a]3 Or *loyal Syzygus*



learned to be content whatever the circumstances. [12]I know what it is to be in need, and I know what it is to have plenty. I have learned the secret of being content in any and every situation, whether well fed or hungry, whether living in plenty or in want. [13]I can do everything through him who gives me strength.

[14]Yet it was good of you to share in my troubles. [15]Moreover, as you Philippians know, in the early days of your acquaintance with the gospel, when I set out from Macedonia, not one church shared with me in the matter of giving and receiving, except you only; [16]for even when I was in Thessalonica, you sent me aid again and again when I was in need. [17]Not that I am looking for a gift, but I am looking for what may be credited to your account. [18]I have received full payment and even more; I am amply supplied, now that I have received from Epaphroditus the gifts you sent. They are a fragrant offering, an acceptable sacrifice, pleasing to God. [19]And my God will meet all your needs according to his glorious riches in Christ Jesus.

[20]To our God and Father be glory for ever and ever. Amen.

*Final Greetings*

[21]Greet all the saints in Christ Jesus. The brothers who are with me send greetings. [22]All the saints send you greetings, especially those who belong to Caesar's household.

[23]The grace of the Lord Jesus Christ be with your spirit. Amen.[a]

# Colossians

1 Paul, an apostle of Christ Jesus by the will of God, and Timothy our brother,

[2]To the holy and faithful[b] brothers in Christ at Colosse:

Grace and peace to you from God our Father.[c]

*Thanksgiving and Prayer*

[3]We always thank God, the Father of our Lord Jesus Christ, when we pray for you, [4]because we have heard of your faith in Christ Jesus and of the love you have for all the saints— [5]the faith and love that spring from the hope that is stored up for you in heaven and that you have already heard about in the word of truth, the gospel [6]that has come to you. All over the world this gospel is bearing fruit and growing, just as it has been doing among you since the day you heard it and understood God's grace in all its truth. [7]You learned it from Epaphras, our dear fellow servant, who is a faithful minister of Christ on our[d] behalf, [8]and who also told us of your love in the Spirit.

[9]For this reason, since the day we heard about you, we have not stopped praying for you and asking God to fill you with the knowledge of his will through all spiritual wisdom and understanding. [10]And we pray this in order that you may live a life worthy of the Lord and may please him in every way: bearing fruit in every good work, growing in the knowledge of God, [11]being strengthened with all power according to his glorious might so that you may have great endurance and patience, and joyfully [12]giving thanks to the Father, who has qualified you[e] to share in the inheritance of the saints in the kingdom of light. [13]For he has rescued us from the dominion of darkness and brought us into the kingdom of the Son he loves, [14]in whom we have redemption,[f] the forgiveness of sins.

*The Supremacy of Christ*

[15]He is the image of the invisible God, the firstborn over all creation. [16]For by him all things were created: things in heaven and on earth, visible and invisible, whether thrones or powers or rulers or authorities; all things were created by him and for him. [17]He is before all things, and in him all things hold together. [18]And he is the head of the body, the church; he is the beginning and the firstborn from among the dead, so that in everything he might have the supremacy. [19]For God was pleased to have all his fullness dwell in him, [20]and through him to reconcile to himself all things, whether things on earth or things in heaven, by making peace through his blood, shed on the cross.

[21]Once you were alienated from God and were enemies in your minds because of[g] your evil behavior. [22]But now he has reconciled you by Christ's physical body through

[a]23 Some manuscripts do not have *Amen.* [b]2 Or *believing* [c]2 Some manuscripts *Father and the Lord Jesus Christ* [d]7 Some manuscripts *your* [e]12 Some manuscripts *us* [f]14 A few late manuscripts *redemption through his blood* [g]21 Or *minds, as shown by*

NEW INTERNATIONAL VERSION

**PHILIPPIANS 4:20—COLOSSIANS 1:18** Means of creation 1468

extent of his riches[a] in glory by means of Christ Jesus. 20 Now to our God and Father be the glory forever and ever.[b] Amen.

21 Give my greetings[c] to every holy one in union[d] with Christ Jesus. The brothers who are with me send YOU their greetings. 22 All the holy ones, but especially those of the household of Caesar, send YOU their greetings.[a]

23 The undeserved kindness of the Lord Jesus Christ [be] with the spirit YOU [show].[b]

TO THE

# COLOSSIANS

1 Paul, an apostle of Christ Jesus through God's will,[a] and Timothy[b] [our] brother 2 to the holy ones and faithful brothers in union[c] with Christ at Co·los′sae:

May YOU have undeserved kindness and peace from God our Father.[d]

3 We thank[e] God the Father of our Lord Jesus Christ always when we pray for YOU,[f] 4 since we heard of YOUR faith in connection with Christ Jesus and the love YOU have for all the holy ones[g] 5 because of the hope[h] that is being reserved for YOU in the heavens.[i] This [hope] YOU heard of before by the telling of the truth of that good news[j] 6 which has presented itself to YOU, even as it is bearing fruit[k] and increasing[l] in all the world[m] just as [it is doing] also among YOU, from the day YOU heard and accurately knew the undeserved kindness[n] of God in truth.[o] 7 That is what YOU have learned from Ep′a·phras[p] our beloved fellow slave, who is a faithful minister of the Christ on our behalf, 8 who also disclosed to us YOUR love[q] in a spiritual way.

9 That is also why we, from the day we heard [of it], have not ceased praying for YOU[r] and asking that YOU may be filled with the accurate knowledge[s] of his will in all wisdom[t] and spiritual comprehension,[u] 10 in order to walk worthily[v] of Jehovah[a] to the end of fully pleasing [him] as YOU go on bearing fruit in every good work[b] and increasing in the accurate[c] knowledge of God, 11 being made powerful with all power to the extent of his glorious might[d] so as to endure[e] fully and be long-suffering with joy, 12 thanking the Father who rendered YOU suitable for YOUR participation in the inheritance[f] of the holy ones[g] in the light.[h]

13 He delivered us from the authority[i] of the darkness and transferred[j] us into the kingdom[k] of the Son of his love,[l] 14 by means of whom we have our release by ransom, the forgiveness of our sins.[m] 15 He is the image[n] of the invisible[o] God, the firstborn[p] of all creation; 16 because by means of him[q] <u>all [other] things</u> were created in the heavens and upon the earth, the things visible and the things invisible, no matter whether they are thrones or lordships or governments or authorities.[r] <u>All [other] things</u> have been created through him[s] and for him. 17 Also, he is before <u>all [other] things</u>[t] and by means of him <u>all [other] things</u> were made to exist,[u] 18 and he is the head of the body, the congregation.[v] He is the beginning, the firstborn from the dead,[w] that he might

1469 Sacred secret. Philosophers, deceivers **COLOSSIANS 1:19—2:10**

become the one who is first[a] in all things; 19 because [God] saw good for all fullness[b] to dwell in him, 20 and through him to reconcile[c] again to himself all [other] things[d] by making peace[e] through the blood[f] [he shed] on the torture stake,[g] no matter whether they are the things upon the earth or the things in the heavens.

21 Indeed, YOU who were once alienated[h] and enemies because YOUR minds were on the works that were wicked,[i] 22 he now has again reconciled[j] by means of that one's fleshly body through [his] death,[k] in order to present YOU holy and unblemished[l] and open to no accusation[m] before him, 23 provided, of course, that YOU continue in the faith,[n] established on the foundation[o] and steadfast[p] and not being shifted away from the hope of that good news which YOU heard,[q] and which was preached[r] in all creation[s] that is under heaven. Of this [good news] I Paul became a minister.[t]

24 I am now rejoicing in my sufferings for YOU,[u] and I, in my turn, am filling up what is lacking of the tribulations[v] of the Christ in my flesh on behalf of his body, which is the congregation.[w] 25 I became a minister[x] of this [congregation] in accordance with the stewardship[y] from God which was given me in YOUR interest to preach the word of God fully, 26 the sacred secret[a] that was hidden from the past systems of things[a] and from the past generations. But now it has been made manifest[b] to his holy ones, 27 to whom God has been pleased to make known what are the glorious riches[c] of this sacred secret[d] among the nations. It is Christ[e] in union with YOU, the hope of [his] glory.[f] 28 He is the one we are publicizing,[g] admonishing every man and teaching every man in all wisdom,[h] that we may present every man complete[a] in union with Christ. 29 To this end I am indeed working hard, exerting myself[b] in accordance with the operation[c] of him and which is at work in me with power.[d]

2 For I want YOU to realize how great a struggle[e] I am having in behalf of YOU and of those at La·o·di·ce′a[f] and of all those who have not seen my face in the flesh, 2 that their hearts may be comforted,[g] that they may be harmoniously joined together in love[h] and with a view to all the riches of the full assurance of [their] understanding,[i] with a view to an accurate knowledge of the sacred secret of God, namely, Christ.[j] 3 Carefully concealed in him are all the treasures of wisdom and of knowledge.[k] 4 This I am saying that no man may delude YOU with persuasive arguments.[l] 5 For though I am absent in the flesh, all the same I am with YOU in the spirit,[m] rejoicing and beholding YOUR good order[n] and the firmness of YOUR faith[o] toward Christ.

6 Therefore, as YOU have accepted Christ Jesus the Lord, go on walking in union[p] with him, 7 rooted[q] and being built up[r] in him and being stabilized in the faith,[s] just as YOU were taught, overflowing with [faith] in thanksgiving.[t]

8 Look out: perhaps there may be someone who will carry[u] YOU off as his prey through the philosophy[v] and empty deception[w] according to the tradition of men, according to the elementary[x] things of the world and not according to Christ; 9 because it is in him that all the fullness[y] of the divine[z] quality[a] dwells bodily. 10 And so YOU are possessed of a fullness by means of him, who is the head of all government and au-

NEW WORLD TRANSLATION

## TABLE OF THE BOOKS OF THE BIBLE

### Books of the Hebrew Scriptures Before the Common (Christian) Era

| Name of Book | Writer(s) | Place Written | Writing Completed (B.C.E.) | Time Covered (B.C.E.) |
|---|---|---|---|---|
| Genesis | Moses | Wilderness | 1513 | "In the beginning" to 1657 |
| Exodus | Moses | Wilderness | 1512 | 1657-1512 |
| Leviticus | Moses | Wilderness | 1512 | 1 month (1512) |
| Numbers | Moses | Wilderness and Plains of Moab | 1473 | 1512-1473 |
| Deuteronomy | Moses | Plains of Moab | 1473 | 2 months (1473) |
| Joshua | Joshua | Canaan | c. 1450 | 1473-c. 1450 |
| Judges | Samuel | Israel | c. 1100 | c. 1450-c. 1120 |
| Ruth | Samuel | Israel | c. 1090 | 11 years of Judges' rule |
| 1 Samuel | Samuel; Gad; Nathan | Israel | c. 1078 | c. 1180-1078 |
| 2 Samuel | Gad; Nathan | Israel | c. 1040 | 1077-c. 1040 |
| 1 Kings | Jeremiah | { Judah and | { 1 roll | c. 1040-580 |
| 2 Kings | Jeremiah | Egypt | 580 | |
| 1 Chronicles | Ezra | Jerusalem (?) | { 1 roll | { After 1 Chronicles 9:44: |
| 2 Chronicles | Ezra | Jerusalem (?) | c. 460 | 1077-537 |
| Ezra | Ezra | Jerusalem | c. 460 | 537-c. 467 |
| Nehemiah | Nehemiah | Jerusalem | a. 443 | 456-a. 443 |
| Esther | Mordecai | Shushan, Elam | c. 475 | 493-c. 475 |
| Job | Moses | Wilderness | c. 1473 | Over 140 years between 1657 and 1473 |
| Psalms | David and others | | c. 460 | |
| Proverbs | Solomon; Agur; Lemuel | Jerusalem | c. 717 | |
| Ecclesiastes | Solomon | Jerusalem | b. 1000 | |
| Song of Solomon | Solomon | Jerusalem | c. 1020 | |
| Isaiah | Isaiah | Jerusalem | a. 732 | c. 778-a. 732 |
| Jeremiah | Jeremiah | Judah; Egypt | 580 | 647-580 |
| Lamentations | Jeremiah | Near Jerusalem | 607 | |
| Ezekiel | Ezekiel | Babylon | c. 591 | 613-c. 591 |
| Daniel | Daniel | Babylon | c. 536 | 618-c. 536 |
| Hosea | Hosea | Samaria (District) | a. 745 | b. 804-a. 745 |
| Joel | Joel | Judah | c. 820 (?) | |
| Amos | Amos | Judah | c. 804 | |
| Obadiah | Obadiah | | c. 607 | |
| Jonah | Jonah | | c. 844 | |
| Micah | Micah | Judah | b. 717 | c. 777-717 |
| Nahum | Nahum | Judah | b. 632 | |
| Habakkuk | Habakkuk | Judah | c. 628 (?) | |
| Zephaniah | Zephaniah | Judah | b. 648 | |
| Haggai | Haggai | Jerusalem rebuilt | 520 | 112 days (520) |
| Zechariah | Zechariah | Jerusalem rebuilt | 518 | 520-518 |
| Malachi | Malachi | Jerusalem rebuilt | a. 443 | |

1546

TABLE OF THE BOOKS OF THE BIBLE 1547

### Books of the Greek Scriptures Written During the Common (Christian) Era

| Name of Book | Writer | Place Written | Writing Completed (C.E.) | Time Covered |
|---|---|---|---|---|
| Matthew | Matthew | Palestine | c. 41 | 2 B.C.E.-33 C.E. |
| Mark | Mark | Rome | c. 60-65 | 29-33 C.E. |
| Luke | Luke | Caesarea | c. 56-58 | 3 B.C.E.-33 C.E. |
| John | Apostle John | Ephesus, or near | c. 98 | After prologue, 29-33 C.E. |
| Acts | Luke | Rome | c. 61 | 33-c. 61 C.E. |
| Romans | Paul | Corinth | c. 56 | |
| 1 Corinthians | Paul | Ephesus | c. 55 | |
| 2 Corinthians | Paul | Macedonia | c. 55 | |
| Galatians | Paul | Corinth or Syrian Antioch | c. 50-52 | |
| Ephesians | Paul | Rome | c. 60-61 | |
| Philippians | Paul | Rome | c. 60-61 | |
| Colossians | Paul | Rome | c. 60-61 | |
| 1 Thessalonians | Paul | Corinth | c. 50 | |
| 2 Thessalonians | Paul | Corinth | c. 51 | |
| 1 Timothy | Paul | Macedonia | c. 61-64 | |
| 2 Timothy | Paul | Rome | c. 65 | |
| Titus | Paul | Macedonia (?) | c. 61-64 | |
| Philemon | Paul | Rome | c. 60-61 | |
| Hebrews | Paul | Rome | c. 61 | |
| James | James (Jesus' brother) | Jerusalem | b. 62 | |
| 1 Peter | Peter | Babylon | c. 62-64 | |
| 2 Peter | Peter | Babylon (?) | c. 64 | |
| 1 John | Apostle John | Ephesus, or near | c. 98 | |
| 2 John | Apostle John | Ephesus, or near | c. 98 | |
| 3 John | Apostle John | Ephesus, or near | c. 98 | |
| Jude | Jude (Jesus' brother) | Palestine (?) | c. 65 | |
| Revelation | Apostle John | Patmos | c. 96 | |

[Names of writers of some books and of places where written are uncertain. Many dates are only approximate, the symbol a. meaning "after," b. meaning "before" and c. meaning "circa," or "about."]

### "YOU" AND VERBS IN THE PLURAL NUMBER

"YOU" printed in all capital letters means that the pronoun is in the plural number. Also, where the plural number of a verb is not certainly apparent to the reader, its plurality is indicated by printing it capitalized.

[ ] Brackets enclose words inserted to complete the sense in the English text; [[ ]] suggest interpolations in original text.

NEW WORLD TRANSLATION, 1984

**COLOSSIANS 1:16—21** 880

εἰκὼν τοῦ θεοῦ τοῦ ἀοράτου, πρωτότοκος
image of the God the invisible, firstborn
πάσης κτίσεως, 16 ὅτι ἐν αὐτῷ
of all creation, because in him
ἐκτίσθη τὰ πάντα ἐν τοῖς οὐρανοῖς
it was created the all (things) in the heavens
καὶ ἐπὶ τῆς γῆς, τὰ ὁρατὰ καὶ
and upon the earth, the (things) visible and
τὰ ἀόρατα, εἴτε θρόνοι εἴτε
the (things) invisible, whether thrones or
κυριότητες εἴτε ἀρχαὶ εἴτε ἐξουσίαι·
lordships or governments or authorities;
τὰ πάντα δι' αὐτοῦ καὶ εἰς αὐτὸν
the all (things) through him and into him
ἔκτισται· 17 καὶ αὐτὸς ἔστιν πρὸ
it has been created; and he is before
πάντων καὶ τὰ πάντα ἐν αὐτῷ
all (things) and the all (things) in him
συνέστηκεν, 18 καὶ αὐτός ἐστιν ἡ
it has stood together, and he is the
κεφαλὴ τοῦ σώματος, τῆς ἐκκλησίας·
head of the body, of the ecclesia;
ὅς ἐστιν ἡ ἀρχή, πρωτότοκος ἐκ
who is the beginning, firstborn out of
τῶν νεκρῶν, ἵνα γένηται ἐν
the dead (ones), in order that might become in
πᾶσιν αὐτὸς πρωτεύων,
all (things) he holding the first place,
19 ὅτι ἐν αὐτῷ εὐδόκησεν πᾶν τὸ
because in him he thought well all the
πλήρωμα κατοικῆσαι 20 καὶ δι' αὐτοῦ
fullness to dwell down and through him
ἀποκαταλλάξαι τὰ πάντα εἰς αὐτόν,
to reconcile the all (things) into him,
εἰρηνοποιήσας διὰ τοῦ αἵματος τοῦ
having made peace through the blood of the
σταυροῦ αὐτοῦ, δι' αὐτοῦ εἴτε
stake of him, through him whether
τὰ ἐπὶ τῆς γῆς εἴτε τὰ ἐν
the (things) upon the earth or the (things) in
τοῖς οὐρανοῖς.
the heavens.
21 καὶ ὑμᾶς ποτὲ ὄντας
And YOU sometime being
ἀπηλλοτριωμένους καὶ ἐχθροὺς τῇ
having been alienated and enemies to the
διανοίᾳ ἐν τοῖς ἔργοις τοῖς
mental perception in the works the

the image of the invisible God, the firstborn of all creation;
16 because by means of him all [other]* things were created in the heavens and upon the earth, the things visible and the things invisible, no matter whether they are thrones or lordships or governments or authorities. All [other] things have been created through him and for him.
17 Also, he is before all [other] things and by means of him all [other] things were made to exist,
18 and he is the head of the body, the congregation. He is the beginning, the firstborn from the dead, that he might become the one who is first in all things;
19 because [God] saw good for all fullness to dwell in him,
20 and through him to reconcile again to himself all [other] things by making peace through the blood [he shed] on the torture stake,* no matter whether they are the things upon the earth or the things in the heavens.
21 Indeed, YOU who were once alienated and enemies because YOUR minds were on the works that were

16* All [other], as in Luke 11:41, 42. 20* See App 3c.

881 **COLOSSIANS 1:22—27**

πονηροῖς, — 22 νυνὶ δὲ ἀποκατήλλαξεν ἐν
wicked, — now but he reconciled in
τῷ σώματι τῆς σαρκὸς αὐτοῦ διὰ τοῦ
the body of the flesh of him through the
θανάτου, — παραστῆσαι ὑμᾶς ἁγίους καὶ
death, — to present YOU holy and
ἀμώμους καὶ ἀνεγκλήτους κατενώπιον αὐτοῦ,
unspotted and unaccusable down in sight of him,
23 εἴ γε ἐπιμένετε τῇ πίστει
if in fact YOU are remaining upon to the faith
τεθεμελιωμένοι καὶ ἑδραῖοι καὶ μὴ
having been founded and settled and not
μετακινούμενοι ἀπὸ τῆς ἐλπίδος τοῦ
being moved elsewhere from the hope of the
εὐαγγελίου οὗ ἠκούσατε, τοῦ
good news of which YOU heard, of the (one)
κηρυχθέντος ἐν πάσῃ κτίσει τῇ ὑπὸ
having been preached in all creation the under
τὸν οὐρανόν, οὗ ἐγενόμην ἐγὼ Παῦλος
the heaven, of which became I Paul
διάκονος.
servant.
24 Νῦν χαίρω ἐν τοῖς παθήμασιν
Now I am rejoicing in the sufferings
ὑπὲρ ὑμῶν, καὶ ἀνταναπληρῶ τὰ
over YOU, and I am filling up instead the
ὑστερήματα τῶν θλίψεων τοῦ χριστοῦ
lacking (things) of the tribulations of the Christ
ἐν τῇ σαρκί μου ὑπὲρ τοῦ σώματος αὐτοῦ,
in the flesh of me over the body of him,
ὅ ἐστιν ἡ ἐκκλησία, 25 ἧς
which is the ecclesia, of which
ἐγενόμην ἐγὼ διάκονος κατὰ τὴν
I became I servant according to the
οἰκονομίαν τοῦ θεοῦ τὴν
house administration of the God the
δοθεῖσάν μοι εἰς ὑμᾶς πληρῶσαι τὸν
having been given to me into YOU to fulfill the
λόγον τοῦ θεοῦ, 26 τὸ μυστήριον τὸ
word of the God, the mystery the
ἀποκεκρυμμένον ἀπὸ τῶν αἰώνων καὶ
having been hidden away from the ages and
ἀπὸ τῶν γενεῶν, — νῦν δὲ ἐφανερώθη
from the generations, — now but it was manifested
τοῖς ἁγίοις αὐτοῦ, 27 οἷς ἠθέλησεν
to the holy (ones) of him, to whom willed
ὁ θεὸς γνωρίσαι τί τὸ πλοῦτος τῆς
the God to make known what the riches of the
δόξης τοῦ μυστηρίου τούτου ἐν τοῖς ἔθνεσιν,
glory of the mystery this in the nations,

wicked,
22 he now has again reconciled by means of that one's fleshly body through [his] death, in order to present YOU holy and unblemished and open to no accusation before him,
23 provided, of course, that YOU continue in the faith, established on the foundation and steadfast and not being shifted away from the hope of that good news which YOU heard, and which was preached in all creation that is under heaven. Of this [good news] I Paul became a minister.
24 I am now rejoicing in my sufferings for YOU, and I, in my turn, am filling up what is lacking of the tribulations of the Christ in my flesh on behalf of his body, which is the congregation.
25 I became a minister of this [congregation] in accordance with the stewardship from God which was given me in YOUR interest to preach the word of God fully,
26 the sacred secret that was hidden from the past systems of things and from the past generations. But now it has been made manifest to his holy ones,
27 to whom God has been pleased to make known what are the glorious riches of this sacred secret among the nations.

THE KINGDOM INTERLINEAR TRANSLATION

servant,[4889] who is a faithful[4103] servant[1249] of Christ on [I]our behalf,
8 and he also informed us of your
[a]love[26] in the Spirit.[4151]
9 For this reason also, [a]since the
day we heard *of it,* [b]we have not ceased
to [ppi]pray[4336] for you and to [ppt]ask that
you may be [asbp]filled with the
[Ic]knowledge[1922] of His will[2307] in all
spiritual[4152] [d]wisdom[4678] and understanding,[4907]
10 so that you may [aint][a]walk[4043]
in a manner worthy of the Lord,
[Ib]to please[699] *Him* in all respects,
[c]bearing fruit in every good[18] work and
[II]increasing in the [III]knowledge[1922] of
God;
11 [a]strengthened[1412] with all
power,[1411] according to [I]His glorious[1391]
might,[2904] [II]for the attaining of all
steadfastness[5281] and [III]patience; [b]joy-
ously[5479]
12 giving thanks[2168] to [a]the Father,
who has [apt]qualified us [I]to share[2427] in

[III]Or, *real knowledge* [a]Eph. 4:1 [b]Eph. 5:10 [c]Rom. 1:13
11 [I]Lit., *the might of His glory* [II]Lit., *unto all* [III]Or, *patience with joy* [a]1Cor. 16:13 [b]Eph. 4:2 12 [I]Lit., *unto the portion of* [a]Eph. 2:18

...lle. 23) was one of Paul's friends and associates,
...soner." Perhaps he may have been imprisoned with
..., but Epaphras is probably not to be identified with
...lized the cities of the Lycus Valley in Phrygia under
...ssae, Hierapolis, and Laodicea. Later he visited Paul
...f conditions in the churches of the Lycus Valley that

...ell as in other contemporary churches was Gnosticism,
...nter this heresy of knowledge, Paul uses a compound
...which is used as an intensive, "on top of, in addition
...ōsis is derived is *ginōskō* (1097), and the verb from
...he difference between these two verbs is that *ginōskō*
...gnize a thing unintentionally," while *epiginōskō* implies
...wn. Compare the use of the two words in Jn. 8:32,
...e who have had full appropriated knowledge" of the
...ō which means not only knowing the truth in its initial

1:27; 14:35; 17:12; Mk. 2:8; 5:30; 6:33,54; Lk. 1:4,22;
12:14; 19:34; 22:24,29; 24:8; 25:10; 27:39; 28:1; Rom.
6:9; 13:5; Col. 1;6; I Tim. 4:3; II Pet. 2:21.
...lated merely as "knowledge" as if it were simply *gnōsis*
...20; 10:2; Eph. 1:17; 4:13; Phil. 1:9; Col. 1:9,10; 2:2;
...b. 10:26; II Pet. 1:2,3,8; 2:20.

1579 COLOSSIANS 1:23

[a]the inheritance[2819] of the [II]saints in
[b]light.[5457]

### The Incomparable Christ

13 For He [ao]delivered[4506] us from
the [I][a]domain[1849] of darkness,[4655] and
[ao]transferred[3179] us to the kingdom[932]
of [II][b]His beloved[26] Son,[5207]
14 [a]in whom we have redemp-
tion,[629] the forgiveness[859] of sins.[266]
15 And He is the [a]image[1504] of the
[b]invisible God,[2316] the [c]first-born[4416] of
all creation.
16 For [I][a]by Him all things were
[aop]created,[2937] [b]*both* in the heavens[3772]
and on earth,[1093] visible and invisible,
whether [c]thrones or dominions[2963] or
rulers[746] or authorities—[1849] [c]all things
have been created[2936] [II]by Him and for
Him.
17 And He [I][a]is before all things, and
in Him all things [pfi][II]hold together.[4921]
18 He is also [a]head of [b]the body,[4983]
the church;[1577] and He is [c]the beginning,[746] [d]the first-born[4416] from the
dead; so that He Himself might come
to have first place in everything.
19 For [I]it was [a]the *Father's* good
pleasure[2106] for all [b]the [II]fulness[4138] to
[aint]dwell[2730] in Him,
20 and through Him to [aint][a]recon-
cile[604] all things to Himself, having made
[apt][b]peace through [c]the blood of His
cross;[4716] through Him, *I say,* [d]whether
things on earth[1093] or things in
[I]heaven.[3772]
21 And although you were [a]formerly
[pfpp]alienated[526] and hostile in mind,[1271]
*engaged* in evil[4190] deeds,
22 yet He has now [ao][a]reconciled[604]
you in His fleshly[4561] [b]body[4983] through
death,[2288] in order to [aint][c]present you
before Him [d]holy[40] and blameless[299] and
beyond reproach—
23 if indeed you continue in [I]the
faith[4102] firmly [pfpp][a]established and
steadfast, and not [ppt]moved away from
the [b]hope[1680] of the gospel[2098] that you

12 [II]Or, *holy ones* [b]Acts 20:32 [c]Acts 26:18
13 [I]Lit., *authority* [II]Lit., *the Son of His love* [a]Eph. 6:12 [b]Eph. 1:6
14 [a]Rom. 3:24
15 [a]2Cor. 4:4 [b]John 1:18 [c]Rom. 8:29
16 [I]Or, *in* [II]Or, *through* [a]Eph. 1:10 [b]Eph. 1:20f.; Col. 2:15 [c]John 1:3; Rom. 11:36; 1Cor. 8:6
17 [I]Or, *has existed prior to* [II]Or, *endure* [a]John 1:1; 8:58
18 [a]Eph. 1:22 [b]Eph. 1:23; Col. 1:24; 2:19 [c]Rev. 3:14 [d]Acts 26:23
19 [I]Or, *all the fulness was pleased to dwell* [II]I.e., *fulness of deity* [a]Eph. 1:5 [b]John 1:16
20 [I]Lit., *the heavens* [a]2Cor. 5:18; Eph. 2:16 [b]Rom. 5:1; Eph. 2:14 [c]Eph. 2:13 [d]Col. 1:16

21 [a]Rom. 5:10; Eph. 2:3, 12 22 [a]2Cor. 5:18; Eph. 2:16 [b]Rom. 7:4 [c]Eph. 5:27; Col. 1:28 [d]Eph. 1:4
23 [I]Or omit, *the* [a]Eph. 3:17; Col. 2:7 [b]Col. 1:5

1:15ff. Here Jesus Christ is presented as the image of God, the invisible One (Jn. 1:18). The order of the Greek text has the word *eikōn* preceding *prōtotokos*. *Eikōn* (1504), "image," means that which resembles an object, which represents it. This word *eikōn* always assumes a prototype, not merely what it resembles, but from which it is drawn. For instance, the reflection of the sun in the water is called by Plato *eikōn*. Paul was telling the Colossians here that Jesus Christ has a "prototype," God the Father who is invisible. He is real because Jesus is real and not imaginary. The relationship between the Son and the Father, Christ and the Father God, is not coincidental as, for instance, two persons being similar, *homoi* (3664). (See also *homoiōma*, 3667, "resemblance.") Paul's teaching to the Colossians was that there was not a mere coincidental resemblance between Jesus Christ and His Father (*homoiōma*), but they were eternally related One to the Other (*eikōn*). The One was the reflection of the Other who was real and not merely the figment of thought or imagination. And this is so in spite of the fact that God is invisible. That which is invisible, nevertheless, can be and is real. See the notes on Jn. 1:18; Phil. 2:6-8.

The other word to which we must turn our attention and which is used twice in this context is the word *prōtotokos* (4416), translated as "first born" or "first begotten." It is used twice in Col. 1:15,18. Elsewhere, it is used in Mt. 1:25; Lk. 2:7; Rom. 8:29; Heb. 1:6; 11:28; 12:23 and Rev. 1:5. What it means here is that Christ holds the same relation to all creation as God the Father and that He is above all creation. It does not mean that He is part of the creation made by God, but that the relation of the whole creation to Him was determined by the fact that He is the cause of the creation of all things (Jn. 1:1; Rev. 3:14) and that without Him there could be no creation (Jn. 1:3,4; Col. 1:16). It is not said of Christ that He was *ktistheis*, "created," from *ktizō* (2936) "to create," a verb used of the creation of the world by Him in Col. 1:16. We never find this verb *ktizō* as referring to Jesus Christ as having been created. The verb is used in Mt. 19:4; Mk. 13:19; Rom. 1:25; I Cor. 11:9; Eph. 2:10; 3:9; 4:24; Col. 1:16 (twice); 3:10; I Tim. 4:3; Rev. 4:11; 10:6. In Rev. 3:14 the Lord Jesus Christ is called "the Beginning of the creation of God." But the word "beginning," *archē* (746), in this instance is not used as the result of God's creation but the cause of God's creation. See the Editor's book on Jn. 1:1-18, entitled *Was Christ God?*.

NEW AMERICAN STANDARD BIBLE, The Hebrew-Greek Key Study Bible, Compiled and edited by Spiros Zodhiates, Th.D. (Chattanooga, TN: AMG Publishers, 1990)

745 Ἀρχέλαος 94 749 ἀρχιερεύς

| Strong's number | Arndt-Gingr. | Greek word | Kittel vol.,pg. | Thayer pg., col. |
|---|---|---|---|---|

Lu. 9: 8. one of the *old* prophets was risen
19. one of the *old* prophets is risen
Acts15: 7. how that a good while ago (lit. from days *of old*)
21. For Moses of *old* time hath in
21:16. one Mnason of Cyprus, an *old* disciple
2Co. 5:17. *old* things are passed away;
2Pet.2: 5. spared not the *old* world, but
Rev.12: 9. that *old* serpent, called the Devil,
20: 2. that *old* serpent, which is the devil,

*745* *111* **Ἀρχέλαος** *76b*
*n.pr.m.* *Archelaus*, son of Herod I, ruler of Judaea, Idumea and Samaria from about 4 BC to 6 AD, Mt 2:22*
Mt 2:22. But when he heard that *Archelaus*

→ *746* *111* **ἀρχή** *1:478* *76b*
*n.f.* *(a) beginning,* *origin,* Mt 19:4; Rv 3:14; *(b) authority, rule, ruler,* Lk 12:11, 20:20; *(c) extremity, corner,* Ac 10:11. ✓756
Mat.19: 4. which made (them) at the *beginning*
8. from the *beginning* it was not so.
24: 8. these (are) the *beginning* of sorrows.
21. since the *beginning* of the world
Mar. 1: 1. The *beginning* of the gospel of
10: 6. from the *beginning* of the creation
13: 8(9). these (are) the *beginnings* of sorrows.
19. as was not from the *beginning*
Lu. 1: 2. from the *beginning* were eyewitnesses,
→ 12:11. unto the synagogues, and (unto) *magistrates*,
→ 20:20. might deliver him unto the *power* and authority of the governor.
Joh. 1: 1. In the *beginning* was the Word,
2. The same was in the *beginning*
2:11. This *beginning* of miracles did
6:64. Jesus knew from the *beginning* who
8:25. I said unto you from the *beginning*.
44. was a murderer from the *beginning*,
15:27. with me from the *beginning*.
16: 4. not unto you at the *beginning*,
Acts10:11. knit at the four *corners*, and let
11: 5. down from heaven by four *corners*;
15. as on us at the *beginning*.
26: 4. which was at *the first* among
Ro. 8:38. nor *principalities*, nor powers, nor
→ 1Co.15:24. have put down all *rule* and all
Eph. 1:21. above all *principality*, and power,
3:10. now unto the *principalities* and
6:12. against *principalities*, against powers,
Phil.4:15. that in the *beginning* of the gospel,
Col. 1:16. dominions, or *principalities*, or
18. who is the *beginning*, the
→ 2:10. the head of all *principality* and
15. having spoiled *principalities* and
2Th. 2:13. God hath from the *beginning* chosen
Tit. 3: 1. subject to *principalities* and powers,
Heb. 1:10. Thou, Lord, in the *beginning*
2: 3. which *at the first* began to
3:14. If we hold the *beginning* of
5:12. the *first* principles of the oracles
6: 1. leaving the *principles* of the doctrine
7: 3. having neither *beginning* of days,
2Pet.3: 4. from the *beginning* of the creation.
1Joh.1: 1. which was from the *beginning*,
2: 7. which ye had from the *beginning*.
— ye have heard from the *beginning*.
1 Joh. 2:13. him (that is) from the *beginning*.
14. known him (that is) from the *beginning*.
24. have heard from the *beginning*.
— ye have heard from the *beginning*
3: 8. the devil sinneth from the *beginning*.
11. that ye heard from the *beginning*,
2Joh. 5. which we had from the *beginning*,
6. as ye have heard from the *beginning*,
Jude 6. angels which kept not their *first estate*,
Rev. 1: 8. the *beginning* and the ending,
3:14. the *beginning* of the creation of God;
→ Rev.21: 6. the *beginning* and the end. I will
22:13. Alpha and Omega, the *beginning* and the end,

→ *747* *112* **ἀρχηγός** *1:478* *77a*
*adj.* only as subst., *(a) leader, ruler,* Ac 5:31; *(b) founder, originator,* Hb 2:10. ✓746 and 71
Acts 3:15. killed the *Prince* of life, whom
5:31. (to be) a *Prince* and a Saviour, for to
Heb. 2:10. to make the *captain* of their salvation
12: 2. Jesus the *author* and finisher of (our) faith;

*748* *112* **ἀρχιερατικός** *77b*
*adj.* *high-priestly,* Ac 4:6* ✓746 and 2413 der.
Ac 4:6. of the kindred *of the high priest*,

*749* *112* **ἀρχιερεύς** *3:221* *78a*
*n.m.* *high priest;* the pl. includes past high priests and members of the high-priestly families, Mk 14:60; Lk 23:13. ✓746 and 4166
Mat. 2: 4. gathered all the *chief priests* and
16:21. the elders and *chief priests* and scribes,
20:18. betrayed unto the *chief priests*
21:15. when the *chief priests* and scribes
23. the *chief priests* and the elders of the
45. the *chief priests* and Pharisees had
26: 3. assembled together the *chief priests*,
— unto the palace of the *high priest*,
14. Iscariot, went unto the *chief priests*,
47. from the *chief priests* and elders of
51. struck a servant of the *high priest's*,
57. away to Caiaphas the *high priest*,
58. unto the *high priest's* palace, and
59. Now the *chief priests*, and elders, and all
62. the *high priest* arose, and said
63. the *high priest* answered and said
65. the *high priest* rent his clothes,
27: 1. all the *chief priests* and elders of
3. silver to the *chief priests* and elders,
6. the *chief priests* took the silver
12. he was accused of the *chief priests*
20. the *chief priests* and elders persuaded
41. also the *chief priests* mocking (him),
62. the *chief priests* and Pharisees came
28:11. shewed unto the *chief priests* all
Mar. 2:26. days of Abiathar the *high priest*,
8:31. (of) the *chief priests*, and scribes,
10:33. be delivered unto the *chief priests*,
11:18. the scribes and *chief priests* heard
27. there come to him the *chief priests*,
14: 1. the *chief priests* and the scribes sought
10. went unto the *chief priests*, to
43. from the *chief priests* and the scribes
47. smote a servant of the *high priest*,

749 ἀρχιερεύς

| Strong's number | Arndt-Gingr. | Greek word | Kittel vol.,pg. | Thayer pg., col. |
|---|---|---|---|---|

Mar. 14:53. led Jesus away to the *high priest*:
— assembled all the *chief priests* and the
54. into the palace of the *high priest*:
55. the *chief priests* and all the council
60. the *high priest* stood up in the
61. Again the *high priest* asked him,
63. the *high priest* rent his clothes,
66. one of the maids of the *high priest*:
15: 1. the *chief priests* held a consultation
3. the *chief priests* accused him
10. the *chief priests* had delivered him
11. the *chief priests* moved the people,
31. also the *chief priests* mocking
Lu. 3: 2. Annas and Caiaphas being the *high priests*,
9:22. *chief priests* and scribes, and be slain,
19:47. the *chief priests* and the scribes
20: 1. the *chief priests* and the scribes
Lu. 20:19. the *chief priests* and the scribes the
22: 2. the *chief priests* and scribes sought
4. communed with the *chief priests*
50. smote the servant of the *high priest*,
52. Jesus said unto the *chief priests*,
54. into the *high priest's* house.
66. the *chief priests* and the scribes
23: 4. said Pilate to the *chief priests*
10. the *chief priests* and scribes stood
13. together the *chief priests* and the rulers
23. of them and of the *chief priests*
24:20. how the *chief priests* and our rulers
Joh. 7:32. the Pharisees and the *chief priests*
45. came the officers to the *chief priests*
11:47. gathered the *chief priests* and the
49. being the *high priest* that same
51. being *high priest* that year,
57. both the *chief priests* and the Pharisees
12:10. the *chief priests* consulted that
18: 3. from the *chief priests* and Pharisees,
10. smote the *high priest's* servant,
13. was the *high priest* that same year.
15. known unto the *high priest*, and
— into the palace of the *high priest*.
16. known unto the *high priest*,
19. The *high priest* then asked Jesus
22. Answerest thou the *high priest* so?
24. bound unto Caiaphas the *high priest*.
26. the servants of the *high priest*,
35. Thine own nation and the *chief priests*
19: 6. the *chief priests* therefore and officers
15. The *chief priests* answered,
21. Then said the *chief priests* of the
Acts 4: 6. Annas the *high priest*, and Caiaphas,
23. the *chief priests* and elders had said
5:17. the *high priest* rose up, and all they
21. the *high priest* came, and they that
24. the *chief priests* heard these things,
27. the *high priest* asked them,
7: 1. Then said the *high priest*, Are
9: 1. went unto the *high priest*,
14. authority from the *chief priests*
21. bound unto the *chief priests*?
19:14. a Jew, (and) *chief of the priests*,
22: 5. also the *high priest* doth bear
30. commanded the *chief priests* and
23: 2. the *high priest* Ananias commanded
4. Revilest thou God's *high priest*?
5. that he was the *high priest*:
14. they came to the *chief priests*
24: 1. Ananias the *high priest* descended

THE NEW ENGLISHMAN'S GREEK CONCORDANCE AND LEXICON, by Jay P. Green
(Peabody, MA: Hendrickson Publishers, 1982)

**PROVERBS 6:30—7:27** A harlot's devices; her persuasions 844

with the wife of his fellowman,[a] no one touching her will remain unpunishable.[b] 30 People do not despise a thief just because he commits thievery to fill his soul when he is hungry. 31 But, when found, he will make it good with seven times as much; all the valuables of his house he will give.[c] 32 Anyone committing adultery with a woman is in want of heart;[d] he that does it is bringing his own soul to ruin.[e] 33 A plague and dishonor he will find,[f] and his reproach itself will not be wiped out.[g] 34 For the rage of an able-bodied man is jealousy,[h] and he will not show compassion in the day of vengeance.[i] 35 He will have no consideration for any sort of ransom, neither will he show willingness, no matter how large you make the present.

7 My son, keep my sayings,[j] and may you treasure up my own commandments with you.[k] 2 Keep my commandments and continue living,[l] and my law like the pupil[m] of your eyes. 3 Tie them upon your fingers,[n] and write them upon the tablet of your heart.[o] 4 Say to wisdom:[p] "You are my sister"; and may you call understanding itself "Kinswoman," 5 to guard you against the woman stranger,[q] against the foreigner who has made her own sayings smooth.[r] 6 For at the window of my house, through my lattice[s] I looked down, 7 that I might peer upon the inexperienced ones.[t] I was interested in discerning among the sons a young man in want of heart,[u] 8 passing along on the street near her corner, and in the way to her house he marches,[v] 9 in the twilight, in the evening of the day,[w] at the approach of the night and the gloom. 10 And, look! there was a woman to meet him, with the garment of a prostitute[x] and cunning of heart. 11 She is boisterous and stubborn.[a] In her house her feet do not keep residing.[b] 12 Now she is outdoors, now she is in the public squares,[c] and near every corner she lies in wait.[d] 13 And she has grabbed hold of him and given him a kiss.[e] She has put on a bold face, and she begins to say to him:

14 "Communion sacrifices were incumbent upon me.[f] Today I have paid my vows.[g] 15 That is why I have come out to meet you, to look for your face, that I may find you. 16 With coverlets I have bedecked my divan, with many-colored things, linen of Egypt.[h] 17 I have besprinkled my bed with myrrh, aloes and cinnamon.[i] 18 Do come, let us drink our fill of love until the morning; do let us enjoy each other with love expressions.[j] 19 For the husband is not in his house; he has gone traveling on a way of some distance.[k] 20 A bag of money he has taken in his hand. On the day of the full moon he will come to his house."

21 She has misled him by the abundance of her persuasiveness.[l] By the smoothness of her lips she seduces him.[m] 22 All of a sudden he is going after her,[n] like a bull that comes even to the slaughter, and just as if fettered for the discipline of a foolish man, 23 until an arrow cleaves open his liver,[o] just as a bird hastens into the trap,[p] and he has not known that it involves his very soul.[q]

24 And now, O sons, listen to me and pay attention to the sayings of my mouth.[r] 25 May your heart not turn aside to her ways. Do not wander into her roadways.[s] 26 For many are the ones she has caused to fall down slain,[t] and all those being killed by her are numerous.[u] 27 The ways to She'ol her house[v] is; they are descend-

r Pr 1:1; s Pr 5:8; 1Pe 2:11; t Ec 7:26; u 1Co 10:8; v Pr 5:5; Pr 9:18.

845 Wisdom prefigured. God's master worker **PROVERBS 8:1—31**

ing to the interior rooms of death.[a]

8 Does not wisdom keep calling out,[b] and discernment keep giving forth its voice?[c] 2 On top of the heights,[d] by the way, at the crossing of the roadways it has stationed itself. 3 At the side of the gates, at the mouth of the town,[e] at the going in of the entrances it keeps crying loudly:[f]

4 "To YOU, O men, I am calling, and my voice is to the sons of men.[g] 5 O inexperienced ones, understand shrewdness;[h] and YOU stupid ones, understand heart.[i] 6 Listen, for it is about the foremost things that I speak;[j] and the opening of my lips is about uprightness.[k] 7 For my palate in low tones utters truth itself;[l] and wickedness is something detestable to my lips.[m] 8 All the sayings of my mouth are in righteousness.[n] Among them there is nothing twisted or crooked.[o] 9 All of them are straight to the discerning one, and upright to the ones finding knowledge.[p] 10 TAKE my discipline and not silver, and knowledge rather than choice gold.[q] 11 For wisdom is better than corals,[r] and all other delights themselves cannot be made equal to it.[s]

12 "I, wisdom, I have resided with shrewdness[t] and I find even the knowledge of thinking abilities.[u] 13 The fear of Jehovah means the hating of bad.[v] Self-exaltation and pride[w] and the bad way and the perverse mouth[x] I have hated. 14 I have counsel[y] and practical wisdom.[z] I—understanding;[a] I have mightiness.[b] 15 By me kings themselves keep reigning, and high officials themselves keep decreeing righteousness.[c] 16 By me princes themselves keep ruling as princes,[d] and nobles are all judging in righteousness.[e] 17 Those loving me I myself love,[f] and those looking for me are the ones that find me.[g] 18 Riches and glory are with me,[h] hereditary values and righteousness.[c] 19 My fruitage is better than gold, even than refined gold, and my produce than choice silver.[d] 20 In the path of righteousness I walk,[e] in the middle of the roadways of judgment,[f] 21 to cause those loving me to take possession of substance;[g] and their storehouses I keep filled.[h]

22 "Jehovah himself produced me as the beginning of his way,[i] the earliest of his achievements of long ago.[j] 23 From time indefinite I was installed,[k] from the start, from times earlier than the earth.[l] 24 When there were no watery deeps I was brought forth as with labor pains,[m] when there were no springs heavily charged with water. 25 Before the mountains themselves had been settled down,[n] ahead of the hills, I was brought forth as with labor pains, 26 when as yet he had not made the earth[o] and the open spaces and the first part of the dust masses of the productive land.[p] 27 When he prepared the heavens I was there;[q] when he decreed a circle upon the face of the watery deep,[r] 28 when he made firm the cloud masses above,[s] when he caused the fountains of the watery deep to be strong,[t] 29 when he set for the sea his decree that the waters themselves should not pass beyond his order,[u] when he decreed the foundations of the earth,[v] 30 then I came to be beside him as a master worker,[w] and I came to be the one he was specially fond[x] of day by day, I being glad before him all the time,[y] 31 being glad at the productive land of his earth,[z]

p Ps 89:11; Ps 90:2; q Ps 33:6; Jer 10:12; Col 1:17; r Ge 1:6; Job 26:10; s Ge 1:7; Job 38:9; t Ge 2:6; Ge 7:11; Ge 8:2; Ps 104:6; u Ge 1:9; Job 38:11; Ps 33:7; Ps 104:9; Jer 5:22; v Ge 1:9; w Ge 1:26; Joh 1:3; Joh 17:5; Col 1:16; x Isa 42:1; Mt 3:17; y Job 38:7; z Ps 8:8; Ps 89:9.

NEW WORLD TRANSLATION

PROVERBS 8:6 846

And, O [b]fools, discern[995]
[II]wisdom.
6 "Listen,[8085] for I shall speak[1696]
[a]noble things;[5057]
And the opening of my lips[8193]
*will produce* [b]right things.[4334]
7 "For my [a]mouth will utter[1897]
truth;[571]
And wickedness[7562] is an
abomination[8441] to my lips.
8 "All the utterances[561] of my
mouth[6310] are in
righteousness;[6664]
There is nothing [a]crooked[6617] or
perverted in them.
9 "They are all [a]straightforward[5228]
to him who understands,[995]
And right[3477] to those who
[b]find knowledge.[1847]
10 "Take my [a]instruction,[4148] and not
silver,
And knowledge rather than
choicest[977] gold.
11 "For wisdom is [a]better[2896] than
[I]jewels;
And [b]all desirable things can not
compare with her.
12 "I, wisdom, [a]dwell[7931] with
prudence,[6195]
And I find [b]knowledge *and*
discretion.[4209]
13 "The [a]fear[3374] of the LORD is to
hate[8130] evil;[7451]
[b]Pride and arrogance and
[c]the evil way,
And the [d]perverted[8419] mouth,
I hate.
14 "[a]Counsel[6098] is mine and
[b]sound wisdom;[8454]
I am understanding,[998]
[c]power is mine.
15 "By me [a]kings[4428] reign,[4427]
And rulers[5081] decree[2710]
justice.[6664]
16 "By me princes[8269] rule,[8323] and
nobles,[5081]
All who judge[8199] rightly.
17 "I [a]love[157] those who love me;
And [b]those who diligently seek
me will find me.
18 "[a]Riches and honor[3519] are with
me,
Enduring [b]wealth and
righteousness.[6666]
19 "My fruit is [a]better than gold,
even pure gold,
And my yield than [b]choicest
silver.
20 "I walk in the way[734] of
righteousness,
In the midst of the paths of
justice,[4941]
21 To endow[5157] those who love me
with wealth,
That I may [a]fill their treasuries.
→ 22 "The LORD possessed me
[a]at the beginning[7225] of His
way,
Before His works [I]of old.[227]
23 "From everlasting[5769] I was
[I][a]established,[5258]
From the beginning,[7218]
[b]from the earliest times of the
earth.
24 "When there were no [a]depths I
was [I]brought forth,[2342]
When there were no springs
abounding[3513] with water.
25 "[a]Before the mountains were
settled,
Before the hills I was [I]brought
forth;[2342]
26 While He had not yet made[6213]
the earth and the [I]fields,
Nor the first dust[6083] of the
world.[8398]
27 "When He [a]established[3559] the
heavens,[8064] I was there,
When [b]He inscribed[2710] a circle
on the face of the deep,
28 When He made firm the skies[7834]
above,
When the springs of the deep
became [I]fixed,
29 When [a]He set for the sea its
boundary,[2706]
So that the water should not
transgress His [I]com-
mand,[6310]
When He marked out[2710]
[b]the foundations[4146] of the
earth;
30 Then [a]I was beside Him, *as* a
master workman;
And I was daily[3117] *His*
delight,
[I]Rejoicing always[6256] before
Him,
31 [I]Rejoicing in the world,[8398] His
earth,
And *having* [a]my delight in the
sons of men.[120]
32 "Now therefore, *O* sons,[1121]
[a]listen[8085] to me,
For [b]blessed[835] are they who
keep[8104] my ways.[1870]
33 "[a]Heed instruction and be
wise,[2449]
And do not neglect *it*.
34 "[a]Blessed is the man who
listens[8085] to me,
Watching daily at my gates,
Waiting at my doorposts.
35 "For [a]he who finds me finds
life,[2416]
And [b]obtains favor[7522] from the
LORD.
36 "But he who [I]sins[2398] against me
[a]injures[2554] himself;[5315]
All those who [b]hate me
[c]love death."[4194]

***Wisdom's Invitation***

9 Wisdom[2454] has [a]built her house,[1004]
She has hewn out[2672] her seven
pillars;
2 She has [I][a]prepared[2873] her
food,[2874] she has [b]mixed her
wine;
She has also [c]set her
table;
3 She has [a]sent out her maidens,
she [b]calls
From the [c]tops of the heights
of the city:
4 "[a]Whoever is [I]naive, let him turn
in here!"
To him who [b]lacks [II]under-
standing[3820] she says,[559]
5 "Come, [a]eat of my food,
And drink of the wine I have
mixed.
6 "[I]Forsake[5800] *your* folly and
[a]live,[2421]

5 [II]Lit., *heart* [b]Prov. 1:22, 32; 3:35
6 [a]Prov. 22:20 [b]Prov. 23:16
7 [a]Ps. 37:30; John 8:14; Rom. 15:8
8 [a]Deut. 32:5; Prov. 2:15; Phil. 2:15
9 [a]Prov. 14:6 [b]Prov. 3:13
10 [a]Prov. 3:14, 15; 8:19
11 [I]Lit., *corals* [a]Job 28:15, 18; Ps. 19:10 [b]Prov. 3:15
12 [a]Prov. 8:5 [b]Prov. 1:4
13 [a]Prov. 3:7; 16:6 [b]1Sam. 2:3; Prov. 16:18; Is. 13:11 [c]Prov. 15:9 [d]Prov. 6:12
14 [a]Prov. 1:25; 19:20; Is. 28:29; Jer. 32:19 [b]Prov. 2:7; 3:21; 18:1 [c]Eccl. 7:19; 9:16
15 [a]2Chr. 1:10; Prov. 29:4; Dan. 2:21; Matt. 28:18; Rom. 13:1
17 [a]1Sam. 2:30; Prov. 4:6; John 14:21 [b]Prov. 2:4, 5; John 7:37; James 1:5
18 [a]Prov. 3:16 [b]Ps. 112:3; Matt. 6:33
19 [a]Job 28:15; Prov. 3:14 [b]Prov. 10:20
21 [a]Prov. 24:4
22 [I]Lit., *from then* [a]Job 28:26-28; Ps. 104:24; Prov. 3:19
23 [I]Or, *conse-crated* [a]John 1:1-3 [b]John 17:5
24 [I]Or, *born* [a]Gen. 1:2; Ex. 15:5; Job 38:16; Prov. 3:20
25 [I]Or, *born* [a]Job 15:7; Ps. 90:2
26 [I]Lit., *outside places*
27 [a]Prov. 3:19 [b]Job 26:10
28 [I]Lit., *strong*
29 [I]Lit., *mouth* [a]Job 38:10; Ps. 104:9 [b]Job 38:6; Ps. 104:5
30 [a]John 1:2, 3

NEW AMERICAN STANDARD BIBLE

## DIALOGUE SEVEN: What Is The Proper Balance Between "Faith" And "Works" In Salvation?



**13 For the one that does not practice mercy will have his judgment without mercy. Mercy exults triumphantly over judgment.**

God will count their good works as evidence of their faith. Jesus Christ, his Son, is the mediator of the new covenant, and it is on the basis of his propitiatory sacrifice that the new covenant is established and that God may carry out the words of that covenant, namely: "I shall forgive their error, and their sin I shall remember no more." (Jer. 31:34) Accordingly, spiritual Israelites under the "law of freedom" conduct themselves, not as though God is one who is looking for a fault in them, but as those who keep "walking" with him, jealously guarding their covenant relationship with him. (Ps. 130:3, 4; Mic. 6:8)

**13 For the one that does not practice mercy will have his judgment without mercy**

James points to a judgment, and he shows the danger into which those showing favoritism were putting themselves. (Rom. 2:6, 16; 14:12; Matt. 12:36) How could they expect mercy from God when they withheld mercy from a man merely because he was "a poor man in filthy clothing"? (Jas. 2:2) How inconsistent and contrary to all reason, that those to whom James wrote included lowly persons, yet they discriminated against the poor man! How would "poor" members feel if they visited another congregation of Christians and were insulted in this way? Proverbs 21:13 reads: "As for anyone stopping up his ear from the complaining cry of the lowly one, he himself also will call and not be answered." Jesus said: "With what judgment you are judging, you will be judged." (Matt. 7:1, 2) He gave a powerful illustration of this point at Matthew 18:23-35.



**14 Of what benefit is it, my brothers, if a certain one says he has faith but he does not have works? That faith cannot save him, can it?**

**Mercy exults triumphantly over judgment**

"Happy are the merciful, since they will be shown mercy," Jesus said. (Matt. 5:7) In a legal court, a man who had exercised mercy toward others would not likely be excused from the penalty for the crime of which he was found guilty, though the punishment might possibly be mitigated somewhat. However, James is not speaking about transgressions under the Mosaic law or under a worldly law. He is here talking about judgment by the "law of freedom." A man in whose mind and heart mercy has been produced by God's spirit, as a result of his faith in Christ, is moved to show mercy in all his dealings. In consequence, he will receive mercy when he comes before judgment. Therefore this merciful person need not be fearful of judgment but can have confidence that he will experience mercy. He will not be condemned. Thus, he triumphs or gains a victory over strict justice or adverse judgment. A notable illustration of merciful concern for others and its effect on judgment is found in the parable of the sheep and the goats, at Matthew 25:32-40. Also, we may consider the mercy that Jehovah exercised toward David, who had in the past shown himself merciful. (2 Sam. 12:13, 14; 22:24-27; Ps. 18:23-26)

**14 Of what benefit is it, my brothers, if a certain one says he has faith but he does not have works?**

It should be noted that James is not contradicting what Paul says, namely, that "a man is declared righteous by faith apart from works of law." (Rom. 3:28) James fully agrees with this

COMMENTARY ON THE LETTER OF JAMES, 1979

teaching, but he writes to refute an abuse or perversion of it. The perversion was the view that a man, by merely holding correct ideas about being justified by faith, without demonstrating that faith at all by doing good works, would be righteous in God's sight and would eventually receive complete salvation. Actually, James pointed out, any so-called faith that does not prompt the person to do good works is not genuine faith. Such a man only *"says* he has faith." The man who claims to have faith in Christ's atonement sacrifice, and says that he is a Christian, but who does not demonstrate that faith by action, is not in reality a Christian. If his "faith" did not make any changes in his personality, his life, his actions, what good would it be? How could he do as Jesus commanded his followers: "Let your light shine before men, that they may see your fine works and give glory to your Father who is in the heavens"? (Matt. 5:16)

**True Faith Will Produce Fine Works**

Would anyone call a man a real doctor, a dedicated physician, who set himself up in office as a doctor and expressed faith in medical treatment, yet never treated or helped another person medically? Jesus said: "Not everyone saying to me, 'Lord, Lord,' will enter into the kingdom of the heavens, but the one doing the will of my Father who is in the heavens will." (Matt. 7:21) What James says in verse 14 ties in with his description at chapter 1:26, 27, where he speaks of the man who "seems to himself" or 'thinks himself' to be a worshiper of God but fails in producing any fruitage of his faith or his form of worship. He fails to "bridle his tongue," discipline it to speak in accord with what is the true state of matters, what he actually is. His form of worship is "futile." He also fails to have works, such



as looking after orphans and widows and keeping himself unspotted from the world. Furthermore, such hollow, futile profession of faith leads a person into such wrongs as the showing of partiality, into failing to fulfill the law of love and neglecting to show mercy. (Jas. 2:8, 9, 13)

**That faith cannot save him, can it?**

Note that James emphasizes, not faith itself, but the particular "faith" in question, *"that* faith," a falsely called faith that is without works. As James recognizes, true faith in God's word can save our souls. (Jas. 1:21) In this, James agrees fully with Paul. They are both in harmony as regards true faith and Christian works. But James is discussing works different from those that Paul writes about in Romans chapters 3 and 4.

Paul, in saying that works cannot bring one a declaration of righteousness, is talking about works of law that a person engaged in, works on which he might rely, thinking that he could *earn* righteousness from God, or, thinking that a Christian's continued good works *of themselves* would be what would gain righteousness for him. (Rom. 4:2-5) But James speaks about Christian works that are *motivated*, not by a law code, but by faith and love. They are a result, a product and a fruitage of that faith and cannot be separated or divorced from true faith. However, Paul, while pointing out that a person is initially declared righteous through faith, also spoke repeatedly of the need for the Christian to do works of faith—works manifesting that faith. He calls Christians a people "zealous for fine works." (Titus 2:14; compare 1 Thessalonians 1:2-7; 1 Timothy 2:10; Titus 2:7; 3:8, 14.) And who performed more works than Paul did? James asks: "That faith [that is, one not having works to show its genuineness] cannot save him, can it?" Clearly, the answer is: No, it cannot.

COMMENTARY ON THE LETTER OF JAMES, 1979

## DIALOGUE EIGHT: Is Eternal Life In The Watchtower Organization A Reality?



may not take advantage of the opportunity to change.—Isaiah 26:10.

[17] To the person who is resurrected, the time period that he was dead would be, to him, only an instant, since death is a nonexistence. It is likened in the Bible to a deep sleep. (John 11:11-14; 1 Thessalonians 4:13, 14; Ecclesiastes 9:5, 10) Thousands of years, or a day, would seem like only a moment of time. To the one resurrected, the experience would be like walking through a doorway out of the present wicked system of things into the righteous, orderly new system of things.

[18] Of course, the person who died many years ago will be surprised to find circumstances on earth so different. He will have to be informed by the members of the "great crowd" of the works that God has performed in the meantime, particularly in giving His Son as the atonement sacrifice. He will also learn how the good conditions are a result of Christ's Kingdom rule. It would be in harmony with God's loving-kindness to assume that family members and friends will be able to receive back their dead loved ones, just as was the case with resurrections reported in the Bible. (Luke 7:12-15; 8:49-56; Hebrews 11:35) Then, after a period of training, the resurrected ones will, in turn, be able to receive and help their yet dead loved ones who are subsequently brought back. Thus no one will be resurrected to a totally unfamiliar world, but, rather, to warm companionship, with no 'communication

17. If a person died centuries ago, will it seem to him that a long time has passed between his death and his resurrection?
18. (a) What will the resurrected ones have to learn? (b) Logically, how will those who are resurrected not be brought back to a totally unfamiliar world, with a 'communication gap'?



gap.' This process will continue until all the ransomed dead are finally resurrected. What a joyous time that will be!

### GOD BECOMES "ALL THINGS TO EVERYONE"

[19] At the end of the thousand years, the last trace of sin and its consequence, death, will have been destroyed. (1 Corinthians 15:26) But does this reaching of perfection by all then on earth mean that such persons cannot sin? No, for the Bible reveals that persons reaching that state will not be assured of *everlasting* life until they prove faithful against a final attack by Satan the Devil. When Christ's kingdom and priesthood accomplish the restoration to perfection, Christ turns the Kingdom back to God, and man again stands in relation to God as Adam did. The situation is restored as it was at the beginning and each man's final, everlasting destiny is for God alone to determine. God permits this attack by Satan and his demon hosts.

[20] Revelation 20:7-10 describes what occurs as a test on earth's inhabitants: "Now as soon as the thousand years have been ended, Satan will be let loose out of his prison [the abyss, where he had been placed just before the thousand years began], and he will go out to mislead those nations in the four corners of the earth, Gog and Magog, to gather them together for the war. The number of these is as the sand of the sea [an unstated, hence humanly undeterminable number]. And they advanced over the breadth of the earth and encircled the camp of the holy ones and the beloved

19. Though perfection comes by Christ's thousand-year rule, when will those on earth be granted everlasting life?
20. What test will come upon the perfect inhabitants of the earth at the end of the thousand years?

ılly do not care. r time, energy, appiness to gain n the world, but od, will find that ," like their life, :thew 6:19, 20;

ıletic game may igorous require- those described

one in the race for athlete?

above, but only for a limited time. Once the games are over, they go back to a normal way of life. They may still train from time to time to maintain their skills, but they no longer follow the same course of severe self-denial, at least not until the next contest is due. It is not so with those who are in the race for life. With them, training and self-denial must be a way of life.—1 Timothy 6: 6-8.

14 "If anyone wants to come after me," said Jesus Christ to a gathering of disciples and others, "let him disown himself (or, "he must say, 'No' to self," *Charles B. Williams*) and pick up his torture stake and follow me continually." (Mark 8:34) When we accept this invitation, we must be prepared to do so "continually," not because there is some special merit in self-denial, but because one moment's indiscretion, one lapse in good judgment, may undo all that has been built up, even jeopardizing our eternal welfare. Spiritual progress is usually made at a rather slow pace, but how quickly it can be nullified if we are not on guard constantly!

15 Furthermore, Paul urged that we must exercise self-control "in all things," that is, we must do so consistently in all aspects of life. This makes good sense because if a trainee overindulges or lives licentiously, what will be the good of all the physical pain and fatigue that he endures? Likewise in our race for life, we must exercise self-control in all things. A person may control himself in such things as drunkenness and fornication, but the value of this diminishes if he is haughty and contentious. Or what if he is long-suffering and kind toward others, but harbors some secret sin in his private life? For self-control to be fully beneficial, it must be exercised "in all things."—Compare James 2:10, 11.

## Run "Not Uncertainly"

16 Seeing the strenuous efforts needed to succeed in the race for life, Paul went on to say: "Therefore, the way I am running is not uncertainly; the way I am directing my blows is so as not to be striking the air." (1 Corinthians 9:26) The word "uncertainly" literally means "unevidently" (*Kingdom Interlinear*), "unobserved, unmarked" (*Lange's Commentary*). Hence, to run "not uncertainly" means that to every observer it should be very evident where the runner is heading. *The Anchor Bible* renders it "not on a zigzag course." If you saw a set of footprints that meanders up and down the beach, circles around now and then, and even goes backward at times, you would hardly think the person was running at all, let alone that he had any idea where he was heading. But if you saw a set of footprints that form a long, straight line, each footprint ahead of the previous one and all evenly spaced, you would conclude that the footprints belong to one who knows exactly where he is going.

17 Paul's life shows clearly that he was running "not uncertainly." He had ample evidence to prove that he was a Christian minister and an apostle. He had but one objective, and he exerted himself vigorously all his life to gain it. He was never sidetracked by fame, power, riches, or comfort, even though he could perhaps have attained any of these. (Acts 20:24; 1 Corinthians 9:2; 2 Corinthians 3:2, 3; Philippians 3:8,

14, 15. Why must a contender in the race for life exercise self-control continually?

16. What does it mean to run "not uncertainly"?
17. (a) How did Paul show that he was running "not uncertainly"? (b) How can we imitate Paul in this regard?

## DIALOGUE NINE: What Must A Person Do In Order To Be Clean In God's Eyes?

their sins in a token way. Thus, they had freedom to approach God in worship. They also had a system of laws and regulations to keep them free from superstitious practices and false worship. Later, they would receive the Promised Land as an inheritance, with the assurance of divine help against their enemies. Their part of the covenant called on the Israelites to keep Jehovah's Law. The Israelites willingly accepted this condition, saying: "All that Jehovah has spoken we are willing to do."—Exodus 19:3-8; Deuteronomy 11:22-25.

11 For more than 1,500 years, the Israelites were in that special relationship with Jehovah. But time after time they failed to keep the covenant. Repeatedly they were seduced by false worship and came into bondage to idolatry and superstition, so God permitted them to be physically enslaved to their enemies. (Judges 2:11-19) Instead of enjoying the liberating blessings that came from keeping the covenant, they were punished because of transgressing it. (Deuteronomy 28:1, 2, 15) Eventually, in 607 B.C.E., Jehovah allowed the nation to become enslaved in Babylon.—2 Chronicles 36:15-21.

12 This was a hard lesson. They should have learned from it the importance of keeping the Law. Nevertheless, when, after 70 years, the Israelites returned to their own land, they still failed to observe the Law covenant properly. Almost a hundred years after their return, Jehovah said to Israel's priests: "You men—you have turned aside from the way. You have caused many to stumble in the law. You have ruined the covenant of Levi." (Malachi 2:8) Indeed, even the most sincere among the Israelites could not measure up to the perfect Law. Instead of being a blessing, it became, in the words of the apostle Paul, "a curse." (Galatians 3:13) Clearly, something more than the Mosaic Law covenant was needed to bring imperfect, faithful humans to the glorious freedom of the children of God.

### The Nature of Christian Freedom

13 That something more was the ransom sacrifice of Jesus Christ. About the year 50 C.E., Paul wrote to the congregation of anointed Christians in Galatia. He described how Jehovah had freed them from slavery to the Law covenant and then said: "For such freedom Christ set us free. Therefore stand fast, and do not let yourselves be confined again in a yoke of slavery." (Galatians 5:1) In what ways did Jesus set men free?

14 After Jesus' death, Jews who accepted him as the Messiah and became his disciples came under a new covenant, which replaced the old Law covenant. (Jeremiah 31:31-34; Hebrews 8:7-13) Under this new covenant, they—and non-Jewish believers who later joined them—became part of a new, spiritual nation that replaced fleshly Israel as God's special people. (Romans 9:25, 26; Galatians 6:16) As such, they enjoyed the freedom that Jesus promised when he said: "The truth will set you free." Apart from setting them free from the curse of the Law of Moses, the truth liberated Jewish Christians from all the onerous traditions that religious leaders had imposed upon them. And it released non-Jewish Christians from the idolatry and superstitions of their former worship. (Matthew 15:3, 6; 23:4; Acts 14:11-13; 17:16) And there was more.

11. What resulted when Israel failed to keep her side of the covenant with Jehovah?
12. What eventually became evident regarding the Mosaic Law covenant?

13. What better basis for freedom was eventually provided?
14, 15. In what wonderful ways did Jesus set believing Jews and non-Jews free?

12 THE WATCHTOWER—JUNE 1, 1992

The fre

15 Jesus,
sets free,
Every doer
8:34) Sinc
individual
and thus a
was Jesus
leased beli
they were
ture. Now
their sins
of Jesus' sa
tions woul
the basis
declared th
proach him
mans 8:33
opened up
endless life
fear of de
2:15.

16 In a w
was opened
what thei

16. How wa
than any fr

; a model **1458**

ere those who had not
rcy, but are now those
shown mercy.[b]
I exhort YOU as aliens
residents[c] to keep ab-
:shly desires,[d] which are
hat carry on a conflict
l.*[e] 12 Maintain YOUR
ıong the nations,[f] that,
which they are speaking
evildoers, they may as
R fine works[g] of which
tnesses glorify God in
] inspection.[h]
ɔrd's* sake subject[i] your-
ıuman creation:[j] wheth-
: being superior 14 or
; being sent by him to
ent on evildoers but to
good.[l] 15 For so the
:hat by doing good YOU
ignorant talk of the un-
ı.[m] 16 Be as free peo-
lding YOUR freedom, not
ɔadness,[o] but as slaves
ɔnor [men] of all sorts,[q]
ıe whole association of
fear of God,[s] have hon-

servants be in subjec-
owners with all [due]
:o the good and reason-
ɔ those hard to please.
eone, because of con-
God, bears up under
and suffers unjustly,
eable thing.[w] 20 For
ıere in it if, when YOU
being slapped,* YOU en-
f, when YOU are doing
suffer,[y] YOU endure it,
greeable with God.[z]
this [course] YOU were
even Christ suffered for
ɔU a model* for YOU to

ıinst the life." Gr., *ka·ta'*
ıt., *ad·ver'sus a'ni·mam;*
*'phesh.* 13* "The Lord's,"
God's"; J[7,8], "Jehovah's."
." 17* "Whole association
"brotherhood." 20* Lit.,
st." 21* Or, "copy." Lit.,
r., *hy·po·gram·mon';* Lat.,

**1459** **Chaste conduct. Weaker vessel. Defense** **1 PETER 2:22—3:19**

follow his steps closely.[a] 22 He committed no sin,[b] nor was deception found
in his mouth.[c] 23 When he was being
reviled,[d] he did not go reviling in return.[e] When he was suffering,[f] he did
not go threatening, but kept on committing himself to the one[g] who judges
righteously. 24 He himself bore* our
sins[h] in his own body upon the stake,*[i]
in order that we might be done with
sins[j] and live to righteousness. And "by
his stripes YOU were healed."[k] 25 For
YOU were like sheep, going astray;[l] but
now YOU have returned to the shepherd[m]
and overseer* of YOUR souls.*

**3** In like manner,[n] YOU wives, be in
subjection[o] to YOUR own husbands,
in order that, if any are not obedient[p] to the word, they may be won*[q]
without a word* through the conduct
of [their] wives,[r] 2 because of having been eyewitnesses of YOUR chaste
conduct[s] together with deep respect.
3 And do not let YOUR adornment be that
of the external braiding of the hair[t] and
of the putting on of gold ornaments[u] or
the wearing of outer garments, 4 but
let it be the secret person*[v] of the
heart in the incorruptible [apparel][w] of
the quiet and mild spirit,[x] which is of
great value in the eyes of God. 5 For
so, too, formerly the holy women* who
were hoping in God used to adorn themselves, subjecting themselves to their
own husbands, 6 as Sarah used to
obey Abraham, calling him "lord."[y] And
YOU have become her children, provided
YOU keep on doing good and not fearing
any cause for terror.[z]
7 YOU husbands, continue dwelling
in like manner[a] with them according to
knowledge,[b] assigning them honor[c] as
to a weaker vessel, the feminine one,
since YOU are also heirs[d] with them of
the undeserved favor of life, in order
for YOUR prayers not to be hindered.[e]

1Pe 2:24* Or, "He himself bore up." 24* Or, "tree." Lit., "wood." Gr., *xy'lon.* See App 5c. 25* "Overseer." Gr., *e·pi'sko·pon;* J[17](Heb.), *peqidh'.* 25* Or, "lives." 3:1* "They may be won," ℵABVg; Sy[p], "you may win them"; J[18], "you may win them to Jehovah." 1* Or, "the word." 4* Or, "the secret man." Lit., "the hidden man." 5* Or, "wives."

**CHAP. 2**
a Mt 16:24; Joh 13:15
b Joh 8:46; Heb 4:15
c Isa 53:9
d Mt 27:39
e Isa 53:7; Ro 12:21
f Heb 5:8
g Jer 11:20; Joh 8:50; Ro 4:24
h Le 16:21; 2Co 5:21
i Php 2:8
j Isa 53:12
k Isa 53:5
l Isa 53:6
m Joh 10:11; Heb 13:20; 1Pe 5:4

**CHAP. 3**
n 1Pe 2:21
o Ro 7:2; 1Co 11:3; 1Co 14:34; Eph 5:22
p Ro 10:16
q Pr 11:30
r 1Co 7:16
s 1Pe 2:12
t 1Ti 2:9
u Pr 11:22
v Ro 7:22; Eph 3:16
w 2Co 4:16; Eph 4:24; Col 3:10
x Pr 25:28; Col 3:12
y Ge 18:12; Eph 5:33
z Pr 3:25; Php 1:28
a 1Pe 2:21
b 1Co 7:3
c Eph 5:25
d Ga 3:28
e La 3:44

**Second Col.**
a 1Co 1:10; Php 2:2
b Ro 12:10; Col 3:12
c Ro 15:5
d Ro 12:17; 1Th 5:15
e 1Pe 2:23
f Ro 12:14; 1Co 4:12
g Ps 34:12
h Jas 3:8
i Ps 34:13; 1Ti 3:11
j Pr 8:13
k Ps 34:14; 1Th 5:13; Jas 3:17; 3Jo 11
l 1Jo 3:22
m Ps 34:15
n Ps 34:16
o Da 6:5; Ro 13:3
p Mt 5:12; Ac 5:41; 1Pe 2:19
q Isa 8:12
r Mt 10:28
s 1Co 1:2
t Col 4:6
u Pr 15:1; 1Ti 6:11; 2Ti 2:25; Tit 3:2

8 Finally, all of YOU be like-minded,[a]
showing fellow feeling,* having brotherly affection, tenderly compassionate,[b]
humble in mind,[c] 9 not paying back
injury for injury[d] or reviling for reviling,[e] but, to the contrary, bestowing a
blessing,[f] because YOU were called to
this [course], so that YOU might inherit
a blessing.
10 For, "he that would love life and
see good days,[g] let him restrain his
tongue[h] from what is bad and [his] lips
from speaking deception,[i] 11 but let
him turn away from what is bad[j] and
do what is good; let him seek peace
and pursue it.[k] 12 For [the] eyes[l] of
Jehovah* are upon the righteous ones,
and his ears are toward their supplication;[m] but [the] face of Jehovah* is
against those doing bad things."[n]
13 Indeed, who is the man that will
harm YOU if YOU become zealous for what
is good?[o] 14 But even if YOU should
suffer for the sake of righteousness,
YOU are happy.[p] However, the object
of their fear do not YOU fear,[q] neither
become agitated.[r] 15 But sanctify the
Christ as Lord* in YOUR hearts,[s] always
ready to make a defense[t] before everyone that demands of YOU a reason for
the hope in YOU, but doing so together
with a mild temper[u] and deep respect.*
16 Hold a good conscience,[v] so that
in the particular in which YOU are spoken against they may get ashamed[w]
who are speaking slightingly of YOUR
good conduct in connection with Christ.[x]
17 For it is better to suffer because
YOU are doing good,[y] if the will of God
wishes it, than because YOU are doing
evil.[z] 18 Why, even Christ died once
for all time concerning sins,[a] a righteous
[person] for unrighteous ones,[b] that he
might lead YOU to God,[c] he being put
to death in the flesh,[d] but being made
alive in the spirit.[e] 19 In this [state]

v Ac 23:1; Ac 24:16; 1Ti 1:5; 1Ti 1:19; 1Ti 3:9; w Tit 2:8; x Ro 12:21; 1Pe 2:12; y 2Co 1:7; Col 1:24; 1Pe 4:12; z Ac 5:9; 1Pe 4:15; a Isa 53:6; Heb 9:28; b Ro 5:6; c 2Co 5:18; d 1Co 15:50; Col 1:22; e 1Ti 3:16.

1Pe 3:8* "Showing fellow feeling." Lit., "sympathetic." Gr., *sym·pa·theis'.* 12* See App 1D. 12* See App 1D. 15* "The Christ as Lord," ℵABC; TR, "the Lord God"; J[7,8,11-14,16,17,24], "Jehovah God." 15* Lit., "fear."

NEW WORLD TRANSLATION - WITH REFERENCES, 1984

people actually not know what these
things mean?' Say, 'Look! The king of
Babylon* came to Jerusalem and proceeded to take its king[a] and its princes
and bring them to himself at Babylon.[b]
13 Furthermore, he took one of the
royal seed[c] and concluded* a covenant
with him and brought him into an oath;[d]
and the foremost men of the land he
took away,[e] 14 in order that the kingdom might become low,[f] unable to lift
itself up, that by keeping his covenant
it* might stand.[g] 15 But he finally rebelled[h] against him in sending his messengers to Egypt, [for it] to give him
horses[i] and a multitudinous people. Will
he have success? Will he escape, he
who is doing these things, and who has
broken a covenant? And will he actually escape?'[j]
16 "'As I am alive,"[k] is the utterance of the Sovereign Lord Jehovah,
"in the place of the king who put in
as king the one that despised his oath[l]
and that broke his covenant, with him
in the midst of Babylon he will die.[m]
17 And by a great military force and
by a multitudinous congregation Phar'-
aoh will not make him effective in the
war,[n] by throwing up a siege rampart
and by building a siege wall, in order to
cut off many souls.[o] 18 And he has
despised an oath[p] in breaking a covenant, and, look! he had given his hand[q]
and has done even all these things. He
will not make his escape."'[r]
19 "'Therefore this is what the Sovereign Lord Jehovah has said: "As I
am alive, surely my oath that he has
despised[s] and my covenant that he has
broken—I will even bring it upon his
head. 20 And I will spread over him
my net, and he will certainly be caught
in my hunting net;[t] and I will bring him
to Babylon and put myself on judgment
with him there respecting his unfaith-
fulness with which he acted against
me.[u] 21 And as regards all the fugi-
tives of his in all his bands, by the
sword they will fall, and the ones left
remaining will be spread abroad even to
every wind.*[a] And YOU people will have
to know that I myself, Jehovah, have
spoken [it]."'[b]
22 "'This is what the Sovereign Lord
Jehovah has said: "I myself will also
take and put some of the lofty tree-
top of the cedar;[c] from the top of its
twigs I shall pluck off a tender one[d]
and I will myself transplant [it] upon a
high and lofty mountain.[e] 23 On the
mountain of the height of Israel I shall
transplant it,[f] and it will certainly bear
boughs and produce fruit[g] and become
a majestic cedar.[h] And under it there
will actually reside all the birds of every wing; in the shadow of its foliage
they will reside.[i] 24 And all the trees
of the field will have to know that I
myself, Jehovah,[j] have abased the high
tree,[k] have put on high the low tree,[l]
have dried up the still-moist tree[m] and
have made the dry tree blossom. I myself, Jehovah, have spoken and have
done[n] [it]."'"

**18** And the word of Jehovah continued to occur to me, saying:
2 "What does it mean to YOU people
that YOU are expressing this proverbial saying on the soil of Israel, saying,
'Fathers are the ones that eat unripe
grapes, but it is the teeth of the sons
that get set on edge'?*[o]
3 "'As I am alive,' is the utterance
of the Sovereign Lord Jehovah, 'it will
no more continue to be YOURS to express this proverbial saying in Israel.
4 Look! All the souls*—to me they belong.[p] As the soul[q] of the father so likewise the soul of the son—to me they
belong.[r] The soul that is sinning[s]—it
itself will die.*[t]

t Ge 2:17; Ge 17:14; Jg 16:30; Job 33:22; Ps 78:50; Isa 53:12; Ac 3:23; Ro 6:23; Re 16:3.

CHAP. 17
a 2Ki 24:12 Jer 22:25
b Isa 39:7 Jer 52:32
c 2Ki 24:17 Jer 37:1
d 2Ch 36:13 Jer 5:2
e 2Ki 24:15 Jer 24:1
f De 28:43 1Sa 2:7
g Jer 27:12 Jer 38:17
h 2Ki 24:20 2Ch 36:13 Jer 52:3 Eze 17:7
i De 17:16 Isa 30:2 Isa 31:1 Jer 37:5
j Pr 19:5 Jer 32:4
k Heb 6:13
l Mal 3:5
m Jer 34:3 Jer 52:11
n Isa 31:1 Jer 37:7 La 4:17 Eze 29:6
o Jer 33:5
p Mt 5:37 Ro 1:31
q La 5:6
r Eze 17:15
s De 5:11 Jer 5:2
t 2Ch 33:11 Eze 12:13 Eze 32:3 Ho 7:12
u Eze 20:36 Mic 6:2

Second Col.
a Eze 5:10 Eze 12:14
b Eze 6:13
c Ps 80:15 Isa 11:1 Jer 23:5 Jer 33:15 Zec 3:8
d Isa 53:2
e Ps 2:6
f Ps 92:13 Da 4:17
g Isa 27:6
h Ps 92:12
i Ps 72:8 Ho 14:7
j Isa 55:12
k 1Sa 2:7 Ps 75:7 Lu 1:52
l Isa 9:6 Eze 21:27 Da 4:17 Am 9:11
m Lu 23:31
n Eze 22:14 Eze 24:14

CHAP. 18
o Jer 15:4 Jer 31:29 La 5:7
p Ps 100:3 Ac 17:26
q Ge 2:7
r De 26:18
s Ro 3:23 Ro 5:12

Eze 17:12* "Babylon," LXXVg; MTSy, "Babel." 13* Lit., "cut." 14* "It," M, fem. sing., referring to the "kingdom"; margin of one Heb. ms, "him," masc. sing., referring to the king.

Eze 17:21* "To every wind," representing direction. Heb., *lekhol-ru'ach;* Gr., *eis pan'ta a'ne·mon;* Lat., *in o'mnem ven'tum.* Compare Ge 1:2 ftn, "Force." 18:2* Lit., "get blunted (dulled)." 4* "The souls." Heb., *han·nepha·shohth';* Gr., *psy·khai';* Lat., *a'ni·mae.* See App 4A. 4* Or, "The soul that is sinning is the one that will die." Heb., *han·ne'phesh ha·cho·te'th' hi' tha·muth'.*



5 "'And as regar
he happens to be ri
executed justice a
6 on the mountains[t]
his eyes he did not
idols of the house
companion's wife he
to a woman in her
not go near;[f] 7 an
maltreat;[g] the pledg
indebtedness, he wou
would he wrest aw
the hungry one he
bread[j] and the nake
er with a garment;[k]
he give on interest[l]
he take;[m] from injus
back his hand;[n] tru
execute between ma
my statutes he kep
judicial decisions h
execute truth,[q] he is
positively keep livin
of the Sovereign Lo
10 "'And [if] one
to a son who is a ro
blood,[u] who has do
of these things* 1
has done none of t
in case he has ea
mountains,[v] and his
he has defiled;[w] 1
poor one he has mal
has wrested away in
thing he would not
dungy idols he lift
detestable thing is
13 On usury he has
he has taken,[d] and h
keep living. All thes
he has done.[e] He wi
to death. On him
come to be.[f]
14 "'And, look! c
ther to a son, who h
sins of his father th
he sees* and does
them.[g] 15 On the
not eaten, and his e

Eze 18:5* Lit., "And a
10* Lit., "done the bro
things," M; T, "done
these things"; SyVg, "d
things." 14* "Sees," M

NEW WORLD TRANSLATION

## DIALOGUE TEN: Doing God's Will—What Does It Mean To "Come To Jesus"?



that God's Word provides, and that is why you have a religion, is that not right?' **Then perhaps add:** 'Here at Matthew 7:13, 14 the Bible provides us some very valuable guidance in the words of Jesus. (Read it.) . . . Why might that be so?'

See also pages 322, 323.

**'As long as you believe in Jesus, it really does not matter what church you belong to'**

**You might reply:** 'There is no question about it, belief in Jesus is vital. And I assume that by that you mean accepting everything that he taught. No doubt you have observed, as I have, that many who say they are Christians really do not live up to what that name represents.' **Then perhaps add:** (1) 'Notice what Jesus said here at Matthew 7:21-23.' (2) 'There is a wonderful future for those who care enough to find out what God's will is and then do it. (Ps. 37:10, 11; Rev. 21:4)'

**'What makes you think there is only one religion that is right?'**

**You might reply:** 'Without doubt, there are sincere people in almost every religion. But what really counts is what God's Word says. How many true faiths does it refer to? Notice what is written here at Ephesians 4:4, 5.' **Then perhaps add:** (1) 'That agrees with what other texts state. (Matt. 7:13, 14, 21; John 10:16; 17:20, 21)' (2) 'So, the challenge that we must face is identifying that religion. How can we do it? (Perhaps use material on pages 328-330.)' (3) (See also what is on pages 199, 200, under the heading "Jehovah's Witnesses.")

**'I just read my Bible at home and pray to God for understanding'**

**You might reply:** 'Have you succeeded in reading the entire Bible as yet?' **Then perhaps add:** 'As you work on that, you will find something very interesting at Matthew 28:19, 20. . . . This is significant because it shows that Christ



uses other humans to help us to understand what is involved in being a real Christian. In harmony with that, Jehovah's Witnesses offer to visit people in their home for an hour or so each week, free of charge, to discuss the Bible. May I take just a few minutes to show you how we go about it?'

See also page 328.

**'I feel that religion is a private affair'**

**You might reply:** 'That is a common view nowadays, and if folks are really not interested in the Bible's message, we gladly go on to other homes. But did you realize that the reason I came to see you was that this is what Jesus instructed his followers to do? . . . (Matt. 24:14; 28:19, 20; 10:40)'

# Resurrection

**Definition:** *A·na'sta·sis,* the Greek word translated "resurrection," literally means "a standing up again" and it refers to a rising up from death. The fuller expression "resurrection of (from) the dead" is used repeatedly in the Scriptures. (Matt. 22:31; Acts 4:2; 1 Cor. 15:12) The Hebrew is *techi·yath' ham·me·thim',* which means "revival of the dead." (Matt. 22:23, ftn, *NW* Reference edition) Resurrection involves a reactivating of the life pattern of the individual, which life pattern God has retained in his memory. According to God's will for the individual, the person is restored in either a human or a spirit body and yet retains his personal identity, having the same personality and memories as when he died. The provision for resurrection of the dead is a magnificent expression of Jehovah's undeserved kindness; it displays his wisdom and power and is a means by which his original purpose regarding the earth will be carried out.

**Is the resurrection a reuniting of an immaterial soul with the physical body?**

For this to be possible, of course, humans would have to have an immaterial soul that could separate from the physical body. The Bible does not teach such a thing. That notion was borrowed from Greek philosophy. The Bible teaching

REASONING FROM THE SCRIPTURES, 1985, 1989 ed

need to make sure that our worship meets God's requirements.

## DOING THE WILL OF THE FATHER

6 Let us read Matthew 7:21-23 and see if we can isolate a crucial factor that determines whether all worship is acceptable to God. Jesus said: "Not everyone saying to me, 'Lord, Lord,' will enter into the kingdom of the heavens, but the one doing the will of my Father who is in the heavens will. Many will say to me in that day, 'Lord, Lord, did we not prophesy in your name, and expel demons [wicked spirit creatures] in your name, and perform many powerful works in your name?' And yet then I will confess to them: I never knew you! Get away from me, you workers of lawlessness."

7 Acknowledging Jesus Christ as Lord is essential in true worship. But something would be missing in the worship of many of those claiming to be Jesus' disciples. He said that some would perform "powerful works," such as supposed miraculous healings. However, they would fail to do what Jesus said is vital. They would not be "doing the will of [his] Father." If we want to please God, we must learn what the will of the Father is and then do it.

## ACCURATE KNOWLEDGE—A PROTECTION

8 Doing God's will requires an accurate knowledge of both Jehovah God and Jesus Christ. Such knowledge leads to everlasting life. Surely, then, all of us will want

6, 7. Why does Jesus not acknowledge some who claim to be his disciples?

8. If we are to do God's will, what is required, and what mistaken views must we avoid?



to take seriously the matter of gaining accurate knowledge from God's Word, the Bible. Some say that there is no need for concern as long as we are sincere and zealous in our worship. Others claim, 'The less you know, the less is expected of you.' Yet, the Bible encourages us to increase in the knowledge of God and his purposes. —Ephesians 4:13; Philippians 1:9; Colossians 1:9.

9 Such knowledge is a protection against contamination of our worship. The apostle Paul spoke of a certain spirit creature who pretends to be "an angel of light." (2 Corinthians 11:14) Thus disguised, this spirit creature—Satan—tries to mislead us into doing things contrary to God's will. Other spirit creatures associated with Satan have also been polluting people's worship, for Paul said: "The things which the nations sacrifice they sacrifice to demons, and not to God." (1 Corinthians 10:20) Likely, many have thought they were worshiping in the right way, although they were not doing what God wanted. They were being misled into unclean false worship. We will learn more about Satan and the demons later, but these enemies of God have definitely been polluting mankind's worship.

10 If you knew that someone had deliberately poisoned your water supply, would you go on drinking from it? Surely, you would take immediate action to find a source of safe, pure water. Well, an accurate knowledge of God's Word equips us to identify true religion and to reject impurities that make worship unacceptable to God.

9. How does accurate knowledge protect us, and why do we need such protection?

10. What would you do if someone deliberately poisoned your water supply, and what does accurate knowledge of God's Word equip us to do?

KNOWLEDGE THAT LEADS TO EVERLASTING LIFE, 1995

ıch one's claims or
feel that *some* of
·e uncanny power,
ho tried them did
no thought of in-
It may have been
esperate desire for
who have been in-
have decided later
al benefit was not

must resolve what
onal matters. Yet,
nber God's coun-
ced puts faith in
wd one considers
5) That applies to

ct God's servants
evil would rejoice
ıg Christians fas-
·sts. He would be
ıey became fasci-
·e, or seem to be,
night draw them
:8.

ıot under the Mo-
attitude toward
changed. As not-
ed the Israelites
ys divination, a
ıne who looks for
e who binds oth-
ı be found among
these things is
ehovah . . . You
itless with Jeho-
)-13.

Christians today
ıit of armor from
a wrestling . . .
rces in the heav-
:11, 12.

# Should You Pray to Jesus?

SOME people consider it proper to pray to Jesus. In Germany many have been taught as children that before their meals they should fold their hands and thank Jesus Christ.

According to the Bible, Jesus indeed occupies a very high position in heaven. Does that, however, mean that we should pray to him? You may be among those who, out of love for Jesus, direct prayers to him, but what does Jesus himself think about such prayers?

First, why do these questions even arise? Because the Bible says that Jehovah God is the "Hearer of prayer." It is hardly surprising, then, that servants of God in ancient times, such as the Israelites, prayed only to Jehovah God, the Almighty.—Psalm 5:1, 2; 65:2.

Did things change when Jesus, the Son of God, came to earth to deliver mankind from sin and death? No, prayers were still directed to Jehovah. When on earth Jesus himself prayed frequently to his heavenly Father, and he taught others to do likewise. Just think of the model prayer, sometimes called the Lord's Prayer or the Our Father, which is one of the best-known prayers in the world. Jesus did not teach us to pray to him; he gave us this model: "Our Father in the heavens, let your name be sanctified." —Matthew 6:6, 9; 26:39, 42.

Now let us look at the subject more thoroughly by examining what prayer actually is.

### What Is a Prayer?

Every prayer is a form of worship. *The World Book Encyclopedia* confirms this, stating: "Prayer is a form of worship in

THE WATCHTOWER—DECEMBER 15, 1994 23

which a person may offer devotion, thanks, confession, or supplication to God."

On one occasion Jesus said: "It is written, 'It is Jehovah your God you must worship, and it is to him alone you must render sacred service.'" Jesus adhered to the fundamental truth that worship—hence also prayers—is to be addressed only to his Father, Jehovah God.—Luke 4:8; 6:12.

**Acknowledging Jesus in Our Prayers**

Jesus died as a ransom sacrifice for mankind, was resurrected by God, and was exalted to a superior position. As you might imagine, all of this did bring about a change regarding acceptable prayers. In what way?

The apostle Paul describes the great influence that Jesus' position exerts on prayer as follows: "For this very reason also God exalted him to a superior position and kindly gave him the name that is above every other name, so that in the name of Jesus every knee should bend of those in heaven and those on earth and those under the ground, and every tongue should openly acknowledge that Jesus Christ is Lord to the glory of God the Father."—Philippians 2:9-11.

Do the words *"in the name* of Jesus every knee should bend" mean that we are to pray to him? No. The Greek phrase here involved "denotes the name upon which those that bow the knee unite, on which united all (πᾶν γόνυ) worship. The name which Jesus has received moves all to united adoration." (*A Grammar of the Idiom of the New Testament,* by G. B. Winer) Indeed, for a prayer to be acceptable, it must be presented "in the name of Jesus," but it is, nevertheless, addressed to Jehovah God and serves to his glorification. For this reason, Paul says: "In everything by prayer and supplication along with thanksgiving let your petitions be made known *to God."* —Philippians 4:6.

Just as a path leads to a goal, so Jesus is the "way" that leads to God the Almighty. "I am the way and the truth and the life. No one comes to the Father except through me," Jesus taught the apostles. (John 14:6) Thus, we should present our prayers to God through Jesus and not directly to Jesus himself.*

'But,' some may ask, 'does the Bible not report that both the disciple Stephen and the apostle John spoke to Jesus in heaven?' That is true. These events, however, did not involve prayers, as Stephen and John each saw Jesus in vision and spoke to him directly. (Acts 7:56, 59; Revelation 1:17-19; 22:20) Bear in mind that simply speaking even to God does not in itself constitute a prayer. Adam and Eve spoke to God, offering excuses for their great sin, when He judged them following their sin in Eden. Their talking to him in that way was not a prayer. (Genesis 3:8-19) Hence, it would be incorrect to cite Stephen's or John's talking to Jesus as evidence that we actually should pray to him.

**How Is the Name of Jesus 'Called Upon'?**

Do you have lingering doubts, still considering it proper to pray to Jesus? One woman wrote to a branch office of the Watch Tower Society: "Unfortunately, I am still not convinced that the first Christians did not pray to Jesus." She had in mind Paul's words at 1 Corinthians 1:2, where he mentioned "all who everywhere are *calling upon* the name of our Lord, Jesus Christ."

* Some might pray to Jesus because they believe that he is God. But Jesus was the *Son* of God, and he himself worshiped Jehovah, his Father. (John 20:17) For a detailed discussion of this subject, see *Should You Believe in the Trinity?,* published by the Watchtower Bible and Tract Society of New York, Inc.



One should note,
inal language, th
can mean things
How was the n
everywhere? One
ers of Jesus of
edged him to be
of the world," p
lous acts in his
3:6; 19:5) There
*ble* states that t
name of our Lor
lordship rather t
Accepting Ch
his shed blood, w
of sins possible,
upon the name
(Compare Acts
literally say Jes
to God through
we can call upon
ble does not indi
him.—Ephesian

**What Je**

Jesus clearly
you ask anythin
Does this requi
asking is addre
in Jesus' name.
petition God th
great power an
How does Je
true followers t
the congregati
may serve as a
it to a body an
The "head" su
spiritual body
"joints and lig
arrangements
tion with spirit
tion. (Colossia
Jesus today us

known *to God."*

a goal, so Je-
to God the Al-
. the truth and
the Father ex-
ught the apos-
should present
Jesus and not

s the Bible not
e Stephen and
sus in heaven?'
owever, did not
and John each
oke to him di-
lation 1:17-19;
mply speaking
lf constitute a
to God, offer-
sin, when He
sin in Eden.
way was not a
ce, it would be
or John's talk-
at we actually

ne
pon'?
ubts, still con-
to Jesus? One
office of the
tunately, I am
rst Christians
had in mind
1:2, where he
ere are *calling*
Jesus Christ."

ause they believe
on of God, and he
her. (John 20:17)
bject, see *Should*
d by the Watch-
York, Inc.

One should note, however, that in the original language, the expression "to call upon" can mean things other than prayer.

How was the name of Christ 'called upon' everywhere? One way was that the followers of Jesus of Nazareth openly acknowledged him to be the Messiah and "Savior of the world," performing many miraculous acts in his name. (1 John 4:14; Acts 3:6; 19:5) Therefore, *The Interpreter's Bible* states that the phrase "to call on the name of our Lord . . . means to confess his lordship rather than to pray to him."

Accepting Christ and exercising faith in his shed blood, which make the forgiveness of sins possible, also constitute a "calling upon the name of our Lord, Jesus Christ." (Compare Acts 10:43 with 22:16.) And we literally say Jesus' name whenever we pray to God through him. So, while showing that we can call upon the name of Jesus, the Bible does not indicate that we should pray to him.—Ephesians 5:20; Colossians 3:17.

### What Jesus Can Do for Us

Jesus clearly promised his disciples: "If you ask anything in my name, I will do it." Does this require praying to him? No. The asking is addressed to Jehovah God—but in Jesus' name. (John 14:13, 14; 15:16) We petition God that His Son, Jesus, apply his great power and authority in our behalf.

How does Jesus communicate with his true followers today? Paul's description of the congregation of anointed Christians may serve as an illustration. He compared it to a body and Jesus Christ to the head. The "head" supplies the members of the spiritual body with their needs by way of "joints and ligaments," or the means and arrangements for supplying his congregation with spiritual nourishment and direction. (Colossians 2:19) In a similar way, Jesus today uses "gifts in men," or spiritually qualified men, to take the lead in the congregation, even administering correction if it becomes necessary. There is no provision for members of the congregation to communicate directly with Jesus or to pray to him, but they certainly should —yes, must—pray to Jesus' Father, Jehovah God.—Ephesians 4:8-12.

### How Do You Honor Jesus?

Concerning the salvation of humans, what a key role Jesus occupies! The apostle Peter exclaimed: "There is no salvation in anyone else, for there is not another name under heaven that has been given among men by which we must get saved." (Acts 4:12) Are you aware of the importance of Jesus' name?

By not directing prayers to Jesus personally, we are not degrading his position. Rather, Jesus is honored when we pray in his name. And just as children honor their parents by being obedient, we honor Jesus Christ by obeying his commandments, especially the new commandment to love one another.—John 5:23; 13:34.

### Acceptable Prayers

Do you desire to offer acceptable prayers? Then direct them to Jehovah God, and do so in the name of his Son, Jesus. Come to know God's will, and let your prayers reflect that understanding. (1 John 3:21, 22; 5:14) Draw strength from the words of Psalm 66: 20: "Blessed be God, who has not turned aside my prayer, nor his loving-kindness from me."

As we have seen, prayers are a form of worship that belongs exclusively to Almighty God. By addressing all our prayers to Jehovah God, we indicate that we have taken to heart Jesus' direction to pray: "Our Father in the heavens."—Matthew 6:9.

worship at the feast; 21 these therefore
came to Philip, who was from Bethsaida of
Galilee, and *began to* ask him, saying, "Sir,
we wish to see Jesus." 22 Philip *came and
*told Andrew; Andrew and Philip *came,
and they *told Jesus. 23 And Jesus *answered them, saying, "The hour has come
for the Son of Man to be glorified.
24 "Truly, truly, I say to you, unless a grain
of wheat falls into the earth and dies, it remains by itself alone; but if it dies, it bears
much fruit. 25 "He who loves his life loses
it; and he who hates his life in this world
shall keep it to life eternal. 26 "If anyone
serves Me, let him follow Me; and where I
am, there shall My servant also be; if anyone serves Me, the Father will honor him.

*Jesus Foretells His Death*

27 "Now My soul has become troubled;
and what shall I say, 'Father, save Me from
this hour'? But for this purpose I came to
this hour. 28 "Father, glorify Thy name."
There came therefore a voice out of
heaven: "I have both glorified it, and will
glorify it again." 29 The multitude therefore, who stood by and heard it, were saying that it had thundered; others were saying, "An angel has spoken to Him."
30 Jesus answered and said, "This voice has
not come for My sake, but for your sakes.
31 "Now judgment is upon this world; now
the ruler of this world shall be cast out.
32 "And I, if I be lifted up from the earth,
will draw all men to Myself." 33 But He
was saying this to indicate the kind of
death by which He was to die. 34 The multitude therefore answered Him, "We have
heard out of the Law that the Christ is to
remain forever; and how can You say, 'The
Son of Man must be lifted up'? Who is this
Son of Man?" 35 Jesus therefore said to
them, "For a little while longer the light is
among you. Walk while you have the light,
that darkness may not overtake you; he
who walks in the darkness does not know
where he goes. 36 "While you have the
light, believe in the light, in order that you
may become sons of light."
These things Jesus spoke, and He departed and hid Himself from them. 37 But
though He had performed so many signs
before them, *yet* they were not believing in
Him; 38 that the word of Isaiah the prophet
might be fulfilled, which he spoke, "LORD,
WHO HAS BELIEVED OUR REPORT? AND TO
WHOM HAS THE ARM OF THE LORD BEEN RE-
VEALED?" 39 For this cause they could not
believe, for Isaiah said again, 40 "HE HAS
BLINDED THEIR EYES, AND HE HARDENED
THEIR HEART; LEST THEY SEE WITH THEIR
EYES, AND PERCEIVE WITH THEIR HEART, AND
BE CONVERTED, AND I HEAL THEM." 41 These
things Isaiah said, because he saw His glory, and he spoke of Him. 42 Nevertheless
many even of the rulers believed in Him,
but because of the Pharisees they were not
confessing *Him*, lest they should be put out
of the synagogue; 43 for they loved the approval of men rather than the approval of
God.
44 And Jesus cried out and said, "He
who believes in Me does not believe in Me,
but in Him who sent Me. 45 "And he who
beholds Me beholds the One who sent Me.
46 "I have come *as* light into the world,
that everyone who believes in Me may not
remain in darkness. 47 "And if anyone
hears My sayings, and does not keep them,
I do not judge him; for I did not come to
judge the world, but to save the world.
48 "He who rejects Me, and does not receive My sayings, has one who judges him;
the word I spoke is what will judge him at
the last day. 49 "For I did not speak on My
own initiative, but the Father Himself who
sent Me has given Me commandment,
what to say, and what to speak. 50 "And I
know that His commandment is eternal
life; therefore the things I speak, I speak
just as the Father has told Me."

*The Lord's Supper*

13 NOW before the Feast of the Passover, Jesus knowing that His hour
had come that He should depart out of this
world to the Father, having loved His own
who were in the world, He loved them to
the end. 2 And during supper, the devil
having already put into the heart of Judas
Iscariot, *the son* of Simon, to betray Him,
3 *Jesus*, knowing that the Father had given
all things into His hands, and that He had
come forth from God, and was going back
to God, 4 *rose from supper, and *laid
aside His garments; and taking a towel, He
girded Himself about.

*Jesus Washes the Disciples' Feet*

5 Then He *poured water into the basin,
and began to wash the disciples' feet, and
to wipe them with the towel with which
He was girded. 6 And so He *came to Simon Peter. He *said to Him, "Lord, do
You wash my feet?" 7 Jesus answered and
said to him, "What I do you do not realize
now, but you shall understand hereafter."
8 Peter *said to Him, "Never shall You
wash my feet!" Jesus answered him, "If I
do not wash you, you have no part with
Me." 9 Simon Peter *said to Him, "Lord,
not my feet only, but also my hands and
my head." 10 Jesus *said to him, "He who
has bathed needs only to wash his feet, but
is completely clean; and you are clean, but
not all *of you*." 11 For He knew the one
who was betraying Him; for this reason He
said, "Not all of you are clean."
12 And so when He had washed their
feet, and taken His garments, and reclined
*at the table* again, He said to them, "Do you
know what I have done to you? 13 "You



call Me Teacher and Lord; and you are
right, for *so* I am. 14 "If I then, the Lord
and the Teacher, washed your feet, you
also ought to wash one another's feet.
15 "For I gave you an example that you
also should do as I did to you. 16 "Truly,
truly, I say to you, a slave is not greater
than his master; neither *is* one who is sent
greater than the one who sent him. 17 "If
you know these things, you are blessed
if you do them. 18 "I do not speak of all of
you. I know the ones I have chosen; but *it*
*is* that the Scripture may be fulfilled, 'HE
WHO EATS MY BREAD HAS LIFTED UP HIS
HEEL AGAINST ME.' 19 "From now on I am
telling you before *it* comes to pass, so that
when it does occur, you may believe that I
am *He*. 20 "Truly, truly, I say to you, he
who receives whomever I send receives
Me; and he who receives Me receives Him
who sent Me."

*Jesus Predicts His Betrayal*

21 When Jesus had said this, He became
troubled in spirit, and testified, and said,
"Truly, truly, I say to you, that one of you
will betray Me." 22 The disciples *began*
looking at one another, at a loss *to know* of
which one He was speaking. 23 There was
reclining on Jesus' breast one of His disciples, whom Jesus loved. 24 Simon Peter
therefore *gestured to him, and *said to
him, "Tell *us* who it is of whom He is
speaking." 25 He, leaning back thus on
Jesus' breast, *said to Him, "Lord, who is
it?" 26 Jesus therefore *answered, "That is
the one for whom I shall dip the morsel
and give it to him." So when He had
dipped the morsel, He *took and *gave it
to Judas, *the son* of Simon Iscariot. 27 And
after the morsel, Satan then entered into
him. Jesus therefore *said to him, "What
you do, do quickly." 28 Now no one of
those reclining *at the table* knew for what
purpose He had said this to him. 29 For
some were supposing, because Judas had
the money box, that Jesus was saying to
him, "Buy the things we have need of for
the feast"; or else, that he should give
something to the poor. 30 And so after receiving the morsel he went out immediately; and it was night.
31 When therefore he had gone out,
Jesus *said, "Now is the Son of Man glorified, and God is glorified in Him; 32 if God
is glorified in Him, God will also glorify
Him in Himself, and will glorify Him immediately. 33 "Little children, I am with
you a little while longer. You shall seek
Me; and as I said to the Jews, I now say to
you also, 'Where I am going, you cannot
come.' 34 "A new commandment I give to
you, that you love one another, even as I
have loved you, that you also love one another. 35 "By this all men will know that
you are My disciples, if you have love for
one another."
36 Simon Peter *said to Him, "Lord,
where are You going?" Jesus answered,
"Where I go, you cannot follow Me now;
but you shall follow later." 37 Peter *said
to Him, "Lord, why can I not follow You
right now? I will lay down my life for
You." 38 Jesus *answered, "Will you lay
down your life for Me? Truly, truly, I say
to you, a cock shall not crow, until you
deny Me three times.

*Jesus Comforts His Disciples*

14 "LET not your heart be troubled;
[23]believe in God, believe also in Me.
2 "In My Father's house are many dwelling
places; if it were not so, I would have told
you; for I go to prepare a place for you.
3 "And if I go and prepare a place for you,
I will come again, and receive you to Myself; that where I am, *there* you may be also.
4 "[24]And you know the way where I am
going." 5 Thomas *said to Him, "Lord, we
do not know where You are going, how do
we know the way?" 6 Jesus *said to him, "I
am the way, and the truth, and the life; no
one comes to the Father, but through Me.

*Oneness with the Father*

7 "If you had known Me, you would have
known My Father also; from now on you
know Him, and have seen Him." 8 Philip
*said to Him, "Lord, show us the Father,
and it is enough for us." 9 Jesus *said to
him, "Have I been so long with you, and
*yet* you have not come to know Me, Philip?
He who has seen Me has seen the Father;
how do you say, 'Show us the Father'?
10 "Do you not believe that I am in the
Father, and the Father is in Me? The
words that I say to you I do not speak on
My own initiative, but the Father abiding
in Me does His works. 11 "Believe Me that
I am in the Father, and the Father in Me;
otherwise believe on account of the works
themselves. 12 "Truly, truly, I say to you,
he who believes in Me, the works that I do
shall he do also; and greater *works* than
these shall he do; because I go to the Father. 13 "And whatever you ask in My
name, that will I do, that the Father may
be glorified in the Son. 14 "If you ask Me
anything in My name, I will do *it*. 15 "If
you love Me, you will keep My commandments.

*Role of the Spirit*

16 "And I will ask the Father, and He will
give you another Helper, that He may be
with you forever; 17 *that is* the Spirit of
truth, whom the world cannot receive, because it does not behold Him or know

[23] *Or, you believe in God*
[24] Many ancient authorities read *And where I go you know, and the way you know*

NEW AMERICAN STANDARD BIBLE

ıing at the table
ıse he said this to
'act, were imagin-
holding the money
telling him: "Buy
. for the festival,"
e something to the
, after he received
out immediately.

: had gone out, Je-
on of man is glori-
ified in connection
God will himself
: will glorify him
ttle children,[f] I am
ger. You will look
: said to the Jews,
ınot come,'[g] I say
nt. 34 I am giv-
andment, that YOU
st as I have loved
love one another.[i]
now that YOU are
have love among

aid to him: "Lord,
'" Jesus answered:
u cannot follow me
llow afterwards."[k]
m: "Lord, why is
ou at present? I
ıl in your behalf."[l]
"Will you surren-
behalf? Most truly
will by no means
disowned me three

UR hearts be trou-
se faith in God,[o]
n me.[p] 2 In the
: there are many
I would have told
going my way to
YOU. 3 Also, if I
re a place for YOU,
: and will receive

:32; Col 1:5; 1Pe 1:4; s Ac

ıns of him." 38* Or,
at., a'ni·mam; J17,18,22
om ne'phesh).



YOU home to myself,[a] that where I am
YOU also may be.[b] 4 And where I am
going YOU know the way."
5 Thomas[c] said to him: "Lord,* we
do not know where you are going.[d] How
do we know the way?"
6 Jesus said to him: "I am the way[e]
and the truth[f] and the life.[g] No one
comes to the Father except through
me.[h] 7 If YOU men had known me,
YOU would have known my Father also;
from this moment on YOU know him and
have seen him."[i]
8 Philip said to him: "Lord, show us
the Father, and it is enough for us."
9 Jesus said to him: "Have I been
with YOU men so long a time, and yet,
Philip, you have not come to know me?
He that has seen me has seen the Father[j] [also]. How is it you say, 'Show us
the Father'?[k] 10 Do you not believe
that I am in union with the Father and
the Father is in union with me?[l] The
things I say to YOU men I do not speak
of my own originality;* but the Father
who remains in union with me is doing
his works.[m] 11 Believe me that I am
in union with the Father and the Father
is in union with me; otherwise, believe
on account of the works themselves.[n]
12 Most truly I say to YOU, He that
exercises faith in me, that one also will
do the works that I do; and he will
do works greater[o] than these, because
I am going my way to the Father.[p]
13 Also, whatever it is that YOU ask in
my name, I will do this, in order that
the Father may be glorified in connection with the Son.[q] 14 If YOU ask*
anything in my name, I will do it.
15 "If YOU love me, YOU will observe
my commandments;[r] 16 and I will request the Father and he will give YOU
another helper* to be with YOU forever,[s]
17 the spirit* of the truth,[t] which the
world cannot receive,[u] because it neither beholds it nor knows it. You know

Joh 14:5* Or, "Master." 10* Lit., "from myself." 14* "Ask," ADIt and in agreement with 15:16 and 16:23; P66ℵBWVgSyh,p, "ask me." 16* Or, "another paraclete (comforter)." Gr., al'lon pa·ra'kle·ton, masc. 17* Or, "the active force." Gr., to pneu'ma, neuter. See Ge 1:2 ftn, "Force."

CHAP. 14
a Joh 17:24; Ro 8:17; 1Co 15:23; Php 1:23; 1Th 4:16; 2Ti 4:8; Heb 10:19
b 1Th 4:17
c Joh 11:16
d Joh 13:36
e Joh 10:9; Ro 5:2; Eph 2:18; Heb 10:20
f Joh 1:17; Ro 15:8; Eph 4:21; Col 2:17
g Joh 1:4; Joh 6:63; Joh 17:3; Ro 6:23; Re 2:10
h Ac 4:12
i Mt 11:27; Joh 1:18; Joh 8:19; 1Jo 4:12
j Joh 5:19; Joh 8:28; Col 1:15; Heb 1:3
k Joh 12:45
l Joh 10:38; Joh 17:21
m Joh 7:16; Joh 8:28; Joh 12:49
n Joh 5:36
o Mt 21:21; Ac 1:8; Ac 2:41; Col 1:23
p Ac 2:33
q Joh 15:16; Joh 16:23
r Joh 13:34; Joh 15:10; Jas 1:22; 1Jo 5:3
s Lu 24:49; Joh 15:26; Joh 16:7; Ac 1:5; Ac 2:4; Ro 8:26
t Mt 10:20; Joh 16:13; 1Co 2:12; 1Jo 2:27
u 1Co 2:14

Second Col.
a Ga 4:6
b Mt 28:20
c Mt 23:39
d Joh 16:16; Joh 17:24
e 1Co 15:22
f Joh 10:38; Joh 17:21
g 1Jo 2:5; 1Jo 5:1
h Lu 6:16; Ac 1:13
i Joh 7:4; Ac 10:41
j Joh 15:10
k 1Jo 2:24; Re 3:20
l Joh 5:19; Joh 7:16; Joh 12:49
m Lu 24:49; Joh 15:26; Joh 16:13; 1Jo 2:27

it,* because it remains with YOU and is
in YOU.[a] 18 I shall not leave YOU bereaved.*[b] I am coming to YOU. 19 A
little longer and the world will behold
me no more,[c] but YOU will behold me,[d]
because I live and YOU will live.[e] 20 In
that day YOU will know that I am in
union with my Father and YOU are in
union with me and I am in union with
YOU.[f] 21 He that has my commandments and observes them, that one is
he who loves me.[g] In turn he that loves
me will be loved by my Father, and I
will love him and will plainly show myself to him."
22 Judas,[h] not Is·car'i·ot, said to him:
"Lord, what has happened that you intend to show yourself plainly to us and
not to the world?"[i]
23 In answer Jesus said to him: "If
anyone loves me, he will observe[j] my
word, and my Father will love him, and
we shall come to him and make our
abode with him.[k] 24 He that does not
love me does not observe my words;
and the word that YOU are hearing is
not mine, but belongs to the Father
who sent me.[l]
25 "While remaining with YOU I have
spoken these things to YOU. 26 But
the helper,* the holy spirit, which the
Father will send in my name, that one*
will teach YOU all things and bring back
to YOUR minds all the things I told
YOU.[m] 27 I leave YOU peace, I give YOU
my peace.[n] I do not give it to YOU the
way that the world gives it. Do not let
YOUR hearts be troubled nor let them
shrink for fear. 28 You heard that I
said to YOU, I am going away and I am
coming [back] to YOU. If YOU loved me,
YOU would rejoice that I am going my
way to the Father, because the Father
is greater[o] than I am. 29 So now I
have told YOU before it occurs,[p] in or-

n Joh 16:33; Eph 2:14; Php 4:7; Col 3:15; 2Th 3:16; o Joh 20:17; 1Co 11:3; 1Co 15:28; Php 2:6; p Joh 13:19; Joh 16:4.

Joh 14:17* "Beholds it . . . . You know it." "It" (Gr., au·to', neuter) refers to "the spirit" (to pneu'ma, neuter). 18* Or, "orphans." Gr., or·pha·nous'; Lat., or'fa·nos. 26* Or, "the paraclete (comforter)." Gr., ho . . . pa·ra'kle·tos, masc. 26* "That one," masc., referring to the "helper," masc.

NEW WORLD TRANSLATION OF THE HOLY SCRIPTURES - WITH REFERENCES
1984

6 λέγει αὐτῷ Ἰησοῦς Ἐγώ εἰμι
Is saying to him Jesus I am
ἡ ὁδὸς καὶ ἡ ἀλήθεια καὶ ἡ ζωή·
the way and the truth and the life;
οὐδεὶς ἔρχεται πρὸς τὸν πατέρα εἰ
no one is coming toward the Father if
μὴ δι' ἐμοῦ. 7 εἰ ἐγνώκειτέ με, καὶ
not through me. If you had known me, also
τὸν πατέρα μου ἂν ᾔδειτε· ἀπ'
the Father of me likely you had perceived; from
ἄρτι γινώσκετε αὐτὸν καὶ ἑωράκατε.
right now you are knowing him and you have seen.
8 Λέγει αὐτῷ Φίλιππος Κύριε, δεῖξον
Is saying to him Philip Lord, show
ἡμῖν τὸν πατέρα, καὶ ἀρκεῖ ἡμῖν.
to us the Father, and it is sufficient to us.
9 λέγει αὐτῷ ὁ Ἰησοῦς Τοσοῦτον χρόνον
Is saying to him the Jesus So much time
μεθ' ὑμῶν εἰμὶ καὶ οὐκ ἔγνωκάς με,
with you I am and not you have known me,
Φίλιππε; ὁ ἑωρακὼς ἐμὲ ἑώρακεν τὸν
Philip? The (one) having seen me has seen the
πατέρα· πῶς σὺ λέγεις Δεῖξον ἡμῖν τὸν
Father; how you are saying Show to us the
πατέρα; 10 οὐ πιστεύεις ὅτι ἐγὼ ἐν
Father? Not you are believing that I in
τῷ πατρὶ καὶ ὁ πατὴρ ἐν ἐμοί ἐστιν; τὰ
the Father and the Father in me is? The
ῥήματα ἃ ἐγὼ λέγω ὑμῖν ἀπ'
sayings which I am saying to you from
ἐμαυτοῦ οὐ λαλῶ· ὁ δὲ πατὴρ ἐν
myself not I am speaking; the but Father in
ἐμοὶ μένων ποιεῖ τὰ ἔργα αὐτοῦ.
me remaining is doing the works of him.
11 πιστεύετέ μοι ὅτι ἐγὼ ἐν τῷ πατρὶ
Be you believing to me that I in the Father
καὶ ὁ πατὴρ ἐν ἐμοί· εἰ δὲ μή, διὰ τὰ
and the Father in me; if but not, through the
ἔργα αὐτὰ πιστεύετε. 12 Ἀμὴν ἀμὴν
works them be you believing. Amen amen
λέγω ὑμῖν, ὁ πιστεύων εἰς ἐμὲ
I am saying to you, the (one) believing into me
τὰ ἔργα ἃ ἐγὼ ποιῶ κἀκεῖνος
the works which I am doing also that (one)
ποιήσει, καὶ μείζονα τούτων ποιήσει,
will do, and greater of these (things) he will do,
ὅτι ἐγὼ πρὸς τὸν πατέρα πορεύομαι·
because I toward the Father am going;
13 καὶ ὅτι ἂν αἰτήσητε ἐν τῷ ὀνόματί
and what likely you should ask in the name

6 Jesus said to him:
"I am the way and
the truth and the life.
No one comes to the
Father except through
me. 7 If YOU men
had known me, YOU
would have known my
Father also; from this
moment on YOU know
him and have seen
him."
8 Philip said to
him: "Lord, show us
the Father, and it is
enough for us."
9 Jesus said to him:
"Have I been with
YOU men so long a
time, and yet, Philip,
you have not come to
know me? He that has
seen me has seen the
Father [also]. How is
it you say, 'Show us
the Father'? 10 Do
you not believe that
I am in union with
the Father and the
Father is in union
with me? The things
I say to YOU men I do
not speak of my own
originality; but the
Father who remains
in union with me
is doing his works.
11 Believe me that I
am in union with the
Father and the Father
is in union with me;
otherwise, believe on
account of the works
themselves. 12 Most
truly I say to YOU, He
that exercises faith
in me, that one also
will do the works that
I do; and he will do
works greater than
these, because I am
going my way to the
Father. 13 Also,
whatever it is that
YOU ask in my name,



μου τοῦτο ποιήσω, ἵνα
of me this I will do, in order that
δοξασθῇ ὁ πατὴρ ἐν τῷ υἱῷ·
might be glorified the Father in the Son;
14 ἐάν τι αἰτήσητέ με ἐν τῷ
If ever anything you should ask me in the
ὀνόματί μου τοῦτο ποιήσω.
name of me this I shall do.
15 Ἐὰν ἀγαπᾶτέ με, τὰς
If ever you may be loving me, the
ἐντολὰς τὰς ἐμὰς τηρήσετε·
commandments the mine you will observe;
16 κἀγὼ ἐρωτήσω τὸν πατέρα καὶ ἄλλον
and I shall request the Father and another
παράκλητον δώσει ὑμῖν ἵνα
paraclete he will give to you in order that
ᾖ μεθ' ὑμῶν εἰς τὸν αἰῶνα, 17 τὸ
it may be with you into the age, the
πνεῦμα τῆς ἀληθείας, ὃ ὁ κόσμος οὐ
spirit of the truth, which the world not
δύναται λαβεῖν, ὅτι οὐ θεωρεῖ αὐτὸ
is able to receive, because not it is beholding it
οὐδὲ γινώσκει· ὑμεῖς γινώσκετε αὐτό,
nor is knowing; you are knowing it,
ὅτι παρ' ὑμῖν μένει καὶ ἐν ὑμῖν
because with you it is remaining and in you
ἐστιν. 18 Οὐκ ἀφήσω ὑμᾶς ὀρφανούς,
it is. Not I shall let go off you orphans,
ἔρχομαι πρὸς ὑμᾶς. 19 ἔτι μικρὸν
I am coming toward you. Yet little (while)
καὶ ὁ κόσμος με οὐκέτι θεωρεῖ, ὑμεῖς
and the world me not yet is beholding, you
δὲ θεωρεῖτέ με, ὅτι ἐγὼ ζῶ καὶ
but are beholding me, because I am living and
ὑμεῖς ζήσετε. 20 ἐν ἐκείνῃ τῇ ἡμέρᾳ ὑμεῖς
you will live. In that the day you
γνώσεσθε ὅτι ἐγὼ ἐν τῷ πατρί μου καὶ
will know that I in the Father of me and
ὑμεῖς ἐν ἐμοὶ κἀγὼ ἐν ὑμῖν. 21 ὁ
you in me and I in you. The (one)
ἔχων τὰς ἐντολάς μου καὶ τηρῶν
having the commandments of me and observing
αὐτὰς ἐκεῖνός ἐστιν ὁ ἀγαπῶν με·
them that (one) is the (one) loving me;
ὁ δὲ ἀγαπῶν με ἀγαπηθήσεται ὑπὸ
the (one) but loving me will be loved by
τοῦ πατρός μου, κἀγὼ ἀγαπήσω αὐτὸν καὶ
the Father of me, and I shall love him and
ἐμφανίσω αὐτῷ ἐμαυτόν.
I shall make apparent in to him myself.

I will do this, in
order that the Father
may be glorified in
connection with the
Son. 14 If YOU ask
anything in my name,
I will do it.
15 "If YOU love
me, YOU will observe
my commandments;
16 and I will request
the Father and he
will give YOU another
helper to be with YOU
forever, 17 the spirit
of the truth, which
the world cannot
receive, because it
neither beholds it
nor knows it. YOU
know it, because it
remains with YOU
and is in YOU. 18 I
shall not leave YOU
bereaved. I am coming
to YOU. 19 A little
longer and the world
will behold me no
more, but YOU will
behold me, because
I live and YOU will
live. 20 In that day
YOU will know that I
am in union with my
Father and YOU are in
union with me and I
am in union with YOU.
21 He that has my
commandments and
observes them, that
one is he who loves
me. In turn he that
loves me will be loved
by my Father, and I
will love him and will
plainly show myself to
him."

THE KINGDOM INTERLINEAR TRANSLATION OF THE GREEK SCRIPTURES, 1985

# DOCUMENTATION FOR SECTION THREE

## *DIALOGUE ONE: Does God's Law On Blood Require No Blood Transfusions? —Parts 1 and 2*

7

THE CHARLOTTE OBSERVER Fri June 25, 1999

## Woman's decision to refuse a transfusion takes her life

# Mother's choice ends life

## True to faith, woman refuses transfusion

By PETER SMOLOWITZ
*Staff Writer*

ROCK HILL — They were prepared for the baby boy to die, but not his mother.

The Peoples family knew that the unborn son of Anthony and Minnie Peoples had a fatal birth defect. And when she delivered Anthony Jr. at a Rock Hill hospital Tuesday night, he was stillborn. But there were complications, and Minnie Peoples needed a blood transfusion.

Peoples

The Peoples are Jehovah's Witnesses, who believe blood is sacred and shouldn't be shared.

Minnie Peoples refused the blood. For her religion, she died Wednesday in intensive care.

"The doctors really tried to plead with me that without blood, she wasn't going to make it," said her husband, Anthony Peoples, 37.

Please see WITNESS / page 9A

**WITNESS** *from 1A*

"They just wanted me to know the risk. But at the same time, I know the Scripture, and I stand by my decision....

"If I had to do it over again, I wouldn't change a thing."

The Rock Hill couple celebrated their 14th anniversary Monday.

Minnie Peoples, 35, declined a transfusion because Jehovah's Witnesses believe sections of the Bible prohibit people from eating blood, and a transfusion would be another form of consuming it.

Deaths such as this happen occasionally across the country, particularly to Witnesses, Christian Scientists and those who practice faith healing. Doctors have long grappled with balancing their oath with their patients' faith.

York County Coroner Doug McKown said Thursday his office considers the death to be from natural causes and closed the investigation.

"She made a decision to die, basically," McKown said. "This lady offered herself to die for her beliefs. I don't fully understand why their God would expect them to die, but I can't question that."

Anthony and Minnie Peoples, who had lived in the Rock Hill area since before their marriage, moved to an apartment two months ago while their three-bedroom house was being built. Minnie Peoples had already selected the carpets and the kitchen decor. Anthony has put construction on hold.

On Thursday, he was surrounded in his living room by family members and friends. He made small talk with some and gave hearty hugs to others. But his mind was on the woman he dated long-distance for three years while she lived in Binghamton, N.Y., and Myrtle Beach.

"What made it special in my mind was we were friends first," he said. "I feel like I lost my best friend."

The Peoples learned from a late winter ultrasound that their son, nicknamed A.J., would not have a fully developed skull. Abortion was not an option because of the Peoples' religious beliefs.

The Peoples' son was born about a month early at Piedmont Medical Center at 7:19 p.m. Tuesday. The family, including the baby's two older sisters and grandparents, took turns holding his lifeless body.

The Peoples did not blame their doctors. Her obstetricians and PMC officials wouldn't comment, citing patient privacy.

About an hour after the birth, doctors started noticing that Minnie's uterus would not contract. While the bleeding continued, they ushered most of the family from the room. The eventually had to perform a hysterectomy.

At about 11:30 p.m., they moved her to intensive care. Her parents, in-laws, brothers, sisters, cousins and others stroked her and told her to hang on.

Anthony said he draws strength from his two daughters, ages 13 and 11, whom his wife homeschooled. As she lay dying, her girls went to her side, kissed her on the cheek and said goodbye.

"They told her they loved her and how much they were going to miss her," he said. "My youngest looked at me and said, 'If you're going to be OK, I'll be OK.' "

Anthony's and Minnie's parents were at the hospital Tuesday night and the couple's apartment Thursday. While others looked through photo albums, the fathers highlighted several sections of the Bible that describe the prohibition from eating blood — passages from the books of Acts and Deuteronomy, and the following passage from Leviticus 7:27:

*Any soul who eats any blood, that soul must be cut off from his people.*

"That's God's laws," said Elijah Peoples, 67, of Fort Mill, Anthony's father. "He knows the sanctity of blood."

The Jehovah's Witness sect began in the United States in the 19th century and in 1996 claimed some 5.2 million believers worldwide. They have little or no association with other denominations and keep separated from all secular governments.

Officials at the Rock Hill Congregation of Jehovah's Witnesses estimate there are 130 Jehovah's Witnesses in Rock Hill and 1,500 in Charlotte.

Courts and hospitals have generally ruled that doctors must abide by patients' wishes even if refusing medical treatment could cause death.

Anthony Peoples' faith remains as strong as his wife's. "I look forward to seeing her in the resurrection," he said, "because she was faithful to the end."

*Staff writer Mark Horvit contributed to this report. Reach Peter Smolowitz at (803) 327-8509 or psmolowitz@charlotte.com.*

**'What if a doctor says, "You will die without a blood transfusion"?'**

**You might reply:** 'If the situation is really that serious, can the doctor guarantee that the patient will not die if he is given blood?' **Then perhaps add:** 'But there is someone who can give a person life again, and that is God. Don't you agree that, when face to face with death, turning one's back on God by violating his law would be a poor decision? I truly have faith in God. Do you? His Word promises a resurrection for those who put faith in his Son. Do you believe that? (John 11:25)'

**Or you could say:** 'It may mean that he personally does not know how to handle the case without the use of blood. If possible, we try to put him in touch with a doctor who has had the needed experience, or we engage the services of another doctor.'

# Born Again

**Definition:** Being born again involves being baptized in water ("born from water") and begotten by God's spirit ("born from . . . spirit"), thus becoming a son of God with the prospect of sharing in the Kingdom of God. (John 3:3-5) Jesus had this experience, as do the 144,000 who are heirs with him of the heavenly Kingdom.

**Why is it necessary for any Christians to be "born again"?**

***God has purposed to associate a limited number of faithful humans with Jesus Christ in the heavenly Kingdom***

Luke 12:32: "Have no fear, little flock, because your Father has approved of giving you the kingdom."

Rev. 14:1-3: "I saw, and, look! the Lamb [Jesus Christ] standing upon the Mount Zion, and with him a hundred and forty-four thousand . . . who have been bought from the earth." (See pages 166, 167, under the heading "Heaven.")



***Humans cannot go to heaven with bodies of flesh and blood***

1 Cor. 15:50: "This I say, brothers, that flesh and blood cannot inherit God's kingdom, neither does corruption inherit incorruption."

John 3:6: "What has been born from the flesh is flesh, and what has been born from the spirit is spirit."

***Only persons who have been "born again," thus becoming God's sons, can share in the heavenly Kingdom***

John 1:12, 13: "As many as did receive him [Jesus Christ], to them he gave authority to become God's children, because they were exercising faith in his name; and they were born, not from blood or from a fleshly will or from man's will, but from God." ("As many as did receive him" does not mean all humans who have put faith in Christ. Notice who is being referred to, as indicated by verse 11 ["his own people," the Jews]. The same privilege has been extended to others of mankind, but only to a "little flock.")

Rom. 8:16, 17: "The spirit itself bears witness with our spirit that we are God's children. If, then, we are children, we are also heirs: heirs indeed of God, but joint heirs with Christ, provided we suffer together that we may also be glorified together."

1 Pet. 1:3, 4: "Blessed be the God and Father of our Lord Jesus Christ, for according to his great mercy he gave us a new birth to a living hope through the resurrection of Jesus Christ from the dead, to an incorruptible and undefiled and unfading inheritance. It is reserved in the heavens for you."

***What will they do in heaven?***

Rev. 20:6: "They will be priests of God and of the Christ, and will rule as kings with him for the thousand years."

1 Cor. 6:2: "Do you not know that the holy ones will judge the world?"

**Can a person who is not "born again" be saved?**

Rev. 7:9, 10, 17: "After these things [after the apostle John heard the number of those who would be "born again,"

REASONING FROM THE SCRIPTURES, 1985, 1989ed

himself without blemish to God, cleanse our consciences from dead works that we may render sacred service to the living God? . . . Unless blood is poured out no forgiveness takes place."

Eph. 1:7: "By means of him [Jesus Christ] we have the release by ransom through the blood of that one, yes, the forgiveness of our trespasses, according to the riches of his undeserved kindness."

**How did those who claimed to be Christians in early centuries C.E. understand the Bible's commands regarding blood?**

Tertullian (c. 160-230 C.E.): "Let your unnatural ways blush before the Christians. We do not even have the blood of animals at our meals, for these consist of ordinary food. . . . At the trials of Christians you [pagan Romans] offer them sausages filled with blood. You are convinced, of course, that the very thing with which you try to make them deviate from the right way is unlawful for them. How is it that, when you are confident that they will shudder at the blood of an animal, you believe they will pant eagerly after human blood?"—*Tertullian, Apologetical Works, and Minucius Felix, Octavius* (New York, 1950), translated by Emily Daly, p. 33.

Minucius Felix (third century C.E.): "So much do we shrink from human blood, that we do not use the blood even of eatable animals in our food."—*The Ante-Nicene Fathers* (Grand Rapids, Mich.; 1956), edited by A. Roberts and J. Donaldson, Vol. IV, p. 192.

## Blood Transfusions

**Does the Bible's prohibition include human blood?**

Yes, and early Christians understood it that way. Acts 15:29 says to "keep abstaining from . . . blood." It does not say merely to abstain from *animal* blood. (Compare Leviticus 17:10, which prohibited eating "any sort of blood.") Tertullian (who wrote in defense of the beliefs of early



Christians) stated: "The interdict upon 'blood' we shall understand to be (an interdict) much more upon *human* blood."—*The Ante-Nicene Fathers*, Vol. IV, p. 86.

**→ Is a transfusion really the same as eating blood?**

In a hospital, when a patient cannot eat through his mouth, he is fed intravenously. Now, would a person who never put blood into his mouth but who accepted blood by transfusion really be obeying the command to "keep abstaining from . . . blood"? (Acts 15:29) To use a comparison, consider a man who is told by the doctor that he must abstain from alcohol. Would he be obedient if he quit drinking alcohol but had it put directly into his veins?

**In the case of a patient that refuses blood, are there any alternative treatments?**

Often simple *saline solution*, *Ringer's solution*, and *dextran* can be used as plasma volume expanders, and these are available in nearly all modern hospitals. Actually, the risks that go with use of blood transfusions are avoided by using these substances. The *Canadian Anaesthetists' Society Journal* (January 1975, p. 12) says: "The risks of blood transfusion are the advantages of plasma substitutes: avoidance of bacterial or viral infection, transfusion reactions and Rh sensitization." Jehovah's Witnesses have no religious objection to the use of nonblood plasma expanders.

***Jehovah's Witnesses actually benefit from better medical treatment because they do not accept blood.*** A doctor writing in the *American Journal of Obstetrics and Gynecology* (June 1, 1968, p. 395) acknowledged: "There is no doubt that the situation where you [the surgeon] are operating without the possibility of transfusion tends to improve your surgery. You are a little bit more aggressive in clamping every bleeding vessel."

***All types of surgery can be performed successfully without blood transfusions.*** This includes open-heart operations, brain surgery, amputation of limbs, and total removal of

REASONING FROM THE SCRIPTURES, 1985, 1989ed

**Commonly asked questions about blood transfusions**

A patient receiving a blood transfusion may ask questions about the transfusion and its aftermath. This chart lists commonly asked questions about transfusions and their answers.

| QUESTION | ANSWER |
| --- | --- |
| → Why am I being given a transfusion? | • The transfusion replaces blood lost from heavy bleeding. Or you may be receiving a transfusion to help treat anemia or another blood disorder. |
| What will happen before the transfusion? | • A blood sample is taken to determine your blood type.<br>• If you have a history of blood transfusion reactions, the nurse will give you medications.<br>• Your vital signs are checked just before the transfusion starts. |
| What will happen during the transfusion? | • Depending on the severity of your condition, transfusions are performed in the hospital or in an outpatient setting.<br>• The blood is delivered into your veins through special tubing.<br>• Commonly, saline solution is used to keep the vein open if the transfusion must be stopped or delayed. |
| What are the possible complications? | • Blood transfusions carry the risk of serious complications, including an acute hemolytic reaction (in which red blood cells are destroyed) or an allergic reaction.<br>• Reactions can occur during, immediately after, or up to 10 days after a blood transfusion but most often occur immediately after the transfusion begins or within an hour after it's completed.<br>• Another serious complication is the transmission of infectious diseases, such as hepatitis C, cytomegalovirus, and AIDS. Because of current techniques for testing donor blood for these diseases, such transmission is uncommon. However, because of these risks, many people elect to donate their own blood so that it can be used subsequently—for example, during a planned surgery.<br>• Certain complications—such as hypothermia and bleeding tendencies—may result from multiple or massive transfusions. |



**Commonly asked questions about blood transfusions** *(continued)*

| QUESTION | ANSWER |
| --- | --- |
| What will happen after the transfusion? | • If the transfusion is being given on an outpatient basis, you'll be observed for at least 2 hours before discharge.<br>• If you're receiving platelets, don't use aspirin. It interferes with platelet function. Use Tylenol or another product that contains acetaminophen for pain relief or fever.<br>• You and your caregiver need to watch for the symptoms of a delayed transfusion reaction and of hepatitis: fever, headache, loss of appetite, nausea, vomiting, and abdominal pain. These symptoms most often occur 3 to 10 days after the transfusion and must be reported to your doctor immediately. |

Before administering a blood product, make sure two nurses have identified the unit of blood as being the correct unit for that patient. Next, positively identify the patient. If the patient is alert and responsive, ask him to state his full name, and always check it against the name and hospital number on his identification wristband or bracelet. When a patient has had a blood sample taken before a transfusion, a wristband or bracelet is placed on his wrist. This identification band lists the patient's full name, medical record number, date and time the sample was drawn, the number of the blood component compatibility tag, and the name of the person who performed the blood collection.

After confirming the patient's identity, two nurses should examine the compatibility tag attached to the unit and the information printed on the bag. Make sure that the ABO group, Rh type, and unit number match. Report discrepancies immediately to the blood bank, and delay the transfusion until those discrepancies are resolved.

You'll also need to make sure the patient has an 18G or 20G venous access catheter in place; smaller catheters may inhibit flow rates. In patients with poor venous access, however, it may be necessary to use 22G or 24G catheters. Don't force blood through small cannulae with a pressure cuff or EID; cell damage may result.

If the patient's existing venipuncture site or infusion don't appear infected or otherwise compromised, proceed with the transfusion.

HANDBOOK OF INFUSION THERAPY (PA: Springhouse Corporation, 1999)

you for writing
namely, "Young
I Survive Without
:2, 1998) It helped
; ability to protect
ur parents. I have
eath, but I often
en to me if they
' Horacio encour-

M. J., Trinidad

'd to express what
article that deals
ive. That was the
titive Strain Inju-
Know." (Decem-
: of injury involv-
do I realize what
iow to deal with
t.

S. T., Yugoslavia

ces equipment to
itive strain injury
osity and contro-
irst-rate. It dealt
sed and indepen-
directors was so
)ies to be sent to
·ut Brazil.

J. P. M., Brazil

outside job that
len boxes. Right
back, arms, and
I started stretch-
utes before get-
exercises would
far more helpful
ire, I will give my
izine.

K. Y., Japan

# Are Blood Transfusions Really Necessary?

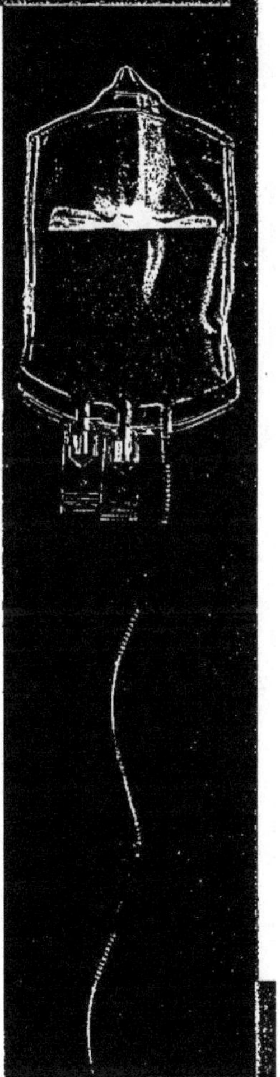

LAST November the above question was raised in a newspaper article written by Dr. Ciril Godec, chairman of urology at Long Island College Hospital, in Brooklyn, New York. He wrote: "Today blood would probably not be approved as a medication, since it would not fulfill safety criteria of the Food and Drug Administration. Blood is an organ of the body, and blood transfusion is nothing less than an organ transplant."

Dr. Godec observed: "Organ transplant is the very last therapeutic option offered to patients. Because of the likelihood of severe side effects, patients are thoroughly informed about all possible alternatives before a transplant is performed." Regarding blood transfusion, he concluded: "The benefit is so questionable that many surgeons have adopted a philosophy of 'transfusion avoidance' not only for medical but also for legal reasons."

A major problem with blood transfusions is that thousands of people have been infected with deadly diseases, including AIDS. Although methods of screening blood have improved in many places, Dr. Godec pointed out: "A potential danger arises from blood donated by individuals who are infected but have not yet developed antibodies that could be detected through screening tests."

Concluding his article, Dr. Godec addressed the question raised above: "As physicians and surgeons develop better understanding of the physiology of oxygen delivery and recognize that hemoglobin levels need not be as high as previously thought, it almost always becomes possible for them to find alternatives to transfusion. As recently as a year ago the demanding surgeries of heart and liver transplantation were fraught with such major blood loss that they were deemed always to require massive amounts of blood replacement. Now, both procedures have been performed without resort to transfusion.

"It is quite possible that in the very near future transfusion will be eliminated altogether. . . . Transfusion is not only costly and dangerous; it simply does not provide the highest quality of care that patients deserve."

Awake! August 22, 1999

8/22/1999 p. 31

**BLOOD—COMPLEX AND UNIQUE**

Whereas some persons may be quick to call the rejection of blood "suicidal," a fair approach to the matter requires acknowledging the fact that there are uncertainties and even dangers associated with blood transfusion.

Doctors know that blood is extremely complex. This is manifested even in just the matter of blood types. Reference works state that there are some fifteen to nineteen known blood group systems. Regarding only one of these, the Rh blood group system, a recent book about blood said that "at the present time nearly three hundred different Rh types may theoretically be recognised."[47]

Another facet of the complexity and uniqueness of each one's blood is the variety of antibodies in it. At a meeting of scientists in Zurich, Switzerland, a group of English criminologists pointed out that the antibodies are so diverse that the blood of each person might be said to be specific and unique. Scientists hope to be able to "reconstruct from a bloodstain the personality image of every person who leaves behind a trace of blood."[48]

The fact that blood is an extremely complex tissue that differs from person to person has a significant bearing on blood transfusion. This is a point Dr. Herbert Silver, from the Blood Bank and Immunohematology Division of the Hartford (Connecticut) Hospital, recently made. He wrote that, considering only those blood factors for which tests can be performed, "there is a less than 1 in 100,000 chance of giving a person blood exactly like his own."[49]



Consequently, whether having religious objections to blood transfusions or not, many a person might decline blood simply because it is essentially an organ transplant that at best is only partially compatible with his own blood.

**BLOOD TRANSFUSIONS —HOW MUCH ACTUAL DANGER?**

Doctors know that with any medical preparation there is a measure of risk, even with medicines as common as aspirin and penicillin. Accordingly, it might well be expected that treatment with a substance as complex as human blood involves some danger. But just how much danger? And what bearing might this have on a physician's view of the stand taken by Jehovah's Witnesses?

*A frank appraisal of the facts proves that blood transfusion must honestly be regarded as a procedure involving considerable danger and even as potentially lethal.*[50]

Dr. C. Ropartz, Director of the Central Department of Transfusions in Rouen, France, commented that "a bottle of blood is a bomb." Since the dangerous results may not appear until some time has passed, he added, "furthermore, it may also be a time bomb for the patient."[51] A United States Government publication carried an article on the dangers of blood and said that

> ". . . donating blood can be compared to sending a loaded gun to an unsuspecting or unprepared person. . . . Like the loaded gun, there is a safety lever or button governing blood transfusions. But, how many persons have died from gun shot wounds as the result of believing the lever was on 'safe'?"[52]

A P P E N D I X

The Witnesses do not feel that the Bible comments directly on organ transplants; hence, decisions regarding cornea, kidney, or other tissue transplants must be made by the individual Witness.

**MAJOR SURGERY POSSIBLE**

Although surgeons have often declined to treat Witnesses because their stand on the use of blood products seemed to "tie the doctor's hands," many physicians have now chosen to view the situation as only one more complication challenging their skill. Since Witnesses do not object to colloid or crystalloid replacement fluids, nor to electrocautery, hypotensive anesthesia,[3] or hypothermia, these have been employed successfully. Current and future applications of hetastarch,[4] large-dose intravenous iron dextran injections,[5,6] and the "sonic scalpel"[7] are promising and not religiously objectionable. Also, if a recently developed fluorinated blood substitute (Fluosol-DA) proves to be safe and effective,[8] its use will not conflict with Witness beliefs.

In 1977, Ott and Cooley[9] reported on 542 cardiovascular operations performed on Witnesses without transfusing blood and concluded that this procedure can be done "with an acceptably low risk." In response to our request, Cooley recently did a statistical review of 1,026 operations, 22% on minors, and determined "that the risk of surgery in patients of the Jehovah's Witness group has not been substantially higher than for others." Similarly, Michael E. DeBakey, MD, communicated "that in the great majority of situations [involving Witnesses] the risk of operation without the use of blood transfusions is no greater than in those patients on whom we use blood transfusions" (personal communication, March 1981). The literature also records successful major urologic[10] and orthopedic surgery.[11] G. Dean MacEwen, MD, and J. Richard Bowen, MD, write that posterior spinal fusion "has been successfully accomplished for 20 [Witness] minors" (unpublished data, August 1981). They add: "The surgeon needs to establish the philosophy of respect for a patient's right to refuse a blood transfusion but still perform surgical procedures in a manner that allows safety to the patient."

Herbsman[12] reports success in cases, including some involving youths, "with massive traumatic blood loss." He admits that "Witnesses are somewhat at a disadvantage when it comes to blood requirements. Nevertheless it's also quite clear that we do have alternatives to blood replacement." Observing that many surgeons have felt restrained from accepting Witnesses as patients out of "fear of legal consequences," he shows that this is not a valid concern.

**LEGAL CONCERNS AND MINORS**

Witnesses readily sign the American Medical Association form relieving physicians and hospitals of liability,[13] and most Witnesses carry a dated, witnessed Medical Alert card prepared in consultation with medical and legal authorities. These documents are binding on the patient (or his estate) and offer protection to physicians, for Justice Warren Burger held that a malpractice proceeding "would appear unsupported" where such a waiver had been signed. Also, commenting on this in an analysis of "compulsory medical treatment and religious freedom," Paris[14] wrote: "One commentator who surveyed the literature reported, 'I have not been able to find any authority for the statement that the physician would incur . . . criminal . . . liability by his failure to force a transfusion on an unwilling patient.' The risk seems more the product of a fertile legal mind than a realistic possibility."

Care of minors presents the greatest concern, often resulting in legal action against parents under child-neglect statutes. But such actions are questioned by many physicians and attorneys familiar with Witness cases, who believe that Witness parents seek good medical care for their children. Not desirous of shirking their parental responsibility or of shifting it to a judge or other third party, Witnesses urge that consideration be given to the family's religious tenets. Dr. A. D. Kelly, former Secretary of the Canadian Medical Association, wrote[15] that "parents of minors and the next of kin of unconscious patients possess the

right to interpret
do not admire th
assembled at 2:0
his parent's custo

It is axiomati
the care of their
risk-benefit pote
or chemotherapy
that go beyond
transfusion,[16] Wi
pies be used that
This accords with
"the whole persor
ble lasting psycho
procedure that vi
beliefs. Often, lar
having experience
cept patient trans
ing to treat Witn

**THE PHYSICIAN**

Understandabl
nesses might seen
physician dedicat
health by employ
disposal. Editorial
ticles about ma
Harvey[17] admitted
beliefs that may i
he added: "Perha
surgery is a craft
technique of indiv
proved."

Professor Bolo
ing report that on
pitals in Dade C
ket policy of refu
pointed out that '
this group of pati
risk than usual." H
geons may feel tha
strument of mode
vinced that by ope
will learn a great d

Rather than co
problem, more an
situation as a me
the challenge they
of practice for this



HOW CAN BLOOD SAVE YOUR LIFE?, 1990

London area there has been reported one death for every 13,000 bottles of blood transfused."—*New York State Journal of Medicine,* January 15, 1960.

Have the dangers since been eliminated so that transfusions are now safe? Frankly, each year hundreds of thousands have adverse reactions to blood, and many die. In view of the preceding comments, what may come to your mind are blood-borne diseases. Before examining this aspect, consider some risks that are less well-known.

## BLOOD AND YOUR IMMUNITY

Early in the 20th century, scientists deepened man's understanding of the marvelous complexity of blood. They learned that there are different blood types. Matching a donor's blood and a patient's blood is critical in transfusions. If someone with type A blood receives type B, he may have a severe hemolytic reaction. This can destroy many of his red cells and quickly kill him. While blood-typing and cross matching are now routine, errors do occur. Every year people die of hemolytic reactions.

The facts show that the issue of incompatibility goes far beyond the relatively few blood types that hospitals seek to match. Why? Well, in his article "Blood Transfusion: Uses, Abuses, and Hazards," Dr. Douglas H. Posey, Jr., writes: "Nearly 30 years ago Sampson described blood transfusion as a relatively dangerous procedure . . . [Since then] at least 400 additional red cell antigens have been identified and characterized. There is no doubt the number will continue to increase because the red cell membrane is enormously complex."—*Journal of the National Medical Association,* July 1989.

***"Approximately 1 in 100 transfusions are accompanied by fever, chills, or urticaria [hives]. . . . Approximately 1 in 6,000 red cell transfusions results in a hemolytic transfusion reaction. This is a severe immunologic reaction that may occur acutely or in a delayed fashion some days after the transfusion; it may result in acute [kidney] failure, shock, intravascular coagulation, and even death." —National Institutes of Health (NIH) conference, 1988.***

Scientists are now studying the effect of transfused blood on the body's defense, or immune, system. What might that mean for you or for a relative who needs surgery?

When doctors transplant a heart, a liver, or another organ, the recipient's immune system may sense the foreign tissue and reject it. *Yet, a transfusion is a tissue transplant.* Even blood that has been "properly" cross matched can suppress the immune system. At a conference of pathologists, the point was made that hundreds of medical papers "have linked blood transfusions to immunologic responses."—"Case Builds Against Transfusions," *Medical World News,* December 11, 1989.

A prime task of your immune system is detecting and destroying malignant (cancer) cells. Could suppressed immunity lead to cancer and death? Note two reports.

The journal *Cancer* (February 15, 1987) gave the results of a study done in the Netherlands: "In the patients with colon cancer, a significant adverse effect of transfusion on long-term survival was seen. In this group there was a cumulative 5-year overall survival of 48% for the transfused and 74% for the nontransfused patients." Physicians at the University of Southern California followed up on a hundred patients who underwent cancer surgery. "The recurrence rate for all cancers of the larynx was 14% for those who did not receive blood and 65% for those who did. For cancer of the oral cavity,

8 *Save Life*

pharynx, and nos
transfusions and 7
*& Laryngology,* Ma
What do such
cle "Blood Transfu
concluded: "The c
geon."—*The Ameri*
Another prim
against infection. S
patients receiving
ter did a study of
25 percent develop
who received no tr
fectious complicati
postoperative infec
en." (*The British Jo*
the American Asso
who received dono
given no blood hac
Dr. John A. C
be ironic indeed if
thing worthwhile s
lems faced by such

DISEASE FREE C

Blood-borne di
disease? Frankly, yo
After discussin
(1982) addresses "c
cytomegalovirus inf

**The pope survived being shot. After leaving the hospital, he was taken back for two months, "suffering a great deal." Why? A potentially fatal cytomegalovirus infection from the blood he received**

HOW CAN BLOOD SAVE YOUR LIFE?, 1990

BROOKLYN, N. Y.

lood is poured out no
ice."—Heb. 9:22.
crifices all foreshad-
r one, a sacrifice that
ve sin and that would
s of eternal life for
sacrifice was not se-
s or the herds of Is-
rist the Son of God,
he Baptist identified
"See, the Lamb of
he sin of the world!"
Jehovah's own pro-
iankind; it was his
e life was given in
this loving arrange-
le for men and wom-
pened to them the
he heavenly courts
ecause these "have
now by his blood."
to this "little flock"
rty-four thousand
vd" of others who
irone on his foot-
themselves of this
g their robes and
the blood of the
ey enjoy the for-
nd are righteous
d.—Rev. 7:14, 15.
of Jesus Christ
need for a sacri-
inful mankind. It
ated. No longer
red; in fact, they
d because they
acrifice that he
refore, the ran-
ist is absolutely
God has author-
i witnesses by
eature may be

e animal sacrifices
d benefit mankind?
our lives depend,



used on behalf of another to save life. "By means of him we have the release by ransom through the blood of that one, yes, the forgiveness of our trespasses, according to the riches of his undeserved kindness." (Eph. 1:7) Our lives depend on our acceptance of this provision, hence on acceptance of the divine arrangement as to the proper use of blood. Wisely, those who want to receive life at God's hands refrain from using blood in any way that has not been authorized by him as the Life-giver.

### LOVING GOD WITH ONE'S WHOLE SOUL

5 On one occasion a certain man versed in the Law inquired of Jesus: "Teacher, by doing what shall I inherit everlasting life?" In his reply Jesus set out a guiding principle that helps us to determine what to do with our present lives in order to gain the reward of everlasting life. He said: " 'You must love Jehovah your God with your whole heart and with your whole soul and with your whole strength and with your whole mind,' and, 'your neighbor as yourself.' " (Luke 10:25-27) Now just what is included in this matter of loving God with our whole soul? It means giving our life to God in dedication, yes, devoting our life to the performance of any work that God may give us to do. Since we have given our life to God in dedication, we ought to realize what the Bible uses to represent life. It is blood, which is the seat of life or soul. So when a life has been taken, it is said that blood has been shed. So fundamentally is blood involved in the life processes that the Bible says that the soul or the life of a person is his blood. When speaking to Noah, God paralleled the expressions soul, or life, and blood, saying: "Only flesh with its soul—its blood—you must not eat." (Gen. 9:4) And to the Israelites he said simply: "The blood is the soul," or, "The blood is the life." (Deut. 12:23, *margin*, 1953 Edition) Consequently, when we dedicate our lives to God we must certainly take care to use that which represents life, our blood, in harmony with his law.

6 This greatest of commandments therefore indicates that a dedicated Christian is not at liberty to donate his lifeblood for use by someone else. Life belongs to God, and we are free to give it only to him in his service. Nor would it be proper to argue that love of neighbor calls for one to give blood. It is not love of neighbor to collaborate with him in violation of the law of God. And since God's Word indicates that it is wrong to take a blood transfusion, it is also wrong to give one's blood for transfusion.

7 Obedience to God is required of his servants; it is also a blessing to them, because it protects them from harm. It is interesting to note that, while the general impression given by organizations that are anxious to have blood donated is that the procedure is perfectly safe, the opinion is not unanimous. For in the book *Physiology and Clinic of Blood Transfusion*,* among others, the statement is made: "As the latest research shows, considerable health disorders can arise on the part of the blood donor." Faithful Christians are spared such hazards that might impair their service to God.

### DANGERS AVOIDED BY OBEDIENCE

8 The position of Jehovah's witnesses in regard to blood transfusion is not one based on the approval or disapproval with

* Published in Jena, Germany, 1960.

5. (a) In answer to an inquirer, what did Jesus say one must do to inherit everlasting life? (b) What is involved in loving God with one's whole soul, and why?

6, 7. Is a Christian free to donate his lifeblood for another person, and is it safe from a medical point of view?

8. Upon what do Jehovah's witnesses base their attitude toward blood transfusion, so why consider medical evidence on the matter?

# Questions From Readers

■ Do Jehovah's Witnesses allow the use of autologous blood (autotransfusion), such as by having their own blood stored and later put back into them?

Medical personnel often distinguish between homologous blood (coming from another person) and autologous blood (the patient's own blood). It is well known that Jehovah's Witnesses do not accept blood from other humans. But what about using autologous blood, a term used regarding a number of procedures?

Some of those procedures are unacceptable to Christians because of being clearly in conflict with the Bible, but others lead to questions. Of course, at the time the Bible was written, transfusions and other such medical uses of blood were unknown. Yet, God provided directions that enable his servants to decide whether certain medical procedures involving blood might displease him.

God's determination is that blood represents life and thus is sacred. He commanded that no human should sustain his life by taking in blood. For instance, God stated: "Every moving animal that is alive may serve as food for you. . . . Only flesh with its soul—its blood—you must not eat." (Genesis 9:3, 4; Leviticus 7:26, 27) According to the Life-Giver, the only acceptable use of blood was in sacrifice: "For the soul of the flesh is in the blood, and I myself have put it upon the altar for you to make atonement for your souls, because it is the blood that makes atonement by the soul in it. That is why I have said to the sons of Israel: 'No soul of you must eat blood.'"—Leviticus 17:11, 12.

Though Christians are not under the Mosaic Law, the Bible says that it is "necessary" for us to 'abstain from blood,' viewing it as sacred. (Acts 15:28, 29) This is understandable, for the sacrifices under the Law foreshadowed Christ's blood, God's means by which we can gain everlasting life.—Hebrews 9:11-15, 22.

How was blood to be dealt with under the Law if it was not used in sacrifice? We read that when a hunter killed an animal for food, "he must in that case pour its blood out and cover it with dust." (Leviticus 17:13, 14; Deuteronomy 12:22-24) So the blood was not to be used for nutrition or otherwise. If taken from a creature and not used in sacrifice, it was to be disposed of on the earth, God's footstool.—Isaiah 66:1; compare Ezekiel 24:7, 8.

This clearly rules out one common use of autologous blood—preoperative collection, storage, and later infusion of a patient's own blood. In such procedure, this is what is done: Prior to elective surgery, some units of a person's whole blood are banked or the red cells are separated, frozen, and stored. Then if it seems that the patient needs blood during or following surgery, his own stored blood can be returned to him. Current anxieties about blood-borne diseases have made this use of autologous blood popular. Jehovah's Witnesses, though, DO NOT accept this procedure. We have long appreciated that such stored blood certainly is no longer part of the person. It has been completely removed from him, so it should be disposed of in line with God's Law: "You should pour it out upon the ground as water."—Deuteronomy 12:24.

In a somewhat different process, autologous blood can be diverted from a patient to a hemodialysis device (artificial kidney) or a heart-lung pump. The blood flows out through a tube to the artificial organ that pumps and filters (or oxygenates) it, and then it returns to the patient's circulatory system. Some Christians have permitted this if the equipment is not primed with stored blood. They have viewed the external tubing as elongating their circulatory system so that blood might pass through an artificial organ. They have felt that the blood in this closed circuit was still part of them and did not need to be 'poured out.'*

What, though, if the flow of such autologous blood stopped briefly, such as if a heart-lung machine is shut down while the surgeon checks the integrity of coronary-bypass grafts?

Actually, the Biblical emphasis is not on the issue of continuous flow. Even aside from surgery, a person's heart might stop briefly and then resume.* His circulatory system would not have to be emptied and his blood disposed of just because blood flow had stopped during the cardiac arrest. Hence, a Christian having to decide whether to permit his blood to be diverted through some external device ought to focus, not primarily on whether a brief interruption in flow might occur, but on whether he conscientiously felt that the diverted blood would still be part of his circulatory system.—Galatians 6:5.

* See *The Watchtower*, June 15, 1978, page 30.

* This might result from a heart attack, an electric shock, or extreme hypothermia, such as from submersion in ice-cold water.



*With a heart-lung device, the circuit includes: (1) tubing from patient's vascular system; (2) recovery suction pumps; (3) bubble oxygenator; (4) hollow-fiber hemofilter; (5) main roller pump; (6) return line to patient's circulatory system*

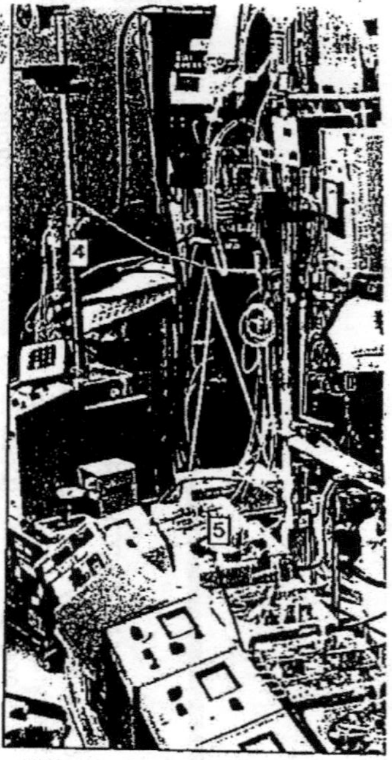


What about induced hemodilution? Some surgeons believe that it is advantageous for a patient's blood to be diluted during surgery. Thus, at the start of an operation, they direct some blood to storage bags outside a patient's body and replace such with nonblood fluids; later, the blood is allowed to flow from the bags back to the patient. Since Christians do not let their blood be stored, some physicians have adapted this procedure, arranging the equipment in a circuit that is constantly linked to the patient's circulatory system. Some Christians have accepted this, others have refused. Again, each individual must decide whether he would consider the blood diverted in such a hemodilution circuit to be similar to that flowing through a heart/lung machine, or he would think of it as blood that left him and therefore should be disposed of.

A final example of autologous blood use involves recovering and reusing blood during surgery. Equipment is used to aspirate blood from the wound, pump it out through a filter (to remove clots or debris) or a centrifuge (to eliminate fluids), and then direct it back into the patient. Many Christians have been very concerned whether in such salvage there might be any brief interruption of blood flow. Yet, as mentioned, a more Biblical concern is whether the blood escaping into a surgical wound is still part of the person. Does the fact that the blood has flowed from his circulatory system into the wound mean that it should be 'poured out,' like the blood mentioned at Leviticus 17:13? If an individual believes so, he would probably refuse to permit such blood salvage. Yet, another Christian (who also would not let blood flow from him, be stored for some time, and later be put back into him) might conclude that a circuit with recovery from a surgical site and ongoing reinfusion would not violate his trained conscience.

As we can see, there is a growing variety of equipment or techniques involving autologous blood. We cannot and should not try to comment on each variation. When faced with a question in this area, each Christian is responsible to obtain details from medical personnel and then make a personal decision.

Though much has been said here about medical aspects, what is of greatest importance are the religious issues. As a Christian

THE WATCHTOW

# Questions From Readers

■ Do Jehovah's Witnesses accept injections of a blood fraction, such as immune globulin or albumin?

Some do, believing that the Scriptures do not clearly rule out accepting an injection of a small fraction, or component, taken from blood.

The Creator first laid upon all mankind the obligation to avoid taking in blood: "Every moving animal that is alive may serve as food for you . . . Only flesh with its soul—its blood—you must not eat." (Genesis 9:3, 4) Blood was sacred and so could be used only in sacrifice. If not used in that way, it was to be disposed of on the ground.—Leviticus 17:13, 14; Deuteronomy 12:15, 16.

This was no mere temporary restriction for Jews. The need to abstain from blood was restated for Christians. (Acts 21:25) Around them in the Roman Empire, God's law was commonly broken, since people ate food made with blood. It was also broken for "medical" reasons; Tertullian reports that some men took in blood thinking that it could cure epilepsy. 'They quaffed with greedy thirst the blood of criminals slain in the arena.' He added: "Blush for your vile ways before the Christians, who have not even the blood of animals at their meals." Jehovah's Witnesses today are just as determined not to violate God's law, no matter how common it is for others to eat food made with blood. In the 1940's, blood transfusions came into widespread use, and the Witnesses saw that obeying God required that they also avoid blood transfusions, even if doctors urged these.

At first, most transfusions were of whole blood. Later, researchers began to separate blood into its primary components, for doctors concluded that a certain patient might not need all major parts of blood. If they gave him only one component, it would be less risky for him, and the doctors could get more use out of the blood available.

Human blood can be separated into dark cellular material and a yellowish fluid (plasma, or serum). The cellular part (45 percent by volume) is made up of what are commonly called red cells, white cells, and platelets. The other 55 percent is the plasma. This is 90 percent water, but it carries small amounts of many proteins, hormones, salts, and enzymes. Today, much of the donated blood is separated into the primary components. One patient may be given a transfusion of plasma (perhaps FFP, fresh-frozen plasma) to treat shock. But an anemic patient might be given packed red cells, that is, red cells that had been stored and then put in a fluid and transfused. Platelets and white cells are also transfused but less commonly.

In Bible times men had not devised such techniques for using these components. God simply commanded: 'Abstain from blood.' (Acts 15:28, 29) But why should anyone think that it would make a difference whether the blood was whole or had been separated into these components? Though some men drank blood, Christians refused even if it meant death. Do you think that they would have responded differently if someone had collected blood, allowed it to separate, and then offered them just the plasma or just the clotted part, perhaps in blood sausage? No, indeed! Hence, Jehovah's Witnesses do not accept transfusions of whole blood or of its primary components (red cells, white cells, platelets, or plasma) used to accomplish a similar purpose.

As the question suggests, though, scientists have learned about specialized blood fractions and how to employ such. A common issue involves the plasma proteins—globulins, albumin, and fibrinogen. Likely, the most widespread therapeutic use of such is injecting immune globulin. Why is that done?

Your body can produce antibodies against certain diseases, giving you active immunity. This is the basis for advance inoculation with a vaccine (toxoid) against polio, mumps, rubella (measles), diphtheria-tetanus-pertussis, and typhoid fever. However, if someone has recently been exposed to certain serious diseases, physicians may recommend an injection of a se-

**In Our Next Issue**

■ **Earth-Wide Security —How?**

■ **Jehovah's People Made Firm in the Faith**

■ **Punctuality and You**

rum (antitoxin) t
mediate passive
til recently such
been made by
mune globulin,
antibodies, fron
ready immune.*
munity gained fr
is not permanen
ed antibodies p
system in time.

In view of the c
stain from bloo
tians have felt t
not accept an i
(protein) injectio
was only a blood
stand is clear a
blood componen
amount.

Others have fe

* With recombina
engineering, technic
developing similar p
made from blood.

## What Is AIDS?

AIDS is an acronym derived from Acquired Immune Deficiency Syndrome. AIDS itself does not kill. But, as its name implies, the victim is left with a crippled immune system. Lacking this protection, a person with the disease will usually die from an infection, such as a unique type of pneumonia or a rare form of skin cancer, Kaposi's sarcoma. Research into detection and diagnosis is in its early stages, and there is, as yet, no known cure for AIDS.

not widely publicized in Britain. The inference always was that donated blood gives no cause for alarm. But two shocking factors have combined, causing *The Daily Telegraph* to conclude: "Britain has lost the battle to prevent the Aids virus infiltrating blood supplies."

The first shock came when press reports revealed that for many years Britain has in fact been buying blood from abroad. "Blood is being bought from people in poor countries where there is a high increase of blood-transmitted diseases," confided a union representative at a blood-products laboratory. Furthermore, some 70 million units of concentrated Factor VIII are imported from the United States and are used to treat British haemophiliacs. Each batch of Factor VIII is made from plasma that is pooled from as many as 2,500 blood donors. It seems that by importing this blood product the AIDS virus was transferred to the British supply.

An additional shock came when AIDS was confirmed as having infected the system from homosexual donors within the British Isles. Although homosexuals have been among those asked not to donate blood because of their higher risk of having AIDS, the warning was not as strongly worded as it should have been, admitted the Department of Health. The warning in their pamphlet on AIDS referred only to "Homosexual men who have many different partners." A current overprinting of the leaflet *A.I.D.S. and how it concerns blood donors* specifies that "Practising male homosexuals and bisexuals" are "particularly susceptible" to AIDS. But the warning came too late. By the beginning of 1985 more than 40 individuals, including a newborn baby, were infected. Furthermore, there is the troubling fact that the AIDS virus has an incubation period of up to two years. So how many more have already been infected? There is a "time-bomb element," as *The Sunday Times* put it. Accordingly, the National Blood Transfusion Service has recently prepared an additional pamphlet for all potential blood donors in Britain, *Some Reasons Why You Should Not Give Blood.*

There have already been some 50 deaths from AIDS in Britain, out of over 100 reported cases. The number of people suffering from the disease is presently doubling every eight months. A medical correspondent for *The Sunday Times* estimated that there could be over 12,000 cases within five years. An even more startling estimate out of the United Kingdom's Royal College of Nursing is that one million people in the British Isles could be affected by the year 1991 if no action is taken to check the spread of AIDS.

The inquirer mentioned above said: "It seems to me that you Jehovah's Witnesses are being proved right on this matter of blood transfusion." More accurately, of course, it is Jehovah God, through his Word, the Bible, who is being vindicated. Centuries ago he commanded Christians to 'abstain from blood.' (Acts 15:29; 21:25) His counsel and standards have certainly proved to be a protection for his people and will continue to be.

30 THE WATCHTOWER—JUNE 15, 1985

(

■ Was Dinah,
it solely an ac

Evidently Sh
lations with D
will. He raped
frequent, frienc
Canaanites put
mising situatic
had led to his s
to her and his c
as his wife.
The account a
reads: "Now Din
out to see the c
land. And Shec
Hamor the Hivit
the land, got to s
took her and lay
and violated her
began clinging
daughter of Jaco
love with the you
spite the efforts c
discourage assoc
immoral people
pitching his camp
of Shechem and
separate water su
"used to go out to s
ters of the land." (G
John 4:12) The
translated "used tc
the imperfect tens
cates continuous
verb in the same
rendered, accordin
ting, "regularly we
"customarily came u
18:13; 1 Kings 10:2
venture was not he
She apparently wan
become better acq
her neighbors in the
On one occasion
regular visits, Sheche
nah] and lay down v
violated her." Regard
brew word rendered

as low as 7 g/dl. Others have found evidence of only moderately impaired function." —*Contemporary Transfusion Practice,* 1987.

While adults accommodate a low hemoglobin level, what of children? Dr. James A. Stockman III says: "With few exceptions, infants born prematurely will experience a decline in hemoglobin in the first one to three months . . . The indications for transfusion in the nursery setting are not well defined. Indeed, many infants seem to tolerate remarkably low levels of hemoglobin concentration with no apparent clinical difficulties."—*Pediatric Clinics of North America,* February 1986.

***"Some authors have stated that hemoglobin values as low as 2 to 2.5 gm./100ml. may be acceptable. . . . A healthy person may tolerate a 50 percent loss of red blood cell mass and be almost entirely asymptomatic if blood loss occurs over a period of time."—"Techniques of Blood Transfusion," 1982.***

Such information does not mean that nothing need be done when a person loses a lot of blood in an accident or during surgery. If the loss is rapid and great, a person's blood pressure drops, and he may go into shock. What is primarily needed is that the bleeding be stopped and the *volume* in his system be restored. That will serve to prevent shock and keep the remaining red cells and other components in circulation.

Volume replacement can be accomplished without using whole blood or blood plasma.* Various nonblood fluids are effective volume expanders. The simplest is saline (salt) solution, which is both inexpensive and compatible with our blood. There are also fluids with special properties, such as dextran, Haemaccel, and lactated Ringer's solution. Hetastarch (HES) is a newer volume expander, and "it can be safely recommended for those [burn] patients who object to blood products." (*Journal of Burn Care & Rehabilitation,* January/February 1989) Such fluids have definite advantages. "Crystalloid solutions [such as normal saline and lactated Ringer's solution], Dextran and HES are relatively nontoxic and inexpensive, readily available, can be stored at room temperature, require no compatibility testing and are free of the risk of transfusion-transmitted disease." —*Blood Transfusion Therapy—A Physician's Handbook,* 1989.

You may ask, though, 'Why do nonblood replacement fluids work well, since I need red cells to get oxygen throughout my body?' As mentioned, you have oxygen-carrying reserves. If you lose blood, marvelous compensatory mechanisms start up. Your heart pumps more blood with each beat. Since the lost blood was replaced with a suitable fluid, the now diluted blood flows more easily, even in the small vessels. As a result of chemical changes, more oxygen is released to the tissues. These adaptations are so effective that if only half of your red cells remain, oxygen delivery may be about 75 percent of normal. A patient at rest uses only 25 percent of the oxygen available in his blood. And most general anesthetics reduce the body's need for oxygen.

## How Can Doctors Help?

Skilled physicians can help one who has lost blood and so has fewer red cells. Once volume is restored, doctors can administer oxygen at high concentration. This makes more of it available for the body and has often had remarkable results. British

* Witnesses do not accept transfusions of whole blood, red cells, white cells, platelets, or blood plasma. As to minor fractions, such as immune globulin, see *The Watchtower* of June 1, 1990, pages 30-1.



**The heart-lung machine has been a great help in heart surgery on patients who do not want blood**

doctors used this
fell to 1.8 g/dl:
centrations and t
*thesia,* January 19
successfully treat

Physicians ca
them iron-contai
making red cells
come available. Y
stimulates bone r
able. Doctors ma
them to form rep

Even during
anesthesiologists
methods. Meticul
minimize bleedin
into a wound car
lation.*

Patients on a
may benefit from
lost.

And there are
oxygen needs du
improve coagulat
time. Laser "scalp
seek to avoid blo

* *The Watchtower* of
salvage and on blood-

HOW CAN BLOOD SAVE YOUR LIFE?, 1990

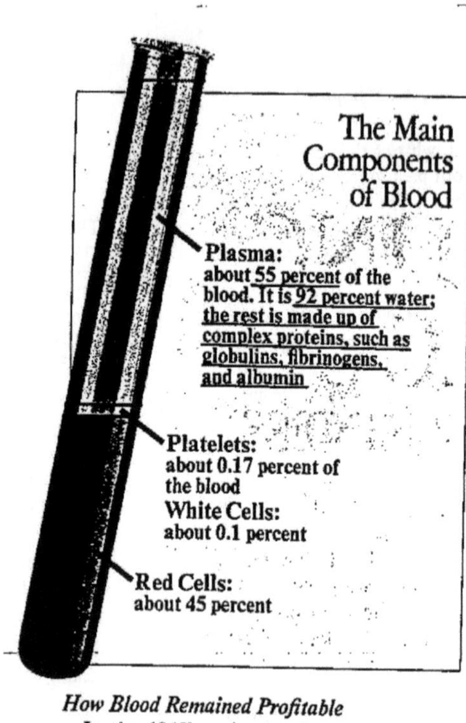
The Main Components of Blood
Plasma: about 55 percent of the blood. It is 92 percent water; the rest is made up of complex proteins, such as globulins, fibrinogens, and albumin
Platelets: about 0.17 percent of the blood
White Cells: about 0.1 percent
Red Cells: about 45 percent

### *How Blood Remained Profitable*

In the 1940's, scientists began to separate blood into its components. The process, now called fractionation, makes blood an even more lucrative business. How? Well, consider: When dismantled and its parts sold, a late-model car may be worth up to five times its value when intact. Similarly, blood is worth much more when it is divided up and its components are sold separately.

Plasma, which makes up about half of the blood's total volume, is an especially profitable blood component. Since plasma has none of the cellular blood parts—red cells, white cells, and platelets—it can be dried and stored. Furthermore, a donor is allowed to give whole blood only five times a year, but he can give plasma up to twice a week by undergoing plasmapheresis. In this process, whole blood is extracted, the plasma separated, and then the cellular components are reinfused into the donor.

The United States still allows donors to be paid for their plasma. Moreover, that country permits donors to give about four times more plasma annually than the World Health Organization recommends! Little wonder, then, that the United States collects over 60 percent of the world's plasma supply. All that plasma in itself is worth about $450 million, but it fetches much more on the market because plasma too can be separated into various ingredients. Worldwide, plasma is the basis for a $2,000,000,000-a-year industry!

Japan, according to the newspaper *Mainichi Shimbun,* consumes about a third of the world's plasma. That country imports 96 percent of this blood component, most of it from the United States. Critics within Japan have

called that cc
world," and tŀ
fare Ministry h
trade, saying tl
from blood. I
that medical in
$200,000,000 i
one plasma coı

The Federal
sumes more bl
Europe combir
country in the
*Blut* (For Inst
products: "Ov
from the U.S..
World. In any c
to improve thei
Some of these
their blood tha

Many comm
tegically locate
the borders of
the impoverish
all too willing t
have ample rea
should or to co
harbor. Such p
countries arour
stopped in one
other. Bribery
gling is not unc

**Awake!**®
October 22, 1990
Vol. 71, No. 20

*Semimonthly Languages Available by Mail:* Afrikaans, Arabic, Cebuano, Danish, Dutch, English, Finnish, French, German, Greek, Iloko, Italian, Japanese, Korean, Norwegian, Portuguese, Spanish, Swedish, Tagalog, Yoruba, Zulu

*Monthly Languages Available by Mail:* Chichewa, Chinese, Cibemba, Croatian, Czech, Hiligaynon, Hungarian, Igbo, Kannada, Malayalam, New Guinea Pidgin, Polish, Russian, Sepedi, Serbian, Sesotho, Sinhalese, Slovak, Slovenian, Swahili, Tahitian, Tamil, Thai, Tswana, Xhosa

Printed in U.S.A.

***Average Printing: 11,930,000*** ***Published in 62 Languages***

*Subscription requests should be sent to the office in your country or to Watchtower, Wallkill, N.Y. 12589, U.S.A.*

*America, United States of,* 25 Columbia Heights, Brooklyn, N.Y. 11201
*Australia,* Box 280, Ingleburn, N.S.W. 2565
*Canada L7G 4Y4,* Box 4100, Halton Hills (Georgetown), Ontario
*England NW7 1RN,* The Ridgeway, London
*New Zealand,* P.O. Box 142, Manurewa
*Nigeria,* P.M.B. 1090, Benin City, Bendel State
*South Africa,* Private Bag 2067, Krugersdorp, 1740

*Changes of address* should reach us 30 days before your moving date. Give us your old and new address (if possible, your old address label).

Unless otherwise indicated, *New World Translation of the Holy Scriptures* is used.

*Would you welcome more information? Write Watch Tower at appropriate address above. This is part of a worldwide Bible educational work supported by voluntary donations.*

*Awake!* (ISSN 0005-237X) is published semimonthly by Watchtower Bible and Tract Society of New York, Inc., 25 Columbia Heights, Brooklyn, N.Y. 11201. Second-class postage paid at Brooklyn, N.Y., and at additional mailing offices. *Postmaster:* Send address changes to *Awake!*, c/o Watchtower, *Wallkill, N.Y. 12589.*

*WHY "AWAKE!" IS*
*AWAKE!* is for tl
how to cope with tc
people in many lan
more. It probes ben
behind current event
not exalt one race al
Most importantly,
promise of a peacefu
saw the events of 19

*Contents: Featu*

AWAKE! 10/22/1990 p.4

what should a Christian consider when deciding on them?

Blood is complex. Even the plasma—which is 90 percent water—carries scores of hormones, inorganic salts, enzymes, and nutrients, including minerals and sugar. Plasma also carries such proteins as albumin, clotting factors, and antibodies to fight diseases. Technicians isolate and use many plasma proteins. For example, clotting factor VIII has been given to hemophiliacs, who bleed easily. Or if someone is exposed to certain diseases, doctors might prescribe injections of gamma globulin, extracted from the blood plasma of people who already had immunity. Other plasma proteins are used medically, but the above mentioned illustrate how a primary blood component (plasma) may be processed to obtain fractions.*

Just as blood plasma can be a source of various fractions, the other primary components (red cells, white cells, platelets) can be processed to isolate smaller parts. For example, white blood cells may be a source of interferons and interleukins, used to treat some viral infections and cancers. Platelets can be processed to extract a wound-healing factor. And other medicines are coming along that involve (at least initially) extracts from blood components. Such therapies are not transfusions of those primary components; they usually involve parts or fractions thereof. Should Christians accept these fractions in medical treatment? We cannot say. The Bible does not give details, so a Christian must make his own conscientious decision before God.

Some would refuse anything derived from blood (even fractions intended to provide temporary passive immunity). That is how they understand God's command to 'abstain from blood.' They reason that his law to Israel required that blood removed from a creature be 'poured out on the ground.' (Deuteronomy 12:22-24) Why is that relevant? Well, to prepare gamma globulin, blood-based clotting factors, and so on, requires that blood be collected and processed. Hence, some Christians reject such products, just as they reject transfusions of whole blood or of its four primary components. Their sincere, conscientious stand should be respected.

Other Christians decide differently. They too refuse transfusions of whole blood, red cells, white cells, platelets, or plasma. Yet, they might allow a physician to treat them with a fraction extracted from the primary components. Even here there may be differences. One Christian may accept a gamma globulin injection, but he may or may not agree to an injection containing something extracted from red or white cells. Overall, though, what might lead some Christians to conclude that they could accept blood fractions?

**SUGGESTED QUESTIONS FOR THE DOCTOR**

*If you face surgery or a treatment that might involve a blood product, ask:*

Do all the medical personnel involved know that, as one of Jehovah's Witnesses, I direct that *no blood transfusions* (whole blood, red cells, white cells, platelets, or blood plasma) be given to me under any circumstances?

*If any medicine to be prescribed may be made from blood plasma, red or white cells, or platelets, ask:*

Has the medicine been made from one of the four primary blood components? If so, would you explain its makeup?

How much of this blood-derived medicine might be administered, and in what way?

If my conscience permits me to accept this fraction, what medical risks are there?

If my conscience moves me to decline this fraction, what other therapy might be used?

After I have considered this matter further, when may I inform you of my decision?

---

* See "Questions From Readers" in *The Watchtower* of June 15, 1978, and October 1, 1994. Pharmaceutical firms have developed recombinant products that are not taken from blood and that may be prescribed in place of some blood fractions used in the past.

30 THE WATCHTOWER • JUNE 15, 2000

"Questions Fro
of June 1, 1990, nc
tions) move from
to the separate b
a mother passes i
providing valuabl
tus' red cells cor
their oxygen-carr
of it becomes bilir
ta to the mother a
wastes. Some Chr
blood fractions ca
natural setting, t
tion derived from
Does the fact t
decisions may di
consequential? N
basic simplicity.
Jehovah's Witne
whole blood and
The Bible direc
things sacrificed
from fornicatior

I out on the ground.' Vhy is that relevant? lobulin, blood-based . requires that blood . Hence, some Chris- , just as they reject or of its four primary conscientious stand

differently. They too ıle blood, red cells, sma. Yet, they might ·m with a fraction ex- mponents. Even here ne Christian may ac- ction, but he may or on containing some- white cells. Overall, ne Christians to con- blood fractions?

R THE DOCTOR

*'ment that might*

·l involved know sses, I direct that blood, red cells, ılasma) be given ?

*ed may be made te cells, or plate-*

· from one of the ts? If so, would

·rived medicine vhat way?

· to accept this there?

to decline this ght be used?

matter further, cision?

"Questions From Readers" in *The Watchtower* of June 1, 1990, noted that plasma proteins (fractions) move from a pregnant woman's blood to the separate blood system of her fetus. Thus a mother passes immunoglobulins to her child, providing valuable immunity. Separately, as a fetus' red cells complete their normal life span, their oxygen-carrying portion is processed. Some of it becomes bilirubin, which crosses the placenta to the mother and is eliminated with her body wastes. Some Christians may conclude that since blood fractions can pass to another person in this natural setting, they could accept a blood fraction derived from blood plasma or cells.

Does the fact that opinions and conscientious decisions may differ mean that the issue is inconsequential? No. It is serious. Yet, there is a basic simplicity. The above material shows that Jehovah's Witnesses refuse transfusions of both whole blood and its primary blood components. The Bible directs Christians to 'abstain from things sacrificed to idols and from blood and from fornication.' (Acts 15:29) Beyond that, when it comes to fractions of any of the primary components, each Christian, after careful and prayerful meditation, must conscientiously decide for himself.

Many people would be willing to accept any therapy that seems to offer immediate benefit, even a therapy having known health risks, as is true of blood products. The sincere Christian endeavors to have a broader, more balanced view that involves more than just the physical aspects. Jehovah's Witnesses appreciate efforts to provide quality medical care, and they weigh the risk/benefit ratio of any treatment. However, when it comes to products derived from blood, they carefully weigh what God says and their personal relationship with our Life-Giver.—Psalm 36:9.

What a blessing for a Christian to have such confidence as the psalmist who wrote: "Jehovah God is a sun and a shield; favor and glory are what he gives. Jehovah himself will not hold back anything good from those walking in faultlessness. O Jehovah . . . , happy is the man that is trusting in you"!—Psalm 84:11, 12.

THE WATCHTOWER 6/15/2000 p. 31

## ers

:d. Platelets and
a also transfused
only.
s men had not de-
hniques for using
nents. God sim-
ed: 'Abstain from
15:28, 29) But
yone think that it
difference wheth-
/as whole or had
d into these com-
ugh some men
Christians refused
nt death. Do you
/ would have re-
ently if someone
blood, allowed it to
hen offered them
a or just the clot-
ips in blood sau-
ed! Hence, Jeho-
s do not accept
f whole blood or
components (red
ells, platelets, or
to accomplish a
.
estion suggests,
sts have learned
zed blood frac-
o employ such. A
involves the plas-
-globulins, albu-
ogen. Likely, the
ead therapeutic
injecting immune
s that done?
an produce anti-
certain diseases,
e immunity. This
advance inocu-
vaccine (toxoid)
mumps, rubella
htheria-tetanus-
typhoid fever.
eone has recent-
ed to certain se-
physicians may
injection of a se-

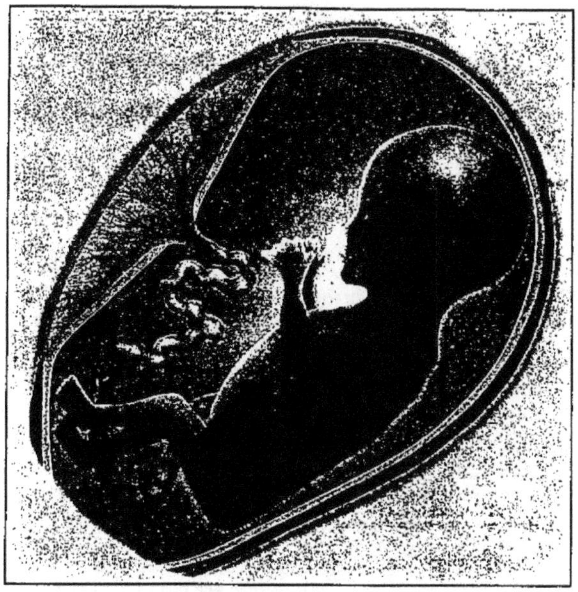

rum (antitoxin) to give him immediate passive immunity. Until recently such injections have been made by extracting immune globulin, which contains antibodies, from a person already immune.* The passive immunity gained from the injection is not permanent, for the injected antibodies pass out of his system in time.

In view of the command to 'abstain from blood,' some Christians have felt that they should not accept an immune globulin (protein) injection, even though it was only a blood fraction. Their stand is clear and simple—no blood component in any form or amount.

Others have felt that a serum (antitoxin), such as immune globulin, containing only a tiny fraction of a donor's blood plasma and used to bolster their defense against disease, is not the same as a life-sustaining blood transfusion. So their consciences may not forbid them to take immune globulin or similar fractions.* They may conclude that for them the decision will rest primarily on whether they are willing to accept any health risks involved in an injection made from others' blood.

It is significant that the blood system of a pregnant woman is separate from that of the fetus in her womb; their blood types are often different. The mother does not pass her blood into the fetus. Formed elements (cells) from the mother's blood do not cross the placental barrier into the fetus' blood, nor does the plasma as such. In fact, if by some injury the mother's and the fetus' blood mingle, health problems can later develop (Rh or ABO incompatibility). However, some substances from the plasma cross into the fetus' circulation. Do plasma proteins, such as immune globulin and albumin? Yes, some do.

A pregnant woman has an active mechanism by which some immune globulin moves from the mother's blood to the fetus'. Because this natural movement of antibodies into the fetus occurs in all pregnancies, babies are born with a degree of normal protective immunity to certain infections.

It is similar with albumin, which doctors may prescribe as a treatment for shock or certain other conditions.* Researchers have proved that albumin from the plasma is also transported, though less efficiently, across the placenta from a mother into her fetus.

That some protein fractions from the plasma do move naturally into the blood system of another individual (the fetus) may be another consideration when a Christian is deciding whether he will accept immune globulin, albumin, or similar injections of plasma fractions. One person may feel that he in good conscience can; another may conclude that he cannot. Each must resolve the matter personally before God.

* With recombinant DNA, or genetic-engineering, techniques, scientists are developing similar products that are not made from blood.

* One example is Rh immune globulin, which doctors may recommend when there is Rh incompatibility between a woman and her fetus. Another is Factor VIII, which is given to hemophiliacs.

* Evidence shows that nonblood volume replacement fluids (such as hetastarch [HES]) can be used effectively to treat shock and other conditions for which an albumin solution might have been used previously.

While the mere acidity of sweat is sufficient to impede the growth of many germs, lysozyme kills them by destroying their cell walls. For that reason, an animal can help heal its wounds simply by licking them.

### Primary Sentinels—White Blood Cells

Let us imagine that bacteria capable of causing disease manage to penetrate our "city" through a wound or by contagion. An army of cells immediately goes into action, with but one purpose—elimination of the invading germ and consequent recovery from illness. The cells that fight to defend the body are called leukocytes, or white blood cells. Three important types of white blood cells in this stage of the struggle are monocytes, neutrophils, and lymphocytes.

When monocytes "hear" chemical signals indicating inflammation in a certain zone, they leave the bloodstream and penetrate the stricken tissue, where they become macrophages, that is, "big eaters." There they devour all that is foreign to the organism. In addition, they secrete important substances called cytokines, which prepare the body to fight the infection. Among their functions, the cytokines provoke fever. Fever is a useful phenomenon in that it is a sign that defensive mechanisms have gone into action. It can accelerate the healing process and also function as a useful diagnostic indicator.

Next, neutrophils "hear" the chemical signal from the inflamed zone and dash to help the macrophages. They too engulf, or swallow, bacteria. When these neutrophils die, they are expelled from the body as pus. Thus, the formation of pus is another type of defense. In this case, the Latin expression used by doctors for centuries would apply: *pus bonum et laudabile.* This means "good and praiseworthy pus." Its formation helps to stem infection. After digesting the germs, our friends the macrophages "present," or display, fragments of the germ to the lymphocytes to warn them of the invader.

The lymphocytes make up a superspecialized elite in the fight against infection. They produce substances called antibodies, which bind specifically to a particular germ fragment. There are two principal teams of lymphocytes with differing abilities. First are the B cells, which release the antibodies that they produce into the bloodstream. The B cells have been called the armed corps of the immune response, and they shoot their arrows, the antibodies, with extreme precision. These antibodies will "seek" the germ they recognize and will strike a vital site on the germ. The other principal team of lymphocytes, the T cells, keep the antibodies that they recognize anchored to their surface. They use them to strike the enemy—engaging in hand-to-hand combat, so to speak.

The story becomes even more complex. A subgroup of T cells, called helper T cells, help their companions, the B cells, to secrete large quantities of antibodies. Before the attack, the helper T cells communicate with one another. Recent research has shown that by means of chemical signals, these cells "talk" excitedly among themselves, exchanging information on the foreign agent, in what has been called vibrant conversation.

Help is lent by another important group, the natural killer cells. These do not produce antibodies, but they are ready to kill cells that

**IN OUR NEXT ISSUE**

**Insurance—Do You Really Need It?**

**The War Did Not Stop Our Preaching**

**What's So Bad About Sneaking Out?**

have become "foı
fected. So natura
to guarding the ir
Finally, by vi
ic memory, lymp
membering the c
though they had
ever that type of
lymphocytes alr
ies to destroy it i
The macropha
immune respons
by staying aroun
flammation. The
the dead cells, c
on the "battlefie
quiet and order t

**When**

The foregoing
the immunolog
work. But defe
reasons: There c
to the immune s
acquired in the
of contracting d
One of the mo

***White blood cells***

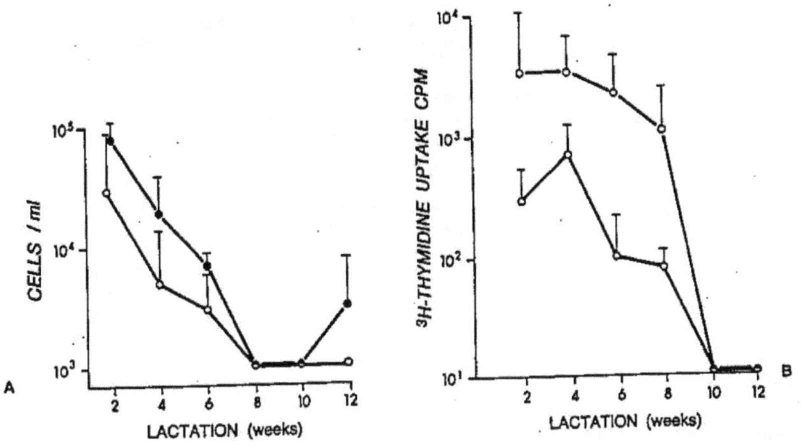


**Fig. 5-2.** Longitudinal study of cells. Same subjects were examined during the second through the twelfth week of lactation. Data are presented as means ± SD of macrophages-neutrophils (●—●) and lymphocytes (○—○) and of stimulated (●—●) and unstimulated (○—○) lymphocytes. **A**, Longitudinal study of numbers of leukocytes. **B**, Longitudinal study of uptake of $^3$H-thymidine in lymphocytes. (From Goldman AS, Garza C, Nichols BL et al: *J Pediatr* 100:563, 1982.)

and Pickering,[8] that the primary function of milk PMNs is as defense of the mammary tissue per se and not to impart maternal immunocompetence to the newborn. This may explain the presence of large numbers of PMNs that are relatively hypofunctional early and then disappear over time.

## Lymphocytes

Both T- and B-lymphocytes are present in human milk and colostrum and are part of the immunologic system in human milk. They synthesize IgA antibody. Human milk lymphocytes respond to mitogens by proliferation, with increased macrophage-lymphocyte interaction and the release of soluble mediators, including MIF. Cells destined to become lymphopoietic cells are derived from two separate influences, the thymus (T) and the bursa (B) or bursal equivalent tissues. The population of cells called B cells comprises the smaller part of the total. The term *B cell* is derived from its origination in a different anatomic site from the thymus; in birds, it has been identified as the bursa of Fabricius. The B cells can be identified by the presence of surface immunoglobulin markers. The B cells in human milk include cells with IgA, IgM, and IgG surface immunoglobulins. B cells transform into plasma cells and remain sessile in the tissues of the mammary gland.

### T-cell system

More rapid mitotic activity occurs in the thymus gland than in any other lymphatic organ, yet 70% of the cells die within the cell substance. Thymosin has been identified as a hormone produced by thymic epithelial cells to expand the peripheral lymphocyte popu-

latio glanc mark lymp lymp ing p gions dent Th man to the gated sensit incite to He corpo ing sh neona Stu have b gators tating exami and th vitro.[4] from tent fi They phocy the T 5-2). shown those i The the fir 10,000 fifth d first da rosette sheep rosette tuted a tenth c The trophil cause t

BREASTFEEDING – A Guide for The Medical Profession, 4th Edition, 1994
by Ruth A. Lawrence (Mosby - Year Book, Inc.)

# Blood Groups and Immunity

**■ Red blood corpuscle** Haemoglobin-carrying cell without a nucleus.

**■ Reticulo-endothelial system** Cells found throughout the body that are concerned with phagocytosis of foreign material, bacteria and broken tissues, and also the development of immunity.

**■ Rhesus factor** Blood antigen found in 85 per cent of the population that is independent of the ABO blood groups

**■ Serum** Liquid that is left after blood has clotted.

**■ Stem cell** Basic, cell from which all blood cells and platelets are formed.

**■ Thoracic duct** Largest lymphatic vessel; it runs from the posterior part of the thorax and joins the venous system in the neck.

**■ Thrombocyte** *See* Platelet

**■ Thymus gland** Gland situated behind the upper sternum that is concerned with the development of immunity, until late adolescence, by the production of a lymphoid-stimulating hormone

**■ Transfusion reaction** Antigen antibody reaction that occurs when an incompatible blood is transfused

**■ Urea** Nitrogen-containing substance formed from ammonia in the liver.

**■ White blood corpuscles** Concerned with fighting infection.

## Blood groups

Although the red cells in different people look the same they are, in fact, dissimilar. They can be divided into four main groups, A, B, AB, and O (*below*). The surface of the cells in each group is different and will act as an antigen to plasma from another group, which carries the antibody. This causes the cells to stick to each other by the process of agglutination. An individual with Group A cells will carry the antibody B in his plasma, those in group AB do not carry either antibody, while those in group O have both antibodies but the cells do not have either antigen. Thus blood from any group can be transferred into those of group AB, as they do not carry antibodies; group AB individuals are known as "universal recipients". A group O recipient can only receive blood from another group O donor, but can give blood to anyone, and thus is known as a "universal donor".

Antibodies in the plasma of the donor blood are quickly diluted by the recipient and the concentration is therefore too low to cause agglutination. The two commonest groups in western Europe are Groups A and O, each found in about 45 per cent of the population, group B in about 10 per cent and group AB is found in less than 5 per cent.

The antigen-antibody reaction not only causes agglutination, but also haemolysis – the breakdown of the red blood cells releasing haemoglobin into the circulation. This is an "incompatible transfusion reaction" and can lead to fever, jaundice, kidney failure from blocking of the tubules with haemoglobin, and even, in some cases, death.

## Rhesus factor

In addition to the four main blood groups there are many other minor ones: Rhesus, NNS, P, Kell Lewis, Duffy, Lutheran, to name a few. The most important is the Rhesus factor, named after the Rhesus monkey, in which it was first discovered. The presence or absence of this antigen makes the individual either Rhesus positive or Rhesus negative. Antibodies are not found in Rhesus negative people unless they have been transfused with Rhesus positive blood. About 15 per cent of the population is Rhesus negative.

It is therefore possible to be Group A Rhesus positive or negative and this is usually written A Rh +ve or A Rh -ve. A true universal donor has to be O Rh -ve. Blood from the recipient and donor are cross-matched before use to check that agglutination does not occur.

## Pregnancy and the Rhesus factor

Particular problems arise in Rhesus negative pregnant mothers with Rhesus positive fathers. In the last weeks of pregnancy small numbers of the baby's red cells escape through the placenta into the mother's circulation. This will not cause trouble in the first pregnancy but in subsequent pregnancies agglutination reactions may occur.

The mother's Rhesus antibodies will invade the baby's circulation, destroying the red cells and leading to anemia; this necessitates an exchange transfusion for the baby at birth with Rhesus negative blood. Provided the possibility is recognized early enough anti-Rhesus immune globulin injections can be given to the mother, to remove Rhesus positive cells from her blood before she develops her own anti-Rhesus globulin antibody.

**Blood: Oxygen and carbon dioxide**

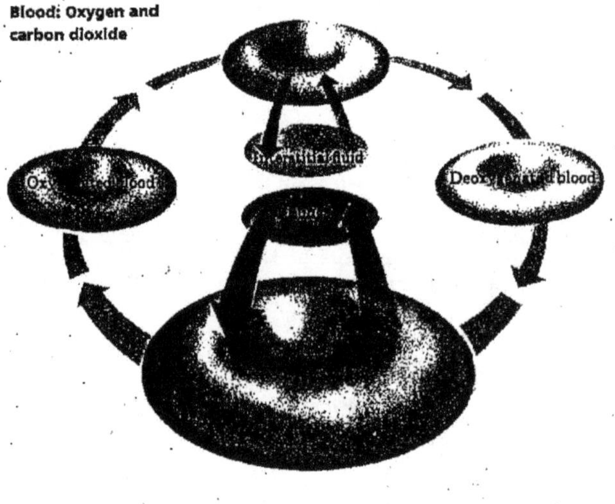

**Blood groups**

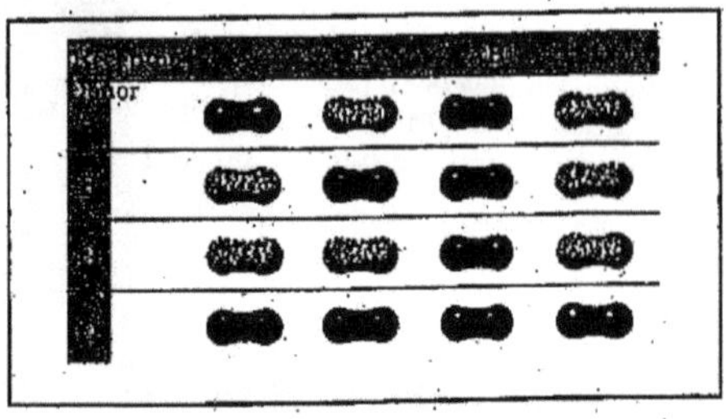

**Blood: Oxygen and carbon dioxide** Oxygen combines with haemoglobin (1) in the red blood corpuscles (*above*) to form oxyhaemoglobin. It would require .75 times as much blood to carry the oxygen if haemaglobin did not exist.

Carbon dioxide (2), from the interstitial fluid, dissolves in the plasma and red cells, where the enzyme – carbonic anhydrase – forms carbonic acid. A little also combines with haemoglobin to form carbamino-haemoglobin. The acidity of carbonic acid forces oxygen out of oxyhaemoglobin (3) into the interstitial fluid with a formation of sodium and potassium bicarbonate. A reverse diffusion occurs in the capillaries of the lung alveoli with loss of carbon dioxide (4) and reoxygenation of the haemoglobin (1).

36 A PICTORIAL HANDBOOK OF ANATOMY AND PHYSIOLOGY, by Dr. James Bevan, 1978

infant infected in utero with Epstein-Barr virus with multiple congenital anomalies, thrombocytopenia, persistent atypical lymphocytosis, and multiple metaphyseal lucencies. Both Epstein-Barr virus and cytomegalovirus were recovered from an infant who died with extensive cerebral calcifications (Joncas et al., 1981). Thrombocytopenia was present prior to the infant's death.

Congenital tuberculosis may produce hepatosplenomegaly in the neonatal period (Pai and Parikh, 1976; Morens et al., 1979). No typical hematologic changes have been described in newborns with this disease.

## PLACENTAL TRANSFER OF FORMED BLOOD ELEMENTS

Accumulated evidence indicates that leukocytes, platelets, and erythrocytes traverse the placental barrier. The transfer of platelets and leukocytes and its consequences are discussed in detail in Chapters Seven and Eight, respectively. Fetal red cells can be demonstrated in the maternal circulation in approximately 50 per cent of all pregnancies (Cohen et al., 1964), and on occasion this form of transplacental hemorrhage may be sufficient to produce severe anemia in the newborn infant, as described in Chapter Three.

### *Maternal-to-Fetal Erythrocyte Transfer*

Maternal red cells may also appear in the fetal circulation, and maternal-to-fetal hemorrhage may be responsible for plethora in the newborn infant.

Hedenstedt and Naeslund (1946) were able to demonstrate elliptocytes in the cord blood after infusing these "naturally" marked cells into the mother. Naeslund (1951) was subsequently able to demonstrate the passage of red cells labeled with phosphorus or iron from the maternal circulation to the fetal circulation.

Mengert and associates (1955) tagged erythrocytes with iron-59 and infused them into mothers 13 minutes to 10 days prior to delivery. In 25 of 29 infants, radioactive red cells could be recovered. Macris and coworkers (1958) infused pregnant women with blood from individuals with sickle cell trait 40 minutes to 153 hours prior to delivery. In 3 of 25 instances sickled cells were found in cord blood specimens. In one mother with naturally occurring sickle cell trait, no sickled cells were observed in her offspring.

Duhring and associates (1960) injected chromium-labeled red cells into pregnant women 13 to 15 hours prior to cesarean section. In 8 of 12 infants, radioactive red cells could be recovered, and transplacental blood loss was estimated to be between 0.3 and 1.0 ml.

Using immunofluorescent techniques, Lee and Vazquez (1962) were able to demonstrate maternal erythrocytes in 2 of 27 infants at term.

Cohen and Zuelzer (1965), using immunofluorescent techniques, searched for maternal cells in the offspring in 154 suitable mother-child pairs. The incidence of positive cells in cord and placental vein blood varied from 36.7 to 11.3 per cent in their two studies, the number of positive cells decreasing markedly as precautions against contamination were increased. In only 2.8 per cent of infants were maternal red cells demonstrable when samples of heel blood were taken within hours after birth. In each positive case, only minute numbers of maternal cells were found. Jennings and Clauss (1978) also observed that maternal erythrocytes could be demonstrated in the circulation of approximately 2 per cent of newborns by the third day of life. Cohen and Zuelzer concluded that generally the presence of maternal cells in the cord blood reflects unavoidable contamination, and that passage of such cells into the fetus is exceptional and of minimal quantitative significance. Donovan and Lund (1966) reached similar conclusions following the injection of chromium-labeled red cells into pregnant women of 12 to 22 weeks' gestation and examination of the abortuses 16 to 24 hours later, at the time of hysterotomy.

Although fetal lymphocytes can be demonstrated in the maternal circulation as early as the tenth week of pregnancy and steadily increase in number as gestation progresses (Kirsch-Volders et al., 1980), the passage of maternal lymphocytes into the fetal circulation can rarely be demonstrated in normal newborns (Turner et al., 1966; Benirschke, 1970; Olding, 1972). Kadowski and coworkers (1965) have described a 16-month-old infant with immunodeficiency, thymic dysplasia, and signs of "runting," in

HEMATOLOGIC PROBLEMS IN THE NEWBORN, 3rd ed. 1982
by Frank A. Oski MD and J. Lawrence Naiman MD

That the pregnant woman and fetus jointly contribute to reproductive outcome is the common knowledge, not always expressed, of obstetricians. Incompatibilities of the Rh and ABO blood groups between the pregnant woman and fetus provide notable examples. For instance, 15 per cent of Caucasians[7] are Rh negative. With random mating (among Caucasians), an Rh negative woman might be fertilized by a man carrying either two genes with the incompatible factor (39 per cent of the population) or one such gene (48 per cent of the population). This means that in Rh negative women about 60 per cent of conceptions can be expected to have incompatible Rh blood types. When fetal blood cells gain access to the maternal bloodstream, as they commonly do in the course of labor, the pregnant woman develops antibodies against Rh positive blood and remains sensitized thereafter. With each subsequent Rh positive fetus, the mother's antibodies become increasingly sensitized and tend to cause increasing degrees of fetal damage in successive pregnancies; the range runs from hemolytic disorder of the newborn, through kernicterus and hydrops fetalis, to perinatal death. Thus, the chance of sensitizing a fetus is influenced not only by the concordance of its Rh type with that of the mother but also by the effects of previous conceptions on her immune state.

Another example of possible interaction between maternal and fetal factors is seen with the recurrence of neural tube defects at birth. Women with one affected pregnancy are at increased risk of having an affected offspring subsequently, and risk is even higher after two affected pregnancies (reviewed in Elwood and Elwood 1980; Seller 1981). This increasing recurrence risk may be due jointly to genetic factors and to environmental factors. On the environmental side, deficiency of specific nutrients is a candidate under hot pursuit as a causal factor.[8] An early randomized trial of folic acid supplementation before conception (Laurence et al. 1981) was too small to permit a conclusion; recurrences occurred in 2 of 60 supplement-treated pregnancies (both to women who had not adhered to the regimen) and in 4 of 51 placebo-treated pregnancies.

A larger but nonrandomized trial carried out in England and Northern Ireland suggests that the risk of recurrence might be reduced by a maternal supplement, before conception, of a mix of vitamins. Vitamins A, B complex, C, and D, folic acid, and iron were all given together. In this trial one cannot be discriminated from another and the hypothesis of a specific folic acid deficiency could not be tested. The favorable result held in two series of women, although not in a third. In the first

[7]Ethnic variation is marked with the Rh blood groups. Only 5 per cent of blacks in the United States are Rh negative.

[8]Several randomized clinical trials (Wald and Polani 1984; Elwood 1983; Czeizel and Rode 1984; reviewed in Rhoads and Mills 1986) are now underway to test whether various vitamin supplements lower the risk of neural tube defects.



two series, the rates of re
were reduced to 0.7 per ce
out of 510) among unsupp
1985; Wild et al. 1986). I
rates were similar betwee
women (4 out of 157 or 2.
(Seller and Nevin 1984).

If the overall beneficial
held in randomized trials,
is possible that persisting n
lihood of neural tube defec
tional state of the woman
genetic constitution of the
predisposition to developm
supplied by the woman. T
experiments in the curly-ta
tible to neural tube defects.
frequency of the defect de
the sex and genotype of th

Few instances of the joir
been analyzed quantitativel
sent, biological interaction i
although the reverse does
that, if we give primacy to
presence or absence or the
If we give primacy to the cc
ceptions would result in m
ferences and produce outcc

In theory, interaction bet
riage implies that the joint
loss is greater or less than t
practice, differences betwee
poorly understood and seld
between the woman and th
the presumption rather tha

The extremely high frequ
initially prompted the notio
riages. Miscarriages, we prop
device for the rejection of ab
tenance of effective reprodu
error at fertilization (Stein e
which an abnormal conceptu
ternal response to a signal
abnormality is lethal in utero
expulsion of the conceptus.

CONCEPTION TO BIRTH - Epidemiology of Prenatal Development, 1989
by Jennie Kline, Zena Stein, Mervyn Susser (Oxford University Press)

more prominent and lie closer to the surface. The stroma of the villi also exhibits changes associated with aging. In placentas of early pregnancy, the branching connective tissue cells are separated by an abundant loose intercellular matrix; later, the stroma becomes denser and the cells more spindly and more closely packed. Another change in the stroma involves the so-called *Hofbauer cells*, which are likely fetal macrophages. These are nearly round cells with vesicular, often eccentric nuclei and very granular or vacuolated cytoplasm. These cells are characterized histochemically by intracytoplasmic lipid and are readily distinguished from plasma cells.

As the placenta grows and ages, certain of the accompanying histological changes are suggestive of an increase in the efficiency of transport to meet the growing fetal metabolic requirements. Such changes involve a decrease in thickness of the syncytium, partial disappearance of Langhans cells, decrease in the stroma, and an increase in the number of capillaries and their approximation to the syncytial surface. By 4 months, the apparent continuity of the cytotrophoblasts is broken, and the syncytium forms knots on the more numerous, smaller villi. At term, the covering of the villi may be focally reduced to a thin layer of syncytium with minimal connective tissue; and the fetal capillaries seem to abut the trophoblast. The villous stroma, Hofbauer cells, and Langhans cells are markedly reduced, and the villi appear filled with thin-walled capillaries. Other changes, however, appear to decrease the efficiency for placental exchange; these changes include the thickening of basement membranes of capillaries and trophoblast, obliteration of certain vessels, deposition of fibrin on the surface of the villi, and deposits of fibrin in the basal and chorionic plates and elsewhere in the intervillous space.

## Immunological Considerations

The success of the fetal semiallogenic graft appears to defy the laws of transplantation immunology. Today, it still is enigmatic that the mother tolerates the fetal graft; but we have reached a time in the investigation of this issue such that a reasonable explanation seems to be very close.

***Immunology of Trophoblasts and Endometrium–Decidua.*** Attempts to explain the survival of the semiallogenic fetal graft have occupied the attention of many outstanding biologists. The first explanation based on antigenic immaturity of the fetus must be discarded in light of Billingham's demonstration (1964) that transplantation antigens (in embryonic tissues) appear very early in life. But ordinarily in the fetal–maternal communication system, only extraembryonic fetal tissues are in direct contact with maternal tissues. And more specifically, trophoblasts are the fetal tissues directly contiguous with maternal blood and decidua. And except for the abnormal passage of fetal blood cellular elements through "breaks" in the placenta, cells of the embryo do not come into direct contact with maternal tissues. Nonetheless, except in parthenogenesis, or in situations in which both parents are genetically identical, the trophoblasts could theoretically confront the mother with foreign paternal antigens.

A second explanation, based on diminished immunological reactivity of the mother during pregnancy, provides at best only an ancillary factor in the prevention of the development of maternal isoimmunization during pregnancy. If the uterus were an immunologically privileged site, as in a third explanation, advanced ectopic pregnancies could never occur. Because transplantation immunity can be evoked and expressed in the uterus as elsewhere, the survival of the homograft must be related to a peculiarity of the conceptus, primarily the trophoblasts, rather than of the uterus.

***Ancillary Immunological Considerations.*** Siiteri and co-workers (1977) demonstrated that the rejection of grafted hamster skin is delayed by the presence of progesterone in high local concentrations.

Maternal lymphocyte function may be altered during pregnancy, as reflected by a reduction in phytohemagglutinin-induced transformation (Finn and colleagues, 1972; Purtilo and associates, 1972). It has been suggested that both trophoblasts and decidua produce agents that suppress lymphocyte immune responses. Sargent and co-workers (1987) reviewed these associations.

***Breaks in the Placental "Barrier."*** The failure of the placenta to maintain absolute integrity of the fetal and maternal circulations is documented by numerous findings of the passage of cells between mother and fetus in both directions, and best exemplified clinically by the occurrence of erythroblastosis fetalis (see Chap. 44, p. 1004). Typically, a few fetal blood cells are found in the mother's blood; and, rarely, the fetus may exsanguinate into the maternal circulation. Leukocytes from the fetus may replicate in the mother; leukocytes bearing a Y chromosome have been identified in women for up to 5 years after giving birth to a son (Ciaranfi and colleagues, 1977). Desai and Creger (1963) labeled maternal leukocytes and platelets with atabrine and found that these cells crossed the placenta from mother to fetus. Lymphocytes passing into the fetus create the possibility of chimerism, the subject of a review by Benirschke (1970).

Cells of fetal origin other than constituents of the blood have also been identified in the maternal circulation. Cells morphologically identical with trophoblast have been identified in uterine venous blood (Douglas and associates, 1959), as well as in cord blood (Salvaggio and co-workers, 1960). The immunological signifi-

Williams Obstetrics, 19th Edition (Appleton + Lange-Norwalk, CT) 1993

from blood transfusions, blood components, and tissue transplants.

But those are mere numbers. They can't begin to convey the depth of the personal tragedies involved. Consider, for instance, the tragedy of Frances Borchelt, 71 years old. She adamantly told doctors that she did not want a blood transfusion. She was transfused anyway. She died agonizingly of AIDS as her family watched helplessly.

Or consider the tragedy of a 17-year-old girl who, suffering from heavy menstrual bleeding, was given two units of blood just to correct her anemia. When she was 19 years old and pregnant, she found out that the transfusion had given her the AIDS virus. At 22 she came down with AIDS. Besides learning that she would soon die of AIDS, she was left wondering if she had passed the disease on to her baby. The list of tragedies goes on and on, ranging from babies to the elderly, all over the world.

In 1987 the book *Autologous and Directed Blood Programs* lamented: "Almost as soon as the original risk groups were defined, the unthinkable occurred: the demonstration that this potentially lethal disease [AIDS] could and was being transmitted by the volunteer blood supply. This was the most bitter of all medical ironies; that the precious life-giving gift of blood could turn out to be an instrument of death."

Even medicines derived from plasma helped to spread this plague around the world. Hemophiliacs, most of whom use a plasma-based clotting agent to treat their illness, were decimated. In the United States, between 60 and 90 percent of them got AIDS before a procedure was set up to heat-treat the medicine in order to rid it of HIV.

Still, to this day, blood is not safe from AIDS. And AIDS is not the only danger from blood transfusion. Far from it.

***The Risks That Dwarf AIDS***

"It is the most dangerous substance we use in medicine," Dr. Charles Huggins says of blood. He should know; he is the director of

the blood tran
setts hospital. I
fusion is as sim
matching bloo
types and the
routinely cross
so other differe
diovascular su
"A blood trans
. . . I think th
bilities in almo

It is not sur
complex subst
it, "confuse" t
fact, a blood tr
nity for as long
most threateni

Then there a
They have exo
ease and cytom
fever and chills
of the Cornell U
there is 1 char

CDC, Atlanta, Ga.

# Is Blood Safe From AIDS Today?

"IT'S Bloody Good News," proclaimed a headline in the New York *Daily News* on October 5, 1989. The article reported that the chances of getting AIDS from a blood transfusion are 1 in 28,000. The process for keeping the virus out of the blood supply, it said, is now 99.9 percent effective.

Similar optimism reigns in the blood-banking industry. 'The blood supply is safer than ever,' they claim. The president of the American Association of Blood Banks said that the risk of acquiring AIDS from blood had been "virtually eliminated." But if blood is safe, why have both courts and doctors slapped it with such labels as "toxic" and "unavoidably unsafe"? Why do some doctors operate wearing what look like space suits, replete with face masks and wading boots, all to avoid contact with blood? Why do so many hospitals ask patients to sign a consent form relieving the hospital of liability for the harmful effects of blood transfusions? Is blood really safe from diseases such as AIDS?

The safety depends on the two measures used to protect blood: screening the donors who supply it and testing the blood itself. Recent studies have shown that in spite of all the efforts to

screen out blooc
them at high ris
who slip throug
answers to the q
Some just want
infected themsel

In 1985 blood
the presence of t
duces to fight th
the test is that a
AIDS virus for s
antibodies that t
cial gap is called

The idea that
getting AIDS fr
from a study pu
*nal of Medicine.'*

e defined, the un-
monstration that
ise [AIDS] could
by the volunteer
most bitter of all
ecious life-giving
t to be an instru-

d from plasma
gue around the
of whom use a
to treat their ill-
e United States,
f them got AIDS
up to heat-treat
it of HIV.
is not safe from
only danger from
it.

substance we use
Huggins says of
is the director of

the blood transfusion service at a Massachusetts hospital. Many think that a blood transfusion is as simple as finding someone with a matching blood type. But besides the ABO types and the Rh factor for which blood is routinely cross-matched, there may be 400 or so other differences for which it is not. As cardiovascular surgeon Denton Cooley notes: "A blood transfusion is an organ transplant. . . . I think that there are certain incompatibilities in almost all blood transfusions."

It is not surprising that transfusing such a complex substance might, as one surgeon put it, "confuse" the body's immune system. In fact, a blood transfusion can suppress immunity for as long as a year. To some, this is the most threatening aspect of transfusions.

Then there are infectious diseases as well. They have exotic names, such as Chagas' disease and cytomegalovirus. Effects range from fever and chills to death. Dr. Joseph Feldschuh of the Cornell University of Medicine says that there is 1 chance in 10 of getting some sort of infection from a transfusion. It is like playing Russian roulette with a ten-chamber revolver. Recent studies have also shown that blood transfusions during cancer surgery may actually increase the risk of recurrence of the cancer.

## Doctors go to great lengths to protect themselves from their patients' blood. But are patients sufficiently protected from transfused blood?

No wonder a television news program claimed that a blood transfusion could be the biggest obstacle to recovery from surgery. Hepatitis infects hundreds of thousands and kills many more transfusion recipients than AIDS does, but it gets little of the publicity. No one knows the extent of the deaths, but economist Ross Eckert says that it may be the equivalent of a DC-10 airliner full of people crashing every month.

ident of the
d Banks said that
n blood had been
lood is safe, why
lapped it with
voidably unsafe"?
wearing what
th face masks and
act with blood?
patients to sign a
pital of liability
l transfusions? Is
such as AIDS?
o measures used
donors who sup-
lf. Recent studies
he efforts to

screen out blood donors whose life-style puts them at high risk for AIDS, there are still some who slip through the screen. They give wrong answers to the questionnaire and donate blood. Some just want to find out discreetly if they are infected themselves.

In 1985 blood banks began to test blood for the presence of the antibodies that the body produces to fight the AIDS virus. The problem with the test is that a person can be infected with the AIDS virus for some time before developing any antibodies that the test would detect. This crucial gap is called the window period.

The idea that there is 1 chance in 28,000 of getting AIDS from a blood transfusion comes from a study published in *The New England Journal of Medicine.* That periodical set the most likely window period at an average of eight weeks. Just months before, though, in June 1989, the same journal published a study concluding that the window period can be much longer—three *years* or more. This earlier study suggested that such long window periods may be more common than once thought, and it speculated that, worse, some infected people may *never* develop antibodies for the virus! The more optimistic study, however, did not incorporate these findings, calling them "not well understood."

No wonder Dr. Cory SerVass of the Presidential Commission on AIDS said: "Blood banks can keep telling the public that the blood supply is as safe as it can be, but the public isn't buying that anymore because they sense it isn't true."

*! October 22, 1990* *Awake! October 22, 1990* 9

*Your* **Health**

# 'Premium' plasma

## *Isn't 'regular' blood safe enough?*

You've probably heard the horror stories about people who go into the hospital for minor surgery and leave with AIDS or hepatitis from a contaminated blood transfusion. One recent response to the frightening prospect of blood-borne illness: brand-name blood.

The American Red Cross and V.I. Technologies, a biotech firm better known as Vitex, recently placed full-page ads in major Sunday newspapers urging people to "ask your physician for it by name!" "It" is PLAS+SD, the first blood-plasma product bearing a brand name and backed by an ambitious marketing campaign. The Red Cross, which supplies roughly half the nation's blood, has an exclusive agreement to supply Vitex with plasma—the liquid part of the blood, rich in antibodies and clotting compounds—then to distribute the finished product nationwide. The new plasma gets washed in chemicals that destroy any viruses that cause AIDS (by far the deadliest risk from blood) or hepatitis C (by far the most common transfusion risk). The price of the Red Cross' premium plasma: roughly 2½ times the price of regular.

**A new test should slash the chance of viral contamination.**

Meanwhile America's Blood Centers, a group of nonprofit blood banks that supply the rest of the nation's blood, has developed a competing product: donor-retested plasma. This plasma is quarantined for several months until the donor is retested for any delayed signs of the worrisome viruses—indicators that might have eluded the first test. Donor-retested plasma costs about 60 percent more than regular. The chance of getting the AIDS or hepatitis C virus from either premium plasma: virtually zero.

But despite all the hubbub about the new plasmas, a third, quieter innovation called nucleic-acid testing (NAT) is actually more important. The new test can detect the virus itself, not just the telltale signs of the virus, which can take weeks or months to appear. So NAT should radically shrink the old testing loophole—the chance of missing a delayed sign of the virus—that created the need to retest the donors or destroy the viruses in the first place. By the time this issue of CONSUMER REPORTS is published, virtually all blood in the U.S. will be screened with the new test.

Moreover, washing and retesting are technically feasible only for plasma. But plasma accounts for only about one of every seven units (pints) of blood transfused in the U.S. (Most of the other units contain either red cells, which transport oxygen, or platelets, which help stop bleeding.) In contrast, NAT can spot viruses in *any* component of the blood and can thus help protect everyone who gets a transfusion.

The new blood and the new test raise two crucial questions: How safe *is* the U.S. blood supply? And is either of the premium plasmas worth the price?

### Dramatic improvement

In the 1970s high rates of hepatitis from transfusions triggered a sweeping re-examination of blood banks' procedures. Most important, the banks stopped collecting blood from paid donors, who were more likely than unpaid donors to be sick.

The advent of AIDS in the early 1980s forced further reforms. The riskiest donors—intravenous-drug abusers and gay men—were asked not to donate or were screened out by questionnaires, interviews, or physical exams. And new tests were developed to detect the AIDS virus in donor blood. The payoffs were huge.

In 1984, the year before blood banks got an AIDS-virus test, 714 transfusion recipients were infected with the disease, according to a 1997 government report. Over the next 12 years, a total of just 38 cases of AIDS were linked to transfusions of blood that had tested negative for the virus—and the vast majority of those cases occurred in the early years,

### What's the risk?

This chart compares the average chances of a hospital patient's being infected from a transfusion against the annual risk of other life-and-death events. Transfusion data are for two units of blood, the amount often given during routine surgery such as knee replacement. (However, some complicated cases—such as heart surgery, care for car-crash victims, or organ transplantation—may require far more units than that.)

The transfusion risks shown here should become even slimmer as nucleic-acid testing is phased in (see story).

As the chart shows, the likelihood of infection from a two-unit blood transfusion is substantially less than the chance of being murdered or of being killed in an auto accident during the year. Indeed, for a hospital patient, the greatest risk shown here is dying from an unexpected adverse reaction to some medication.

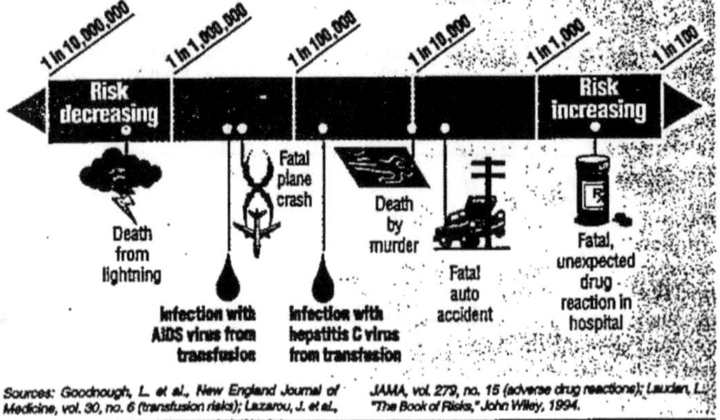


*Sources: Goodnough, L. et al., New England Journal of Medicine, vol. 30, no. 6 (transfusion risks); Lazarou, J. et al., JAMA, vol. 279, no. 15 (adverse drug reactions); Lauden, L. "The Book of Risks," John Wiley, 1994.*

Illustrations by Jack Tom

seriously sick, but the scare highlighted one of the shortcomings of PLAS+SD. For all its purported safety, it's a "pooled" product: Each lot mixes together nearly a pint of plasma from each of up to 2,500 donors. Undetected pathogens from just one donor can spoil the whole batch and, potentially, spread to thousands of transfusion recipients. (Vitex says it has added extra testing to detect parvovirus and the hepatitis A virus, which is also impervious to the washing process.) But other, more obscure viruses theoretically could slip through.

Cerus, another high-tech company, is currently testing a different process that potentially offers wider protection than PLAS+SD. Cerus uses chemicals energized by ultraviolet light, which theoretically can inactivate *any* pathogens in *any* blood components by attacking their genetic material.

**See if you can use your own blood for transfusions.**

### Recommendations

Transfusions save nearly 10,000 lives a day: trauma and burn victims, surgery patients who lose lots of blood, cancer patients who undergo blood-depleting chemotherapy and radiation, and people with deadly anemias and clotting disorders. On average, that benefit far outweighs the extremely small risk of getting a serious disease from tainted blood.

Due to the higher cost of the premium plasmas and the introduction of NAT, most hospitals so far have not chosen to stock the new plasmas. So if you're among the minority of transfusion recipients who do need plasma, you probably won't be automatically offered a choice between regular and premium. Hospitals generally will order a premium plasma if your doctor asks for it. However, our medical consultants are wary of PLAS+SD because it combines the blood of so many donors. The labeling warns against using PLAS+SD in pregnant women because of possible risk. People with suppressed immunity, such as chemotherapy or AIDS patients, should also be especially concerned about the risk, we think.

Donor-retested plasma might be useful as an extra safety measure if you're one of the few people who need lots of plasma, usually for a severe clotting disorder that requires multiple transfusions. For everyone else, there's no particular need for premium plasma—even though insurance will generally cover the extra cost, which could run to hundreds of dollars.

If you or your family has the luxury of planning your procedure, the safest options are to reduce or eliminate the need for other people's blood by using your own—or, better yet, to see if you can avoid the transfusion altogether. Consider these possibilities:

**Avoid the transfusion.** "In many ways, the best transfusion is the transfusion not given," says the Red Cross' Davey. New drugs that stimulate blood-cell production may help some patients do without a transfusion. Other patients may not actually need the blood they're given.

"Plasma is one of the most misused items," says Bianco of America's Blood Centers. Many times an electrolyte solution will do as well as plasma to make up lost blood volume, without the risks. But some hospitals are three times as likely as others to transfuse patients during coronary-bypass surgery. The implication: Some of those transfusions aren't needed.

If you're facing elective surgery, ask how low your hematocrit (part of the blood count) can go before your surgeon orders a transfusion. Most people don't need one until their hematocrit drops to 25 percent or lower, depending on the clinical circumstances.

**Autologous transfusion.** You may be able to bank your own blood—which includes all the components you may need—weeks before a planned operation. That option, which eliminates all risk of transfusion-borne infection or adverse reactions to a stranger's blood, is generally best of all when you may need a transfusion. But some individuals may not be healthy enough or strong enough to give blood.

**Hemodilution.** Just before surgery, some blood is withdrawn and saved. The missing blood is replaced with intravenous solutions. If you need blood during or after surgery, you'll first get your own blood back. The technique is not practical for all operations or all patients, and it may still expose you to strangers' blood if you need more than the amount withdrawn. Other methods allow just your red cells to be removed before surgery and then stored for subsequent use, if necessary.

**Cell salvage.** Blood lost during surgery can be collected, washed, filtered, and returned to you during or after the operation. Most hospitals, particularly large ones, can perform this technique. As with hemodilution, cell salvage may not be practical in all operations, and it may not eliminate the need to receive standard transfusions. CR

# Recalls

## Vehicles and equipment

**'91-96 Chevrolet and GMC light trucks, sport-utility vehicles, and vans**
Antilock brake system (ABS) could malfunction, resulting in increased stopping distances.

**Models:** Approx. 1.1 million '91-96 4-wheel-drive vehicles, including Chevrolet Blazer and S-10, and GMC Jimmy and Sonoma. Also subject to corrective action are about 2.4 million 2-wheel-drive vehicles, including '93-96 Chevrolet Blazer and GMC Jimmy, '94-96 Chevrolet S-10 and GMC Sonoma, and '92-95 Chevrolet Astro and GMC Safari. According to General Motors, braking problems are much less likely to occur in the 2-wheel-drive vehicles because of a combination of unusual circumstances necessary to precipitate them.
**What to do:** Have dealer replace sensor switch in ABS system of 4-wheel-drive vehicles. With 2-wheel-drive models, dealer will modify computer-control unit in ABS system.

## Household products

**Cosco Arriva and Turnabout infant safety seat/carrier**
When used as carrier, handle could release unexpectedly, causing child to fall.

**Products:** 670,000 child safety seats made 3/1/95 to 9/9/97 including the following models: Arriva—02-665, 02-729, 02-731, 02-732, 02-733, 02-751, 02-756, 02-757. Turnabout—02-667, 02-758, 02-759, 02-760, 02-761, 02-762, 02-763, 02-764, 02-765. Manufacture date and model no. are on seat shell. Seats were sold at juvenile-product, mass-merchandise, and discount department stores as stand-alone product for about $30 to $60, and with stroller for about $89 to $140.
**What to do:** Stop using seat as infant carrier and call Cosco at 800 221-6736 for free repair kit. Information is also available at company's web site, *www.coscoinc.com.* Note: Consumers may continue to use the product to restrain child in car or in conjunction with stroller.

**Pool dive sticks (various brands)**
In shallow water, child could be impaled on hard plastic implements. Child could also cut face or eye on stick when attempting to retrieve it.

**Products:** 19 million cylindrical or shark-shaped dive sticks sold since 1979 at grocery, drug, pool, and discount department stores for $4 to $7 per set. Toys were sold under various brand names, which may or may not appear on sticks themselves. Recall includes, but is not limited to, 9 million dive sticks distributed by Florida Pool and sold at Wal-Mart; 2 million sticks distributed by Poolmaster and bearing company name on device; 897,000 sticks distributed by J&M Industries, identifiable by words "Made in USA." Dive sticks are colorful pool toys that sink to the bottom and stand upright so child can swim or dive to retrieve them. Cylinder-shaped items measure 4 to 8 inches long and about 1 inch in diameter. Shark-shaped ones are about 7 inches long and have egg-shaped bottom. Most were sold in packages of three to six; some came with other pool diving games.

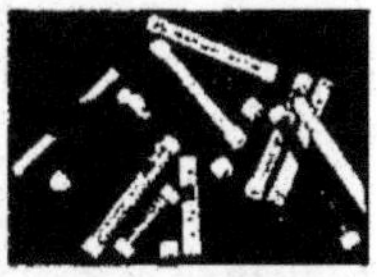

**What to do:** Wal-Mart is offering free repair kit for Florida Pool dive sticks. Owners of Poolmaster sticks can call 800 854-1492 for replacement. J&M Industries dive sticks can be returned to place of purchase for replacement. Return all other sticks to place of purchase for refund or repair. To report an injury or ask questions about the recall, call the CPSC hotline at 800 638-2772.

**▶ For more information**

To report a dangerous vehicle or auto product, call the National Highway Traffic Safety Administration at 800 424-9393. To report a dangerous household product, call the Consumer Product Safety Commission at 800 638-2772, then press 1, followed by 777. Past recalls are available free in searchable form at Consumer Reports Online, at *www.ConsumerReports.org.*

## DIALOGUE TWO: Does Christian Love For Brother Demand Abstinence From War?

shed in 75 Languages

**ocaust**
**ɔoke Out?**
**versary of**
**he Camps**
**3-15**

ɔ those who
i concentra-
ɔorrified by
ie voice had
Nazi atroc-
t who failed
y were they
cles include
esented at a
: U.S. Holo-
al Museum,
ngton, D.C.



# One Voice in the Midst of Silence

FIFTY years ago a monster was slain. When the world finally drew aside the curtain to look on the fallen Third Reich, the ghastly sight was too much of a nightmare to comprehend. Soldiers and civilians alike could only stare in silent horror at the gruesome remains of a monstrous killing machine.

U.S. National Archives photo

Earlier this year thousands celebrated the 50th anniversary of the liberation of the concentration camps by quietly tramping through their desolate grounds. They struggled to fathom the enormity of the crime. Why, some 1,500,000 people had been killed in the death camp at Auschwitz alone! It was a time for silence, a time to reflect on man's inhumanity to man. Haunting questions echoed in the cold ovens, in the empty barracks, across the undisturbed mountains of plundered shoes.

Today there is horror; there is outrage. The Holocaust, during which several million were systematically murdered, reveals what a monstrous evil Nazism was. But what about then? Who spoke out? Who did not?

For many, their first knowledge of the mass slayings came only at the close of World War II. The book *Fifty Years Ago—Revolt Amid the Darkness* explains: "The still photographs and newsreel films of the killing centers and camps liberated by the Allies in 1944 and 1945 first brought the shocking reality to the broad public, especially in the west."

Yet, *even before* the death camps were set up, a voice was proclaiming the dangers of Nazism, through *Awake!*, the magazine you hold in your hands. It was first known as *The Golden Age* and was renamed *Consolation* in 1937. Beginning in 1929, these magazines, published by Jehovah's Witnesses, boldly warned of the perils of Nazism, living up to the proclamation on the cover, "A Journal of Fact, Hope and Courage."

"How can one remain silent," asked *Consolation* in 1939, "about the horrors of a land where, as in Germany, 40,000 innocent persons are arrested at one time; where 70 of them were executed in a single night in one prison; . . . where all homes, institutes and hospitals for the aged, the poor, and the helpless, and all orphanages for the children, are destroyed?"

How, indeed, could one remain silent? While the world in general was unaware or skeptical of the horrific reports trickling out of Germany and occupied lands, Jehovah's Witnesses could not keep quiet. They knew firsthand the cruelties of the Nazi regime, and they were not afraid to speak out.

Awake! August 22, 1995 3

# Why Unafraid to Speak Out

IN RETROSPECT, it could be said that the clash between Jehovah's Witnesses and Nazism, or National Socialism, was all but inevitable. Why? Because of the Nazis' unyielding demands that conflicted with three of the Witnesses' fundamental Bible-based beliefs. These are: (1) *Jehovah God is the Supreme Sovereign.* (2) *True Christians are politically neutral.* (3) *God will resurrect those who have proved faithful to him until death.*

These Bible-based beliefs determined the steadfast stand of Jehovah's Witnesses against the Nazis' ungodly demands. Thus, they courageously spoke out and exposed Nazism as the evil that it was.

Jehovah's Witnesses refused to heil Hitler. They refused because they attribute their salvation to God and have dedicated their lives to him alone. The Bible says of Jehovah: "You alone are the Most High over all the earth."—Psalm 83:18.

Actually, "Heil Hitler" implied that salvation was by Hitler. So the Witnesses could not be faithful to God and at the same time heil any human. Their lives as well as their loyalty and allegiance belonged to God.

Jehovah's Witnesses had clear precedents for refusing to obey Hitler's wrongful demands. For example, when Jesus' first-century apostles were ordered to cease declaring the good news about Christ, they

Awake!

**Why *Awake!* Is Published** *Awake!* is for the enlightenment of the entire family. It shows how to cope with today's problems. It reports the news, tells about people in many lands, examines religion and science. But it does more. It probes beneath the surface and points to the real meaning behind current events, yet it always stays politically neutral and does not exalt one race above another. Most important, this magazine builds confidence in the Creator's promise of a peaceful and secure new world before the generation that saw the events of 1914 passes away.

**Would you welcome more information? Write Watch Tower at the appropriate address on page 5. Publication of *Awake!* is part of a worldwide Bible educational work supported by voluntary donations.**

Unless otherwise indicated, *New World Translation of the Holy Scriptures—With References* is used.

*Awake!* (ISSN 0005-237X) is published semimonthly by Watchtower Bible and Tract Society of New York, Inc., 25 Columbia Heights, Brooklyn, NY 11201-2483. Second-class postage paid at Brooklyn, N.Y., and at additional mailing offices. ***Postmaster:*** Send address changes to *Awake!*, c/o Watchtower, ***Wallkill, NY 12589.***
Vol. 76, No. 16
Printed in U.S.A.

Awake! August 22, 1995

refused. The
ruler rather t
for their det
"flogged the
speaking up
Yet, the apos
defying orde
up teaching
—Acts 5:29,

Many earl
obeyed God
ished in Ro
fused, in effe
an act of wo
sons it was a
faithful to G
valiant soldi
half of his cc

Because J
only one gc
some have v
nothing cou
In imitation
part of the w
litically neut
God, they ob
human gover
plary in their
thorities." (F
advocated re
ernment!

There is, h
crossed und

**Semimonthly**
Afrikaans, Arabic, Ce
atian, Czech, Danish,
Greek, Hungarian, Ilo
Norwegian, Portugue
Swedish.

**Monthly La**
Chichewa, Cibemba, E
Kannada, New Guinea
Sesotho, Shona, Sin
Tsonga, Tswa

* Au

belongs to Him. (Matthew 22:21) If anyone tries to exact from them what belongs to God, that attempt will fail.

What if a Witness is threatened with death? Well, Jehovah's Witnesses have unshakable confidence in God's ability to restore them to life. (Acts 24:15) So Witnesses have the same attitude as did three young Hebrews in ancient Babylon. When threatened with death in a fiery furnace, they told King Nebuchadnezzar: "If it is to be, our God whom we are serving is able to rescue us. . . . Let it become known to you, O king, that your gods are not the ones we are serving, and the image of gold that you have set up we will not worship." —Daniel 3:17, 18.

Thus, as noted earlier, when Hitler began to climb onto his pedestal as a self-appointed god, an ideological battle was inevitable. The Third Reich, sword drawn, found itself face-to-face with a tiny band of Jehovah's Witnesses who had sworn loyalty to the true God, the Almighty God, Jehovah. Even before the battle began, however, the outcome was decided.

# The Evils of Nazism Exposed

IN THE 1920's, as Germany struggled to recover from its defeat in World War I, Jehovah's Witnesses were busy distributing tremendous amounts of Bible literature. Not only did this offer comfort and hope to the German people but it alerted them to the rising power of militarism. Between 1919 and 1933, the Witnesses delivered an average of eight books, booklets, or magazines to each of the approximately 15 million families in Germany.

The *Golden Age* and *Consolation* magazines often drew attention to the militaristic stirrings in Germany. In 1929, more than three years before Hitler came to power, the German edition of *The Golden Age* boldly stated: *"National Socialism is . . . a movement that is acting . . . directly in the service of man's enemy, the Devil."*

On the eve of Hitler's taking power, *The Golden Age* of January 4, 1933, said: "There looms forth the menacing promontory of the National Socialist movement. It seems incredulous that a political party so insignificant in its origin, so heterodox in its policies, can, in the space of a few years, develop into proportions that overshadow the structure of a national government. Yet Adolf Hitler and his national socialist party (the Nazis) have accomplished this rare feat."

**→ An Appeal for Understanding**

Hitler became prime minister of Germany on January 30, 1933, and a couple of months later, on April 4, 1933, the Magdeburg branch office of Jehovah's Witnesses was seized. However, the order was rescinded on April 28, 1933, and the property was returned. What would happen next?

In spite o
ler regime, J
convention
1933. Some
Witnesses p
clear: "Our
any sense. '
Word of Je
that withou
Thus Jeh
faith effort
the consequ

The imm
Witnesses, a
Kingdom, v
government
tolerate any
ogy.
Immedia
tion conclu
branch offi
1933. They
made arrest
dismissed f
raids on the

Awake! August 22, 1995

ds are not the
: image of gold
l not worship."

hen Hitler be-
estal as a self-
al battle was in-
sword drawn,
a tiny band of
ad sworn loyal-
ghty God, Jeho-
egan, however,

n

33, said: "There
promontory of
ment. It seems
party so insig-
rodox in its pol-
few years, de-
at overshadow
overnment. Yet
al socialist par-
lished this rare

**standing**

ister of Germa-
nd a couple of
'33, the Magde-
vah's Witnesses
der was rescind-
e property was
en next?

***The 150 workers at the Magdeburg branch office of Jehovah's Witnesses in 1931***

In spite of the evident hostility of the Hitler regime, Jehovah's Witnesses organized a convention in Berlin, Germany, on June 25, 1933. Some 7,000 persons assembled. The Witnesses publicly made their intentions clear: "Our organization is not political in any sense. We only insist on teaching the Word of Jehovah God to the people, and that without hindrance."

Thus Jehovah's Witnesses made a good-faith effort to state their case. What were the consequences?

**The Attack Begins**

The immovable neutral position of the Witnesses, along with their loyalty to God's Kingdom, was unacceptable to the Hitler government. The Nazis did not intend to tolerate any refusal to support their ideology.

Immediately after the Berlin convention concluded, the Nazis again seized the branch office at Magdeburg, on June 28, 1933. They broke up Witness meetings and made arrests. Soon Witnesses began to be dismissed from their jobs. They suffered raids on their homes, beatings, and arrests. By early 1934 the Nazis had seized from the Witnesses 65 tons of Bible literature and had burned it outside Magdeburg.

**Witnesses' Resolute Stand**

Despite these initial attacks, Jehovah's Witnesses stood their ground and publicly denounced the oppression and injustice. The November 1, 1933, issue of *The Watchtower* featured the article "Fear Them Not." It was prepared especially for the German Witnesses, exhorting them to take courage in the face of mounting pressure.

On February 9, 1934, J. F. Rutherford, the president of the Watch Tower Society, sent a letter of protest to Hitler stating: "You may successfully resist any and all men, but you cannot successfully resist Jehovah God. . . . In the name of Jehovah God and His anointed King, Christ Jesus, I demand that you give order to all officials and servants of your government that Jehovah's witnesses in Germany be permitted to peaceably assemble and without hindrance worship God."

Rutherford set March 24, 1934, as the deadline. He said that if by that time relief

**Awake! August 22, 1995**

will meet together
d, and will worship
commanded."
vah's Witnesses in
n special assembly
elegram to Hitler:
Jehovah's witness-
le of earth and dis-
frain from further
itnesses; otherwise
ind your national

almost immediate-
persecution. Hitler
; brood will be ex-
" But as opposition
nation of the Wit-
ondingly.
*ge* exposed the In-
thods of the Nazi
m. It also revealed
ie Hitler Youth or-

ganization to purge Germany's youths of their belief in God. The following year a nationwide Gestapo campaign resulted in the arrests of thousands of Witnesses. Soon after, on December 12, 1936, the Witnesses answered with their own campaign, blanketing Germany with tens of thousands of copies of a resolution protesting the persecution of Jehovah's Witnesses.

On June 20, 1937, the Witnesses who were still free distributed another message that was unsparing in its detail about the persecution. It named officials and cited dates and places. The Gestapo were appalled at this exposure and the ability of the Witnesses to carry it off.

Love of neighbor is what compelled the Witnesses to warn the people of Germany not to be fooled by the grandiose vision of a glorious thousand-year rule by the Third Reich. "We must tell the truth and give the warning," said the booklet *Face the Facts,* published in 1938. "We recognize the totalitarian government . . . as the product of Satan brought forth as the substitute for God's kingdom." Jehovah's Witnesses were among the first targets of Nazi abuse, but they also loudly decried atrocities against Jews, Poles, the handicapped, and others.

The resolution "Warning!," adopted at a 1938 convention of Jehovah's Witnesses in Seattle, Washington, U.S.A., said: "The Fascists and Nazis, radical political organizations, have wrongfully seized control of many countries of Europe . . . All the people will be regimented, all their liberties taken away, and all will be compelled to yield to the rule of an arbitrary dictator and then the ancient Inquisition will be fully revived."

Rutherford regularly took to the airwaves, delivering powerful lectures on the satanic nature of Nazism. The lectures were rebroadcast globally and were printed for distribution by the millions. On October 2, 1938, he delivered the address "Fascism or Freedom," in which he denounced Hitler in no uncertain terms.

"In Germany the common people are peace-loving," Rutherford proclaimed. "The Devil has put his representative Hitler in control, a man who is of unsound mind, cruel, malicious and ruthless . . . He cruelly persecutes the Jews because they were once Jehovah's covenant people and

### Witnesses Exposed Existence of Camps

ALTHOUGH Auschwitz, Buchenwald, Dachau, and Sachsenhausen were names unknown to most people until after World War II, they were well known to readers of *The Golden Age* and *Consolation.* The reports of Jehovah's Witnesses, smuggled out of the camps at great risk and publicized in Watch Tower literature, exposed the murderous intent of the Third Reich.

In 1933, *The Golden Age* carried the first of many reports of the existence of concentration camps in Germany. In 1938, Jehovah's Witnesses published the book *Crusade Against Christianity,* in French, German, and Polish. It carefully documented the vicious Nazi attacks on the Witnesses and included diagrams of the Sachsenhausen and Esterwegen concentration camps.

Nobel prize winner Dr. Thomas Mann wrote: "I have read your book and its terrible documentation with deepest emotion. I cannot describe the mixed feeling of abhorrence and loathing which has filled my heart while perusing these records of human degradation and abominable cruelty. . . . To keep quiet would serve only the moral indifference of the world . . . *You have done your duty in publishing this book* and bringing these facts to light."—Italics ours.

Awake! August 22, 1995 9

bore the name of Jehovah, and because Christ Jesus was a Jew."

As the Nazi rage against Jehovah's Witnesses reached new heights, the Witnesses' denunciations became ever more scathing. The May 15, 1940, issue of *Consolation* stated: "Hitler is such a perfect child of the Devil that these speeches and decisions flow through him like water through a well-built sewer."

**Horrors of Camps Exposed**

Although the public was largely unaware of the existence of the concentration camps until 1945, detailed descriptions of them appeared often in Watch Tower publications in the 1930's. In 1937, for example, *Consolation* told of experiments with poison gas at Dachau. By 1940, Witness publications had named 20 different camps and had reported on their unspeakable conditions.

Why were Jehovah's Witnesses so well acquainted with the concentration camps? When World War II started in 1939, there were already 6,000 Witnesses confined in camps and prisons. German historian Detlef Garbe estimates that the Witnesses constituted at that time between 5 and 10 percent of the total camp population!

At a seminar on the Witnesses and the Holocaust, Garbe stated: "Of the 25,000 persons who admitted to being Jehovah's Witnesses at the beginning of the Third Reich, about 10,000 were imprisoned for any length of time. Of these, over 2,000 were admitted to concentration camps. This means that the Jehovah's Witnesses were, with the exception of the Jews, the worst persecuted by the SS of all the religious based groups."

In June 1940, *Consolation* said: "There were 3,500,000 Jews in Poland when Germany began its Blitzkrieg . . . , and if reports which reach the Western world are correct their destruction seems well under way." In 1943, *Consolation* noted: "Whole nations like the Greeks, Poles and Serbs are being exterminated systematically." By 1946, *The Golden Age* and *Consolation* had identified 60 different prison and concentration camps.

**Witnesses Among First in the Camps**

MADAME Geneviève de Gaulle, niece of former president of France Charles de Gaulle, was a member of the French Resistance. Upon her capture and her later imprisonment in the Ravensbrück concentration camp in 1944, she met Jehovah's Witnesses. After World War II, Madame de Gaulle lectured throughout Switzerland and spoke often of the Witnesses' integrity and courage. In an interview on May 20, 1994, she said of them:

"They were among the first deportees in the camp. Many had already died . . . We recognized them by their distinctive badge. . . . It was absolutely forbidden for them to talk about their beliefs or to have any religious books, and especially the Bible, which was considered the supreme book of sedition. . . . I know of [one of Jehovah's Witnesses], and there were others I was told, who was executed for having a few pages of Bible texts. . . .

"What I admired a lot in them was that they could have left at any time just by signing a renunciation of their faith. Ultimately, these women, who appeared to be so weak and worn out, were stronger than the SS, who had power and all the means at their disposal. [Jehovah's Witnesses] had their strength, and it was their willpower that no one could beat."

10 Awake! August 22, 1995

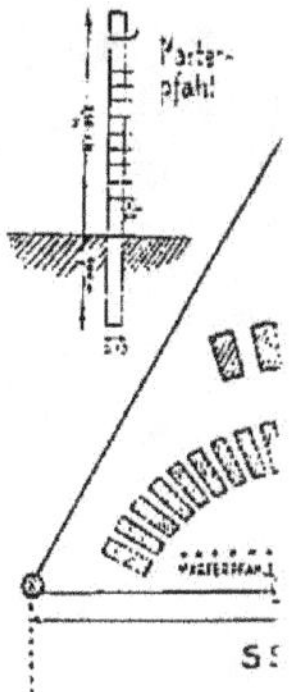

KONZENTR
SACHSENHAU
1936 n

**Nazis F**

Although t
of Watch Tc
ficial admitte
cret places in
dents' literatu
carries name
trays another

Despite th
were never al
the total num

OUT OF love o
their spiritual f

A Jew who s
*scher.* They cc
their God. The
to the camp o
round with a br
four days."

Similarly, a J
a brave people
to us, these w
family, and beg

Christian neutrality, but they failed miserably. The book *The Theory and Practice of Hell* said: "One cannot escape the impression that, psychologically speaking, the SS was never quite equal to the challenge offered them by Jehovah's Witnesses."

Indeed, the Witnesses, backed up by God's spirit, won the battle. Historian Christine King, chancellor of Staffordshire University in England, described the opponents in the conflict: "One [the Nazis] enormous, powerful, seemingly invincible. One [the Witnesses] very, very tiny . . . with only their faith, no other weapon . . . Jehovah's Witnesses brought morally to their knees the might of that Gestapo power."

Jehovah's Witnesses were a small, peaceable enclave within the Nazi realm. Yet, they waged and won a battle in their own way—a battle for the right to worship their God, a battle to love their neighbor, and a battle to tell the truth.

**Efforts to Deny the Holocaust Predicted**

IN ITS September 26, 1945, issue, *Consolation* noted that future attempts might be made to revise history and deny what had happened. The article "Has Nazism Been Destroyed?" said:

"Propagandists think the people have short memories. It is their intention to erase past history, presenting themselves in the modern disguise of benefactors, their incriminating record being covered up."

The magazine gave this perceptive warning: "Until Jehovah does fight Armageddon, Nazism will continue to raise its ugly head."

# Why the Churches Kept Silent

ON DECEMBER 8, 1993, Dr. Franklin Littell of Baylor University spoke at the United States Holocaust Memorial Museum about a troublesome "concrete truth." What was that?

The truth, Littell said, was that "six million Jews were targeted and systematically murdered in the heart of Christendom, by baptized Roman Catholics, Protestants, and Eastern Orthodox who were never rebuked, let alone excommunicated." One voice, however, did consistently speak out about clergy involvement with Hitler's regime. And the voice, as we have seen, was that of Jehovah's Witnesses.

Hitler was a baptized Roman Catholic, as were many of the leaders in his government. Why weren't they excommunicated? Why didn't the Catholic Church condemn the horrors that these men were committing? Why did Protestant churches also keep silent?

Did the churches really remain silent? Is there proof that they supported Hitler's war efforts?

**Role of Catholic Church**

Catholic historian E. I. Watkin wrote: "Painful as the admission must be, we cannot in the interest of a false edification or dishonest loyalty deny or ignore the historical fact that Bishops have consistently sup-

Awake! August 22, 1995

ported all wars
their country. .
alism is concei
mouthpiece of
When Watk
Catholic Churc
by the governr
cluded the war
ler. As Roman
at Vienna Univ
ted: "In the col
Cross and the
gether, until t
message of vic
man cathedra
round altars a
theologians, p.
men welcomec
Catholic Cl
qualified supp
Roman Cathc
wrote: "The C
to his religiou
ance and direc
ler's wars rec
swers he woul
ruler himself.'
That Catho!
rection of thc
mented by Pı

*New York Post*
August 27, 1940, Blu
Final Edition, page 1!

*The New York Times*,
September 25,
1939, Late City
Edition, page 6

GERMA
RALLI
Protesta
to Reich

time." Contrasting such pastors with Jehovah's Witnesses, Johnson wrote: "The bravest were the Jehovah's Witnesses, who proclaimed their outright doctrinal opposition from the beginning and suffered accordingly. They refused any cooperation with the Nazi state."

Back in 1939, the year World War II began, *Consolation* quoted T. Bruppacher, a Protestant minister, as saying: "While men who call themselves Christians have failed in the decisive tests, these unknown witnesses of Jehovah, as Christian martyrs, are maintaining unshakable opposition against coercion of conscience and heathen idolatry. The future historian must some day acknowledge that not the great churches, but these slandered and scoffed-at people, were the ones who stood up first against the rage of the Nazi demon . . . They refuse the worship of Hitler and the Swastika."

Similarly, Martin Niemoeller, a Protestant church leader who himself had been in a Nazi concentration camp, later confessed: 'It may be truthfully recalled that Christian churches, throughout the ages, have always consented to bless war, troops, and arms and that they prayed in a very unchristian way for the annihilation of their enemy.' He admitted: "All this is our fault and our fathers' fault, but obviously not God's fault."

Niemoeller then added: "And to think that we Christians of today are ashamed of the so-called sect of the serious scholars of the Bible [Jehovah's Witnesses], who by the hundreds and thousands have gone into concentration camps and died because they refused to serve in war and declined to fire on human beings."

Susannah Heschel, a professor of Judaic studies, uncovered church documents proving that the Lutheran clergy were willing, yes anxious, to support Hitler. She said they begged for the privilege of displaying the swastika in their churches. The overwhelming majority of clergymen were not coerced collaborators, her research showed, but were enthusiastic supporters of Hitler and his Aryan ideals.

As a lecturer, Heschel is frequently asked by church members, "What could we have done?"

"You could have been like Jehovah's Witnesses," she replies.

**Why They Were Silent**

The reason the churches were silent becomes clear. It is because Christendom's clergy and their flocks had abandoned the teachings of the Bible in favor of supporting the political state. In 1933 the Roman Catholic Church concluded a concordat with the Nazis. Roman Catholic cardinal Faulhaber wrote to Hitler: "This handshake with the Papacy . . . is a feat of immeasurable blessing. . . . May God preserve the Reich Chancellor [Hitler]."

Indeed, the Catholic Church and other churches as well became handmaidens of the evil Hitler government. Even though Jesus Christ said his true followers "are no part of the world," the churches and their parishioners became an integral part of Hitler's world. (John 17:16) As a result, they failed to speak out about the horrors against humanity that were committed by the Nazis in their death camps.

True, a few courageous individuals from the Catholic, Protestant, and various other religions stood up against the Nazi State. But even as some of them paid with their lives, their spiritual leaders, who claimed to serve God, were serving as puppets of the Third Reich.

There was, however, one voice that consistently spoke out. Though the news media, by and large, overlooked the churches as major players in the Nazi drama, Jehovah's Wit-



nesses felt com
ery and hypocr
of their behind
pages of the fo
well as other
1930's and 19
dictments of re
came Nazism's

**Identifying**

Jehovah's W
from the relig
part of the wo
wars of the na
instructions, 't
into plowshare
ence to Christ'
another. (John
er go to war a
other.

When it co
worshipers of
in saying: "*The*
*dren of the D*
Everyone who
ness does not
does he who d

:s. The overwhelm-
n were not coerced
arch showed, but
rters of Hitler and

is frequently asked
hat could we have

like Jehovah's Wit-

**e Silent**

ies were silent be-
se Christendom's
ad abandoned the
avor of supporting
l the Roman Cath-
concordat with the
ardinal Faulhaber
indshake with the
easurable blessing.
Reich Chancellor

Church and other
: handmaidens of
t. Even though Je-
followers "are no
hurches and their
tegral part of Hit-
As a result, they
he horrors against
itted by the Nazis

individuals from
and various oth-
nst the Nazi State.
n paid with their
s, who claimed to
ıs puppets of the

e voice that con-
h the news media,
e churches as ma-
ia, Jehovah's Wit-

nesses felt compelled to expose the treachery and hypocrisy of the clergy, with details of their behind-the-scenes collusion. In the pages of the forerunner of this magazine as well as other publications throughout the 1930's and 1940's, they printed strong indictments of religious organizations that became Nazism's handmaidens.

**Identifying Christ's True Followers**

Jehovah's Witnesses are totally different from the religions of the world. Being no part of the world, they take no part in the wars of the nations. In obedience to God's instructions, 'they have beaten their swords into plowshares.' (Isaiah 2:4) Yes, in obedience to Christ's instructions, they love one another. (John 13:35) This means they never go to war and intentionally hurt one another.

When it comes to identifying the true worshipers of God, the Bible is very plain in saying: *"The children of God and the children of the Devil are evident by this fact:* Everyone who does not carry on righteousness does not originate with God, neither does he who does not love his brother. For this is the message which you have heard from the beginning, *that we should have love for one another; not like Cain, who originated with the wicked one and slaughtered his brother.*"—1 John 3:10-12.

Yes, history reveals that Jehovah's Witnesses have always shown love for their fellowman, even in the face of intense pressure. When Hitler waged war throughout Europe, the Witnesses stood firm in the face of the Nazis' brutal attempts to make them join in the orgy of killing. Professor Christine King well summed up the matter: "Jehovah's Witnesses did speak out. They spoke out from the beginning. They spoke out with one voice. And they spoke out with a tremendous courage, which has a message for all of us."

Until this world is safely under the loving rule of Jehovah's government and is free from war and wickedness, Jehovah's Witnesses will continue to speak out. As long as it is the will of the Sovereign Lord Jehovah, this magazine will expose the evils of this satanic world and herald the only true hope for mankind, God's Kingdom.—Matthew 6: 9, 10.

***Unlike the churches, Jehovah's Witnesses spoke out against Nazism***

15

# 1934 YEAR BOOK

of

JEHOVAH'S WITNESSES

Containing

Report of the Year 1933

with

Daily Texts and Comments

for 1934

*Corporate Publishers:*

Watch Tower Bible and Tract Society
Peoples Pulpit Association
International Bible Students Association
Brooklyn, New York, U.S.A.
Branch Offices appear on last page

year 1921. After being thus legally admitted as a
corporation a large sum of money was spent in erect-
ing buildings, machinery, etc. The Society has always
respected the laws of the German government and has
never done anything that might be interpreted as
being contrary to the same. The Society has never
had any affiliation directly or indirectly with commu-
nists or any other political body. All of its literature
shows positively that it is against such. The Society's
work is devoted exclusively to teaching the Scriptures,
and not at any time to anything political.

A treaty exists between the United States and German governments, which treaty guarantees to American citizens the right to have and maintain property
in Germany and to carry forward their work in harmony with German laws. The action of the German
government has been directly in violation of this
treaty. The State Department has acted together with
the Society to have these violations removed. From
June, 1933, to the first part of October the Society's
property at Magdeburg was in possession of the state
police and the machines were sealed, and most of the
180 workers there were compelled to leave the prem-
ises. During that time the government police seized
and carried away and burned over $25,000 worth of
literature, books, booklets, paintings, Bibles and other
material of the Society. The government has forbidden any meetings of the various companies of Jehovah's witnesses throughout Germany, seized and confiscated all the literature and completely stopped the
distribution of the same.

In June, the president of the Society visited Germany to take some action to get the Society's property
restored to our possession and to carry on the work
further. Knowing that the enemy has misrepresented



the facts to the government, a Declaration of Facts was prepared, and on the 25th day of June, 1933, more than 7,000 of Jehovah's witnesses assembled at Berlin and unanimously adopted the resolution, millions of which were printed and distributed throughout Germany. That resolution is as follows, to wit:

### Declaration of Facts

"This company of German people, who are peaceable and law-abiding citizens representing many others from every part of Germany, all of whom are earnestly laboring for the highest welfare of the people of this land, being now duly assembled at Berlin this 25th day of June, A.D. 1933, do joyfully declare our complete devotion to Jehovah, the Almighty God, and to his kingdom under Christ Jesus, whose shed blood bought the human race. We declare that the holy Scriptures set forth in the Bible constitute the Word of Jehovah God given to men for their guidance in righteousness, and that the Word of God is the truth, and that it is of greatest importance that man have a knowledge of his relationship to God. We ask to be judged by the standard of the Word of God.

"Christ Jesus is Jehovah God's great Witness to the truth, and as his faithful and devoted followers we are, by His grace, witnesses to the truth. The purpose of this Declaration is that we may present a true and faithful witness before the rulers and the people as to the name and purpose of Jehovah God and our relation thereto.

"We are wrongfully charged before the ruling powers of this government and before the people of this nation; and in order that the name of Jehovah God may be exalted in the minds of the people, and that his benevolent purposes be better understood and

of God and thus bear witness against themselves. The same materialistic spirit that caused the persecution of Jesus Christ now exists and is back of the persecution of us as his faithful followers.

"It is falsely charged by our enemies that we have received financial support for our work from the Jews. Nothing is farther from the truth. Up to this hour there never has been the slightest bit of money contributed to our work by Jews. We are the faithful followers of Christ Jesus and believe upon Him as the Savior of the world, whereas the Jews entirely reject Jesus Christ and emphatically deny that he is the Savior of the world sent of God for man's good. This of itself should be sufficient proof to show that we receive no support from Jews and that therefore the charges against us are maliciously false and could proceed only from Satan, our great enemy.

"The greatest and the most oppressive empire on earth is the Anglo-American empire. By that is meant the British Empire, of which the United States of America forms a part. It has been the commercial Jews of the British-American empire that have built up and carried on Big Business as a means of exploiting and oppressing the peoples of many nations. This fact particularly applies to the cities of London and New York, the stronghold of Big Business. This fact is so manifest in America that there is a proverb concerning the city of New York which says: 'The Jews own it, the Irish Catholics rule it, and the Americans pay the bills.' We have no fight with any of these persons mentioned, but, as the witnesses for Jehovah and in obedience to his commandment set forth in the Scriptures, we are compelled to call attention to the truth concerning the same in order that the people may be enlightened concerning God and his purpose.



Our Literature

"It is said that our books and like literature, when circulated amongst the people, constitute a danger to the peace and safety of the nation. We are certain that this conclusion is due to the fact that our books and other literature have not been carefully examined by the rulers and hence are not properly understood. We respectfully call attention to the fact that these books and other literature were written originally in America and the language therein used has been adapted to the American style of plainness of speech and, when translated into the German, the same appears to be harsh. We admit that the same truths might be stated in a less blunt and more pleasing phrase, and yet the language of these books follows closely the language of the Bible.

"It should be borne in mind that in the British Empire and in America the common people have suffered and are now suffering greatly because of the misrule of Big Business and conscienceless politicians, which misrule has been and is supported by political religionists, and hence the writers of our books or literature have endeavored to employ plain language to convey to the people the proper thought or understanding. The language used, however, is not as strong or emphatic as that used by Jesus Christ in denouncing the oppressors and false teachers of his time.

"The present government of Germany has declared emphatically against Big Business oppressors and in opposition to the wrongful religious influence in the political affairs of the nation. Such is exactly our position; and we further state in our literature the reason for the existence of oppressive Big Business and the wrongful political religious influence, because the Holy Scriptures plainly declare that these oppressive

instruments proceed from the Devil, and that the complete relief therefrom is God's kingdom under Christ. It is therefore impossible for our literature or our work to in any wise be a danger or a menace to the peace and safety of the state.

"Our organization is not political in any sense. We only insist on teaching the Word of Jehovah God to the people, and that without hindrance. We do not object to or try to hinder anyone's teaching or believing what he desires, but we only ask the freedom to believe and teach what we conceive the Bible to teach, and then let the people decide which they wish to believe.

"To know Jehovah God and his gracious provision for humankind is of most vital importance to all persons, because God has declared in His Word that where there is no vision or understanding of his Word the people perish. (Proverbs 29:18) We have devoted our lives and our material substance to the work of enabling the people to gain a vision or understanding of God's Word, and therefore it is impossible for our literature and our work to be a menace to the peace and safety of the nation. Instead of being against the principles advocated by the government of Germany, we stand squarely for such principles, and point out that Jehovah God through Christ Jesus will bring about the full realization of these principles and will give to the people peace and prosperity and the greatest desire of every honest heart.

"Our organization seeks neither money nor members, but we are a company or organized body of Christian people engaged solely in the benevolent work of teaching the Word of God to the people at the least possible cost to them. Our organization was originally incorporated in the United States of America in 1884 under the name of the WATCH TOWER BIBLE & TRACT SOCIETY, and in 1914 incorporated under the laws of Great Britain by the name of the INTERNATIONAL BIBLE STUDENTS ASSOCIATION. These are merely the corporate names of our organization for legally carrying forward its work. The Scriptural name by which we are known is 'Jehovah's witnesses'. We are engaged solely in a benevolent work. The purpose of our organization is to aid the people to understand the Bible, which discloses the only possible way for the complete relief and blessing for mankind. Our organization has extended its work throughout the earth. The education, culture and upbuilding of the people must and will come through the agency of God's kingdom concerning which we teach as set forth in the Bible. The salvation of the people depends upon the true knowledge of and obedience to Jehovah God and his righteous ways.

"The people are in great distress and in need of help to understand the reason for their unhappy condition and what is the means of relief. The Scriptures, when understood, make this matter clear. Instead of collecting money from the people and using the same to erect great buildings and to support men in luxury, we print the gospel message of God's kingdom and carry it to the homes of the people that they may, at the least inconvenience to themselves, gain a knowledge of God's purposes concerning them.

"A careful examination of our books and literature will disclose the fact that the very high ideals held and promulgated by the present national government are set forth in and endorsed and strongly emphasized in our publications, and show that Jehovah God will see to it that these high ideals in due time will be at-

the world. They do not interfere with what others do about sharing in patriotic ceremonies, serving in the armed forces, joining a political party, running for a political office, or voting. But they themselves worship only Jehovah, the God of the Bible; they have dedicated their lives unreservedly to him and give their full support to his Kingdom.

**What scriptures have had a bearing on the attitude of Christians toward the authority of secular governments?**

Rom. 13:1, 5-7: "Let every soul be in subjection to the superior authorities [governmental rulers], for there is no authority except by God . . . There is therefore compelling reason for you people to be in subjection, not only on account of that wrath but also on account of your conscience. . . . Render to all their dues, to him who calls for the tax, the tax; to him who calls for the tribute, the tribute; to him who calls for fear, such fear; to him who calls for honor, such honor." (No government could exist without God's permission. Regardless of the conduct of individual officials, true Christians have shown them respect because of the office they occupied. For example, regardless of the use that governments have made of tax money, worshipers of Jehovah have made honest payment of their taxes in return for those services from which everyone could benefit.)

Mark 12:17: "Jesus then said: 'Pay back Caesar's things to Caesar, but God's things to God.'" (So Christians have always recognized that they must not only "pay back" money in the form of taxes to the secular government but also fulfill the superior obligations they have toward God.)

Acts 5:28, 29: "[A spokesman for the Jewish high court] said: 'We positively ordered you [the apostles] not to keep teaching upon the basis of this name [of Jesus Christ], and yet, look! you have filled Jerusalem with your teaching, and you are determined to bring the blood of this man upon us.' In answer Peter and the other apostles said: 'We must obey God as ruler rather than men.'" (When there has been a direct conflict between the commands of human rulers and the requirements of God, true Christians have imitated the example of the apostles by putting obedience to God first.)



**What scriptures have always had a bearing on the attitude of true Christians toward participation in carnal warfare?**

Matt. 26:52: "Jesus said to him: 'Return your sword to its place, for all those who take the sword will perish by the sword.'" (Could there have been any higher cause for which to fight than to safeguard the Son of God? Yet, Jesus here indicated that those disciples were not to resort to weapons of physical warfare.)

Isa. 2:2-4: "It must occur in the final part of the days that the mountain of the house of Jehovah will become firmly established above the top of the mountains . . . And he will certainly render judgment among the nations and set matters straight respecting many peoples. And they will have to beat their swords into plowshares and their spears into pruning shears. Nation will not lift up sword against nation, neither will they learn war anymore." (Individuals out of all nations must personally decide what course they will pursue. Those who have heeded Jehovah's judgment give evidence that he is their God.)

2 Cor. 10:3, 4: "Though we walk in the flesh, we do not wage warfare according to what we are in the flesh. For the weapons of our warfare are not fleshly, but powerful by God for overturning strongly entrenched things." (Paul here states that he never resorted to fleshly weapons, such as trickery, high-sounding language, or carnal weapons, to protect the congregation against false teachings.)

Luke 6:27, 28: "I [Jesus Christ] say to you who are listening, Continue to love your enemies, to do good to those hating you, to bless those cursing you, to pray for those who are insulting you."

***Is it not true that Jehovah allowed ancient Israel to engage in warfare?***

Jehovah directed ancient Israel to use warfare to take possession of the land that he himself designated as their inheritance and to execute people whose depraved practices and defiance of the true God caused Jehovah to view them as being no longer fit to live. (Deut. 7:1, 2, 5; 9:5; Lev. 18:

REASONING FROM THE SCRIPTURES, 1985, 1989ed

24, 25) Nevertheless, mercy was shown to Rahab and to the Gibeonites because they demonstrated faith in Jehovah. (Josh. 2:9-13; 9:24-27) In the Law covenant God laid down rules for warfare that he would approve, stipulating exemptions and the manner in which this warfare was to be carried out. Such were truly holy wars of Jehovah. That is not true of the carnal warfare of any nation today.

***With the establishing of the Christian congregation, a new situation came into existence.*** Christians are not under the Mosaic Law. Christ's followers were to make disciples of people of all nations; so worshipers of the true God would in time be found in all those nations. However, what is the motive of those nations when they go to war? Is it to carry out the will of the Creator of all the earth or is it to further some nationalistic interest? If true Christians in one nation were to go to war against another nation, they would be fighting against fellow believers, against people who prayed for help to the same God that they did. Appropriately, Christ directed his followers to lay down the sword. (Matt. 26:52) He himself, glorified in the heavens, would henceforth carry out the execution of those who showed defiance of the true God and His will.—2 Thess. 1:6-8; Rev. 19:11-21.

***As to serving in the armed forces, what does secular history disclose about the attitude of early Christians?***

"A careful review of all the information available goes to show that, until the time of Marcus Aurelius [Roman emperor from 161 to 180 C.E.], no Christian became a soldier; and no soldier, after becoming a Christian, remained in military service."—*The Rise of Christianity* (London, 1947), E. W. Barnes, p. 333.

"We who were filled with war, and mutual slaughter, and every wickedness, have each through the whole earth changed our warlike weapons,—our swords into ploughshares, and our spears into implements of tillage,—and we cultivate piety, righteousness, philanthropy, faith, and hope, which we have from the Father Himself through Him who was crucified."—Justin Martyr in "Dialogue With Trypho, a Jew" (2nd century C.E.), *The Ante-Nicene Fathers* (Grand



Rapids, Mich.; reprint of 1885 Edinburgh edition), edited by A. Roberts and J. Donaldson, Vol. I, p. 254.

"They refused to take any active part in the civil administration or the military defence of the empire. . . . it was impossible that the Christians, without renouncing a more sacred duty, could assume the character of soldiers, of magistrates, or of princes."—*History of Christianity* (New York, 1891), Edward Gibbon, pp. 162, 163.

**What scriptures have always had a bearing on the attitude of true Christians toward involvement in political issues and activities?**

John 17:16: "They are no part of the world, just as I [Jesus] am no part of the world."

John 6:15: "Jesus, knowing they [the Jews] were about to come and seize him to make him king, withdrew again into the mountain all alone." Later, he told the Roman governor: "My kingdom is no part of this world. If my kingdom were part of this world, my attendants would have fought that I should not be delivered up to the Jews. But, as it is, my kingdom is not from this source."—John 18:36.

Jas. 4:4: "Adulteresses, do you not know that the friendship with the world is enmity with God? Whoever, therefore, wants to be a friend of the world is constituting himself an enemy of God." (Why is the matter so serious? Because, as 1 John 5:19 says, "the whole world is lying in the power of the wicked one." At John 14:30, Jesus referred to Satan as being "the ruler of the world." So, no matter what worldly faction a person might support, under whose control would he really come?)

***Regarding political involvement, what do secular historians report as being the attitude of those known as early Christians?***

"Early Christianity was little understood and was regarded with little favor by those who ruled the pagan world: . . . Christians refused to share certain duties of Roman citizens. . . . They would not hold political office."—*On the Road to*

REASONING FROM THE SCRIPTURES, 1985, 1989ed

l the gold
nine,' fails
will under-
the publi-

cost five
still costs
te of much
g costs. It
of a few
ion copies
ld that not
and power-
viewpoint
emphasized
ones.

x years of
is constant-
es of Jeho-
. Many per-
*Vatchtower*
ve come to
s attention
eryone else,
ancial prob-
for them to
regation of
l never be
of their in-
al money-
m them. It
unobtrusive
for use by
give money
ongregation.
quarters of
re also un-
ry.

s that have
not simply
c problems.
ey have lost
use they no
but, rather,
support to
those who
iritual good.



WHAT IS THE BIBLE'S VIEW?

# Should You Defend Yourself?

IN MANY parts of the earth crime and violence are on the increase. Especially in the larger cities, people do not feel secure even in their own homes. What if you were threatened with violence? Should you 'turn the other cheek'?

Jesus Christ did speak about 'turning the other cheek.' But we need to consider whether he was actually talking about serious threats to a person's life. He said: "Do not resist him that is wicked; but whoever slaps you on your right cheek, turn the other also to him." (Matt. 5:39) Now, a slap is an insult, often designed to provoke a fight. By not retaliating when subjected to insulting speech or action, the Christian may prevent trouble. "An answer, when mild," says the Bible, "turns away rage."—Prov. 15:1.

The situation, however, is very different when one is threatened with serious bodily harm. In his Law to Israel, Jehovah God revealed that the individual had the right of self-defense. For example, regarding a thief who broke into a house at night, the Law stated: "If a thief should be found in the act of breaking in and he does get struck and die, there is no bloodguilt for him." (Ex. 22:2) At night it would be very hard to determine the intentions of the intruder. To protect himself from possible harm, the homeowner had the right to inflict hard blows. And if these blows proved fatal, he was considered to be free from bloodguilt.

Actually, it is inherent in man to prevent injury to his body. If an object is hurled at him, he instinctively tries to get out of the way or, if that is impossible, to shield the head from injury. Similarly, if a beloved relative—wife or child—comes under attack, a man will instinctively do what he can to help, even if doing so could cost him his life. Such action is also in harmony with what Jesus Christ himself did in sacrificing his life for the congregation.—Eph. 5:25.

So if you or one of your loved ones were confronted by a man or a woman carrying a weapon, what could you do? To the extent that time and human ability allow, you must assess matters, judging whether the individual merely wants money and other valuables or is bent on inflicting serious bodily injury. It would certainly be foolhardy to sacrifice one's life in an effort to protect perishable material possessions. Giving up money or other valuables without putting up resistance may well remove any threat to life. Then, too, the Mosaic law considered as bloodguilty the person taking the life of a thief in the daytime. (Ex. 22:3) Why? Evidently because, in the daytime, the thief could be identified to the Law. Since the Mosaic law sets forth God's view, we can appreciate that a Christian could not claim self-defense if, in reality, only property defense against an identifiable criminal was involved.

On the other hand, the armed person may definitely want to kill. What then?

When flight is possible, that is to be preferred. The Bible relates a number of instances involving Jesus' doing just that. There was the time when certain Jews 'picked up stones to hurl at him; but Jesus hid and went out of the temple.' (John 8:59) Regarding another occasion, we

read: "They tried again to seize him; but he got out of their reach."—John 10:39.

If flight is impossible, the individual may be able to reason with the assailant. But, at other times, trying to reason with a person determined to inflict injury may lead to loss of valuable time. The situation may be such that the only thing a person can do is to use whatever is at hand to protect himself or others. As a result, the attacker may receive a fatal blow. From the Scriptural standpoint, the one acting in self-defense would not thereby incur bloodguilt.

In view of increasing crime and violence, some Christians may wonder whether they should not arm themselves in preparation for a possible attack. Jesus' apostles were known to have had at least two swords. (Luke 22:38) This was not something unusual, for Jews at that time were under the Mosaic law that allowed for armed conflict. Also, swords were of value in warding off wild beasts. And they could serve a utilitarian purpose, much like that of an ax or a large knife.

However, as developments on Nisan 14, 33 C.E., show, Jesus Christ did not want his Jewish followers to use swords under circumstances that might provoke armed resistance against authorities of the land. When Peter, for example, used one of the swords against the mob that had come to arrest his Lord, Jesus commanded: "Return your sword to its place, for all those who take the sword will perish by the sword." (Matt. 26:52) Peter's action in this case was not a matter of self-defense, but, rather, resistance to authorities and even against God's will. The intent of the mob was to arrest Jesus and to bring him to trial.

It is good to keep in mind that we simply cannot prepare ourselves for everything that might happen. The Christian, therefore, is wise when he does not become overanxious about his material needs and safety. Jesus Christ cautioned: "Stop being anxious about your souls as to what you will eat or what you will drink, or about your bodies as to what you will wear." (Matt. 6:25) Jesus was not here saying that a person should not work for life's necessities, but he was simply pointing out that this should not become a matter of undue concern. Similarly, it is right to take precautions about one's personal safety, but it is an entirely different matter when one allows this to become a cause for great anxiety.

A Christian, therefore, should give serious consideration to the potential dangers that come with procuring a deadly weapon, such as a gun, for self-defense. Not infrequently availability of a gun, coupled with panic or overreaction, has led to needless deaths. There was the forty-year-old man in Arkansas who loaded his shotgun for the first time in four years. Because of robberies that had been taking place in the neighborhood, he was determined to protect his property. Early the next morning he heard what he thought to be a prowler stumbling outside his home. He took hold of his gun and fired at the front door. Then he turned on the light. There in the doorway lay his thirteen-year-old daughter—dead.

Accordingly, before buying a deadly weapon, one should certainly weigh both aspects—one potential danger against the other potential danger. He must decide which would be the greater risk.

From the foregoing it is evident that the Scriptures give a person the right to defend himself or others against bodily harm. However, they give no authorization for armed conflicts or the taking of human life in efforts during daytime to protect material possessions.

**First Greek** ...
◆ Despite ... from the Gr... gy, Jehoval... Greece held ... assembly, at ... um near Atl... to 13. This "... ty" Assembl... 19,211. The ... and its newl... tion made ... blies of Je... possible for ... a few week... courts also ... riages amo... nesses were ... legal and c... unions legit... gy influenc... nition by t... ously been ... witnesses.

**Court Back**...
◆ A woma... by a Texas ... that atten... business m... pulsory, fo... be paid. Bu... ing she sav... a religious ... a Baptist ... that her fr... was being ... solved not ... meetings, ... were comp... she left th... cuit Court ... that she ...

# DIALOGUE THREE: Is Political Neutrality Christian? —Part I and 2

my wheelchair." And that is exactly what she did. Our beloved brothers from Bethel sent us many encouraging letters. Martha was repeatedly reminded of the words at Psalm 41:3: "Jehovah himself will sustain him upon a divan of illness; all his bed you will certainly change during his sickness."

Because of these serious health problems, in 1986 it was decided that it would be appropriate for me to serve as a special pioneer in Kaválla, where I live near the family of our dear daughter. Last March my dear Martha passed away, faithful to the end. Before she died, when brothers would ask her: "How are you?" she usually replied: "Since I am close to Jehovah, I am very well!" When we prepared for the meetings or received tempting invitations to serve in areas where the harvest is plentiful, Martha used to say: "John, let us go to serve where the need is greater." She never lost her zealous spirit.

Some years ago, I too had to cope with a severe health problem. In March 1994, I was diagnosed with a life-threatening heart problem, and surgery was imperative. Once again I felt Jehovah's loving hand supporting me through a critical period. I will never forget the prayer that a circuit overseer offered at my bedside when I got out of intensive care, as well as the celebration of the Memorial that I conducted right there in my hospital room with four patients who had shown some interest in the truth.

### Jehovah Has Been Our Helper

Time flies, and our flesh weakens, but our spirit is renewed through study and service. (2 Corinthians 4:16) It has now been 39 years since I said, "Here I am! Send me." It has been a full, happy, and rewarding life. Yes, sometimes I feel that "I am afflicted and poor," but then I can say with confidence to Jehovah: "You are my assistance and the Provider of escape for me." (Psalm 40:17) He has indeed been a God of loving-kindness to me.

## QUESTIONS FROM READERS

***How do Jehovah's Witnesses view voting?***

There are clear principles set out in the Bible that enable servants of God to take a proper view of this matter. However, there appears to be no principle against the practice of voting itself. For example, there is no reason why a board of directors should not take a vote in order to arrive at decisions affecting their corporation. Congregations of Jehovah's Witnesses often make decisions about meeting times and the use of congregation funds by voting with a show of hands.

What, though, of voting in political elections? Of course, in some democratic lands, as many as 50 percent of the population do not turn out to vote on election day. As for Jehovah's Witnesses, they do not interfere with the right of others to vote; neither do they in any way campaign against political elections. They respect and cooperate with the authorities who are duly elected in such elections. (Romans 13:1-7) As to whether they will personally vote for someone running in an election, each one of Jehovah's Witnesses makes a decision based on his Bible-trained conscience and an understanding of his responsibility to God and to the State. (Matthew 22:21; 1 Peter 3:16) In making this personal decision, the Witnesses consider a number of factors.

First, Jesus Christ said of his followers: "They are no part of the world, just as I am no part of the world." (John 17:14) Jehovah's Witnesses take this principle seriously. Being "no part of the world," they are neutral in the political affairs of the world.—John 18:36.

Second, the apostle Paul referred to himself as



an "ambassado
ple of his day. (
20) Jehovah's
sus is now the e
Kingdom, and
nounce this to t
elation 11:15)
neutral and not
of the countries
sentatives of Go
Witnesses feel c
in the politics of

A third factor
a part in voting
responsible for
thy 5:22, The N
to consider care
der that respon

Fourth, Jehov
Christian unity.
get involved in
sion among the
Christ, Jehovah
volved in politic
unity.—Matthew

Fifth and finc
gives Jehovah'
to approach pe
with the importa
brews 10:35.

In view of th
above, in many
a personal deci
tions, and their
supported by th
if the law requir
each Witness is
tious, Bible-base
the situation. If
ing booth, that i
polling booth is

The Novembe
tower, on page
Caesar makes i
. . . [Witnesses]

eatening heart
ıperative. Once
hand support-
iod. I will nev-
ircuit overseer
[ got out of in-
lebration of the
ɡht there in my
ients who had
ruth.

ır Helper
ɜakens, but our
study and ser-
as now been 39
a! Send me." It
rewarding life.
m afflicted and
rith confidence
ıstance and the
'salm 40:17) He
oving-kindness

respect and co-
are duly elected
-7) As to wheth-
someone running
ovah's Witnesses
Bible-trained con-
his responsibility
iew 22:21; 1 Pe-
nal decision, the
factors.
followers: "They
as I am no part
ovah's Witnesses
g "no part of the
political affairs of

red to himself as

an "ambassador" representing Christ to the people of his day. (Ephesians 6:20; 2 Corinthians 5:20) Jehovah's Witnesses believe that Christ Jesus is now the enthroned King of God's heavenly Kingdom, and they, like ambassadors, must announce this to the nations. (Matthew 24:14; Revelation 11:15) Ambassadors are expected to be neutral and not to interfere in the internal affairs of the countries to which they are sent. As representatives of God's heavenly Kingdom, Jehovah's Witnesses feel a similar obligation not to interfere in the politics of the countries where they reside.

A third factor to consider is that those who have a part in voting a person into office may become responsible for what he does. (Compare 1 Timothy 5:22, *The New English Bible.*) Christians have to consider carefully whether they want to shoulder that responsibility.

Fourth, Jehovah's Witnesses greatly value their Christian unity. (Colossians 3:14) When religions get involved in politics, the result is often division among their members. In imitation of Jesus Christ, Jehovah's Witnesses avoid becoming involved in politics and thus maintain their Christian unity.—Matthew 12:25; John 6:15; 18:36, 37.

Fifth and finally, their keeping out of politics gives Jehovah's Witnesses freeness of speech to approach people of all political persuasions with the important message of the Kingdom.—Hebrews 10:35.

In view of the Scriptural principles outlined above, in many lands Jehovah's Witnesses make a personal decision not to vote in political elections, and their freedom to make that decision is supported by the law of the land. What, though, if the law requires citizens to vote? In such a case, each Witness is responsible to make a conscientious, Bible-based decision about how to handle the situation. If someone decides to go to the polling booth, that is his decision. What he does in the polling booth is between him and his Creator.

The November 15, 1950, issue of *The Watchtower,* on pages 445 and 446, said: "Where Caesar makes it compulsory for citizens to vote . . . [Witnesses] can go to the polls and enter the voting booths. It is here that they are called upon to mark the ballot or write in what they stand for. The voters do what they will with their ballots. So here in the presence of God is where his witnesses must act in harmony with his commandments and in accordance with their faith. It is not our responsibility to instruct them what to do with the ballot."

What if a Christian woman's unbelieving husband insists that she present herself to vote? Well, she is subject to her husband, just as Christians are subject to the superior authorities. (Ephesians 5:22; 1 Peter 2:13-17) If she obeys her husband and goes to the polling booth, that is her personal decision. No one should criticize her.—Compare Romans 14:4.

What of a country where voting is not mandated by law but feelings run high against those who do not go to the voting booth—perhaps they are exposed to physical danger? Or what if individuals, while not legally obliged to vote, are severely penalized in some way if they do not go to the polling booth? In these and similar situations, a Christian has to make his own decision. "Each one will carry his own load."—Galatians 6:5.

There may be people who are stumbled when they observe that during an election in their country, some Witnesses of Jehovah go to the polling booth and others do not. They may say, 'Jehovah's Witnesses are not consistent.' People should recognize, though, that in matters of individual conscience such as this, each Christian has to make his own decision before Jehovah God.—Romans 14:12.

Whatever personal decisions Jehovah's Witnesses make in the face of different situations, they take care to preserve their Christian neutrality and freeness of speech. In all things, they rely on Jehovah God to strengthen them, give them wisdom, and help them avoid compromising their faith in any way. Thus they show confidence in the words of the psalmist: "You are my crag and my stronghold; and for the sake of your name you will lead me and conduct me."—Psalm 31:3.

THE WATCHTOWER—NOVEMBER 1, 1999 29

"I am YHWH, that is My Name, and My glory will I not five to another. . ." (Isaiah 42:8)

3. THE LAW OF YHWH AND THE GRACE OF YHWHHOSHUA

We believe that we are saved by the grace of YHWHHOSHUA, in that He shed his blood for the remission of our sins; and that we accept this grace by faith in what He did and taught as well as what He teaches today. We do not misconstrue this grace as a license to continue in our sin by disobeying YHWH's laws, but rather the strength to repent from our former lives of sin. It is by repentance and the keeping of YHWH's laws that we have access to His Holy Spirit.

4. IMMERSION (BAPTISM)

Once an individual decides that he or she is willing to dedicate their life of obedience to YHWH, it is required that one be baptized by full immersion in a natural body of water (lake, river or sea), by a minister of YHWHHOSHUA, as a token of the covenant that he is going to cleanse his life. We believe that YHWHHOSHUA honors this token of faith by applying the redeeming value of the blood that He shed to the individual's soul; cleansing him from all the sins that were committed previous to baptism. "He that believeth and is immersed shall be saved; but he that believeth not shall be damned." (Mark 16:16) "Repent and be immersed every one of you in the Name of YHWHHOSHUA the Messiah, for the remission of sins, and ye shall receive the gift of the Holy Spirit." (Acts 2:38) "Except a man be born of water and of the Spirit, he can not enter into the kingdom of YHWH". (John 3:5)

5. THE GIFT OF THE HOLY SPIRIT

Once a believer totally yields his heart, mind, body and soul to the perfect will of YHWH, he will receive the gift of the Holy Spirit, the Power of the Almighty, which will be initially evidenced by a marked improvement in the individual's life in the way of love, joy, peace, longsuffering, gentleness, faith, meekness, temperance, and a willingness to obey the laws of YHWH. When one receives the fullness and infilling of the Holy Spirit, he will speak in a heavenly tongue as the Spirit moves in him. "For with stammering lips and another tongue will He speak to this people." To whom He said, "This is the rest wherewith ye may cause the weary to rest; and this is the refreshing: yet they should not hear." (Isaiah 28:11-12) "And these signs shall follow them that believe; in My Name shall they cast out demons; they shall speak with new tongues:" (Mark 16:17)

6. MINISTERS

A minister or pastor of YHWHHOSHUA is a man (not a woman) who is in obedience to the doctrine of YHWHHOSHUA. "... ordain elders in every city. . ., If any be blame less, the husband of one wife. . ." (Titus 5:6) "That the man of YHWH may be perfect, thoroughly furnished unto all good works." (Timothy 3:17) "Let your women keep silence in the assemblies: for it is not permitted unto them to speak; but they are commanded to be under obedience, as also saith the law." (I Corinthians 14:34) "But I do not allow a woman to preach, nor to usurp authority over the man, but to be quiet. " (I Timothy 2:12)

7. SANCTIFICATION

The members of the assembly of YHWHHOSHUA are to be separate from the institutions, customs, traditions, styles and carnal pleasures of the United States as well as the world. A member in no way should participate into the affairs and practices of the world.

8. GOVERNMENT

YHWHHOSHUA is our government. He is our counselor, our welfare, medicare. He is our social security and old age care, our employment. Through YHWHHOSHUA all things are provided. The widows and orphans, the elderly and sick, those who are unable to work are to be supported by the assembly as a whole; the men working and giving out of the generosity of their hearts. It is the duty of every member of the assembly to help all those members of the assembly of YHWHHOSHUA who are in need. In no way should we participate in the charities of the world, for these charities are not for YHWH'S people. Thus a servant of YHWH can not vote or contribute to or accept any benefits from the institutions of the United States, such as Social Security, Medicare, Unemployment Compensation, etc. . . . nor shall he be allowed to be a government official, to be a juror, or to serve in the Armed Forces.

9. INCOME TAX

Members of the assembly of YHWHHOSHUA are not to pay the Federal Income Tax. The income tax of the United States is used to pay for such things that are contrary to the law of YHWH. Such as, the armed forces of America, "Thou shalt not kill." (Exodus 20) Numerous government medical benefits are provided by the income tax (abortion clinics, birth control research grants, experimental animal killing, etc . . .) These things are contrary to the law of YHWH. The lists seems endless, these are just a few of the atrocities the income tax encourages. "Render therefore unto Caesar (United States) the things which are Caesar's; and unto YHWH the things that are YHWH's." (Matthew 22:21) The money that the servants of YHWH earn belongs to YHWH and is to be used to supply the needs of YHWH's people, not those of the world. "And the multitude of them that believed were of one heart and of one soul; neither was there any among them that lacked; for as many as were possessors of lands or houses sold them and brought the prices of the things that were sold, and laid them down at the apostles' feet; and distribution was made unto every man according as he had need." (Acts 4:32, 34, 35) "Come out of her, My people, that ye be not partakers of her sins, and that ye received not of her plagues." (Rev. 18:4) "YHWHHOSHUA spoke to him, saying, What thinkest thou, Simon? of whom do the kings of the earth take custom or tribute? of their own children, or of strangers? Peter saith unto Him, Of strangers. YHWHHOSHUA saith unto him, Then are the children free." (Matthew 17:25-26)

10. HOLIDAYS

Christmas (Saturnalia), Easter (Ishtar), New Years, Independence Day, Thanksgiving, and any other heathen holiday are



THE ENCYCLOPEDIA OF AMERICAN RELIGIONS: RELIGIOUS CREEDS, Vol. 2
J. Gordon Melton, Editor (Gale Research Company, 1988)

24, 25) Nevertheless, mercy was shown to Rahab and to the Gibeonites because they demonstrated faith in Jehovah. (Josh. 2:9-13; 9:24-27) In the Law covenant God laid down rules for warfare that he would approve, stipulating exemptions and the manner in which this warfare was to be carried out. Such were truly holy wars of Jehovah. That is not true of the carnal warfare of any nation today.

***With the establishing of the Christian congregation, a new situation came into existence.*** Christians are not under the Mosaic Law. Christ's followers were to make disciples of people of all nations; so worshipers of the true God would in time be found in all those nations. However, what is the motive of those nations when they go to war? Is it to carry out the will of the Creator of all the earth or is it to further some nationalistic interest? If true Christians in one nation were to go to war against another nation, they would be fighting against fellow believers, against people who prayed for help to the same God that they did. Appropriately, Christ directed his followers to lay down the sword. (Matt. 26:52) He himself, glorified in the heavens, would henceforth carry out the execution of those who showed defiance of the true God and His will.—2 Thess. 1:6-8; Rev. 19:11-21.

***As to serving in the armed forces, what does secular history disclose about the attitude of early Christians?***

"A careful review of all the information available goes to show that, until the time of Marcus Aurelius [Roman emperor from 161 to 180 C.E.], no Christian became a soldier; and no soldier, after becoming a Christian, remained in military service."—*The Rise of Christianity* (London, 1947), E. W. Barnes, p. 333.

"We who were filled with war, and mutual slaughter, and every wickedness, have each through the whole earth changed our warlike weapons,—our swords into ploughshares, and our spears into implements of tillage,—and we cultivate piety, righteousness, philanthropy, faith, and hope, which we have from the Father Himself through Him who was crucified."—Justin Martyr in "Dialogue With Trypho, a Jew" (2nd century C.E.), *The Ante-Nicene Fathers* (Grand



Rapids, Mich.; reprint of 1885 Edinburgh edition), edited by A. Roberts and J. Donaldson, Vol. I, p. 254.

"They refused to take any active part in the civil administration or the military defence of the empire. . . . it was impossible that the Christians, without renouncing a more sacred duty, could assume the character of soldiers, of magistrates, or of princes."—*History of Christianity* (New York, 1891), Edward Gibbon, pp. 162, 163.

**What scriptures have always had a bearing on the attitude of true Christians toward involvement in political issues and activities?**

John 17:16: "They are no part of the world, just as I [Jesus] am no part of the world."

John 6:15: "Jesus, knowing they [the Jews] were about to come and seize him to make him king, withdrew again into the mountain all alone." Later, he told the Roman governor: "My kingdom is no part of this world. If my kingdom were part of this world, my attendants would have fought that I should not be delivered up to the Jews. But, as it is, my kingdom is not from this source."—John 18:36.

Jas. 4:4: "Adulteresses, do you not know that the friendship with the world is enmity with God? Whoever, therefore, wants to be a friend of the world is constituting himself an enemy of God." (Why is the matter so serious? Because, as 1 John 5:19 says, "the whole world is lying in the power of the wicked one." At John 14:30, Jesus referred to Satan as being "the ruler of the world." So, no matter what worldly faction a person might support, under whose control would he really come?)

***Regarding political involvement, what do secular historians report as being the attitude of those known as early Christians?***

"Early Christianity was little understood and was regarded with little favor by those who ruled the pagan world: . . . Christians refused to share certain duties of Roman citizens. . . . They would not hold political office."—*On the Road to*

REASONING FROM THE SCRIPTURES, 1985, 1989ed

# WHO REALLY RULES THE WORLD?

Many people would answer the above question with a single word—God. But significantly, nowhere does the Bible say that either Jesus Christ or his Father are the real rulers of this world. On the contrary, Jesus said: "The ruler of this world will be cast out." And he added: "The ruler of the world is coming. And he has no hold on me."—John 12:31; 14:30; 16:11.

So the ruler of this world is in opposition to Jesus. Who could this be?

### A Clue From World Conditions

Despite the efforts of well-meaning humans, the world has suffered terribly throughout history. This causes thinking persons to wonder, as did the late editorial writer David Lawrence: "'Peace on earth'—nearly everybody wants it. 'Good will toward men'—almost all the peoples of the world feel it toward one another. Then what's wrong? Why is war threatened despite the innate desires of peoples?"

It seems a paradox, doesn't it? When the natural desire of people is to live at peace, they commonly hate and kill one another—and with such viciousness. Consider the cold-blooded excesses in monstrous cruelty. Humans have used gas chambers, concentration camps, flamethrowers, napalm bombs, and other heinous methods to torture and slaughter one another mercilessly.

Do you believe that humans, who long for peace and happiness, are capable, in themselves, of such gross wickedness against others? What forces drive men to such loathsome deeds or maneuver them into situations where they feel

2

compelled to commit atrocities? Have you ever wondered whether some wicked, invisible power is influencing people to commit such acts of violence?

### The Rulers of the World Identified

There is no need to guess at the matter, for the Bible clearly shows that an intelligent, unseen person has been controlling both men and nations. It says: "The whole world is lying in the power of the wicked one." And the Bible identifies him, saying: "The one called Devil and Satan . . . is misleading the entire inhabited earth."—1 John 5:19; Revelation 12:9.

On an occasion when Jesus was "*tempted* by the Devil," Jesus did not question Satan's role as the ruler of this world. The Bible explains what happened: "The Devil took him along to an unusually high mountain, and showed him all the kingdoms of the world and their glory, and he said to him: 'All these things I will give you if you fall down and do an act of worship to me.' Then Jesus said to him: 'Go away, Satan!'"—Matthew 4:1, 8-10.

Think about this. Satan *tempted* Jesus by offering him "*all the kingdoms of the world.*" Yet, would Satan's offer have been a real *temptation* if Satan was not actually the ruler of these kingdoms? No, it would not. And note, Jesus did not deny that all these worldly governments were Satan's, which he would have done if Satan did not have power over them. So, then, Satan the Devil really is the unseen ruler of the world! The Bible, in fact, calls him "the god of this system of things." (2 Corinthians 4:4) Yet, how did such a wicked person ever come into this powerful position?

The one who became Satan had been an angel created by God, but he became envious of God's position. He challenged God's rightful rulership. To this end he used a serpent as a mouthpiece to deceive the first woman, Eve, and was thus able to get her and her husband, Adam, to do his bidding

3

rather than obey God. (Genesis 3:1-6; 2 Corinthians 11:3) He also claimed he could turn all of Adam and Eve's yet unborn offspring away from God. So God allowed time for Satan to try to prove his claim, but Satan has not succeeded.—Job 1:6-12; 2:1-10.

Significantly, Satan is not alone in his rulership of the world. He was successful in persuading some of the other angels to join him in rebellion against God. These became demons, his spirit accomplices. The Bible speaks of them when it urges Christians: "Stand firm against the machinations of the Devil; because we have a wrestling, not against blood and flesh, but . . .

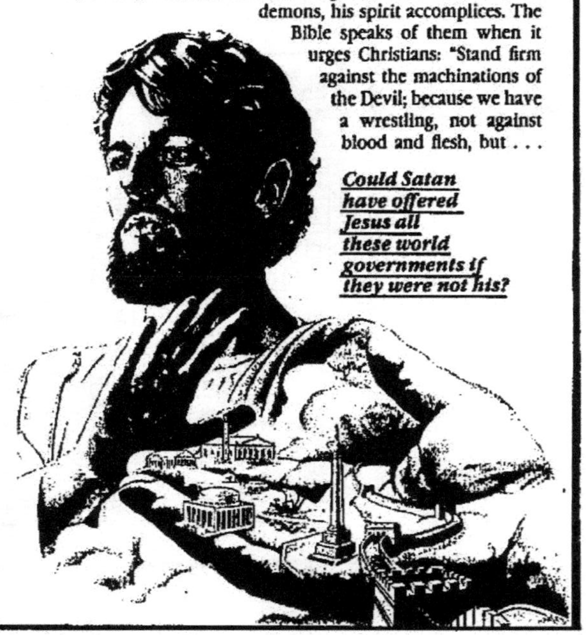

***Could Satan have offered Jesus all these world governments if they were not his?***

banded 1096

n before me Daniel,
te-shaz'zar[a] accord-
of my god[b] and in
spirit of the holy
him I said what the

zar the chief of the
ests,[d] because I my-
t the spirit of the
[e] and that there is
t is troubling you,[f]
of my dream that
s interpretation.[g]
sions of my head
ened to be behold-
ee[i] in the midst of
t of which was im-
e grew up and be-
very height finally
and it was visible*
the whole earth.[k]
fair, and its fruit
here was food for
e beast[l] of the field
and on its boughs
vens would dwell,[n]
would feed itself.
eholding in the vi-
pon my bed, and,
even a holy one,[p]
he heavens them-
calling out loudly,*
vas saying: "CHOP
cut off its boughs.
e, and scatter its
ast flee from un-
from its boughs.[r]
ts rootstock itself
a banding of iron
the grass of the
ew of the heavens
h the beast let its
vegetation of the
heart be changed
, and let the heart
it,[t] and let seven

9* "Secret." Aram.,
n; Lat., sa·cra·men'-
sight of it was."
'ir; LXX[Bagster](Gr.),
ngel"; Lat., vi'gil.
gy."



times*[a] pass over it. 17 By the decree
of watchers*[b] the thing is, and [by] the
saying of holy ones the request is, to
the intent that people living may know
that the Most High is Ruler* in the
kingdom of mankind[Δc] and that to the
one whom he wants to, he gives it[d] and
he sets up over it even the lowliest one
of mankind."[■e]
18 "'This was the dream that I myself, King Neb·u·chad·nez'zar, beheld;
and you yourself, O Bel·te·shaz'zar, say
what the interpretation is, forasmuch
as all the [other] wise men of my kingdom are unable to make known to me
the interpretation itself.[f] But you are
competent, because the spirit of holy
gods* is in you.'[g]
19 "At that time Daniel himself,
whose name is Bel·te·shaz'zar,[h] was astonished for a moment, and his very
thoughts began to frighten him.[i]
"The king was answering and saying, 'O Bel·te·shaz'zar, do not let the
dream and the interpretation themselves
frighten you.'[j]
"Bel·te·shaz'zar was answering and
saying, 'O my lord,* may the dream
[apply] to those hating you, and its interpretation to your adversaries.[k]
20 "'The tree that you beheld, that
grew great and became strong and the
height of which finally reached the
heavens and which was visible to all the
earth,[l] 21 and the foliage of which
was fair, and the fruit of which was
abundant, and on which there was food
for all; under which the beasts of the
field would dwell, and on the boughs of

Da 4:16* Or, "appointed (definite) times"; or, "time periods." Aram., 'id·da·nin'; Gr., e'te, "years"; LXX[Bagster](Gr.), kai·roi', "appointed times"; Lat., tem'po·ra, "times." "Years," BDB, p. 1105; KB, p. 1106; *Lexicon Linguae Aramaicae Veteris Testamenti*, by E. Vogt, Rome, 1971, p. 124. "Seven times" as seven years are twice three and a half times. Compare 7:25 ftn, "Time"; 12:7 ftn, "Half." 17* "Watchers." Aram., 'i·rin'; LXX[Bagster](Gr.), *eir*; Lat., *vi'gi·lum*. 17* Or, "is ruling." Aram., *shal·lit'*. 17[Δ] "Mankind." Aram., *'anow·sha'*. 17[■] "And . . . the lowliest one of **mankind**." Aram., *u·shephal' 'ana·shim'* (pl. of *'enash'*). 18* "Spirit of . . . gods." Aram., *ru·ach-'ela·hin'*; Lat., *spi'ri·tus de·o'rum*. 19* "O my lord." Aram., *ma·ri'y'*.

CHAP. 4
a Da 7:25, Da 12:7, Lu 21:24, Re 12:14
b Da 4:13
c Ps 83:18, Jer 16:21, Da 4:34
d Ps 75:7, Ps 89:36, Mt 25:31, Lu 1:32, Lu 1:33
e 1Sa 2:8, Eze 17:24, Zec 9:9, Mt 11:29
f Isa 47:13, Da 5:8, Da 5:15
g Ge 41:16, Da 2:28, Da 4:8
h Da 1:7
i Da 7:28
j 1Sa 3:17
k 2Sa 18:32
l Eze 31:3, Da 4:10

Second Col.
a Da 4:12
b Da 2:37
c Isa 14:13, Isa 14:14
d Da 2:38
e Nu 22:32, De 33:2, Ps 89:7, Da 4:13, Da 8:13, Mt 18:10, Ac 10:3, Ac 12:23
f Da 4:16, Da 5:21, Lu 21:24
g Isa 23:9, Isa 55:11, Da 4:17
h Ps 83:18
i Job 34:19, Ps 107:40
j Da 4:32, Da 5:21
k Ps 106:20
l Da 4:16, Lu 21:24
m Ps 83:18
n Job 34:24, Jer 27:5, Da 2:21, Da 5:21, Da 7:14
o Da 4:15
p Ps 11:4, Isa 66:1
q Ps 119:46
r Pr 16:6, Pr 28:13, Isa 55:7, Eze 18:21, Mt 3:8
s Ps 41:1, Isa 58:7, Mic 6:8, 1Jo 3:17
t 1Ki 21:29, Joe 2:14, Jon 3:10
u Nu 23:19, Pr 10:24, Isa 55:11
v Ps 73:9

which the birds of the heavens would
reside,[a] 22 it is you, O king,[b] because
you have grown great and become
strong, and your grandeur has grown
great and reached to the heavens,[c] and
your rulership to the extremity of the
earth.[d]
23 "'And because the king beheld
a watcher,* even a holy one,[e] coming
down from the heavens, who was also
saying: "CHOP the tree down, and RUIN
it. However, LEAVE its rootstock itself
in the earth, but with a banding of iron
and of copper, among the grass of the
field, and with the dew of the heavens
let it become wet, and with the beasts
of the field let its portion be until
seven times* themselves pass over it,"[f]
24 this is the interpretation, O king,
and the decree[g] of the Most High[h] is
that which must befall my lord* the
king.[i] 25 And you they will be driving
away from men, and with the beasts of
the field your dwelling will come to be,[j]
and the vegetation is what they will
give even to you to eat just like bulls;[k]
and with the dew of the heavens you
yourself will be getting wet, and seven
times*[l] themselves will pass over you,
until you know that the Most High is
Ruler* in the kingdom of mankind,[Δm]
and that to the one whom he wants to
he gives it.[n]
26 "'And because they said to leave
the rootstock of the tree,[o] your kingdom will be sure to you after you
know that the heavens are ruling.[p]
27 Therefore, O king, may my counsel
seem good to you,[q] and remove your
own sins by righteousness,[r] and your
iniquity by showing mercy to the poor
ones.[s] Maybe there will occur a length-
ening of your prosperity.'"[t]
28 All this befell Neb·u·chad·nez'zar
the king.[u]
29 At the end of twelve lunar months
he happened to be walking upon the
royal palace of Babylon. 30 The king
was answering and saying:[v] "Is not

Da 4:23* "A watcher." Aram., *'ir*; LXX[Bagster](Gr.), *eir*; Lat., *vi'gi·lem*. 23* See vs 16 ftn. 24* "My lord." Aram., *ma·ri'y'*. 25* See vs 16 ftn. 25* Or, "ruling." 25[Δ] Or, "men." Aram., *'ana·sha'*.

NEW WORLD TRANSLATION OF THE HOLY SCRIPTURES - WITH REFERENCES, 1984

18 In Nebuchadnezzar's dream, the great tree was felled and its stump was banded to prevent growth upward for seven times. Similarly, Nebuchadnezzar "was brought down from the throne of his kingdom" when Jehovah struck him with madness. (Daniel 5:20) In effect, this changed the king's heart from that of a man to that of a bull. Yet, God reserved Nebuchadnezzar's throne for him until the seven times ended. While Evil-merodach possibly acted as the temporary head of government, Daniel served as "the ruler over all the jurisdictional district of Babylon and the chief prefect over all the wise men of Babylon." His three Hebrew companions continued to share in administering that district's affairs. (Daniel 1:11-19; 2:48, 49; 3:30) The four exiles awaited Nebuchadnezzar's restoration to the throne as a sane king who had learned that "the Most High is Ruler in the kingdom of mankind, and that to the one whom he wants to he gives it."

## NEBUCHADNEZZAR'S RESTORATION

19 Jehovah restored Nebuchadnezzar's sanity at the end of seven times. Then acknowledging the Most High God, the king said: "At the end of the days I, Nebuchadnezzar, lifted up to the heavens my eyes, and my own understanding began to return to me; and I blessed the Most High himself, and the One living to time indefinite I praised and glorified, because his rulership is a rulership to time indefinite and his kingdom is for generation after generation. And all the inhabitants of the earth are being considered as merely nothing, and he is doing according to his own will among the army of the heavens and the inhabitants of the earth. And there exists no one that can

18. During the seven times, what took place with regard to Babylon's throne?
19. After Jehovah restored Nebuchadnezzar's sanity, what did the Babylonian king come to realize?



check his hand or that can say to him, 'What have you been doing?' " (Daniel 4:34, 35) Yes, Nebuchadnezzar did come to realize that the Most High is indeed the Sovereign Ruler in the kingdom of mankind.

20 When Nebuchadnezzar returned to his throne, it was as though the metal bands around the dream tree's rootstock had been removed. Concerning his restoration, he said: "At the same time my understanding itself began to return to me, and for the dignity of my kingdom my majesty and my brightness themselves began to return to me; and for me even my high royal officers and my grandees began eagerly searching, and I was reestablished upon my own kingdom, and greatness extraordinary was added to me." (Daniel 4:36) If any court officials had despised the deranged king, now they were "eagerly searching" for him in complete subservience.

21 What "signs and wonders" the Most High God had performed! It should not surprise us that the restored Babylonian king said: "Now I, Nebuchadnezzar, am praising and exalting and glorifying the King of the heavens, because all his works are truth and his ways are justice, and because those who are walking in pride he is able to humiliate." (Daniel 4:2, 37) Such an acknowledgment, however, did not make Nebuchadnezzar a Gentile worshiper of Jehovah.

## IS THERE SECULAR EVIDENCE?

22 Some have identified Nebuchadnezzar's madness with lycanthropy. Says one medical dictionary:

20, 21. (a) How did the removal of the metal bands around the dream tree's rootstock find a parallel in what happened to Nebuchadnezzar? (b) What acknowledgment did Nebuchadnezzar make, and did this make him a worshiper of Jehovah?
22. With what disorder have some identified Nebuchadnezzar's madness, but what should we realize regarding the cause of his deranged state?

of the world were Satan's to give. Later, he called Satan "the ruler of this world." (John 12:31; 16:11) Toward the end of the first century C.E., the apostle John wrote: "We know we originate with God, but the whole world is lying in the power of the wicked one." (1 John 5:19) This does not mean that Jehovah has relinquished his sovereignty over the earth. Remember that Satan, when offering Jesus rulership over the political kingdoms, stated: "I will give you all this authority . . . because it has been delivered to me." (Luke 4:6) Satan exercises authority over the kingdoms of the world only by God's permission.

[3] Similarly, the State exercises its authority only because God as Sovereign Ruler permits it to do so. (John 19:11) Thus, "the existing authorities" can be said to "stand placed in their relative positions by God." Relative to Jehovah's supreme sovereign authority, theirs is by far a lesser authority. However, they are "God's minister," "God's public servants," in that they provide necessary services, maintain law and order, and punish evildoers. (Romans 13: 1, 4, 6) So Christians need to understand that just because Satan is the invisible ruler of this world, or system, they are not subjecting themselves to him when they recognize their relative subjection to the State. They are obeying God. In this year, 1996, the political State is still a part of "the arrangement of God," a temporary arrangement that God permits to exist, and it should be recognized as such by Jehovah's earthly servants. —Romans 13:2.

*When Satan offered him political power, Jesus turned it down*

3. (a) What position do the governments of the nations hold before Jehovah? (b) How can we say that subjection to the governments of this world does not mean subjecting ourselves to Satan, the god of this world?

10 THE WATCHTOWER—MAY 1, 1996

Je
of

[4] In pre-Ch
mitted some
prominent pc
For example,
Joseph becar
second only t
esis 41:39-43
evident that
that Joseph
in preservin
descendants,
poses. Of cou
that Joseph
and he lived
had neither t
the Christ."-
latians 6:2.

[5] Centurie
Jeremiah wa
Jewish exiles
in exile in Ba
peace of that
wrote: "This
God of Israel
ple, . . . 'Seek
I have caused
in its behalf
there will pr
selves.'" (Jer
hovah's peop
for themselv
live, in orde
Jehovah.—1

[6] During

4. Why did
prominent in
5. Why were
the peace" of
6. Although g
in what ways
ions refuse to
vah's Law?

God, but now have been shown mercy because of their disobedience, 31 so these also
now have been disobedient, in order that
because of the mercy shown to you they
also may now be shown mercy. 32 For God
has shut up all in disobedience that He
might show mercy to all.
33 Oh, the depth of the riches both of the
wisdom and knowledge of God! How un-
searchable are His judgments and unfath-
omable His ways! 34 For WHO HAS KNOWN
THE MIND OF THE LORD, OR WHO BECAME
HIS COUNSELOR? 35 OR WHO HAS FIRST GIV-
EN TO HIM THAT IT MIGHT BE PAID BACK TO
HIM AGAIN? 36 For from Him and through
Him and to Him are all things. To Him *be*
the glory forever. Amen.

### *Dedicated Service*

12 I URGE you therefore, brethren, by
the mercies of God, to present your
bodies a living and holy sacrifice, acceptable to God, *which is* your spiritual service
of worship. 2 And do not be conformed to
this world, but be transformed by the re-
newing of your mind, that you may prove
what the will of God is, that which is good
and acceptable and perfect.
3 For through the grace given to me I
say to every man among you not to think
more highly of himself than he ought to
think; but to think so as to have sound
judgment, as God has allotted to each a
measure of faith. 4 For just as we have
many members in one body and all the
members do not have the same function,
5 so we, who are many, are one body in
Christ, and individually members one of
another. 6 And since we have gifts that differ according to the grace given to us, *let
each exercise them accordingly:* if prophecy,
according to the proportion of his faith; 7 if
service, in his serving; or he who teaches,
in his teaching; 8 or he who exhorts, in his
exhortation; he who gives, with [14]liberality;
he who leads, with diligence; he who shows
mercy, with cheerfulness.
9 Let love be without hypocrisy. Abhor
what is evil; cling to what is good. 10 Be
devoted to one another in brotherly love;
give preference to one another in honor;
11 not lagging behind in diligence, fervent
in spirit, serving the Lord; 12 rejoicing in
hope, persevering in tribulation, devoted to
prayer, 13 contributing to the needs of the
saints, practicing hospitality. 14 Bless those
who persecute [15]you; bless and curse not.
15 Rejoice with those who rejoice, and
weep with those who weep. 16 Be of the
same mind toward one another; do not be
haughty in mind, but associate with the
lowly. Do not be wise in your own estima-
tion. 17 Never pay back evil for evil to anyone. Respect what is right in the sight of all
men. 18 If possible, so far as it depends on
you, be at peace with all men. 19 Never
take your own revenge, beloved, but leave
room for the wrath *of God,* for it is written,
"VENGEANCE IS MINE, I WILL REPAY," says
the Lord. 20 "BUT IF YOUR ENEMY IS HUN-
GRY, FEED HIM, AND IF HE IS THIRSTY, GIVE
HIM A DRINK; FOR IN SO DOING YOU WILL
HEAP BURNING COALS UPON HIS HEAD."
21 Do not be overcome by evil, but overcome evil with good.

### *Be Subject to Government*

13 LET every person be in subjection to
the governing authorities. For there
is no authority except from God, and those
which exist are established by God.
2 Therefore he who resists authority has
opposed the ordinance of God; and they
who have opposed will receive condemnation upon themselves. 3 For rulers are not
a cause of fear for good behavior, but for
evil. Do you want to have no fear of authority? Do what is good, and you will
have praise from the same; 4 for it is a minister of God to you for good. But if you do
what is evil, be afraid; for it does not bear
the sword for nothing; for it is a minister of
God, an avenger who brings wrath upon
the one who practices evil. 5 Wherefore it
is necessary to be in subjection, not only
because of wrath, but also for conscience'
sake. 6 For because of this you also pay
taxes, for *rulers* are servants of God, devoting themselves to this very thing. 7 Render
to all what is due them: tax to whom tax *is
due;* custom to whom custom; fear to
whom fear; honor to whom honor.
8 Owe nothing to anyone except to love
one another; for he who loves his neighbor
has fulfilled *the* law. 9 For this, "YOU SHALL
NOT COMMIT ADULTERY, YOU SHALL NOT
MURDER, YOU SHALL NOT STEAL, YOU SHALL
NOT COVET," and if there is any other commandment, it is summed up in this saying,
"YOU SHALL LOVE YOUR NEIGHBOR AS YOUR-
SELF." 10 Love does no wrong to a neighbor; love therefore is the fulfillment of *the*
law.
11 And this *do,* knowing the time, that it
is already the hour for you to awaken from
sleep; for now [16]salvation is nearer to us
than when we believed. 12 The night is almost gone, and the day is at hand. Let us
therefore lay aside the deeds of darkness
and put on the armor of light. 13 Let us
behave properly as in the day, not in ca-
rousing and drunkenness, not in sexual
promiscuity and sensuality, not in strife
and jealousy. 14 But put on the Lord Jesus
Christ, and make no provision for the flesh
in regard to *its* lusts.

[14] Or, *simplicity*
[15] Some ancient mss. do not contain *you*
[16] Or, *our salvation is nearer than when*



### *Principles of Conscience*

14 NOW accept the one who is weak in
faith, *but* not for *the purpose of* passing judgment on his opinions. 2 One man
has faith that he may eat all things, but he
who is weak eats vegetables *only.* 3 Let not
him who eats regard with contempt him
who does not eat, and let not him who does
not eat judge him who eats, for God has
accepted him. 4 Who are you to judge the
servant of another? To his own master he
stands or falls; and stand he will, for the
Lord is able to make him stand. 5 One man
regards one day above another, another regards every day *alike.* Let each man be fully convinced in his own mind. 6 He who
observes the day, observes it for the Lord,
and he who eats, does so for the Lord, for
he gives thanks to God; and he who eats
not, for the Lord he does not eat, and gives
thanks to God. 7 For not one of us lives for
himself, and not one dies for himself; 8 for
if we live, we live for the Lord, or if we die,
we die for the Lord; therefore whether we
live or die, we are the Lord's. 9 For to this
end Christ died and lived *again,* that He
might be Lord both of the dead and of the
living. 10 But you, why do you judge your
brother? Or you again, why do you regard
your brother with contempt? For we shall
all stand before the judgment seat of God.
11 For it is written,
"AS I LIVE, SAYS THE LORD, EVERY
KNEE SHALL BOW TO ME,
AND EVERY TONGUE SHALL GIVE
PRAISE TO GOD."
12 So then each one of us shall give account
of himself to God.
13 Therefore let us not judge one another
anymore, but rather determine this—not to
put an obstacle or a stumbling block in a
brother's way. 14 I know and am convinced
in the Lord Jesus that nothing is unclean in
itself; but to him who thinks anything to be
unclean, to him it is unclean. 15 For if because of food your brother is hurt, you are
no longer walking according to love. Do
not destroy with your food him for whom
Christ died. 16 Therefore do not let what is
for you a good thing be spoken of as evil;
17 for the kingdom of God is not eating and
drinking, but righteousness and peace and
joy in the Holy Spirit. 18 For he who in
this *way* serves Christ is acceptable to God
and approved by men. 19 So then [17]let us
pursue the things which make for peace
and the building up of one another. 20 Do
not tear down the work of God for the sake
of food. All things indeed are clean, but
they are evil for the man who eats and
gives offense. 21 It is good not to eat meat
or to drink wine, or *to do anything* by which
your brother stumbles. 22 The faith which
you have, have as your own conviction before God. Happy is he who does not condemn himself in what he approves. 23 But
he who doubts is condemned if he eats, because *his eating is* not from faith; and whatever is not from faith is sin.

### *Self-denial on Behalf of Others*

15 NOW we who are strong ought to
bear the weaknesses of those without
strength and not *just* please ourselves. 2 Let
each of us please his neighbor for his good,
to his edification. 3 For even Christ did not
please Himself; but as it is written, "THE
REPROACHES OF THOSE WHO REPROACHED
THEE FELL UPON ME." 4 For whatever was
written in earlier times was written for our
instruction, that through perseverance and
the encouragement of the Scriptures we
might have hope. 5 Now may the God who
gives perseverance and encouragement
grant you to be of the same mind with one
another according to Christ Jesus; 6 that
with one accord you may with one voice
glorify the God and Father of our Lord
Jesus Christ.
7 Wherefore, accept one another, just as
Christ also accepted us to the glory of God.
8 For I say that Christ has become a servant to the circumcision on behalf of the
truth of God to confirm the promises *given*
to the fathers, 9 and for the Gentiles to glorify God for His mercy; as it is written,
"THEREFORE I WILL GIVE PRAISE TO
THEE AMONG THE GENTILES,
AND I WILL SING TO THY NAME."
10 And again he says,
"REJOICE, O GENTILES, WITH HIS PEO-
PLE."
11 And again,
"PRAISE THE LORD ALL YOU GENTILES,
AND LET ALL THE PEOPLES PRAISE
HIM."
12 And again Isaiah says,
"THERE SHALL COME THE ROOT OF
JESSE,
AND HE WHO ARISES TO RULE OVER
THE GENTILES,
IN HIM SHALL THE GENTILES HOPE."
13 Now may the God of hope fill you with
all joy and peace in believing, that you may
abound in hope by the power of the Holy
Spirit.
14 And concerning you, my brethren, I
myself also am convinced that you yourselves are full of goodness, filled with all
knowledge, and able also to admonish one
another. 15 But I have written very boldly
to you on some points, so as to remind you
again, because of the grace that was given
me from God, 16 to be a minister of Christ
Jesus to the Gentiles, ministering as a
priest the gospel of God, that *my* offering of
the Gentiles might become acceptable,
sanctified by the Holy Spirit. 17 Therefore
in Christ Jesus I have found reason for
boasting in things pertaining to God.
18 For I will not presume to speak of anything except what Christ has accomplished

[17] Many ancient mss. read *we pursue*

NEW AMERICAN STANDARD BIBLE

part with them, when I
ıway."[a] 28 True, with
e good news they are
R sakes,[b] but with ref-
] choosing* they are be-
ce of their forefathers.[c]
: and the calling of God
e will regret.[d] 30 For
e once disobedient* to
ow been shown mercy[f]
disobedience,[g] 31 so
have been disobedient
lting to YOU,[h] that they
nay now be shown mer-
l has shut them all up
edience,[i] that he might
. mercy.[j]
pth of God's riches[k]
knowledge![m] How un-
lgments[n] [are] and past
ways [are]! 34 For
to know Jehovah's*
s become his counsel-
Vho has first given to
ıst be repaid to him?"[q]
. him and by him and
hings.[r] To him be the
nen.
ıtly I entreat YOU by
ssions of God, broth-
UR bodies[t] a sacrifice[u]
eptable to God,[x] a sa-
h YOUR power of rea-
being fashioned[a] after
ıings,* but be trans-
YOUR mind over,[b] that
yourselves[c] the good
l perfect will[d] of God.
the undeserved kind-
I tell everyone there
· think more of him-
essary to think;[e] but
have a sound mind,[f]

41:11; r 1Co 8:6; s Ga 1:5; Re :3; 1Co 6:20; u Heb 13:13; v Ro Le 22:19; y Php 3:3; Heb 9:14; :25; Eph 4:23; c 1Ti 4:15; d 1Th Co 4:6; Ga 6:3; Eph 4:2; 1Pe

oosing." Or, "the choos-en." 34* See App 1D. ce." Gr., *la·trei'an;* J[17] -*khem'*, "your service 2:25 ftn. 2* Or, "order ; Lat., *sae'cu·lo.*



each one as God has distributed to him
a measure* of faith.[b] 4 For just as we
have in one body many members,[c] but
the members do not all have the same
function, 5 so we, although many, are
one body[d] in union with Christ, but
members belonging individually to one
another.[e] 6 Since, then, we have gifts
differing[f] according to the undeserved
kindness[g] given to us, whether prophecy, [let us prophesy] according to the
faith proportioned [to us]; 7 or a ministry, [let us be] at this ministry;[h] or
he that teaches,[i] [let him be] at his
teaching;[j] 8 or he that exhorts, [let
him be] at his exhortation;[k] he that
distributes, [let him do it] with liberal-
ity;[l] he that presides,*[m] [let him do it]
in real earnest; he that shows mercy,[n]
[let him do it] with cheerfulness.
9 Let [YOUR] love[o] be without hypocrisy.[p] Abhor what is wicked,[q] cling to
what is good.[r] 10 In brotherly love[s]
have tender affection for one another. In showing honor[t] to one another take the lead. 11 Do not loiter at
YOUR business.[u] Be aglow with the spirit.[v] Slave for Jehovah.*[w] 12 Rejoice
in the hope.[x] Endure under tribulation.[y] Persevere in prayer.[z] 13 Share
with the holy ones according to their
needs.[a] Follow the course of hospitality.[b] 14 Keep on blessing those who
persecute;[c] be blessing[d] and do not be
cursing.[e] 15 Rejoice with people who
rejoice;[f] weep with people who weep.
16 Be minded the same way toward
others as to yourselves;[g] do not be
minding lofty things,[h] but be led along
with the lowly things.[i] Do not become
discreet in YOUR own eyes.[j]
17 Return evil for evil[k] to no one.
Provide fine things in the sight of all
men. 18 If possible, as far as it depends upon YOU, be peaceable[l] with all
men. 19 Do not avenge[m] yourselves,
beloved, but yield place to the wrath;[n]
for it is written: "Vengeance is mine;
I will repay, says Jehovah."*[o] 20 But,
"if your enemy is hungry, feed him;
if he is thirsty, give him something to

Ro 12:8* Or, "that acts as leader." 11* See App 1D. 19* See App 1D.

CHAP. 12
a Eph 4:7
b Eph 2:8
c 1Co 12:12
d Col 3:15
e 1Co 12:25 Eph 4:25
f 1Co 12:4 Eph 3:7
g 1Pe 4:10
h 1Pe 4:11
i Ga 6:6
j 1Ti 5:17
k 2Ti 4:2
l De 15:11 Pr 11:25 2Co 8:2
m 1Th 5:12 1Pe 5:2
n Eph 4:32
o 1Co 13:4
p 1Ti 1:5 Jas 3:17 1Pe 1:22
q Ps 97:10 Pr 8:13
r Ps 34:14 Heb 1:9
s 1Th 4:9
t Php 2:3
u Pr 13:4
v Ac 18:25
w Ro 6:22
x 1Th 1:3
y Ac 14:22
z Php 4:6 1Th 5:17
a Pr 3:27 1Jo 3:17
b 1Pe 4:9 3Jo 8
c Mt 5:44
d Lu 6:28 1Co 4:12
e Jas 3:9
f Lu 1:58
g Mt 22:39 1Pe 3:8
h Mr 10:42 Lu 22:24
i Lu 14:10 Joh 13:14 Eph 4:2 Php 2:3
j Job 37:24 Pr 3:7 Jas 3:13
k 1Th 5:15 1Pe 2:23 1Pe 3:9
l 2Ti 2:24 Heb 12:14 Jas 3:18
m Heb 10:30
n Mt 5:39
o Le 19:18 De 32:35 Ps 99:8 Na 1:2 Heb 10:30

Second Col.
a Pr 25:21
b Pr 25:22
c Ex 23:4 Mt 5:44 Lu 6:27

CHAP. 13
d Tit 3:1
e 1Pe 2:13
f Lu 4:6 Re 13:4
g Joh 19:11
h Mt 22:21 Ac 5:29 1Co 11:3
i De 32:8 Ac 17:26

drink;[a] for by doing this you will heap
fiery coals upon his head."[b] 21 Do not
let yourself be conquered by the evil,
but keep conquering the evil with the
good.[c]

13 Let every soul* be in subjection[d]
to the superior authorities,[e] for
there is no authority[f] except by God;[g]
the existing authorities stand placed
in their relative[h] positions* by God.[i]
2 Therefore he who opposes* the authority has taken a stand against the
arrangement of God; those who have
taken a stand against it will receive
judgment to themselves.[j] 3 For those
ruling are an object of fear, not to the
good deed, but to the bad.[k] Do you,
then, want to have no fear of the authority? Keep doing good,[l] and you will
have praise from it;* 4 for it* is God's
minister* to you for your good.[m] But if
you are doing what is bad,[n] be in fear:
for it is not without purpose that it
bears the sword; for it is God's minister, an avenger[o] to express wrath upon
the one practicing what is bad.
5 There is therefore compelling reason* for YOU people to be in subjection,
not only on account of that wrath but
also on account of [YOUR] conscience.[p]
6 For that is why YOU are also paying taxes; for they are God's public
servants*[q] constantly serving this very
purpose.* 7 Render* to all their dues,
to him who [calls for] the tax, the tax;[r]
to him who [calls for] the tribute, the
tribute; to him who [calls for] fear,
such fear;[s] to him who [calls for] hon-
or, such honor.[t]
8 Do not YOU people be owing anybody a single thing,[u] except to love one

j Ec 8:4; k 1Pe 2:14; l 1Pe 3:13; m Heb 13:21; n Ps 34:16; o Isa 10:5; Isa 45:1; p 1Pe 2:19; 1Pe 3:16; q Ro 15:27; r Mt 22:21; Mr 12:17; Lu 20:25; s Pr 24:21; t 1Pe 2:13; 1Pe 2:17; u Ps 37:21.

Ro 13:1* Or, "every living person." See App 4A. 1* "Stand placed in their relative positions." Lit., "having been set in order they are." 2* Lit., "the (one) setting self against." 3* Or, "her," that is, the "authority." 4* Or, "she," that is, the "authority." 4* Lit., "servant." 5* Lit., "necessity." 6* "Public servants." Gr., *lei·tour·goi'*. 6* Or, "devoting themselves to this very thing." 7* Lit., "Give you back."

NEW WORLD TRANSLATION OF THE HOLY SCRIPTURES - WITH REFERENCES, 1984.

except by God." Who are the "superior authorities"? Paul's words in succeeding verses show that they are human governmental authorities. (Romans 13:1-7; Titus 3:1) Jehovah did not originate man's governmental authorities, but they exist by his permission. So Paul could write: "The existing authorities stand placed in their relative positions by God." What does this indicate about such earthly authority? That it is subordinate, or inferior, to God's authority. (John 19:10, 11) Therefore, when there is a conflict between man's law and God's law, Christians must be guided by their Bible-trained conscience. They "must obey God as ruler rather than men."—Acts 5:29.

8 Much of the time, however, the governmental superior authorities act as 'God's minister to us for our good.'

8. How do you benefit from the superior authorities, and how can you show your subjection to them?



(Romans 13:4) In what ways? Well, think of the numerous services the superior authorities provide, such as mail delivery, police and fire protection, sanitation, and education. "That is why you are also paying taxes," wrote Paul, "for they are God's public servants constantly serving this very purpose." (Romans 13:6) With regard to taxes or any other legal obligation, we should "conduct ourselves honestly."—Hebrews 13:18.

9 At times, the superior authorities misuse their power. Does this absolve us of our responsibility to remain in subjection to them? No, it does not. Jehovah sees the misdeeds of these authorities. (Proverbs 15:3) His toleration of man's rule does not mean that he winks at its corruption; nor does he expect us to do so. Indeed, God will soon "crush and put an end to all these kingdoms," replacing them with the rule of his own righteous government. (Daniel 2:44) But until this occurs, the superior authorities serve a useful purpose.

10 Paul explained: "He who opposes the authority has taken a stand against the arrangement of God." (Romans 13:2) The superior authorities are God's "arrangement" in that they preserve a measure of order, without which chaos and anarchy would reign. Opposing them would be unscriptural and senseless. To illustrate: Imagine that you had undergone surgery and stitches were securing the wound. Though the stitches are foreign to the body, they serve a purpose for a limited time. Removing them prematurely could be harmful. Similarly, human governmental authorities were not part of God's original purpose. Until his Kingdom is ruling the earth completely, however, human governments hold society together, performing a function that fits in with God's will for the present

9, 10. (a) How do the superior authorities fit into God's arrangement? (b) Why would it be wrong to oppose the superior authorities?

KNOWLEDGE THAT LEADS TO EVERLASTING LIFE, 1995

or Chal·de'an. **11** But the thing that
the king himself is asking is difficult,
and nobody else exists who can show
it before the king except the gods,*[a]
whose own dwelling does not exist with
flesh at all."[b]
**12** Because of this the king himself
became angry and got very furious,[c]
and he said to destroy all the wise men
of Babylon.*[d] **13** And the order itself
went out, and the wise men were about
to be killed;* and they looked for Daniel and his companions, for them to be
killed.
**14** At that time Daniel,* for his part,
addressed himself with counsel and sen-
sibleness[e] to Ar'i·och the chief of the
king's bodyguard, who had gone out to
kill the wise men of Babylon. **15** He
was answering and saying to Ar'i·och
the officer of the king: "For what reason is there such a harsh order on the
part of the king?" Then it was that Ar'-
i·och made known the matter itself to
Daniel.[f] **16** So Daniel himself went in
and asked from the king that he should
give him time expressly to show the
very interpretation to the king.[g]
**17** After that Daniel went to his
own house; and to Han·a·ni'ah, Mish'a·el
and Az·a·ri'ah his companions he made
known the matter, **18** even [for them]
to ask for mercies[h] on the part of the
God* of heaven[i] concerning this secret,*[j]
in order that they might not destroy
Daniel and his companions with the remainder of the wise men of Babylon.[k]
**19** Then it was that to Daniel in a
night vision the secret was revealed.[l]
Consequently Daniel himself blessed[m]
the God of heaven.* **20** Daniel was
answering and saying: "Let the name
of God* become blessed[n] from time indefinite even to time indefinite, for wisdom and mightiness—for they belong

CHAP. 2

a Da 2:23, Da 2:28, Da 2:47
b 2Ch 6:18
c Pr 16:14, Pr 19:12, Pr 20:2
d Da 2:24
e Ec 10:4
f Da 2:9
g Ge 41:16
h Ps 116:5
i Ps 115:3, Ps 115:16
j Ps 50:15, Pr 3:5, Mt 18:19
k Ge 18:23, Mal 3:18, 2Pe 2:9
l Nu 12:6, Job 33:15, Ps 25:14, Da 2:28, 1Co 2:11
m Ps 50:15, Ps 145:10
n 1Ch 29:20, Ps 34:1, Ps 72:18, Ps 113:2

Second Col.

a 1Ch 29:11, Job 12:13, Ps 147:5, Jer 32:18
b Isa 60:22, Da 7:25, Ac 1:7
c 1Sa 2:7, Ps 75:7, Pr 8:15, Jer 27:5, Da 4:17
d Pr 2:6, Ec 2:26, Eph 1:17, Jas 1:5
e Job 12:22, Jer 33:3, 1Co 2:10
f Ps 139:12, Heb 4:13
g Ps 36:9, Ps 112:4, 1Jo 1:5
h Ps 145:3, Da 2:28
i Ec 7:19, Da 1:17
j Am 3:7
k Da 2:15
l Da 2:12
m Da 1:19, Da 2:16
n Ne 7:6, Da 1:6, Da 6:13
o Da 1:7, Da 4:8, Da 4:19, Da 5:12
p Da 4:18, Da 5:16
q Isa 47:12, Da 2:10
r Ge 40:8, Da 1:17
s Da 10:14
t Job 33:15

to him.[a] **21** And he is changing times*
and seasons,[b] removing kings and setting up kings,[c] giving wisdom to the wise
ones and knowledge to those knowing
discernment.[d] **22** He is revealing the
deep things and the concealed things,[e]
knowing what is in the darkness;[f] and
with him the light[g] does dwell. **23** To
you, O God of my forefathers, I am giving praise and commendation,[h] because
wisdom[i] and mightiness you have given
to me. And now you have made known
to me what we requested of you, for
you have made known to us the very
matter of the king."[j]
**24** Because of this Daniel himself
went in to Ar'i·och,[k] whom the king had
appointed to destroy the wise men of
Babylon.[l] He went, and this is what he
said to him: "Do not destroy any wise
men of Babylon. Take me in before the
king,[m] that I may show the interpretation itself to the king."
**25** Then it was that Ar'i·och, in a
hurry, took Daniel in before the king,
and this is what he said to him: "I
have found an able-bodied man of the
exiles*[n] of Judah who can make known
the interpretation itself to the king."
**26** The king was answering and saying
to Daniel, whose name was Bel·te·shaz'-
zar:*[o] "Are you competent enough to
make known to me the dream that I beheld, and its interpretation?"[p] **27** Daniel was answering before the king and
saying: "The secret that the king himself is asking, the wise men, the conjur-
ers, the magic-practicing priests [and]
the astrologers themselves are unable
to show to the king.[q] **28** However,
there exists a God* in the heavens who
is a Revealer of secrets,[r] and he has
made known to King Neb·u·chad·nez'-
zar* what is to occur in the final part of
the days.[s] Your dream and the visions
of your head upon your bed—this it is:
**29** "As for you, O king, on your bed[t]
your own thoughts came up as regards

**Da 2:11*** "Gods." Aram., *'ela·hin'*. **12*** "Babylon," LXX[Bagster]Vg; MSy, "Babel." **13*** Lit., "were being killed." **14*** "Daniel." Aram., *Da·ni·yel'*, spelled the same in Heb. See Title ftn. **18*** "God of." Aram., *'Elah'*; Syr., *'A·la·ha'*. **18*** "Secret." Aram., *ra·zah'*; Gr., *my·ste·ri'ou*. **19*** "The God of heaven." Aram., *le·'Elah' shemai·ya'*. **20*** Or, "of the [true] God." Aram., *di-'Ela·ha'*; LXX[Bagster](Gr.), *tou The·ou'*; SyVg, "Jehovah."

**Da 2:21*** Or, "appointed times." Aram., *'id·da·nai·ya'*, "the times." Compare 4:16 ftn. **25*** Lit., "sons of the Exile." **26*** "Belteshazzar." Aram., *Bel·tesha'ts·tsar'*. **28*** "God." Aram., *'Elah'*. **28*** "Nebuchadnezzar." Aram., *Nevu·khadh·nets·tsar'*.



what is to occur aft
One who is the Revea
made known to you v
**30** And as for me, it i
wisdom that exists i
in any others alive tl
revealed to me,[b] exce
that the interpretatic
known to the king hin
thoughts of your hear
**31** "You, O king, ha
holding, and, look! a
image. That image, v
and the brightness of
traordinary, was stan
you, and its appearan
**32** As regards that im
of good gold,[d] its brea
were of silver,[e] its bel
were of copper,[f] **33**
iron,[g] its feet were pa
partly of molded clay.
on looking until a stor
not by hands,[i] and it s
on its feet of iron and
and crushed them.[j] 3
the iron, the molded c
the silver and the gold
er, crushed and becam
from the summer thres
the wind* carried them
trace at all was found c
for the stone that struc
became a large mounta
whole earth.[m]
**36** "This is the drear
pretation we shall say b
**37** You, O king, the kin
to whom the God of h
en the kingdom,[o] the
strength and the dignity
whose hand he has gi
the sons of mankind ar
beasts of the field and tl
tures of the heavens, an
made ruler over all of t
self are the head of gold
**39** "And after you the

**Da 2:34*** "Stone." Aram., *'e*
Lat., *la'pis*. **34*** "Cut out,'
'cut out of a mountain."
Aram., *ru·cha'*; LXX[Bagster](
*los*; Lat., *ven'to*. See Ge 1:

NEW WORLD TRANSLATION OF THE HOLY SCRIPTURES - WITH REFERENCES, 1984

nothing
the per-

was im-
the two
myself.
nger and
me any
e to as-
not take
prepared
at public
has been
officials?

he situa-
Instead,
ive cam-
religious
en waged
find this
lowing.

OR
lide

January
l: "West-
oth Mala-
nnot con-
eports of
ts reach-
it of Wit-
give them

75, Colin
r of Lon-
s against
g savage
d torture,
dozens of

'H 22, 1976

villages in Malawi. . . . Detailed evidence of this new reign of terror rests on statements collected by the Witnesses' Watchtower Society, but is also independently corroborated by reports coming out of the villages."

Outside Malawi, voices have been raised in expressions of shocked disapproval. In the United States, for instance, the *Public Employee Press* of January 16, 1976, said this about the sufferings of Jehovah's Witnesses under the headline "Nazi-Like Tactics in Central Africa":

"*'Ufulu, ufulu!'* This shout rang out on July 6, 1964, in the Republic of Malawi, a land previously called Nyasaland, in Central Africa. This was its birth shout. It was now free of European domination. Translated, that shouted word means 'freedom.' The new name it took [Malawi] means 'flaming waters.' In 1975 there is, indeed, a flame in the land; yes, a fire that once again has taken *ufulu* away from a minority of Malawians. In its wake one sees rape, torture, unspeakable indignities, and destruction of property—all against law-abiding citizens."

### A Decade of Terror

The history of these atrocities against peace-loving Christians is a long and sordid one. It was back in 1964 that the first wave of persecution came upon Jehovah's Witnesses in Malawi. The reason then was the same as now. Jehovah's Witnesses know Christ Jesus' statement that 'his kingdom was not of this world' and that his followers would not be of this world. (John 18:36; 15:19) So, because of conscience and Bible-based principles Jehovah's Witnesses—not only in Malawi but world wide—do not engage in politics or join political parties. For that reason and that reason alone, in 1964 some 1,081 of their homes and over a hundred of their Kingdom Halls, or meeting places, in Malawi were burned or otherwise ruined.

In 1967, *The Times* of Malawi announced that the government had banned Jehovah's Witnesses. This triggered a new country-wide assault. Burnings of Witness homes and Kingdom Halls were accompanied by beatings and jailings. Thousands of Jehovah's Witnesses fled to neighboring Zambia and Mozambique to find refuge until the violence subsided.

Five years later, the Malawi Congress Party went to the extreme of formally adopting a resolution calling for the dismissal of all Witnesses from their places of employment, the discouraging of their farming and business activities and their violent ouster from the very villages in which they had their homes. The savagery of the assaults this resolution provoked took on new proportions. Young girls were repeatedly raped, men were beaten to the point of unconsciousness and forms of torture were employed—all in an effort to make Jehovah's Witnesses abandon their religious convictions, violate their conscience and buy membership cards for the dominant political party. Their homes burned, their crops destroyed, their livestock stolen or killed, the Witnesses made a mass exodus from the country. In time, some 36,000, including children, had settled in ten different refugee camps set up in neighboring Mozambique.

Came 1975 and the majority of these camps were shut down by the new Mozambique government, forcing thousands of Witnesses back across the border into Malawi. The horrifying account of the depraved attacks they experienced following this forced repatriation has been made known in the December 8, 1975, issue of *Awake!* magazine, as well as in newspapers, magazines and radio and television reports around the world. A new element was added to the list of cruelties. Along

AWAKE! — MARCH 22, 1976 5

tial campaign of 1936 also stressed the *grass roots* theme and doubtless did much to bring the phrase to wide popular recognition and use.

**politics/politician.** *Politics* has its origin in the Greek words *polis* (city) and *polites* (citizen). From the same source, incidentally, came the word *police.* Originally *politics* meant whatever had to do with the rights and status of a citizen. Gradually it has come to have at least two clearly defined meanings: the art and science of government, sometimes called "political science," and the day-to-day professional management of political affairs from the city precinct to the White House. An expert manipulator of political affairs, especially one who regards the great game of politics as his career, is known as a *politician.* This word has always had somewhat unsavory connotations, with, as one authority puts it, "implications of seeking personal or partisan gain." For this reason even the most skilled political operators often shun the label *politician,* much preferring to be called "statesmen."

**politics makes strange bedfellows,** one of the most widely quoted of American aphorisms, originally appeared in print in *My Summer in a Garden* (1870) by Charles Dudley Warner, editor of the *Hartford* (Conn.) *Courant* as well as brother-in-law and collaborator of Mark Twain. According to some authorities, it was Warner, not Twain, who first wrote: "Everybody talks about the weather, but nobody does anything about it."

**polka dot.** One dictionary, which shall here be nameless, suggests that *polka dot* may be "perhaps a respelling of 'poke a dot.' " Well, the story behind this expression is by no means as dull as that editor's imagination. It all started in the nineteenth century when dancing the polka was all the rage in America. Just as the Charleston swept the country in the 1920s and the Frug and Watusi in the 1960s, so the polka was once the dance for everyone with any pretensions to style. At the time, there was no radio or TV, not even phonograph records, so fashions in music as well as in dress tended to last much longer than they do today. Fabric manufacturers and dress designers often named their products after the songs most in vogue at the time. And so it was that those years saw "polka gauze," "polka hats" and fabrics printed with *polka dots.* Only the *polka dots* lasted, though.

**poll.** The first *polls* were elections held by counting heads, for *pol, polle* in Middle English simply meant "head." One still, of course, goes to the *polls* to cast ballots in elections. The first so called straw or unofficial *polls* were held in the United States in 1824. They consisted chiefly of man-in-the-street interviews or door-to-door canvassing by newspaper reporters. Since the mid 1930s, with the debacle of the *Literary Digest* mail poll, which predicted a victory for Landon over Roosevelt, techniques have been greatly improved. Now such *polls* as the Gallup, Harris and Roper surveys are used not only to gauge probable election results but also to test public reaction to new products.

**poltergeist**—from the German *Polter,* meaning "uproar," and *Geist,* "spirit or ghost"—is a prankish sort of spirit, the Middle European equivalent of Erin's elves, leprechauns and little men.



**pompadour** is a style of hairdre
the hair is brushed straight
Marquise de *Pompadour,* m
said, *"Après moi le déluge"*

**pomp and circumstance,** which
heard at high school gradua
and circumstance of glorio
words, *circum* and *stare,* a
came to mean an event at
around. By Shakespeare's d
meaning is now archaic.

**pooh-pooh** goes back centuries.
or contempt even in the tim
century, people began doubl
more apparent. Now it simp
for something other people

**poor/rich.** "I've been *poor* and
This observation, nearly as c
different," was first made by
the twentieth century, Sophi
Sophie, known as "The L
to make that statement. A hi
the end of her life, she had
traveling burlesque shows an
ninth birthday she made thes
century: "From birth to age
teen to thirty-five, she needs
needs a good personality. Fr

**poor as Job's turkey.** If there we
it would not refer to *turkey*—
the turkey is a uniquely Ame
coined in the early nineteent
Slick." It was intended to in
Biblical Job, who was the ve
name was Thomas Chandler

**poor as Lazarus.** In Luke 19:31
was clothed in purple and fine
there was a certain beggar na
of sores and desiring to be fed
table . . ."
To paraphrase the story in l
do nothing to help Lazarus,
Abraham's bosom." The rich
with Abraham to be spared hi
all the good things during his

MORRIS DICTIONARY OF WORD AND PHRASE ORIGINS, 2nd edition by William and Mary Morris (New York: Harper and Row Publishers, 1988)

ıl (in optics), borrowed from French
d from New Latin *polaris* polar +
. As used by Faraday and others, said
English from *polar* + *-ize*, but surely
e earlier and continuous use of *polar-*
· figurative sense of divide into oppos-
ions appeared in 1949, in Koestler's
*filment*, from the earlier use of "give
cial application to" (1860, in Oliver
' writings).

nder piece of wood, etc. Before 1325
. surname *Waghepol* (1218); also, *pole*
*ite of Inwyt*); developed from Old
050) *pāl* stake; borrowed from Latin
*gslos*) stake, related to *pangere* fasten;
ıglish *pāl* is cognate with Old Frisian
*ıl* stake, Middle Dutch *pael*, Old High
l Old Icelandic *pāll*. Doublet of PALE[2]
furnish with poles; later, push with a
ı the noun. —**pole vaulting** sport of
ıe aid of a pole. (1877, American

.d of the earth's axis. About 1380 *pool*,
ıslation of Boethius' *De Consolatione*
:er *pole* (1391); borrowed perhaps
nch *pole*, *pol*, or directly from Latin
ıxis, the sky, from Greek *pólos* pivot,
WHEEL. —**polestar** *n.* the North Star,

7 *poleax* (more commonly *polax*, *pol-*
attle-ax; formed from *pol* head (see
ıe modern spelling *poleax* was in-
.l.

: related to the ferret, fitch. 1320 *pol-*
med through Anglo-French *pol*, *pul*,
ı *poule*, *pol* fowl, hen; see PULLET +
*at*, reinforced by Middle English *cat;*
. because it preys on poultry. Another
ıt the first element *pol-*, later *pul-*, is
. *pulent* stinking, because of the pole-
ıd while this seems plausible, the form
ppear in the record of English before

k) *n.* argument, dispute, controversy.
Drummond's *Works;* borrowed prob-
:h *polémique*, from Middle French
disputatious or controversial; or per-
:ances, directly from Greek *polemikós*
ent, from *pólemos* war, related to
*in* to shake, see FEEL; for suffix see -IC.
ıt or dispute, controversial. 1641, bor-
'rom French *polémique*, from Middle
*ıe;* or perhaps, in some instances, di-
:k *polemikós*.

mol'əjē) *n.* study of war. 1938, formed
Greek *pólemos* war (see POLEMIC) +
-**polemologist** *n.* 1970, formed from
*ɔgy* + *-ist*.

ıblic order, civil administration, regu-
ine of a community enforced through
ıf Police (1714); found in the earlier
: sense of civil organization (1530, *po-*
ıtiated from earlier use in the form
· before 1439, in Lydgate's *Falls of*
ıaps about 1390, in Chaucer's *Canter-*
POLICY[1]). The English form *police* in
the modern sense of law enforcement was borrowed from modern French *police*, but in its older sense of civil organization was borrowed from Old French *policie* civil organization; see POLICY[1].

The first recorded use of *police* in specific reference to those concerned with enforcing the law and maintaining public order is found from about 1730 in Scotland.

—*v.* 1589 (implied in *policing*), keep order in; borrowed from Middle French *policer*, from *police*, n. The sense of keep order in by use of a police force (1841) is probably from later use of the noun in English.

An earlier sense of make policies or improve land is first recorded in 1535, in Scottish. The meaning of make clean and orderly, clean up (a camp, etc.) is first found in American English (1851).

—**police dog** (1908) —**police force** (1838, in Dickens' writings) —**policeman** *n.* (1801) —**police officer** (1800) —**police station** (1858) —**policewoman** *n.* (1853)

**policy**[1] *n.* way of management. About 1385 *policye* the art, study or practice of government, in Usk's *The Testament of Love;* also *policie* organized government, civil administration (1390, in Chaucer's *Canterbury Tales*); borrowed from Old French *policie*, learned borrowing from Late Latin *polītīa* settled order of government, the State, from Latin *polītīa* the State, from Greek *politeíā* state, administration, government, citizenship, from *polī́tēs* citizen, from *pólis* city; cognate with Lithuanian *pilìs* citadel, and Sanskrit accusative *púram* (nominative *pū́r*) citadel, town, from Indo-European **pel-* (root *pel-* heap up) stronghold (Pok.799); for suffix see -Y[3]. Doublet of POLITY. The general meaning of a plan of action, way of management is first recorded probably about 1406.

**policy**[2] *n.* written agreement about insurance. 1565 *police of assuraunce* insurance policy; borrowed from Middle French *police* contract or bill of lading, from Italian *pòlizza*, from Old Italian *pòliza* written evidence of a transaction, alteration of Medieval Latin *apodissa*, *apodixa* receipt or security for money, from Greek *apódeixis* proof, publication, declaration (*apo-* off + *deiknýnai* to show; see DICTION); for suffix see -Y[3]. According to the OED, the form development *apódissa*, *pódissa*, *pólissa* is supported by Portuguese *apólice* (from Latin *apódixem*) and the Provençal form *pódiza*.

**poliomyelitis** (pō'lēōmī'əlī'tis) *n.* infantile paralysis. 1878, New Latin, formed from Greek *poliós* gray (see FALLOW[2]) + *myelós* marrow (probably related to *mýs* muscle; see MYO- and MOUSE) + New Latin *-itis* inflammation; so called because the disease involves inflammation of the gray matter in the spinal cord, causing paralysis of various muscles; earlier called infantile paralysis, 1843, because it affected chiefly the young. The shortened form *polio* is first recorded in 1931.

**polish** *v.* Before 1325 *polisen* make smooth and shiny, in *Cursor Mundi;* later *polishen* (probably before 1400); borrowed from Old French *poliss-*, stem of *polir*, from Latin *polīre* to polish, make smooth, of uncertain origin; for suffix see -ISH[2]. The figurative sense of free from coarseness, cleanse, refine, is first recorded about 1340, in an early psalter. —*n.* 1597, absence of coarseness, refinement; from the verb. The literal sense of the act of polishing is first recorded in Newton's *Optics* (1704), and that of a substance used for polishing is first found in 1819.

**politburo** (pol'ətbyûr'ō) *n.* Communist Party executive committee. 1927, borrowed from Russian *Politbyuro*, shortened form of *Polit(icheskoe) Byuro* Political Bureau.

**polite** *adj.* Before 1398 *polit* polished, burnished, in Trevisa's translation of Bartholomew's *De Proprietatibus Rerum;* earlier as a surname *Polyte* (1263); borrowed from Latin *polītus* refined, polished, elegant, from past participle of *polīre* to polish.

The figurative meaning of refined, elegant, cultured, is first recorded in English in 1501; the weakened sense of courteous, behaving properly, is first found in Goldsmith's *Citizen of the World* (1762, from the earlier use of civilized, cultivated in respect of art or scholarship, 1629).

**politic** *adj.* 1427 *pollitique* of or having to do with public affairs, political; also 1436 *politik* prudent, judicious; borrowed from Middle French *politique*, and directly from Latin *politicus* of or having to do with citizens or the State, civil, civic, from Greek *politikós* having to do with citizens or the State, from *polī́tēs* citizen, from *pólis* city; see POLICY[1]; for suffix see -IC. —*v.* Now usually *politick*. engage in political activity, campaign. 1917, back formation from *politics* or *political*. —**political** *adj.* 1551, having to do with citizens or government; formed in English probably from Latin *politicus* political + English *-al*[1], and, perhaps in some instances, from *politic*, adj. + *-al*[1]. —**political science** (1779, in Hume's writings) —**politician** *n.* 1588, shrewd person; 1589, person skilled in politics; formed from English *politic*, adj. + *-ian*. —**politics** *n.* Before 1529, in Skelton's *Poetical Works;* formed from English *politic*, adj. + *-s*[1], and also found in 1450 as *Polettiques* Aristotle's book on the subject of governing and government.

**politico** (pəlit'əkō) *n.* politician. 1630, borrowed from Italian *politico* or Spanish *político*, noun use of adjective, political, from Latin *politicus* POLITIC.

**polity** *n.* government. 1538, civil organization, borrowed from Late Latin *polītīa* organized government, civil administration; see the doublet POLICY[1]; for suffix see -TY[2]. The meaning of a particular form of government is first recorded in 1597, and that of a community with a government, in 1650.

**polka** (pōl'kə) *n.* kind of lively dance of Bohemian origin. 1844, borrowing of French *polka*, from German *Polka*, from Czech *polka*, the dance; literally, Polish woman; also found in Polish *Polka* Polish woman, feminine of *Polak* a Pole. The dance was introduced in Prague in 1831 (in tribute to the unsuccessful Polish rebellion against the Russians in 1830) and quickly spread through Europe and into England. It has also been suggested that Czech *polka* was, at least in part, an alteration of *pulka* half, in reference to the half steps of the original Bohemian peasant dance.

The term *polka dot* (pō'kə), meaning a pattern of dots of uniform size and arrangement, is first recorded in 1884 and was named after the dance, whose popularity in the mid-1800's was such that it was reputedly prefixed as a trade name to many articles of food, clothing, and ornament.

—*v.* dance a polka. 1846, in Dickens' *Letters;* from the noun.

**poll** *n.* 1625, collection of votes; extended from earlier counting of heads (1607, in Shakespeare's *Coriolanus*); developed from Middle English (about 1300) *polle* hair of the head; later *pol* person or individual, head (before 1325); borrowed from Middle Low German or Middle Dutch *pol* head, top; probably cognate with Latin *bulla*



THE BARNHART DICTIONARY OF ETYMOLOGY, Robert K. Barnhart, editor
(The H.W. Wilson Company, 1988)

## DIALOGUE FOUR: Are Holiday And Birthday Celebrations Pagan?

by a number of
n very effectively
60 million acres
been converted
'and and pasture
cactorum, intro-
'25. By 1933 the
er control.
use of biolog-
California, where
l Klamath weed
n by three insect
insects continued
Fort being carried
l Idaho by 1950.
fter introduction
hat some 2.5 mil-
res) of rangeland
isects of the genus
enus Agrilus have
Johnswort is con-
y state of suppres-
tionships are now
inces of successful

nimals have been
cific weeds. Sheep
nployed to con-
gelands in many
ess is evident in
and Africa where
have been almost
ing goats. In these
iveness of the goats
ness in plant pest
need for rational
t weed control.
control weeds in
and in mint plan-
fishes are useful in
der control; exam-
, the Israeli carp,
Florida manatee is
aquatic plants, and
is feeds on alligator
r hyacinth.
irable than chemi-
standpoint of time
il weed control has
ideal for situations
ation in Australia
introduced free of
e are places where
coping with serious
iple, the control of
plant covering mil-
land, and Canada
n-central and north-
ere millions of acres
gricultural lands are
ind, the control by
iny of the common
n crops is out of the
nber and variety of
submit to safe intro-
ors.
intages to biological
ects is limited almost
its. Few insects can
t of the annual cycle
n the plant is dead
. Biological control
eeds of uncultivated
m of weed species
ds in the soil, and
l seeds will live for
litate against success
ncipal annual crop
l effective herbicide

en organisms is ha-
e organisms may be
abitat. Kikuyu grass
to California to pro-
lsides and roadways
rds, turf, and crop
serious weed.

Biological weed control tends to be only periodically effective. Experience has proved that the weed species, when subjected to control by insects, may be reduced initially to a very low level. The insects then die off for lack of food. Soon the weed recovers or becomes reestablished from seed. The predators then flourish; the weed is reduced and so on, through reciprocal cycles.

**Weed, Thurlow** (b. Nov. 15, 1797, Cairo, N.Y., U.S.—d. Nov. 22, 1882, New York, N.Y.), American journalist and politician who helped form the Whig Party in New York.

Weed learned the printer's trade, worked on various upstate New York newspapers, and became a leader in the Anti-Masonic Party (1828). When the Masons forced him out of his management of the *Rochester Telegraph*, he started an anti-Masonic campaign paper but soon realized that anti-Masonry was not a strong enough issue for a national party. Hence he became active with the Whig organization. His paper, the *Albany Evening Journal*, founded in 1830 to support anti-Masonry, became a leading Whig organ.

Weed allied himself with William H. Seward, a leading New York Whig, and was influential in Seward's election as governor of the state (1838). When the Whig Party disintegrated, Weed joined the new Republican Party and helped manage Seward's unsuccessful campaign for the Republican presidential nomination in 1860; he eventually became a staunch supporter of President Abraham Lincoln. In 1861 Seward, then Lincoln's secretary of state, sent Weed as a special agent to England, where he was a propagandist for the United States. Following Lincoln's death (1865) and the rise of the Radical Republicans, Weed's influence in the Republican Party declined. In 1863 he sold his paper and retired from politics.

**Weehawken,** township, Hudson county, northeastern New Jersey, U.S. It lies immediately north of Jersey City and opposite New York City, on the Hudson River. An industrial port, coal depot, and railroad centre, it is the western terminal of the Lincoln Tunnel. It was settled by the Dutch about 1647, when Maryn Adriadsen received patent for 80 morgens (169 acres [68 hectares]) of land. Prior to 1840, when Hudson county was formed, Weehawken was part of the Old Township of Bergen. Weehawken Township was incorporated in 1859. There are various theories about the derivation of its Indian place-name; one holds that it means "corn (maize) land," others allude to "rocks" and "gulls." Highwood, the estate of New York banker James Gore King, was the scene in 1804 of the duel in which Alexander Hamilton was fatally wounded by Aaron Burr. A bronze bust of Hamilton marks the site. The semicircular wall surrounding the Hamilton monument was built by King to protect his guest, author Washington Irving, from falling off the promontory where he liked to nap. Pop. (1990) 12,385.

**week,** period of seven days, a unit of time artificially devised with no astronomical basis. The origin of the term is generally associated with the ancient Jews and the biblical account of the Creation, according to which God laboured for six days and rested on the seventh. Evidence indicates, however, that the Jews may have borrowed the idea of the week from Mesopotamia, for the Sumerians and the Babylonians divided the year into weeks of seven days each, one of which they designated a day of recreation.

The Babylonians named each of the days after one of the five planetary bodies known to them and after the Sun and the Moon, a custom later adopted by the Romans. For a time the Romans used a period of eight days in civil practice, but in AD 321 Emperor Constantine established the seven-day week in the Roman calendar and designated Sunday as the first day of the week. Subsequent days bore the names Moon's-day, Mars's-day, Mercury's-day, Jupiter's-day, Venus'-day, and Saturn's-day. Constantine, a convert to Christianity, decreed that Sunday should be a day of rest and worship.

The days assigned by the Romans to the Sun, Moon, and Saturn were retained for the corresponding days of the week in English (Sunday, Monday, and Saturday) and several related languages. The other weekday names in English are derived from Anglo-Saxon words for the gods of Teutonic mythology. Tuesday comes from Tiu, or Tiw, the Anglo-Saxon name for Tyr, the Norse god of war. Tyr was one of the sons of Odin, or Woden, the supreme deity after whom Wednesday was named. Similarly, Thursday originates from Thor's-day, named in honour of Thor, the god of thunder. Friday was derived from Frigg's-day, Frigg, the wife of Odin, representing love and beauty, in Norse mythology.

**Weeki Wachee Spring,** spring in Hernando county, west-central Florida, U.S., 55 miles (89 km) north of St. Petersburg. One of the state's most popular attractions, the spring, with a depth of more than 140 feet (43 m), produces a crystal clear water flow of more than 168 million gallons (638 million litres) daily at a temperature of 70°–72° F (21°–22° C). With the development of underwater breathing techniques consisting of occasional trips by the underwater performers to free-floating air hoses, the spring (once a swimming and boating hole) was engineered and promoted as a showcase for an underwater ballet of "mermaids"—*i.e.*, female underwater swimmers. A large auditorium was built 16 feet (5 m) below the water's surface with thick plate-glass windows for viewing, and the first underwater show was presented in 1947. The spring, whose name derives from the Creek Indian words *wekiwa* ("spring") and *chee* ("little"), forms a river which meanders through the Weeki Wachee Swamp for 12 miles (19 km) to the Gulf of Mexico.

**Weelkes, Thomas** (b. *c.* 1570—d. Nov. 30, 1623, London, Eng.), English organist and composer, one of the most important of the English madrigal composers.

Nothing definite is known of Weelkes's early life. His later career suggests that he came from southern England. He may have been the Thomas Wikes who was a chorister at Winchester College from 1583 to 1584, since he was organist there from about 1598 to 1601. His finest work is in the two books of madrigals, of five and six parts, respectively, that appeared in 1600. He was appointed organist of Chichester Cathedral probably late in 1601. In 1602 he received the degree of bachelor of music at the University of Oxford, and the following year he married. From the time of his appointment at Chichester he composed mainly sacred works. In his last volume of madrigals (1608) he claimed the title "Gentleman of the Chapel Royal." From 1609 he was frequently reprimanded at Chichester for a variety of reasons, including bad language and drunkenness.

Nearly 100 of his madrigals survive. They have been said to combine the elegance of Luca Marenzio and the firm sense of tonality characteristic of Thomas Morley with the verbal sensitivity of William Byrd. Weelkes is noted for his word painting, lively rhythms, and highly developed sense of form and structure. He also wrote music for virginal, viol, and organ. His sacred compositions, largely unpublished, suffered much loss and destruction. Of Weelkes's 10 Anglican services none survives complete; three that have been reconstructed blend the solo writing of the English verse anthem with the massive antiphonal style of the Venetian school. Twenty-five of Weelkes's 41 anthems are either complete or



restorable; the "full" anthems (with no solo verses) show him deploying large numbers of voices. His range of expression is illustrated by the airy song in the Italian madrigal style, the *balletto* "On the Plains Fairy Trains." Examples of the graver manner include the madrigal "O Care, Thou Wilt Despatch Me," noted for its chromaticism (use of notes outside the basic scale, for effects of colour or intensity), and the massive anthem *O Lord, Arise.*

The madrigals of Weelkes are published in vol. 9 to 13 of *The English Madrigal School,* ed. by E.H. Fellowes (1913–24).

**Weems, Mason Locke,** byname PARSON WEEMS (b. Oct. 11, 1759, Anne Arundel county, Md. [U.S.]—d. May 23, 1825, Beaufort, S.C.), American clergyman, itinerant book agent, and fabricator of the story of George Washington's chopping down the cherry tree. This fiction was inserted into the fifth edition (1806) of Weems's book *The Life and Memorable Actions of George Washington* (1800).

Weems was ordained in the Anglican church in 1784 and served as a pastor in Maryland until 1792. From 1794 he hawked books throughout the country as an agent for the publisher Mathew Carey. Weems also wrote a biography (1809) of General Francis Marion that, like that of Washington, was more noted for its apocryphal anecdotes and readability than its accuracy.

**weever,** any of four species of small marine fishes of the family Trachinidae (order Perciformes). Weevers are long-bodied fishes that habitually bury themselves in the sand. They have large, upwardly slanted mouths and eyes near the top of the head. There is a sharp spine on each gill cover; these spines, like those of the first dorsal fin, are associated with venom glands and can produce very painful wounds.

Three species of weevers are found in the Old World, and one in the New World, along the Chilean coast. Well-known species include the greater and lesser weevers (*Trachinus draco* and *T. vipera*), of both Europe and the Mediterranean.

**weevil,** also called SNOUT BEETLE, true weevil of the insect family Curculionidae. This family is not only the largest family of the order Coleoptera (about 40,000 species) but is also the largest family in the animal kingdom. Most weevils have long, elbowed antennae that may fold into special grooves on the prominent snout, which has mouthparts at its end. Many have no wings; others are excellent fliers. Most are less than 6 mm (0.25 inch) in length, although the largest exceed 80 mm (3 inches). Most are plainly coloured and marked; however, a few (*e.g.*, the diamond beetle *Entimus* of Brazil) are brightly coloured.

The majority of weevils feed exclusively on plants. The fleshy, legless larvae of most species feed only on a certain part of a plant—the flower head, seeds, fleshy fruits, stems, or roots. Many larvae feed either on a single plant species or on closely related ones. Adult weevils tend to be less specialized in their feeding habits.

Weevils have probably been successful because of the development of the snout, which is used not only for penetration and feeding but also for boring holes for eggs. This family includes some extremely destructive pests (*e.g.*, the grain weevil *Sitophilus granarius* and the rice weevil *S. oryzae*).

**Wefers, Bernard J., Sr.,** byname BERNIE WEFERS (b. Feb. 19, 1873, Lawrence, Mass., U.S.—d. April 18, 1957, New York, N.Y.), American sprinter who held the world record for the 200-metre dash (straightaway; 1896–1921, though tied by five other runners) and

THE NEW ENCYCLOPAEDIA BRITANNICA, Vol. 12, 1998

# Are They Idolatrous Decorations?

IN May 1976 a New York newspaper advertised as a gift for 'the woman in your life' a necklace that should show her "that she's as dear to your heart as you are to hers." On a silver chain hung the pendant, a "porcelain heart embedded in silver."

Many who saw that advertisement had no objection to the pendant's shape. But some persons might feel strongly that a Christian woman should not wear a heart-shaped decoration. Why not?

Well, objectors might consider the heart to be an idolatrous decoration, having learned that it formerly was used in non-Christian worship. They may sincerely want to apply this Bible advice: "What agreement does God's temple have with idols? . . . 'Therefore get out from among them, and separate yourselves,' says Jehovah, 'and quit touching the unclean thing'; 'and I will take you in.' "—2 Cor. 6:15-17.

Frankly, this touches on a broader and more basic question that can arise with many designs and decorations. It is: What should be a Christian's attitude toward shapes and designs that have at some time or place been connected with false religion?

This question may be involved when you choose wallpaper for your home, the print on a necktie or dress, or jewelry such as cuff links, a bracelet or a necklace to purchase. It may even be of concern regarding the design of lamps or dishes. You might wonder, 'Is this design somehow connected with idolatrous worship?' Or some acquaintance may start you thinking by asking that question. You want to do what is right, but just what is the right thing?

Let's consider a few examples of such decorations. Alexander Hislop's book *The Two Babylons* points out:

> "The 'Heart' was one of the sacred symbols of [the Egyptian god] Osiris when he was born again, and appeared as Harpocrates, or the infant divinity . . . The veneration of the 'sacred heart' seems also to have extended to India, for there Vishnu, . . . is represented as wearing a *heart* suspended on his breast . . . Now, the worship of the 'Sacred Heart' was just, under a symbol, the worship of the 'Sacred Bel,' that mighty one of Babylon."

Similarly, the first printing of the *New World Translation of the Christian Greek Scriptures* presented this captioned drawing:

Heart of the Babylonian God Bel





The anci
symbols. F
or Winged
in Phoenic
However,
G. d'Alviel
good reaso
Egyptian
you have
signs.

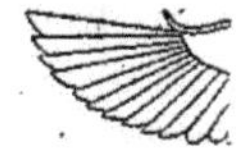

The Eg
gious sym
them. Reg
*The Worl*
reports: "
the scarab
resurrecti
They carv
sects out o
used them
Certain
religious s
thology m
such as "
cypress, t
(French,
up to mor
in ancient
of the her
royal hou
France ir
fleurs-de-li
Holy Tri
*ca,* 1976

recent use
those past
ly come to
ay. As this
swastika
evil asso-
ained con-

taking on
in another
*might lose*
book *The*

a symbol
from one
a symbol
ornament
value, or
y, it is re-
acquainted

particular
place. The
exemplifies
might still
symbol of
. In other
relatively
n view a
et or a tie
(Compare
places nei-
generally
over were
llpaper or
night con-
lecoration,
eaves and
used deco-

primarily
at a cer-
eant thou-
might be
the world,
ost people

*ER 22, 1976*

***In Practice***

What does all of this mean in practice? Obviously, some ancient religious symbols are still venerated or held to have a religious significance, in the same religion or a different one. Take the cross for example.

The *Encyclopædia Britannica* (1976) mentions: "Cross forms were used as symbols, religious or otherwise, long before the Christian era in almost every part of the world." And d'Alviella reports: "When the Spaniards took possession of Central America, they found in the native temples real Crosses, which were regarded as the symbol . . . of a divinity at once terrible and beneficent."

Jehovah's Witnesses have often pointed to Biblical evidence that establishes that Jesus actually was not put to death on a stake with a crossbeam. (Acts 5:30) Accordingly, they do not link the cross with the death of Jesus. Nonetheless, the cross *still has* a religious significance in most parts of the earth. So, were a Witness to wear a cross with the view that it was a mere decoration, observers would understandably view it differently. They would most probably conclude that the Christian was wearing it because of its *current* religious significance. Thus, the Witnesses avoid displaying this religious symbol.

But, as another example, let us return to the heart-shape. Though this was a religious symbol in ancient Babylon, does it now have such a meaning where you live? Most likely not. It may be nothing more than a decoration that calls to mind the human heart or, at most, suggests "love." In that case, some Christians might feel free to use the heart-shape simply as a decorative design.

However, take into consideration another aspect: Even though the heart is not a religious symbol in many parts of the earth today, it might be where you live. Or perhaps around the celebration of a certain holiday, such as Valentine's Day, cards or jewelry with that design on them would suggest to others that you are sharing in that religious celebration. So you might conclude that even if Christians elsewhere or at other times could freely use this decoration, your situation recommends that you avoid it, or at least avoid it at that time of year.

***Concentrate on What?***

With so many different designs having been used in false worship, if a person went to the trouble and took the time he might find an undesirable connection with almost every design he sees around him. But why do that? Would it not be needlessly upsetting? And is that the best use of one's time and attention?

If a particular design or shape is commonly understood where you live to be a religious symbol, there is good reason to avoid it. Or if *many* people locally have become especially sensitive about some shape or decoration, the mature Christian might choose to shun it so as to avoid needless disturbance or stumbling. The apostle Paul wisely wrote: "Let us pursue the things making for peace and the things that are upbuilding to one another. It is well not to eat flesh or to drink wine or do anything over which your brother stumbles."—Rom. 14:19, 21.

Paul, however, also showed the value of concentrating on the things that are of real importance instead of getting involved in controversy over petty meanings and possible connections that are not of obvious significance. (1 Cor. 10:25, 26; 2 Tim. 2:14, 23) In that way the Christian can concentrate on "righteousness and peace and joy with holy spirit," which help a person to get to the core of what the kingdom of God means.—Rom. 14:17.

*AWAKE! — DECEMBER 22, 1976* 15

May and June are popular months for weddings in the United States, but Italians traditionally believed that marrying in May would end in widowhood because May was the Virgin Mary's month and so was unsuitable for marriage. In many rural cultures weddings took place after the harvest when there was a lull in the workload and plenty of food available for the festivities. In the same spirit, an Irish proverb held that marriage during the harvest meant, "You'll have no rest from worries or work." Instead, for the Irish, winter was matchmaking time and marriages were expected to take place during Shrovetide (the three days prior to Lent), as the sacrament of matrimony was prohibited during Lent. The Chinese usually considered the first new moon of the year or the season of the first peach blossom an auspicious time for marriage while in Japan the tenth, eleventh, or twelfth lunar months were favored.

Although for Americans covering the bride's face with a veil has come to represent innocence and purity, the practice was originally used in other cultures as protection from harm or molestation and was one of many rituals adopted out of concern for the happiness, safety, and fertility of the bride and groom. Covering the heads of the bridal couple in many cultures serves such a purpose—to protect them from descending malice. In a Jewish wedding the *chuppah*, or marriage canopy, offers shelter to the wedding party (and symbolically establishes a new home) whereas traditional Chinese weddings employ umbrellas as canopies. Conversely, raised chairs, red carpets, special shoes and other forms of insulation or protection have been used to defend against malicious spirits on the ground. For example, in China the bride, heavily veiled, walked gingerly in her father's shoes to the bridal sedan, and in Western societies it is customary for the groom to carry the bride over the threshhold. The current Western practice of having a bridal party to attend the couple evolved from a Roman tradition, in which the bridesmaids and ushers dressed exactly like the bride and groom, to protect the wedding couple by confusing evil spirits.

Above:
Sikh. Richmond Hill, NY 1984
Before the Sikh wedding ceremony, the bride's *palu* is pulled well forward to shadow her face.

Right:
Jewish. Dobbs Ferry, NY 1982
A Jewish couple share a cup of wine under the *chuppah*.

8

SOMETHING OLD, SOMETHING NEW ETHNIC WEDDINGS IN AMERICA, 1987

Some states require both the man and
ave a blood test before they can obtain a
e. Several states test to determine if a
ilis, a sexually transmitted disease (see
states test the blood for immunity to
ates require both tests. In some states,
d the woman must also have a medical
ore they can get a marriage license.
quire a waiting period of three to five
e day a couple apply for a license and
rry. This period gives both people time
ey want to marry. The waiting period de-
Roman Catholic custom that required a
nce their engagement publicly on each
days before the wedding day. Between
cement and the wedding, anyone who
e couple should not marry was expected
, some couples announce their engage-
services or through church bulletins.
ments are called *banns.*

**of the United States population**
s 18 years old and over

| Married | Single | Widowed | Divorced |
|---|---|---|---|
| 62.7 | 28.6 | 8.1 | 0.6 |
| 64.8 | 25.7 | 8.5 | 1.0 |
| 65.6 | 24.5 | 8.5 | 1.4 |
| 65.8 | 24.1 | 8.6 | 1.5 |
| 72.2 | 16.8 | 9.0 | 2.0 |
| 73.9 | 14.7 | 8.9 | 2.5 |
| 71.7 | 16.2 | 8.9 | 3.2 |
| 69.6 | 17.5 | 8.3 | 4.6 |
| 65.5 | 20.3 | 8.0 | 6.2 |
| 63.0 | 21.5 | 7.9 | 7.6 |
| 61.9 | 22.2 | 7.6 | 8.3 |
| 60.9 | 22.9 | 7.0 | 9.2 |
| 59.7 | 23.6 | 6.9 | 9.8 |

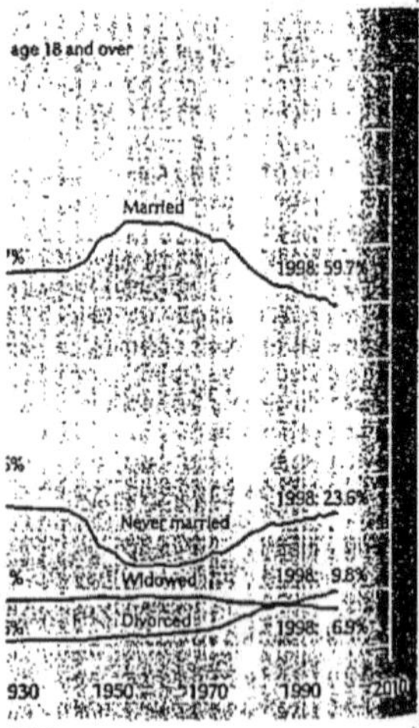


Census.

If an unmarried couple live together as husband and wife, a court may declare them married after a certain period of time. The time period varies among the states that permit such *common-law marriages.* It is usually several years. A couple do not have to have a license or wedding ceremony for a common-law marriage.

Most states have laws forbidding people of the same sex to marry. However, many homosexual couples establish long-term relationships that are similar to marriage and consider themselves married. Some countries of Europe, as well as the state of Vermont, have passed laws that grant same-sex couples many of the same legal rights as husbands and wives.

**Wedding ceremonies and customs.** Most wedding ceremonies involve two requirements. First, the man and woman must say that they want to become husband and wife. Second, the ceremony must have witnesses, including the official who marries the couple. If the couple have a religious ceremony, it is conducted by a member of the clergy, such as a minister, priest, or rabbi. If a couple are married in a *civil* (nonreligious) ceremony, a judge or some other authorized official performs it. During the days of long sea voyages, the captain of a ship was authorized to conduct a marriage ceremony while the ship was at sea.

Many couples prefer a traditional religious ceremony, though some people depart from custom. Some even write their own wedding service. A traditional marriage ceremony begins with the bridesmaids and ushers walking slowly down a center aisle to the altar. They stand on each side of the altar throughout the ceremony. The groom enters and waits for the bride at the altar. The bride then walks down the aisle with her father, another male relative, or a family friend. She wears a white dress and veil and carries a bouquet. At the altar, the bride and groom exchange marriage vows and accept each other as husband and wife. The groom puts a wedding ring on the ring finger of the bride's left hand, and the bride may also give the groom a ring. After the ceremony, the bride and groom kiss and then leave down the aisle.

People of many backgrounds follow the traditional wedding ceremony, but certain religious groups add their own features to it. For example, different Protestant groups have their own versions of the ceremony. Many Roman Catholic weddings take place during a Mass, and the bride and groom receive Holy Communion. Marriage is a *sacrament* (important religious ceremony) in the Roman Catholic and Eastern Orthodox churches (see Sacrament).

Most Jewish weddings are held under a special canopy that represents the couple's future home. At the end of the ceremony, an empty glass or other breakable object is placed on the floor and the groom breaks it with his foot. This act symbolizes the destruction of the ancient Jewish Temple in Jerusalem and reminds the couple that a marriage can also break if it is not protected.

Mormon weddings are held privately in Mormon temples. Only church members in good standing can attend these ceremonies. Mormons believe that marriage and family life continue after death.

A Quaker man and woman marry at a public gathering where they declare their commitment to each other. Quakers believe that God makes a couple husband and

J. M. Bertrand, Shustal

**Some societies permit** ***polygamy,*** the practice of having more than one wife or husband. This photograph shows a prince from the African country of Benin with five of his wives.

wife, and so a minister or other official is not required.

Many wedding customs have been popular since ancient times. For example, Roman brides probably wore veils more than 2,000 years ago. Bridal veils became popular in Britain and the New World during the late 1700's. The custom of giving a wedding ring dates back to the ancient Romans. The roundness of the ring probably represents eternity, and the presentation of wedding rings symbolizes that the man and woman are united forever. Wearing the wedding ring on the ring finger of the left hand is another old custom. People once thought that a vein or nerve ran directly from this finger to the heart. An old superstition says that a bride can ensure good luck by wearing "something old, something new, something borrowed, and something blue." Another superstition is that it is bad luck for a bride and groom to see each other before the ceremony on their wedding day.

The bride may toss her bouquet to the unmarried female guests. The woman who catches the flowers will supposedly be the next to marry. This custom probably started in France in the 1300's. The bride may also throw her garter to the unmarried men. The man who catches it will supposedly be the next male to marry.

**Marriage problems.** A man and woman expect certain things of each other even before they marry. After marriage, some husbands and wives cannot satisfy their partner's expectations. They may become disappointed and unhappy with each other and have problems with their marriage.

A couple may argue about almost anything, such as how to spend their money or how to treat their children. If they do not work out their differences, they may find it difficult to be friends, romantic partners, or good parents.

Couples with marriage problems should seek help from a trained marriage counselor. Only a few states require marriage counselors to be licensed. A couple can obtain the names of qualified counselors in their area from the American Association for Marriage and Family

THE WORLD BOOK ENCYCLOPEDIA, vol. 13, 2000

:d'ər-bûrn, Alexander, 1st
ɪн and 1st Earl of Rosslyn
ɪtesman: b. Edinburgh, Scot
; d. near Windsor, England
as a member of the Scottish
1757, and thereafter of the
ected to the House of Com
nber for Ayr, he subsequently
constituencies and was by
g as expediency suited him.
olicitor general in 1771, and
ı 1778, by Lord North, of
ican policies he strongly ap
was created baron and made
Court of Common Pleas. He
ı until 1792, when he became
ı retirement in 1801, he was
ɪsslyn. As judge he displayed
gment; but as politician, de
oratorical powers, he was

ɪrriage, History of.

ERSARY, wĕd'ĭng ăn-ə-vûr'-
orative celebration of a wed
date each year. Such celebra
l in most parts of the world;
ping track of the anniversary
rate familiarity with a calen
ıot possible among nonliterate
ıtries where a majority of the
. The Shi'ite Muslims of Iran
ıiversary of the marriage of
of Mohammed, with Ali, his
rks a major event in the history
ion, and is part of the ritual
ched over by the priests.
ctice of observing wedding an
to have grown up in western
est references in English litera
17th century: In the *Diary* of
659 there is mention of an in
y-first wedding-day feast," and
ıis *Diary*, wrote of going home
ing my sixth wedding night."
urch record of 1624 mentions
the silver wedding anniversary
ot widely celebrated (perhaps
le in those days lived so long),
796 felt it necessary to explain
ast" was the 25th wedding an
s. Anna Letitia Barbauld, friend
ınson, writing in 1806, attribut
er feast" to the Germans. The
the golden wedding appears in
newspaper, and the first to a
in *Punch* in 1872. The sym
ıiversaries seem to have evolved
ently. But whereas Pepys' and
es to the 6th and 41st wedding
t in 17th century England every
he occasion for a party of family
esent-day United States the 2d,
0th, 25th, and 50th are the most
s for parties, although husband
celebrate annually with an ex
or a special meal or entertain

for wedding anniversaries are:
otton, calico; 3d–leather; 4th–
books; 5th–wood; 6th–candy,
–wool, copper, brass, bronze;
ctrical appliances; 9th–pottery;



10th–tin, aluminum; 11th–steel; 12th–linen, silk, nylon; 13th–lace; 14th–ivory; 15th–crystal; 20th –china; 25th–silver; 30th–pearl; 35th–coral, jade; 40th–ruby; 45th–sapphire; 50th–golden; 55th–emerald; 60th or 75th (formerly the 60th, now more often the 75th)–diamond.

Elizabeth E. Bacon.

**WEDDING CAKE,** a large cake, iced and elaborately ornamented, which is served to guests at the repast or reception following a wedding. Small pieces are often sent to absent friends. In modern American usage figures of a bride and groom often top the confectionery edifice, and the bride, assisted by the groom, makes the first cut into the cake. Until recently, pieces of cake in tiny containers were given to unmarried girls to take home in the belief that if the cake was placed under the girl's pillow she would dream of her future husband.

The wedding cake has its origins far back in time. Among many peoples throughout the world the sharing of food by bride and groom is a significant part of the marriage rite. In ancient Greece the eating of a cake of sesame seed meal mixed with honey was the final act of the ritual, and such cakes were distributed among the guests. In Rome the early marriage rite was called *confarreatio* from the cake of wheat (*farreus panis*) which the couple first offered to the gods, then ate together.

The serving of cakes was also an important part of the marriage celebration in western Europe. The early cake was a small, unleavened biscuit. With the development of baking technology, the small biscuits evolved into a large bride cake, increasingly rich and elaborately ornamented, but always an essential part of the wedding feast.

Elizabeth E. Bacon.

**WEDEKIND,** vä'də-kint, **Frank,** German Dramatist: b. Hannover, Germany, July 24, 1864; d. Munich, March 9, 1918. The son of a physician and reared in Switzerland, he spent his mature years mainly in Munich. He was active as dramatist, poet, short-story writer, cofounder of the satiric periodical *Simplicissimus*, inspirer of the Munich *Überbrettl* or supervaudeville, and actor primarily in his own plays. Abused by some as a pornographic clown and satanic sensualist, he was hailed by others as literary creator of a freer world wherein beauty was not marred by taboos, and natural impulses of body and soul were not stifled by social and moral conventions. His characters are smoldering volcanoes that erupt with elemental power under the impact of inner urges.

In his most famous heroine, Lulu, the central character of *Erdgeist* (1895; Eng. tr., *Earth Spirit*, 1914) and of *Die Büchse der Pandora* (1903; Eng. tr., *Pandora's Box*, 1918), he depicted womanhood per se, sex desire that demanded satiety, instinct that demoniacally rushed on to fulfillment and destruction. He maintained that in Lulu, the wild, untamed, beautiful, sweet, female primitive, he reproduced the eternal feminine, woman's primary configuration, more faithfully than did his contemporaries Henrik Ibsen and Gerhart Hauptmann with their well-groomed, continually jabbering domestic creatures. Wedekind's *Frühlings Erwachen* (1891; Eng. tr., *Spring's Awakening*, 1909) dealt with the devastating effect which the imposition of artificial adult restraints had upon adolescents in whom the stifled cry for life had to find morbid, miserable outlets.

German expressionism was strongly influenced by Wedekind's nervous dramatic dialogue which stressed the mutual unintelligibility of people who could not bridge the chasm between soul and soul; by his substitution of types for individuals, of oversimplified demonic personalities for complex real beings; by his hatred of sham and cant; by his ridicule of monarchy and bourgeoisie; and by his flight to the lower depths of human society, to harlots, criminals, and charlatans.

Sol Liptzin, *Author of "A Historical Survey of German Literature"*

**WEDEMEYER,** wed'ə-mī-ər, **Albert Coady,** American army officer: b. Omaha, Nebr., July 9, 1897; d. Fort Belvoir, Va., Dec. 17, 1989. He graduated from West Point in 1919 and later studied at both the Command and General Staff School and, just prior to World War II, the Kriegsakademie (German General Staff School). His service included duty in the Philippines and China. A lieutenant general at war's end, Wedemeyer received the rank of general by act of Congress in 1954.

In 1940, Wedemeyer was assigned to Washington, D.C., and the next year he joined the war planning branch of the General Staff under Gen. George C. Marshall, whose protégé he became. In 1943, Wedemeyer was decorated with the Distinguished Service Medal for his outstanding work as chief of the strategy and policy group of the operations division.

In the same year, Wedemeyer was appointed American deputy chief of staff of the Southeast Asia Command, then operating under Admiral Lord Louis Mountbatten against the Japanese in Burma. He was transferred to Chungking, China, in 1944 to succeed the controversial Gen. Joseph Stilwell in command of U.S. Army forces in China and to serve as chief of staff to Chiang Kai-shek. Promoted to the temporary rank of lieutenant gerneral in 1945, he remained in China in command of U.S. troops until the summer of 1946. His 1947 report on conditions in China and Korea became so controversial in U.S. Asian policy-making circles that it was not published until 1951, when he retired from active service and became an executive in an aircraft-manufacturing company.

Wedemeyer's book, *Wedemeyer Reports*, was published in 1958. In 1985, he was awarded the Medal of Freedom.

**WEDGE,** wĕdj, a double inclined plane having two or more tapering sides, thick at the head and coming to a sharp edge or point. The most common wedges are of wood or metal. They are usually actuated by percussion, as from a hammer, applied to the head along the direction of the length. Friction is important in the tool's effectiveness, for without it the resistance of the object through or against which the wedge is being driven would force it back out of the crevice it makes. Because of this great friction, it is difficult to determine mechanical advantage accurately, but in general it depends upon the ratio of length to thickness. Ordinary uses include splitting wood and rock, exerting great pressure, and raising heavy bodies. Axes, knives, chisels, nails, carpenter's planes, and other cut-

THE ENCYCLOPEDIA AMERICANA, vol. 28, 1999

But all fair signs appear
Within the chamber here.
Juno here, far off doth stand,
Cooling sleep with charming wand.

Early fairy-tales throw much light on the ideas of primitive peoples regarding marriage. Most of the well-known tales occur in some form or other among every race and nation, and the main idea is always the same. The hero has to attempt some heroic deed, the heroine to fulfil some well-nigh impossible task. If they succeed in passing through these ordeals with courage and skill with tact and loyalty, in the end they receive their reward—the hand of the beloved whose heart has been already won. The intrinsic truth of these fairy-tales makes them the very best initiation for children into the mysteries of love and marriage. The myths enshrine some essential facts, put in a form so perfect that a high ideal is held up before the child, and is never afterwards forgotten. It is no exaggeration to say that tales like *The White Cat, Cinderella, The Sleeping Beauty in the Wood, Beauty and the Beast,* and many others are legacies from early civilisations, when the winning of the bride and the deserving of the bridegroom were no easy task, but dependent on high moral qualities tested and strained to their utmost proof. It is a very excellent thing that marriage should not be made too easy, and our ancestors embodied this in beautiful and immortal romances.

In these early tales we also note the ideal of love, as leading to marriage, gradually emerging from a more barbaric conception. The fairy prince always chooses the right sister out of many; the fairy princess can single out one from several brothers all alike. The



hero often has to reject some substitute thrust upon him as his lawful bride. The machinations of sorcerers or of wicked step-mothers have constantly to be met and overcome by the will, or by the talisman of the supernatural guide, in the form of a good fairy, or a fairy godmother. All these ideas belong to primitive civilisations, and abound in the folk-lore of every country. The reason why modern fairy-tales are so seldom convincing, is that they are not founded on the verities of the primitive tales, and therefore ring false. The real old fairy-tale is the descendant of actual customs once observed in primitive communities.

The supernatural element prevailing in these tales is the outcome of the superstitions always closely connected with marriage, superstitions which we shall see extend to the observance of the day and hour, the dresses and colours appropriate, the ritual feast, the groomsmen and bridesmaids, the wedding-ring, the knot, the other rites of marriage, and the behaviour of both the bride and the groom. There is not a single point connected with marriage which is not shrouded in innumerable superstitions, some of them dating back to hoary antiquity.

*Lucky Months for Marriage*

Married in January's hoar and rime,
Widowed you'll be before your prime.
Married in February's sleepy weather,
Life you'll tread in time together.
Married when March winds shrill and roar,
Your home will lie on a distant shore.
Married 'neath April's changeful skies,
A chequered path before you lies.
Married when bees o'er May-blossoms flit,
Strangers around your board will sit.

as a merchant captain until he died, unmarried, in 1834, but he left no accounts of any further explorations.

FINN RONNE,
*Captain, United States Naval Reserve.*

**WEDDELL SEA,** arm of the South Atlantic Ocean (latitude 73° S., longitude 45° W.), forming a large indentation in the coastline of Antarctica between Coats Land and the Palmer Peninsula. To the north its basin is partially blocked by a loop of the submerged Scotia Ridge, a continuation of the Andes Mountains of South America, which emerges in Antarctica as the Palmer Peninsula. The ridge breaks the surface as the South Shetland, South Orkney, and South Sandwich islands.

In the north the Weddell Sea averages 16,000 feet in depth, with a maximum of 27,108 feet in the South Sandwich Trench. The bottom shoals regularly toward the Palmer Peninsula and the continent, the continental shelf being steeper and deeper than is normal. This shelf is transversely breached beneath the Filchner Ice Shelf by the Crary Trough about 3,500 feet deep, which was probably glacially cut during lower stages of sea level.

The southern portion of the sea is covered by the Filchner Ice Shelf (also called Lassiter Ice Shelf), an area of 160,000 square miles and 750 to 1,600 feet thick. It is grounded near its center by ice-covered Berkner Island. The shelf is fed by adjacent continental glaciers and local precipitation. Almost the entire sea contains pack ice. Along the east coast a westerly setting current removes the pack ice in summer and allows ship access to the coast. The current originates in the Indian Ocean where it attains high salinity and temperature. This current is cooled as it flows along the continental shelf. It then flows downslope becoming significant as Antarctic bottom water—the Cold Deep Current of the Weddell Sea.

Precipitation varies from 7.8 inches on the ice shelf to 14 inches at Cape Norvegia. The variation is due to the Filchner area being a preferred breakout position for the inland high pressure system which forces easterly moving moisture-laden cyclones to seaward until they hit Cape Norvegia. The average annual temperature is −26° C. (−14.8° F.).

The Weddell Sea has been a focus of exploration. Early expeditions include those of James Weddell (Great Britain, 1823); Nils Otto Gustaf Nordenskjöld (Sweden, 1901–1903); William S. Bruce (Scotland, 1902–1904); Wilhelm Filchner (Germany, 1911–1912); Ernest Henry Shackleton (United Kingdom, 1914–1916), and whaling expeditions of Carl Anton Larsen (Norway, 1892–1924).

During the International Geophysical Year, 1957–1958, scientific stations were set up in the Coats Land-Filchner Ice Shelf area at Ellsworth (United States), General Belgrano (Argentina), Shackleton (United Kingdom), Halley Bay (United Kingdom), and Norway. Halley Bay and Ellsworth stations (now under Argentine administration) remain in operation.

See also ANTARCTIC REGIONS; POLAR EXPLORATION, SOUTH; and individual biographies of the explorers.

WILLIAM W. VICKERS,
*Institute of Polar Studies, The Ohio State University.*

**WEDDERBURN,** wĕd'ər-bûrn, **Alexander, 1st BARON LOUGHBOROUGH and 1st EARL OF ROSSLYN,** British judge and statesman: b. Edinburgh, Scotland, Feb. 13, 1733; d. near Windsor, England, Jan. 2, 1805. He was a member of the Scottish bar from 1754 until 1757, and thereafter of the bar of England. Elected to the House of Commons in 1761 as member for Ayr, he subsequently represented various constituencies and was by turn Tory and Whig as expediency suited him. He was appointed solicitor general in 1771, and attorney general in 1778, by Lord North, of whose North American policies he strongly approved. In 1780 he was created baron and made chief justice of the Court of Common Pleas. He served on the bench until 1792, when he became lord chancellor. On retirement in 1801, he was made 1st earl of Rosslyn. As judge he displayed great clarity of judgment; but as politician, despite considerable oratorical powers, he was widely distrusted.

**WEDDING.** See MARRIAGE, HISTORY OF.

**WEDDING ANNIVERSARY,** wĕd'ĭng ăn-ə-vûr'-sə-rĭ, the commemorative celebration of a wedding, on the same date each year. Such celebrations are not found in most parts of the world; for one reason, keeping track of the anniversary date requires a literate familiarity with a calendar, a familiarity not possible among nonliterate peoples or in countries where a majority of the people are illiterate. The Shī'ite Muslims of Iran celebrate the anniversary of the marriage of Fatima, daughter of Mohammed, with Ali, his cousin, but this marks a major event in the history of the Shī'ite religion, and is part of the ritual lunar calendar watched over by the priests.

The family practice of observing wedding anniversaries seems to have grown up in western Europe. The earliest references in English literature occur in the 17th century: In the *Diary* of John Evelyn for 1659 there is mention of an invitation to a "forty-first wedding-day feast," and Samuel Pepys, in his *Diary*, wrote of going home "to be merry, it being my sixth wedding night."

Although a church record of 1624 mentions "sylver brydells," the silver wedding anniversary was apparently not widely celebrated (perhaps because few people in those days lived so long), for an author in 1796 felt it necessary to explain that the "silver-feast" was the 25th wedding anniversary, and Mrs. Anna Letitia Barbauld, friend of Dr. Samuel Johnson, writing in 1806, attributed the term "silver feast" to the Germans. The first reference to the golden wedding appears in an 1860 London newspaper, and the first to a diamond wedding in *Punch* in 1872. The symbols for other anniversaries seem to have evolved comparatively recently. But whereas Pepys' and Evelyn's references to the 6th and 41st wedding feasts suggest that in 17th century England every anniversary was the occasion for a party of family and friends, in present-day United States the 2d, 5th, 10th, 15th, 20th, 25th, and 50th are the most frequent occasions for parties, although husband and wife often celebrate annually with an exchange of gifts or a special meal or entertainment.

The symbols for wedding anniversaries are: 1st—paper; 2d—cotton, calico; 3d—leather; 4th—fruit, flowers, books; 5th—wood; 6th—candy, sugar, iron; 7th—wool, copper, brass, bronze; 8th—rubber, electrical appliances; 9th—pottery; 10th—tin, aluminum; 11th—steel; nylon; 13th—lace; 14th—ivory; 15 —china; 25th—silver; 30th—pea jade; 40th—ruby; 45th—sapphire 55th—emerald; 60th or 75th (for now more often the 75th)—dian

ELIZA

**WEDDING CAKE,** a large cake, orately ornamented, which is serv the repast or reception followi Small pieces are often sent to ab modern American usage figures groom often top the confectione the bride, assisted by the groom, cut into the cake. Until recently, in tiny containers were given to to take home in the belief that i placed under the girl's pillow sh of her future husband.

The wedding cake has its orig time. Among many peoples t world the sharing of food by br is a significant part of the ma ancient Greece the eating of a seed meal mixed with honey wa of the ritual, and such cakes w among the guests. In Rome the rite was called *confarreatio* fron wheat (*farreus panis*) which tl offered to the gods, then ate toget

The serving of cakes was alsc part of the marriage celebratic Europe. The early cake was a sm biscuit. With the development o nology, the small biscuits evolve bride cake, increasingly rich ar ornamented, but always an essent wedding feast.

ELIZAB

**WEDEKIND,** vā'də-kint, **Frank,** G atist: b. Hannover, Germany, Jul Munich, March 9, 1918. The son and reared in Switzerland, he spe years mainly in Munich. He was a atist, poet, short-story writer, cof satiric periodical *Simplicissimus*, i Munich *Überbrettl* or supervaudev primarily in his own plays. Abuse a pornographic clown and satanic was hailed by others as literary cre world wherein beauty was not mar and natural impulses of body and stifled by social and moral conv characters are smoldering volcano with elemental power under the in urges.

In his most famous heroine, Lul character of *Erdgeist* (1895; En *Spirit*, 1914) and of *Die Büchse* (1903; Eng. tr., *Pandora's Box*, 1 picted womanhood per se, sex de manded satiety, instinct that demon on to fulfillment and destruction. H that in Lulu, the wild, untamed, be female primitive, he reproduced feminine, woman's primary config faithfully than did his contempo Ibsen and Gerhart Hauptmann wit groomed, continually jabbering d tures. Wedekind's *Frühlings Erwa* Eng. tr., *Spring's Awakening*, 190 the devastating effect which the i

THE ENCYCLOPEDIA AMERICANA, VOL. 28, 1999

book of the Bible, was completed in 1513 B.C.E. Did you know that, after Genesis was written, some 2,900 years passed before the complete Bible was translated into English? And over 200 more years elapsed before translation of the *King James Version* was completed (1611 C.E.).' (3) 'Since the 17th century, English has undergone many changes. We have seen that in our own lifetime, haven't we? . . . So we appreciate modern translations that carefully express the same original truths in the language that we speak today.'

**'You have your own Bible'**

See the main heading "New World Translation."

# Birthday

**Definition:** The day of one's birth or the anniversary of that day. In some places the anniversary of one's birth, especially that of a child, is celebrated with a party and the giving of gifts. *Not a Biblical practice.*

**Do Bible references to birthday celebrations put them in a favorable light? The Bible makes only two references to such celebrations:**

Gen. 40:20-22: "Now on the third day it turned out to be Pharaoh's birthday, and he proceeded to make a feast . . . Accordingly he returned the chief of the cupbearers to his post of cupbearer . . . But the chief of the bakers he hung up."

Matt. 14:6-10: "When Herod's birthday was being celebrated the daughter of Herodias danced at it and pleased Herod so much that he promised with an oath to give her whatever she asked. Then she, under her mother's coaching, said: 'Give me here upon a platter the head of John the Baptist.' . . . He sent and had John beheaded in the prison."

Everything that is in the Bible is there for a reason.



(2 Tim. 3:16, 17) Jehovah's Witnesses take note that God's Word reports unfavorably about birthday celebrations and so shun these.

**How did early Christians and Jews of Bible times view birthday celebrations?**

"The notion of a *birthday festival* was far from the ideas of the Christians of this period in general."—*The History of the Christian Religion and Church, During the Three First Centuries* (New York, 1848), Augustus Neander (translated by Henry John Rose), p. 190.

"The later Hebrews looked on the celebration of birthdays as a part of idolatrous worship, a view which would be abundantly confirmed by what they saw of the common observances associated with these days."—*The Imperial Bible-Dictionary* (London, 1874), edited by Patrick Fairbairn, Vol. I, p. 225.

**What is the origin of popular customs associated with birthday celebrations?**

"The various customs with which people today celebrate their birthdays have a long history. Their origins lie in the realm of magic and religion. The customs of offering congratulations, presenting gifts and celebrating—complete with lighted candles—in ancient times were meant to protect the birthday celebrant from the demons and to ensure his security for the coming year. . . . Down to the fourth century Christianity rejected the birthday celebration as a pagan custom."—*Schwäbische Zeitung* (magazine supplement *Zeit und Welt*), April 3/4, 1981, p. 4.

"The Greeks believed that everyone had a protective spirit or *daemon* who attended his birth and watched over him in life. This spirit had a mystic relation with the god on whose birthday the individual was born. The Romans also subscribed to this idea. . . . This notion was carried down in human belief and is reflected in the guardian angel, the fairy godmother and the patron saint. . . . The custom of lighted candles on the cakes started with the Greeks. . . . Honey

REASONING FROM THE SCRIPTURES, 1989

important change took place in
after the Exile. Leviticus 10:10-11
ests responsibility for both moral
and ceremonial matters, but the
ching role seemed to disappear
ile. Only one mention of a priestly
:urs after the Exile (Hag. 2:10-13).
prophet Malachi complained that
of his time failed in this important
al. 2:7-8). Levites other than the
ucted the people concerning the
8:7). The high priest became a
ity, combining functions of both
state. (*See* "Jews in New Testa-
.")

s atmosphere of the earlier rituals
one of great seriousness and re-
ritual feasts had been primarily
; now they became awe-inspiring
ntrospection. After the Exile, the
ere seeking to learn how they
re obedient to God's covenant.
and more joyous festival—the
m—was added to the ceremonial
during this period. This festival
Adar 14-15 to commemorate the
rance from Haman while they
Persian rule. (*See* "The Per-
e the time of the Exile, Jews have
is feast in recognition of God's
liverance of His people.

n observance followed a fixed
13 was a day of fasting. On the
at day (which is the beginning of
h day), the Jews assembled for a
eir synagogues. Following the
Book of Esther was read.

name of Haman was read, the
. "Let his name be blotted out,"
e of the wicked shall rot." The
man's sons were all read in one
phasize the fact that they were all
: same time.

orning the people again went to
e to finish the formal religious
The rest of the day was a time for
g. As in other festival obser-
ich were called on to provide for

. Alexander the Great began his
Syria, the Middle East, and
his death in 323 B.C., his generals
ands among themselves. After
f political turmoil, a line of Syrian
s the Seleucids gained control of
he Seleucid ruler named An-
forced his will upon the Jews by
m to engage in sacrifices, rites,
orship of any kind.

**Samaritan sacrifice.** The Samaritans still make sacrifices in accordance with the Law of Moses, much as their ancestors did. Here lambs are offered on Mount Gerizim in celebration of the Passover.

In 167 B.C., a Syrian officer brought an unnamed Jew to the temple and forced him to make a sacrifice to Zeus. A priest named Mattathias witnessed the event. He slew them both, called for all faithful Jews to follow him, and fled for the hills outside Jerusalem. There he and his sons organized for war against the Seleucids. They swept over Jerusalem, defeated the Syrian army, and secured the city. The Syrian leaders were forced to repeal their ordinances against worship in Israel. Now the temple could be cleansed and true worship could resume. (The biblical account of this period in Israel's history can be found in the deuterocanonical books of 1 and 2 Maccabees. *See also* "Jews in New Testament Times" and "The Greeks and Hellenism" for more detailed account of the history of this period.) Modern Jews remember this great event at the Feast of Dedication or Hanukkah. Jesus Himself was in Jerusalem at the time of a Hanukkah celebration near the end of His earthly ministry (John 10:22). This 8-day feast is celebrated on the twenty-fifth of the month Chislev. Also known as the Feast of Lights, it is marked by the lighting of 8 candles—one on each day of the feast. The celebration features the singing of the Hallel Psalms and is somewhat similar to the Feast of Booths.

Under the Maccabees, the Jews worshiped in a nationalistic manner. Their hopes for a God-ruled earth brought new emphasis to their worship, such as the use of apocalyptic literature. (*See* "The Literature of the Bible.") Prophecy gradually diminished as apocalyptic took its place. One apocalyptic writer expressed his hopes for an earthly kingdom of God in this fashion: "And now, O Lord, behold, these heathen, which have ever been reputed as nothing, have begun to be lords over us, and to devour us. But we thy



people, whom thou hast called thy firstborn, thy only begotten, and thy fervent lover, are given into their hands. If the world now is made for our sakes, why do we not possess an inheritance with the world? how long shall this endure?" (2 Esdras 6:57-59). During this period, however, the seer or apocalyptist spoke for God. He spoke of demons and angels, dark and light, evil and good. He predicted the final triumph of the nation of Israel. This hope flowed as the undercurrent of Jewish worship.

One other feature of worship that became more prominent in this period was the study of the Law. It was primarily a priestly duty, on which the Hasidim (Pharisees) concentrated. They produced many new teachings and doctrines in the process, notably the doctrine of the resurrection of dead.

**V. The New Testament Era.** In 47 B.C., Julius Caesar selected Herod Antipater, a Jew of Idumea (the area south of Judea), to be governor of Judea. His son, Herod the Great, inherited the position and called himself "king of the Jews." Realizing the history of unrest among the people, Herod wanted to gain their favor and faith in some way. To do this, he announced the building of a third temple at Jerusalem. Priests specially trained in construction skills did much of the work to make sure the new building followed Moses' floor plan. Most of the construction was completed in about 10 years (*ca.* 20–10 B.C.), but not all was finished until about A.D. 60. (In fact, some scholars feel the new temple had not been completed at the time Jerusalem fell to the Roman general Titus in A.D. 70.) Most worship activities occurred here.

Yet during the persecutions and exiles of Israel, many Jews found themselves too far from Jerusalem to worship there. Did this mean that they were not able to worship at all? By no means! Rather they instituted the custom of local synagogue worship. Although the Old Testament uses the word *synagogue* only once (Psa. 74:8), many of these informal worship places surely existed during the Exile. The New Testament mentions them often (e.g., Matt. 4:23; 23:6; Acts. 6:9), but gives us little descriptive information about them. (*See* "Judaism in New Testament Times.") We do know something of the early synagogues from rabbinic sources. We also know that the Law was studied and pronounced there: "For Moses of old time hath in every city them that preach him, being read in the synagogues every sabbath day" (Acts 15:21). Many prayers were recited in synagogue worship (Matt. 6:5). Sources outside the Bible tell us

ILLUSTRATED MANNERS AND CUSTOMS OF THE BIBLE, J. I. Paker, M.C. Tenney, editors (Nashville, TN: Thomas Nelson Publishers, 1980)

"The notion of a *birthday festival* was far from the ideas of the Christians of this period in general."—*The History of the Christian Religion and Church, During the Three First Centuries* (New York, 1848), by Augustus Neander (translated by Henry John Rose), page 190.

"Of all the holy people in the Scriptures, no one is recorded to have kept a feast or held a great banquet on his birthday. It is only sinners (like Pharaoh and Herod) who make great rejoicings over the day on which they were born into this world below."—*The Catholic Encyclopedia* (New York, 1911), Volume X, page 709 (quoting Origen Adamantius of the third century).

Additionally, birthday celebrations tend to give excessive importance to an individual, no doubt one reason why early Christians shunned them. (Ecclesiastes 7:1) So you will find that Jehovah's Witnesses do not share in birthday festivities (the parties, singing, gift giving, and so forth).

***Christmas:*** As you are probably aware, December 25 was not the birthday of Jesus Christ. You may feel that this does not matter—that the event is the important thing. But the way the Christmas holiday developed shows that there is more to it than that. The following encyclopedias explain:

"The observance of Christmas is not of divine appointment, nor is it of N[ew] T[estament] origin. The day of Christ's birth cannot be ascertained from the N[ew] T[estament], or, indeed, from any other source. The fathers of the first three centuries do not speak of any special observance of the nativity."—*Cyclopedia of Biblical, Theological, and Ecclesiastical Literature* (Grand Rapids, Michigan, 1981 reprint), by John McClintock and James Strong, Volume II, page 276.

"Most of the Christmas customs now prevailing in Europe, or recorded from former times, are not genuine Christian customs, but heathen customs which have been absorbed or tolerated by the Church. . . . The Saturnalia in Rome provided the model for most of the *merry* customs of the Christmas time."—*Encyclopœdia of Religion and Ethics* (Edinburgh, 1911), edited by James Hastings, Volume III, pages 608, 609.

It is commonly known that Christmas was not originally a celebration of Christ's birth. *U.S. Catholic* of

18

December 19[...]
separate Chri[...]
azine explains

"The Roma[...]
began on Dec[...]
unconquered
Somewhere i[...]
savvy official[...]
25 would ma[...]
the 'sun of ri[...]

When lear[...]
have some b[...]
*pedia* (1982)
1600's . . . Cl[...]
parts of the [...]
in the past r[...]
its pagan ori[...]
hovah's Witn[...]
part in Chris[...]
of gifts, or in
with Christm[...]
Jehovah's
tal nonpartic[...]
holidays that
is that these
Christian wo[...]
worship ofte[...]
following ex[...]

***Easter:*** A[...]
memorate C[...]
thorities say

"Easter. [...]
Teutonic g[...]
Saxon as E[...]
was transfe[...]
festival desi[...]
—*The West*[...]
1944), by J[...]

"Everywh[...]
brought by
play, but t[...]

SCHOOL AND JEHOVAH'S WITNESSES, 1983

THE BIBLE'S VIEWPOINT

# A Balanced View of Popular Customs

"THERE IS NO POSSIBLE LINE OF CONDUCT WHICH HAS NOT AT SOME TIME AND PLACE BEEN CONDEMNED, AND WHICH AT SOME OTHER TIME AND PLACE BEEN ENJOINED AS A DUTY."

WITH this observation, the Irish historian William Lecky sums up the fickle nature of people. His comments might also apply to customs and traditions down through the ages. Indeed, many practices that were once viewed as an essential part of daily life have in later times been condemned. This is not surprising, for as the Christian apostle Paul noted, "the scene of this world is changing."—1 Corinthians 7:31.

Yes, human society is in a constant state of flux. This is often reflected in wide shifts in attitudes and social habits. Christians are to be "no part of the world"—that is, they remain separate from human society that is alienated from God. Still, the Bible acknowledges that Christians are "in the world," and it does not command them to be isolationists. Hence, a balanced view of customs is vital.—John 17:11, 14-16; 2 Corinthians 6:14-17; Ephesians 4:17-19; 2 Peter 2:20.

### What Are Customs?

Customs are practices that apply to social life and are common to a particular place or class of people. Some customs, such as table manners and etiquette, may have arisen out of a need to regulate people's behavior in group activities, enabling them to interact in a civil and mutually respectful manner. In such cases, social courtesies can be likened to oil, in that they lubricate the wheels of human relationships.

Customs have been profoundly influenced by religion. Many, in fact, arose from old superstitions and non-Biblical religious ideas. For instance, giving flowers to bereaved ones may have had its origin in religious superstition.* In addition, the color blue—often associated with baby boys—was thought to frighten away demons. Mascara served as a protection against the evil eye, while lipstick

* According to some anthropologists, flower bouquets were at times used as offerings to the dead to prevent them from haunting the living.

**Some ancient customs, such as covering the mouth while yawning and giving flowers to the bereaved, have lost their original significance**

26

was used to di
ing a woman'
Even a custom
mouth while y
the idea that o
a wide-open m
the religious a
day these prac
gious significa

**The (**

When a Ch
not to follow
cern should b
expressed in t
demned certa
tolerated in
cluded child
and various
13, 14; 18:1-30
certain custo
clearly not in
Among these
nected with r
mas and Eas
tices related

But what
have been li
but that tod
cial etiquett
wedding cus
of rings and
pagan origi
tians are for
Are Christia
lously each
whether sor
negative co

Paul poir
Jehovah is,
ans 3:17; Ja
this freedor
ish cravings
ers to disti
tians 5:13; F
in a matter

AWAKE! January 8, 2000

)T AT
SOME

**ns?**
apply to social
ticular place or
ıs, such as table
ıave arisen out
ɔ's behavior in
ːn to interact in
ful manner. In
can be likened
ıe wheels of hu-

ndly influenced
ıse from old su-
religious ideas.
) bereaved ones
igious supersti-
blue—often as-
ʋas thought to
ara served as a
ɔ, while lipstick

ts, flower bouquets
ead to prevent them

**and**
**e**

was used to discourage demons from entering a woman's mouth and possessing her. Even a custom as innocuous as covering the mouth while yawning may have arisen from the idea that one's soul could escape through a wide-open mouth. Over the years, however, the religious associations have faded, and today these practices and customs have no religious significance.

### The Concern of Christians

When a Christian must decide whether or not to follow a certain custom, his main concern should be, What is God's viewpoint as expressed in the Bible? In the past God condemned certain practices that may have been tolerated in some communities. These included child sacrifice, the misuse of blood, and various sexual practices. (Leviticus 17:13, 14; 18:1-30; Deuteronomy 18:10) Likewise, certain customs that are common today are clearly not in harmony with Bible principles. Among these are non-Biblical traditions connected with religious holidays such as Christmas and Easter or with superstitious practices related to spiritism.

But what about customs that may once have been linked to questionable practices but that today are primarily viewed as social etiquette? For example, many popular wedding customs—including the exchanging of rings and the eating of cake—may have pagan origins. Does this mean that Christians are forbidden to observe such customs? Are Christians required to scrutinize meticulously each custom of the community to see whether somewhere or at some time it had negative connotations?

Paul points out that "where the spirit of Jehovah is, there is freedom." (2 Corinthians 3:17; James 1:25) God wants us to use this freedom, not as an inducement for selfish cravings, but to train our perceptive powers to distinguish right from wrong. (Galatians 5:13; Hebrews 5:14; 1 Peter 2:16) Hence, in a matter where there is no clear violation of Bible principles, Jehovah's Witnesses do not create a hard-and-fast rule. Instead, each Christian must weigh the circumstances at hand and make a personal decision.

### Seek Others' Advantage

Does this mean that it is always proper to participate in a certain custom as long as it does not directly violate Bible teachings? No. (Galatians 5:13) Paul indicated that a Christian should seek not only his own advantage "but that of the many." He should "do all things for God's glory" and not become a cause for stumbling. (1 Corinthians 10:31-33) So a person seeking God's approval would want to ask himself: 'How do others view this custom? Does the community attach any objectionable meaning to it? Would my participation imply that I am in agreement with practices or ideas that are displeasing to God?' —1 Corinthians 9:19, 23; 10:23, 24.

Though generally innocuous, some customs may be practiced locally in ways that are contrary to Bible principles. For instance, on specific occasions the giving of flowers may take on special meaning that conflicts with Bible teachings. So, what should a Christian primarily be concerned about? Although there may be reason to examine the origin of a particular custom, in some cases it is more important to consider *what the custom means to people at the time and in the place where one now lives.* If a custom has unscriptural or otherwise negative connotations during a particular period of the year or under certain circumstances, Christians may wisely decide to avoid it at that time.

Paul prayed that Christians continue letting their love abound with accurate knowledge and full discernment. By keeping a balanced view of popular customs, Christians "make sure of the more important things, so that [they] may be flawless and not be stumbling others." (Philippians 1:9, 10) At the same time, they will let their "reasonableness become known to all men."—Philippians 4:5.

## DIALOGUE FIVE: Is Hell Real and the Human Soul Immortal? —Parts 1 and 2



ord's
t. 18:23
t. 18:24; 9:13
ord 24:45, 23
12:44; Rev. 21:7
t. 18:24; 9:13
t. 24:45, 21
t. 18:24; 9:13
to the s
tt. 13:12; 1:25; 1:18; John
tt. 8:12; Luke
tt.
s. 4:16; s. 1:7; 9:28; 14; Rev.
latt. 19:28
tt. 13:49; 5:10
34:17,
n. 2:19; 9 [b]Eccl.
tt. 5:3; Luke 1Cor. 5:50; Gal. James 2:5
13:35; 11:50; 17:24; 1:4; Heb. 1:26; 1Pet. Rev. 13:8;
58:7; 18:7, 16; s 2:15, 16 31:32; 13:2
58:7; 18:7, 16; s 2:15, 16 es 1:27 1. 1:16f.
att. 25:34; 19:38; 17:14; [b]Prov. Matt. Heb.
att. 7:23 k 9:48; 16:24; 7 [c]Matt. Rev. 12:9

30 "And [aim]cast out the worthless[888] slave into [a]the outer darkness;[4655] in that place there shall be weeping and gnashing[1030] of teeth.

### The Judgment

31 "But when [a]the Son of Man comes in His glory,[1391] and all the angels with Him, then [b]He will sit on His glorious throne.

32 "And all the nations[1484] will be [a]gathered before Him; and He will separate[873] them from one another, [b]as the shepherd[4166] separates the sheep from the goats;

33 and He will put the sheep [a]on His right,[1188] and the goats [b]on the left.

34 "Then the King[935] will say to those on His right, 'Come, you who are blessed[2127] of My Father, [aim] [a]inherit[2816] the kingdom prepared for you [b]from the foundation[2602] of the world.

35 'For [a]I was hungry,[3983] and you gave Me *something* to eat; I was thirsty, and you gave Me drink; [b]I was a stranger, and you invited[4863] Me in;

36 [a]naked,[1131] and you clothed Me; I was sick,[770] and you [b]visited[1980] Me; [c]I was in prison, and you came to Me.'

37 "Then the righteous[1342] will answer Him, saying, 'Lord, when did we see You [ppt]hungry,[3983] and feed You, or [ppt]thirsty, and give You drink?

38 'And when did we see You a stranger, and invite You in, or naked, and clothe You?

39 'And when did we see You sick,[770] or in prison, and come to You?'

40 "And [a]the King[935] will [apt]answer and say to them, 'Truly I say to you, [b]to the extent that you did it to one of these brothers[80] of Mine, *even* the least *of them*, you did it to Me.'

41 "Then He will also say to those on His left, [pim] [a]'Depart from Me, accursed ones,[2672] into the [art] [b]eternal fire which has been prepared for [c]the devil and his angels;[32]

42 for I [ao]was hungry,[3983] and you gave Me *nothing* [ainf]to eat; I was [ao]thirsty, and you gave Me nothing to drink;

43 I was a stranger, and you did not invite[4863] Me in; naked,[1131] and you did not clothe Me; sick, and in prison, and you did not visit[1980] Me.'

44 "Then they themselves also will answer, saying, 'Lord, when did we see You [ppt]hungry,[3983] or [ppt]thirsty, or a stranger, or naked, or sick, or in prison, and did not [1]take care[1247] of You?'

45 "Then He will answer them, saying, 'Truly I say to you, to the extent that you did not do it to one of the least of these, you did not do it to Me.'

46 "And these will go away into [a]eternal punishment,[2851] but the righteous[1342] into [b]eternal life."[2222]

### The Plot to Kill Jesus

26 [a]And it came about that when Jesus had finished all these words,[3056] He said to His disciples,

2 "[a]You know that after two days [b]the Passover[3957] is coming, and the Son of Man is *to be* [c]delivered up for crucifixion."[4717]

3 [a]Then the chief priests and the elders[4245] of the people were gathered together[4863] in [b]the court of the high priest, named [c]Caiaphas;

4 and they [a]plotted together to seize Jesus by stealth, and kill *Him*.

5 But they were saying, "Not during the festival, [a]lest a riot occur among the people."[2992]

### The Precious Ointment

6 [a]Now when Jesus was[1096] in [b]Bethany, at the home of Simon the leper,

7 [a]a woman came to Him with an alabaster vial of very costly perfume, and she poured it upon His head as He [ppt]reclined *at the table*.

8 But the disciples were indignant when they saw *this*, and said, "Why this waste?[684]

9 "For this *perfume* might have been sold for a high price and *the money* given to the poor."



44 [1]Or, *serve*
46 [a]Dan. 12:2; John 5:29; Acts 24:15 [b]Matt. 19:29; John 3:15f., 36; 5:24; 6:27, 40, 47, 54; 17:2f.; Acts 13:46, 48; Rom. 2:7; 5:21; 6:23; Gal. 6:8; 1John 5:11
1 [a]Matt. 7:28
2 [a]Matt. 26:2-5; *Mark 14:1, 2; Luke 22:1, 2* [b]John 11:55; 13:1 [c]Matt. 10:4
3 [a]John 11:47 [b]Matt. 26:58, 69; 27:27; Mark 14:54, 66; 15:16; Luke 22:55; John 18:15 [c]Matt. 26:57; Luke 3:2; John 11:49; 18:13, 14, 24, 28; Acts 4:6
4 [a]Matt. 12:14
5 [a]Matt. 27:24
6 [a]Matt. 26:6-13; *Mark 14:3-9;* Luke 7:37-39; John 12:1-8 [b]Matt. 21:17
7 [a]Luke 7:37f.
11 [a]Deut. 15:11; Mark 14:7; John 12:8
12 [a]John 19:40
13 [a]Mark 14:9
14 [a]Matt. 26:14-16; *Mark 14:10, 11; Luke 22:3-6* [b]Matt. 10:4; 26:25, 47; 27:3; John 6:71; 12:4; 13:26; Acts 1:16
15 [I]Lit., *and I will* [II]Or, *betray* [III]Or, *silver shekels* [a]Matt. 10:4 [b]Ex. 21:32; Zech. 11:12
16 [I]Or, *deliver Him up*
17 [a]Matt. 26:17-19; *Mark 14:12-16; Luke 22:7-13* [b]Ex. 12:18-20
18 [a]Mark 14:13; Luke 22:10 [b]John 7:6, 8
20 [a]Matt. 26:20-24; *Mark 14:17-21*
21 [a]Luke 22:21-23; John 13:21f.
22 [I]Or, *one after another*

10 But Jesus, aware of this, said to them, "Why do you bother[2873] the woman? For she [ao]has done[2038] a good deed[2041] to Me.

11 "For [a]the poor you have with you always; but you do not always have Me.

12 "For when she [apt]poured this perfume upon My body, she did it [a]to prepare Me for burial.

13 "Truly[281] I say to you, [a]wherever this gospel[2098] is preached[2784] in the whole world,[2889] what this woman has [ao]done shall also be spoken of in memory of her."

### Judas' Bargain

14 [a]Then one of the twelve, named [b]Judas Iscariot, [apt]went to the chief priests,

15 and said, "What are you willing[2309] to [ainf]give me [I]to [II][a]deliver Him up to you?" And [b]they weighed out[2476] to him thirty [III]pieces of silver.

16 And from then on he *began* [ipf]looking for a good opportunity[2120] to [I]betray Him.

17 [a]Now on the first *day* of [b]Unleavened Bread[106] the disciples came to Jesus, saying, "Where do You want us to prepare for You to eat the Passover?"

18 And He said, "Go into the city to [a]a certain man, and say to him, 'The Teacher says, "[b]My time[2540] is at hand;[1451] I *am to* [pin]keep the Passover at your house with My disciples." ' "

19 And the disciples did as Jesus had directed them; and they prepared the Passover.

### The Last Passover

20 [a]Now when evening had come, He was reclining *at the table* with the twelve disciples.

21 And as they were [ppt]eating, He said, "[a]Truly I say to you that one of you will betray Me."

22 And being deeply [ppt]grieved, they [I]each one began to [pinf]say to Him, "Surely not [epn]I, Lord?"

23 And He answered[611] and said,

NEW AMERICAN STANDARD BIBLE

**MATTHEW 25:20—44** **Sheep from goats. Do good to brothers** **1250**

20 So the one that had received five talents came forward and brought five additional talents, saying, 'Master,
you committed five talents to
me; see, I gained five talents
more.'[a] 21 His master said to
him, 'Well done, good and faithful slave![b] You were faithful[c]
over a few things. I will appoint you over many things.[d]
Enter into the joy[e] of your master.' 22 Next the one that had
received the two talents came
forward and said, 'Master, you
committed to me two talents;
see, I gained two talents more.'[f]
23 His master said to him, 'Well
done, good and faithful slave!
You were faithful over a few
things. I will appoint you over
many things.[g] Enter into the
joy[h] of your master.'
24 "Finally the one that had
received the one talent came
forward[i] and said, 'Master, I
knew you to be an exacting
man, reaping where you did not
sow and gathering where you
did not winnow. 25 So I grew
afraid[j] and went off and hid
your talent in the ground. Here
you have what is yours.' 26 In
reply his master said to him,
'Wicked and sluggish slave, you
knew, did you, that I reaped
where I did not sow and gathered where I did not winnow?
27 Well, then, you ought to
have deposited my silver mon-
ies with the bankers, and on
my arrival I would be receiving
what is mine with interest.[k]
28 "'Therefore TAKE away
the talent from him and give
it to him that has the ten talents.[l] 29 For to everyone that
has, more will be given and he
will have abundance; but as for
him that does not have, even
what he has will be taken away
from him.[m] 30 And throw the
good-for-nothing slave out into
the darkness outside. There is
where [his] weeping and the
gnashing of [his] teeth will be.'[n]
31 "When the Son of man[o]
arrives in his glory, and all the
angels with him,[a] then he will
sit down on his glorious throne.[b]
32 And all the nations will be
gathered before him,[c] and he
will separate[d] people one from
another,[e] just as a shepherd
separates the sheep from the
goats. 33 And he will put the
sheep on his right[f] hand, but
the goats on his left.[g]
34 "Then the king will say
to those on his right, 'Come,
YOU who have been blessed by
my Father,[h] inherit[i] the kingdom[j] prepared for YOU from
the founding of the world.[k]
35 For I became hungry and
YOU gave me something to eat;[l]
I got thirsty and YOU gave me
something to drink. I was a
stranger and YOU received me
hospitably;[m] 36 naked,[n] and
YOU clothed me. I fell sick
and YOU looked after me. I
was in prison[o] and YOU came
to me.' 37 Then the righteous
ones will answer him with the
words, 'Lord, when did we see
you hungry and feed you, or
thirsty,[p] and give you something to drink?[q] 38 When did
we see you a stranger and receive you hospitably, or naked,
and clothe you? 39 When did
we see you sick or in prison
and go to you?' 40 And in reply the king[r] will say to them,
'Truly I say to YOU, To the extent that YOU did it to one of
the least[s] of these my brothers,[t]
YOU did it to me.'[u]
41 "Then he will say, in turn,
to those on his left, 'Be on YOUR
way from me,[v] YOU who have
been cursed, into the everlasting fire[w] prepared for the Devil and his angels.[x] 42 For I
became hungry, but YOU gave
me nothing to eat,[y] and I
got thirsty,[z] but YOU gave me
nothing to drink. 43 I was a
stranger, but YOU did not receive me hospitably; naked, but
YOU did not clothe[a] me; sick
and in prison,[b] but YOU did not
look after me.' 44 Then they

CHAP. 25
a Lu 19:16
b Lu 19:17
c Pr 28:20; Lu 16:10
d Pr 12:24; Lu 12:44
e Heb 12:2
f Lu 19:18
g Lu 19:19
h Heb 12:2
i Lu 19:20
j Pr 26:13; Lu 19:21; Re 21:8
k Lu 19:23
l Lu 19:24
m Mt 13:12; Mr 4:25; Lu 8:18; Joh 15:2
n Ps 112:10; Mt 8:12
o Da 7:13; Mt 16:27; Ac 1:11; Re 1:7

Second Col.
a Zec 14:5; Mt 13:41; Mt 19:28
b Re 3:21
c 2Co 5:10
d Eze 34:17; Mt 13:49
e Eze 20:38
f Joh 10:16
g Mt 25:41
h Ps 115:15
i Ro 8:17
j 1Th 2:12; Re 5:10
k Mt 13:35; Heb 9:26; 1Pe 1:20; Re 13:8
l Isa 58:7; Eze 18:16
m Heb 13:2; 3Jo 5
n Eze 18:7; Jas 2:15
o 2Ti 1:16
p Mt 10:42
q Mt 6:3
r Lu 19:38; Re 17:14
s Pr 19:17; Mt 10:40; Mr 9:41
t 2Co 5:20; Heb 2:11
u Heb 6:10
v Mt 7:23; Lu 13:27
w Mt 18:8; Re 20:10
x Re 12:9
y Isa 58:7; Eze 18:16
z Mt 10:42
a Eze 18:7; Jas 2:15
b 2Ti 1:16

**1251** **Last Passover. Lord's Evening Meal** **MATTHEW 25:45—26:26**

also will answer with the words,
'Lord, when did we see you
hungry or thirsty or a stranger
or naked or sick or in prison
and did not minister to you?'
45 Then he will answer them
with the words, 'Truly I say to
YOU, To the extent that YOU did
not do it to one of these least
ones,[a] YOU did not do[b] it to me.'[c]
46 And these will depart into
everlasting cutting-off,[d] but the
righteous ones into everlasting
life."[e]

26 Now when Jesus had finished all these sayings, he
said to his disciples: 2 "YOU
know that two days from now
the passover occurs,[f] and the
Son of man is to be delivered
up to be impaled."[g]
3 Then the chief priests and
the older men of the people
gathered together in the courtyard of the high priest who was
called Ca'ia·phas,[h] 4 and took
counsel[i] together to seize Jesus
by crafty device and kill him.
5 However, they kept saying:
"Not at the festival, in order
that no uproar may arise among
the people."[j]
6 While Jesus happened to
be in Beth'a·ny[k] in the house of
Simon the leper,[l] 7 a woman
with an alabaster case of costly
perfumed oil[m] approached him,
and she began pouring it upon
his head as he was reclining
at the table. 8 On seeing this
the disciples became indignant
and said: "Why this waste?[n]
9 For this could have been sold
for a great deal and been given
to poor[o] people." 10 Aware of
this,[p] Jesus said to them: "Why
do YOU try to make trouble for
the woman? For she did a fine
deed toward me.[q] 11 For YOU
always have the poor[r] with YOU,
but YOU will not always have
me.[s] 12 For when this woman put this perfumed oil upon
my body, she did it for the
preparation of me for burial.[t]
13 Truly I say to YOU, Wherever
this good news is preached in
all the world, what this woman did shall also be told as a
remembrance of her."[a]
14 Then one of the twelve,
the one called Judas Is·car'i-
ot,[b] went to the chief priests
15 and said: "What will YOU
give me to betray him to YOU?"[c]
They stipulated to him thirty silver pieces.[d] 16 So from
then on he kept seeking a good
opportunity to betray him.[e]
17 On the first day of the
unfermented cakes[f] the disciples came up to Jesus, saying: "Where do you want us
to prepare for you to eat the
passover?"[g] 18 He said: "Go
into the city to So-and-so[h] and
say to him, The Teacher says,
'My appointed time is near; I
will celebrate the passover with
my disciples at your home.'"[i]
19 And the disciples did as Jesus ordered them, and they got
things ready for the passover.[j]
20 When, now, it had become
evening,[k] he was reclining at
the table with the twelve disciples.[l] 21 While they were eating, he said: "Truly I say to YOU,
One of YOU will betray me."[m]
22 Being very much grieved at
this, they commenced each and
every one to say to him: "Lord,
it is not I, is it?"[n] 23 In reply
he said: "He that dips his hand
with me in the bowl is the one
that will betray me.[o] 24 True,
the Son of man is going away,
just as it is written[p] concerning him, but woe[q] to that man
through whom the Son of man
is betrayed![r] It would have been
finer for him if that man had
not been born." 25 By way of
reply Judas, who was about to
betray him, said: "It is not I,
is it, Rabbi?" He said to him:
"You yourself said [it]."
26 As they continued eat-
ing, Jesus took a loaf[s] and, after saying a blessing, he broke
it[t] and, giving it to the disci-

CHAP. 25
a De 23:4; 2Co 5:20; Heb 2:11
b Zec 2:8
c Ac 9:5
d Da 12:2; 2Pe 2:9
e Ro 2:7

CHAP. 26
f Ex 12:14; Mr 14:1; Lu 22:1; Joh 13:1
g Mt 16:21; Mt 20:19; Mt 27:26; Mr 15:15; Joh 19:16
h Mt 26:57; Lu 3:2; Lu 22:2; Joh 18:13; Joh 18:24
i Ps 2:2; Mr 14:1; Joh 11:49
j Mr 14:2
k Mt 21:17
l Mt 8:2
m Mr 14:3; Joh 12:3
n Mr 14:4; Joh 12:4
o Mr 14:5; Joh 12:5
p Joh 12:6
q Mr 14:6
r De 15:11; Mr 14:7
s Mt 9:15; Joh 12:8; Joh 17:11
t Mr 14:8; Joh 12:7

Second Col.
a Mr 14:9
b Mt 10:4; Lu 22:3; Joh 13:2
c Mr 14:10; Joh 11:57; 1Ti 6:10
d Ex 21:32; Zec 11:12; Mt 27:3; Mr 14:11; Lu 22:5
e Mr 14:11; Lu 22:6
f Ex 12:18; Ex 23:15; Le 23:6; Mr 14:12; Lu 22:7
g Lu 22:9
h Mt 21:3; Mr 14:13; Lu 22:10
i Mr 14:14; Lu 22:11
j Mr 14:16; Lu 22:13
k De 16:6
l Mr 14:17; Lu 22:14
m Mr 14:18; Joh 6:70; Joh 13:21
n Mr 14:19; Joh 13:22

o Ps 41:9; Mr 14:20; Lu 22:21; Joh 13:26; p Mt 5:17; q De 27:25; Lu 22:22; r Mr 14:21; Joh 17:12; s 1Co 11:23; t 1Co 10:16; 1Co 11:24.

NEW WORLD TRANSLATION

usually means 'life,' or 'vitality,' or, at times, 'the self.'" —*The Encyclopedia Americana* (1977), Vol. 25, p. 236.

## What sort of people go to the Bible hell?

### *Does the Bible say that the wicked go to hell?*

Ps. 9:17, *KJ:* "The wicked shall be turned into hell,* and all the nations that forget God." (*"Hell," 9:18 in *Dy;* "death," *TEV;* "the place of death," *Kx;* "Sheol," *AS, RS, NE, JB, NW.*)

### *Does the Bible also say that upright people go to hell?*

Job 14:13, *Dy:* "[Job prayed:] Who will grant me this, that thou mayst protect me in hell,* and hide me till thy wrath pass, and appoint me a time when thou wilt remember me?" (God himself said that Job was "a man blameless and upright, fearing God and turning aside from bad."—Job 1:8.) (*"The grave," *KJ;* "the world of the dead," *TEV;* "Sheol," *AS, RS, NE, JB, NW.*)

Acts 2:25-27, *KJ:* "David speaketh concerning him [Jesus Christ], . . . Because thou wilt not leave my soul in hell,* neither wilt thou suffer thine Holy One to see corruption." (The fact that God did not "leave" Jesus in hell implies that Jesus was in hell, or Hades, at least for a time, does it not?) (*"Hell," *Dy;* "death," *NE;* "the place of death," *Kx;* "the world of the dead," *TEV;* "Hades," *AS, RS, JB, NW.*)

### *Does anyone ever get out of the Bible hell?*

Rev. 20:13, 14, *KJ:* "The sea gave up the dead which were in it; and death and hell* delivered up the dead which were in them: and they were judged every man according to their works. And death and hell were cast into the lake of fire." (So the dead will be delivered from hell. Notice also that hell is not the same as the lake of fire but will be cast into the lake of fire.) (*"Hell," *Dy, Kx;* "the world of the dead," *TEV;* "Hades," *NE, AS, RS, JB, NW.*)

### *Why is there confusion as to what the Bible says about hell?*

"Much confusion and misunderstanding has been caused



through the early translators of the Bible persistently rendering the Hebrew Sheol and the Greek Hades and Gehenna by the word hell. The simple transliteration of these words by the translators of the revised editions of the Bible has not sufficed to appreciably clear up this confusion and misconception."—*The Encyclopedia Americana* (1942), Vol. XIV, p. 81.

Translators have allowed their personal beliefs to color their work instead of being consistent in their rendering of the original-language words. For example: (1) The *King James Version* rendered *she'ohl'* as "hell," "the grave," and "the pit"; *hai'des* is therein rendered both "hell" and "grave"; *ge'en·na* is also translated "hell." (2) *Today's English Version* transliterates *hai'des* as "Hades" and also renders it as "hell" and "the world of the dead." But besides rendering "hell" from *hai'des* it uses that same translation for *ge'en·na.* (3) *The Jerusalem Bible* transliterates *hai'des* six times, but in other passages it translates it as "hell" and as "the underworld." It also translates *ge'en·na* as "hell," as it does *hai'des* in two instances. Thus the exact meanings of the original-language words have been obscured.

## Is there eternal punishment for the wicked?

Matt. 25:46, *KJ:* "These shall go away into everlasting punishment ["lopping off," *Int;* Greek, *ko'la·sin*]: but the righteous into life eternal." (*The Emphatic Diaglott* reads "cutting-off" instead of "punishment." A footnote states: "*Kolasin* . . . is derived from *kolazoo,* which signifies, 1. *To cut off;* as lopping off branches of trees, to prune. 2. *To restrain, to repress.* . . . 3. *To chastise, to punish.* To cut off an individual from life, or society, or even to restrain, is esteemed as *punishment;*—hence has arisen this *third* metaphorical use of the word. The primary signification has been adopted, because it agrees better with the second member of the sentence, thus preserving the force and beauty of the antithesis. The righteous go to *life,* the wicked to the *cutting off* from life, or *death.* See 2 Thess. 1.9.")

2 Thess. 1:9, *RS:* "They shall suffer the punishment of *eternal destruction** and exclusion from the presence of the Lord and from the glory of his might." (*"Eternal ruin,"

REASONING FROM THE SCRIPTURES, 1985, 1989 ed.

***Will some be raised simply to have judgment pronounced and then be consigned to second death?***

*What is the meaning of John 5:28, 29?* It says: "All those in the memorial tombs will hear his voice and come out, those who did good things to a resurrection of life, those who practiced vile things to a resurrection of judgment." What Jesus said here must be understood in the light of the later revelation that he gave to John. (See Revelation 20:12, 13, quoted on page 337.) Both those who formerly did good things and those who formerly practiced bad things will be "judged individually according to their deeds." What deeds? If we were to take the view that people were going to be condemned on the basis of deeds in their past life, that would be inconsistent with Romans 6:7: "He who has died has been acquitted from his sin." It would also be unreasonable to resurrect people simply for them to be destroyed. So, at John 5:28, 29a, Jesus was pointing ahead to the resurrection; then, in the remainder of verse 29, he was expressing the outcome after they had been uplifted to human perfection and been put on judgment.

***What does Revelation 20:4-6 indicate as to those who will be resurrected on earth?***

Rev. 20:4-6: "I saw thrones, and there were those who sat down on them, and power of judging was given them. Yes, I saw the souls of those executed with the ax for the witness they bore to Jesus and for speaking about God . . . And they came to life and ruled as kings with the Christ for a thousand years. (The rest of the dead did not come to life until the thousand years were ended.) This is the first resurrection. Happy and holy is anyone having part in the first resurrection; over these the second death has no authority, but they will be priests of God and of the Christ, and will rule as kings with him for the thousand years."

The parentheses are used in *NW* and *Mo* to help the reader to connect what follows the parenthetical statement with what precedes it. As clearly stated, it is not "the rest of the dead" who share in the first resurrection. That resurrection is for those who rule with Christ for the thousand years. Does this mean that no others of mankind will live during



the thousand years except the ones who rule in heaven with Christ? No; because, if such were the case, it would mean that there was no one on behalf of whom they were serving as priests, and their domain would be a desolate globe.

*Who, then, are "the rest of the dead"?* They are all those of mankind who died as a result of Adamic sin and those who, though survivors of the great tribulation or those who may be born during the Millennium, need to be relieved of the death-dealing effects of such sin.—Compare Ephesians 2:1.

*In what sense do they not "come to life" until the end of the thousand years?* This does not mean their resurrection. This 'coming to life' involves much more than merely existing as humans. It means attaining to human perfection, free from all effects of Adamic sin. Notice that the reference to this in verse 5 occurs immediately after the preceding verse says that those who will be in heaven "came to life." In their case it means life free from all effects of sin; they are even specially favored with immortality. (1 Cor. 15:54) For "the rest of the dead," then, it must mean the fullness of life in human perfection.

**Who will be included in the earthly resurrection?**

John 5:28, 29: "Do not marvel at this, because the hour is coming in which all those in the memorial tombs will hear his voice [the voice of Jesus] and come out." (The Greek word translated "memorial tombs" is not the plural form of *ta'phos* [grave, an individual burial place] or *hai'des* [gravedom, the common grave of dead mankind] but is the plural dative form of *mne·mei'on* [remembrance, memorial tomb]. It lays stress on preserving memory of the deceased person. Not those whose memory was blotted out in Gehenna because of unforgivable sins but persons remembered by God will be resurrected with the opportunity to live forever. —Matt. 10:28; Mark 3:29; Heb. 10:26; Mal. 3:16.)

Acts 24:15: "I have hope toward God . . . that there is going to be a resurrection of both the righteous and the unrighteous." (Both those who lived in harmony with God's righteous ways and people who, out of ignorance, did unrigh-

REASONING FROM THE SCRIPTURES, 1985, 1989 edition

teous things will be resurrected. The Bible does not answer all our questions as to whether certain specific individuals who have died will be resurrected. But we can be confident that God, who knows all the facts, will act impartially, with justice tempered by mercy that does not ignore his righteous standards. Compare Genesis 18:25.)

Rev. 20:13, 14: "The sea gave up those dead in it, and death and Hades gave up those dead in them, and they were judged individually according to their deeds. And death and Hades were hurled into the lake of fire. This means the second death, the lake of fire." (So, those whose death was attributable to Adamic sin will be raised, whether they were buried at sea or in Hades, the common earthly grave of dead mankind.)

See also the main heading "Salvation."

### If billions are to be raised from the dead, where will they all live?

A very liberal estimate of the number of people who have ever lived on earth is 20,000,000,000. As we have seen, not all of these will be resurrected. But, even if we assume that they would be, there would be ample room. The land surface of the earth at present is about 57,000,000 square miles (147,600,000 sq km). If half of that were set aside for other purposes, there would still be just a little less than an acre (c. 0.37 ha) per person, which can provide more than enough food. At the root of present food shortages is not any inability of the earth to produce sufficient but, rather, political rivalry and commercial greed.

See also page 116, under the heading "Earth."

## Return of Christ

**Definition:** Before leaving the earth, Jesus Christ promised to return. Thrilling events in connection with God's Kingdom are associated with that promise. It should be noted that there is a difference between *coming* and *presence*. Thus, while a person's coming (associated with his arrival or return) occurs at a given time, his presence may thereafter extend over a period of years. In the Bible the Greek word *er'kho·mai* (meaning "to come") is also used with reference to Jesus' directing his attention to an important task at a specific time *during* his presence, namely, to his work as Jehovah's executioner at the war of the great day of God the Almighty.



### Do the events associated with Christ's presence take place in a very brief time or over a period of years?

Matt. 24:37-39: "Just as the days of Noah were, so the presence ["coming," *RS, TEV;* "presence," *Yg, Ro, ED;* Greek, *pa·rou·si'a*] of the Son of man will be. For as they were in those days before the flood, eating and drinking, men marrying and women being given in marriage, until the day that Noah entered into the ark; and they took no note until the flood came and swept them all away, so the presence of the Son of man will be." (The events of "the days of Noah" that are described here took place over a period of many years. Jesus compared his presence with what occurred back then.)

At Matthew 24:37 the Greek word *pa·rou·si'a* is used. Literally it means a "being alongside." Liddell and Scott's *Greek-English Lexicon* (Oxford, 1968) gives *"presence,* of persons," as its first definition of *pa·rou·si'a.* The sense of the word is clearly indicated at Philippians 2:12, where Paul contrasts his presence (*pa·rou·si'a*) with his absence (*a·pou·si'a*). On the other hand, in Matthew 24:30, which tells of the "Son of man *coming* on the clouds of heaven with power and great glory" as Jehovah's executioner at the war of Armageddon, the Greek word *er·kho'me·non* is used. Some translators use 'coming' for both Greek words, but those that are more careful convey the difference between the two.

### Will Christ return in a manner visible to human eyes?

John 14:19: "A little longer and the world will behold me no more, but you [Jesus' faithful apostles] will behold me, because I live and you will live." (Jesus had promised his

REASONING FROM THE SCRIPTURES, 1985, 1989 ed.

of him that can destroy both soul and body in Gehenna." What does it mean? Notice that there is no mention here of *torment* in the fires of Gehenna; rather, he says to 'fear him that can *destroy* in Gehenna.' By referring to the "soul" separately, Jesus here emphasizes that God can destroy all of a person's life prospects; thus there is no hope of resurrection for him. So, the references to the 'fiery Gehenna' have the same meaning as 'the lake of fire' of Revelation 21:8, namely, destruction, "second death."

***What does the Bible say the penalty for sin is?***

Rom. 6:23: "The wages sin pays is death."

***After one's death, is he still subject to further punishment for his sins?***

Rom. 6:7: "He who has died has been acquitted from his sin."

***Is eternal torment of the wicked compatible with God's personality?***

Jer. 7:31: "They [apostate Judeans] have built the high places of Topheth, which is in the valley of the son of Hinnom, in order to burn their sons and their daughters in the fire, a thing that I had not commanded and that had not come up into my heart." (If it never came into God's heart, surely he does not have and use such a thing on a larger scale.)

*Illustration:* What would you think of a parent who held his child's hand over a fire to punish the child for wrongdoing? "God is love." (1 John 4:8) Would he do what no right-minded human parent would do? Certainly not!

## By what Jesus said about the rich man and Lazarus, did Jesus teach torment of the wicked after death?

*Is the account, at Luke 16:19-31, literal or merely an illustration of something else? The Jerusalem Bible,* in a footnote, acknowledges that it is a "parable in story form without reference to any historical personage." If taken literally, it would mean that those enjoying divine favor could all fit at the bosom of one man, Abraham; that the



water on one's fingertip would not be evaporated by the fire of Hades; that a mere drop of water would bring relief to one suffering there. Does that sound reasonable to you? If it were literal, it would conflict with other parts of the Bible. If the Bible were thus contradictory, would a lover of truth use it as a basis for his faith? But the Bible does not contradict itself.

*What does the parable mean?* The "rich man" represented the Pharisees. (See verse 14.) The beggar Lazarus represented the common Jewish people who were despised by the Pharisees but who repented and became followers of Jesus. (See Luke 18:11; John 7:49; Matthew 21:31, 32.) Their deaths were also symbolic, representing a change in circumstances. Thus, the formerly despised ones came into a position of divine favor, and the formerly seemingly favored ones were rejected by God, while being tormented by the judgment messages delivered by the ones whom they had despised.—Acts 5:33; 7:54.

## What is the origin of the teaching of hellfire?

In ancient Babylonian and Assyrian beliefs the "nether world . . . is pictured as a place full of horrors, and is presided over by gods and demons of great strength and fierceness." (*The Religion of Babylonia and Assyria,* Boston, 1898, Morris Jastrow, Jr., p. 581) Early evidence of the fiery aspect of Christendom's hell is found in the religion of ancient Egypt. (*The Book of the Dead,* New Hyde Park, N.Y., 1960, with introduction by E. A. Wallis Budge, pp. 144, 149, 151, 153, 161) Buddhism, which dates back to the 6th century B.C.E., in time came to feature both hot and cold hells. (*The Encyclopedia Americana,* 1977, Vol. 14, p. 68) Depictions of hell portrayed in Catholic churches in Italy have been traced to Etruscan roots.—*La civiltà etrusca* (Milan, 1979), Werner Keller, p. 389.

But the real roots of this God-dishonoring doctrine go much deeper. The fiendish concepts associated with a hell of torment slander God and originate with the chief slanderer of God (the Devil, which name means "Slanderer"), the one whom Jesus Christ called "the father of the lie."—John 8:44.

REASONING FROM THE SCRIPTURES, 1985, 1989 edition

*Strong's number · Arndt-Gingr. · Greek word · Kittel vol.,pg. · Thayer pg., col.*

*3634 565* **οἷος** *442b*
*rel. pron. (a) which, (such) as,* Mt 24:21; Mk 9:3; *(b) what kind of, what sort of,* 1 Th 1:5.

Mat.24:21. tribulation, *such as* was not since
Mar 9: 3. *so as* no fuller on earth can white them.
13:19. affliction, *such as* was not from the
Lu. 9:55. Ye know not *what manner of* spirit
Ro. 9: 6. Not *as* though the word of God
1Co.15:48. *As* (is) the earthy, such (are) they
— *as* (is) the heavenly, such (are) they
2Co.10:11. *such as* we are in word by letters
12:20. I shall not find you *such as* I would,
— unto you *such as* ye would not:
Phi. 1:30. Having the same conflict *which* ye saw
1Th. 1: 5. ye know *what manner of* men we were
2Ti. 3:11. afflictions, *which* came unto me at
— *what* persecutions I endured:
Rev.16:18. *such as* was not since men were

*3635 565* **ὀκνέω** *442b*
*vb. to be slow, delay,* Ac 9:38* ✓ **ὄκνος** *(hesitation)*
Ac 9:38. that he would not *delay* to come

*3636 565* **ὀκνηρός** *5:166 442b*
*adj. tardy,* i.e., *indolent,* Rm 12:11; *slothful,* Mt 25:25; fig., *irksome, troublesome,* Php 3:1* ✓3635
Mat.25:26. (Thou) wicked and *slothful* servant,
Ro. 12:11. Not *slothful* in business; fervent
Phi. 3: 1. to me indeed (is) not *grievous,*

*3637 565* **ὀκταήμερος** *442b*
*adj. on the eighth day,* Php 3:5* ✓3638/2250
Php 3:5. Circumcised *the eighth day*

*3638 565* **ὀκτώ** *443a*
*numeral. eight,* Lk 2:21.
Lu. 2:21. when *eight* days were accomplished
9:28. about an *eight* days after
13: 4. Or those *eighteen,* upon whom
11. a spirit of infirmity *eighteen* years,
16. lo, these *eighteen* years,
Joh. 5: 5. an infirmity thirty and *eight* years.
20:26. after *eight* days again his disciples
Acts 9:33. which had kept his bed *eight* years,
1Pet.3:20. *eight* souls were saved by water.

→ *3639 566* **ὄλεθρος** *5:167 443a*
*n.m. destruction, ruin,* 1 Co 5:5; 1 Th 5:3.
1Co. 5: 5. for the *destruction* of the flesh,
1Th. 5: 3. then sudden *destruction* cometh
2Th. 1: 9. with everlasting *destruction* from
1Ti. 6: 9. which drown men in *destruction* and

*3640 566* **ὀλιγόπιστος** *6:174 443a*
*n.f. lacking trust, having little faith,* Mt 6:30; 8:26; 14:31; 16:8; Lk 12:28* ✓3641 and 4102
Mat. 6:30. O ye *of little faith?*
8:26. Why are ye fearful, O ye *of little faith?*
14:31. O thou *of little faith,* wherefore didst
16: 8. O ye *of little faith,* why reason ye
Lu. 12:28. (will he clothe) you, O ye *of little faith?*

*3641 566* **ὀλίγος** *5:171 443a*
*adj. little, small, few;* as subst., *a few,* Mk 1:19; 6:31; Ac 12:28; 1 Tm 5:23; Mt 15:34; Mt 7:14.
Mat. 7:14. and *few* there be that find it.
9:37. but the labourers (are) *few;*
15:34. and a *few* little fishes.
20:16. for many be called, but *few* chosen.
22:14. but *few* (are) chosen.
25:21. hast been faithful over a *few* things,
23. hast been faithful over a *few* things,
Mar 1:19. when he had gone a *little* farther
6: 5. he laid his hands upon a *few* sick
31. and rest *a while:*
8: 7. And they had a *few* small fishes:
Lu. 5: 3. thrust out *a little* from the land.
7:47. to whom *little* is forgiven, (the same) loveth *little.*
10: 2. but the labourers (are) *few:*
Lu. 12:48. shall be beaten with *few* (stripes).
13:23. Lord, are there *few* that be saved?
Acts12:18. there was no *small* stir among the
14:28. there they abode long (lit. not a *little*) time with
15: 2. no *small* dissension and disputation
17: 4. and of the chief women not a *few.*
12. and of men, not a *few.*
19:23. there arose no *small* stir
24. no *small* gain unto the craftsmen;
26:28. Almost (lit. in a *little*) thou persuadest me
29. were both almost, and altogether (lit. in a *little,* and in much)
27:20. and no *small* tempest lay on (us),
2Co. 8:15. he that (had gathered) *little* had no lack.
Eph. 3: 3. as I wrote afore in *few* words,
1Ti. 4: 8. bodily exercise profiteth *little:*
5:23. but use a *little* wine
Heb 12:10. for a *few* days chastened (us)
Jas. 3: 5. how great a matter a *little* fire
4:14. appeareth for a *little* time,
1Pet.1: 6. though now for a *season,*
3:20. wherein *few,* that is, eight souls
5:10. after that ye have suffered *a while,*
12. I have written *briefly,*
Rev. 2:14. I have a *few* things against thee,
20. I have a *few* things against thee,
3: 4. Thou hast a *few* names even in Sardis
12:12. that he hath but a *short* time.
17:10. he must continue a *short space.*

*3642 567* **ὀλιγόψυχος** *9:608 443a*
*adj.* pl. as subst., *little-spirited;* i.e., *faint-hearted,* 1 Th 5:14* ✓3641 and 5590
1 Th 5:14. comfort the *feebleminded*

*3643 567* **ὀλιγωρέω** *443a*
*vb. to have little regard for, despise,* Hb 12:5* ✓3641 and **ὥρα** *(care)*
Hb 12:5. *despise* not thou the chastening of the Lord,

*3644 567* **ὀλοθρευτής** *5:167 443b*
*n.m. destroyer, ruiner,* 1 Co 10:10* ✓3645. Cf. Ex 12:23; Hb 11:28
1 Co 10:10. were destroyed of the *destroyer*



*Strong's number · Arndt-Gingr. · Greek word · Kittel vol.,pg.*

*3645 567* **ὀλοθρεύω**
*vb. to spoil, destroy,* i.e., *slay;* pt. as sub
*destroyer* (the angel who destroyed the firs
Egypt), Hb 11:28. Cf. Ex 12:23. ✓3639
Hb 11:28. lest he *that destroyed* the firstborn

*3646 567* **ὁλοκαύτωμα**
*n.nt. wholly-burned offering,* in which th
animal is consumed, Mk 12:33: Hb 10:6,
Mar 12:33. is more than all *whole burnt offerings*
Heb 10: 6. In *burnt offerings* and (sacrifices) fo
8. and *burnt offerings* and (offering) fo
thou wouldest not,

*3647 567* **ὁλοκληρία** *3:758*
*n.f. wholeness, perfect health,* Ac 3:16*
Ac 3:16. hath given him this *perfect soundness*

*3648 567* **ὁλόκληρος** *3:758*
*adj. complete* in every part, *whole,* 1 Th 5
1:4* ✓3650 and 2819
1 Th 5:23. (I pray God) your *whole* spirit and
Js 1:4. that ye may be perfect and *entire*

*3649 567* **ὀλολύζω** *5:173*
*vb. to howl, wail,* Js 5:1*
Js 5:1. weep and *howl* for your miseries

*3650 567* **ὅλος** *5:174*
*adj. complete, whole, all,* Mt 1:22; 4:23; 5
*adv., completely,* Jn 9:34.
Mat. 1:22. Now *all* this was done, that
4:23. Jesus went about *all* Galilee,
24. his fame went throughout *all* Syria:
5:29. and not (that) thy *whole* body shoul
30. and not (that) thy *whole* body shoul
6:22. thy *whole* body shall be full of light.
23. thy *whole* body shall be full of darkn
9:26. fame hereof went abroad into *all* that
31. his fame in *all* that country.
13:33. till the *whole* was leavened.
14:35. they sent out into *all* that country
16:26. if he shall gain the *whole* world,
20: 6. Why stand ye here *all* the day idle?
21: 4. *All* this was done, that
22:37. love the Lord thy God with *all* thy
and with *all* thy soul, and with *all*
40. hang *all* the law and the prophets.
24:14. In *all* the world for a witness
26:13. be preached in the *whole* world,
56. But *all* this was done, that
59. and *all* the council, sought false
27:27. gathered unto him the *whole* band
Mar 1:28. throughout *all* the region round Galilee.
33. *all* the city was gathered
39. synagogues throughout *all* Galilee,
6:55. ran through that *whole* region
8:36. if he shall gain the *whole* world,
12:30. love the Lord thy God with *all* thy
and with *all* thy soul, and with a
mind, and with *all* thy strength:
33. to love him with *all* the heart, and w
*all* the understanding, and with *all*
soul, and with *all* the strength,

THE NEW ENGLISHMAN'S GREEK CONCORDANCE AND LEXICON by Jay P. Green, Sr, 1982

2005, 2006

their ancestors. Still other religions teach that the dead go to an underworld to be judged and are then reincarnated, or reborn in another body.

4 Such religious teachings all share one basic idea—that some part of us survives the death of the physical body. According to almost every religion, past and present, we somehow live on forever with the ability to see, hear, and think. Yet, how can that be? Our senses, along with our thoughts, are all linked to the workings of our brain. At death, the brain stops working. Our memories, feelings, and senses do not continue to function independently in some mysterious way. They do not survive the destruction of our brain.

## WHAT REALLY HAPPENS AT DEATH?

5 What happens at death is no mystery to Jehovah, the Creator of the brain. He knows the truth, and in his Word, the Bible, he explains the condition of the dead. Its clear teaching is this: *When a person dies, he ceases to exist.* Death is the opposite of life. The dead do not see or hear or think. Not even one part of us survives the death of the body. We do not possess an immortal soul or spirit.*

6 After Solomon observed that the living know that they will die, he wrote: "As for the dead, they are conscious of *nothing at all.*" He then enlarged on that basic truth by saying that the dead can neither love nor hate and that "there is no work nor devising nor knowledge nor wisdom in [the grave]." (Ecclesiastes 9:5, 6, 10) Similarly, Psalm 146:4 says that when a man dies, "his

* For a discussion of the words "soul" and "spirit," please see the Appendix, pages 208-11.

4. What basic idea do many religions share concerning death?
5, 6. What does the Bible teach about the condition of the dead?



thoughts do perish." We are mortal and do not survive the death of our body. The life we enjoy is like the flame of a candle. When the flame is put out, it does not *go* anywhere. It is simply gone.

**Where did the flame go?**

## WHAT JESUS SAID ABOUT DEATH

7 Jesus Christ spoke about the condition of the dead. He did so with regard to Lazarus, a man whom he knew well and who had died. Jesus told his disciples: "Lazarus our friend has gone to rest." The disciples thought that Jesus meant that Lazarus was resting in sleep, recovering from an illness. They were wrong. Jesus explained: "Lazarus has died." (John 11:11-14) Notice that Jesus compared death to rest and sleep. Lazarus was neither in heaven nor in a burning hell. He was not meeting angels or ancestors. Lazarus was not being reborn as another human. He was at rest in death, as though in a deep sleep without dreams. Other scriptures also compare death to sleep. For example, when the disciple Stephen was stoned to death, the Bible says that he "fell asleep." (Acts 7:60) Similarly, the apostle Paul wrote about some in his day who had "fallen asleep" in death.—1 Corinthians 15:6.

8 Was it God's original purpose for people to die? Not at all! Jehovah made man to live forever on earth. As we learned earlier in this book, God placed the first human couple in a delightful paradise. He blessed them with

7. How did Jesus explain what death is like?
8. How do we know that it was not God's purpose for people to die?

## KNOWING THE TRUTH ABOUT DEATH IS BENEFICIAL

15 What the Bible teaches about the condition of the dead is comforting. As we have seen, the dead do not suffer pain or heartache. There is no reason to be afraid of them, for they cannot harm us. They do not need our help, and they cannot help us. We cannot speak with them, and they cannot speak with us. Many religious leaders falsely claim that they can help those who have died, and people who believe such leaders give them money. But knowing the truth protects us from being deceived by those who teach such lies.

16 Does your religion agree with what the Bible teaches about the dead? Most do not. Why? Because their teachings have been influenced by Satan. He uses false religion to get people to believe that after their body dies, they will continue to live in the spirit realm. This is a lie that Satan combines with other lies to turn people away from Jehovah God. How so?

17 As noted earlier, some religions teach that if a person lives a bad life, after death he will go to a place of fiery torment to suffer forever. This teaching dishonors God. Jehovah is a God of love and would never make people suffer in this way. (1 John 4:8) How would you feel about a man who punished a disobedient child by holding his hands in a fire? Would you respect such a man? In fact, would you even want to get to know him? Definitely not! You would likely think that he was very cruel. Yet, Satan wants us to believe that Jehovah tortures people in fire forever—for countless billions of years!

15. Why is it comforting to know the truth about death?
16. Who has influenced the teachings of many religions, and in what way?
17. Why does the teaching of eternal torment dishonor Jehovah?



18 Satan also uses some religions to teach that after death people become spirits who must be respected and honored by the living. According to this teaching, the spirits of the dead can become powerful friends or terrible enemies. Many people believe this lie. They fear the dead and give them honor and worship. In contrast, the Bible teaches that the dead are sleeping and that we should worship only the true God, Jehovah, our Creator and Provider.—Revelation 4:11.

19 Knowing the truth about the dead protects you from being misled by religious lies. It also helps you to understand other Bible teachings. For example, when you realize that people do not pass on to the spirit realm at death, the promise of everlasting life on a paradise earth takes on real meaning for you.

20 Long ago, the righteous man Job raised this question: "If an able-bodied man dies can he live again?" (Job 14:14) Can a lifeless person who is sleeping in death be brought back to life? What the Bible teaches about this is deeply comforting, as the next chapter will show.

18. Worship of the dead is based on what religious lie?
19. Knowing the truth about death helps us to understand what other Bible teaching?
20. What question will we consider in the next chapter?

### WHAT THE BIBLE TEACHES

- The dead do not see or hear or think. —Ecclesiastes 9:5.
- The dead are at rest; they do not suffer. —John 11:11.
- We die because we inherited sin from Adam. —Romans 5:12.

***Will those raised to heavenly life eventually have glorified physical bodies there?***

Phil. 3:20, 21: "The Lord Jesus Christ . . . will refashion our humiliated body to be conformed to his glorious body according to the operation of the power that he has." (Does this mean that it is their body of flesh that will eventually be made glorious in the heavens? Or does it mean that, instead of having a lowly body of flesh, they will be clothed with a glorious spirit body when raised to heavenly life? Let the following scripture answer.)

1 Cor. 15:40, 42-44, 47-50: "There are heavenly bodies, and earthly bodies; but the glory of the heavenly bodies is one sort, and that of the earthly bodies is a different sort. So also is the resurrection of the dead. . . . It is sown a physical body, it is raised up a spiritual body. . . . The first man [Adam] is out of the earth and made of dust; the second man [Jesus Christ] is out of heaven. As the one made of dust is, so those made of dust are also; and as the heavenly one is, so those who are heavenly are also. And just as we have borne the image of the one made of dust, we shall bear also the image of the heavenly one. However, this I say, brothers, that flesh and blood cannot inherit God's kingdom." (There is no allowance here for any mixing of the two sorts of bodies or the taking of a fleshly body to heaven.)

**How did Jesus demonstrate what resurrection will mean for mankind in general?**

John 11:11, 14-44: "[Jesus said to his disciples:] 'Lazarus our friend has gone to rest, but I am journeying there to awaken him from sleep.' . . . Jesus said to them outspokenly: 'Lazarus has died.' . . . When Jesus arrived, he found he [Lazarus] had already been four days in the memorial tomb. . . . Jesus said to her [Martha, a sister of Lazarus]: 'I am the resurrection and the life.' . . . He cried out with a loud voice: 'Lazarus, come on out!' The man that had been dead came out with his feet and hands bound with wrappings, and his countenance was bound about with a cloth. Jesus said to them: 'Loose him and let him go.'" (If Jesus had thus called



Lazarus back from a state of bliss in another life, that would have been no kindness. But Jesus' raising Lazarus up from a lifeless state was a kindness both to him and to his sisters. Once again Lazarus became a living human.)

Mark 5:35-42: "Some men from the home of the presiding officer of the synagogue came and said: 'Your daughter died! Why bother the teacher any longer?' But Jesus, overhearing the word being spoken, said to the presiding officer of the synagogue: 'Have no fear, only exercise faith.' . . . He took along the young child's father and mother and those with him, and he went in where the young child was. And, taking the hand of the young child, he said to her: *'Tal'i·tha cu'mi,'* which, translated, means: 'Maiden, I say to you, Get up!' And immediately the maiden rose and began walking, for she was twelve years old. And at once they were beside themselves with great ecstasy." (When the general resurrection takes place on earth during Christ's Millennial Reign, doubtless many millions of parents and their offspring will be overjoyed when they are reunited.)

**What prospects will await those raised to life on earth?**

Luke 23:43: "Truly I tell you today, You will be with me in Paradise." (All the earth will be transformed into a paradise under the rule of Christ as King.)

Rev. 20:12, 13: "I saw the dead, the great and the small, standing before the throne, and scrolls were opened. But another scroll was opened; it is the scroll of life. And the dead were judged out of those things written in the scrolls according to their deeds. . . . They were judged individually according to their deeds." (The opening of scrolls evidently points to a time of education in the divine will, in harmony with Isaiah 26:9. The fact that "the scroll of life" is opened indicates that there is opportunity for those who heed that education to have their names written in that scroll. Ahead of them will be the prospect of eternal life in human perfection.)

See also pages 227-232, under "Kingdom."

REASONING FROM THE SCRIPTURES, 1985, 1989ed.

that God's Word provides, and that is why you have a religion, is that not right?' **Then perhaps add:** 'Here at Matthew 7:13, 14 the Bible provides us some very valuable guidance in the words of Jesus. (Read it.) . . . Why might that be so?'

See also pages 322, 323.

### 'As long as you believe in Jesus, it really does not matter what church you belong to'

**You might reply:** 'There is no question about it, belief in Jesus is vital. And I assume that by that you mean accepting everything that he taught. No doubt you have observed, as I have, that many who say they are Christians really do not live up to what that name represents.' **Then perhaps add:** (1) 'Notice what Jesus said here at Matthew 7:21-23.' (2) 'There is a wonderful future for those who care enough to find out what God's will is and then do it. (Ps. 37:10, 11; Rev. 21:4)'

### 'What makes you think there is only one religion that is right?'

**You might reply:** 'Without doubt, there are sincere people in almost every religion. But what really counts is what God's Word says. How many true faiths does it refer to? Notice what is written here at Ephesians 4:4, 5.' **Then perhaps add:** (1) 'That agrees with what other texts state. (Matt. 7:13, 14, 21; John 10:16; 17:20, 21)' (2) 'So, the challenge that we must face is identifying that religion. How can we do it? (Perhaps use material on pages 328-330.)' (3) (See also what is on pages 199, 200, under the heading "Jehovah's Witnesses.")

### 'I just read my Bible at home and pray to God for understanding'

**You might reply:** 'Have you succeeded in reading the entire Bible as yet?' **Then perhaps add:** 'As you work on that, you will find something very interesting at Matthew 28:19, 20. . . . This is significant because it shows that Christ



uses other humans to help us to understand what is involved in being a real Christian. In harmony with that, Jehovah's Witnesses offer to visit people in their home for an hour or so each week, free of charge, to discuss the Bible. May I take just a few minutes to show you how we go about it?'

See also page 328.

### 'I feel that religion is a private affair'

**You might reply:** 'That is a common view nowadays, and if folks are really not interested in the Bible's message, we gladly go on to other homes. But did you realize that the reason I came to see you was that this is what Jesus instructed his followers to do? . . . (Matt. 24:14; 28:19, 20; 10:40)'

# Resurrection

**Definition:** *A·na'sta·sis,* the Greek word translated "resurrection," literally means "a standing up again" and it refers to a rising up from death. The fuller expression "resurrection of (from) the dead" is used repeatedly in the Scriptures. (Matt. 22:31; Acts 4:2; 1 Cor. 15:12) The Hebrew is *techi·yath' ham·me·thim',* which means "revival of the dead." (Matt. 22:23, ftn, *NW* Reference edition) Resurrection involves a reactivating of the life pattern of the individual, which life pattern God has retained in his memory. According to God's will for the individual, the person is restored in either a human or a spirit body and yet retains his personal identity, having the same personality and memories as when he died. The provision for resurrection of the dead is a magnificent expression of Jehovah's undeserved kindness; it displays his wisdom and power and is a means by which his original purpose regarding the earth will be carried out.

### Is the resurrection a reuniting of an immaterial soul with the physical body?

For this to be possible, of course, humans would have to have an immaterial soul that could separate from the physical body. The Bible does not teach such a thing. That notion was borrowed from Greek philosophy. The Bible teaching

REASONING FROM THE SCRIPTURES, 1985, 1989 ed.

## DIALOGUE SIX: Is The Cross A Pagan Symbol?



through me, resulting in the obedience of the Gentiles by word and deed, 19 in the power of signs and wonders, in the power of the Spirit; so that from Jerusalem and round about as far as Illyricum I have fully preached the gospel of Christ. 20 And thus I aspired to preach the gospel, not where Christ was *already* named, that I might not build upon another man's foundation; 21 but as it is written,

"THEY WHO HAD NO NEWS OF HIM SHALL SEE,
AND THEY WHO HAVE NOT HEARD SHALL UNDERSTAND."

22 For this reason I have often been hindered from coming to you; 23 but now, with no further place for me in these regions, and since I have had for many years a longing to come to you 24 whenever I go to Spain—for I hope to see you in passing, and to be helped on my way there by you, when I have first enjoyed your company for a while— 25 but now, I am going to Jerusalem serving the saints. 26 For Macedonia and Achaia have been pleased to make a contribution for the poor among the saints in Jerusalem. 27 Yes, they were pleased *to do so,* and they are indebted to them. For if the Gentiles have shared in their spiritual things, they are indebted to minister to them also in material things. 28 Therefore, when I have finished this, and have put my seal on this fruit of theirs, I will go on by way of you to Spain. 29 And I know that when I come to you, I will come in the fulness of the blessing of Christ.

30 Now I urge you, brethren, by our Lord Jesus Christ and by the love of the Spirit, to strive together with me in your prayers to God for me, 31 that I may be delivered from those who are disobedient in Judea, and *that* my service for Jerusalem may prove acceptable to the saints; 32 so that I may come to you in joy by the will of God and find *refreshing* rest in your company. 33 Now the God of peace be with you all. Amen.

*Greetings and Love Expressed*

16 I COMMEND to you our sister Phoebe, who is a servant of the church which is at Cenchrea; 2 that you receive her in the Lord in a manner worthy of the saints, and that you help her in whatever matter she may have need of you; for she herself has also been a helper of many, and of myself as well.

3 Greet Prisca and Aquila, my fellow workers in Christ Jesus, 4 who for my life risked their own necks, to whom not only do I give thanks, but also all the churches of the Gentiles; 5 also *greet* the church that is in their house. Greet Epaenetus, my beloved, who is the first convert to Christ from Asia. 6 Greet Mary, who has worked hard for you. 7 Greet Andronicus and Junias, my kinsmen, and my fellow prisoners, who are outstanding among the apostles, who also were in Christ before me. 8 Greet Ampliatus, my beloved in the Lord. 9 Greet Urbanus, our fellow worker in Christ, and Stachys my beloved. 10 Greet Apelles, the approved in Christ. Greet those who are of the *household* of Aristobulus. 11 Greet Herodion, my kinsman. Greet those of the *household* of Narcissus, who are in the Lord. 12 Greet Tryphaena and Tryphosa, workers in the Lord. Greet Persis the beloved, who has worked hard in the Lord. 13 Greet Rufus, a choice man in the Lord, also his mother and mine. 14 Greet Asyncritus, Phlegon, Hermes, Patrobas, Hermas and the brethren with them. 15 Greet Philologus and Julia, Nereus and his sister, and Olympas, and all the saints who are with them. 16 Greet one another with a holy kiss. All the churches of Christ greet you.

17 Now I urge you, brethren, keep your eye on those who cause dissensions and hindrances contrary to the teaching which you learned, and turn away from them. 18 For such men are slaves, not of our Lord Christ but of their own appetites; and by their smooth and flattering speech they deceive the hearts of the unsuspecting. 19 For the report of your obedience has reached to all; therefore I am rejoicing over you, but I want you to be wise in what is good, and innocent in what is evil. 20 And the God of peace will soon crush Satan under your feet.

The grace of our Lord Jesus be with you.

21 Timothy my fellow worker greets you, and *so do* Lucius and Jason and Sosipater, my kinsmen. 22 I, Tertius, who write this letter, greet you in the Lord. 23 Gaius, host to me and to the whole church, greets you. Erastus, the city treasurer greets you, and Quartus, the brother. 24 [[a]The grace of our Lord Jesus Christ be with you all. Amen.]

25 Now to Him who is able to establish you according to my gospel and the preaching of Jesus Christ, according to the revelation of the mystery which has been kept secret for long ages past, 26 but now is manifested, and by the Scriptures of the prophets, according to the commandment of the eternal God, has been made known to all the nations, *leading* to obedience of faith; 27 to the only wise God, through Jesus Christ, be the glory forever. Amen.

[a] Many mss. do not contain this verse

THE FIRST EPISTLE OF PAUL TO THE

### CORINTHIANS

*Appeal to Unity*

1 PAUL, called *as* an apostle of Jesus Christ by the will of God, and Sosthenes our brother, 2 to the church of God which is at Corinth, to those who have been sanctified in Christ Jesus, saints by calling, with all who in every place call upon the name of our Lord Jesus Christ, their *Lord* and ours: 3 Grace to you and peace from God our Father and the Lord Jesus Christ.

4 I thank [1]my God always concerning you, for the grace of God which was given you in Christ Jesus, 5 that in everything you were enriched in Him, in all speech and all knowledge, 6 even as the testimony concerning Christ was confirmed in you, 7 so that you are not lacking in any gift, awaiting eagerly the revelation of our Lord Jesus Christ, 8 who shall also confirm you to the end, blameless in the day of our Lord Jesus Christ. 9 God is faithful, through whom you were called into fellowship with His Son, Jesus Christ our Lord.

10 Now I exhort you, brethren, by the name of our Lord Jesus Christ, that you all agree, and there be no divisions among you, but you be made complete in the same mind and in the same judgment. 11 For I have been informed concerning you, my brethren, by Chloe's *people,* that there are quarrels among you. 12 Now I mean this, that each one of you is saying, "I am of Paul," and "I of Apollos," and "I of Cephas," and "I of Christ." 13 Has Christ been divided? Paul was not crucified for you, was he? Or were you baptized in the name of Paul? 14 [2]I thank God that I baptized none of you except Crispus and Gaius, 15 that no man should say you were baptized in my name. 16 Now I did baptize also the household of Stephanas; beyond that, I do not know whether I baptized any other. 17 For Christ did not send me to baptize, but to preach the gospel, not in cleverness of speech, that the cross of Christ should not be made void.

*The Wisdom of God*

18 For the word of the cross is to those who are perishing foolishness, but to us who are being saved it is the power of God. 19 For it is written,

"I WILL DESTROY THE WISDOM OF THE WISE,
AND THE CLEVERNESS OF THE CLEVER I WILL SET ASIDE."

20 Where is the wise man? Where is the scribe? Where is the debater of this age? Has not God made foolish the wisdom of the world? 21 For since in the wisdom of God the world through its wisdom did not *come to* know God, God was well-pleased through the foolishness of the message preached to save those who believe. 22 For indeed Jews ask for signs, and Greeks search for wisdom; 23 but we preach [3]Christ crucified, to Jews a stumbling block, and to Gentiles foolishness, 24 but to those who are the called, both Jews and Greeks, Christ the power of God and the wisdom of God. 25 Because the foolishness of God is wiser than men, and the weakness of God is stronger than men.

26 For consider your calling, brethren, that there were not many wise according to the flesh, not many mighty, not many noble; 27 but God has chosen the foolish things of the world to shame the wise, and God has chosen the weak things of the world to shame the things which are strong, 28 and the base things of the world and the despised, God has chosen, the things that are not, that He might nullify the things that are, 29 that no man should boast before God. 30 But by His doing you are in Christ Jesus, who became to us wisdom from God, and righteousness and sanctification, and redemption, 31 that, just as it is written, "LET HIM WHO BOASTS, BOAST IN THE LORD."

*Paul's Reliance upon the Spirit*

2 AND when I came to you, brethren, I did not come with superiority of speech or of wisdom, proclaiming to you the [4]testimony of God. 2 For I determined to know nothing among you except Jesus Christ, and Him crucified. 3 And I was with you in weakness and in fear and in much trembling. 4 And my message and my preaching were not in persuasive words of wisdom, but in demonstration of the Spirit and of power, 5 that your faith should not rest on the wisdom of men, but on the power of God.

6 Yet we do speak wisdom among those who are mature; a wisdom, however, not of this age, nor of the rulers of this age, who are passing away; 7 but we speak God's wisdom in a mystery, the hidden *wisdom,* which God predestined before the ages to our glory; 8 *the wisdom* which none of the rulers of this age has understood; for if they had understood it, they would not have crucified the Lord of glory; 9 but just as it is written,

"THINGS WHICH EYE HAS NOT SEEN AND EAR HAS NOT HEARD,
AND *which* HAVE NOT ENTERED THE HEART OF MAN,

[1] Some ancient mss. do not contain *my*
[2] Some ancient mss. read *I give thanks that*
[3] I.e., Messiah [4] Some ancient mss. read *mystery*

NEW AMERICAN STANDARD BIBLE

**1 CORINTHIANS 1:11—2:7** **Not be divisions. God's wisdom** **1372**

agreement,[a] and that there should not
be divisions*[b] among YOU, but that YOU
may be fitly united in the same mind and
in the same line of thought.[c] 11 For
the disclosure[d] was made to me about
YOU, my brothers, by those of [the house
of] Chlo'e, that dissensions exist among
YOU. 12 What I mean is this, that each
one of YOU says: "I belong to Paul,"
"But I to A·pol'los,"[e] "But I to Ce'phas,"
"But I to Christ." 13 The Christ exists divided.[f] Paul was not impaled* for
YOU, was he? Or were YOU baptized[g] in
the name of Paul? 14 I am thankful
I baptized none of YOU except Cris'pus[h]
and Ga'ius,[i] 15 so that no one may
say that YOU were baptized in my name.
16 Yes, I also baptized the household
of Steph'a·nas.[j] As for the rest, I do not
know whether I baptized anybody else.
17 For Christ dispatched me,[k] not to go
baptizing, but to go declaring the good
news, not with wisdom of speech,[l] that
the torture stake* of the Christ should
not be made useless.
18 For the speech about the torture
stake is foolishness[m] to those who are
perishing,[n] but to us who are being
saved[o] it is God's power.[p] 19 For it is
written: "I will make the wisdom of the
wise [men] perish,[q] and the intelligence
of the intellectual[r] [men] I will shove
aside."[s] 20 Where is the wise man?
Where the scribe?[t] Where the debater[u]
of this system of things?*[v] Did not God
make the wisdom of the world foolish?[w]
21 For since, in the wisdom of God, the
world through its wisdom[x] did not get
to know God,[y] God saw good through
the foolishness[z] of what is preached to
save those believing.
22 For both the Jews ask for signs[a]
and the Greeks look for wisdom;[b]
23 but we preach Christ impaled,[c] to
the Jews a cause for stumbling[d] but to
the nations foolishness;[e] 24 however,
to those who are the called, both Jews

1Co 1:10* Or, "splits." Gr., *skhi'sma·ta,* "schisms"; Lat., *sci'sma·ta.* 13* Or, "fastened on a stake (pole)." See App 5c. 17* See App 5c. 20* Or, "order of things." Gr., *ai·o'nos;* Lat., *sae'cu·li;* J17,22(Heb.), *ha·'oh·lam' haz·zeh',* "this order of things."

CHAP. 1
a 2Co 13:11 Php 2:2
b Ro 16:17 Eph 4:3
c Ro 15:5 2Co 13:11
d Le 5:1 1Co 5:1
e Ac 18:24 1Co 3:4 1Co 3:21
f Eph 4:5
g Ac 2:38
h Ac 18:8
i Ro 16:23
j 1Co 16:15
k Ac 9:15
l 1Co 2:1
m Ac 17:18 1Co 2:14
n 1Jo 2:17
o 1Co 15:2
p Ro 1:16
q Ps 33:10 1Co 3:19
r Jer 8:9 1Ti 6:20
s Isa 29:14
t Isa 33:18
u Ac 17:18
v Eph 2:2
w Job 12:17 Ro 1:22
x Col 2:8
y Mt 11:25 Lu 10:21
z Ac 17:19 1Co 2:14 1Co 3:18
a Mt 12:38 Lu 11:29
b Ac 17:18
c 1Co 2:2
d Isa 8:14
e Ac 17:32

Second Col.
a Mr 13:26
b 1Co 1:30 Col 2:3
c 2Co 13:4
d Ac 4:13
e Ro 8:30
f Joh 7:48 Jas 2:5
g Lu 16:8
h Mt 11:25
i Ro 4:17
j 1Co 2:6
k Ro 3:27 1Co 4:7
l Jer 23:5 Re 5:12
m Ro 10:4 2Co 5:21
n Joh 17:19 Heb 10:10
o Ro 3:24 Col 1:14
p Jer 9:24 2Co 10:17

CHAP. 2
q 1Co 1:17 2Co 10:10 2Co 11:6
r Eph 3:5 Col 2:2
s Ga 6:14 Php 3:8
t 2Co 10:1 Ga 4:13
u Ro 15:19 1Co 4:20 1Th 1:5 2Pe 1:16
v Eph 1:17

and Greeks, Christ the power[a] of God
and the wisdom[b] of God. 25 Because
a foolish thing* of God is wiser than
men, and a weak thing# of God is stronger than men.[c]
26 For YOU behold his calling of YOU,
brothers, that not many wise[d] in a fleshly way were called,[e] not many powerful,[f]
not many of noble birth; 27 but God
chose the foolish things of the world,[g]
that he might put the wise men to
shame; and God chose the weak things
of the world, that he might put the
strong things to shame;[h] 28 and God
chose the ignoble things of the world
and the things looked down upon, the
things that are not,[i] that he might bring
to nothing[j] the things that are, 29 in
order that no flesh might boast[k] in the
sight of God. 30 But it is due to him
that YOU are in union with Christ Jesus,
who has become to us wisdom[l] from
God, also righteousness[m] and sanctification[n] and release by ransom;[o] 31 that
it may be just as it is written: "He that
boasts, let him boast in Jehovah."*[p]

**2** And so I, when I came to YOU,
brothers, did not come with an ex-
travagance* of speech[q] or of wisdom declaring the sacred secret[r] of God to YOU.
2 For I decided not to know anything
among YOU except Jesus Christ,[s] and
him impaled. 3 And I came to YOU in
weakness and in fear and with much
trembling;[t] 4 and my speech and what
I preached were not with persuasive
words of wisdom but with a demonstration of spirit and power,[u] 5 that YOUR
faith might be, not in men's wisdom,[v]
but in God's power.[w]
6 Now we speak wisdom among those
who are mature,*[x] but not the wisdom[y]
of this system of things nor that of the
rulers of this system of things,#[z] who are
to come to nothing.[a] 7 But we speak
God's wisdom in a sacred secret,[b] the

w 2Co 4:7; 2Co 6:7; x 1Co 14:20; Eph 4:13; Heb 5:14; y 1Co 3:20; 2Co 1:12; 1Ti 6:20; z Mt 20:25; a 1Co 15:24; b Ge 3:15; Ro 16:25; Eph 3:9.

1Co 1:25* Or, "the foolishness." 25# Or, "the weakness." 31* See App 1D. 2:1* Or, "superiority." 6* Or, "full grown." Lit., "perfect (ones)." 6# See 1:20 ftn.

**1373** **Physical ma**

hidden wisdom, which Go
before the systems[a] of t
glory. 8 This [wisdom]
rulers[b] of this system of
know,[c] for if they had k
would not have impaled
Lord. 9 But just as it is
has not seen and ear h
neither have there been
the heart of man the th
has prepared for those w
10 For it is to us God
them through his spirit,[g]
searches into all things,
things of God.
11 For who among m
things of a man except th
that is in him? So, too, n
to know the things of G
spirit[k] of God. 12 Now
not the spirit[l] of the worl
it[m] which is from God,
know the things that ha
given us by God.[n] 13 T
also speak, not with wo
human wisdom,[o] but wit
by [the] spirit,[p] as we co
[matters] with spiritual
14 But a physical* ma
ceive the things of the sp
they are foolishness to hi
not get to know [them],
are examined spirituall
er, the spiritual[s] man* ex
all things, but he himsel
ined[t] by any man. 16
come to know the mind
that he may instruct him
have the mind[w] of Chris

**3** And so, brothers, I
speak to YOU as to
but as to fleshly men, a
Christ. 2 I fed YOU m
thing to eat,[z] for YOU

1Co 2:7* Or, "orders of th
aon; Lat., *sae'cu·la;* J22(Heb.)
"the **orders of things.**"
match spiritual [matters] to
14* Or, "soulical." Gr., *psy·k*
*ma'lis.* 15* Lit., "the **spiri**
ko . . . ***pneu·ma·ti·kos';***
*ri·tu·a'lis.* 16* See App 1
P46אACVgSypJ17,18,22; BD'It, "

NEW WORLD TRANSLATION, 1984 edition

·t from these, however,
. were intended to cover
ɔut any punitive addition.
from goring by a vicious
nily was to be paid what-
to be fair in the light of
Exod 21:30)—unless the
usly been known to its
ıs. Or if a woman suffered
some assailant brawling
hen the man responsible
reed upon by the husband
: whom the case was tried
who deflowered a virgin
eduction, since rape was a
l to pay her father the
ıat would normally go to
ntly fifty shekels, according
2:29), unless the father
arrying her (Exod 22:16,
ages of unspecified amount
e offense of seducing a be-
ı; in such a case she would
lic scourging, and the man
to present a guilt offering
v 19:20-22).

This was for a term of years
in the case of an Israelite
was prescribed as the pen-
ɔ could not repay the two-
nages required for the theft
Other types of enslavement
: civil actions rather than
or the non-payment of debts
leh 5:5; Amos 2:6). Volun-
scussed (Lev 25:39ff.), as a
ɔ under economic pressures.
ıg to do with criminal law.

. A. Alt, "Die Ursprünge des
" (1934), revised in "Kleine
hichte des Volkes Israel" 1
B. Clark, *Biblical Law*, (2nd
endenhall, *Law and Covenant
ar East* (1955); J. Pritchard,
· *Eastern Texts*, 2nd ed. (1955),
.x, *Ancient Israel, Its Life and*
ch. 10 ("Law and Justice").

G. L. ARCHER

·. (KJV) of three words in
·:30); תּוֹלָע (Isa 1:18); and
; (cochineal). Pliny described
l shading from the dark rose
.e (Nat. Hist. XXI, 45, 46).
ım the body of the female
·imson cochineal of Armenia
the Hebrews after Sargon II
ech. IV, 102). The cochineal
crimson in the Tabernacle.

H. G. STIGERS

;EASE, DISEASES.

. The KJV tr. of חרימים in
/ has *satchels* and RSV *hand*

*bags*. Other trs. have also been suggested. Crisping pins are pins for crisping, or curling, the hair.

S. BARABAS

**CRISPUS** (Κρίσπος, from Lat. "curled," "curly") a superintendent of the Corinthian synagogue and an early convert there with his family (Acts 18:8), baptized by Paul (who baptized very few Corinthians, 1 Cor 1:14). Despite his Lat. name, he was not necessarily a proselyte; a Rabbi Crispus occurs in Talmud Jer. *Yebamoth* 12.2. Most Corinthian Jews opposed the Gospel, and synagogue preaching became impossible (Acts 18:4-8, 12); the conversion of a prominent synagogue official must have been striking. He occurs, mistakenly, for Crescens in some ancient VSS of 2 Timothy 4:10.

A. F. WALLS

**CRITICISM AND ARCHEOLOGY.** *See* ARCHEOLOGY.

**CRITICISM OF THE BIBLE.** *See* BIBLICAL CRITICISM.

**CROCODILE** (לִוְיָתָן, *Leviathan* [KJV, ASV, RSV]; *crocodile* [RSVmg.] Job 41:1). There is general agreement that the subject of Job 41 is the Nile crocodile (*Crocodilus niloticus*). The passage is highly fig., but contains several points that confirm the identification and suggest personal knowledge: v. 7, "Can you fill his skin with harpoons?" and v. 26 "Though the sword reaches him, it does not avail." The skin is indeed very hard to penetrate: v. 13, "his double coat of mail" and v. 15, "His back is made of rows of shields." These vv. well describe the heavily armored back. Verse 31, "He makes the deep boil like a pot." A wounded crocodile can make a tremendous disturbance. This ch. can hardly refer to another aquatic animal.

In historic times the Nile crocodile was found from the mouth to the source of the Nile, but powered river craft and then rifles quickly reduced its numbers and range. By a cent. ago it had almost gone from Egypt. Its former status N of Egypt is hard to determine, but Pleistocene remains have been found in the Mt. Carmel caves and some lived in the Zerka river, still known as Crocodile River, near Caesarea, until the first decade of the twentieth cent. and perhaps rather later. Thus the crocodile would be well-known to the Israelites before the Exodus and familiar to at least some of the writers throughout the Biblical era.

In Egypt it was venerated as a symbol of sunrise. Crocodiles were sometimes reared and cared for in the temples, and embalmed when they died; because they fed on corpses and carrion they were regarded as utterly unclean by the Israelites. These two facts, and esp. their place in pagan worship, could explain why crocodiles are not specifically mentioned. A few scholars, including Bodenheimer, see the Nile crocodile in Ezekiel 29:3ff.; most regard this dragon as fig. of Pharaoh.

Although its average size is smaller today, an occasional individual reaches sixteen ft. and may weigh up to a ton. It is entirely carnivorous, feeding at first on aquatic insects and then fish, later taking birds and mammals, both dead and alive. Crocodiles sometimes become man-eaters but in some parts of Africa this habit does not develop. Throughout their range their numbers are decreasing, mainly because of hunting.

G. S. CANSDALE

**CROCUS** (חֲבַצֶּלֶת, *delight*). A young man complimenting his girl friend would be more likely to use the names of flowers than cities. Therefore Moffatt's tr. of Tirzah as "crocus" seems right. The v. therefore reads: "You are as beautiful as a crocus, my darling, and as lovely as the Lily of the Valley" (S of Sol 6:4).

There were fifteen different types of crocuses known in Pal, and four were found in the Lebanon area—where Solomon prob. wrote the Song of Solomon.

These four are: the gray-blue *Crocus cancelatus damascenus*; the pale blue *C. zonatus*; the white and lilac, orange-throated *C. lyemalis*; and the orange yellow *C. vitellinus*.

W. E. SHEWELL-COOPER

**CROOK-BACKED, CROOKBACKT.** *See* DISEASE, DISEASES.

**CROOKED SERPENT.** *See* ASTRONOMY.

**CROP.** As a Heb. noun, (מֻרְאָה, Lev 1:16), crop refers to the craw of a bird and was to be removed in sacrificial rites. As a Heb. verb, (קָטַף, Ezek 17:4, 22), crop means "to strip off" or "plucking," hence it does not fully conceptualize modern agricultural use where the idea is gathering the yield of cultivated plants. Harvest is the common Biblical term referring to agricultural products as well as attending activity in reaping or gathering. Major crops in Biblical culture were wheat, barley, grapes, olives, figs, and pomegranates (Deut 8:8). Supplementary crops included products from fields as flax, lentils, millet, sesame, and spelt ("rye"); from gardens as beans, chick peas, cucumbers, garlic, leeks, melons, and onions; and from trees as almonds, dates, pistachio nuts, and walnuts (*see* AGRICULTURE).

*BIBLIOGRAPHY.* H. N. and A. L. Moldenke, *Plants of the Bible* (1952).

G. JENNINGS

→ **CROSS (CROSS-BEARING)** (σταυρός, *pale, stake, cross*). **1. Background.** The word *stauros* comes from the Gr. verb *histēmi* (root *sta*), "to stand," and originally meant an "upright pointed stake" or "pale." Criminals were either tied to or impaled upon it. *Stauros* in the NT,

ditor,
ology

ditor,
llege.

ulting
Semi-
vinity

ditor,
enant
uri.

ditor,
meri-
Wil-

g Ed-
ligion
ry in

ditor,
ity of

THE ZONDERVAN PICTORIAL ENCYCLOPEDIA OF THE BIBLE, Vol. 1, 1976

however, apparently was a pole sunk into the ground with a cross-bar fastened to it giving it a "T" shape. Often the word "cross" referred only to the cross-bar.

Death by crucifixion originated somewhere in the E. Alexander the Great seems to have learned of it from the Persians. Rome borrowed the idea from the Phoenicians through Carthage, and perfected it as a means of capital punishment.

The Romans reserved crucifixion, however, for slaves, robbers, assassins, and the like, or for rebellious provincials. Only rarely were Rom. citizens subjected to this kind of treatment (Cicero, In Ver. 1. 5. 66). The tradition, therefore, which relates the beheading of Paul, and Peter's crucifixion accords well with this distinction between peoples.

Upon receiving the sentence of death the condemned person was flogged with a leather whip loaded with metal or bone so cruelly that it became known as the intermediate death. He was then required to shoulder the crossbar upon which he was to be extended and carry it to the place of his crucifixion (Plutarch, De Ser. Num. Vind. 9.554A). He wore about his neck a placard naming his crime. At the execution site he was stripped and tied or nailed to the crossbar, which then was fastened to an upright post. A projecting peg gave the condemned a place to sit to relieve the strain on his arms. Death, therefore, was slow in coming, except when it was hurried by soldiers breaking the crucified man's legs (John 19:31).

According to Josephus crucifixion in Pal. was a most common sight (Antiq. 17. 10. 10; 20. 5. 2; Wars, 2. 12. 6, 13. 2, 14. 9; 5. 11. 1). The fact that two robbers were crucified with Jesus in Jerusalem tends to confirm this claim.

The Jewish nation, unlike the Rom., did not crucify living persons. Frequently, however, they did suspend the bodies of the executed upon a tree to intensify their punishment and to expose them to public shame (Num 25:4; Josh 10:26; 1 Sam 31:10). Men thus hanged were considered accursed by God (Deut 21:22, 23).

Crucifixion, therefore, was abhorrent to the Jew (1 Cor 1:23; Gal 3:13), but no less so to the Rom. Cicero wrote: "Let the very name of the cross be far away not only from the body of a Roman citizen, but even from his thoughts, his eyes, his ears" (Pro Rab. 5).

**2. Jesus' cross.** In the NT, when used of Jesus, the word *staurós* has both a literal and figurative meaning. Literally it meant that physical instrument by which Jesus was put to death. After being flogged (Matt 27:26) and forced to carry His own cross (=crossbar, John 19:17), which, though not a heavy piece of wood, was, nevertheless, too heavy for Him in His weakened condition (Mark 15:21; cf. 2 Cor 13:4), He was fastened to it by nails (cf. John 20:25), and hoisted then with it up onto the upright stake already in place at the execution site (Matt 27:35). Here He was left to die, a death which Jesus Himself had anticipated (20:18, 19), and from which He could not escape (Mark 15:32).

Figuratively Jesus' cross became the mark of God's redemptive action in history. It was symbolic of the means God employed for releasing into this world a power for good sufficiently strong to save men (1 Cor 1:18), to break down otherwise insurmountable barriers between man and man, thus making it possible for him to live at one with his brother (Eph 2:16), to bring everything back into peace and harmony with God (Col 1:20), to effect for mankind forgiveness of sins and a release from that which continually made him feel his guilt (2:14), and to free him forever from the cosmic forces of evil which everywhere surrounded him (2:15).

Since the cross was reserved for criminals and those accursed by God (see above), it symbolized, too, the suffering, shame and humiliation Jesus endured (Heb 12:2) for the human race, indicating the depths to which He was willing to go to lift up the worst and lowest of men.

Jesus' cross also stood as the symbol of God's unique purpose for Him. That is to say, since dying was planned by God as Jesus' supreme mission (Acts 2:23; cf. Matt 16:21 with 20:18, 19 and John 18:11), the cross, therefore, becomes a metonym for mission, a symbol both of the divine will for Jesus, and Jesus' voluntary submission to that will (Mark 14:36; Phil 2:8).

**3. The Christian's cross: crossbearing.** The cross was used also of the followers of Jesus, both literally and metaphorically. Because crucifixion was a frequent occurrence, and because the spectacle of condemned men carrying their crosses to the place of execution was common, Jesus' words about taking up the cross and following Him (Matt 16:24; cf. John 12:26) must first of all have been interpreted literally. These words must have been understood as a prediction of the same physical means of death for Jesus' followers as for Him (Matt 23:34). This prediction was soon fulfilled in the early years of the Church's history (cf. the tradition about Peter's crucifixion and see also Ignatius, Rom. 5.3; Hermas, Vis. 3.2.1).

Jesus also interpreted metaphorically the cross His followers must bear. It was for Him the symbol of their self-sacrifice: "If any man wills to come after me," He said, "let him deny (perhaps, 'lose sight of') himself, and take up his cross (Luke adds, 'daily'), and [continually] follow me" (Mark 8:34-36). "To bear the cross," therefore, means a continuing loyalty to Christ along with a continuing death to self. It means "we must refuse, abandon, deny self altogether as a ruling or determining or originating element in us. It is to be no longer the regent of our action. We are no more to think

Various types of crosses, particularly

'What should I like to do?' but 'What wou Living One have me do?' " (George Mac ald).

If in the experience of Jesus the cross metonym for His mission, there is a sense in which the cross also stands for that m in life to which the Christian has been c "To bear the cross," therefore, means fu that the Christian is called upon to in Jesus' commitment to doing that particular assigned him by God and doing it compl (Luke 14:27, noting esp. the words "*his* cross"; cf. John 17:4). The cross is a sy then, of life lived under Christian disci marked by voluntary obedience to the w God.

The cross is also a symbol of the shame humiliation which the Christian must be pared to endure for the sake of Christ ( 12:2 with 13:12, 13; cf. also Ign. Trall. 1 Hermas, Vis. 3. 2. 1). It is a symbol, fur of the destruction of everything which i poses itself between man and God, whether an institutionalized religion, as in the cas Paul (Gal 6:14), or material things, as in case of Ignatius (Rom 7:2), or whatever there might be. The cross, too, is a symbo that mystical union of the Christian Christ, wherein one's old evil impulses are cified with Christ, and new desires and po are released in his life (Gal 2:19b, 20; 1 6:6).

The Christian's cross is always a volun thing. Unlike the convict he never is c pelled to carry it: "If any man wills to do Jesus said (Mark 8:34). Nor is there ever

THE ZONDERVAN PICTORIAL ENCYCLOPEDIA OF THE BIBLE, Vol. 1, 1976

ıt stake already in place at the
Matt 27:35). Here He was left
: which Jesus Himself had an-
8, 19), and from which He
e (Mark 15:32).
Jesus' cross became the mark of
ve action in history. It was sym-
ans God employed for releasing
a power for good sufficiently
nen (1 Cor 1:18), to break down
nountable barriers between man
making it possible for him to
th his brother (Eph 2:16), to
g back into peace and harmony
l 1:20), to effect for mankind
sins and a release from that
ally made him feel his guilt
free him forever from the cos-
vil which everywhere surround-

oss was reserved for criminals
ırsed by God (see above), it
, the suffering, shame and humil-
ured (Heb 12:2) for the human
: the depths to which He was
lift up the worst and lowest of

also stood as the symbol of
urpose for Him. That is to say,
as planned by God as Jesus'
n (Acts 2:23; cf. Matt 16:21
and John 18:11), the cross,
mes a metonym for mission, a
: the divine will for Jesus, and
submission to that will (Mark
).

**tian's cross: crossbearing.** The
also of the followers of Jesus,
id metaphorically. Because cru-
requent occurrence, and because
: condemned men carrying their
lace of execution was common,
out taking up the cross and fol-
Matt 16:24; cf. John 12:26)
l have been interpreted literally.
ıust have been understood as a
e same physical means of death
wers as for Him (Matt 23:34).
was soon fulfilled in the early
ıurch's history (cf. the tradition
rucifixion and see also Ignatius,
ias, Vis. 3.2.1).
interpreted metaphorically the
wers must bear. It was for Him
their self-sacrifice: "If any man
fter me," He said, "let him deny
sight of') himself, and take up
adds, 'daily'), and [continually]
Mark 8:34-36). "To bear the
e, means a continuing loyalty
with a continuing death to self.
nust refuse, abandon, deny self
ruling or determining or origin us. It is to be no longer the
ction. We are no more to think

Various types of crosses, particularly the type used in crucifying Jesus.

'What should I like to do?' but 'What would the Living One have me do?'" (George MacDonald).

If in the experience of Jesus the cross was a metonym for His mission, there is a sense then in which the cross also stands for that mission in life to which the Christian has been called. "To bear the cross," therefore, means further that the Christian is called upon to imitate Jesus' commitment to doing that particular task assigned him by God and doing it completely (Luke 14:27, noting esp. the words *"his own* cross"; cf. John 17:4). The cross is a symbol, then, of life lived under Christian discipline, marked by voluntary obedience to the will of God.

The cross is also a symbol of the shame and humiliation which the Christian must be prepared to endure for the sake of Christ (Heb 12:2 with 13:12, 13; cf. also Ign. Trall. 11:2: Hermas, Vis. 3. 2. 1). It is a symbol, further, of the destruction of everything which interposes itself between man and God, whether it be an institutionalized religion, as in the case of Paul (Gal 6:14), or material things, as in the case of Ignatius (Rom 7:2), or whatever else there might be. The cross, too, is a symbol of that mystical union of the Christian with Christ, wherein one's old evil impulses are crucified with Christ, and new desires and powers are released in his life (Gal 2:19b, 20; Rom 6:6).

The Christian's cross is always a voluntary thing. Unlike the convict he never is compelled to carry it: "If any man wills to do so," Jesus said (Mark 8:34). Nor is there ever any hint that the Christian, like Christ, by bearing his cross acts redemptively or becomes accursed in behalf of others or thereby atones for another's sins. Yet there is a sense in which the Christian who bears the cross fills up (supplements) on his part the things lacking of the afflictions of Christ (Col 1:24), i.e. by continued acts of self-denial on the part of successive individuals through the years in the interest of God and humanity, the work which Christ began continues even to the present.

*BIBLIOGRAPHY.* H. Cremer, *Biblico-Theological Lexicon of NT Greek* (1892); F. W. Dillistone, *Jesus Christ and His Cross* (1953); L. Morris, *The Apostolic Preaching of the Cross* (1955); J. Schneider, σταυρός, in G. Kittel, ed., *Theologisches Wörterbuch zum NT* (1962); *Theological Dictionary of the NT*, tr. and ed. by G. W. Bromiley (1971).

G F. HAWTHORNE

**CROW.** *See* RAVEN.

**CROWN** (קדקד, *top of the head*, RSV Job 2:7; נזר, *chaplet, wreath*, Exod 29:6; זר, *border, ring*, Exod 25:11; עטרה, *royal crown*, 2 Sam 12:30 RSV *molding*; כתר, *royal crown*, Esth 1:11; עטר [verb], *to crown*, Ps 8:5; διάδημα, *diadem, crown of royalty*, Rev 19:12; στέφανος, *garland, wreath*, Matt 27:29; στεφανόω [verb] *to crown*, 2 Tim 2:5).

1. **Non-symbolic use of crown.** As used in Job 2:7 (of the top of Job's head) and in Exodus 25:11, etc. (of a part of the ornamentation of the Ark of the Covenant), "crown" merely connotes something of a particular form or shape, with prob. no symbolic meaning.

THE ZONDERVAN PICTORIAL ENCYCLOPEDIA OF THE BIBLE, vol. 1, 1976

### What is the origin of the raw material of which the universe is made?

Scientists have learned that matter is a concentrated form of energy. This is demonstrated with the explosion of nuclear weapons. Astrophysicist Josip Kleczek states: "Most and possibly all elementary particles may be created by materialization of energy."—*The Universe* (Boston, 1976), Vol. 11, p. 17.

From where could such energy come? After asking, "Who has created these things [the stars and planets]?", the Bible states regarding Jehovah God, "Due to the abundance of dynamic energy, he also being vigorous in power, not one of them is missing." (Isa. 40:26) So God himself is the Source of all the "dynamic energy" that was needed to create the universe.

### Was all physical creation accomplished in just six days sometime within the past 6,000 to 10,000 years?

The facts disagree with such a conclusion: (1) Light from the Andromeda nebula can be seen on a clear night in the northern hemisphere. It takes about 2,000,000 years for that light to reach the earth, indicating that the universe must be at least millions of years old. (2) End products of radioactive decay in rocks in the earth testify that some rock formations have been undisturbed for billions of years.

Genesis 1:3-31 is not discussing the original creation of matter or of the heavenly bodies. It describes the preparation of the already existing earth for human habitation. This included creation of the basic kinds of vegetation, marine life, flying creatures, land animals, and the first human pair. All of this is said to have been done within a period of six "days." However, the Hebrew word translated "day" has a variety of meanings, including 'a long time; the time covering an extraordinary event.' (*Old Testament Word Studies*, Grand Rapids, Mich.; 1978, W. Wilson, p. 109) The term used allows for the thought that each "day" could have been thousands of years in length.

# Cross

**Definition:** The device on which Jesus Christ was executed is referred to by most of Christendom as a cross. The expression is drawn from the Latin *crux.*

### Why do Watch Tower publications show Jesus on a stake with hands over his head instead of on the traditional cross?

The Greek word rendered "cross" in many modern Bible versions ("torture stake" in *NW*) is *stau·ros'*. In classical Greek, this word meant merely an upright stake, or pale. Later it also came to be used for an execution stake having a crosspiece. *The Imperial Bible-Dictionary* acknowledges this, saying: "The Greek word for cross, [*stau·ros'*], properly signified a *stake*, an upright pole, or piece of paling, on which anything might be hung, or which might be used in impaling [fencing in] a piece of ground. . . . Even amongst the Romans the *crux* (from which our *cross* is derived) appears to have been originally an upright pole."—Edited by P. Fairbairn (London, 1874), Vol. I, p. 376.

Was that the case in connection with the execution of God's Son? It is noteworthy that the Bible also uses the word *xy'lon* to identify the device used. *A Greek-English Lexicon*, by Liddell and Scott, defines this as meaning: "*Wood* cut and ready for use, *firewood, timber,* etc. . . . *piece of wood, log, beam, post* . . . *cudgel, club* . . . *stake* on which criminals were impaled . . . of live wood, *tree.*" It also says "in *NT*, of the *cross,*" and cites Acts 5:30 and 10:39 as examples. (Oxford, 1968, pp. 1191, 1192) However, in those verses *KJ, RS, JB,* and *Dy* translate *xy'lon* as "tree." (Compare this rendering with Galatians 3:13; Deuteronomy 21:22, 23.)

The book *The Non-Christian Cross,* by J. D. Parsons (London, 1896), says: "There is not a single sentence in any of the numerous writings forming the New Testament, which, in the original Greek, bears even indirect evidence to the effect that the stauros used in the case of Jesus was



REASONING FROM THE SCRIPTURES

other than an ordinary stauros; much less to the effect that it consisted, not of one piece of timber, but of two pieces nailed together in the form of a cross. . . . It is not a little misleading upon the part of our teachers to translate the word stauros as 'cross' when rendering the Greek documents of the Church into our native tongue, and to support that action by putting 'cross' in our lexicons as the meaning of stauros without carefully explaining that that was at any rate not the primary meaning of the word in the days of the Apostles, did not become its primary signification till long afterwards, and became so then, if at all, only because, despite the absence of corroborative evidence, it was for some reason or other assumed that the particular stauros upon which Jesus was executed had that particular shape." —Pp. 23, 24; see also *The Companion Bible* (London, 1885), Appendix No. 162.

Thus the weight of the evidence indicates that Jesus died on an upright stake and not on the traditional cross.

**What were the historical origins of Christendom's cross?**

"Various objects, dating from periods long anterior to the Christian era, have been found, marked with crosses of different designs, in almost every part of the old world. India, Syria, Persia and Egypt have all yielded numberless examples . . . The use of the cross as a religious symbol in pre-Christian times and among non-Christian peoples may probably be regarded as almost universal, and in very many cases it was connected with some form of nature worship." —*Encyclopædia Britannica* (1946), Vol. 6, p. 753.

"The shape of the [two-beamed cross] had its origin in ancient Chaldea, and was used as the symbol of the god Tammuz (being in the shape of the mystic Tau, the initial of his name) in that country and in adjacent lands, including Egypt. By the middle of the 3rd cent. A.D. the churches had either departed from, or had travestied, certain doctrines of the Christian faith. In order to increase the prestige of the apostate ecclesiastical system pagans were received into the churches apart from regeneration by faith, and were permitted largely to retain their pagan signs and symbols. Hence the Tau or T, in its most frequent form, with the cross-piece lowered, was adopted to stand for the cross of Christ."—*An Expository Dictionary of New Testament Words* (London, 1962), W. E. Vine, p. 256.



"It is strange, yet unquestionably a fact, that in ages long before the birth of Christ, and since then in lands untouched by the teaching of the Church, the Cross has been used as a sacred symbol. . . . The Greek Bacchus, the Tyrian Tammuz, the Chaldean Bel, and the Norse Odin, were all symbolised to their votaries by a cruciform device."—*The Cross in Ritual, Architecture, and Art* (London, 1900), G. S. Tyack, p. 1.

"The cross in the form of the 'Crux Ansata' . . . was carried in the hands of the Egyptian priests and Pontiff kings as the symbol of their authority as priests of the Sun god and was called 'the Sign of Life.'"—*The Worship of the Dead* (London, 1904), Colonel J. Garnier, p. 226.

"Various figures of crosses are found everywhere on Egyptian monuments and tombs, and are considered by many authorities as symbolical either of the phallus [a representation of the male sex organ] or of coition. . . . In Egyptian tombs the crux ansata [cross with a circle or handle on top] is found side by side with the phallus."—*A Short History of Sex-Worship* (London, 1940), H. Cutner, pp. 16, 17; see also *The Non-Christian Cross*, p. 183.

"These crosses were used as symbols of the Babylonian sun-god, ⊕, and are first seen on a coin of Julius Cæsar, 100-44 B.C., and then on a coin struck by Cæsar's heir (Augustus), 20 B.C. On the coins of Constantine the most frequent symbol is ☧; but the same symbol is used without the surrounding circle, and with the four equal arms vertical and horizontal; and this was the symbol specially venerated as the 'Solar Wheel'. It should be stated that Constantine was a sun-god worshipper, and would not enter the 'Church' till some quarter of a century after the legend of his having seen such a cross in the heavens."—*The Companion Bible*, Appendix No. 162; see also *The Non-Christian Cross*, pp. 133-141.

REASONING FROM THE SCRIPTURES

This biblical sanction against allowing a corpse to hang more than one day, together with the accursed state of the one so hung (whatever exactly that meant), probably mirrors and at the same time accounts for the failure of Jews to employ this cruel form of torture. The resort to crucifixion among them for high treason in the Hasmonean period and a puzzling exception of its use in the Mishnah (ca. 180 C.E.) will be dealt with below. But, for the moment, one can see why the claim for a messiah who was crucified would be thoroughly repulsive to the Jewish ear. Paul calls the cross a scandal (in translations, commonly, "stumbling block") to Jews and an absurdity to Gentiles. He does this in writing to the once pagan but now believing communities of Corinth (1 Cor. 1:23) and the highlands of the province of Galatia (Gal. 5:11). Paul makes capital of Jesus' presumably accursed condition in the latter epistle by posing the paradox that his "becoming a curse for us" extended "the blessing of Abraham to the Gentiles through Christ Jesus."[15] More of that later; the point for now is that one might have expected the earliest believers in Jesus to avoid or at least soft-pedal the fact that Jesus died as a convicted felon.

They did quite otherwise. They wrote at length not simply that it happened and hence was bound to be remembered, but, for a reason that seemed good to them, they identified this unqualified evil as somehow a good. Christian apologists like Lactantius (d. ca. 320) and Arnobius (d. ca. 330) would puzzle over why God had not proposed an honorable (*honestum*) kind of death for Jesus, but there it was. He died on what the ancient world invariably called in Greek the "criminal wood," as also later in Latin (*mala crux*). The anonymous Epistle (actually a treatise) to the Hebrews unblinkingly calls the cross a sign of "shame" (*aischýnēs*), saying that Jesus endured it for the sake of the joy that lay before him.[16]

## The Torture of Crucifixion

The origins of crucifixion are hard to trace. Not only Jews but Greeks, Romans, and those that both of them denoted barbarians considered it an obscene form of punishment. It is commonly called Persian or Medean in its origins, probably because Herodotus (d. after 44 B.C.E.) frequently has these peoples employing it. He generally uses one verb for crucifying living men (*anaskolopízein*) and another for corpses (*anastaurízein*), a distinction later lost.[17] The Homeric mythic tradition does not mention it. From the full range

15. Gal. 3:13–14.
16. See Heb. 12:2.
17. For exhaustive detail on how and by whom crucifixion was administered in the ancient world see Martin Hengel, *Crucifixion*, trans. John Bowden (London: SCM; Philadelphia: Fortress Press, 1977), a revised and enlarged version of the author's "*Mors turpissima crucis:* Die Kreuzigung in der antiken Welt und die 'Torheit' des 'Wortes vom Kreuz,'" *Rechtfertigung:*



of texts it is impossibl
*lops* or *staurós*) or ha
whether the victims w
in individual citations
crossbeam also was us
tus supplies is the adm
Xanthippus to the satr
offenses: "They nailed
son, they stoned him t
Detailed descriptio
refers to a variety of
some victims are thru
genitals (*obscena*), still
The Jewish historian J
explicit about Jews ca
before they died, and t
that Titus, father of Jo
not keep Titus from le
day: "The soldiers, out
those they caught, in di
their number was so g
and not enough cros
wretched of deaths." H
the east shore of the D
oner with crucifixion.[2
An especially grim c
ers, highwaymen, and
poem: "Punished with
they are fastened, naile
prey and grim scraps f
Much later in Latin
the speaker thought th

*Festschrift für Ernst Käsema*
Göttingen: Vandenhoeck un
cient world are found in Urb
*ex Archaeologia Romana ill*
printed from *Verbum Domin*
18. Herodotus 9.120 (E
Median impaled (*aneskolóp*
suaded him to let Cyrus go f
19. Seneca *To Marcia on*
20. Josephus *Jewish War*
21. Ibid., 7.202–3 (3.563
22. Pseudo-Manetho *Ap*
(translation adapted).

THE CRUCIFIXION OF JESUS: History, Myth, Faith, by Gerard S. Sloyan (Minneapolis MN: Augsburg Fortress Publishers, 1995).

›se to hang more than one
so hung (whatever exactly
me accounts for the failure
resort to crucifixion among
ınd a puzzling exception of
ılt with below. But, for the
h who was crucified would
:alls the cross a scandal (in
Jews and an absurdity to
an but now believing com-
.nds of the province of Ga-
umably accursed condition
. "becoming a curse for us"
.es through Christ Jesus."[15]
e might have expected the
ft-pedal the fact that Jesus

ǥth not simply that it hap-
ıt, for a reason that seemed
as somehow a good. Chris-
rnobius (d. ca. 330) would
orable (*honestum*) kind of
ıt the ancient world invari-
later in Latin (*mala crux*).
the Hebrews unblinkingly
ng that Jesus endured it for

ion

only Jews but Greeks, Ro-
arians considered it an ob-
ɨ Persian or Medean in its
B.C.E.) frequently has these
› for crucifying living men
*urízein*), a distinction later
ıtion it. From the full range

n was administered in the ancient
.ondon: SCM; Philadelphia: For-
or's "*Mors turpissima crucis:* Die
es vom Kreuz,'" *Rechtfertigung:*



of texts it is impossible to be sure whether impaling corpses on a stake (*skólops* or *staurós*) or hanging the condemned up to die is in question. Again, whether the victims were affixed by nails or lashed with thongs is not clear in individual citations, any more than whether an upright stake alone or a crossbeam also was used. The only detailed account of a crucifixion Herodotus supplies is the administration of the punishment by the Athenian general Xanthippus to the satrap (*hýparchos*) Artaÿctes for what are called religious offenses: "They nailed him to planks and hanged him aloft; and as for his son, they stoned him to death before his father's eyes."[18]

Detailed descriptions come only from Roman times. Seneca (d. 65 C.E.) refers to a variety of postures and different kinds of tortures on crosses: some victims are thrust head downward, others have a stake impale their genitals (*obscena*), still others have their arms outstretched on a crossbeam.[19] The Jewish historian Josephus, writing of the Jewish War of the late 60s, is explicit about Jews captured by the Romans who were first flogged, tortured before they died, and then crucified before the city wall. The pity he reports that Titus, father of Josephus's imperial patron Vespasian, felt for them did not keep Titus from letting his troops dispatch as many as five hundred in a day: "The soldiers, out of the rage and hatred they bore the prisoners, nailed those they caught, in different postures, to the crosses for the sport of it, and their number was so great that there was not enough room for the crosses and not enough crosses for the bodies."[20] Josephus calls it "the most wretched of deaths." He tells of the surrender of the fortress Machaerus on the east shore of the Dead Sea when the Romans threatened a Jewish prisoner with crucifixion.[21]

An especially grim description of this punishment, meted out to murderers, highwaymen, and other gross offenders, is the following from a didactic poem: "Punished with limbs outstretched, they see the stake as their fate; they are fastened, nailed to it with sharpest spikes, an ugly meal for birds of prey and grim scraps for dogs."[22]

Much later in Latin speech "*Crux!*" became a curse, to indicate the way the speaker thought the one accursed should end. Other epithets among the

*Festschrift für Ernst Käsemann zum 70. Geburtstag*, ed. J. Friedrich, et al. (Tübingen: Mohr; Göttingen: Vandenhoeck und Ruprecht, 1976), 125–84. Some of the same data from the ancient world are found in Urbanus Holzmeister, S. I., *Crux Domini atque Crucifixio; quomodo ex Archaeologia Romana illustrantur* (Rome: Pontificium Institutum Biblicum, 1934), 32, reprinted from *Verbum Domini* 14 (1934): 149–55, 241–49, 257–63.

18. Herodotus 9.120 (ET, A. D. Godley, 1924; 4.298). See also 1.128, where Astyages the Median impaled (*aneskolópise*) the Magians (*mágoi*), interpreters of dreams, who had persuaded him to let Cyrus go free.

19. Seneca *To Marcia on Consolation* 20.3 (ET, John W. Basore, 1935; 2.68).

20. Josephus *Jewish War* 5.451 (ET, H. St. J. Thackeray, 1928; 3.340).

21. Ibid., 7.202–3 (3.563).

22. Pseudo-Manetho *Apotelesmatica* 4.198ff., as cited by Hengel, *Crucifixion*, 9, n. 20 (translation adapted).

THE CRUCIFIXION OF JESUS: History, Myth, Faith, by Gerard S. Sloyan (Minneapolis, MN: Augsburg Fortress Publishers, 1995)

a trio of Jewish leaders—Rabbi Herschel Schacter, chairman of the American Jewish Conference on Soviet Jewry; Dr. William Wexler, chairman of the Conference of Presidents of Major American Jewish Organizations, and Detroit multimillionaire Max Fisher, a heavy contributor to the Republican Party—went to Washington on Dec. 30, Secretary of State William Rogers told them he was opposed to a public government protest against the Soviet Union. "When the U.S. takes a strong stand on an internal Soviet issue," Rogers said, "the Russian rulers feel they cannot back down because they fear that it may look as though they are doing so under power pressure."

**Mercy:** In response to Rogers's caution, the three Jewish leaders settled for a private meeting with Richard Nixon and a mild public expression of Presidential "concern." But the Administration did apply substantial indirect pressure on the Soviets. First, as Jewish leaders had advised, Washington urged the Spanish Government to commute the sentences of the six Basque rebels who had been condemned to death (NEWSWEEK, Jan. 11) in the hope that a show of mercy by Madrid would set a strong example for Moscow. Next, American diplomats advised Russian officials that a harsh handling of the convicted Jews would cool U.S.-Soviet relations.

Not all U.S. Jews were willing to put their faith in conventional political pressure, however. In Washington and in New York City, the militant Jewish Defense League spent two weeks noisily demonstrating outside the Soviet Embassy and other Russian agencies. And on Long Island, hundreds of Jewish militants, many of them young and eleven of them dressed as inmates of a Soviet prison camp, paraded near a Russian-owned estate in Glen Cove. "The Jewish Establishment works through the medium of telegrams, petitions and politics," says Cantor Lawrence Fine, the JDL's husky executive director. "We don't believe in that. If we don't bury respectability at a time when Jewish survival is at stake, respectability will bury us."

But the majority of Jewish groups in the U.S. remain committed to the respectable approach, fearing that the JDL's tactics—not to speak of the bombing of Soviet buildings in the U.S.—will prove counterproductive. And the Israeli Government, which has privately asked the JDL to cool it somewhat (page 34), apparently agrees. Still, the JDL's militancy has clearly influenced the thinking of many Jewish organizations. Next month, representatives from 50 countries will hold a Jewish summit conference in Brussels to coordinate a massive campaign aimed at winning the right of emigration for Soviet Jews. "The one miracle in all of this is the bold new assertiveness on the part of Soviet Jews themselves," says Rabbi Schacter. "Could it be the mighty Soviet Government will ultimately yield to some little 'Yid' on the street who refuses to shut up?"

Rogers and Schacter: Pressure AP

## Papal Politics

There are some things that liberal Catholics—even in Holland—cannot do without approval from Rome. One of them is to choose a bishop, and last week, in the first direct effort by Rome to turn back the trend toward functional democracy in the church's tense Dutch province, the Vatican announced the appointment of an eminent conservative priest, Adrianus Johannes Simonis, as the new Bishop of Rotterdam.

At 39, Simonis is the youngest man to head a diocese in the entire Roman Catholic Church. And in his opposition to birth control, married clergy and democratic sharing of church authority, he is clearly to the right of the aging Dutch primate, Bernard Cardinal Alfrink. One of his aims, Simonis said after his appointment, is to convert what is now "a talking church into a praying church."

Some liberals fear Simonis's conversion effort could trigger a fatal schism in the Dutch church. Shortly after the appointment was announced, the diocesan pastoral council of Rotterdam, which, according to custom, had secretly recommended five priests for the Rotterdam see, passed an irate resolution charging the Vatican with attempting to "drive a wedge between the Dutch bishops." More directly, all fourteen deans of the diocese publicly urged Father Simonis to reject his appointment. But Simonis, with the Vatican's support, is not likely to heed his critics. "It is claimed that there was a power move from Rome," says one of Simonis's supporters. "There was—but it was a legitimate one."

## SCIENCE AND SPACE

## The Rite of Crucifixion

Few methods of death by torture were quite so agonizing and protracted as crucifixion—and the ancients, accordingly, reserved the punishment for what they regarded as the worst offenders. Crucifixion is known to have been practiced by the Phoenicians. In 519 B.C., the Persian King Darius I crucified 3,000 Babylonians. In A.D. 66, the Romans crucified 3,600 Jews, thereby igniting the Jews in revolt, and by the time the Romans had got things under control again, so many Jews had been crucified that the executioners ran out of wood for crosses.

Among the unnumbered thousands of Jews crucified over the years, of course, was the most famous martyr in history: Jesus Christ. And it is the depiction of Christ's crucifixion by later artists (none known to have been done earlier than approximately A.D. 440) on which the modern world's knowledge of the technique of the rite is based. But last week, Israeli archeologists revealed that they have discovered in a hillside cave near Jerusalem the first remains of a victim—the skeleton, including spike-pierced heel bones, of a young man executed just about 2,000 years ago.

The question immediately arose: could the skeleton be that of Christ? "I cannot prove that it is not Christ," says Dr. Avraham Biran, director of the Israeli Government's Department of Antiquities and Museums, "but the statistical odds against it are overwhelming." Most Christian experts agree emphatically, noting besides that Roman Catholic dogma holds that Christ ascended bodily into heaven after his death.

**Jehohannan:** The only identification of the crucified man was an inscription on the ossuary that read, in part, "Jehohannan Ben." Jehohannan was a common Hebrew name of that long-ago era and "Ben" means "son of." The remainder of the inscription was too illegible for the Israeli scientists to decipher.

Jehohannan's bones had deteriorated over the centuries, but not so badly as to prevent Israeli scientists from drawing a tentative sketch of the man. They saw him as a lithe, graceful individual of average height and apparent good health; he had never been subjected to either major injury or heavy physical labor during the 24 to 28 years that he lived prior to crucifixion. He did have a slightly misshapen head, a malformation caused probably by some major change in his mother's diet during the time she carried him in her womb. But on balance, according to Dr. Nicu Haas, the senior lecturer in anatomy at the Hebrew University-Hadassah Medical Center who examined Jehohannan's skeleton, the young man had a "gracious, almost feminine allure; [he] reminds us of the Hellenistic ideal youth."

Judging from various artifacts found

Bettmann Archive

Albrecht Dürer's version of crucifixion; Jehohannan's spike-pierced heel bones; sketch of his posture on cross

UPI

in the tomb that contained the crucified man's skeleton, Vasilius Tzaferis, a Greek-born Israeli archeologist who was one of the excavators of the burial site, concludes that Jehohannan was most likely crucified around A.D. 7. That was when the Jews had rebelled at a Roman census—presumably because they thought the census presaged forced military service in Roman legions, compulsory labor or increased taxes.

Though there are no clues whatever to the crime for which Jehohannan was executed, the Roman penal code is known to have reserved crucifixion for non-Roman murderers, brigands and insolent or rebellious slaves. What particularly interested the scholars were the marks found on the crucified man's bones. They indicate that the crucifixion position was not the erect, cruciform pose so commonly depicted by the artists. As the scholars see it, Jehohannan was probably held down by soldiers while his outstretched arms were fastened first to the cross bar—with the spikes driven not through the palms of his hands, but between the ulnar and radial bones of his forearms. Scratches on these two sets of bones are clearly discernible just above the wrist.

**Sedecula:** Once the victim's arms were immobilized, the Roman executioners most likely then turned to his legs, pressing them together and twisting them to one side, somewhat in the position of a deep-knee bend. Then the executioners drove a large iron spike approximately 7 inches long through his two calcaneal (or heel) bones, and into the wood. To prevent the victim from sagging—and possibly tearing himself loose from the cross—a small crosspiece called a "sedecula" was nailed to the upright member of the cross; it provided a support shelf for the condemned man's buttocks. In most cases, the experts think, death on the cross came within a span of several hours to a day or more, either from loss of blood or from suffocation as the victim's rib cage collapsed over his diaphragm.

What really preserved the evidence of crucifixion is the fact that the spike hammered through Jehohannan's heels struck a knot in the wood of the cross, bent and became so tightly stuck that the attendants were later unable to extract the valuable spike from his heels after death. So the executioners took an ax and chopped the feet off above the ankles. The relatives or friends who buried Jehohannan placed his amputated, but still-pierced, feet in the 3- by 2- by 2-foot limestone ossuary, or bone box, along with the rest of the body—and also that of a 3- or 4-year-old child. The box was then slipped into one of four small tunnels extending out from the closet-size burial cave, somewhat like the vaults found in modern morgues.

Fourteen ossuaries similar to that of Jehohannan's were found in the tunnels of four caves on, or near, Giv'at Ha-Mivtar (the Hebrew phrase means "Hill of the Cut"). It was there, in 1968, that bulldozers digging the foundations for a new Israeli housing project scraped away the accumulated centuries of dirt and rubble—and exposed the large slabs sealing the burial caves of Jehohannan and some 34 others. Though the scientists who made the find agree that there is no chance at all that the bones they found could be Christ's, they also noted quietly that the question is one that may well be around for a very long time. "An initial anthropological approach to the first material evidence of a crucifixion," Haas wrote in the Israel Exploration Journal, "does not exclude a certain emotional concern."

## Pollutants of the Week

For more than a year, four prestigious conservation groups had battled through the courts to force the government to widen the present partial ban on the use of DDT. Last week, the conservationists won the fight, though whether their victory is final remains to be seen. In Washington, the U.S. Court of Appeals ordered the newly established Federal Environmental Protection Agency to ban almost all further use of the pesticide and also to decide if DDT is enough of a health hazard to warrant a new ban on interstate shipments of the stuff.

Since the partial ban on DDT proclaimed in November 1969, the authority to regulate pesticides has been shifted from the Department of Agriculture to the EPA, which indicated that it probably wouldn't appeal the court's decision. In the past, Agriculture Department officials had argued vigorously that DDT posed no threat to human safety. Now, the agricultural experts insist, one immediate result of the extended ban could be a vast increase of boll-weevil infestation in Southern cotton fields.

**Ban:** But it seems likely that further litigation may be necessary before a complete ban on DDT takes effect. This is because the court left a loophole for DDT supporters, admitting that additional inquiry might show that certain uses of the poison should be permitted even despite a substantial degree of risk.

■ Researchers at the New York State Department of Environmental Conservation announced some disquieting news. Tests on 43-year-old preserved fish showed levels of mercury more than twice as high as the amount currently regarded as safe for human consumption. The significance of this bizarre finding was not immediately clear, but it obviously raises a number of new questions about the amount of mercury Americans may have ingested over the years; it also seemed to suggest that a great deal more research will be necessary before scientists have enough data in hand to enable them to decide what pollutants and how much of them are dangerous and what the average person's chances are of ingesting a dangerous dose.

January 18, 1971 53

ıe Word."
ı.
earth by
womb of
ı human
t inherit
sent Je-
ıs: (1) To
John 18:
ntegrity,
ow (1 Pe-
ıis life to
.th. Why
0:28.
mmand,
ed what
ntenced
9) He no
's stan-
nymore.
l. Adam
en. That
ick, and
saved?

***Jesus' ministry included teaching, performing miracles, and even offering up his life for us***

4. Jesus was a perfect human just like Adam. Unlike Adam, though, Jesus was perfectly obedient to God under even the greatest test. He could therefore sacrifice his perfect human life to pay for Adam's sin. This is what the Bible refers to as the "ransom." Adam's children could thus be released from condemnation to death. All who put their faith in Jesus can have their sins forgiven and receive everlasting life.—1 Timothy 2:5, 6; John 3:16; Romans 5:18, 19.

5. When on earth Jesus cured the sick, fed the hungry, and calmed storms. He even raised the dead. Why did he perform miracles? (1) He felt pity for people who were suffering, and he wanted to help them. (2) His miracles proved that he was God's Son. (3) They showed what he will do for obedient mankind when he rules as King over the earth. —Matthew 14:14; Mark 2:10-12; John 5:28, 29.

6. Jesus died and was resurrected by God as a spirit creature, and he returned to heaven. (1 Peter 3:18) Since then, God has made him a King. Soon Jesus will remove all wickedness and suffering from this earth. —Psalm 37:9-11; Proverbs 2:21, 22.

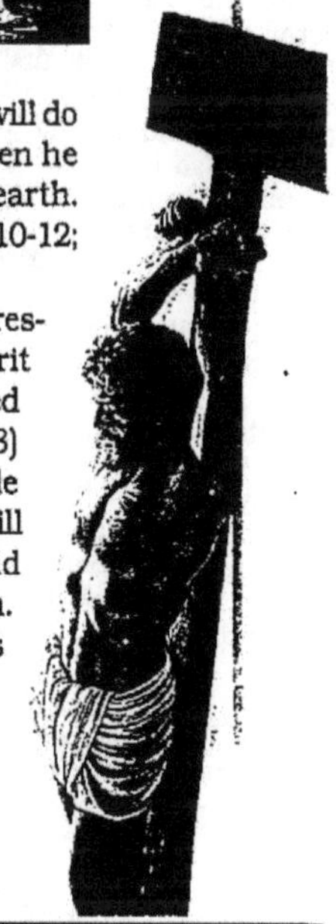

*What Does God Require of Us?*

nging a roll* of myrrh
ut a hundred pounds*
they took the body of
d it up with bandages
,[b] just the way the Jews
n of preparing for burial.
, at the place where he
ere was a garden, and
a new memorial tomb,[c]
e had ever yet been laid.
, on account of the prep-
Jews, they laid Jesus,
morial tomb was nearby.

first day[e] of the week
Mag'da·lene came to the
early, while there was
and she beheld the stone
away from the memorial
refore she ran and came
r and to the other dis-
om Jesus had affection,
them: "They have tak-
ord* out of the memorial
do not know where they
"

er[i] and the other disci-
and started for the me-
4 Yes, the two together
; but the other disciple
Peter with greater speed
he memorial tomb first,
g forward, he beheld the
g,[j] yet he did not go in.
Peter also came follow-
e entered into the memo-
he viewed the bandages
o the cloth that had been
not lying with the ban-
arately rolled up in one
that time, therefore, the
who had reached the me-
irst also went in, and he
ved. 9 For they did not
e scripture that he must
dead.[l] 10 And so the
back to their homes.
owever, kept standing out
e memorial tomb, weep-

ll," א*B; P[66]א[c]AVgSy[p], "mix
unds." Gr., li'tras, generally
e Roman pound that weighed
Lat., li'bras. 20:2* Or, "Mas



ing. Then, while she was weeping, she
stooped forward to look into the memorial tomb 12 and she viewed two angels[a] in white sitting one at the head and
one at the feet where the body of Jesus
had been lying. 13 And they said to
her: "Woman, why are you weeping?"
She said to them: "They have taken my
Lord away, and I do not know where
they have laid him." 14 After saying these things, she turned back and
viewed Jesus standing, but she did not
discern it was Jesus.[b] 15 Jesus said
to her: "Woman, why are you weeping? Whom are you looking for?"[c] She,
imagining it was the gardener, said to
him: "Sir, if you have carried him off,
tell me where you have laid him, and I
will take him away." 16 Jesus said to
her: "Mary!"[d] Upon turning around, she
said to him, in Hebrew: *"Rab·bo'ni!"**[e]
(which means "Teacher!") 17 Jesus
said to her: "Stop clinging to me. For
I have not yet ascended to the Father.
But be on your way to my brothers[f]
and say to them, 'I am ascending to
my Father[g] and YOUR Father and to my
God[h] and YOUR God.'"[i] 18 Mary Mag'-
da·lene came and brought the news to
the disciples: "I have seen the Lord!"
and that he said these things to her.[j]
19 Therefore, when it was late on
that day, the first of the week,[k] and, although the doors were locked where the
disciples were for fear[l] of the Jews, Jesus came[m] and stood in their midst and
said to them: "May YOU have peace."[n]
20 And after he said this he showed
them both his hands and his side.[o]
Then the disciples rejoiced[p] at seeing
the Lord. 21 Jesus, therefore, said to
them again: "May YOU have peace. Just
as the Father has sent me forth,[q] I
also am sending YOU."[r] 22 And after
he said this he blew upon them and said
to them: "Receive holy spirit.[s] 23 If
YOU forgive the sins of any persons,[t]
they stand forgiven to them; if YOU retain those of any persons, they stand
retained."[u]
24 But Thomas,[v] one of the twelve,
who was called The Twin,* was not
with them when Jesus came. 25 Consequently the other disciples would say
to him: "We have seen the Lord!" But
he said to them: "Unless I see in his
hands the print of the nails and stick
my finger into the print of the nails
and stick my hand into his side,[a] I will
certainly not believe."[b]
26 Well, eight days later his disciples were again indoors, and Thomas
with them. Jesus came, although the
doors were locked, and he stood in their
midst and said: "May YOU have peace."[c]
27 Next he said to Thomas: "Put your
finger here, and see my hands, and take
your hand[d] and stick it into my side, and
stop being unbelieving but become believing." 28 In answer Thomas said to
him: "My Lord and my God!"[e] 29 Jesus said to him: "Because you have
seen me have you believed? Happy are
those who do not see and yet believe."[f]
30 To be sure, Jesus performed many
other signs also before the disciples,
which are not written down in this
scroll.[g] 31 But these have been written down[h] that YOU may believe that
Jesus is the Christ the Son of God, and
that, because of believing,[i] YOU may
have life by means of his name.

**21** After these things Jesus manifested himself again to the disciples at the sea of Ti·be'ri·as; but he
made the manifestation in this way.
2 There were in company Simon Peter
and Thomas, who was called The Twin,[j]
and Na·than'a·el[k] from Ca'na of Gal'i-
lee and the sons of Zeb'e·dee[l] and two
others of his disciples. 3 Simon Peter
said to them: "I am going fishing." They
said to him: "We also are coming with
you." Out they went and got aboard the
boat, but during that night they caught
nothing.[m]
4 However, just as it was getting to
be morning, Jesus stood on the beach,
but the disciples did not, of course, discern that it was Jesus.[n] 5 Then Jesus
said to them: "Young children, YOU do

Joh 20:16* *"Rabboni!"* J[18](Heb.), *Rib·boh·ni'*.

Joh 20:24* Or, "Didymous." Gr., *Di'dy·mos;* Lat., *Di'dy·mus.*

CHAP. 20
a Mr 16:5, Heb 1:14, Re 19:14
b Lu 24:16, Lu 24:31, Joh 21:4
c Joh 1:38
d Joh 10:3
e Mr 10:51, Joh 1:38
f Ps 22:22, Mt 12:50, Mt 25:40, Mt 28:10, Ro 8:29, Heb 2:11
g Joh 14:28, Joh 16:28
h 1Co 11:3, Eph 1:17, Col 1:3
i Ge 17:7, Heb 11:16
j Mt 28:10, Lu 24:10
k Lu 24:1
l Joh 9:22
m 1Co 15:5
n Mt 10:12, Lu 10:5, Lu 24:36
o Joh 19:34, 1Jo 1:1
p Joh 16:22
q Isa 61:1, Joh 5:36
r Mt 28:19, Joh 17:18, 2Ti 2:2
s Lu 1:67, Lu 2:25, Ac 2:2, Ac 2:4
t Mt 16:19
u Ac 13:11
v Joh 11:16

Second Col.
a Joh 19:34
b 2Co 5:7
c Joh 20:19
d 1Jo 1:1
e Isa 9:6, Joh 1:1, Joh 1:18, Joh 14:28, Joh 20:17, Joh 20:31
f 2Co 5:7, 1Pe 1:8
g Joh 21:25
h Lu 1:4
i Joh 3:15, Joh 5:24, 1Pe 1:9, 1Jo 5:13

CHAP. 21
j Joh 11:16, Joh 20:24
k Joh 1:45
l Mt 4:21
m Lu 5:5
n Lu 24:16, Joh 20:14

NEW WORLD TRANSLATION, 1984 edition

**JOHN 21:6—25** **Jesus appears in Galilee. 'Peter, Feed my sheep'** **1312**

not have anything to eat, do YOU?" They
answered "No!" to him. **6** He said to
them: "Cast the net on the right side
of the boat and YOU will find [some]."[a]
Then they cast it, but they were no
longer able to draw it in because of the
multitude of the fishes.[b] **7** Therefore
that disciple whom Jesus used to love*[c]
said to Peter:[d] "It is the Lord!"#
Hence Simon Peter, upon hearing that it was
the Lord, girded about himself his top
garment, for he was naked, and plunged
into the sea. **8** But the other disciples
came in the little boat, for they were
not a long way from land, only about
three hundred feet* away, dragging the
net of fishes.
**9** However, when they disembarked
onto land they beheld lying there a
charcoal fire[e] and fish lying upon it and
bread. **10** Jesus said to them: "Bring
some of the fish YOU just now caught."
**11** Simon Peter, therefore, went on
board and drew the net to land full of big
fishes, one hundred and fifty-three of
them. But although there were so many
the net did not burst. **12** Jesus said
to them: "Come, take YOUR breakfast."[f]
Not one of the disciples had the courage to inquire of him: "Who are you?"
because they knew it was the Lord.
**13** Jesus came and took the bread and
gave it to them,[g] and the fish likewise.
**14** This was now the third time[h] that
Jesus appeared to the disciples after his
being raised up from the dead.
**15** When, now, they had breakfasted,
Jesus said to Simon Peter: "Simon son
of John,* do you love# me more than
these?"[i] He said to him: "Yes, Lord, you
know I have affection for you."△[j] He said
to him: "Feed my lambs."[k] **16** Again
he said to him, a second time: "Simon
son of John, do you love*[l] me?" He said
to him: "Yes, Lord, you know I have
affection for you."# He said to him:
"Shepherd my little sheep."[a] **17** He
said to him the third time: "Simon son
of John, do you have affection for me?"*
Peter became grieved that he said to
him the third time: "Do you have affection for me?" So he said to him: "Lord,
you know all things;[b] you are aware
that I have affection for you."# Jesus
said to him: "Feed my little sheep.[c]
**18** Most truly I say to you, When you
were younger, you used to gird yourself and walk about where you wanted.
But when you grow old you will stretch
out your hands and another [man] will
gird[d] you and bear you where you do
not wish."[e] **19** This he said to signify
by what sort of death[f] he would glorify
God.[g] So, when he had said this, he said
to him: "Continue following me."[h]
**20** Upon turning about Peter saw
the disciple whom Jesus used to love*[i]
following, the one who at the evening meal had also leaned back upon
his breast and said: "Lord, who is the
one betraying you?" **21** Accordingly,
when he caught sight of him, Peter said
to Jesus: "Lord, what will this [man
do]?" **22** Jesus said to him: "If it is
my will for him to remain until I come,[j]
of what concern is that to you? You
continue following me." **23** In consequence, this saying went out among the
brothers, that that disciple would not
die. However, Jesus did not say to him
that he would not die, but: "If it is my
will for him to remain[k] until I come, of
what concern is that to you?"
**24** This is the disciple[l] that bears
witness about these things and that
wrote these things, and we know that
the witness he gives is true.[m]
**25** There are, in fact, many other
things also which Jesus did, which, if
ever they were written in full detail, I
suppose, the world itself could not contain the scrolls written.*[n]

CHAP. 21
a Lu 5:4
b Lu 5:6
c Joh 13:23, Joh 19:26, Joh 20:2
d Mt 14:29
e 1Ki 19:6
f Ac 10:41
g Lu 24:30
h Joh 20:19, Joh 20:26
i Joh 21:12
j Mt 26:33, Joh 17:26
k Lu 22:32, Ac 20:28, 1Pe 5:2
l Joh 14:21

Second Col.
a Ps 95:7, Mt 10:6, Ac 1:15, Ac 2:14, Heb 13:20, 1Pe 2:25
b Mr 2:8, Joh 2:24, Joh 2:25, Joh 16:30
c Joh 10:3, Joh 10:16
d Ac 21:11
e Ac 12:3
f 2Pe 1:14
g Php 1:20
h Mt 19:28, Joh 12:26, Re 14:4
i Joh 13:23, Joh 20:2
j Mt 16:27, Mt 25:31, 1Co 4:5, Re 1:10, Re 22:20
k Re 1:1, Re 1:9
l Joh 13:23, Joh 19:26, Joh 20:2, Joh 21:7
m Joh 19:35, 3Jo 12
n Joh 20:30

Joh 21:7* Or, "prefer." 7# Or, "Master." 8* Lit., "about two hundred cubits." See App 8A. 15* "John," BVg; ASy[p,s], "Jona." See 1:42 ftn, "John." 15# Lit., "are you loving." Gr., *a·ga·pais'*. 15△ Lit., "I am having affection for you." Gr., *phi·lo' se*. 16* Lit., "are you loving." Gr., *a·ga·pais'*. 16# Lit., "I am having affection for you." Gr., *phi·lo' se*.

Joh 21:17* Lit., "are you having affection for me?" Gr., *phi·leis' me*. 17# Lit., "I am having affection for you." Gr., *phi·lo' se*. 20* Or, "prefer." 25* Vs 25 is contained in ℵ[c]ABCVgSy[p,s]; ℵ* omits.

**1** The first account,
I composed about
sus started both to d
**2** until the day that
up,[c] after he had give
through holy spirit to th
he chose.[d] **3** To thes
positive proofs he show
after he had suffered,
them throughout forty
ing the things about
God.[f] **4** And while h
with them he gave th
"Do not withdraw from
keep waiting for what
promised,[h] about which
me; **5** because John,
with water, but YOU wi
holy spirit[i] not many
**6** When, now, they
they went asking him:
restoring the kingdom[j]
time?" **7** He said to
not belong to YOU to
of the times or seaso
Father has placed in h
tion;#[l] **8** but YOU will
when the holy spirit ar
and YOU will be witness
in Jerusalem[o] and in all
mar'i·a[p] and to the most
the earth."[q] **9** And af
these things, while the
on, he was lifted up[r] and
him up from their visio
they were gazing into t
was on his way,[t] also, l
white*[u] garments stood
**11** and they said: "Men
do YOU stand looking int

Ac 1:6* Or, "Master."
times." Gr., *kai·rous'*. 7#
Gr., *e·xou·si'ai*. 8* "Witne
*ty·res*; Lat., *te'stes*. 8# "M
Or, "extremity." Gr., *e·skha*
*qetseh'*. See Jer 25:31, 33
12:42 ftn. 10* Or, "bright.

NEW WORL TRANSLATION, 1984ed

ɪl set a price, 10 and
for the potter's[a] field,
at Jehovah[#] had com-

stood before the gover-
ernor put the question
the king of the Jews?"[b]
You yourself say [it]."[c]
he was being accused[d]
ests and older men, he
[e] 13 Then Pilate said
n not hear how many
estifying against you?"[f]
ot answer him, no, not
the governor wondered

festival to festival it
of the governor to re-
to the crowd, the one
16 Just at that time
ng a notorious prison-
bas.[i] 17 Hence when
ed together Pilate said
n one do YOU want me
U, Bar·ab'bas or Jesus
rist?"[j] 18 For he was
envy[k] they had handed
Moreover, while he was
idgment seat, his wife
saying: "Have nothing
righteous[m] man,* for I
lay in a dream[n] because
it the chief priests and
persuaded the crowds
b'bas,[o] but to have Je-
21 Now in responding
id to them: "Which of
want me to release to
"Bar·ab'bas."[p] 22 Pi-
m: "What, then, shall
the so-called Christ?"
Let him be impaled!"
hy, what bad thing did
ey kept crying out all
him be impaled!"[r]
at it did no good but
ar was arising, Pilate
washed his hands be-
saying: "I am innocent

gave," A[c]B'CItVg; ℵB
10* See App 1D. 19* Se
fastened on a stake (pole)



of the blood of this [man].* YOU yourselves must see to it." 25 At that all
the people said in answer: "His blood
come upon us and upon our children."[a]
26 Then he released Bar·ab'bas to them,
but he had Jesus whipped[b] and handed
him over to be impaled.[c]
27 Then the soldiers of the governor
took Jesus into the governor's palace
and gathered the whole body of troops
together to him.[d] 28 And disrobing
him, they draped him with a scarlet
cloak,[e] 29 and they braided a crown
out of thorns and put it on his head and
a reed in his right hand. And, kneeling
before him, they made fun[f] of him, saying: "Good day, you King of the Jews!"[g]
30 And they spit[h] upon him and took
the reed and began hitting him upon
his head. 31 Finally, when they had
made fun[i] of him, they took the cloak
off and put his outer garments upon
him and led him off for impaling.[j]
32 As they were going out they found
a native of Cy·re'ne named Simon.[k]
This man they impressed into service
to lift up his torture stake. 33 And
when they came to a place called *Gol'-
go·tha,*[1] that is to say, Skull Place,[#]
34 they gave him wine mixed with
gall[m] to drink; but, after tasting it, he
refused to drink.[n] 35 When they had
impaled[o] him they distributed his outer
garments[p] by casting lots,[q] 36 and, as
they sat, they watched over him there.
37 Also, they posted above his head the
charge against him, in writing: "This is
Jesus the King of the Jews."[r]
38 Then two robbers were impaled
with him, one on his right and one on
his left.[s] 39 So the passersby began
speaking abusively[t] of him, wagging[u]
their heads 40 and saying: "O you
would-be thrower-down of the temple[v]
and builder of it in three days, save
yourself! If you are a son of God, come
down off the torture stake!"[w] 41 In
like manner also the chief priests with
the scribes and older men began making
fun of him and saying:[a] 42 "Others
he saved; himself he cannot save! He
is King[b] of Israel; let him now come
down off the torture stake and we will
believe on him.[c] 43 He has put his
trust in God; let Him now rescue[d] him
if He wants him, for he said, 'I am God's
Son.'"[e] 44 In the same way even the
robbers that were impaled together with
him began reproaching him.[f]
45 From the sixth hour* on a darkness fell[g] over all the land, until the
ninth hour.[#][h] 46 About the ninth hour
Jesus called out with a loud voice,
saying: *"E'li, E'li, la'ma sa·bach·tha'-
ni?"** that is, "My God, my God, why
have you forsaken me?"[i] 47 At hearing this, some of those standing there
began to say: "This man is calling
E·li'jah."[j] 48 And immediately one of
them ran and took a sponge and soaked
it with sour[k] wine and put it on a reed
and went giving him a drink.[l] 49 But
the rest of them said: "Let him be! Let
us see whether E·li'jah comes to save
him."[m] [[Another man took a spear and
pierced his side, and blood and water
came out.]]*[n] 50 Again Jesus cried
out with a loud voice, and yielded up
[his] spirit.*[o]
51 And, look! the curtain[p] of the
sanctuary was rent in two, from top to
bottom,[q] and the earth quaked, and the
rock-masses were split.[r] 52 And the
memorial tombs were opened and many
bodies of the holy ones that had fallen
asleep were raised up, 53 (and persons,* coming out from among the memorial tombs after his being raised up,
entered into the holy city,)[s] and they became visible to many people. 54 But
the army officer* and those with him
watching over Jesus, when they saw the
earthquake and the things happening,

**CHAP. 27**
a De 19:10; Jos 2:19; Ac 5:28; 1Th 2:15
b Lu 18:33; Joh 19:1
c Mr 15:15; Lu 23:25
d Mr 15:16
e Joh 19:2
f Jg 16:25
g Mr 15:19; Joh 19:3
h Isa 49:7; Isa 50:6; Mt 26:67
i Isa 53:7; Mt 20:19
j Mr 15:20
k Mr 15:21; Lu 23:26; Joh 19:17
l Lu 23:33; Joh 19:17
m Ps 69:21
n Mr 15:23
o Ps 22:16; Joh 19:18
p Ps 22:18; Lu 23:34; Joh 19:23
q Mr 15:24
r Mr 15:26; Lu 23:38; Joh 19:19
s Isa 53:12; Mr 15:27; Lu 23:33; Joh 19:18
t Lu 18:32; Heb 12:3
u Ps 22:7; Ps 109:25; Lu 23:35
v Mt 26:61; Joh 2:19
w Mr 15:30; Lu 4:3

**Second Col.**
a Mr 15:31; Lu 23:35
b Joh 1:49; Joh 12:13
c Mr 15:32
d Ps 3:2; Ps 22:8; Ps 42:10
e Mr 14:62; Joh 5:18; Joh 10:36
f Mr 15:32; Lu 23:39
g Am 8:9
h Mr 15:33; Lu 23:44
i Ps 22:1; Isa 53:10; Mr 15:34
j Mr 15:35
k Ps 69:21
l Lu 23:36; Joh 19:29
m Mr 15:36
n Joh 19:34
o Mr 15:37; Lu 23:46; Joh 19:30
p Ex 26:31; Heb 9:3; Heb 10:20
q Mr 15:38; Lu 23:45
r 1Sa 14:15
s Mt 4:5

**Mt 27:24*** Or, "innocent of this blood." **33*** *"Golgotha."* Gr., *Gol·go·tha';* Lat., *Gol'-go·tha;* J[17,18](Heb.), *Gol·gol·ta'*. **33**[#] "Skull Place." Gr., *Kra·ni'ou To'pos;* Lat., *Cal·va'ri·ae lo'cus;* J[17](Heb.), *meqohm' Gul·go'leth.*

**Mt 27:45*** "Sixth hour," that is, about 12 noon. **45**[#] "Ninth hour," that is, about 3 p.m. **46*** *"Eli, Eli, lama sabachthani?"* Compare Ps 22:1 ftn, "Me." **49*** "Another man . . . came out," ℵBC; ADWItVgSy[h,p,s]Arm omit. **50*** Or, "ceased to breathe." Lit., "he let go off the spirit." Gr., *a·phe'ken to pneu'ma.* **53*** Or, "they," not referring to the "bodies." **54*** Lit., "the centurion," that is, the one in command of 100 soldiers.

NEW WORLD TRANSLATION, 1984ed

:oncern re-
dishes. You
. somehow
rship?'. Or
ou thinking
want to do
the right

es of such
book *The*

acred sym-
s when he
as Har-
The vener-
lso to have
is
spended on
hip of the
ymbol, the
nighty one

of the *New*
*tian Greek*
oned draw-

Sel

ER 22, 1976

The ancients used many other religious symbols. For instance, the Winged Globe or Winged Disk was used in various forms in Phoenicia, Assyria and other nations. However, *The Migration of Symbols* by G. d'Alviella says: "It has been said, with good reason, that the Winged Globe is the Egyptian symbol *par excellence.*" Likely you have seen it in Egyptian art or designs.

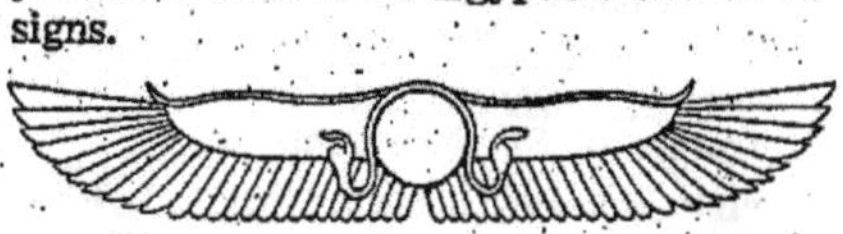

The Egyptians also employed as religious symbols things in nature around them. Regarding the scarab or dung beetle, *The World Book Encyclopedia* reports: "For the Egyptians, the scarab also symbolized the resurrection and immortality. They carved figures of the insects out of stone or metal, and used them as charms."

Certain plants, too, have been taken as religious symbols. In their religion or mythology many nations had a Sacred Tree, such as "the palm, the pomegranate, the cypress, the vine, etc." The fleur-de-lis (French, "flower of the lily") brings this up to more recent times. This design, used in ancient India and Egypt, became part of the heraldic design on the shield of the royal house of France. "Charles V of France in 1376 limited the number of fleurs-de-lis to three, in honour of the Holy Trinity."—*Encyclopædia Britannica*, 1976 edition, Volume IV, page 182.

A similar religious connection may arise with the shamrock or three-leaf clover. Regarding this plant or design, one encyclopedia reports:

"Shamrock (Ir. *seamròg*, 'little clover'), any of several [three-leaf] clovers . . . , all of which are native to Ireland. The shamrock was originally chosen as the national emblem of Ireland because of the legend that Saint Patrick used the plant to illustrate the doctrine of the Trinity. Most shamrocks . . . have been considered by the Irish as good-luck symbols since earliest times, and this superstition has persisted in modern times among people of many nationalities."

***Need to Determine***

Snakes, crosses, stars, birds, flowers . . . yes, there is an almost endless number of designs and symbols that have at some time or other been linked with idolatrous worship. So how can the sincere Christian know what to avoid or what to overlook as unimportant?

It certainly is not as if it makes no difference as to what decoration a Christian uses in his home or on his person. Illustrating this is the law Jehovah God gave to the Israelites about not cutting the side locks and extremities of their beards. (Lev. 19:27) Evidently some of the pagan nations around them at the time practiced cutting their beards in a certain fashion, doing so in connection with the worship of their gods. (Jer. 9:26; 25:23) If an Israelite adopted the same style, observers might well take it to be a symbol of his religious beliefs, signifying that he upheld pagan worship. Obediently, God's people avoided this style of grooming or personal decoration. So it is appropriate to avoid decorations that would link a person with idolatrous worship.

On the other hand, just because idol worshipers at some time or place might

*AWAKE!—DECEMBER 22, 1976* 13

use a certain design, that does not automatically mean that true worshipers must always shun it. For instance, figures of palm trees, pomegranates and bulls were incorporated in the design of Jehovah's temple in Jerusalem. (1 Ki. 6:29-35; 7:15-18, 23-25) The fact that other religions might take these natural things that God created and use them as symbols in idol worship did not make it wrong for true worshipers to use them decoratively. Anyone visiting the temple could tell that God's people were not worshiping these decorations or venerating them as sacred symbols.

Another factor to consider is a design's meaning where you are.

### *Things Change*

Many times a design will change in significance according to location and time. A certain shape may have a particular meaning to an observer at one time and place, but a different meaning to an observer elsewhere or in another age. Note this example:

What does this design bring to your mind? Actually, the gammadion, or swastika, is an old religious symbol used in nations around the globe. *The World Book Encyclopedia* says of it:

> "An ancient symbol often used as an ornament or a religious sign. . . . The swastika has been found on Byzantine buildings, Buddhist inscriptions, Celtic monuments, and Greek coins. Swastikas were widely used symbols among the Indians of North America and South America."



However, because of its more recent use as a symbol in Nazi Germany, those past religious meanings do not readily come to the mind of most observers today. As this encyclopedia explains, now the swastika has come "to stand for all the evil associated with the Nazis as they gained control of Europe."

This matter of a symbol's taking on different significance can work in another way. *A pagan religious symbol might lose its religious connotation.* As the book *The Migration of Symbols* explains:

> "It frequently happens that a symbol changes its meaning in passing from one country to another. In this manner a symbol can very well become a mere ornament when, on account of its æsthetic value, or simply by reason of its originality, it is reproduced by artists who are unacquainted with its primitive acceptation."

Also, the significance of a particular design may vary from place to place. The shamrock or three-leaf clover exemplifies this point. In some localities it might still be commonly looked on as a symbol of the unscriptural Trinity doctrine. In other areas that connection might be relatively unknown, but people may often view a shamrock displayed on a bracelet or a tie as being a "good luck" symbol. (Compare Isaiah 65:11, 12.) In yet other places neither of these significances may generally come to mind; if a three-leaf clover were part of the design of some wallpaper or piece of clothing, most persons might consider it just a pleasant natural decoration, even as flowers, colored tree leaves and other attractive vegetation are used decoratively.

So the Christian needs to be primarily concerned about what? Not what a certain symbol or design possibly meant thousands of years ago or how it might be thought of on the other side of the world, but what it means now to most people where he lives.



*In Practic*
What do
Obviously,
bols are st
religious s
gion or a c
example.
The *En*
mentions:
bols, relig
the Christ
the world.'
the Spani
America, t
real Cross
symbol . .
and benefi
Jehovah
to Biblica
Jesus actu
stake with
cordingly,
the death
*still has* a
parts of th
wear a cr
a mere de
standably
most prob
was weari
gious sign
avoid disp
But, as
to the hea
ligious sy
now have
Most likel
than a de
human he
In that c
free to u
decorative
Howeve
other asp
not a rel
the earth

**Is veneration of the cross a Scriptural practice?**

1 Cor. 10:14: "My beloved ones, flee from idolatry." (An idol is an image or symbol that is an object of intense devotion, veneration, or worship.)

Ex. 20:4, 5, *JB:* "You shall not make yourself a carved image or any likeness of anything in heaven or on earth beneath or in the waters under the earth; you shall not bow down to them or serve them." (Notice that God commanded that his people not even *make an image* before which people would bow down.)

Of interest is this comment in the *New Catholic Encyclopedia:* "The representation of Christ's redemptive death on Golgotha does not occur in the symbolic art of the first Christian centuries. The early Christians, influenced by the Old Testament prohibition of graven images, were reluctant to depict even the instrument of the Lord's Passion." —(1967), Vol. IV, p. 486.

Concerning first-century Christians, *History of the Christian Church* says: "There was no use of the crucifix and no material representation of the cross."—(New York, 1897), J. F. Hurst, Vol. I, p. 366.

**Does it really make any difference if a person cherishes a cross, as long as he does not worship it?**

How would you feel if one of your dearest friends was executed on the basis of false charges? Would you make a replica of the instrument of execution? Would you cherish it, or would you rather shun it?

In ancient Israel, unfaithful Jews wept over the death of the false god Tammuz. Jehovah spoke of what they were doing as being a 'detestable thing.' (Ezek. 8:13, 14) According to history, Tammuz was a Babylonian god, and the cross was used as his symbol. From its beginning in the days of Nimrod, Babylon was against Jehovah and an enemy of true worship. (Gen. 10:8-10; Jer. 50:29) So by cherishing the cross, a person is honoring a symbol of worship that is opposed to the true God.



As stated at Ezekiel 8:17, apostate Jews also 'thrust out the shoot to Jehovah's nose.' He viewed this as "detestable" and 'offensive.' Why? This "shoot," some commentators explain, was a representation of the male sex organ, used in phallic worship. How, then, must Jehovah view the use of the cross, which, as we have seen, was anciently used as a symbol in phallic worship?

# Dates

**Definition:** Dates mark the time at which events occur. The Bible expresses dates in relation to the lifetime of individuals, the period during which certain rulers were in office, or other notable events. It contains the only complete chronology reaching back to the time of Adam's creation. Bible chronology also pinpointed in advance the time when certain important events in the fulfillment of God's purpose would take place. The Gregorian calendar, which is now popular in much of the world, did not come into use until 1582. In secular sources there is disagreement on dates given for events in ancient history. However, certain key dates, such as 539 B.C.E. for the fall of Babylon, and hence 537 B.C.E. for the Jews' return from captivity, are well established. (Ezra 1:1-3) Using such dates as starting points, it is possible to express in terms of current calendars the dates for ancient Biblical events.

**Have scientists proved that humans have been on earth for millions of years, not merely some thousands of years as the Bible indicates?**

The dating methods used by scientists are built on assumptions that can be useful but that often lead to very contradictory results. So, dates given by them are constantly being revised.

A report in *New Scientist* of March 18, 1982, reads: "'I am staggered to believe that as little as a year ago I made the statements that I made.' So said Richard Leakey, before the elegant audience of a Royal Institution evening discourse last Friday. He had come to reveal that the conven-

REASONING FROM THE SCRIPTURES

## DIALOGUE SEVEN: Your Decision To Serve God—Loyalty To Jehovah Or Loyalty To An Organization?

/S

ghter that she was
u get baptized, I
e," responded An-
ever, did not deter
ondition, she was

act to this? There
repared a special
aptism. Then she
ou are baptized,
y? "Like a new-

sses met a retired
Union. Since he
ed a Bible study,
ney made rapid
aptized publish-
ne former officer
t love for spiritu-
nent to all in the
expended them-
a local residence

# HAVE YOU MADE THE TRUTH YOUR OWN?

*"Be transformed by making your mind over, that you may prove to yourselves the good and acceptable and perfect will of God."*—ROMANS 12:2.

TO BE a true Christian in these last days—these "critical times hard to deal with"—is not easy. (2 Timothy 3:1) The fact is that to follow Christ's example, one must conquer the world. (1 John 5:4) Recall what Jesus said about the Christian way: "Go in through the narrow gate; because broad and spacious is the road leading off into destruction, and many are the ones going in through it; whereas narrow is the gate and cramped the road leading off into life, and few are the ones finding it." He also said: "If anyone wants to come after me, let him disown himself and pick up his torture stake day after day and follow me continually."—Matthew 7:13, 14; Luke 9:23.

2 Having found the cramped road to life, a Christian's next challenge is to stay on it. Why is that a challenge? It is because our dedication and baptism make us a target of Satan's crafty acts, or subtle machinations. (Ephesians 6:11; footnote) He takes note of our weaknesses and seeks to exploit them in an effort to subvert our spirituality. After all, he attempted to break down Jesus, so why should he leave us alone?—Matthew 4:1-11.

### Satan's Crafty Tactics

3 One ploy that Satan uses is to plant doubts in our mind. He looks for weaknesses in our spiritual armor. In the very beginning, he used that tactic with Eve, asking: "Is it really so that God said you must not eat from every tree of the garden?" (Genesis 3:1) In other words, Satan was saying, 'Is it really possible that God could have placed such a prohibition on you? Would he hold back something so good from you? Why, God knows that in the very day of your eating from the tree your eyes are bound to be opened and you are bound to be like God, knowing good and bad!' Satan planted a seed of doubt and waited for it to germinate.—Genesis 3:5.

4 How does Satan use this tactic today? If we neglect our Bible reading, our personal study, our prayers, and our Christian ministry and meetings, we may leave ourselves open to doubts raised by others. For example: "How do we know that this is the truth as Jesus taught it?" "Are these really the last days? After all, we are already in the 21st century." "Are we on the threshold of Armageddon, or is it a long way off?" If such doubts should arise, what can we do to remove them?

5 James gave practical counsel when he wrote: "If any one of you is lacking in wisdom, let him keep on asking God, for he gives generously to all and without reproaching; and it will be given him. But let him keep on asking in faith, not doubting at all, for he who doubts is like a wave of the sea driven by the wind and blown about. In fact, let not that man suppose that he will receive anything from Jehovah; he is an indecisive man, unsteady in all his ways."—James 1:5-8.

1, 2. Why is it not easy to be a true Christian today?
3. How did Satan plant doubts in Eve's mind?
4. What doubts might affect some today?
5, 6. What must we do if doubts should arise?

THE WATCHTOWER • FEBRUARY 1, 2001 9

*Regular Bible study and prayer can help us dispel doubts*

6 What, then, must we do? We should "keep on asking God" in prayer for faith and understanding and bolster our efforts in personal study regarding any questions or doubts. We can also ask for help from those who are strong in the faith, never doubting that Jehovah will give us the support we need. James also said: "Subject yourselves, therefore, to God; but oppose the Devil, and he will flee from you. Draw close to God, and he will draw close to you." Yes, our doubts will dissipate as we draw close to God through study and prayer.—James 4:7, 8.

7 Take, for example, the question: How do we know that we are practicing the form of worship that Jesus taught? To answer this, what criteria must be considered? The Bible points out that authentic Christians must have true love among themselves. (John 13: 34, 35) They must sanctify God's name, Jehovah. (Isaiah 12:4, 5; Matthew 6:9) And they must make known that name.—Exodus 3:15; John 17:26.

8 Another identifying feature of true worship is respect for God's Word, the Bible. It is the unique book that reveals God's personality and his purposes. (John 17:17; 2 Timothy 3: 16, 17) Additionally, true Christians proclaim the Kingdom of God as man's only hope for everlasting life on a paradise earth. (Mark 13: 10; Revelation 21:1-4) They keep separate from this world's corrupt politics and its defiling way of life. (John 15:19; James 1:27; 4:4) Who today have really met these criteria? The facts establish that there is only one answer—Jehovah's Witnesses.

### What if Doubts Linger?

9 What if we do find ourselves in a tunnel of doubts? What should we do then? Wise King Solomon provides the answer: "My son, if you will receive my sayings and treasure up my own commandments with yourself, so as to pay attention to wisdom with your ear, that you may incline your heart to discernment; if, moreover, you call out for understanding itself and you give forth your voice for discernment itself, if you keep seeking for it as for silver, and as for hid treasures you keep searching for it, in that case you will understand the fear of Jehovah, and you will *find the very knowledge of God.*"—Proverbs 2:1-5.

10 Is that not a staggering thought? If we are willing to pay earnest attention to God's wis-

7, 8. What are some basic criteria for determining the form of worship that was taught by Jesus, and who meet these criteria?
9, 10. What can we do to overcome lingering doubts?

dom, we will '
God." Yes, the
Lord of the uni
are willing to re
That means tur
through person
of his Word can
see the light of t

11 A clear exa
fearful and dou
at 2 Kings 6:11
spiritual percep
that heavenly
God's prophet,
Syrian army. In
"Alas, my mast
did Elisha resp
there are more
who are with t
dant to be con
heavenly hosts.

12 "Elisha beg
vah, open his e

11. How was Elis
12. (a) How wer
(b) How can we
have?

ch first-century
imothy: "Shun
e what is holy;
more and more
ord will spread
s and Philetus
very men have
. . and they are
e." "Alexander
ny injuries . . .
for he resisted
gree."—2 Tim.

nings given by
ing identifying
es emerge:

h of some and
ter themselves
sheep's cover-

uits; they 'ad-
e ungodliness'
ant to enable
y to identify
guard against

ater
ne"

"already at
apostles were
later periods
r death. The
reasingly ap-
tury on and
rth century.
to occur be-
Lord Jesus
' Jehovah."

itures of typical
oretold by what

UGUST 1, 1980

8 But other scriptures make it clear that even during "the last days" of the present system of things, cases of apostasy would occur within the true Christian congregation. The apostle Peter wrote:

"In the last days there will come ridiculers with their ridicule, proceeding according to their own desires and saying: 'Where is this promised presence of his?' . . . You, therefore, beloved ones, having this advance knowledge, be on your guard that you may not be led away with them by the error of the law-defying people and fall from your own steadfastness."—2 Pet. 3:3, 4, 17.

9 Peter was not merely warning his brothers against "ridiculers" and "law-defying people" in the world. Christians have always been well aware of danger from that quarter. Peter was also speaking of the danger of being "led away" by some within the Christian congregation who would become "ridiculers," making light of the fulfillment of prophecies concerning Christ's "presence" and adopting a law-defying attitude toward "the faithful and discreet slave," the Governing Body of the Christian congregation and the appointed elders.

8, 9. (a) What warning did Peter give concerning the last days? (b) Would these "ridiculers" and "law-defying people" be exclusively outside the Christian congregation?

## Causes and Effects of Apostasy

10 Among the various causes of apostasy, one of the foremost is unquestionably a *lack of faith* through doubt. (Heb. 3:12) Interestingly, *The New International Dictionary of New Testament Theology* supplies the following information on the Greek verb that is often translated by "to doubt": "*Diakrinō*, make a distinction, judge, . . . ; doubt, waver. . . . In some [New Testament] passages doubt appears as a lack of faith and thus as sin (Rom. 14:23). . . . In Rom. 4:20f. doubt comes close to disbelief. . . . Doubt is thus a lack of trust in the act of God which he has still to perform and which men are to await. . . . In the NT the doubter sins against God and his promises, because he judges God falsely."

11 Thus, the one who doubts to the point of becoming an apostate sets himself up as a judge. He thinks he knows better than his fellow Christians, better also than the "faithful and discreet slave," through whom he has learned the best part, if not all that he knows about Jehovah God and his purposes. He develops a *spirit of in-*

10, 11. (a) What is one important cause of apostasy? (b) What are some parallel meanings of the Greek word translated "to doubt," and how does the apostate set himself up as a judge?

**CAUSES**

Lack of faith

Spirit of independence

Ingratitude

Presumption

**EFFECTS**

Loss of joy

Rebelliousness

Lack of spiritual nourishment

Works of the flesh

THE WATCHTOWER — AUGUST 1, 1980

19

THE WATCHTOWER 8/1/1980

*dependence,* and becomes "proud in heart . . . something detestable to Jehovah." (Prov. 16:5) Some apostates even think they know better than God, as regards his ordering of events in the outworking of his purposes. Two other causes of apostasy are therefore *ingratitude* and *presumption.*—2 Pet. 2:10b-13a.

[12] As to the effects of a course of apostasy, one immediate result is a loss of joy. The apostate becomes hardened in his rebellious ways. Another is he fails to take in the spiritual food provided by "the faithful and discreet slave"—this leading to spiritual weakness and breakdown of spirit. Contrasting the happiness of his loyal servants with the sad condition of apostates, Jehovah stated prophetically:

> "Look! My own servants will eat, but you yourselves will go hungry. Look! My own servants will drink, but you yourselves will go thirsty. Look! My own servants will rejoice, but you yourselves will suffer shame. Look! My own servants will cry out joyfully because of the good condition of the heart, but you yourselves will make outcries because of the pain of heart and you will howl because of sheer breakdown of spirit."—Isa. 65:13, 14.

[13] After having yielded to such works of the flesh as "enmities, strife, jealousy, fits of anger, contentions, divisions, sects," apostates often fall victim to other fleshly works such as "drunken bouts," "loose conduct" and "fornication." (Gal. 5:19-21) Peter warns us against those who "look down on lordship" by despising theocratic order, who "speak abusively" of those entrusted with responsibility within the Christian congregation, and so 'abandon the straight path.' He says that their "final conditions have become worse for them than the first."—Read carefully 2 Peter, chapter 2.

12. What are some of the effects of rebellion and apostasy?
13. What is meant by 'looking down on lordship,' and in what does this result? (Jude 8, 10)

20

## How to Avoid 'Falling Away from the Faith'

[14] We have seen that one of the basic causes of apostasy is a lack of faith through destructive doubt, and that the word translated "doubt" also means "to distinguish." The apostate makes himself a decider of what is true and what is false, of what is "good and bad" in the way of spiritual food. He becomes presumptuous. —Compare Genesis 2:17; 3:1-7.

[15] So to avoid falling away from the faith, the Christian should beware of a lack of faith, "the sin that easily entangles us," and "run with endurance the race that is set before us." (Heb. 12:1; 3:12, 19) Paul gives us this advice: "Keep testing whether you are in the faith, keep proving what you yourselves are." (2 Cor. 13:5) Paul is not inviting us to have doubts about "the faith," but to question ourselves, as to whether we are living up to the faith or not. Such honest self-examination should fill us with modesty and humility, thus protecting us from the *independent spirit* and *presumptuousness* of the apostate.

[16] To avoid falling away from the faith, we also need to guard against *ingratitude.* We should be thankful for the abundant spiritual food we are receiving through the "faithful and discreet slave." (Matt. 24:45) This does not mean that we should not convince ourselves of things as we go along. In this respect, a twofold lesson can be learned from the Beroean Jews. To be sure, they 'carefully examined the Scriptures daily as to whether these things were so,' but they were also "noble-minded" because "they received the word [being preached to them by Paul and Silas] *with the greatest eagerness of mind.*"—Acts 17:11.

14, 15. How can we avoid presumptuousness?
16. (a) What other pitfall should we avoid? (b) What twofold lesson can we learn from the Beroean Jews?

THE WATCHTOWER — AUGUST 1, 1980

[17] Such *gr*
help us to c
curate know
cernment. T
in turn, ena
things of ma
lesser impor
trouble in un
Does it affec
we have lea
"slave" class
selves and p
vent us from

[18] Paul cou
tinue praying
yet more and
edge and full
make sure of
so that you
stumbling oth
and may be
which is thro
glory and pr

17, 18. What shou
what advice does

"Sav

THE WATCHTOWER –

Do those associated with your organization seek political positions or reforms? Those in the early congregation had a more permanent hope centered in God's kingdom. (2 Pet. 3:13, 14) Do national or racial barriers exist within your organization? There were none in first-century congregations. (Gal. 3:28; Rev. 7:9) Is discrimination practiced? Early Christians abided by the principle that "there is no partiality with God" but his "will is that all sorts of men should be saved and come to an accurate knowledge of truth." —Rom. 2:11; 1 Tim. 2:4; Jas. 2:1-4.

#### IDENTIFYING THE THEOCRATIC ORGANIZATION

18 Those in the apostolic organization did not fulfill these requirements for the Christian congregation in just a token way. They viewed their position in Jehovah's chosen visible channel as sacred and would allow nothing to jeopardize their standing with God. They had no fear of this world. (Matt. 10:26-28) Their only concern was to provide for the safety and well-being of the flock of God. Jesus pointed to this mark of the true visible organization in connection with a detailed prophecy relating to this time of the end. He said: "Who really is the faithful and discreet slave whom his master appointed over his domestics, to give them their food at the proper time? Happy is that slave if his master on arriving finds him doing so. Truly I say to you, He will appoint him over all his belongings."—Matt. 24:45-47.

19 Evidences are now conclusive that Jesus Christ was enthroned in heaven in 1914 C.E. and that he accompanied Jehovah to his temple in 1918 C.E., when judgment began with the house of God.* (1 Pet. 4:17) After cleansing those belonging to this house who were alive on earth, Jehovah poured out his spirit upon them and assigned them the responsibility of serving as his sole visible channel, through whom alone spiritual instruction was to come. Those who recognize Jehovah's visible theocratic organization, therefore, must recognize and accept this appointment of the "faithful and discreet slave" and be submissive to it.

20 Today those thus charged with this grand privilege and responsibility are called Jehovah's witnesses, and have been since 1931. As a group they have been separated more and more from the sectarianism of Christendom from the 1870's onward. Since 1879 the *Watch Tower* magazine has been used by this collective group to dispense spiritual food regularly to those of this "little flock" of true Christians. (Luke 12:32) In 1884 they formed a legal servant, a corporation, called Zion's Watch Tower Tract Society, now known as the Watch Tower Bible and Tract Society of Pennsylvania. By 1919, having survived the fiery trials of World War I, this "faithful and discreet slave" class was no novice organization. True, the apostles were no longer in its midst, but they had left behind written instructions as part of Jehovah's great Record Book. Additionally, the modern-day members of this 1900-year-old Christian congregation had received from the days of the apostles onward a rich heritage of Christian loyalty and integrity, long and patient suffering of persecution, abiding faith in Jehovah's precious promises, con-

18. What mark of the true visible organization did Jesus identify, and what reward did he say he would give?
19. What must those who recognize Jehovah's visible organization accept?

* See the book *You May Survive Armageddon into God's New World*, Chapter 6, entitled "A·do·nay' Comes to His Temple." Published by the Watch Tower Bible & Tract Society in 1955.

20, 21. Who today are charged with the responsibility of representing Jehovah's King, and what record provides their recommendation?

10/1/1967

OCTOBER

fidence i
Lord an
ence to i
witnesses
21 In t
they wel
tually sh

Fa

JEHOVA
freedor
earth for
under wa
developme
pending d
of things
thousand-
mediately
ceive life
fort. Not
alone. Ja
century
"Faith, if
in itself.
breath is d
is dead."
must prov
action, by

1. How and
gift of life?

food. Suppose he never bothered to wash his hands or comb his hair—was never really prepared for the meal—and then sat at the table and just pushed the food around his plate, food that you had worked so hard to prepare, even refusing to pass anything. Suppose you had a guest for dinner that night; would you feel proud of Junior? Would you not, rather, be mortified at his inconsiderate, disrespectful attitude? And yet, we have a guest, yes, more than a guest, at all our congregation's spiritual feasts. Not just the stranger or newly interested person of good will who attends, but our Lord Jesus Christ, who said: "Where there are two or three met together in my name, there I am in their midst." Not one of Jehovah's witnesses would deliberately insult either our heavenly Father or his motherly organization, would he? Then why should we do it by our thoughtlessness? Our brothers have worked hard and spent many busy hours preparing the spiritual feasts our heavenly Father has provided for us. And they continue to do it gladly, too, because by far the majority of the New World society are heeding Paul's counsel to the Thessalonians: "Now we request you, brothers, to have regard for those who are working hard among you and presiding over you in the Lord and admonishing you, and to give them more than extraordinary consideration in love because of their work."—Matt. 18:20; 1 Thess. 5:12, 13, *NW*.

#### RELYING ON JEHOVAH'S DIRECTIVE POWER

14 Showing respect for Jehovah's organization really resolves itself down to our attitude toward God's visible channel and the trust that we place in our proved, faithful brothers. If we have become thoroughly convinced that this is Jehovah's organization, that he is guiding and directing his people, then we shall not be unsettled by anything that happens. If something comes up that we do not understand we will wait patiently until it is made thoroughly clear to us. If we feel sure something is wrong we will 'keep the commandment' of our Father and take whatever theocratic steps are open to us and then wait on Jehovah. We will not 'forsake our mother's teaching' by immediately beginning to criticize and find fault. We will realize that Jehovah knows what is going on in his organization, and if he is willing to permit it, who are we to insist it should be different? If we really have faith, we will know that if it is wrong he will straighten it out eventually, and we are far safer inside his organization even with these minor difficulties than we would be on the outside where only chaos and destruction await us.

15 When we consider the tender care of our heavenly Father as manifested through his loving, motherly organization, how can our hearts but be refreshed and warmed with an overflowing appreciation? When we taste the rich and sumptuous food he provides and observe the careful attention to detail with which our mother has served it, how can we speak anything but praise for such worthy parents? And when we truly see the great motherly organization of God arrayed with the heavenly light of truth and righteousness, walking in the pathway of divine light, with perfect organizational light brightening and adorning her mind, how happily we can exclaim: 'This woman is the spouse of the universal King of whom it is written, "God is light," and in her heavenly position she can worthily bring forth his royal heavenly creation.' What a privilege to be her children and to share in the beautiful

14. Why is it safe to trust our proved, faithful brothers, and what should be our attitude if we believe something has gone wrong?

15, 16. What reasons has Jehovah given us for praising him and our motherly organization?

MAY 1, 

name sh
ness"! (J
ours in 
beaming
person 
ones fro
to come

A V
fr
many w
Knowing
changed
the very
appeared
officer as
with a re
on her w
not. She
using th
truth by
the mini
In thi
dent. Di
by both
ham, Isa
the truth
tile enem
do we r
doing so
termed
Their ac
counsel:
as sheep
yourselv
innocent
Perha
the line
theocrat
truth ar
let it be
an oath

* For de

5/1/1957

than opposing and rejecting it and presumptuously taking the position that we are more likely to be right than the discreet slave. We should meekly go along with the Lord's theocratic organization and wait for further clarification, rather than balk at the first mention of a thought unpalatable to us and proceed to quibble and mouth our criticisms and opinions as though they were worth more than the slave's provision of spiritual food. Theocratic ones will appreciate the Lord's visible organization and not be so foolish as to pit against Jehovah's channel their own human reasoning and sentiment and personal feelings.

[12] Now some may ask, Should we accept as from the Lord and true the food provided through the discreet slave, or should we withhold acceptance until we have proved it for ourselves? If we have gained our present understanding of the Bible by feeding at the table set by the slave, if we have been thereby freed from false doctrines and built up in the clean and undefiled worship of God and given a new world hope, we should have some confidence in the slave's provisions. After being nourished to our present spiritual strength and maturity, do we suddenly become smarter than our former provider and forsake the enlightening guidance of the organization that mothered us? "Forsake not the law of thy mother." (Prov. 6:20-23) And if the heavenly Father would not give a stone or serpent or scorpion to a child who asked for bread or fish or an egg from him, are we to take the spiritual food he provides through the slave into our hands as if we were going to be bruised by a stone or bitten by a serpent or stung by a scorpion? (Matt. 7:7-11; Luke 11:9-13, *NW*) Are we to be doubtful and suspicious about each new provision? "He who doubts is like a wave of the sea driven by the wind and blown about. In fact, let not that man suppose that he will receive anything from Jehovah." (Jas. 1:6, 7, *NW*) Even the Beroeans first received Paul's preaching "with the greatest readiness of mind", and then went to "carefully examining the Scriptures daily as to whether these things were so". (Acts 17:11, *NW*) This was the first real contact the Beroeans had with Paul's preaching, yet they received it readily and then studied the Scriptural support for themselves. How much more readily we can receive the slave's provisions with confidence, since, unlike the Beroeans, we have much past experience with the precious provisions from the slave. After receiving these food supplies we prove their Scripturalness for ourselves to make the message our own, in a spirit of meekness and trustfulness and not combativeness.

### THE FOLLY OF SPECULATING

[13] There are some who seem to dote on speculations. They love to be the talking center of little groups, voicing their theories on how or when this or that is going to happen. They may not be deliberately rebellious about what the slave provides, but if they can offer only what the slave has already supplied they do not stand out. How can they shine personally if they merely reflect what all others of Jehovah's witnesses are reflecting? So they seek for something more sensational, for some "new light" to dazzle unwary listeners. As they feed the open-mouthed listeners their line of new theories, the listeners by their rapt attention feed the ego of the speculators. When someone else begins to do the talking and occupies the spotlight, the speculator loses interest in the conversing group and drifts on. These speculating ones may acknowledge that some of their past theories were wrong, but they do not show they have learned the lesson from these mis-

12. In view of our past experience, in what attitude can we receive the slave's provisions?

13. Why do some habitually speculate and theorize?

FEBRUARY 1, 1

takes by refra
new theories. '
as an indeper
stronger than t

[14] Some of th
rebellious thai
matically with
sions, exalting
established ch
theocratic org
been right, an
the organizatic
and thus imply
will likewise l
never mention
they have adv
never adopted
campaign to g
bled up. What
is that the vis
has never cl
knows the mess
fied by the elir
that it expects
fest as more p
gradually the
more until the
clarifications
creet slave an
tors. (Prov. 4:
It is a continu
"to keep givi
food supplies
12:42, *NW*) D
that are not pu
earlier may ha
have been "at t
the Lord.

[15] But wheth
ly or only thou
They place the
of becoming p
importance, o

14. How do some
does their conceit l
15. What harm can
and how will theoc

February 1, 1952

observer noted that these men "were critical of the articles in *The Watchtower,* not wanting to accept it as . . . God's channel of truth, always trying to influence others in their way of thinking." However, loyal elders never try to influence others to reject any of the spiritual food provided by God through the faithful slave.

[8] As Jehovah's dedicated Witnesses, all of us must be loyal to him and to his organization. We should never even contemplate turning aside from God's wonderful light, pursuing an apostate course that can lead to spiritual death now and eventual destruction. (Jeremiah 17:13) But what if it is hard for us to accept or fully appreciate some Scriptural point presented by the faithful slave? Then let us humbly acknowledge where we learned the truth and pray for wisdom to deal with this trial until it comes to an end with some published clarification of matters.—James 1:5-8.

### Appreciate the Christian Brotherhood

[9] *Heartfelt appreciation for the spirit of fellowship existing within our Christian brotherhood furnishes another incentive to serve Jehovah loyally.* In fact, our relationship with God and Christ cannot be spiritually sound without this spirit. The apostle John told anointed Christians: "That which we have seen and heard we are reporting also to you, that you too may be having a sharing ["fellowship," *Diaglott*] with us. Furthermore, this sharing of ours is with the Father and with his Son Jesus Christ. . . . If we make the statement: 'We are having a sharing with him,' and yet we go on walking in the darkness, we are lying and are not practicing the truth." (1 John 1:3-6) This principle applies to all Christians, whether their hope is heavenly or earthly.

[10] Effort is required to maintain a spirit of fellowship. For instance, the Christian women Euodia and Syntyche apparently found it difficult to resolve a problem between them. Paul thus exhorted them "to be of the same mind in the Lord." He added: "I request you too, genuine yokefellow, keep assisting these women who have striven side by side with me in the good news along with Clement as well as the rest of my fellow workers, whose names are in the book of life." (Philippians 4:2, 3) Those godly women had fought side by side with Paul and others "in the good news," and he was sure that they were among those 'whose names were in the book of life.'

[11] Christians do not wear an insignia to show what they have been privileged to do in Jehovah's organization and how they have served him loyally. If they have a spiritual problem, how unloving it would be to ignore their years of loyal service to Jehovah! Likely, the one called "genuine yokefellow" was a loyal brother eager to assist others. If you are an elder, are you a "genuine yokefellow," ready to give help in a compassionate way? May all of us consider the good done by fellow believers, even as God does, and lovingly help them to bear their burdens.—Galatians 6:2; Hebrews 6:10.

8. What if we do not fully appreciate some Scriptural point presented by the faithful and discreet slave?
9. How does 1 John 1:3-6 show that Christians must have a spirit of fellowship?
10. Though Euodia and Syntyche apparently had difficulty resolving a personal problem, how did Paul view these women?
11. If a loyal Christian encounters a spiritual problem, what would it be fitting to keep in mind?

No
[12] *We will be ally with his that there is n nal.* When Jes disciples to go asked his apos also, do you?" shall we go av everlasting lif come to know God."—John 6
[13] "Sayings found in Judai Its principal si as the Messial Judaism based Scriptures. Th tence of angel resurrection. agreed with tl sinfully made G their unscriptu 1-11; Acts 23:6- the Jews and r accept Jesus C for 'the traditio (Paul) in his ig cutor of Christ'. 14, 23.
[14] Judaism la vah blessed the Son's followers works.' (Titus exists, and of it vah said: "If one tant to me, it ha

12. When Jesus' ples to go off to tl did Peter take?
13, 14. (a) Why divine favor? (b) of Jehovah say ab

zealous about their faith and obviously thought they had a good relationship with God but who did not understand what was really required in order to have God's approval.—Rom. 10:2-4.

Could we have a good personal relationship with God if we treated as of little importance his commandments? One of these is that we regularly assemble with fellow believers. —Heb. 10:24, 25.

***If we personally read the Bible, is that sufficient?***

It is true that many people can learn a great deal by reading the Bible personally. If their motive is to learn the truth about God and his purposes, what they are doing is highly commendable. (Acts 17:11) But, being honest with ourselves, are we truly going to grasp the full significance of it all without help? The Bible tells about a man who held a prominent position but who was humble enough to acknowledge his need for help in understanding Bible prophecy. That help was provided by a member of the Christian congregation.—Acts 8:26-38; compare other references to Philip in Acts 6:1-6; 8:5-17.

Of course, if a person reads the Bible but does not apply it in his life, it does him little good. If he believes it and acts on it, he *will* associate with God's servants in regular congregation meetings. (Heb. 10:24, 25) He will also join with them in sharing the "good news" with other people.—1 Cor. 9:16; Mark 13:10; Matt. 28:19, 20.

**How can a person know which religion is right?**

**(1) On what are its teachings based?** Are they from God, or are they largely from men? (2 Tim. 3:16; Mark 7:7) Ask, for example: Where does the Bible teach that God is a Trinity? Where does it say that the human soul is immortal?

**(2) Consider whether it is making known the name of God.** Jesus said in prayer to God: "I have made your name manifest to the men you gave me out of the world." (John 17:6) He declared: "It is Jehovah your God you must worship, and it is to him alone you must render sacred service."



(Matt. 4:10) Has your religion taught you that 'it is Jehovah you must worship'? Have you come to know the Person identified by that name—his purposes, his activities, his qualities—so that you feel you can confidently draw close to him?

**(3) Is true faith in Jesus Christ being demonstrated?** This involves appreciation of the value of the sacrifice of Jesus' human life and of his position today as heavenly King. (John 3:36; Ps. 2:6-8) Such appreciation is shown by obeying Jesus—sharing personally and zealously in the work that he assigned to his followers. True religion has such faith that is accompanied by works.—Jas. 2:26.

**(4) Is it largely ritualistic, a formality, or is it a way of life?** God strongly disapproves of religion that is merely a formalism. (Isa. 1:15-17) True religion upholds the Bible's standard of morality and clean speech instead of weakly going along with popular trends. (1 Cor. 5:9-13; Eph. 5:3-5) Its members reflect the fruits of God's spirit in their lives. (Gal. 5:22, 23) So, those who adhere to true worship can be identified because they sincerely endeavor to apply Bible standards in their lives not only at their places of meeting but in their family life, at their secular work, in school, and in recreation.

**(5) Do its members truly love one another?** Jesus said: "By this all will know that you are my disciples, if you have love among yourselves." (John 13:35) Such love reaches across racial, social, and national boundaries, drawing people together in genuine brotherhood. So strong is this love that it sets them apart as being truly different. When the nations go to war, who have enough love for their Christian brothers in other lands that they refuse to take up arms and kill them? That is what early Christians did.

**(6) Is it truly separate from the world?** Jesus said that his true followers would be "no part of the world." (John 15:19) To worship God in a manner that he approves requires that we keep ourselves "without spot from the world." (Jas. 1:27) Can that be said of those whose clergy and other members are involved in politics, or whose lives are largely built around materialistic and fleshly desires?—1 John 2:15-17.

REASONING FROM THE SCRIPTURES

·bs 27:11) Call
ayer, knowing
. as one of his
ıe understand-
ɔath of life with
.bove all, do not
l. When things
that Jehovah is

ıswer?
ake, but
ɔut mistakes
why should
oid becom
ıovah?

LY

UEL 22:26.

g (paralleling
ɾah as "the Pro-
prayer. (2 Sam-
ıly temple, God
. servant from
David was thus
upright course
ɜ. (Verses 20-27)
ds done in God-

sented in David's
pter 22?

given strength. (Verses 28-43) Last, David cited deliverance from faultfinders at home and from enemies abroad and gave thanks to Jehovah as "the One doing great acts of salvation for his king and exercising loving-kindness to his anointed one." (Verses 44-51) Jehovah can deliver us too if we pursue an upright course and rely on him for strength.

### What It Means to Be Loyal

[3] David's song of deliverance gives us this comforting assurance: "With someone loyal you [Jehovah] will act in loyalty." (2 Samuel 22:26) It is the Hebrew adjective *cha·sidh'* that denotes "someone loyal," or "one of loving-kindness." (Psalm 18:25, footnote) The noun *che'sedh* contains the thought of kindness that lovingly attaches itself to an object until its purpose in connection therewith is realized. Jehovah expresses that sort of kindness for his servants, even as they express it for him. This righteous, holy loyalty is rendered "loving-kindness" and "loyal love." (Genesis 20:13; 21:23) In the Greek Scriptures, "loyalty" carries the idea of holiness and reverence, expressed in the noun *ho·si·o'tes* and the adjective *ho'si·os.* Such loyalty includes faithfulness and devotion and means being devout and carefully performing all duties toward God. To be loyal to Jehovah means to stick to him with devotion so strong that it acts like a powerful adhesive.

[4] Jehovah's own loyalty is shown in many ways. For example, he takes judicial action against the wicked because of loyal love for his people and loyalty to justice and righteousness. (Revelation 15:3, 4; 16:5) Loyalty to his covenant with Abraham moved him to be long-suffering toward the Israelites. (2 Kings 13:23) Those loyal to God can count on his help to the end of their loyal course and can be sure that he will remember them. (Psalm 37:27, 28; 97:10) Jesus was strengthened by the knowledge that as God's chief "loyal one," his soul would not be left in Sheol.—Psalm 16:10; Acts 2:25, 27.

[5] Since Jehovah God is loyal, he requires loyalty of his servants. (Ephesians 4:24) For example, men must be loyal to qualify for appointment as congregation elders. (Titus 1:8) What factors should move Jehovah's people to serve him loyally?

### Appreciation for the Things Learned

[6] *Gratitude for the Scriptural things we have learned should move us to serve Jehovah loyally.* The apostle Paul urged Timothy: "Continue in the things that you learned and were persuaded to believe, knowing from what persons you learned them and that from infancy you have known the holy writings, which are able to make you wise for salvation through the faith in connection with Christ Jesus." (2 Timothy 3:14, 15) Remember that such knowledge came from God through "the faithful and discreet slave."—Matthew 24:45-47.

[7] Especially should appointed elders appreciate the nourishing spiritual food provided by God through the faithful slave. Years ago a few elders lacked such appreciation. One

3. From a Scriptural standpoint, what does it mean to be loyal?
4. How is Jehovah's loyalty shown?

5. Since Jehovah is loyal, what does he require of his servants, and what question will be given consideration?
6. How should we feel about the Scriptural things we have learned, and what should we remember about such knowledge?
7. How should elders feel about spiritual food provided by God through the faithful slave?

Ve are having a
e go on walking
ıg and are not
hn 1:3-6) This
ıtians, whether
thly.
ntain a spirit of
Christian wom-
ırently found it
between them.
be of the same
led: "I request
keep assisting
en side by side
ong with Clem-
fellow workers,
k of life." (Phi-
ly women had
l and others "in
sure that they
mes were in the

an insignia to
privileged to do
and how they
ey have a spir-
it would be to
ervice to Jeho-
"genuine yoke-
eager to assist
re you a "genu-
e help in a com-
us consider the
's, even as God
n to bear their
brews 6:10.

yche apparently
ıal problem, how

nters a spiritual
ting to keep in

### Nowhere Else to Go

[12] *We will be impelled to serve Jehovah loyally with his organization if we remember that there is nowhere else to go for life eternal.* When Jesus' statements caused 'many disciples to go off to the things behind,' he asked his apostles: "You do not want to go also, do you?" Peter replied: "Lord, whom shall we go away to? You have sayings of everlasting life; and we have believed and come to know that you are the Holy One of God."—John 6:66-69.

[13] "Sayings of everlasting life" were not found in Judaism of the first century C.E. Its principal sin was the rejection of Jesus as the Messiah. In none of its forms was Judaism based exclusively on the Hebrew Scriptures. The Sadducees denied the existence of angels and did not believe in the resurrection. Though the Pharisees disagreed with them in these respects, they sinfully made God's Word invalid because of their unscriptural traditions. (Matthew 15:1-11; Acts 23:6-9) These traditions enslaved the Jews and made it difficult for many to accept Jesus Christ. (Colossians 2:8) Zeal for 'the traditions of his fathers' caused Saul (Paul) in his ignorance to be a vicious persecutor of Christ's followers.—Galatians 1:13, 14, 23.

[14] Judaism lacked God's favor, but Jehovah blessed the organization made up of his Son's followers—'a people zealous for fine works.' (Titus 2:14) That organization still exists, and of it a longtime Witness of Jehovah said: "If one thing has been most important to me, it has been the matter of keeping close to Jehovah's visible organization. My early experience taught me how unsound it is to rely on human reasoning. Once my mind had been resolved on that point, I determined to stay by the faithful organization. How else can one get Jehovah's favor and blessing?" There is nowhere else to go for divine favor and life eternal.

[15] Our hearts should impel us to cooperate with Jehovah's organization because we know that it alone is directed by his spirit and is making known his name and purposes. Of course, those shouldering responsibility in it are imperfect. (Romans 5:12) But "Jehovah's anger got to be hot" against Aaron and Miriam when they found fault with Moses and forgot that he, not they, was entrusted with God-given responsibility. (Numbers 12:7-9) Today, loyal Christians cooperate with "those who are taking the lead" because that is what Jehovah requires. (Hebrews 13:7, 17) Evidence of our loyalty includes attending Christian meetings regularly and making comments that 'incite others to love and fine works.'—Hebrews 10:24, 25.

### Be Upbuilding

[16] *A desire to be upbuilding to others should also motivate us to serve Jehovah loyally.* Paul wrote: "Knowledge puffs up, but love builds up." (1 Corinthians 8:1) Since a certain kind of knowledge puffed up its possessors, Paul must have meant that love also upbuilds those showing that quality. A book by Professors Weiss and English says: "The person who has the capacity to love is usually loved in return. The capacity to

12. When Jesus' statements caused 'many disciples to go off to the things behind,' what position did Peter take?
13, 14. (a) Why did first-century Judaism lack divine favor? (b) What did one longtime Witness of Jehovah say about God's visible organization?

15. Why cooperate with Jehovah's visible organization and with those shouldering responsibility in it?
16. A desire to do what for others should also move us to serve Jehovah loyally?

# Religion

**Definition:** A form of worship. It includes a system of religious attitudes, beliefs, and practices; these may be personal, or they may be advocated by an organization. Usually religion involves belief in God or in a number of gods; or it treats humans, objects, desires, or forces as objects of worship. Much religion is based on human study of nature; there is also revealed religion. There is true religion and false.

## Why are there so many religions?

A recent tabulation concluded that there are 10 main religions and some 10,000 sects. Of these, some 6,000 exist in Africa, 1,200 in the United States, and hundreds in other lands.

Many factors have contributed to the development of new religious groups. Some have said that the various religions all represent different ways of presenting religious truth. But a comparison of their teachings and practices with the Bible indicates, rather, that the diversity of religions is because people have become followers of men instead of listening to God. It is noteworthy that, to a large extent, teachings they hold in common, but that differ from the Bible, originated in ancient Babylon. (See pages 50, 51, under the heading "Babylon the Great.")

Who is the instigator of such religious confusion? The Bible identifies Satan the Devil as "the god of this system of things." (2 Cor. 4:4) It warns us that "the things which the nations sacrifice they sacrifice to demons, and not to God." (1 Cor. 10:20) How vitally important, then, to make sure that we really are worshiping the true God, the Creator of heaven and earth, and that our worship is pleasing to him!

## Are all religions acceptable to God?

Judg. 10:6, 7: "The sons of Israel again proceeded to do what was bad in the eyes of Jehovah, and they began to serve the Baals and the Ashtoreth images and the gods of Syria and the gods of Sidon and the gods of Moab and the gods of

322

RELIGION 323

the sons of Ammon and the gods of the Philistines. So they left Jehovah and did not serve him. At this Jehovah's anger blazed against Israel." (If a person worships any thing or any person other than the true God, the Creator of heaven and earth, it is evident that his form of worship is not acceptable to Jehovah.)

Mark 7:6, 7: "He [Jesus] said to them [the Jewish Pharisees and scribes]: 'Isaiah aptly prophesied about you hypocrites, as it is written, "This people honor me with their lips, but their hearts are far removed from me. It is in vain that they keep worshiping me, because they teach as doctrines commands of men."'" (Regardless of whom a group *profess* to worship, if they hold to doctrines of men instead of the inspired Word of God, their worship is in vain.)

Rom. 10:2, 3: "I bear them witness that they have a zeal for God; but not according to accurate knowledge; for, because of not knowing the righteousness of God but seeking to establish their own, they did not subject themselves to the righteousness of God." (People may have God's written Word but lack accurate knowledge of what it contains, because they have not been taught properly. They may feel that they are zealous for God, but they may not be doing what he requires. Their worship is not going to please God, is it?)

### *Is it true that there is good in all religions?*

Most religions do teach that a person should not lie or steal, and so forth. But is that sufficient? Would you be happy to drink a glass of poisoned water because someone assured you that *most* of what you were getting was water?

2 Cor. 11:14, 15: "Satan himself keeps transforming himself into an angel of light. It is therefore nothing great if his ministers also keep transforming themselves into ministers of righteousness." (Here we are cautioned that not everything that originates with Satan may appear hideous. One of his chief methods of deceiving mankind has been false religion of all kinds, to some of which he gives a righteous appearance.)

2 Tim. 3:2, 5: "Men will be . . . having a form of godly devotion but proving false to its power; and from these turn away." (Regardless of their outward professions of love for

REASONING FROM THE SCRIPTURES, 1985, 1989 ed

le a choice that
m and for their
y demonstrates
:ntelligent crea-
ntrary to their
And since "God
ıe only dedica-
.e based on love,
ıeerfulness, one
ice. (2 Corinthi-
ınacceptable.
ıis requirement,
ıcate the dedi-
but they never
such a dedica-
ıildren. In con-
he Witnesses do
as infants, as if
em into dedica-
personal choice.
ollow is the one
Timothy. As an
ıstle Paul: "Con-
ou learned and
knowing from
them and that
n the holy writ-
ke you wise for
ı in connection
othy 3:14, 15.
Timothy knew
ə he had been
. He had been
ı believe Chris-
ıer and grand-
a result, Timo-
ming a follower
the *personal*
ion. In modern

e as a pattern for
ıat has his exam-

***In ancient Israel, dedication to God was a matter of birth***

times, tens of thousands of young men and women whose parents are Jehovah's Witnesses have followed this example. (Psalm 110:3) Others have not. It is a matter of personal choice.

### Choosing to Be a Slave of Whom?

14 No human is totally free. Everyone is restricted in his freedom by physical laws, such as the law of gravity, which cannot be ignored with impunity. Also in a spiritual sense, no one is totally free. Paul reasoned: "Do you not know that if you keep presenting yourselves to anyone as slaves to obey him, you are slaves of him because you obey him, either of sin with death in view or of obedience with righteousness in view?"—Romans 6:16.

15 The idea of being someone's slave strikes most people as unpleasant. Yet, in today's world the reality is that people often let themselves be manipulated and influenced in so many subtle ways that they end up *involuntarily* doing what others want them to do. For instance, the advertising industry and the entertainment world endeavor to press people into a mold, establishing standards for them to follow. Political and religious organizations get people to support their ideas and goals, not always

14. What does Romans 6:16 tell us about total freedom?
15. (a) How do people feel about being slaves, but what do most end up doing? (b) What appropriate questions might we ask ourselves?

***Christian dedication is a matter of choice***

by means of convincing arguments, but often by appealing to a sense of solidarity or loyalty. Since Paul noted that 'we are the slaves of those whom we obey,' each of us does well to ask himself, 'Of whom am I a slave? Who exercises the greatest influence on my decisions and my way of life? Do religious clergymen, political leaders, financial tycoons, or entertainment personalities? Whom do I obey—God or men?'

[16] Christians do not view obedience to God as an unwarranted infringement upon personal freedom. They willingly exercise their freedom in the manner of their Exemplar, Jesus Christ, bringing personal desires and priorities into line with God's will. (John 5:30; 6:38) They develop "the mind of Christ," submitting themselves to him as Head of the congregation. (1 Corinthians 2:14-16; Colossians 1:15-18) This is much like a woman who marries and willingly cooperates with the man she loves. In fact, the body of anointed Christians is spoken of as a chaste virgin promised to the Christ in marriage.—2 Corinthians 11:2; Ephesians 5:23, 24; Revelation 19:7, 8.

[17] Each of Jehovah's Witnesses, whether he has a heavenly hope or an earthly one, has made a *personal* dedication to God to do his will and to obey him as Ruler. For each Witness, dedication has been a *personal* choice to become a slave of God in preference to remaining a slave of men. This is in harmony with the apostle Paul's counsel: "You were bought with a price; stop becoming slaves of men."—1 Corinthians 7:23.

16. In what sense are Christians slaves of God, and what is the proper view of such slavery?

17. What have all of Jehovah's Witnesses chosen to become?



**Learnin**

[18] Before a
one of Jehova
Scriptural qu
care in dete
ness truly un
Christian ded
be one of Jeh
ing to live up
he is ineligib

[19] If an ind
ments, howe
cized for volu
cision to let
and by His i
ceptable to
God than by
benefit? Jeho
so. They who
words writte
am your God,
efit yourself,
in the way in
iah 48:17.

[20] Bible tru
ing false reli
nal torment i
5, 10) Instead
itude for the
resurrection
Jesus Christ'
20:28; Acts 24
frees people
ing on politic
fall short. Ins
overflow with

18. When does
baptism?
19. Why is the
who decides t
God?
20. In what re
truth?

Printed in the USA
CPSIA information can be obtained
at www.ICGtesting.com
LVHW082313150424
777488LV00041B/300